F. SCOTT FITZGERALD IN CONTEXT

The fiction of F. Scott Fitzgerald serves as a compelling and incisive chronicle of the Jazz Age and Depression eras. This collection explores the degree to which Fitzgerald was in tune with, and keenly observant of, the social, historical, and cultural contexts of the 1920s and 1930s. Original essays from forty international scholars survey a wide range of critical and biographical scholarship published on Fitzgerald, examining how it has evolved in relation to critical and cultural trends. The essays also reveal the micro-contexts that have particular relevance for Fitzgerald's work – from the literary traditions of naturalism, realism, and high modernism to the emergence of youth culture and prohibition, early twentieth-century fashion, architecture and design, and Hollywood – underscoring the full extent to which Fitzgerald internalized the world around him.

BRYANT MANGUM is Professor of English at Virginia Commonwealth University in Richmond, Virginia. He is author of *A Fortune Yet: Money in the Art of F. Scott Fitzgerald's Short Stories* and editor of *The Best Early Short Stories of F. Scott Fitzgerald*.

F. Scott Fitzgerald at his desk, ca. 1921 (Princeton University Library).

F. SCOTT FITZGERALD IN CONTEXT

EDITED BY

BRYANT MANGUM

Virginia Commonwealth University

CAMBRIDGE
UNIVERSITY PRESS

32 Avenue of the Americas, New York NY 10013-2473, USA

Cambridge University Press is part of the University of Cambridge.

It furthers the University's mission by disseminating knowledge in the pursuit of education, learning, and research at the highest international levels of excellence.

www.cambridge.org
Information on this title: www.cambridge.org/9781107009196

First published 2013
Reprinted 2013

A catalog record for this publication is available from the British Library.

Library of Congress Cataloging in Publication data
F. Scott Fitzgerald in context / [edited by] Bryant Mangum,
Virginia Commonwealth University.
pages cm
Includes bibliographical references and index.
ISBN 978-1-107-00919-6
1. Fitzgerald, F. Scott (Francis Scott), 1896–1940 – Criticism and interpretation.
I. Mangum, Bryant, 1943– editor of compilation.
PS3511.I9Z6153 2013
813′.52–dc23 2012033996

ISBN 978-1-107-00919-6 Hardback

Contents

PART VI. THE DEPRESSION ERA (1929–1940)

Illustrations

Contributors

CHRISTOPHER AMES is Professor of English at Washington College. He is the author of *The Life of the Party: Festive Vision in Modern Fiction* and *Movies About the Movies: Hollywood Reflected.* He has published articles on literary modernism, the Hollywood novel, and Woody Allen.

CATHY W. BARKS is Associate Director of the Honors College at the University of Maryland, where she teaches American literature. She is the coeditor of *Dear Scott/Dearest Zelda: The Love Letters of F. Scott and Zelda Fitzgerald.*

RONALD BERMAN is Distinguished Professor of Literature Emeritus, University of California at San Diego. He has been Executive Officer for the District Intelligence Office, FIRST Naval District, and Chairman of the National Endowment for the Humanities. His books include The Great Gatsby *and Modern Times*; The Great Gatsby *and Fitzgerald's World of Ideas*; and *Fitzgerald, Hemingway, and the Twenties.* He has been awarded the Medal of the City of New York.

ANTHONY J. BERRET, S. J., is a member of the English Department at St. Joseph's University, Philadelphia. Author of *Mark Twain and Shakespeare: A Cultural Legacy*, he has written articles on Mark Twain and on music and literature in the works of Toni Morrison and F. Scott Fitzgerald.

ROBERT BEUKA is Professor of English at Bronx Community College, City University of New York. He has published on nineteenth- and twentieth-century American literature, as well as film, popular culture, nature writing, and suburban studies. His first book, *SuburbiaNation* (2004), examined the depiction of American suburbia in fiction and film, and his latest book, *American Icon* (2011), traces the critical reception and cultural impact of Fitzgerald's classic *The Great Gatsby.*

WILLIAM BLAZEK is Senior Lecturer in English at Liverpool Hope University, where he teaches courses on nineteenth- and twentieth-century American and European literature. He has published essays and articles on the work of E. E. Cummings, John Dos Passos, Louise Erdrich, F. Scott Fitzgerald, Ernest Hemingway, Henry James, Herman Melville, and Edith Wharton. He is currently writing a book of themed essays on Wharton and Fitzgerald. A founding coeditor of the *F. Scott Fitzgerald Review*, he has also coedited the essay collections *American Mythologies: New Essays on American Literature* (2005) and *Twenty-First-Century Readings of* Tender Is the Night (2007).

ELISABETH BOUZONVILLER is Associate Professor at Jean Monnet University in St. Etienne, France, where she teaches American literature and civilization. She has published two books on F. Scott Fitzgerald, *Francis Scott Fitzgerald ou la plénitude du silence* and *Francis Scott Fitzgerald, écrivain du déséquilibre*. She is a member of the F. Scott Fitzgerald Society and has published various articles and reviews in the *F. Scott Fitzgerald Review*. She has taken part in several French national radio programs devoted to the Fitzgeralds. She has also contributed to collected works with articles on Fitzgerald and other American novelists such as Ernest Hemingway, William Faulkner, and John Steinbeck. She is currently conducting research and writing on Native American writers, especially Louise Erdrich, whose novels she has dealt with in various recent publications.

JACKSON R. BRYER is Professor Emeritus of English at the University of Maryland and cofounder and president of the F. Scott Fitzgerald Society. Among the books by or about Fitzgerald he has written, edited, or coedited are *Approaches to Teaching Fitzgerald's* The Great Gatsby (2009); *F. Scott Fitzgerald in the Twenty-First Century* (2003); *Dear Scott, Dearest Zelda: The Love Letters of F. Scott and Zelda Fitzgerald* (2002); *New Essays on F. Scott Fitzgerald's Neglected Stories* (1996); *The Critical Reputation of F. Scott Fitzgerald: A Bibliographical Study* (1967, 1984); *F. Scott Fitzgerald: The Critical Reception* (1978); *The Basil and Josephine Stories by F. Scott Fitzgerald* (1973); *Dear Scott/Dear Max: The Fitzgerald-Perkins Correspondence* (1971); and *F. Scott Fitzgerald in His Own Time: A Miscellany* (1971).

DEBORAH CLARKE is Professor of English at Arizona State University, specializing in twentieth-century American fiction. She is the author of *Robbing the Mother: Women in Faulkner* and *Driving Women: Fiction and Automobile Culture in Twentieth-Century America*. She is currently working on a new book project, "Alternative Economies: Credit, Debt, and Barter in 20th Century American Fiction."

GRETCHEN COMBA is Teaching Assistant Professor of English at Virginia Commonwealth University. Her work on William Maxwell has appeared in *Resources for American Literary Study* and *MidAmerica: The Yearbook of the Society for the Study of Midwestern Literature*. Her fiction has appeared in numerous journals, including *Alaska Quarterly Review*, *North American Review*, and *The South Carolina Review*. She is a recipient of the F. Scott Fitzgerald Award for Short Fiction.

KIRK CURNUTT is Professor and Chair of English at Troy University's Montgomery, Alabama, campus. He serves as vice president of the F. Scott Fitzgerald Society and managing editor of the *F. Scott Fitzgerald Review*. His publications include *The Cambridge Introduction to F. Scott Fitzgerald*, the novels *Breathing Out the Ghost* and *Dixie Noir*, and *Brian Wilson*, a volume in Equinox Publishing's Icons of Pop Music series. He is currently at work on a reader's guide to Ernest Hemingway's *To Have and Have Not*, forthcoming from Kent State University Press.

LINDA DE ROCHE is Professor of English and American Studies at Wesley College in Dover, Delaware. She has published numerous articles on American literature, most recently in *Edith Wharton in Context*, as well as books on Willa Cather and F. Scott Fitzgerald. She is currently conducting research for a biography of Mrs. Victor Bruce.

SUZANNE DEL GIZZO is Assistant Professor of English at Chestnut Hill College in Philadelphia. She has written numerous articles, most of them on Ernest Hemingway and F. Scott Fitzgerald, that have appeared in journals such as *Modern Fiction Studies*, the *Hemingway Review*, and the *F. Scott Fitzgerald Review*. She is also coeditor of *Hemingway's* The Garden of Eden*: Twenty-Five Years of Criticism* and *Ernest Hemingway in Context*.

KATHLEEN DROWNE is Associate Professor of English at the Missouri University of Science and Technology in Rolla, Missouri. Her research focuses on the intersection of literature and popular culture in the American 1920s, and her published work includes *Spirits of Defiance: National Prohibition and Jazz Age Literature, 1920–1933* and *The 1920s*. She is currently working on a book, "Flappers of Color: Multiethnic Modern Women in Jazz Age Literature."

RICHARD FINE is Professor of English and Coordinator of the American Studies Program at Virginia Commonwealth University. He is the author of two books about Hollywood and the profession of authorship: *West of Eden: Writers in Hollywood, 1928–1940* and *James M. Cain and the American Authors' Authority.* He is currently at work on a book about the American media and the military during World War II.

EDWARD GILLIN is Professor of English and American Studies at the State University College of New York at Geneseo. His articles on F. Scott Fitzgerald have appeared in the *Fitzgerald Review*, *F. Scott Fitzgerald in the Twenty-First Century*, *F. Scott Fitzgerald: New Perspectives*, the *Journal of Aesthetic Education*, *Resources for American Literary Study*, *The Neglected Short Fiction of F. Scott Fitzgerald*, and the *F. Scott Fitzgerald Newsletter.*

MICHAEL K. GLENDAY is the author of *F. Scott Fitzgerald.* His other publications include *Saul Bellow and the Decline of Humanism* and *Norman Mailer and American Mythologies: Essays on Contemporary Literature* (coedited with William Blazek).

RICHARD GODDEN is Professor of English at the University of California, Irvine. His publications include *Fictions of Capital: The American Novel from James to Mailer, Fictions of Labor: William Faulkner and the South's Long Revolution,* and *William Faulkner: An Economy of Complex Words* (2007). He currently works on the relation between narrative poetics and financial forms in recent American fiction.

STEVEN GOLDLEAF is Professor and Associate Chair of the Department of English at Pace University in New York City, as well as senior editor at Pace University Press. He is the author of *Richard Yates* (with David Castronovo) and of *John O'Hara: The Short Fiction.* He is currently editing a collection of O'Hara's New York stories, collecting a series of memoirs under the title "Only Mostly True," and writing a novel about the death of F. Scott Fitzgerald.

PETER L. HAYS is Professor Emeritus at the English Department of the University of California, Davis. His most recent book is *The Critical Reception of Hemingway's* The Sun Also Rises; he is also a contributor to *Hemingway in Context*, as well as editor of "News and Notes" for the *Fitzgerald Newsletter.*

PEARL JAMES is Assistant Professor in the Department of English at the University of Kentucky. Her interdisciplinary research on American modernism has been published in journal articles and in the collection of essays that she edited for the University of Nebraska entitled *Picture This: World War I Posters and Visual Culture* (2009). She is currently working on a book, "The New Death: World War I and American Modernism."

JOEL KABOT is an MFA candidate at Virginia Commonwealth University. A Fulbright Fellow who will study next year in Ukraine, he is originally from Manlius, New York, a suburb of Syracuse, and is currently working on a novel about regional and ancestral identity in the American South, upstate New York, and Eastern Europe.

HEIDI M. KUNZ is Professor and Chair of the Department of English at Randolph College in Lynchburg, Virginia. She has written numerous articles on literature of the United States, most recently including chapters in *Edith Wharton in Context* and *Scientific Discourses and Cultural Difference.* She is currently at work on a book, "The Mitchell Phenomenon: Celebrity Science and Cultural Memory."

JAROM LYLE MCDONALD is Associate Professor of Humanities Technology at Brigham Young University. He specializes in digital humanities and American literature, having published print and electronic articles on F. Scott Fitzgerald, Emily Dickinson, and other writers. He is the author of *Sports, Narrative, and Nation in the Fiction of F. Scott Fitzgerald.*

PHILIP MCGOWAN is Senior Lecturer in American Literature at The Queen's University of Belfast. He has published on, among others, F. Scott Fitzgerald, Saul Bellow, Nelson Algren, Anne Sexton, and William Maxwell. He is currently completing work on two books, "Reading Las Vegas" and an illustrated life of Dorothy Parker.

BONNIE SHANNON MCMULLEN is the author of many scholarly articles on English and American fiction of the nineteenth and twentieth centuries. Her most recent publications have focused on Edgar Allan Poe, F. Scott Fitzgerald, and Edith Wharton, including a chapter in *Edith Wharton in Context.* She lives in Oxford, England.

BRYANT MANGUM is Professor of English at Virginia Commonwealth University. In addition to *F. Scott Fitzgerald in Context,* he is the editor of Modern Library's *The Best Early Stories of F. Scott Fitzgerald.* He is also the author of *A Fortune Yet: Money in the Art of F. Scott Fitzgerald's*

Short Stories. His essays have appeared in *Resources for American Literary Study*, the *F. Scott Fitzgerald Review*, the *Fitzgerald/Hemingway Annual*, *The Cambridge Companion to F. Scott Fitzgerald*, *New Essays on F. Scott Fitzgerald's Neglected Stories*, and many other books and journals.

LAUREN RULE MAXWELL is Assistant Professor of English and Director of the MAT English Program at The Citadel in Charleston, South Carolina. She has published articles in *Modern Fiction Studies*, *Margaret Atwood Studies*, and the *F. Scott Fitzgerald Review*. Her book "Romantic Revisions in Novels from the Americas" is forthcoming from Purdue University Press.

JAMES H. MEREDITH, Lieutenant Colonel and Professor of English at the U.S. Air Force Academy (ret.), is president of the Ernest Hemingway Foundation and Society and serves on the board of the F. Scott Fitzgerald Society. He is the author of *Understanding the Literature of World War II* and has published articles on Fitzgerald, Hemingway, Stephen Crane, and Andre Dubus, among others. Most recently he has written an essay that will appear in *Ernest Hemingway in Context*.

LINDA PATTERSON MILLER is Professor of English at Penn State Abington and most recently has been appointed as the 2011–12 Penn State Laureate for the Humanities. She publishes in all areas of American literature, but her specialty is the cultural milieu of the American expatriate artists of the 1920s. Her books in this field include *Letters from the Lost Generation* and "Reading Hemingway's *In Our Time*" (forthcoming). She is completing a group biography of the Lost Generation artists on the French Riviera. Miller is head of the editorial board for the *Hemingway Complete Letters Project* (Cambridge University Press), and she continues to serve as a scholarly consultant for public broadcasting projects and museum exhibitions that focus on twentieth-century life and art.

JAMES NAGEL is the Eidson Distinguished Professor of American Literature at the University of Georgia and the president of the Society for the Study of the American Short Story. Early in his career he founded the scholarly journal *Studies in American Fiction* and the widely influential series *Critical Essays on American Literature*, which published 156 volumes of scholarship. Among his twenty-three books are *Stephen Crane and Literary Impressionism*; *Hemingway in Love and War* (which was made into a Hollywood film starring Sandra Bullock); *Hemingway: The Oak Park Legacy*; *The Contemporary American*

Short-Story Cycle; *Anthology of The American Short Story*, published by Houghton Mifflin; *The Blackwell Companion to the American Short Story*, edited with Alfred Bendixen; and the forthcoming "Race and Culture in Stories of New Orleans." He has been a Fulbright Professor as well as a Rockefeller Fellow. He has published some eighty articles in the field and lectured on American literature in fifteen countries.

MICHAEL NOWLIN is Professor of English at the University of Victoria, Canada. Alongside several articles in the field of modern American literature, he is the author of *F. Scott Fitzgerald's Racial Angles and the Business of Literary Greatness* (Palgrave, 2007) and the editor of the Broadview Editions of *The Great Gatsby* (2007) and Edith Wharton's *The Age of Innocence* (2002). He is currently working on a book tentatively titled "Literary Ambition and the African American Novel from Chesnutt to Ellison."

RUTH PRIGOZY is Professor of English at Hofstra University and executive director and cofounder of the F. Scott Fitzgerald Society. She is the author of *F. Scott Fitzgerald: An Illustrated Life* and *The Life of Dick Haymes*. She is editor of *The Great Gatsby* and *This Side of Paradise*, and coeditor of *F. Scott Fitzgerald: New Perspectives* and *F. Scott Fitzgerald in the Twentieth-First Century*. She has also written many articles on Fitzgerald, Hemingway, J. D. Salinger. D. W. Griffith, and Billy Wilder, among many others.

LAURA RATTRAY is Senior Lecturer in American Literature at the University of Hull. Her recent Fitzgerald work includes editing – with William Blazek – *Twenty-First-Century Readings of* Tender Is the Night (Liverpool University Press, 2007) and acting as program director for the Eleventh International F. Scott Fitzgerald Society Conference in Lyon (2011). She is editor of the two-volume *The Unpublished Writings of Edith Wharton* (Pickering and Chatto, 2009), *Edith Wharton's* The Custom of the Country*: A Reassessment* (Pickering and Chatto, 2010), and *Edith Wharton in Context* (Cambridge University Press, 2012). She is currently working on a study of 1930s American fiction.

WALTER RAUBICHECK is Professor of English at Pace University. He recently coauthored *Scripting Hitchcock*, which was nominated for an Edgar Award. He is the coeditor with Ruth Prigozy of *Going My Way: Bing Crosby and American Culture* and has published a number of articles on American authors, among them Fitzgerald, T. S. Eliot, and Walt Whitman. He has also written extensively on film and popular music.

DEBORAH DAVIS SCHLACKS is Professor of English at the University of Wisconsin-Superior. She is the author of *American Dream Visions: Chaucer's Surprising Influence on F. Scott Fitzgerald* (Peter Lang, 1994) and "Echoes of the Middle Ages: Teaching the Medieval in *The Great Gatsby*," a chapter of *Approaches to Teaching Fitzgerald's* The Great Gatsby, ed. Jackson R. Bryer and Nancy P. VanArsdale (Modern Language Association, 2009).

GAIL D. SINCLAIR is Executive Director and Scholar in Residence of Winter Park Institute at Rollins College. Her publications include coediting *Key West Hemingway: A Reassessment* (2009), essays in *Approaches to Teaching Fitzgerald's* The Great Gatsby (2009), and *Teaching Hemingway's* A Farewell to Arms (2008). She is currently on the board of directors for the F. Scott Fitzgerald Society and the Ernest Hemingway Foundation and Society.

ROBERT SKLAR was Professor Emeritus in New York University's Department of Cinema Studies until his death on July 2, 2011. He was author of F. *Scott Fitzgerald: The Last Laocoön* (1967) and *Movie Made America: A Cultural History of American Movies* (1975), among numerous other books and articles in the field of Fitzgerald studies and cinema studies. He completed work on "Heroes and Hollywood," his essay in this volume, in June 2011.

LINDA WAGNER-MARTIN has been Hanes Professor of English and Comparative Literature at the University of North Carolina at Chapel Hill since 1988; she recently retired. The recipient of Guggenheim, Rockefeller, National Endowment for the Humanities, and other fellowships, she received the Hubbell Medal for lifetime work in American literature in 2011. She wrote several books on Wharton for the Twayne series and edited *The Portable Edith Wharton* for Penguin (2003). Her biographies include books on Zelda Fitzgerald, Sylvia Plath, Gertrude Stein, Barbara Kingsolver, and Ernest Hemingway.

JAMES L. W. WEST III is Edwin Erle Sparks Professor of English at Pennsylvania State University. He is a biographer, book historian, and scholarly editor. Two recent books, both published by Random House, are *William Styron: A Life* (1998) and *The Perfect Hour: The Romance of F. Scott Fitzgerald and Ginevra King* (2005). West has held fellowships from the Guggenheim Foundation, the National Humanities Center, and NEH. He has had Fulbright appointments in England (at Cambridge University) and in Belgium (at the Université de Liège), and he has been a visiting Fellow at the American Academy in Rome. He is the general editor of the Cambridge Fitzgerald Edition; his edition of *Trimalchio: An Early Version of* The Great Gatsby appeared in 2000.

DONI M. WILSON is Associate Professor of English at Houston Baptist University as well as an adjunct faculty member of the Cameron School of Business MBA program at the University of Saint Thomas in Houston, Texas. She has published on American Transcendentalism and American Modernism and is writing "Understanding Mary Oliver" for the University of South Carolina Press.

Preface

F. Scott Fitzgerald, defining as he did the Jazz Age, and creating and chronicling as he did the flapper in fiction, has become himself an important context virtually inseparable from two of the most exciting, complex, and turbulent eras in American history: The Jazz Age and the Great Depression. From the moment of his marriage to Zelda Sayre in 1920, Scott and Zelda became linked in the public consciousness as an idealized image of the glittering Jazz Age couple, and Fitzgerald's writings came to represent postcards from the heart of the popular culture that had, often with the Fitzgeralds' help, constructed the image. As the Roaring Twenties moved toward the stock market crash of 1929 and the Great Depression that followed, the Fitzgeralds, too, faded for a time from the public eye, riding the crest of the mid-decade wave of prosperity and seeking, as did many Americans, some personal "Carnival by the Sea," then drifting aimlessly as they awaited a change for the better following the collapse of the stock market. Fitzgerald had sent public messages from time to time from Europe, where the Fitzgeralds mostly were, and from a variety of spots in America, to which they sometimes returned, in the form of his popular magazine stories of the mid- to late 1920s that contained tales of exotically decadent, wandering expatriates in Europe. The Fitzgeralds did not emerge again as cultural emblems until the publication of Zelda's *Save Me the Waltz* in 1932 and Scott's *Tender Is the Night* in 1934. Both novels told tales of personal failure, depression, and alcoholism, and when Scott and Zelda reentered the popular imagination it was as symbols of post-Crash loss and regret. As a writer Fitzgerald became a generational spokesman who wrote with what he himself called "the authority of failure."[1] In the end, of course, he spoke with an insider's knowledge from Hollywood, where so many writers went to get rich quick or, as in Fitzgerald's case, to die, even as he eulogized its Golden Age in the incomplete *The Last Tycoon*.

In the cases of both the Jazz Age and Depression eras Fitzgerald internalized and embodied, both reflected and shaped as well as recorded, many aspects of the cultural and intellectual contexts of his time, crossing as he did many social and geographical boundaries in the process. Part of his success as a writer for "the youth of his own generation, the critics of the next and the schoolmaster of ever afterwards,"[2] as he phrased it, came from his gift of being able to capture with absolute accuracy the subtleties within a wide variety of social and cultural contexts. In John O'Hara's words, Fitzgerald was a writer who would "come right out and say Locomobile instead of high-powered car, Shanley's instead of gay cabaret, and George, instead of François, the *chasseur* at the Paris Ritz. These touches guaranteed that the writer knew what he was talking about."[3] Part of the secret of what Malcolm Cowley labeled Fitzgerald's "double vision" lies in his ability to enter many contexts with apparent ease, rendering them authentic, while at the same time retaining the capacity to see them objectively and often critically – in what Fitzgerald referred to when he characterized the "test of a first-rate intelligence" as "the ability to hold two opposed ideas in the mind at the same time, and still retain the ability to function" (*Crack-Up* 69). Fitzgerald himself, in fact, possessed the ability to hold in his mind many observed and imagined worlds in which the social and cultural contexts differed radically from each other. Again, as John O'Hara notes, he was "a sort of class secretary, except that the class included – at my guess 50,000 men and women" (O'Hara xi). *F. Scott Fitzgerald in Context* addresses the social, historical, and cultural contexts that are a part of Fitzgerald's actual and fictional worlds, but it also addresses other contexts that were very much a part of the cultures of the Jazz Age and Depression eras, some of them signaled rather loudly, if in passing, in Fitzgerald's writings, and many brought into high relief by their omission.

There has long been popular interest in the Jazz Age and Depression eras in America, an interest evident early in Frederick Lewis Allen's *Only Yesterday: An Informal History of the Nineteen-Twenties*[4] and in his history of the 1930s, *Since Yesterday: The Nineteen-Thirties in America*.[5] More recently, fascination with the two decades has intensified, as is evident in the many cultural studies and popular culture articles and books on the subject, among them, Kate Drowne and Patrick Huber's 2004 *American Popular Culture through History: The 1920s*,[6] which includes comprehensive lists and discussions of many of the important contexts of the Jazz Age. The popular interest in historical and cultural contexts in Fitzgerald's writing has been intense at least since the beginning of the Fitzgerald Revival in the early 1950s, but especially so since the mid-1970s. In response to a question as to why this has been true, Fitzgerald's daughter, Scottie, responded in this way in a 1974 article in *Family Circle*: "People read him now for clues and guidelines, as if by understanding him and his beautiful and damned period, they could see more clearly what's wrong" – a comment that addressed her own belief that World War II had taken away an earlier sense of idealism that had existed in America, a lost idealism the causes of which, readers believed, Fitzgerald might help them understand.[7]

Until a few years ago, the study of Fitzgerald, to the degree that it had concerned itself with contexts, had tended to work from the inside of Fitzgerald's writings outward toward a construction of cultural contexts that could be inferred from his work. More recently, with *The Cambridge Companion to F. Scott Fitzgerald*, edited by Ruth Prigozy,[8] and Oxford's *A Historical Guide to F. Scott Fitzgerald*, edited by Kirk Curnutt,[9] a solid foundation has been established for considering from the outside inward many of the social, historical, and cultural contexts of Fitzgerald's world, both those alluded to in his writings and those most notable in their omission. *F. Scott Fitzgerald in Context* contains careful analyses by established scholars of many, if not most, of the important social, historical, and cultural contexts of Fitzgerald's time viewed through the window of the twenty-first century. The volume is divided into six sections. The first two sections, Life and Works and An Author's Formation, are foundational: their purpose is not only to survey the critical and biographical scholarship that has been published on Fitzgerald's life and works, but also to examine how and why it has evolved as it has in relationship to critical and cultural trends. The following four sections – Jazz Age Literary and Artistic Movements, Historical and Social Contexts in the Jazz Age, Popular and Material Culture in the Jazz Age, and The Depression Era – examine elements of both high culture (in section III) and popular culture (in sections IV, V, and VI) in order to identify and analyze those contexts of the Jazz Age and Depression eras that have particular relevance to Fitzgerald's work. As one of the most comprehensive collections of its kind, *F. Scott Fitzgerald in Context* is an indispensable resource for Fitzgerald scholars, as well as for instructors and graduate or advanced undergraduate students conducting research on Fitzgerald and/or the literature and culture of the Jazz Age and Depression eras.

I am deeply indebted to Ray Ryan of Cambridge University Press for his encouragement and continuing support from the beginning of *F. Scott Fitzgerald in Context* to the end. This volume would not have come into existence without his steady guidance and direction. I also want to thank Louis Gulino for his patience, generosity, and grace in responding to my many queries as this volume moved from typescript into production. I greatly appreciate the guidance of Bindu Vinod at Newgen, and I am especially grateful for the sharp editorial eye and vigilance of John Edwards of PETT Fox, Inc. From the moment that the idea for this volume was conceived, I received invaluable suggestions and help from these colleagues and friends: James L. W. West III, Kirk Curnutt, Heidi Kunz, Kate Drowne, Michael Nowlin, Laura Rattray, Cathy Barks, Suzanne del Gizzo, James Meredith, Catherine Ingrassia, Susann Cokal, Patrick Vickers, Judith Baughman, Richard Layman, Marcel Cornis-Pope, and Richard Fine. For help with the images in this volume I am indebted to Maurice Duke; and for great assistance in the final stages of this project, I am indebted to Heather Fox. And as is true for every Fitzgerald project I have ever been involved in – this one especially – I have relied on the wisdom, advice, and experience of Ruth Prigozy and Jackson R. Bryer.

From the beginning of my work I have received the generous support of Terry Oggel, former chair of the English Department of Virginia Commonwealth University, and I am grateful to him for his encouragement. Margret Vopel of the English Department and Katherine Bassard, chair of the department, have provided much appreciated assistance in the preparation of this volume. James Coleman, Dean of the College of Humanities and Sciences at Virginia Commonwealth University, has been generous and encouraging during the preparation of *F. Scott Fitzgerald in Context*, and I am grateful for his ongoing support. I have been graced throughout by the assistance of Joel Kabot, whose chapter is contained in the volume, and who has come behind me on every line finding, more often than not, things that I had overlooked. Gretchen Comba, my colleague at Virginia Commonwealth University, has given me her support on this project from the beginning. She has constructed the chronology for this volume and has brought her sharp editorial eye to bear on every chapter. I am extraordinarily grateful to her for her careful and untiring work with me on this book. Robert Sklar (1936–2011), who contributed the final chapter, was an early inspiration to me in my study of Fitzgerald's work. And finally, in virtually every chapter I was reminded of the extraordinary body of scholarship on Fitzgerald of my mentor, Matthew J. Bruccoli (1931–2008). I am grateful for the love of Fitzgerald that he passed on to me. This volume is dedicated to Robert Sklar and Matthew J. Bruccoli.

NOTES

1 E. Wilson (ed.), *The Crack-Up* (New York: New Directions, 1945), 93–242. See 81. Subsequent references to this work are included in the text.
2 See F. S. Fitzgerald, "The Author's Apology" in M. J. Bruccoli, *F. Scott Fitzgerald: A Descriptive Bibliography*, rev. edn. (Pittsburgh, PA: University of Pittsburgh Press, 1987), 19.
3 J. O'Hara, "Introduction" in *The Portable F. Scott Fitzgerald*, selected by Dorothy Parker (New York: Viking, 1945), xii. Subsequent references to this work are included in the text.
4 F. L. Allen, *Only Yesterday: An Informal History of the Nineteen-Twenties* (New York: Harper & Row, 1957 [1931]).
5 F. L. Allen, *Since Yesterday: The Nineteen-Thirties in America* (New York: Bantam, 1961 [1939]).
6 K. Drowne and P. Huber, *American Popular Culture through History: The 1920s* (Westport, CT: Greenwood, 2004).
7 S. F. Smith, "Notes About My Now-Famous Father," *Family Circle* 84 (May 1974), 118–120. See 120.
8 R. Prigozy (ed.), *The Cambridge Companion to F. Scott Fitzgerald* (Cambridge: Cambridge University Press, 2002).
9 K. Curnutt (ed.), *A Historical Guide to F. Scott Fitzgerald* (New York: Oxford University Press, 2004).

Picture Acknowledgments

The editor would like to thank the following libraries, historical societies, collections, estates, and individuals for assistance with the images reproduced in this volume: F. Scott Fitzgerald Papers, Manuscripts Division, Department of Rare Books and Special Collections of Princeton University Library; Matthew J. and Arlyn F. Bruccoli Collection of Thomas Cooper Library of the University of South Carolina; Alderman Library of the University of Virginia; Minnesota Historical Society; estate of Sheilah Graham Westbrook; and Mark A. Vieira and the Starlight Studio of Los Angeles, California.

Abbreviations

PRIMARY SOURCE ABBREVIATIONS

ASYM — *All the Sad Young Men*, ed. James L. W. West III (New York: Cambridge University Press, 2007)

B&J — *The Basil, Josephine, and Gwen Stories*, ed. James L. W. West III (New York: Cambridge University Press, 2009)

B&D — *The Beautiful and Damned*, ed. James L. W. West III (New York: Cambridge University Press, 2008)

CU — *The Crack-Up*, ed. Edmund Wilson (New York: New Directions, 1945)

F&P — *Flappers and Philosophers*, ed. James L. W. West III (New York: Cambridge University Press, 2000)

FSFL — *F. Scott Fitzgerald's Ledger: A Facsimile*, ed. Matthew J. Bruccoli (Washington: Bruccoli Clark/NCR, 1973)

GG — *The Great Gatsby*, ed. Matthew J. Bruccoli (New York: Cambridge University Press, 1991)

LD — *The Lost Decade: Short Stories from "Esquire," 1936–1941*, ed. James L. W. West III (New York: Cambridge University Press, 2008)

LT — *The Love of the Last Tycoon: A Western*, ed. Matthew J. Bruccoli (New York: Cambridge University Press, 1993)

MLC — *My Lost City: Personal Essays, 1920–1940*, ed. James L. W. West III (New York: Cambridge University Press, 2005)

N — *The Notebooks of F. Scott Fitzgerald*, ed. Matthew J. Bruccoli (New York: Harcourt Brace Jovanovich/Bruccoli Clark, 1978)

P — *The Price Was High: The Last Uncollected Stories of F. Scott Fitzgerald*, ed. Matthew J. Bruccoli (New York: Harcourt Brace Jovanovich/Bruccoli Clark, 1979)

S	*The Short Stories of F. Scott Fitzgerald*, ed. Matthew J. Bruccoli (New York: Charles Scribner's Sons, 1989)
S&G	*Spires and Gargoyles: Early Writings, 1909–1919*, ed. James L. W. West III (New York: Cambridge University Press, 2010)
T	*Trimalchio: An Early Version of "The Great Gatsby,"* ed. James L. W. West III (New York: Cambridge University Press, 2000)
TAR	*Taps at Reveille* (New York: Charles Scribner's Sons, 1935)
TITN	*Tender Is the Night* (New York: Charles Scribner's Sons, 1934)
TJA	*Tales of the Jazz Age*, ed. James L. W. West III (New York: Cambridge University Press, 2002)
TSOP	*This Side of Paradise*, ed. James L. W. West III (New York: Cambridge University Press, 1995)

LETTERS VOLUMES ABBREVIATIONS

AE	*As Ever, Scott Fitz–: Letters Between F. Scott Fitzgerald and His Literary Agent Harold Ober, 1919–1940,* ed. Matthew J. Bruccoli (Philadelphia: J. B. Lippincott, 1972)
C	*Correspondence of F. Scott Fitzgerald*, eds. Matthew J. Bruccoli and Margaret M. Duggan (New York: Random House, 1980)
S&M	*Dear Scott/Dear Max: The Fitzgerald-Perkins Correspondence,* eds. John Kuehl and Jackson R. Bryer (New York: Charles Scribner's Sons, 1971)
S&Z	*Dear Scott, Dearest Zelda: The Love Letters of F. Scott and Zelda Fitzgerald*, eds. Jackson R. Bryer and Cathy W. Barks (New York: St. Martin's, 2002)
L	*The Letters of F. Scott Fitzgerald*, ed. Andrew Turnbull (New York: Charles Scribner's Sons, 1963)
LL	*F. Scott Fitzgerald: A Life in Letters*, ed. Matthew J. Bruccoli (New York: Charles Scribner's Sons, 1994)
LTD	*Letters to His Daughter,* ed. Andrew Turnbull (New York: Charles Scribner's Sons, 1965)

Fitzgerald was a notoriously bad speller. Quotations in this volume taken from Fitzgerald's letters and the *Ledger* preserve his misspellings without signaling them with the notation 'sic.' There are no silent emendations of quotations from Fitzgerald's letters or the *Ledger*.

Chronology

Gretchen Comba

This chronology situates F. Scott Fitzgerald's personal and professional life within a broader historical, political, cultural, literary, and artistic context. When both biographical and contextual details are represented in a single entry marked by year, the biographical details related to Fitzgerald are listed first and are followed by the contextual details.[1]

1896 Francis Scott Key Fitzgerald is born to Edward and Mary ("Mollie") McQuillan Fitzgerald on September 24 in St. Paul, Minnesota.

The National Association of Colored Women is formed.

1898 The Fitzgeralds move to Buffalo, New York, where Edward takes a job with Proctor & Gamble.

1900 Zelda Sayre is born to Anthony D. and Minnie Machen Sayre on July 24 in Montgomery, Alabama.

A hurricane kills more than 6,000 people in Galveston, Texas. William McKinley is elected president. Joseph Conrad's *Lord Jim* is published. Theodore Dreiser's *Sister Carrie* is published. Sigmund Freud's *The Interpretation of Dreams* is published.

1901 Edward's job takes the family to Syracuse, New York. Annabel Fitzgerald, sister of Fitzgerald, is born in Syracuse. William McKinley is assassinated. Theodore Roosevelt assumes presidency. Alabama adopts a constitution with provisions to bar African Americans from voting.

1902 Conrad's *Heart of Darkness* is published. Henry James's *The Wings of the Dove* is published.

1903 The Fitzgeralds return to Buffalo. Theodore Roosevelt is elected president. W. E. B. DuBois' *The Souls of Black Folk: Essays and Sketches* is published. James's *The Golden Bowl* is published. Jack London's *The Call of the Wild* is published. The film *The Great Train Robbery* is released.

1904 Conrad's *Nostromo* is published.

1905 Mary Harris ("Mother") Jones helps found the Industrial Works of the World, a prominent U.S. labor organization. Edith Wharton's *The House of Mirth* is published.

1906 An earthquake and fire kill more than 3,000 people in San Francisco, California. Emma Goldman publishes the first issue of *Mother Earth*. A race riot erupts in Atlanta, Georgia, and the city is placed under martial law.

1907 A downturn in the stock market touches off the Panic of 1907. Henry Adams's *The Education of Henry Adams* is published.

1908 The Fitzgeralds return to St. Paul. Fitzgerald enrolls in the St. Paul Academy and begins to write plays and short stories.

King Leopold II is forced to relinquish control of the Congo Free State. William Howard Taft is elected president. A race riot occurs in Springfield, Illinois. The Model T is introduced by the Ford Motor Company. E. M. Forster's *A Room with a View* is published.

1909 The National Association for the Advancement of Colored People is founded. Gertrude Stein's *Three Lives* is published.

1910 The Mexican Revolution begins after Francisco Madero calls for an end to the Díaz regime. International Women's Day is established. DuBois publishes the first issue of *Crisis*. Forster's *Howards End* is published.

1911 Fitzgerald enrolls in the Newman School in Hackensack, New Jersey. Dreiser's *Jennie Gerhardt* is published. Wharton's *Ethan Frome* is published.

1912 Fitzgerald meets Father Cyril Sigourney Webster Fay and Shane Leslie. The Bread and Roses Strike occurs in Lawrence, Massachusetts. Woodrow Wilson is elected president.

1913 Fitzgerald enters Princeton University as a member of the class of 1917. He meets Edmund Wilson and John Peale Bishop.

More than 8,000 people march in Washington, D.C., for women's suffrage. Leo Frank is tried and convicted, and later lynched, in Atlanta. The Anti-Defamation League is formed. Henry Ford introduces the assembly-line model of production. Willa Cather's *O Pioneers!* is published. The Armory Show opens in New York City.

1914 World War I begins when Archduke Ferdinand of Austria is assassinated in Sarajevo. Margaret Sanger publishes the first issue of *Woman Rebel*. The Ludlow Massacre occurs in Ludlow, Colorado. Edgar Rice Burroughs's *Tarzan of the Apes* is published.

1915 Fitzgerald meets Ginevra King. The *Nassau Literary Magazine* publishes "The Ordeal," which is later revised and published as "Benediction" in the *Smart Set* in 1919. Fitzgerald drops out of Princeton.

T. S. Eliot's "The Love Song of J. Alfred Prufrock" is published. Franz Kafka's "The Metamorphosis" is published. The film *The Birth of a Nation* is released.

1916 Fitzgerald returns to Princeton as a member of the class of 1918.

Pancho Villa raids Columbus, New Mexico. Woodrow Wilson is reelected. James Joyce's *A Portrait of the Artist as a Young Man* is published. The Cabaret Voltaire opens in Zurich.

1917 Fitzgerald receives commission as infantry second lieutenant in the U.S. Army. He begins "The Romantic Egotist," an early draft of *This Side of Paradise*, while stationed in Fort Leavenworth, Kansas.

Czar Nicholas II is overthrown in the Russian Revolution. The United States enters World War I. Margaret Sanger publishes the first issue of the *Birth Control Review*.

1918 While stationed at Camp Sheridan, Fitzgerald meets Zelda Sayre of Montgomery, Alabama. Charles Scribner's Sons rejects "The Romantic Egotist." Scribners editor Maxwell Perkins encourages Fitzgerald to revise the manuscript and resubmit it.

In 1918 and 1919, the Spanish influenza pandemic kills between 50 million and 100 million people worldwide. World War I ends with Germany's surrender. Woodrow Wilson proposes the formation of the League of Nations. Cather's *My Ántonia* is published.

1919 Fitzgerald is discharged from the army. He moves to New York, where he works for the Barron Collier advertising agency. Zelda breaks their engagement. Fitzgerald returns to St. Paul, where he rewrites "The Romantic Egotist." The *Smart Set* publishes "Babes in the Woods." Scribners accepts "The Romantic Egotist," now titled *This Side of Paradise*. Fitzgerald becomes a client of Harold Ober at the Paul Revere

Reynolds Agency. The *Saturday Evening Post* buys "Head and Shoulders."

The Treaty of Versailles is signed. Congress passes the Eighteenth Amendment, prohibiting the manufacture, sale, and transportation of intoxicating liquors. May Day Riots erupt in a number of U.S. cities, including Boston, Cleveland, and New York. A race riot erupts in Chicago, Illinois. Emma Goldman is deported. The Chicago Black Sox scandal occurs. Sherwood Anderson's *Winesburg, Ohio* is published.

1920 On April 3, Fitzgerald marries Zelda Sayre in New York City. Scribners publishes *This Side of Paradise.* Scribners publishes *Flappers and Philosophers.* Fitzgerald begins work on *The Beautiful and Damned.*

The American Civil Liberties Union is established. The Department of Justice arrests 4,000 suspected Communists and radicals. Congress passes the Nineteenth Amendment, which grants women the right to vote. Warren G. Harding is elected president. Wharton's *The Age of Innocence* is published.

1921 The Fitzgeralds travel to Europe. Upon their return, they rent a house at Dellwood, White Bear Lake in Minnesota. On October 26, Frances Scott ("Scottie") Fitzgerald is born in St. Paul. Fitzgerald finishes *The Beautiful and Damned.*

A race riot erupts in Tulsa, Oklahoma. The Second International Congress of Eugenics is held in New York City; during the Congress, the Eugenics Committee of the U.S.A. (later the American Eugenics Society) is formed. The American Birth Control League is founded. The films *The Kid* and *The Sheik* are released.

1922 The Fitzgeralds rent a house in Great Neck, Long Island, New York. Fitzgerald develops a friendship with Ring Lardner. Scribners publishes *The Beautiful and Damned* and *Tales of the Jazz Age.*

Benito Mussolini and the Fascist Party rise to power in Italy. Eliot's *The Waste Land* is published. Joyce's *Ulysses* is published. Emily Post's *Etiquette in Society, in Business, in Politics and at Home* is published.

1923 Scribners publishes *The Vegetable.* The play fails at a tryout in Atlantic City, New Jersey.

Warren G. Harding dies in office. Calvin Coolidge assumes presidency. The National Women's Party proposes the Lucretia Mott Amendment. Jean Toomer's *Cane* is published.

1924 The Fitzgeralds travel to Paris, and then the French Riviera. Zelda has an affair with French aviator Edouard Jozan. The Fitzgeralds meet Gerald and Sara Murphy at Cap d'Antibes. Fitzgerald writes *The Great Gatsby.*

V. I. Lenin dies. Joseph Stalin rises to power in the USSR. Congress passes the National Origins Act, which restricts the annual number of European immigrants and prohibits all Asian immigration. Congress passes the Indian Citizen Act. Calvin Coolidge is elected president. Leopold and Loeb are sentenced to life imprisonment. Forster's *A Passage to India* is published. The Bureau for Surrealist Research opens in Paris.

1925 The Fitzgeralds move to Paris. Fitzgerald meets Ernest Hemingway at the Dingo Bar. Scribners publishes *The Great Gatsby.* Fitzgerald plans Francis Melarky version of *Tender Is the Night.*

The Ku Klux Klan holds a rally in Washington, D.C. The *Tennessee v. Scopes* trial takes place in Dayton, Tennessee, culminating in Scopes's conviction. Dreiser's *An American Tragedy* is published. Hemingway's *In Our Time* is published. Alain Locke's anthology *The New Negro* is published. The Decorative Art Exhibition is held in Paris.

1926 The Fitzgeralds spend the summer on the Riviera with Gerald and Sara Murphy and with Hemingway and his first wife, Hadley Richardson. Scribners publishes *All the Sad Young Men.*

Hemingway's *The Sun Also Rises* is published. Langston Hughes's *The Weary Blues* is published.

1927 The Fitzgeralds go to Hollywood. They meet Lois Moran. The Fitzgeralds move to "Ellerslie" near Wilmington, Delaware, where Zelda studies ballet.

Following the Shanghai Massacre, the Chinese Civil War begins. Charles Lindbergh flies solo across the Atlantic Ocean. The *Buck v. Bell* case is decided, and Virginia's right to sterilize a poverty-stricken woman involuntarily is upheld. Sacco and Vanzetti are executed in Massachusetts. Virginia Woolf's *To the Lighthouse* is published. The films *The General* and *It* are released.

1928 The Fitzgeralds move to Paris, where Zelda studies ballet under Lubov Egorova of the Ballets Russes, and then return to the United States.

Herbert Hoover is elected president. Babe Ruth bats .625 for the New York Yankees in the World Series.

1929 The Fitzgeralds return to Europe.

The U.S. stock market crashes. The St. Valentine's Day Massacre occurs in Chicago. William Faulkner's *The Sound and the Fury* is published. Hemingway's *A Farewell to Arms* is published. Thomas Wolfe's *Look Homeward, Angel* is published. Woolf's *A Room of One's Own* is published.

1930 Zelda suffers a nervous breakdown. She is admitted to the Malmaison Clinic outside Paris; then the Val-Mont Clinic in Glion, Switzerland; and then the Prangins Clinic in Nyon, Switzerland.

John Dos Passos's *42nd Parallel* is published. Faulkner's *As I Lay Dying* is published. The Colonial Exhibition is held in Paris. The film *All Quiet on the Western Front* is released.

1931 Fitzgerald's father dies. Zelda is released from the Prangins Clinic. The Fitzgeralds return to Montgomery, Alabama. Fitzgerald returns to Hollywood in order to make money in the motion picture industry. The *Saturday Evening Post* publishes "Babylon Revisited," which would become Fitzgerald's most widely anthologized, read, and studied short story.

Hoover signs bill making "The Star-Spangled Banner" the national anthem. Pearl S. Buck's *The Good Earth* is published. Henry Miller's *Tropic of Cancer* is published. The films *Dracula*, *Frankenstein*, and *Svengali* are released.

1932 Zelda enters the Phipps Clinic in Baltimore, where she writes *Save Me the Waltz.* Fitzgerald lives in Towson, a town outside Baltimore. Zelda is discharged from the Phipps Clinic. Scribners publishes *Save Me the Waltz.*

Mahatma Gandhi begins his nonviolent campaigns for the poverty-stricken. Franklin Delano Roosevelt is elected president. The Lindberghs' son is kidnapped and murdered. Amelia Earhart flies solo across the Atlantic Ocean. Dos Passos's *Nineteen-Nineteen* is published. Faulkner's *Light in August* is published. The film *Tarzan the Ape Man* is released.

1933 Zelda's play *Scandalabra* opens to poor reviews in Baltimore.

Adolf Hitler and the Nazi Party rise to power in Germany. Congress passes the Twenty-First Amendment, which repeals Prohibition. The NAACP unsuccessfully sues the University of North Carolina on behalf of Thomas Hocutt. Stein's *The Autobiography of Alice B. Tolkas* is published. Nathanael West's *Miss Lonelyhearts* is published. The films *42nd Street*, *Gold Diggers of 1933*, and *King Kong* are released.

1934 Zelda returns to the Phipps Clinic, then moves to Craig House in Beacon, New York, and then transfers to Sheppard-Pratt Hospital outside Baltimore. Scribners publishes *Tender Is the Night*.

John O'Hara's *Appointment in Samara* is published. The films *Babes in Toyland* and *It Happened One Night* are released.

1935 Scribners publishes *Taps at Reveille*. Fitzgerald, while staying at a hotel in Hendersonville, North Carolina, writes "The Crack-Up," the first of three confessional articles that appear in *Esquire* in consecutive months the following year.

1936 Zelda enters Highland Hospital in Asheville, North Carolina. Fitzgerald's mother dies.

The Spanish Civil War begins with a military uprising against the Popular Front government. Roosevelt is reelected. Djuna Barnes's *Nightwood* is published. Faulkner's *Absalom, Absalom!* is published. Margaret Mitchell's *Gone with the Wind* is published.

1937 Fitzgerald returns to Hollywood, where he meets Sheilah Graham. He works under a six-month contract with Metro-Goldwyn-Mayer.

Zora Neale Hurston's *Their Eyes Were Watching God* is published. Steinbeck's *Of Mice and Men* is published.

1938 Scottie enters Vassar. Metro-Goldwyn-Mayer does not renew Fitzgerald's contract.

Joe Louis defeats Max Schmeling.

1939 Fitzgerald travels to Dartmouth College with Budd Schulberg to work on the film *Winter Carnival*. He is fired for drunkenness and then hospitalized in New York City. Fitzgerald's relationship with Harold Ober ends. In Hollywood, he begins work on *The Last Tycoon*.

World War II begins when Germany invades Poland. The NAACP Legal Defense and Education Fund is organized.

West's *The Day of the Locust* is published. Steinbeck's *The Grapes of Wrath* is published. The films *Gone with the Wind*, *The Hunchback of Notre Dame*, and *The Wizard of Oz* are released.

1940 Zelda is released from Highland Hospital and returns to Montgomery. Fitzgerald dies of a heart attack in Sheilah Graham's apartment in Hollywood on December 21.

Roosevelt wins third presidential term. Hemingway's *For Whom the Bell Tolls* is published. Richard Wright's *Native Son* is published.

1941 Scribners publishes the unfinished novel *The Last Tycoon* in a volume together with *The Great Gatsby* and selected short stories.

The Nazi plan known as "The Final Solution" begins. Japan bombs Pearl Harbor and the United States enters World War II. James Agee's *Now Let Us Praise Famous Men* is published.

1942 Roosevelt signs Executive Order 9066, authorizing the internment of Japanese and Japanese Americans on the Pacific Coast and in Hawaii. Albert Camus' *The Stranger* is published.

1944 Roosevelt wins fourth presidential term.

1945 Edmund Wilson edits and publishes *The Crack-Up*, in effect inaugurating the Fitzgerald revival.

Roosevelt dies in office. Harry S. Truman assumes presidency. The United States drops atomic bombs on Hiroshima and Nagasaki. World War II ends with Germany's and Japan's surrender.

1947 India wins freedom from British rule and is partitioned.

Jackie Robinson plays for the Brooklyn Dodgers.

1948 Zelda dies in a fire at Highland Hospital on March 10.

NOTE

1 In the biographical entries, selected details related to Fitzgerald's personal life (listed chronologically) appear first and are followed by selected details related to his professional life (listed chronologically). In the contextual entries, selected details appear in the following order: global historical events; U.S. historical events (listed chronologically); U.S. political events (listed chronologically); U.S. cultural events (listed chronologically); European and U.S. publications (listed alphabetically by author); European and U.S. art events and openings; U.S. film releases (listed alphabetically by title).

PART I

Life and Works (1896–Present)

Figure 1.1. F. Scott Fitzgerald, study by Gordon Bryant (*Shadowland*, January 1921).

I

Biography

Cathy W. Barks

Fitzgerald (Figure 1.1.) participated unreservedly in the world he wrote about. He saw his life as a vivid example of American aspirational themes and as representative of a turning point in American history, the extreme prosperity and social changes of the 1920s followed by the Crash of 1929. In attaching himself so seamlessly to America's grand mythology and depicting that mythology's allure and corruption in his fiction, the link between life and work is not only appropriate; it is also key.[1]

Born in St. Paul, Minnesota, in 1896 to an Irish-Catholic family, Fitzgerald was named after a famous distant cousin, Francis Scott Key, author of "The Star-Spangled Banner." His father's inability to earn a reliable income caused the family to move around during Fitzgerald's childhood, first to Buffalo, then Syracuse, then back to Buffalo, and finally back to St. Paul, where they would remain. The Summit Hill neighborhood in which he grew up included St. Paul's social elite. Fitzgerald's family, by contrast, once upper middle class, was now a family in decline, moving from one lackluster rental property to another while his classmates lived seemingly charmed lives in charmed houses that carried their family names. Although his mother's inheritance provided the family with a comfortable life, Fitzgerald knew he had no family name or money to back him, and to compensate, he became an expert observer of markers of social class: differences in manners, taste, speech, and whether one projected confidence or insecurity. As Scott Donaldson argues in his biography of Fitzgerald, "he was driven to please other people," and "he tried to prove his worth by exercising his charm."[2]

Like most Americans, Fitzgerald believed in self-improvement, but he also believed that early experiences determined the fundamentals of character. In a letter to the *Princeton Alumni Weekly* in 1932, Fitzgerald expressed his conviction that the "salient points of character" were "*fixed by the age of twelve*," and that "the deeper matters of whether [a person is] weak or strong, strict or easy with himself, brave or timid" were "arranged in the home, almost in the nursery" (qtd. in Donaldson, 179; emphasis added). Andrew Turnbull's poignant memoir/biography, *Scott Fitzgerald*, provides an insightful rendering of two of Fitzgerald's childhood memories that seem to have been formative. Twelve is exactly the age Fitzgerald was when his father, Edward, lost his job with Procter & Gamble, and he vividly remembered how traumatic this event was for him. "I felt that disaster had come to us," Fitzgerald recalled: "'Dear God,' I prayed, 'please don't let us go to the poorhouse.'" He remembered his father had left home that morning "comparatively young" and "full of confidence" and had returned "a completely broken man."[3] In the same vein, Fitzgerald recalled an even earlier memory about a "nursery book" depicting a fight between "large animals, like the elephant" and "small animals, like the fox." Even though the small animals were winning the battle at first, the large animals eventually overpowered them. Fitzgerald's sympathies were with the fox. "I wonder if even then," he said, "I had a sense of the wearing down power of big, respectable people. I can almost weep now when I think of that poor fox." Fitzgerald believed that this story was "one of the big sensations" of his life, and he remembered how it had filled him "with the saddest most yearning emotion" (Turnbull 14). Fitzgerald's father, a kind, well-mannered but defeated man, surely seemed to him like one of the small foxes, and being his father's son put the younger Fitzgerald in a precarious situation from the beginning.

Whether Fitzgerald's memory was actual or imagined, it nevertheless provides a basis for understanding his ambivalence about success. Although Fitzgerald always dreamed of being wildly successful, and in his early twenties realized that dream, it was the story of failure, not success, that appealed to him as a writer. Fitzgerald was as suspicious of making it big as he was desirous of it. When years later he would write in his notebook, "I talk with the authority of failure – Ernest [Hemingway] with authority of success" (*N*, no. 191, 318), he was not feeling sorry for himself so much as he was asserting the authenticity of his experience and vision as a writer. His distrust of American versions of success puts him in the same camp as other American writers whose work he knew well, writers such as Mark Twain, Henry James, Sherwood Anderson, and Theodore Dreiser. Fitzgerald's most famous character, Jay Gatsby, embodies America's divided nature, transcendental idealism versus the crass worship of success. Although Fitzgerald is a modernist writer, his conviction that the accidents of birth, the family and home one is born into, mold one's character, which, coupled with his deeply ingrained vision of the powerful in society crushing the more vulnerable, account for the deterministic themes that persist in his fiction.

The role that Fitzgerald's mother played in his early life was as uncomfortable for him as that of his father. Mollie Fitzgerald adored, pampered, and spoiled her only son. She also embarrassed him. When Fitzgerald's pioneering biographer, Arthur Mizener, interviewed Fitzgerald's childhood friends, they remembered Mollie "as a witchlike old lady who carried an umbrella, rain or shine."[4] She was also known to have worn one old shoe and one new shoe (each a different color) to a dressy social event because she wanted to break in one shoe at a time (Mizener 3). Such behavior must have horrified her son, who at the time wanted nothing as much as he wanted to be popular. He began putting on airs and imagined that he was secretly the son of royalty and that he had been dropped off on his parents' doorstep by some stroke of misfortune.[5] Fitzgerald enjoyed living in his imagination, creating idealized versions of himself, and inventing stories wherein he demonstrated courage, athletic prowess, and all manner of exceptional abilities.[6]

In addition to the rich world of his imagination, he also enjoyed a highly active social life in St. Paul: toboggan parties, dances, and playing post office with pretty girls. Even as a young boy, he knew he was handsome, and he felt that he was destined for something great. Mollie kept his baby book with loving care, recording the things he did and said as if each were exceptionally clever and important. A page entitled "Progressive Record of Autographs" in his baby book preserves a visual record of Fitzgerald's invention of the person he wanted to become.[7] His autograph at five is simply *Scott*, scrawled in large, uneven letters; soon he becomes *Scott Fitzgerald*, written in careful cursive. At age fifteen, he plays with signing his name *Francis Scott Fitzgerald*. At seventeen, he settles on *F. Scott Fitzgerald*, written in a more mature but still unremarkable hand. At age twenty-one, his name finally appears in the elegant, confident cursive he would use the rest of his life. This was the signature of what Fitzgerald called a "personage," a person of distinction.

Well-off relatives paid Fitzgerald's tuition so that he could attend private schools. A bright boy and an enthusiastic reader, he nevertheless did not like to study and was always a poor student. What he *did* like to do was write, and he began publishing stories in his school's magazine when he was thirteen. Fitzgerald failed the admissions test to Princeton but was close enough to passing and persuasive enough to argue his way in. He soon fell in with a literary group as excited about literature as he was. He wrote poetry, plays, and stories for Princeton publications and the lyrics for two musicals for the Triangle Club. Poor grades disqualified him from being president of the Triangle Club, a position that he very much wanted. According to Matthew J. Bruccoli, his definitive biographer, "Fitzgerald established a pattern of having to make up for past failures while failing current courses. It was a predicament that would get worse every term."[8] He also lost the girl he had his heart set on winning. A Lake Forest, Illinois, socialite, Ginevra King was popular, pretty, and rich.[9] Fitzgerald idealized her and conducted an ardent courtship mostly through letters. During the time of an unsatisfactory visit with Ginevra in Lake Forest near the end of their relationship, Fitzgerald overheard this comment that he recorded in his *Ledger*: "Poor boys shouldn't think of marrying rich girls" (*FSFL* 170). Highly sensitive to rejection and class distinctions, Fitzgerald would always remember the role Ginevra's wealth seemed to play in the breakup, and the corrupting power of money over love in American life became one of the great themes in his fiction.

Realizing he would not be graduating from Princeton, Fitzgerald joined the army and wrote melodramatic letters to his family, stating he felt certain that he would be killed in war. He also wrote an autobiographical novel, "The Romantic Egotist," which, although the publisher encouraged him to revise and resubmit it, was still turned down. Fitzgerald's disappointments – Princeton, Ginevra, his manuscript, and even his impending death – did not dampen his spirit for long. Although he had a self-confessed tendency to take disappointments hard, he was also often surprisingly resilient, even to the point of exuberance. For example, while waiting in New York to leave for training camp, Fitzgerald enjoyed a continuous round of parties. And while having a drink at the elegant Bustanoby's on Broadway, he suddenly exhibited his elation by turning cartwheels from the bar all the way into the ladies' room (Mizener 83).

His training camp was outside of Montgomery, Alabama, where he met Zelda Sayre, the most beautiful, sought-after girl in three states. Just two months after meeting Zelda, Fitzgerald wrote in his *Ledger*, "Sept: Fell in love on the 7th," and on his birthday, he summed up his twenty-first year: "A year of enormous importance. Work, and Zelda. Last year as a Catholic" (*FSFL* 172–73). The essentials of his future – matters of vocation, love, and faith – had been decided. Fitzgerald saw in Zelda a spirit that matched his own, but unlike himself, Zelda seemed absolutely fearless, a trait he found especially attractive but also unsettling. After their marriage, as Zelda's behavior became increasingly erratic, Fitzgerald would see those traits that originally charmed him in a different light. But he was at the time, as he would be throughout his life, firmly committed to Zelda.

In a letter just prior to their marriage, Fitzgerald wrote this about his love of Zelda: "My friends are unanimous in frankly advising me not to marry a wild, pleasure loving girl like Zelda ... but ... I love her and that's the beginning and end of everything" (*C* 53). Fitzgerald believed in romantic and lasting love even though he also believed that ugly money and class issues fought against it. Zelda reassured him that her passion matched his own: "Scott – there's nothing in the world I want but you – and your precious love," she wrote to him. "All the material things are nothing ... Don't ever think of the things you can't give me. You've trusted me with the dearest heart of all." (*S&Z* 15–16).

The war ended before Fitzgerald was scheduled to go overseas, and he went to New York to start a career, hoping to send for Zelda. He landed a job in advertising, hated it, and made very little money. Worst of all, he and Zelda seemed to have reached a dead end in their plans to be married. Fitzgerald went on a three-day bender, then went back home to St. Paul and, with astonishing discipline, revised his novel. Scribners immediately accepted the new version, and Fitzgerald was so ecstatic that he literally stopped strangers on the street to tell them that he was officially an author. *This Side of Paradise* is an autobiographical coming-of-age novel. It tells the story of a new generation liberated from their parents' Victorian ideas, and it virtually became a handbook for the new ways of talking, dressing, and even thinking. Fitzgerald was not only an important new author; he was a spokesman for the new flappers and philosophers, an *enfant terrible*, and though he would later see the folly clearly, at the time, no one could have played this role better or enjoyed it more.

Once Fitzgerald's novel was accepted for publication, Zelda quickly joined him in New York, where they were married at St. Patrick's Cathedral. Passionately in love, and giddy with sudden celebrity, the couple already exhibited unsustainable patterns: endless parties, drinking, reckless spending, and outrageous behavior designed to garner attention. In 1921, the Fitzgeralds went to Europe for the first time, and then they returned to St. Paul for the birth of their only child, Scottie, a healthy daughter with a cheerful disposition. But the Fitzgeralds continued to move restlessly about and never settled anywhere long enough to establish a real sense of home.

Fitzgerald's second novel, *The Beautiful and Damned* (1922), lacks the vitality that runs through *This Side of Paradise*, but Fitzgerald wanted to develop new themes – the new novel presented a bleak portrait of a glamorous young married couple, Anthony and Gloria Patch, who, while waiting to inherit the Patch fortune, slip into dissipation and alcoholism.

Anthony and Gloria represented New York's young socialites who were turning the city into their playground. It is a cautionary story about waste, but it is also a portrayal of humiliation, an experience that Fitzgerald would come to know all too well because of his own alcoholism.

The Fitzgeralds moved to Great Neck, New York, hoping that Scott could settle into a productive writing routine. They continued their party life instead, and Fitzgerald's drinking accelerated. He and Zelda were still viewed as beautiful young celebrities, but their extravagant lifestyle and the magazine stories Fitzgerald churned out to support it began to wear on him. Fitzgerald had a complex relationship with the magazines that published his stories. Their massive circulation contributed to his fame and success, and they paid well. Additionally, Scribners published a book of Fitzgerald's stories after each novel; Fitzgerald, always borrowing against future work, needed additional income. Even though he often disparaged the stories, Fitzgerald produced approximately 175 of them, and they played an important role in his development as a writer. Many of his finest stories – "May Day," "The Diamond as Big as the Ritz," "Winter Dreams," and "Babylon Revisited," for example – remain a vital part of his canon. Still, he resented the time they took away from his work on his novels.[10]

The Fitzgeralds' lives in Great Neck soon became so chaotic that they embarked on yet another geographic cure, this time to France, where Fitzgerald wrote his third novel, *The Great Gatsby* (1925), a beautifully crafted meditation on human longing. The Jazz Age setting contrasts with the imaginative promise the New World first represented. Gatsby's (and early America's) idealism gives way to rapacious materialism. One of Fitzgerald's great achievements is to expose the ugly, predatory underside of what the dream had become under capitalism while preserving the beauty and promise of the original aspiration: to begin again and achieve perfection.

Living in Paris in 1925 brought Fitzgerald into the company of writers, artists, and intellectuals such as Gertrude Stein, Man Ray, Picasso, Jean Cocteau, and Erik Satie, who were casting off the old ideas and art forms and experimenting with new ones more indicative of life in the twentieth century. Fitzgerald's French biographer, André LeVot, describes the attraction Paris held for Fitzgerald in this way:

> Paris was then the capital of the imagination, the promised land of artists from all over the world … This was the place where all the world's scattered and repressed aspirations converged and flowered … Except for Jazz, the arts were stagnating in the United States. The whole country had eyes only for Wall Street, where financial speculation had reached fever pitch.[11]

While living in France, Fitzgerald met Ernest Hemingway, generously championed his writing, and remained a loyal if uneasy friend over the years as Hemingway condescendingly played the role of superior big brother.[12] If France first appeared to these expatriates to be paradise, Fitzgerald still sensed the clock was ominously ticking down the minutes to when it would be spoiled. He later wrote that "by 1928 Paris had grown suffocating" and that with "each new shipment of Americans spewed up by the boom the quality fell off, until towards the end there was something sinister about the crazy boatloads" (*CU* 20).

When the Fitzgeralds returned to America, Fitzgerald tried his hand at screenwriting in Hollywood, without success. The couple then moved to Delaware and rented an elegant old mansion, Ellerslie, which was rumored to be haunted. When guests arrived, Fitzgerald had stationed the butler out of sight with instructions to make ghostlike noises and rattle a chain. Meanwhile, he told everyone that it must be the ghost of Ellerslie. Fitzgerald enjoyed this stunt so much that one night when friends were sleeping over, he slipped into their bedroom with a sheet over his head and moaned until the husband awoke with start and took a swing at him. Suddenly, flames appeared. Fitzgerald, tipsy, had foolishly been smoking a cigarette under the sheet.[13] Episodes like this made for good stories, but between parties, drinking, and arguments with Zelda, Fitzgerald made little progress on his next novel.

When the Fitzgeralds returned to France in 1929, Zelda devoted herself obsessively to ballet classes, suffered her first breakdown, and entered a hospital in Switzerland for treatment. Although Zelda's parents never talked about it, there was a family history of mental illness.[14] Zelda had always been impulsive, but by this time, it was clear that she was seriously ill. The year 1929 marked a crash for the Fitzgeralds as dramatic as the economic crash in America. Fitzgerald's own health declined, earning a living became increasingly difficult, and he worried constantly about Zelda. He paid endless medical bills and, again, borrowed money against future work.

The Fitzgeralds left Europe for good in 1931. Zelda suffered another breakdown in 1932 and entered Johns Hopkins Hospital, and later Sheppard Pratt Hospital, in Baltimore. While in Hopkins, she hurriedly wrote an autobiographical novel, *Save Me the Waltz* (1932), based on her marriage, the same material that Fitzgerald was using in his novel in progress. Fitzgerald believed that its publication would greatly diminish the public's response to his own. Moreover, he argued, he was the professional writer, and their living depended on his income. Fitzgerald hoped to reestablish his reputation with the new novel, *Tender Is the Night* (1934), a study of the American expatriate scene in France based on his own experience.[15] But as Arthur Mizener suggests, Fitzgerald had even more than money and reputation at stake: Fitzgerald was desperately hoping that the novel's reception would restore "his ability to believe in himself" (280). Critics, though generally positive, still expressed disappointment that the novel was not as good as they had anticipated, a judgment that has changed since Fitzgerald's death, but one that had a disastrous effect on Fitzgerald at the time.

As Fitzgerald's belief in himself spiraled downward, he tried to examine what had gone wrong in his life in a series of autobiographical essays for magazines. In "Sleeping and Waking" (1934), Fitzgerald writes candidly about his insomnia, which caused him to obsess over his least heroic moments and conclude this: "Waste and horror – what I might have been and done that is lost, spent, gone, dissipated, unrecapturable." He writes about "night-cap[s]" and "luminol" (at the time a commonly prescribed barbiturate now known to be addictive and to exacerbate alcoholism), his "intense fatigue of mind," and "the perverse alertness of [his] nervous system" (*CU* 66, 67). Fitzgerald's advanced alcoholism resulted in the onset of rapid physical deterioration. He entered the hospital for treatment, but any small progress was soon blotted out by humiliating relapses. In 1935, Fitzgerald hit his lowest point and wrote the three essays in the "Crack-Up" sequence, published in *Esquire* in 1936. As the country was still in the Depression, it seemed appropriate to Fitzgerald to describe his own deterioration in economic metaphors. "I began to realize," he wrote, "that for two years my life had been a drawing on resources that I did not possess, that I had been mortgaging myself physically and spiritually up to the hilt" (*CU* 72). As Mizener concludes, although "Fitzgerald's crack-up was not so final as he supposed ... he was a scared man whose success was of a very different order from what the man he had been before he went emotionally bankrupt had desired and, to a large matter achieved. For the rest of his life he continued to think of himself as living on what he had saved out of a spiritual forced sale" (291).

Fitzgerald returned to Hollywood in 1937 and, writing for Metro-Goldwyn-Mayer (MGM), he earned a steady salary, slowly repaid his debts, and provided for Zelda's care while she lived intermittently between her mother's home in Montgomery and Highland Hospital in North Carolina, to which she returned during periods of relapse. Zelda was never well enough to join Fitzgerald in Hollywood. They stayed in touch, sharing each other's daily lives through letters, not knowing that they would never live together again. While living alone in Hollywood, Fitzgerald fell in love with Sheilah Graham, who, along with his secretary, Frances Kroll, had a steadying influence on his life. Graham would later write a loving memoir about their time together, saying that during the last year of his life he did not drink, his morale was high, and he was absorbed in writing another novel.[16] By that time, however, alcoholism had done its damage. On December 21, 1940, Fitzgerald suffered a sudden and fatal heart attack at the age of forty-four. Zelda was too ill to attend the funeral. Eight years later, at midnight on March 10, 1948, Highland Hospital caught fire, and Zelda perished in the flames. Scott and Zelda are buried together in St. Mary's Catholic Church cemetery in Rockville, Maryland. Neither of them had lived to see fifty.

During Fitzgerald's final years in Hollywood, he understood that he was a forgotten man, but he nonetheless died fully engaged in and optimistic about his writing. "I'm deep in the novel," he wrote to Zelda two months before his death, "living in it, and it makes me happy ... Two thousand words today and all good" (*S&Z* 373). Published posthumously, *The Last Tycoon* (1941), even in its incomplete form, is still considered one the best fictional treatments of Hollywood. The themes of Fitzgerald's final novel – love, aspiration, the conflict between American ideas and American life – are consistent with his previous work. But Fitzgerald was an artist whose work never fell into safe patterns of repetition. As he experienced new situations, he tried new things in his fiction. *The Last Tycoon* retains Fitzgerald's characteristic verbal sparkle while it also reveals a more deeply mature point of view and a writer in control of his art.

The Fitzgerald legend – that he was a casualty of the Jazz Age, a playboy who threw away a fortune and drank away his talent – has given unsympathetic biographers grist for biographies that emphasize the worst aspects of Fitzgerald's life with less than judicious accuracy.[17] Bruccoli has corrected the part of the legend that damaged his reputation with painstaking documentary evidence of Fitzgerald's conscientious attention to craftsmanship. The fact that Fitzgerald has for decades now been a writer whose work continues to speak to new readers and aspiring writers like few other voices attests to the depth and authenticity of the work itself, independent of the legend. Paul Auster, for example, is only one of the writers who have acknowledged the profound power Fitzgerald's work has had in his own life:

> I first read *The Great Gatsby* as a high school student more than thirty years ago, and even now I don't think I have fully recovered from the experience ... it cuts to the heart of storytelling itself – and the result is a work of such simplicity,

power, and beauty that one is marked by it forever. I realize that I am not alone in my opinion, but I can't think of another twentieth-century American novel that has meant as much to me.[18]

Many readers from all over the globe might say nearly the same thing. Fitzgerald's fiction has a way of becoming personal: His readers recognize the sense of infinite longing even while at the same time they internalize his cautionary voice. In Fitzgerald's world, to desire and to imagine are as close to greatness as one will ever get. History, individual and collective, is the story of dreams made material and thereby corrupted.

Although Fitzgerald's reputation as a writer has been restored, two additional correctives to the legend are still needed. First, the role alcoholism played in his life is still sometimes used as an excuse either to dismiss Fitzgerald as a drunk or to romanticize his drinking. Alcoholism is a complicated and devastating disease, and Fitzgerald lived and wrote in a state of extreme physical and emotional discomfort brought on by an illness almost no one understood or sympathized with, including himself. Fitzgerald channeled his experience into his fiction. His characters are drawn to alcohol even as it destroys them: The material world once again, alcohol in this case, first intensifies the imagination, then corrupts it. The fact that alcoholism is a disease makes the role it plays in human history and life no less real and no less a significant and moving subject for fiction. Everything Fitzgerald experienced and felt as a result of his drinking went into his work and is part of what makes that work important and lasting.[19]

Another important corrective to the legend, which over the past decades has understandably emphasized the tragic elements of Fitzgerald's life, is to remember that he also enjoyed much of his life. Exuberance characterized his personality as much as melancholy: He loved pranks and was quick to laugh, his friendships tended to be heartfelt and lifelong, and he was doggedly true to his vaulting ambition to become a first-rate writer. He had the satisfaction of knowing that at his best he had been a great one. Yet Fitzgerald could still laugh at himself. His college friend Edmund Wilson, for example, tells a story about Fitzgerald overhearing some of his friends making fun of a "bathetic" passage in an early version of *The Beautiful and Damned*: "But ... he had not really seen Anthony. For Maury had indulged his appetite for alcoholic beverage once too often: he was now stone-blind!" According to Wilson, Fitzgerald, who had been entirely serious when he wrote the passage, laughed as hard as anyone and improvised an even worse Fitzgeraldian passage on the spot: "It seemed to Anthony that Maury's eyes had a fixed stare, his legs moved stiffly as he walked and when he spoke his voice was lifeless. When Anthony came nearer, he saw that Maury was dead."[20]

In addition to humor, Fitzgerald also had a gift for friendship. Frances Kroll Ring writes in her memoir of Fitzgerald's last year that when he died, his daughter, Scottie, wrote asking her to set something in his possession aside for Margaret Turnbull. "[M]aybe just a pencil," Scottie suggested. Ring remembers that she "was struck by the trail of warmth Scott left behind so that a memento – even a pencil – would have such sentimental value for a friend."[21] Fitzgerald's life and fiction are indisputably tragic, but they also convey an all-too-often-missed sense of honor and a spirit of generosity and goodwill. What Fitzgerald once said was America's defining characteristic – "a willingness of heart"[22] – was ultimately his own.

NOTES

1 Although Fitzgerald never wrote an autobiography, he kept meticulous personal records in a variety of forms over the course of his life: *The Thoughtbook of Francis Scott Key Fitzgerald,* J. Kuehl, ed. (Princeton, NJ: Princeton University Library, 1965) reproduces Fitzgerald's account of his social life, romances, and popularity when he was fourteen; *F. Scott Fitzgerald's Ledger*, intro. by M. J. Bruccoli (Washington: Bruccoli Clark/NCR, 1973) is a facsimile of the ledger in which Fitzgerald recorded summary notes for each year of his life to 1937, along with a complete list of his works, and a year-by-year list of his earnings; *The Romantic Egoists: A Pictorial Autobiography from the Scrapbooks and Albums of F. Scott and Zelda Fitzgerald*, M. J. Bruccoli, S. F. Smith, and J. P. Kerr, eds. (New York: Charles Scribner's Sons, 1974), is an invaluable compilation of the baby books, scrapbooks, photographs, reviews, letters, and other memorabilia the Fitzgeralds preserved to document their lives; *The Notebooks of F. Scott Fitzgerald*, M. J. Bruccoli, ed. (New York: Harcourt Brace Jovanovich/Bruccoli Clark, 1978), contains fragments of conversations, quips, observations and descriptions he might use in his writing, along with brief of notes of self-analysis. In addition, the personal essays Fitzgerald wrote between 1931 and 1937, collected in *The Crack-Up*, E. Wilson, ed. (New York: New Directions, 1945), are, as Wilson claims, "an autobiographical sequence which vividly puts on record his state of mind and his point of view during the later years of his life" (11). As chapter 3 in this volume suggests, Fitzgerald was also a tireless writer of letters.

2 S. Donaldson, *A Biography of F. Scott Fitzgerald: Fool for Love* (New York: Congdon & Weed, 1983), x. Subsequent references to this biography are included in the text.

3 A. Turnbull, *Scott Fitzgerald* (New York: Charles Scribner's Sons, 1962), 17. Subsequent references to this work are included in the text.

4 A. Mizener, *The Far Side of Paradise* (Boston: Houghton Mifflin, 1965), 3. Subsequent references to this biography are cited parenthetically in the text.
5 F. S. Fitzgerald, "Author's House," *Afternoon of an Author*, A. Mizener, ed. (New York: Charles Scribner's Sons, 1958), 185.
6 In "Sleeping and Waking" (1934), *The Crack-Up*, E. Wilson, ed. (New York: New Directions, 1945), Fitzgerald writes that his daydream of heroically winning a football game for Princeton against Yale has finally "worn thin" (66).
7 Reproduced in *The Romantic Egoists: A Pictorial Autobiography from the Scrapbooks and Albums of F. Scott and Zelda Fitzgerald*, M. J. Bruccoli, S. F. Smith, and J. P. Kerr, eds. (New York: Charles Scribner's Sons, 1974), 6.
8 M. J. Bruccoli, *Some Sort of Epic Grandeur: The Life of F. Scott Fitzgerald*, 2nd rev. edn. (Columbia, SC: University of South Carolina Press, 2004), 46. Subsequent references to this biography are included in the text.
9 See J. L. W. West III, *The Perfect Hour: The Romance of F. Scott Fitzgerald and Ginevra King, His First Love* (New York: Random House, 2006) for an account of this relationship and for letters Ginevra King wrote to Fitzgerald.
10 For a discussion of the role short stories played in Fitzgerald's life and work, see B. Mangum, *A Fortune Yet: Money in the Art of F. Scott Fitzgerald's Short Stories* (New York: Garland, 1991).
11 A. LeVot, *F. Scott Fitzgerald: A Biography* (New York: Doubleday, 1983), 185.
12 For full discussions of their relationship, see M. J. Bruccoli, *Scott and Ernest: The Authority of Failure and the Authority of Success* (New York: Random House, 1978) and *Fitzgerald and Hemingway: A Dangerous Friendship* (New York: Carroll & Graff, 1994); also S. Donaldson, *Hemingway and Fitzgerald: The Rise and Fall of a Literary Friendship* (Woodstock, NY: Overlook Press, 1999).
13 E. Wilson, "A Weekend at Ellerslie," *The Shores of Light: A Literary Chronicle of the 1920s and 1930s* (Boston: Northeastern University Press, 1985), 383.
14 In *Epic Grandeur*, Bruccoli writes that Zelda's maternal grandmother committed suicide (93), her father "suffered a nervous breakdown" (92–93), her sister Marjorie "was subject to nervous illness most of her life" (91), and her brother, Anthony, committed suicide in 1933 (296).
15 See H. D. Piper, *F. Scott Fitzgerald: A Critical Portrait* (New York: Holt, 1965). Piper contends that the pair of novels depicts the Fitzgeralds' different viewpoints of their marriage and that "the disturbing thing about both novels is their authors' mutual failure to comprehend the other's point of view" (192, 204).
16 S. Graham and G. Frank, *Beloved Infidel* (New York: Holt, 1958), 311.
17 J. R. Mellow, for example, in his preface to *Invented Lives: F. Scott and Zelda Fitzgerald* (1984), admits his antipathy toward his subjects and states his intention "not to let the glamorous Fitzgeralds get away with anything" (xvii). J. Myers seems determined to depict Fitzgerald in the worst possible light in his biography *Scott Fitzgerald* (1994). Sally Cline in *Zelda Fitzgerald: Her Voice in Paradise* (2002) pursues a line of tawdry speculation into the Fitzgeralds' sex lives.

18 Qtd. in M. J. Bruccoli, *F. Scott Fitzgerald's "The Great Gatsby": A Literary Reference* (New York: Carroll & Graff Publishers, 2000), 308.

19 For the role that alcohol and alcoholism have played in American history and in the 1920s in particular, see D. Okrent, *Last Call: The Rise and Fall of Prohibition* (New York: Charles Scribner's Sons, 2011) and *Prohibition*, dir. K. Burns and L. Novak (Walpole, NH: Florentine Films, 2011), DVD.

20 E. Wilson, "F. Scott Fitzgerald," *The Shores of Light: A Literary Chronicle of the 1920s and 1930s* (Boston: Northeastern University Press, 1985), 33.

21 F. K. Ring, *Against the Current: As I Remember F. Scott Fitzgerald* (San Francisco: Ellis/Creative Arts, 1985), 128.

22 "The Swimmers" [1929] in M. J. Bruccoli, ed., *The Short Stories of F. Scott Fitzgerald* (New York: Charles Scribner's Sons, 1989), 512.

2

Interpreting Fitzgerald's Ledger

James L. W. West III

F. Scott Fitzgerald's ledger is a mongrel document – part bibliography, part business record, part sourcebook, part autobiographical self-assessment. Theodore Dreiser, E. M. Forster, André Gide, Virginia Woolf, Franz Kafka, Anaïs Nin, John Cheever, and a great many other authors left behind journals and diaries, but Fitzgerald's ledger is something else again, an unclassifiable portmanteau of information about his life, writings, and literary career. The ledger has been consulted by bibliographers to establish Fitzgerald's oeuvre, by book historians to study the profession of authorship, by biographers to give an overview of Fitzgerald's career, by critics to discover sources for his stories and novels, and by teachers to show how a writer's life is organized. The ledger can also be regarded as a literary work, a verbal construction that is unfinished but is enormously revealing when read as if it were a story, from the first page through to the last.

Copies of Fitzgerald's novels, stories, and essays can be borrowed from libraries or purchased in bookstores. The ledger, however, is somewhat more difficult to access. A black-and-white reproduction of the original was issued in 1972, edited by Matthew J. Bruccoli and published by NCR/Microcard Editions. The book was entitled *F. Scott Fitzgerald's Ledger: A Facsimile.* One thousand copies were printed, according to the copyright page, each copy bearing a handwritten number. Most Fitzgerald scholars own this facsimile. NCR/Microcard Editions no longer exists as a publishing entity, but their unsold back stock is available for purchase. As of July 2011, one could still acquire an unopened copy of the facsimile for less than forty dollars through Alibris or Amazon. It is also possible to borrow a copy on interlibrary loan. A search of WorldCat indicates that 278 copies of the facsimile reside in libraries; these libraries are located in forty-seven of the fifty U.S. states and in Puerto Rico, Australia, Canada, Germany, Ireland, Israel, and the United Kingdom. As for the original ledger (measuring 8½ × 13¾ inches), it is preserved in the Matthew J.

and Arlyn Bruccoli Collection of F. Scott Fitzgerald, Irvin Department of Rare Books and Special Collections, Ernest F. Hollings Special Collections Library, University of South Carolina. This original bears layers of Fitzgerald's handwriting in different inks and pencil colors. Its pages are smudged by his fingers; its binding is worn at the extremities by his handling. Perhaps a full-color digital scan of this original will someday be available online.[1]

From internal evidence it appears that Fitzgerald acquired his ledger toward the end of 1922, probably to help him keep track of literary earnings. He conceived a structure for the ledger and, to judge from ink colors and foliation, began to fill in the pages immediately after purchase, bringing the record up to January 1923. In the years that followed he made new entries regularly, adding story and novel titles, fees collected, commissions paid, events attended, and travels undertaken. He divided the ledger into five parts and listed them on a contents page:

> Record of Published Fiction; Novels, Plays, Stories
> (Not including unpaid-for juvenilia)
> Record of Other Published Work, Paid for.
> Earnings by years
> Geneological Table
> Autobiographical Chart
>
> (*FSFL* 1)

Fitzgerald took great care with the ledger entries during the first ten years of his career. He kept the pages in meticulous order, correcting mistakes with ink eradicator or pasting a blank slip of paper over an error and writing the correct information onto the substituted slip. Fitzgerald was assembling a curriculum vitae of sorts, updating it from time to time, ensuring its completeness and accuracy, and fussing with its appearance. During the 1930s he was less careful: The entries for these years are corrected by cancellations and interlinear substitutions, but the purpose is still the same: to maintain a record of composition, publication, payment, and disposal for every piece of writing that he generated. It must be remembered that Fitzgerald wrote for money. He had no trust fund on which to draw and no inherited capital or property. He did not marry into money. Fitzgerald and his wife and daughter lived on what he earned with his pen. The ledger, carefully maintained, was his scorecard.

For a bibliographer intent on tracking down every item published by Fitzgerald, the ledger is a valuable resource, especially for locating fugitive items. It is easy for a bibliographer to find a story such as "The Diamond as Big as the Ritz," which appeared first in the *Smart Set* for June 1922 and was reprinted a few months later in Fitzgerald's second collection of short fiction, *Tales of the Jazz Age* (1922). Without the ledger, however, it would be hard to find (or even be aware of) Fitzgerald's review of Woodward Boyd's forgotten novel *The Love Legend*. Fitzgerald published this notice in the *New York Evening Post* for October 28, 1922. He logged that item in with the rest in a subsection of "Published Miscelani" that begins on page 103 of the ledger. His bibliographers have been grateful for this entry and for records in the ledger of other similarly obscure pieces of writing.

Fitzgerald has recorded the publication history of each item, noting reprints in newspapers, appearances in English magazines, and inclusions in anthologies. He has been careful to note the disposal of subsidiary rights. The movie rights to *This Side of Paradise*, for example, fetched $10,000 from Famous Players; drama and cinema rights to *The Great Gatsby* brought $26,000, some of it from the Broadway producer Sam Harris and the rest from Famous Players. These payments illustrate an important principle of professional authorship: Writers are successful financially if they can make their work continue to produce income *after* the initial act of publication. A large payment for the first appearance is welcome, but when a literary property continues to generate money, the author is not thrown constantly upon fresh invention. The possibilities for such recycling were not as numerous in Fitzgerald's time as they are today. There were, for example, no paperback publishers as we know them; the first true American paperback house, Pocket Books, issued its initial list in 1939, a year before Fitzgerald died. Likewise, there were no television adaptations, audio books, or digital rights. Still, Fitzgerald did profit from what was available to him – from magazine serialization of his novels before they appeared between cloth covers, from book-club editions and cheap reprints and newspaper "second serials," from stage and movie rights, from anthology appearances, from British editions, and (for *The Great Gatsby*) from a translation into French.

The existence of the ledger makes it possible to calculate Fitzgerald's total earnings for his career – or at least until 1937, when the entries cease. (Fitzgerald went to Hollywood in June 1937 to work as a scriptwriter for Metro-Goldwyn-Mayer (MGM) and did not update the ledger after that.) Through 1937 he earned around $360,000 for his magazine work but only about $66,000 in book royalties.[2] These figures show that the most dependable money for Fitzgerald came from high-paying magazines such as the *Saturday Evening Post*, *Redbook*, and *Metropolitan* – not from the novels and short-story collections that were issued by Charles

Scribner's Sons, his book publisher. The rhythm of writing for "the slicks," as these magazines were called, was relatively straightforward. Fitzgerald produced his stories in short bursts of energy, marketed them through his literary agent, Harold Ober, and was paid immediately for his labor. Novel writing, by contrast, was done at a slower pace, and advances from the publisher, negotiations for serialization rights, and payment of royalties came many months after publication. For immediate gold, Fitzgerald relied on the magazines.

In March and April 1932, Fitzgerald became involved in a bitter dispute with his wife, Zelda Sayre, over her novel *Save Me the Waltz*. The ledger bears evidence of their disagreement. Fitzgerald believed that the first version of *Save Me the Waltz*, now lost, was a personal attack on him and an attempt by Zelda to destroy their marriage. He insisted on playing a role in the revision of the novel. Zelda balked. Until that point, they had published rather many items under the shared byline "F. Scott and Zelda Fitzgerald." Most of the work on these stories and articles was Zelda's; Fitzgerald typically rewrote and polished what she had produced in her first drafts. (The magazines would pay more if his name was attached.) Zelda seems not to have been bothered at first by this arrangement, but by 1932 she had determined to write and publish on her own. Probably in response to her stance, Fitzgerald made some changes in the ledger. He struck through the heading "Geneological Table" on the contents page and substituted the word "Zelda." He sliced out pages 145–50, which probably contained genealogical information. Then on page 143, a blank, he set down a record of Zelda's earnings. He also went back through the previous ledger pages and marked which of the items were collaborations. A story called "Our Own Movie Queen," published in the magazine section of the *Chicago Sunday Tribune* on June 7, 1925, under Fitzgerald's name only, was designated "half Zelda" on page 55 of the ledger and "half mine" on page 143. "Paint and Powder," an editorial that Zelda wrote for *Photoplay*, was rejected by that magazine and subsequently published under Fitzgerald's name only in the May 1929 issue of the *Smart Set*. Fitzgerald marked this editorial as entirely Zelda's work on the ledger page numbered 61–63. (Some of the pages have combination numbers to account for leaves that Fitzgerald removed.) These markings, together with the entries on page 143, have helped biographers and editors to sort out the collaborations and have led to publication of a volume of Zelda Fitzgerald's collected writings.[3]

Biographers have found the ledger valuable for the picture it gives of Fitzgerald's literary career, which flourished in the 1920s, peaked around

1931, and almost flickered out after he went to Hollywood in 1937. It is instructive to page through the ledger entries and watch Fitzgerald's income rise from $879 in 1919, to $28,759 in 1923, to a high of $37,599 in 1931, and then drop to $16,328 in 1933 and to $10,180 in 1936 – still a great deal more than most Americans were making during the Great Depression. One learns a lesson that is still true today: The emoluments of authorship are irregular and unpredictable. Most authors need another source of income, a steady source.

Fitzgerald did not bother to fill in his earnings for 1937. He published five manuscripts in *Esquire* magazine that year at $250 apiece and collected a few more dollars for some miscellaneous exercises in nonfiction, but his main source of money was his screenwriting job at MGM. He was paid $1,000 per week, from June to December. He performed well enough at the studio to have his contract renewed for the following year at $1,250 a week, money that he became accustomed to having and that allowed him to pay off large debts to Scribners and to Ober. He resumed work as a freelance in January 1939 but did not record his publications or earnings in his ledger. He died in December 1940 without ever bringing the ledger up to date. One likes to imagine that, had he lived, Fitzgerald would have scored a success with *The Last Tycoon*, the novel he was writing at his death, and that he would have returned to his ledger keeping to write down several more years of sales and earnings during the comeback that he surely deserved.

Critics of Fitzgerald's work have found the ledger helpful as a record of source material for his stories and novels. That is how Fitzgerald himself used the section entitled "Autobiographical Chart." He seems to have combed through this section repeatedly in search of incidents and memories that he could transform into fiction. In this year-by-year and month-by-month record of his life, he wrote down events and trips and experiences as a quasi-ceremonial act, beginning each year not in January but in September, the month of his birth. At some point he entered summations of these twelve-month periods. For September 1918 to September 1919, for example, he wrote (with a typical misspelling), "The most important year of life. Every emotion and my life work decided. Miserable and exstatic but a great success" (*FSFL* 173). For the following year, 1919–1920: "Revelry and marriage. The rewards of the year before. The happiest year since I was 18" (*FSFL* 174). For 1924–1925, the year during which he published *The Great Gatsby*: "Zelda's sickness and resulting depression. Drink, loafing + the Murphys" (*FSFL* 179). For 1928–1929 Fitzgerald wrote the word "Ominous" and underlined it three times and "No Real Progress in any way + wrecked myself with dozens of people" (*FSFL* 183). The last of these comments is for 1933–1934: "Zelda breaks, the novel finished. Hard times begin for me slow but sure" (*FSFL* 188).[4]

Reading through this autobiographical material, one spots the following reference in the entry for January 1909: "Freshest boy in school 'Will someone poison Scotty or find some means to shut his mouth'" (*FSFL* 163). If one is familiar with the Basil Duke Lee stories, a series that Fitzgerald published in the *Saturday Evening Post* in 1928 and 1929, one remembers immediately the fictional incident that Fitzgerald fashioned from this memory. When the author was twelve and attending St. Paul Academy, the snippet about "Scotty's" freshness appeared in the school newspaper, the whimsically titled *Now and Then* – because of its irregular publication schedule. In 1928 Fitzgerald transferred the incident into one of the Basil stories, the one entitled "The Freshest Boy." Basil is mortified by the printed remark, as young Scott Fitzgerald had been in 1909. The mature Fitzgerald, however, spins this incident into a lesson for Basil. In "The Freshest Boy," Basil comes to realize that he must control his vanity and talkativeness, especially when he is among his peers. If he is to grow past adolescence into a self-confident adulthood, he must limit the loquaciousness and soft-pedal the braggadocio.

In the entry for May 1919 one finds a reference to "Mr. In and Mr. Out – and other parties" (*FSFL* 173). Fitzgerald's novella "May Day" comes to mind. It was published first in the *Smart Set* for May 1920 and collected in *Tales of the Jazz Age* (1922). Toward the end of a long night of revelry in that narrative, two of Fitzgerald's characters, Peter Himmel and Philip Dean,[5] commandeer the signs for ingress and egress from the coat room at Delmonico's, affix them to their shirt fronts, and perform a vaudeville routine as "Mr. In" and "Mr. Out" – this to amuse themselves and their bibulous companions. Fitzgerald based this bit of fictional fun on an escapade in May 1919 in which he was "Mr. In" and his friend Ludlow Fowler, the model for Anson Hunter in "The Rich Boy" (1926), was "Mr. Out." Before a year had elapsed, Fitzgerald had turned "Mr. In" and "Mr. Out" into fictional characters.

Paging onward to July 1930, one encounters a reference to "Paris with Scotty" (*FSFL* 184) – the afternoon and evening in the city with his daughter, Scottie, that gave rise to Fitzgerald's best-known story, "Babylon Revisited," published in the *Post* for February 21, 1931, and collected in *Taps at Reveille* (1935).[6] In that story the protagonist, Charlie Wales, passes a memorable few hours in Paris with his daughter, Honoria. Fitzgerald based that part of the narrative on the time he had spent in the city with

Scottie in July 1930. "Babylon Revisited" has other sources as well. While Zelda was hospitalized for mental illness in 1930, Fitzgerald temporarily left Scottie with Zelda's sister, Rosalind. Fitzgerald absorbed heavy criticism from Rosalind, who blamed him for Zelda's breakdown. Fitzgerald's revenge was to write "Babylon Revisited" and to use Rosalind as the model for Marion Peters, one of his most repellent characters. After he had completed "Babylon Revisited" but before it had appeared in the *Post*, he made certain to send a carbon typescript of the story to Rosalind. Today this typescript, like the ledger, is among the holdings at South Carolina.

It is easy to cherry-pick phrases and sentences from among the ledger entries and to match them with particular Fitzgerald stories or with incidents in his novels. This, however, can lead to the misconception that Fitzgerald merely transferred material from his life into his writings – a mistake often made by apprentices in the Fitzgerald field. In fact, Fitzgerald rarely worked directly from life. The longer one studies his career and work, the blurrier becomes the line between reality and fiction. Nothing in the ledger suggests a strictly one-to-one relationship between life and writings.

Most of the references in the ledger, in fact, are cryptic. The great majority must have had meaning only for Fitzgerald – names and phrases and snippets of speech that triggered images and memories in his mind. Why did he organize his boyhood friends into "an army with curven swords" (May 1906)? What was "the cruelty to animals society" (September 1908)? What was special about "Little Marjorie King + her smile" (August 1916)? Might a short-story plot have been constructed around "the cigarette case and the purse" (December 1918)? Why does Fitzgerald say, "I should have asked Julian Everson if he wanted the suitcase for the silver" (April 1923)? What happened during the "Party with Gloria Swanson" (January 1924)? Could a minor but odiferous character have been created from "the smelly maid" (November 1929)? What occurred during "my trip South by myself in the car" (May 1933)? And why was "Scottie very gay" (March 1935)? A potential character or scene or plot twist seems to lurk in almost every line of the "Autobiographical Chart." Alas, Fitzgerald did not live to create these characters or manufacture these narratives.

Teachers can put the ledger to good use. Students are curious to learn about the mechanics of literary authorship. The ledger shows Fitzgerald working and thinking as a professional, keeping a year-by-year record of his earnings, tracking the republication and adaptation of his work, and building a repository of memories on which to draw for inspiration. Unless educated to the contrary, most undergraduates seem to think that writers are fed by the crows and that a literary work springs into being fully formed from its author's brow. A document like Fitzgerald's ledger will disabuse them of these notions and give them a more realistic picture of a writer's life – and earnings.

Read as a literary work, Fitzgerald's ledger is a remarkable blend of business data, publishing history, and autobiographical commentary. It is a serial work, proceeding chronologically, written from a single point of view. The narrative voice grows older and becomes more introspective as the years advance. The life moves from early childhood and adolescence through uncertain apprenticeship to mid-career success; it peaks around 1931 and then starts to disintegrate. Fitzgerald is initially setting down this record for himself, but as he matures he seems to sense that other eyes might someday read the entries. Even during the discouraging last years, Fitzgerald knew that he had been among the most original writers of his era. He suspected, correctly, that the story of his life would someday command attention. Close reading and study of the ledger can deepen one's understanding of Fitzgerald and his work. One comes to comprehend much more fully the balance between art and commerce that he sought – a balance that is quite difficult to achieve. Fitzgerald did it as well as any writer of his generation.

NOTES

1 The Hollings Library is developing a plan to make such a scan available, together with images of other Fitzgerald manuscripts and artifacts. For updates the reader should consult http://library.sc.edu/spcoll/rarebook.html.

2 For a sketch of the career, see J. L.W. West III, "F. Scott Fitzgerald, Professional Author" in K. Curnutt (ed.), *A Historical Guide to F. Scott Fitzgerald* (New York: Oxford University Press, 2004), 49–68. To calculate the buying power of these amounts in twenty-first-century dollars, one should multiply by a factor of ten or eleven. A useful website for making such comparisons is www.measuringworth.com.

3 Z. Fitzgerald, *Zelda Fitzgerald: The Collected Writings*, ed. M. J. Bruccoli, intro. M. Gordon (New York: Charles Scribner's Sons, 1991).

4 The novel that Fitzgerald has finished in the last of these summations is *Tender Is the Night*. One is reminded of the melancholy Samuel Johnson's habit in his journals of reviewing the past year's accomplishments each Easter morning. On Easter 1779, for example, he wrote, "Little but dismal vacuity, neither business nor pleasure; much intended, and little done. My health is much broken; my nights afford me little rest ... Last week I published the Lives of the Poets." (S. Johnson, *Prayers and Meditations*. London: T. Cadell, 1785.)

5 In the *Smart Set* version Philip Dean is named Philip Cory.

6 Fitzgerald sometimes spelled his daughter's name "Scotty."

3

Letters

Bryant Mangum

Since 1963, seven substantial scholarly volumes of Fitzgerald's correspondence have been published, each containing large samplings of the more than 3,000 letters he wrote that have been located. Several of the volumes also contain many of the thousands of letters written to Fitzgerald, and each provides extensive editorial apparatus. With three exceptions, the titles and subtitles of these seven collections suggest the scope and focus of each volume: *The Letters of F. Scott Fitzgerald* (1963); *Letters to His Daughter* (1965); *Dear Scott/Dear Max: The Fitzgerald–Perkins Correspondence* (1971); *As Ever. Scott Fitz–: Letters Between F. Scott Fitzgerald and His Literary Agent Harold Ober, 1919–1940* (1972); *Correspondence of F. Scott Fitzgerald* (1980); *F. Scott Fitzgerald: A Life in Letters* (1994); and *Dear Scott, Dearest Zelda: The Love Letters of F. Scott and Zelda Fitzgerald* (2002). Of these seven volumes, four, as is evident from their titles, contain only letters between Fitzgerald and four of the most important people in his life: his wife, Zelda; his daughter, Scottie; his friend and editor at Scribners, Maxwell Perkins; and his agent, Harold Ober. The three other collections include letters from a wide range of correspondents and differ from each other in ways that are sometimes obvious from each volume's introduction, ways determined, among numerous other considerations, by editorial parameters regarding which letters were to be included or excluded. *Correspondence*, for example, includes no letters that had been included in previous volumes, although it does include letters written to Fitzgerald, unlike *Letters*, which includes only letters written by Fitzgerald and those included in Edmund Wilson's *The Crack-Up* (1945). More subtle differences in the volumes involve editorial decisions regarding transcription of the letters, particularly concerning whether Fitzgerald's spelling should or should not be tampered with.

The climate that prepared the way for publication of his extensive correspondence was established in the five years following Fitzgerald's death, during the time usually referred to as the first phase of the Fitzgerald revival, or "resurrection." Mentioned, but rarely emphasized, in discussions of the Fitzgerald revival is the importance of Wilson's decision to include a large section of Fitzgerald's letters in *The Crack-Up*. By including more than fifty pages of letters written by Fitzgerald, Wilson took a first important step in bringing Fitzgerald into the public consciousness as a prolific and gifted letter writer. In his headnote to "The Letters" section he expresses a wish regarding the future publication of Fitzgerald's correspondence: "It is to be hoped that Scott Fitzgerald's letters will be eventually collected and published" (*CU* 243). Perhaps through viewing Wilson's layout as a template of sorts and understanding his rationale for selecting letters for his collection one can best understand the logic behind the organization of the subsequent volumes of Fitzgerald's correspondence.

Wilson includes in his "Letters to Friends" section what he describes as "merely a handful [of letters] that happened to be easily obtainable and which throw light on Fitzgerald's literary activities and interests" (*CU* 243). This group of letters illustrates personal qualities in Fitzgerald that subsequent volumes of correspondence have fully documented – qualities that allow the reader to see him in many different lights: as a man of letters; as a prose stylist; as an informed student of history; as a husband, father, and friend; and as simply a complex and curious human being. It also points to the need for establishing some sort of standard for inclusion and criteria for organizing and editing Fitzgerald's letters. It is not surprising that Wilson chose to reprint over twenty of Fitzgerald's letters to him in the "Letters to Friends" section, since they were "easily obtainable." Seven of the letters in the section were from John Peale Bishop, a close Princeton friend of Fitzgerald. One letter to Ernest Hemingway, two to Gerald and Sara Murphy, one to his friend Beatrice Dance, and one to a casual acquaintance whose book Fitzgerald had reviewed are also included. Finally, Wilson included a second section of letters from Fitzgerald to his daughter, Scottie, many of them written in the last year of his life.

The way in which the letters sections of *The Crack-Up* provide an implicit suggestion for direction of subsequent correspondence volumes, as well as a solid foundation for examining the role of letter writing in Fitzgerald's life, is nicely illustrated by examining the way in which Wilson's collection of letters and the later correspondence volumes come to complement each other, especially in the case of the Fitzgerald–Wilson correspondence itself. The beauty of the twenty-one letters to Wilson in the first section, particularly given that Wilson included notes explaining some obscure details, is that they span the years of their friendship

(1917–1940) and cover the entirety of Fitzgerald's professional career. Wilson was able to provide with these letters a full and rounded picture of Fitzgerald from the beginning of his professional career, a picture that would be filled out in even greater detail in later letter volumes. When Andrew Turnbull assembled his *Letters* volume in 1963, he included all of the letters from the Wilson volume and added to them a dozen letters that Wilson had not included. In 1980, Matthew J. Bruccoli and Margaret M. Duggan further augmented the record in *Correspondence*, which did not reprint the previously published letters but added seven new letters, all relatively brief. By the time Bruccoli assembled *A Life in Letters*, a kind of "single-volume collection that would organize the best of the collected and unpublished Fitzgerald letters in chronological order," Bruccoli was able to pick and choose those letters that, to him, best represented the Fitzgerald–Wilson friendship from many available sources (*LL* xvi). His goal, similar to that of all editors of the Fitzgerald correspondence volumes after Turnbull, was to reproduce the letters as Fitzgerald had written them: in full and with misspellings. In Turnbull's volume, the letters had, in many cases, been corrected by the editor.

Although on a much more limited scale than that of the Fitzgerald–Wilson correspondence, the Fitzgerald–Bishop correspondence chosen by Wilson and the subsequent augmentation of it by editors of later volumes reveal a similar pattern. The letters from Fitzgerald to Bishop in *The Crack-Up* hint at the subtleties of their complex friendship, although much of the complexity of their relationship became clear only when additional letters from both correspondents were published in later volumes. Turnbull published all of the letters that Wilson included in *The Crack-Up* and added four new ones; Bruccoli and Duggan then rounded out the picture of the relationship by publishing nine substantive letters from Bishop to Fitzgerald – and by cross-referencing these letters to relevant ones in the earlier volumes. A reader of both sides of the discourse is able to see that Bishop was as relentless in his criticism of Fitzgerald's work as Fitzgerald was of Bishop's.

Finally, in his section of "Letters to Frances Scott Fitzgerald," Wilson included approximately twenty letters dating from 1933 to 1940, as well as numerous undated fragments. Apart from demonstrating Fitzgerald's involvement through letters in his daughter's life, the correspondence convincingly demonstrates Fitzgerald's intellectual acumen and his erudition as a literary critic. Scottie, his daughter, had noted these qualities to Perkins just weeks after her father's death, when she had tried unsuccessfully to convince him to include a selection of the letters in *The Last*

Tycoon: "[T]hese letters are so far beyond the average literary critic that they're incomparable" (*C* xv). Indeed, the letters indicate the broad range of Fitzgerald's reading as well as demonstrate his wish to be involved in shaping Scottie's life, even if often only through letters and from a distance. Finally, Fitzgerald's letters to his daughter contain many names that are known to readers familiar with Fitzgerald's biography, names such as Zelda Fitzgerald, Harold Ober, and Maxwell Perkins. The doorway Wilson provided with the "Letters" section of *The Crack-Up* begged to be opened wider.

Slightly less than two decades after *The Crack-Up* was published, Turnbull began to open this doorway with the publication of *Letters* (1963), the first book-length collection of Fitzgerald's correspondence. Turnbull estimated the volume contained only half of the letters available to him. The number of letters that Turnbull had to choose from was vast compared to those relatively few "easily obtainable" ones from which Wilson made his selection, but the influence of Wilson's letters section in *The Crack-Up* on this first full volume of Fitzgerald's letters is noteworthy. Turnbull organized his volume into twelve sections of letters to important individuals in Fitzgerald's life and one section of "Miscellaneous Letters." Two of the sections discussed above – those devoted to the Fitzgerald–Wilson and Fitzgerald–Bishop letters – demonstrate the importance of Wilson's foundation in the shaping of the Turnbull volume, which in turn provided direction for future correspondence collections. Perhaps the most dramatic illustration, however, of the way in which Turnbull built on Wilson's section of letters in *The Crack-Up* is his treatment of Fitzgerald's letters to his daughter in a section titled, as was Wilson's section, "Letters to Frances Scott Fitzgerald." Turnbull included those nearly two dozen letters to Scottie printed by Wilson and added approximately fifty new ones to her from Fitzgerald's last Hollywood years (1937–1940). These new letters are filled with details that provide insight into Fitzgerald's frame of mind during this time and into his strict regimen for work on *The Last Tycoon*. Although they do not substantially alter the impression of Fitzgerald as a man of letters, a literary critic, and an involved father that could be gleaned from his letters to Scottie in the Wilson collection, they do deepen the reader's understanding of him in these various roles, even as they provide a wealth of valuable biographical information about his last years in Hollywood. Within two years after the publication of *Letters* Turnbull reprinted the entire section of Fitzgerald's letters to Scottie in a separate volume entitled *Letters to His Daughter*. Fifteen years later Bruccoli and Duggan added approximately a dozen new letters to Scottie to those that had been published in *The Crack-Up* and in the two Turnbull volumes with the publication of *Correspondence*, which did not reprint those letters to Scottie that had been previously published. In 1994 Bruccoli selected fewer than two dozen letters to Scottie that he considered the most important from those previously published and included them in his *A Life in Letters*. The way in which the publication of Fitzgerald's letters to his daughter has evolved provides an excellent illustration of both the wealth of information available in Fitzgerald's published correspondence and of the challenge to general readers and scholars who wish to use the various volumes of correspondence to best advantage. There is much overlap in the publication of these letters, particularly among the Wilson volume and the two Turnbull volumes. In addition, the editorial styles of Wilson, Turnbull, and Bruccoli are different enough in many cases to create substantively different versions of the same letter.

In the approximately fifty years since Turnbull's *Letters* and *Letters to His Daughter* appeared the five subsequent collections of Fitzgerald's letters mentioned earlier have been published. With the exception of Fitzgerald's letters to Scottie, the most important letters contained in Turnbull's *Letters* have been reprinted with editorial eyes focused more carefully than were Turnbull's on accurate transcriptions of Fitzgerald's original texts. Turnbull's *Letters* volume, however, is especially important because it made Fitzgerald's correspondence widely accessible to scholars and general readers. Whereas Wilson's collection in *The Crack-Up* provided a first step toward collection and publication of Fitzgerald's letters as well as a direction for future volumes, Turnbull's *Letters* expanded various sections of the correspondence that Wilson had published and added new ones. The single letter to Hemingway in *The Crack-Up*, for example, was expanded to a twenty-page section in *Letters*; the two letters to Gerald and Sara Murphy were expanded to six letters. After 1980, both *Correspondence* and *A Life in Letters* added substantially to the record of Fitzgerald's correspondence with Hemingway, the Murphys, and many others.

One of the most intriguing possibilities regarding Turnbull's *Letters* and his *Letters to His Daughter* is the degree to which his organizational and conceptual framework for both volumes foreshadows the direction of three of the correspondence volumes that follow. In the case of *Letters*, Turnbull grouped letters by their recipients, rather than chronologically, as had Wilson in the "Letters to Friends" section of *The Crack-Up* or as in *Correspondence* and *A Life in Letters*. In the "Letters to Frances Scott

Fitzgerald" section of *Letters* and then in his *Letters to His Daughter* volume, Turnbull focused on a single recipient, Scottie Fitzgerald. The letters within each section are themselves arranged in chronological sequence – an arrangement that follows Wilson's pattern exactly. The three remaining volumes of correspondence, excluding the two Bruccoli collections, follow Turnbull's lead, at least to a point: They organize Fitzgerald's letters by individual correspondents and they are arranged chronologically. Moreover, each volume builds on and expands one of the single sections in Turnbull's *Letters*. *Dear Scott/Dear Max*, for example, builds on Turnbull's "Letters to Maxwell Perkins"; *As Ever, Scott Fitz–* builds on Turnbull's "Letters to Harold Ober"; and *Dear Scott, Dearest Zelda* builds on Turnbull's "Letters to Zelda Fitzgerald." The point of departure from Turnbull is that each of these three volumes includes letters Fitzgerald wrote to and received from an individual. The result in each case is a volume that provides careful transcriptions of the texts of the letters and sequences them to form a linear discourse that is fully annotated and documents the relationship between Fitzgerald and either Perkins, Ober, or Zelda – individuals who have become a familiar part of the Fitzgerald narrative.

To read through the extensive correspondence between Fitzgerald and Perkins in *Dear Scott/Dear Max* is to grasp immediately the truth of the assertion of editors John Kuehl and Jackson R. Bryer that "the professional relationship between the two men was as considerate and constructive as their remarkable friendship" (*S&M* 15). The volume begins with Fitzgerald's July 26, 1919, letter to Perkins announcing that he had just the day before finished a new draft of a novel called "The Education of a Personage" that he had submitted to Scribners in another form in 1918. The novel Fitzgerald referred to in this early letter was shortly to become *This Side of Paradise*, the novel that Scribners published in 1920 and that launched Fitzgerald's career as chronicler of the flapper and poet laureate of the Jazz Age. For his part, by encouraging Fitzgerald to submit and resubmit his first novel and insisting that the conservative Charles Scribner's Sons publish Fitzgerald's book, Perkins at this early point in his career took the first step toward his own ultimate position as "dean of American editors."[1] As letter after letter in the Fitzgerald–Perkins correspondence demonstrates, Perkins never wavered in his loyalty to Fitzgerald. In the financially difficult time a year before Fitzgerald's death, when he was working steadily to finish *The Last Tycoon* with very little predictable income, Perkins offered to loan him "another thousand dollars," one of many loans and advances over the course of their friendship, and Fitzgerald acknowledged it by calling the offer "the kindest thing I ever heard of … Max, you are so kind" (*S&M* 260). But of all the wonderful letters between Fitzgerald and Perkins the most fascinating to many will likely be those exchanges that took place during the crucial revision stages of *The Great Gatsby,* which led Perkins to make this comment: "You once told me you were not a natural writer my God! You have plainly mastered the craft, of course; but you needed far more than craftsmanship for this" (*S&M* 84). Fitzgerald remained ever grateful for Perkins's many suggestions, particularly regarding the structure of *Gatsby,* which in Fitzgerald's mind so strengthened the novel that he told Perkins in a 1924 letter: "With the aid you've given me I can make 'Gatsby' perfect" (*S&M* 89). Aside from the extraordinary collection of letters from Fitzgerald to Perkins from Turnbull's volume that Kuehl and Bryer reprinted after creating more exact transcriptions and adding new letters, *Dear Scott/Dear Max* also included Perkins's side of the correspondence, along with copious notes explaining obscure references and cross-referencing allusions in the letters. Bruccoli and Duggan then added to this rich collection additional previously unpublished letters with their 1980 *Correspondence* volume.

There is a nice symmetry in the fact that the publication in 1971 of Fitzgerald's letters to and from Perkins, the only editor at Scribners he ever had, was followed in 1972 by the publication of *As Ever, Scott Fitz–*, a collection of his letters to and from Harold Ober, the only literary agent he had during his career. Ober handled the sale of Fitzgerald's commercial writing, excluding the books he published with Scribners through 1939, when the two had a falling out and parting of ways professionally over Ober's unwillingness to advance money to Fitzgerald any longer. After his break with Ober, Fitzgerald wrote the following to Kenneth Littauer, an editor at *Collier's* to whom he was presenting work as his own agent: "I've very seldom taken [Ober's] advice on stories. I have regarded him as a mixture of friend, bill collector and for a couple of sick years as backer" (*AE* 406–07). The hundreds upon hundreds of letters and cables contained in *As Ever* bear out Fitzgerald's assessment, and virtually the only correspondence that hints at feelings of warmth between the two involves Fitzgerald's daughter, Scottie, whom Ober and his wife accepted into their home on holidays from the time she became a student at the Ethel Walker School in Connecticut. The lack of a close personal relationship between Fitzgerald and Ober, however, does not detract from the fact that it is in their letters that one learns about the composition and marketing history of virtually everything Fitzgerald wrote for sale on the open market, including alterations of titles for various stories, revisions that Fitzgerald made in his commercial work, and reactions from editors who had either accepted or rejected a given piece. For those interested in Fitzgerald's career as a professional writer there is no more valuable collection of documents than the Fitzgerald–Ober correspondence. His interactions with Ober from 1919 through 1939, documented so fully in *As Ever*, bring Fitzgerald's "metamorphosis from amateur into professional" writer into high relief (*CU 86*). Later, in *A Life in Letters*, Bruccoli, who also edited *As Ever*, reprinted the most important of the hundreds of Fitzgerald–Ober letters and allowed the story of Fitzgerald's transition from amateur into professional writer to blend into the larger Fitzgerald narrative – or, as it has more often seemed, the Fitzgerald myth or legend.

To many, this Fitzgerald narrative has been from the beginning inseparable from the legend or myth of Scott and Zelda Fitzgerald, and there is considerable irony in the fact that the voices of Zelda and Scott in their letters have been among the last to be heard as Fitzgerald's correspondence was published. Wilson, for example, did not include a single letter from Fitzgerald to Zelda in *The Crack-Up*; Turnbull only included a relatively brief section of thirty-five letters from Scott to Zelda in his *Letters* volume – all of them from the period 1939 to 1940. It was not until the publication of Nancy Milford's 1969 *Zelda: A Biography*, the first and still most authoritative biography of Zelda Fitzgerald, that readers were made aware of what Milford describes as the "hundreds of letters," presumably letters from both sides of the correspondence, that would have been among the documents that are, in Milford's words, "the backbone" of her book.[2] The glimpses Milford gives into the Fitzgeralds' correspondence with each other are tantalizing, but since these glimpses are provided through short quotations from the letters or through paraphrase, the reader must often assume contextual information that one would have to have in order to assess the value of the fragments and paraphrases in relation to the main themes of Milford's book. In 1980, with the publication of *Correspondence*, Bruccoli and Duggan provided readers "twenty-three Scott-to-Zelda letters and sixty-two Zelda-to-Scott letters" (*C* xvi). All of these letters in *Correspondence* were previously unpublished, including the remarkable forty-two page letter Zelda wrote to Scott charting and describing the ways in which she believed they destroyed each other. When the *Correspondence* letters are added to the thirty-five contained in Turnbull's *Letters*, the reader is able to form from the balanced sample of letters contained in the two volumes an objective sense of the relationship between Scott and Zelda.

The most recent addition to the Scott–Zelda narrative, and a fitting anchor for the correspondence volumes published thus far, is *Dear Scott, Dearest Zelda*, which takes an important step toward providing readers with a collection of letters that demonstrates beyond a doubt that "the most important relationship that either F. Scott or Zelda Sayre Fitzgerald had was that with each other" (*S&Z* xiii). With this volume, editors Bryer and Cathy W. Barks honor both Scott and Zelda's relationship and the legacy of solid, careful scholarship that has characterized the editing of the Fitzgerald correspondence volumes leading up to *Dear Scott, Dearest Zelda*. Their relationship has been honored by the editors through their contextualizing of the letters, both in their introduction and through notes and discursive explanatory sections accompanying the letters from each phase of the relationship. The notes are without any sense of judgment toward two of the dominant forces in Scott and Zelda's relationship: his alcoholism and her mental illness. These two forces have led various biographers to take polarized stands as to whether Scott's drinking drove Zelda to insanity or whether Zelda's insanity drove Scott to drink. Bryer and Barks argue in their preface for a less reductive, more moderate position that supports a conclusion that "the most enduring impression of the Fitzgeralds that emerges from their letters is the courage, beauty, and insight born of their deep but tormented love" (*S&Z* xvi). *Dear Scott, Dearest Zelda* also builds on existing scholarship, noting precisely which of the letters in the volume have been published previously (fifty-eight letters from Scott to Zelda; sixty-three from Zelda to Scott) and inventorying the remaining unpublished Scott–Zelda letters in the Princeton University Library (twenty-two from Scott to Zelda and approximately 430 from Zelda to Scott). *Dear Scott, Dearest Zelda* includes all of Scott's known letters to Zelda as well as many of the important letters from Zelda previously published; it also includes 189 of the 430 letters from Zelda to Scott. Having the Scott–Zelda letters in a single collection allows the reader to see the harsh and accusatory letters, which are in a minority, scattered among the more frequent loving ones in which Scott remains "Sweetheart" or "Dearest Do-Do" and Zelda continues most often to be "Darling" or "Dearest." And though the following sentiment was expressed by Scott in the dark days of 1934 when Zelda was in Craig House, it reflects a sentiment that weaves its way through both sides of their exchanges to the very end: "The good things we had two years ago in Montgomery will stay with me forever, and you should feel like I do that they can be renewed, if not in a new spring, then in a new summer. I love you my darling, darling" (*S&Z* 194).

From Hollywood on December 13, 1940, Scott wrote Zelda, who was living with her mother in Montgomery, Alabama, a cheerful letter in which he recalled an episode from their lives together just before and shortly after the stock market crash of 1929, updated her on news about mutual friends including Maxwell Perkins, and reported optimistically on his novel-in-progress. He then told her of medical tests that indicated his damaged heart was improving slowly, and he promised to write again the next week, "in time for Christmas" (*S&Z* 382). On that same day he wrote Perkins to say, "I just wanted to tell you the book is coming along and that comparatively speaking all is well" (*LL* 474). Two days later he wrote to Scottie encouraging her to "be sweet to your mother at Xmas" (*LL* 475). On December 19 he wrote again to Zelda, wishing her and her friends and family "a fine time at Christmas" (*S&Z* 383). Then, two days later, on December 21, he took a break from writing his novel, which had "become of absorbing interest" (*LL* 474), and from writing the letters to those he cared for across the continent in the East. That day in the Hollywood apartment of Sheilah Graham, his companion, as he read in the alumni magazine about the Princeton football team he so faithfully followed, he stood up from his chair, reached for the mantelpiece, and fell dead of a heart attack onto the floor. On Christmas Eve, Zelda expressed in a letter to Harold Ober her love for Scott, her appreciation of him, and her grief over her loss of him in her distinctive voice with its own cadences, its own rules of spelling and punctuation, and its own lexicon: "I am heart-broken over Scott: he loved people and had deadicated so much of his life to the moral sustenance of many that I am sure that he must have left many friends. Many nights, he has worked on somebody elses manuscript, transposing a paragraph or giving a bit of advice *when he was too sick to take care of his own* He was as spiritually generous a soul as ever was; and he gave as freely of his soul as he did of whatever hospitality a hard life left him to dispose" (*AE* 424). Evidence of the generosity of Fitzgerald's soul and an abundant helping of the sustenance it provided others during his lifetime are now available for all to see in the hundreds upon hundreds of pages of Fitzgerald's letters now filling seven substantial scholarly volumes that are both a tribute to the man who wrote the letters and a gift to those they will continue to sustain.

NOTES

1 A. S. Berg, *Max Perkins: Editor of Genius* (New York: E. P. Dutton/Thomas Congdon Books, 1978), 9.

2 N. Milford, *Zelda: A Biography* (New York: Harper & Row, 1970), xiii.

4
Literary Style

Kirk Curnutt

From the moment he burst on the literary scene in 1920, F. Scott Fitzgerald was hailed as a stylist. The praise was not unmitigated, however; it often came with the qualification that his subject matter – whether the mores of the rising generation in his early novels and short stories, the adulterous triangle in *The Great Gatsby* (1925), or the expatriate dissolution of *Tender Is the Night* (1934) – was frivolous. "Whew! How That Boy Can Write!" effused the headline of a *Chicago Daily News* review of *This Side of Paradise* (1920) that likened the gusto of his prose to the pizzazz of advertising.[1] Of *Flappers and Philosophers* (1920), another commentator declared, "The stories in it are unusually well written – it seems impossible for Mr. Fitzgerald not to write well; they are clever and amusing; but that is all" (*Critical Reception* 36). And in H. L. Mencken's notoriously wrong-headed assessment of *Gatsby*, the sage of Baltimore dismisses the plot as a "glorified anecdote" while effusing over the polish of the prose: "There are pages so artfully contrived that one can no more imagine improvising them than one can imagine improvising a fugue. They are full of little delicacies, charming turns of phrase, penetrating second thoughts" (*Critical Reception* 213). (Despite that praise, Mencken's review remains risibly alone in its insistence that *Gatsby* "is certainly not to be put on the same shelf with, say, *This Side of Paradise*.") The idea that Fitzgerald's natural gift for eloquence was his greatest strength would remain a refrain throughout obituaries, memorials, and the posthumous response to *The Last Tycoon* (1941). "Nobody, of all the writers of our time, could write as well as he," concluded *Esquire* editor Arnold Gingrich in his remembrance. "Scott Fitzgerald drew the finest and purest tone from the English language of any writer since Walter Pater."[2]

The persistence of such acclaim raises questions that illustrate the difficulties of defining "fine writing." Those difficulties begin with the long-held prejudice against "little delicacies" and "charming turns of phrase" that allow an "artfully contrived" style to be denigrated as at best "a harmless bit of window dressing" and "at worst as a polite name for fraud."[3] Styles that hew close to what Roland Barthes famously called *le degré zéro de l'écriture*, or "zero-degree" writing – one thinks of Frank Norris's naturalism or Ernest Hemingway's minimalism – often boast of subverting linguistic niceties and politesse with their supposed transparency and rugged frankness. Defining themselves against literary or poetic language, they insist that writers who prefer some charm or delicacy traffic in frills and fripperies instead of exposing cold, hard truths. Authors of "fine writing" thus frequently find themselves accused of perpetuating style over substance. Among Fitzgerald's many early critics, it was Edmund Wilson – a friend if not exactly a supporter in Fitzgerald's lifetime – who invoked this idea most nastily. Wilson begins a 1922 *Bookman* estimation, "F. Scott Fitzgerald," with a sardonic putdown purportedly provided by his lover, Edna St. Vincent Millay: "It has been said by a celebrated person that to meet F. Scott Fitzgerald is to think of a stupid old woman with whom someone left a diamond; she is extremely proud of the diamond and shows it to everyone who comes by, and everyone is surprised that such an ignorant old woman should possess so valuable a jewel; for in nothing does she appear so inept as in the remarks she makes about the diamond" (*In His Own Time*, 404–09; 404). In this formulation, the jewel is Fitzgerald's "exhilaratingly clever" facility with words, a bauble that on the surface enchants by glittering, but one whose gauche, gaudy display in his prose demonstrates that the author "has been given a gift for expression without many ideas to express." Such criticism would inspire in Fitzgerald a career-long defensiveness toward being labeled a "facile" writer.[4]

Perhaps sensitive as well to this charge, enthusiasts have generally shied away from assessing Fitzgerald's style in favor of explicating its thematic significance – arguing, for example, that the lapidary prose of *Gatsby* reflects a conservative nostalgia for social order, or that the more oblique discursiveness of *Tender* marks the author's floundering faith in imagination.[5] To be sure, there is no shortage of testimonials to the beauty of his writing. The late Matthew J. Bruccoli was fond of quoting Raymond Chandler's 1950 comments: "He had one of the rarest qualities in all of literature ... [T]he word is charm – charm as Keats would have used it ... It's not a matter of pretty writing or clear style. It's a kind of subdued magic, controlled and exquisite, the sort of thing you get from good string quartets."[6] Despite such encomia, the sources of that "charm" and "magic" mostly go unelaborated – in part, again, for fear of overemphasizing the comeliness of Fitzgerald's prose. Yet what if we admitted that part of the appeal of his writing is indeed its "prettiness"? What might we learn about the gratifications of polish and craft that might make the finery of style seem more substantial than the cut of a suave tuxedo or the sophisticated slake of a martini?

As much as how one uses words, style constitutes a rhetorical stance: It bespeaks not only how a writer addresses the audience but the effect he or she hopes to achieve. Rebel writers set out to shock and offend, moralists to redeem, and still others aim for no further goal than to entertain. Fitzgerald's goal, simply stated, was to move the reader through what he called "the chime" of words, "their most utter value for evocation, persuasion or charm" (*L* 88). As he wrote paraphrasing Conrad to Hemingway in 1934, "[T]he purpose of fiction is to appeal to the lingering after-effects in the reader's mind as differing from, say, the purpose of oratory or philosophy which respectively leave people in a fighting or thoughtful mood" (*L* 309) – a line that seemingly defines language as an emotional stimulant, one whose enduring power lies in its inability to be shaken long after the initial arousal has worn off. But one need not look to Fitzgerald's scattered and often abstract aesthetic pronouncements to infer his purpose. It is present in his style's fervid appeal to pathos. As a devotee of Romantic poetry, Fitzgerald believed in dramatizing the intensity of emotion, often depicting his characters as overcome by reveries that compel them to profoundly morose insights into the intangibility of romance, dreams, and identity. These are moments Milton R. Stern describes as passages of "lyrical intoxication" that convey "the lush expression of internalities … excited sensibilities, feeling and response, mood for its own sake and" – in a description that again suggests how an elaborate style can seem indulgent and extraneous – "luxurious literary showing off."[7]

As examples of what another critic calls Fitzgerald's propensity for the "verbal swoon," one might cite Amory Blaine's pondering of the spires and gargoyles of Princeton in the closing paragraphs of *Paradise*, which leads to his realization that his generation has "grown up to find all Gods dead, all wars fought, all faiths in man shaken" (*TSOP* 269).[8] Or one might note Dexter Green's sudden awareness in "Winter Dreams" (1922) that Judy Jones no longer symbolizes his aspiration: "The dream was gone. Something had been taken from him … The gates were closed, the sun was gone down, and there was no beauty but the grey beauty of steel that withstands all time …" (*ASYM* 65). Rhythmically propulsive, these passages are often built out of chains of conjoined sentences, sometimes periodic and sometimes cadenced for parallelism, or else they link appositives and subordinate clauses to structure a crescendo in emotion.

Such rhapsodies are more diverse than we might expect. Not only are they not necessarily confined to the final page of a text, as the preceding examples suggest, but they draw from various genres and serve a range of purposes. In some cases, they may evoke a "Kubla Khan"-style hallucination, as when the disoriented Southern belle Sally Carrol Happer in "The Ice Palace" (1920) imagines perishing in the inhospitable Minnesota winter (*F&P* 58–59). In others, the rhythm of the prose builds from an itemizing of historical details, as when Dick Diver elaborates upon the "whole-souled sentimental equipment" accounting for the significance of the Somme battlefield he walks in *Tender Is the Night* (75), or when Fitzgerald spends upwards of 300 words on Nicole Diver's shopping spree to demonstrate how she "illustrate[s] very simple principles" of consumerism (*TITN* 71–72). Still elsewhere, the building oratory may conclude with a maxim indicative of didactic or moralizing literature – *The Beautiful and Damned* (1922) is peppered with dozens of these interjected wisdoms on everything from aging to concupiscence to the inexorability of melancholy.

More felicitously, the ecstasy may culminate in an epiphany, as when Josephine Perry in "Emotional Bankruptcy" (1931) realizes she has squandered her capacity to love (*B&J* 286). In rarer instances, the passage is capped by a device borrowed directly from Romantic poetry, such as the apostrophe at the end of the posthumously published tribute to New York, "My Lost City": "Come back O glittering and white – " (*MLC* 115). Most famously, the oratory will climax in a beguiling image, as in the quintessential moment when Nick Carraway celebrates Gatsby for embodying the peculiarly resilient American capacity for wonder and optimism: "It eluded us then, but that's no matter – tomorrow we will run faster, stretch out our arms farther ... And one fine morning – So we beat on, boats against the current, borne ceaselessly into the past" (*GG* 180).

More often than *Gatsby*'s arresting final symbol, however, these "lush internalities" tend to revel in a metaphor dramatizing its own rumbling intensity, as in the conclusion of "Jacob's Ladder" (1927): "The wave [of realization] appeared far off, sent up whitecaps, rolled toward him with the might of pain, washed over him. 'Never any more. Never any more.' The wave beat upon him, drove him down, pounding with the hammer of agony on his ears ..." (*S* 371). As in "Winter Dreams," such passages can seem overwritten, if not overtly melodramatic. The worry that Fitzgerald could lay it on a little too thick pinpoints the critical concern with his style in general: Its appeal to pathos violates a fundamental precept of modernism. As T. S. Eliot declared in "Tradition and the Individual

Talent" (1919), "Poetry [and literature in general] is not a turning loose of emotion, but an escape from emotion."[9] In fiction, that escape might be accomplished through any number of means. It might be achieved through what James Joyce called the "scrupulous meanness" of style, the unadorned realism of *Dubliners* (1914) that refuses either to moralize or make pretty.[10] Or it might occur through the spectatorial detachment of the narrative stance, as when Frederic Henry in *A Farewell to Arms* (1929) or the camera eye in John Dos Passos's *Nineteen-Nineteen* (1932) can only comprehend violence and brutality with detached stoicism. More experimentally, emotion might be discharged through the objective correlative of symbolism or allusion, or bracketed in layers of narrative irony through the use of free indirect discourse or interior monologue (a particular strength of Katherine Anne Porter). It might even be diffused through a chosen technique or two, as in Gertrude Stein's incantatory use of repetition and rhythm in *Three Lives* (1909) or *The Making of Americans* (1925), in which style lulls the reader into a hypnotic (some might say somnambulistic) state. Whatever their method, most modernists scrupulously eschewed what Fitzgerald himself sometimes regarded as the "blankets," "ruminations," and even "sideshows" within his "poetic prose." He had a simple reason for loosening emotion through such passages, however: these "sideshows," he admitted, "often turn out to be highspots" (*AE* 411).

Modernist histories teach that Eliot, Ezra Pound, Hemingway, and others avoided dramatizing emotional frenzies because they regarded feeling as corrupt and vulgar, as too redolent of the shriek and sentimentality of mass culture to serve an artistic aim. And while escaping emotion proved easier in theory than practice – plenty of sentimentality churns through *Dubliner*'s "The Dead" and *To the Lighthouse* (1927) – Fitzgerald's overt soliciting of it is one reason in his own day he was as often compared to authors such as Robert W. Chambers, Harold McGrath, and even O. Henry as he was to Joyce, Virginia Woolf, or Dos Passos. It is also the reason that for decades critics such as James E. Miller argued that his artistic maturity was incumbent upon his learning to harness his lyrical reveries to demonstrate "an absolute certainty of authorial control."[11] Equating "authorial control" with suppressing emotion does not merely reflect the modernist aversion to Romanticism, however. It also reflects a need to inoculate Fitzgerald from any association with a genre that established itself in the marketplace as a durably popular form in the same early 1920s in which he first emerged: romance fiction. While a great deal of critical effort has gone into ameliorating Fitzgerald's affinities with the exclamatory impulses of Keats, Byron, Shelley, and even Swinburne and Brooke, comparatively little has been done even to begin measuring his stylistic affinities with a mode whose loosened emotion is often mockingly derided as its sole raison d'être. Consider a passage from *The Great Gatsby* that comes dangerously close to cloying:

> One autumn night, five years before, [Gatsby and Daisy] had been walking down the street when the leaves were falling, and they came to a place where there were no trees and the sidewalk was white with moonlight. They stopped here and turned toward each other. Now it was a cool night with that mysterious excitement in it which comes at the two changes of the year. The quiet lights in the houses were humming out into the darkness and there was a stir and bustle among the stars. Out of the corner of his eye Gatsby saw that the blocks of the sidewalks really formed a ladder and mounted to a secret place above the trees – he could climb to it, if he climbed alone, and once there he could suck the pap of life, gulp down the incomparable milk of wonder.
>
> His heart beat faster and faster as Daisy's white face came up to his own. He knew that when he kissed this girl, and forever wed his unutterable visions to her perishable breath, his mind would never romp again like the mind of God. So he waited, listening for a moment longer to the tuning fork that had been struck upon a star. Then he kissed her. At his lips' touch she blossomed for him like a flower and the incarnation was complete. (*GG* 111)

Moonlight, stars, ladders to the heavens, flowers, trees, and even breath are all stock imagery in popular/pulp-fiction tableaux of passion in the 1920s, where they serve to create a romantic atmosphere that both legitimizes and elevates sexual desire into the "higher" realm of love. Two constituent elements make such scenes vulnerable to derisive stereotyping: the manner by which images and metaphors serve as euphemisms for physiological urges (sucking the pap of life) and the way in which their rapid concatenation seems to mimic the frenzied rhythm of sexual climax. To appreciate how compatible Fitzgerald's style at such moments is with romance fiction, one can extract a passage from a representative work published in the same year in which *Gatsby* is set, Joan Conquest's *The Hawk of Egypt* (1922), a self-advertised "novel without asterisks" that belonged to a deluge of tales of exotic Middle Eastern romance inspired by the massive success of E. M. Hull's *The Sheik* (1919). Here is the obligatorily swarthy Arab prince, Hugh Carden Ali, pining for the obligatorily fetching English heroine, Damaris:

> The floods of love drown me, the full-blossomed trees of passion throw their shade upon the surging waters, and, behold, the shade is that of tenderness. From the midst of the flood where I am likely to drown, I stretch my arms to the rocky shore where stands, looking towards me, the desire of my soul. Behold,

my eyes have seen her, and behold, her hair is white, with hair like the desert at sunset, and eyes even as the pools of Lebanon. She is as a rod to be bent, and as a vase of perfume to be broken upon a night of love ... a doe to be hunted at dawn, a mare to be spurred through the watches of night – [12]

Of course, an argument can be made that through *Gatsby*'s incarnating kiss Fitzgerald critiques, if not subtly parodies, just this sort of overripe, metaphorical excess. And yet, despite the deeper resonances that reassure more literary-minded readers that his kiss is not maudlin or sappy, countless other romantic passages in Fitzgerald *do not* qualify the language of love in this manner. In "The Ice Palace," Sally Carrol Happer kisses Harry Bellamy "until the sky seemed to fade out and all her smiles and tears to vanish in an ecstasy of eternal seconds" (*F&P* 43). In *The Beautiful and Damned*, Anthony Patch finds a kiss from future wife Gloria "a flower held against the face, never to be described" – despite Fitzgerald's having just spent about a hundred words describing it – "scarcely to be remembered; as though her beauty were giving off emanations of itself which settled transiently and already dissolving upon his heart" (*B&D* 91). Even in *The Last Tycoon*, the unfinished novel in which Fitzgerald claimed he was assiduously restraining his floridity, one finds sentences that would fit as well in a romance novel as they would any literary contemporary this side of D. H. Lawrence: "Stahr's eyes and Kathleen's met and tangled. For an instant they made love as no one ever dares to after. Their glance was closer than an embrace, more urgent than a call" (*LT* 64).

These examples all illustrate a point Richard D. Lehan succinctly made in the mid-1960s: "[T]he key to Fitzgerald's style is overstatement."[13] The emotional intensity is evident not just in elaborate passages of "lyrical intoxication" but in far more compact scenic evocations of mood. When Hemingway wanted to convey a striking detail, he would fix on it with literal precision, as when Jake Barnes comments on Brett Ashley's pallor during a Parisian taxi ride: "[The Avenue des Gobelins] was torn up and men were working on the car-tracks by the light of the acetylene flares. Brett's face was white and the long line of her neck showed in the bright light of the flares."[14] Fitzgerald, by contrast, never simply notes a "bright light" but emblazons it through elaboration, as in a comparable scene from *Tender Is the Night* when Dick Diver and Rosemary Hoyt steal a kiss: "[T]hey fell ravenously on the quick seconds while outside the taxi windows the green and cream twilight faded, and the fire-red, gas-blue, ghost-green signs began to shine smokily through the tranquil rain. It was nearly six, the streets were in movement, the bistros gleamed, the Place de la Concorde moved by in pink majesty as the cab turned north" (*TITN*

97). Not only would Hemingway blanch at the regality and effeminacy of "pink majesty"; he would pencil out any adverb such as "ravenously" as undisciplined in its dramatizing of desire. It is the seemingly gratuitous "fire-red, gas-blue, ghost-green" that would strike him as indicative of the ornamentation or "scrollwork" that for him was better implied than enumerated, however. Yet this intensification – what Fitzgerald himself would call "surcharg[ing]" the mood (*TITN* 18, 40) – is essential to the vibrancy we associate with him. An earlier passage in *Tender*, for example, describes the sea "as mysteriously colored as the agates and cornelians of childhood, green as green milk, blue as laundry water, wine dark" (*TITN* 19). In addition to concatenated appositives, Fitzgerald might intensify the emotion by employing color dissociation (the "blue lawn" of Gatsby's mansion) or even synesthesia (the "yellow cocktail music" at his parties, the "scherzo of color" in *Tender* [*TITN* 33]). Whatever the particular technique, as Lehan notes, his "prose is inflated to create a moonlit, magically heightened world," one in which details never simply "show" but "glitter," "gleam," "smolder," "tremble," "flower," "throb," "quaver," and "exude" (42). To use another favorite Fitzgerald word that is too ostentatious for most modernists, his style insists on educing the *splendor* of experience.

In some instances, Fitzgerald was so intent on enlivening the emotion of a scene or passage that he resorted to an extreme personification that can be equal parts absurd and precious. "Head and Shoulders" (1920) includes a transitional passage depicting spring's blossoming: "March mellowed into April. May read a gorgeous riot act to the parks and waters of Manhattan, and they were very happy" (*F&P* 77). Even more surreally, "The Ice Palace" describes shadows on Southern street corners as "twilight play[ing] at somnolent black-and-white checkers with the end of day" (*F&P* 43). Nor is it only nature that receives this treatment. "Rags Martin-Jones and the Pr-nce of W-les" (1924) opens with a luxury liner called *The Majestic* entering New York with all the haughty pomp its name suggests: "She sniffed at the tugboats and turtle-gaited ferries, winked at a gaudy young yacht, and ordered a cattle-boat out of her way with a snarling whistle of steam" (*S* 273). As tempting as it is to dismiss the use of personification and the pathetic fallacy as pandering to the commercial marketplace's demand for writing that is "clever and amusing, but that is all," these devices appear throughout *Gatsby, Tender*, and his "serious" efforts. One famous closing paragraph anthropomorphizes Long Island as "the fresh, green breast of the new world" (*GG* 180), while the picturesque opening vista of another describes the Gausse Hotel on the Riviera as so "proud" that its "flushed" façade must be shaded by "deferential" palms (*TITN* 3). Fitzgerald's land- and cityscapes are rarely inert backdrops – more often they are animated, in some cases dramatizing the poetry of vivacity, in others the poetry of melancholy, but always insisting that the world is fundamentally alive.

The desire to elevate and animate, then, is what motivates the "fine," "pretty," and even "delicate" qualities of Fitzgerald's style. Even when evoking modernism's favorite theme of aridity and sterility, he emphasizes the poetic over the imagistic, employing devices that call attention to the constructed musicality of his prose instead of passing off language as a verbal icon, the thing in itself: "This is a valley of ashes – a fantastic farm where ashes grow like wheat into ridges and hills and grotesque gardens; where ashes take the forms of houses and chimneys and rising smoke and, finally, with transcendent effort, of men who move dimly and already crumbling through the powdery air" (*GG* 23). Alliteration was hardly a taboo for the modernist fiction writer, of course, yet it tends to appear in Joyce, Dos Passos, and Faulkner either as a satirical device emphasizing the pomposity of official, bureaucratized language, or, conversely, in internalized modes of discourse (stream of consciousness) to convey associative as opposed to logical patterns of thought. Relatively few fiction writers – Virginia Woolf is the major exception – employed it as Fitzgerald does here: as a linguistic dollop. (The reason for modernists' aversion was simple: Alliteration sounded like Victorian artifice.) Of course, Fitzgerald modifies *farms* with *fantastic* and *gardens* with *grotesque* here to dramatize the *irreality* of this vista, which is itself hardly a rarity among modernists. Yet hallucinatory glimpses of Eliot's "unreal city" for most are apt to be phantasmagoric rather than picturesque, which again is Fitzgerald's characteristic instinct. If a "throbbing" urban environ makes Nick Carraway imagine New Yorkers "hurrying toward gayety" (*GG* 57), it is more likely to drive the nocturnal denizens of Djuna Barnes's *Nightwood* (1936) to despair. Barnes's transvestite soliloquist, Dr. Matthew O'Connor, can only conceive of emotion as terror and alienation; for him, "the very constitution of twilight is a fabulous reconstruction of fear, fear bottom-out and wrong side up."[15] Even in Fitzgerald's most unrelentingly despondent novel, *Tender Is the Night*, the specters haunting expatriate life pause for the romantic possibilities. For every image of madness and disfigurement, there are sentences that seem present solely to suggest the sentience of setting, as if characters may at any moment be "drowned and engulfed in love" (*TITN* 203): "The river shimmered with lights from the bridges and cradled many cold moons" (*TITN* 79); "Two thousand feet below [Nicole] saw the necklace and bracelet of lights that were Montreux and Vevey, beyond them a dim pendant of Lausanne" (*TITN* 160); "[T]hey swam in Beaulieu in a roofless cavern of white moonlight formed by a circlet of pale boulders about a cup of phosphorescent water ... " (*TITN* 384).

In the end, the beauty of such images suggests that other concept that many modernists claimed they were escaping: *sensibility.* Perhaps the best statement on Fitzgerald's temperament – with one caveat – comes from Lionel Trilling: "Even in Fitzgerald's early, cruder books, even in his commercial stories, and even when his style is careless, there is a tone and pitch to the sentences which suggest his warmth and tenderness, and what is rare nowadays and not likely to be admired, his gentleness without softness."[16] While that final prepositional phrase seems an unfortunate euphemism for assuring us that a male writer who is neither tight-lipped nor stoic is not perforce effeminate, Trilling's other characteristics – "warmth," "tenderness," and "gentleness" – are themselves pitch-perfect. Above all, Fitzgerald's style conveys a sensitivity or receptiveness to emotion that suggests a pining for the sublime elevation of art. For him, language was neither a tool of incitement nor a form of containment. It was a means to rhapsody, and like the titular nightingale of the Keats poem he adored so much, he wanted his words to sing.

NOTES

1 H. Hansen, "Whew! How That Boy Can Write!" in J. R. Bryer (ed.), F. *Scott Fitzgerald: The Critical Reception* (New York: Burt Franklin, 1978), 1–2; 1. Subsequent references to this work are included in the text.

2 A. Gingrich, "Salute and Farewell to F. Scott Fitzgerald" in M. J. Bruccoli and J. R. Bryer (eds.), *F. Scott Fitzgerald In His Own Time* (Kent, OH: Kent University Press, 1941), 477–81; 478. Subsequent references to works in this collection are included in the text.

3 F. N. Thomas, *Clear and Simple as the Truth: Writing Classic Prose* (Princeton, NJ: Princeton University Press), 9.

4 See, for example, "Afternoon of an Author" (1936): "[T]hey said he had 'fatal facility,' and he labored like a slave over every sentence so as not to be like that" (*S* 738).

5 Examples include J. Giltrow and D. Stouck, "Style as Politics in *The Great Gatsby*," *Studies in the Novel* 29 (Winter 1997), 476–90, and G. Toles, "The Metaphysics of Style in *Tender Is the Night*," *American Literature* 62 (September 1990), 423–44.

6 R. Chandler, *The Raymond Chandler Papers: Selected Letters and Nonfiction, 1909–1959*, qtd. in T. Hiney and F. McShane, eds. (Boston: Atlantic Monthly Press, 2002), 140.

7 M. R. Stern, "*The Last Tycoon* and Fitzgerald's Last Style," in J. R. Bryer, R. Prigozy, and M. R. Stern (eds.), *F. Scott Fitzgerald in the Twenty-First Century* (Tuscaloosa: University of Alabama Press, 2003), 317–32; 318.
8 For the "verbal swoon" line, see D. Monk, "Fitzgerald: The Tissue of Style," *Journal of American Studies* 17.1 (1983), 77–94; 77.
9 T. S. Eliot, *Selected Prose of T. S. Eliot*, F. Kermode, ed. (New York: Houghton Mifflin Harcourt, 1975), 43.
10 J. Joyce, *Letters of James Joyce, Volume II*, R. Ellmann, ed. (New York: Viking, 1966), 134.
11 J. E. Miller, *F. Scott Fitzgerald: His Art and His Technique* (New York: New York University Press), 139.
12 J. Conquest, *The Hawk of Egypt* (New York: Macaulay, 1922), 61.
13 R. D. Lehan, *F. Scott Fitzgerald and the Craft of Fiction* (Carbondale: Southern Illinois University Press, 1966), 42. Subsequent references to this work are included in the text.
14 E. Hemingway, *The Sun Also Rises* (New York: Charles Scribner's Sons, 1926), 25.
15 D. Barnes, *Nightwood* (London: Faber and Faber, 1936), 80.
16 L. Trilling, *The Liberal Imagination: Essays on Literature and Society*, L. Menad, ed. (New York: New York Review of Books, 2008), 244.

5

Literary Influences

William Blazek

F. Scott Fitzgerald declared to himself: "Great art is the contempt of a great man for small art" (*N* 162). His literary influences reflect that maxim, in that the writing he most admired and the work he most often adapted for his own fiction were of lasting quality. John Keats and Joseph Conrad are the most frequently cited of his literary exemplars. Fitzgerald's art steadily evolved through each of his five novels, demonstrating how consciously he aspired for greatness and how assiduously he crafted his literary influences toward a distinctive personal style and particular structural and thematic aims. While Fitzgerald could be caustic about some of the publications of his contemporaries and offered specific reasons for their failings in his critiques,[1] he was just as often an enthusiastic advocate of those among his fellow writers who had broken new ground in ways that further stretched and enhanced the canon. The novelist demanded excellence and a sense of legacy from his fellow writers (and critical understanding from his readers, beyond those "curious children nosed at the slime of Mr. Tiffany Thayer in the drug-store libraries" [*MLC* 148]). John Dos Passos and Archibald MacLeish, among others, testified to his acuity in matters of technique and narrative structure, and Ernest Hemingway benefited from his advice on drafts of both *The Sun Also Rises* and *A Farewell to Arms*.[2] Fitzgerald's conception of his place in literary history was announced early on, in his first successful short story, "Tarquin of Cheapside," with its clever revelation about a young William Shakespeare.[3] Frances Kroll Ring's memoir includes this supportive comment: "His hope was to attain a measure of immortality in the literary world and that stubborn objective repeated itself throughout his lifetime."[4] Lionel Trilling also emphasizes the reach of Fitzgerald's ambition: "[H]e put himself, in all modesty, in the line of greatness, he judged himself in a large way."[5] "My whole theory of writing," Fitzgerald wrote in May 1920, "I can sum up in one sentence: An author ought to write for the youth of his own generation, the critics of the next, and the schoolmasters of ever afterward."[6] The statement is both callow and perceptive, for Fitzgerald was highly conscious of the permanent mark he might make, and he was a confident critic of the American writers of his generation; only two others, Hemingway and Thomas Wolfe, did he consider his rivals. Instead, Fitzgerald looked mainly toward England and its literary tradition when he envisioned his career. However, applying Harold Bloom's conception of literary influence does not sit particularly well in Fitzgerald's case. Bloom argues from a long history of English poetry and prose that authors engage in "creative misreading" of their literary predecessors in order to unlock new technical paradigms and achieve canonical ascendancy.[7] The dominant feeling that emerges from Fitzgerald's comments on literary artists is that he was a novelist striving to enter the guild of prestigious authors. Nevertheless, in comparing himself with and utilizing the lessons from other writers, Fitzgerald most often employed creative reading, not so much to argue with or denigrate the work of others but to capture the most useful elements of their craft, apply it to his own plans, and discard or avoid influences that no longer served his purposes.

The emergence of Fitzgerald's distinctive balance of romantic lyricism and realist determinism can be traced to foundational sources in poetry and prose. Fitzgerald thought of his reading as both career- and character-forming, stating, "one's first influences are largely literary but the point where the personal note emerges *can* come very young (*vidé* Keats)" (*L* 593). Keats provided him with a touchstone, a model for a controlled romantic style and thematic juxtapositions of the imaginary and the real. The poet also demonstrated how, as André Le Vot explains, the writer's presence in the world could be affirmed through language that is sumptuous and musical as well as focused on ideas.[8] Fitzgerald's love for Romantic poetry was instilled in him during his childhood, when his father would recite to him from Byron's *The Prisoner of Chillon*. At Princeton he was unimpressed by his poetry tutors, but he spent months intensely discussing Wordsworth, Lord Byron, Percy Bysshe Shelley, and Keats with his Princeton classmate John Peale Bishop, who would be characterized in *This Side of Paradise* and epigraphed in *The Great Gatsby* as Thomas Parke D'Invilliers. "You need, at the beginning, some enthusiast who also knows his way around," he wrote to his daughter, Scottie, while she was beginning her undergraduate courses at Vassar, "– John Peale Bishop performed that office for me at Princeton." He elaborated on his ideas about poetry to Scottie in this way:

> Poetry is either something that lives like fire in you … or else it is nothing, an empty formalized bore around which pedants can endlessly drone their notes

and explanations. The Grecian Urn is unbearably beautiful with every syllable as inevitable as the notes in Beethoven's Ninth Symphony or it's just something you don't understand ... Likewise with The Nightingale which I can never read through without tears in my eyes; ... and The Eve of St. Agnes, which has the richest, most sensuous imagery in English, not excepting Shakespeare. And finally his three of four great sonnets, Bright Star and the others.

Knowing those things very young and granted an ear, one could scarcely every afterwards be unable to distinguish between gold and dross in what one read. In themselves those eight poems are a scale of workmanship for anybody who wants to know truly about words, their most utter value for evocation, persuasion or charm. For awhile after you quit Keats all other poetry seems to be only whistling or humming. (*LL* 460)

The evaluation, written within the last five months of his life, reveals Fitzgerald's own artistic aims to evoke, persuade, and charm in his prose; to use lyricism pointedly within structural imagery and metaphor; to provoke readers to both feel and think. Creating something "unbearably beautiful" requires more than self-indulgent aestheticism; it demands a richer poignancy, associated with the losses and failures of life. Great writers, Fitzgerald implies, also need to discriminate between gold and dross in their own work by weighing it against the excellence of others.

Setting himself up against the youthful Romantic poets in his own early success, Fitzgerald also drew upon more contemporary sources, most of which he abandoned as he grew in confidence about his ability and as he developed the range of his material. Aestheticism flowed through his youthful reading of Wilde and Swinburne while the social reform literature of Wells and Shaw served as counterpoint. Compton Mackenzie's *Sinister Street* was an inspiration for a generation of American Ivy Leaguers, including Dos Passos at Harvard; certainly for the aspiring Fitzgerald the appeal of this narrative of Cambridge undergraduate life was embedded in the formation of *This Side of Paradise* (although "much more in intention than in literal fact," he later explained, adding that "my literary taste was so unformed that *Youth's Encounter* [*Sinister Street*'s first volume in the American edition] was still my 'perfect book'" [*L* 468–69]). Booth Tarkington's novel *Seventeen* (1916) and Owen Johnson's *Stover at Yale* (1912) were also backdrops for his exuberant debut, with its vaudeville mixtures of form and technique. "I am a professed literary thief," he admitted in what was probably a self-penned newspaper interview shortly after the novel was published. Writing about style as "color," Fitzgerald announced his intentions while revealing his admirations: "I want to be able to do anything with words: handle slashing, flaming descriptions like Wells, and use the paradox with the clarity of Samuel Butler, the breadth of Bernard Shaw and the wit of Oscar Wilde. I want to do the wide sultry heavens of Conrad, the rolled-gold sundowns and crazy-quilt skies of Hichens and Kipling, as well as the pastelle dawns of Chesterton."[9] In correspondence with Edmund Wilson in 1918 about the first draft called "The Romantic Egotist," Fitzgerald confessed "It shows traces of Tarkington, Chesterton, Chambers[,] Wells, Benson (Robert Hugh), Rupert Brooke and includes Compton-Mckenzie like love-affairs" (*LL* 17). A more stable influence was Samuel Butler's *Notebooks* (1912), from which he derived narrative sketch-patterns and confessional passages, but also a professional manual for gathering material for later reflection and composition. When he described the novel as "A Romance and a Reading List" he was not so much denigrating its naivety as acknowledging its eclectic form – since the rest of that entry in his *Notebooks* reads "Sun Also Rises. A Romance and a Guide Book" (*N* 158). Despite what seems a hodgepodge of youthful enthusiasms and immediate associations, *This Side of Paradise* nevertheless exhibits a distinctive American voice and energy that shows how the author was able to mold literary sources to his own ends.

Fitzgerald took that first effort in novel writing to a different level with *The Beautiful and Damned* two years later. Originally he planned to use the title *The Beautiful Lady Without Mercy* (*L* 464), and Keatsian rhythms run through the first half of the finished novel. But by early 1921 the name and focus of the project had altered, as he turned to new inspirations – novels by American naturalists, especially Theodore Dreiser, Frank Norris, and his brother, Charles G. Norris, along with the work of Joseph Conrad – sources introduced to him by H. L. Mencken, the co-editor (with George Jean Nathan) of the *Smart Set* literary magazine, where Fitzgerald first announced himself as the spokesman for the Jazz Age. In large measure, *The Beautiful and Damned* can be seen as a repudiation of the fruitless indulgences behind his generation's new freedoms that he wrote about in *This Side of Paradise* and his early stories. He chronicles in his second novel the physical and moral deterioration of the wealthy and glamorous central characters, Anthony Patch and Gloria Gilbert. He explained to his editor at Scribners, Maxwell Perkins, how the new perspective arrived: "I've fallen lately under the influence of an author who's quite changed my point of view. He's a chestnut to you, no doubt, but I've just discovered him – Frank Norris" (*S&M* 28), citing the naturalist novels *McTeague* (1899) and *Vandover and the Brute* (1914). Fitzgerald would add them to his store of deterministic fiction, along with Charles G. Norris' *Salt* (1917) and Dreiser's *Sister Carrie* (1900).

Moreover, a new discovery appeared who would come to play a key role in how the young novelist thought about his approach to writing, as he told Perkins: "I'm not so cocksure about things as I was last summer [1919] – this fellow Conrad seems to be pretty good after all" (*S&M* 28). Although Conrad's influence would later be integrated with modernist techniques and ideas in *The Great Gatsby* and more fully in *Tender Is the Night*, it already demonstrates its sway in *The Beautiful and Damned*'s pessimistic mood and its characters' spiral into anomie.[10]

Those qualities reappear in *The Great Gatsby*, but Conrad's structural and stylistic presence is more prominent in this text. The narrative focus of Nick Carraway, who is both "within and without" as both secondary character and observer-narrator, is paralleled by Marlow in *Heart of Darkness* – although Jay Gatsby is much more at the center of action than is Kurtz in Conrad's more psychologically refined study. The stylistic similarities emerge from a deeper vein, as Fitzgerald often expressed a debt to Conrad's preface to *The Nigger of the 'Narcissus,'* with its delineation of new aesthetic objectives. The preface asserts that "A work that aspires, however humbly, to the condition of art should carry its justification in every line," and because it "appeals primarily to the senses" it should achieve "the perfect blending of form and substance; it is only through an unremitting, never-discouraged care for the shape and ring of sentences that an approach can be made to plasticity, to color, and that the light of magic suggestiveness may be brought to play for an evanescent instant over the commonplace surface of words: of the old, old words, worn thin, defaced by ages of careless usage."[11] Andrew Hook argues that reading Conrad's preface "could only have resulted in an enormous renewal of Fitzgerald's artistic self-confidence,"[12] after the relative disappointment of *The Beautiful and Damned*; certainly Conrad's revivalist artistic credo, formal devices, and emphasis on sensual colorings and nuances would have appealed to Fitzgerald's judgment of his own strengths. His older contemporary also had an enviable record of critically acclaimed success; Conrad's arguably five most distinguished novels appeared within eleven years, from 1904 to 1915.[13] As he began what would become his third novel within five years, Fitzgerald consciously looked toward the critics and his reputation when he composed *The Great Gatsby* with a tight structure and a sophisticated narrative form ("in protest against my own formless two novels," he told Mencken). As the manuscript neared completion in 1924 he exclaimed to Perkins that "My book is wonderful" and "I think my novel is about the best American novel ever written" (*LL* 110, 77, 80).

Proof of Fitzgerald's maturation as an artist in *The Great Gatsby* is that he was able to draw upon a number of literary pathfinders in the achievement of his own goal. Besides the crucial template provided by Conrad, he also found inspiration from Mark Twain's explorations of Western myth in the face of America's new commercial and industrial forces. From Henry James came the international theme, converted to an East-West divide within the borders of the United States, the Atlantic gap condensed to the Long Island inlet separating East and West Egg. "Daisy Miller" provided the first name for the femme fatale of Gatsby's dreams. For Fitzgerald, James also represented – along with Conrad, Edith Wharton, H. G. Wells, and W. M. Thackeray – the epitome of career achievement, a figure to be emulated, as James himself viewed Balzac and Flaubert. More specifically, the plot of Charles Dickens's *Great Expectations* is centered on a poor boy's pursuit of a beautiful rich girl, and Trimalchio's ostentatious feast in *The Satyricon* by the Latin satirist Petronius was updated into the descriptions of Gatsby's parties. Fitzgerald also came under the spell of Fyodor Dostoevsky's *The Brothers Karamazov*, shown in the tussle of egos between Carraway and Gatsby, the merging of their social consciousnesses into a mutual understanding of the weight of American ideals. In addition, modernist techniques of time bending, layered narrative, color symbolism, and omission are applied in the text. Fitzgerald completed the *Gatsby* manuscript in Europe during his first major exposure to modernist thinkers and practitioners,[14] and a revealing comment from April 1923 welds two sides of his outlook, citing Conrad's *Nostromo* as "The great novel of the past fifty years, as 'Ulysses' is the great novel of the future" (qtd. in Bruccoli, *Epic Grandeur* 173). Joyce was the modern master for him along with T. S. Eliot, "the greatest living poet in any language" (*LL* 137). Fitzgerald famously drew upon *The Waste Land* and related poetic visions of sterile landscapes and hollow lives when he included the Valley of Ashes setting in *Gatsby*, yet it was also more generally Eliot and Joyce's daring technical and aesthetic innovations combined with the self-belief that drove them toward greatness that inspired the American novelist. His later meetings with Joyce and Eliot (as well as with Edith Wharton and an attempted audience with Conrad) illustrate his tendency to hero-worship famous literary contemporaries but also demonstrate how Fitzgerald saw himself as a worthy member of their company. Following the publication of *Gatsby*, he reveled in receiving insightful letters of admiration from Eliot, Wharton, and Willa Cather, treating their correspondence as if he had been awarded badges of honor for admission to the pantheon.

While Conrad remained a constant presence in his thinking about literary art, Fitzgerald was also mindful of maintaining his own originality, not only in subject matter but in his own contribution to a distinctive modern form. Thus he warned himself and Hemingway to "beware Conrad rhythms in direct quotation from characters" (*L* 300). Yet it was Conrad and Keats as standards of excellence whom he referred to when working through the nine-year gestation of *Tender Is the Night*. Fitzgerald took the title from, and quoted for an epigraph, the fourth stanza of "Ode to a Nightingale," omitting key lines to highlight loss and doubt over invocations of literary immortality. He explained to Perkins not long after the publication of *Gatsby* that his fourth novel would be "something really NEW in form, idea, structure – the model for the age that Joyce and Stien are searching for, that Conrad didn't find" (*S&M* 104). Entering his second decade as a professional writer, as one of the most highly paid American authors for his short stories in popular magazines, with one modern American classic novel to his credit already, by the early 1930s Fitzgerald had made three false starts on the new novel but had integrated his aesthetic guides within its plan. Rather than specific technical borrowings, he turned to broad conceptual frameworks, intellectually to Oswald Spengler's historical theories, and artistically to past masters who delivered social criticism through character study. Comparing his two best novels after the publication of *Tender*, he wrote this to Bishop: "Gatsby was shooting at something like Henry Esmond while this was shooting at something like Vanity Fair. The dramatic novel has cannons quite different from the philosophical, now called psychological novel. One is a kind of tour de force and the other a confession of faith" (*LL* 255). The shift in genres was bold, aided by Fitzgerald's thorough assimilation of modernist narrative disjunction and multiple perspectives derived from *Ulysses* and Virginia Woolf's novels, especially *Mrs. Dalloway*. Demonstrating his ability to control the disparate technical and philosophical elements in *Tender*, Fitzgerald would also assuage the structural shortcomings of his first two novels. He emphasized to Perkins how *Tender* "conformed to a definite intention" and that "the motif of the 'dying fall' was absolutely deliberate . . . from a definite plan." He further explained: "That particular trick is one that Ernest Hemmingway and I worked out – probably from Conrad's preface to 'The Nigger' – and it has been the greatest 'credo' of my life, ever since I decided that I would rather be an artist than a careerist" (*LL* 256).[15] Thus, Conrad's prototype in authorship gave Fitzgerald the impetus to stake out new ground for the American novel. He shared that artistic goal with Hemingway; and while *Tender*'s dying fall in Book

III and the final chapter outlining Dick Diver's life after his divorce can be compared with the constrained closure of *A Farewell to Arms*, what seems more pertinent is these two authors' larger efforts to fashion individual voices within what had become an increasingly commercial and fashion-conscious literary marketplace from the 1920s, meaning that they faced challenges unknown to their predecessors in creating work that would last.

Fitzgerald's head-hunting of Hemingway for Scribners and the editorial assistance given on *The Sun Also Rises* point to the initially one-sided nature of the two authors' relationship, but Hemingway soon became for Fitzgerald in literary judgment "as near as I know for a final reference," his "artistic conscience," as Edmund Wilson was always his "intellectual conscience" (*S&M* 219; *MLC* 148–49). What Hemingway also reinforced in his fellow novelist was integrity of artistic purpose and a determination to overcome life's vicissitudes for the ultimate pursuit of literature. Fitzgerald had to avoid the influence of Hemingway's distinctive style, remarking after the publication of *Tender* that he did not read Hemingway's work for a year and a half "because I was afraid that your particular rhythms were going to creep in on mine by process of infiltration" (*LL* 263). What came to dominate Fitzgerald's thinking was the *idea* of Hemingway, as his once-close friend became the most important public figure in American literature of the 1930s. Planning a historical novel tentatively entitled "Philippe, Count of Darkness," Fitzgerald sketched his theme: "Just as Stendahl's portrait of a Byronic man made *Le Rouge et Noir* so couldn't *my* portrait of Ernest as Phillipe make the real modern man" (*N* 159). Literary history surely benefited from the abandonment of that novel, but Hemingway's fame and artistic example also helped to stir Fitzgerald in his last major effort, the unfinished novel *The Last Tycoon*.

The author, struggling with his health and residual financial debt in Hollywood, found another heroic figure in Monroe Stahr to ground *Tycoon*'s narrative of social change and moral choice. One vital note in Fitzgerald's letters indicates the new direction he intended: "It is a novel a la Flaubert without 'ideas' but only people moved singly and in mass through what I hope are authentic moods" (*LL* 470). He told Perkins that he was "digging it out of myself like uranium," but in a letter to Zelda Fitzgerald he was firm in his conviction that "It is a constructed novel like Gatsby, with passages of poetic prose when it fits the action, but no ruminations or side-shows like Tender. Everything must contribute to the dramatic movement" (*LL* 470, 467). The remaining evidence of his achievement of this aim is compelling, but bittersweet in what is absent. Yet the letters about *Tycoon* also record the lasting influence of classic literary models, of Conrad's lesson in evoking moods and feelings, and of modern narrative structure as an essential foundation for novels that employ idealized characters as ideas. While he was writing, Fitzgerald was also was thinking about an ideal curriculum for reading in classic (mainly English) literature: Giving tutorial instruction to his mistress Sheilah Graham, he devised what they called the "College of One."

That the most informative letters about *Tycoon* were sent to his wife and to his editor also reveals the limits of the present essay on Fitzgerald's literary influences, focused as it is on important writers that the author connected with his novels' formal design and style, and with his quest for artistic distinction. Another study might conclude that Perkins should be called to center stage, for his discovery and management of Fitzgerald's talent, his editorial suggestions about the arrangement of chapters in *Gatsby* and the characterization of Gatsby, his dubious influence in rushing *Tender* into print, and his casual proofreading of Fitzgerald's manuscripts. A different interpretation might place Zelda in the foreground, not for her role as muse (or, as she and others would consider it, his plagiarism of her notebooks and of events in their lives together), but as her husband's most ardent and attentive reader. Finishing *Gatsby* in southern France, for instance, Fitzgerald explained her role as more than just a sounding board for his writing: "Zelda + I are contemplating a careful revision after a weeks complete rest" (*LL* 79).

However, a conclusion based on what writers of significant merit, with long and productive careers, contributed to Fitzgerald's standing in the art of the novel must emphasize how thoughtfully he took what he wanted and needed from them, while applying what he was most capable of achieving from his own natural creative gifts. By the mid-1930s Fitzgerald had relinquished "[t]he old dream of being an entire man in the Goethe-Byron-Shaw tradition, with an American touch" (*MLC* 153). Yet at about the same time he would emphasize to Bishop: "I believe that the important thing about a work of fiction is that the essential reaction shall be profound and enduring" (*L* 362), and the "writer only" in him continued to strive for the next best work. Edmund Wilson introduced him to the novels of Franz Kafka, and a week before his death Fitzgerald wrote to Perkins: "He will never have a wide public but 'The Trial' and 'America' are two books that writers are never able to forget." Considering that Fitzgerald included the poignant comment that he had "been doing a lot of ruminating as to what this whole profession is about" (*LL* 474), his analysis of Kafka as a writer to be admired by writers signifies how much his own desire for literary legacy was a marker against oblivion.

NOTES

1 A sampling might include Fitzgerald's view that "Dorothy Canfield as a novelist is certainly of no possible significance" (*L* 571). Fitzgerald's rant in 1925 about some recently published novels is equally blunt. He writes that a group including Sinclair Lewis's *Arrowsmith*, Edith Wharton's *The Mother's Recompense*, and Sherwood Anderson's *Dark Laughter* "were just lousy," while others including Willa Cather's *The Professor's House* were "almost as bad" (*LL* 132). See also his comments on work by Thomas Boyd and Thomas Wolfe (*LL* 118–19, 280, 473).

2 See A. Turnbull, *Scott Fitzgerald* (London: Vintage, 2004), 234. Hemingway's gratitude for Fitzgerald's assistance became increasingly subdued. "Kiss my ass" was his initial written response to Fitzgerald's revision notes for *A Farewell to Arms* (*LL* 167).

3 This was first published in the *Nassau Literary Magazine* (April 1917) as "Tarquin of Cheepside," revised and expanded for the *Smart Set* (Feb. 1921) as "Tarquin of Cheapside," and reprinted in *Tales of the Jazz Age* (*TJA* 196–203).

4 F. K. Ring, *Against the Current: As I Remember F. Scott Fitzgerald* (Los Angeles: Figueroa Press, 2005), 35.

5 L. Trilling, *The Liberal Imagination: Essays on Literature and Society* (New York: Charles Scribner's Sons, 1950), 249–50.

6 See F. S. Fitzgerald, "The Author's Apology," in M. J. Bruccoli, *F. Scott Fitzgerald: A Descriptive Bibliography*, rev. edn. (Pittsburgh: University of Pittsburgh Press, 1987), 19.

7 H. Bloom, *The Anxiety of Influence: A Theory of Poetry* (New York: Oxford University Press, 1973).

8 A. Le Vot, *F. Scott Fitzgerald: A Biography*, trans. William Byron (London: Allen Lane, 1984), 40.

9 H. Broun, "Books," *New York Tribune*, May 7, 1920, 14. Qtd. in M. J. Bruccoli, *Some Sort of Epic Grandeur: The Life of F. Scott Fitzgerald*, 2nd rev. edn. (Columbia, SC: University of South Carolina Press, 2002), 137–38; and see n. 50, p. 587. Subsequent references to Bruccoli's *Epic Grandeur* are included in the text.

10 In a June 3, 1920, letter from F. S. Fitzgerald to J. G. Hibben, president of Princeton University, Fitzgerald replies to an earlier letter from Hibben with what reads as dramatized world-weariness beyond his years: "My view of life, President Hibben, is the view of Theodore Dreisers and Joseph Conrads – that life is too strong and remorseless for the sons of men" (*LL* 40).

11 J. Conrad, Preface, *The Nigger of the 'Narcissus': A Tale of the Sea*, The Works of Joseph Conrad, vol. 3 (London: William Heineman, 1921), vii, ix–x.

12 A. Hook, *F. Scott Fitzgerald: A Literary Life* (New York: Palgrave Macmillan, 2002), 59.

13 *Nostromo* (1904), *The Secret Agent* (1907), *Under Western Eyes* (1911), *Chance* (1911), and *Victory* (1915).

14 In an August 1926 letter, F. S. Fitzgerald explained to M. Perkins: "God, how much I've learned in these two and a half years in Europe" (*S&M* 145).

15 See *LL* 263–64 for Fitzgerald's comment to Hemingway about taking from Conrad the theory "that the purpose of a work of fiction is to appeal to the lingering after-effects in the reader's mind."

6

Intellectual Influences

Ronald Berman

Throughout his career, F. Scott Fitzgerald discussed ideas and their institutions with the two leading critics of his time, H. L. Mencken and Edmund Wilson. One of Wilson's mentorial letters of 1919 advises him to come to New York City to begin his writing career. As usual, Wilson gives Fitzgerald a reading list. He then advises him to get ready for the new intellectual world by dropping his "*Saturday Evening Post*" mentality – and also his remaining attachment to "the decaying Church of Rome."[1] Wilson thought that Scott's Catholicism (and his own Protestantism) had lost explanatory powers to science and to the big secular systems of Marx and Freud. In this case, Fitzgerald agreed, later telling a St. Paul friend that his heroes were secular. In fact, "the Rosseaus, Marxes, Tolstois" did more good for the world than believers in "the silly and cruel old God" of our imaginings (*LL* 45). In an interview of 1923, he stated that Freud "has had the widest influence on the younger generation. You cannot begin to conceive how far his theories have spread in America ... Why, Freud at third-hand ran over this country like wildfire."[2] Years later, he told his daughter, Scottie, to "read the terrible chapter in Das Kapital on The Working Day, and see if you are ever quite the same" (*LL* 436). Yet he was also committed, as he wrote to Max Perkins, to "the intellectual pleasures of the world we live in." His own advice to Wilson as the 1930s began? Less politics, then "Back to Mallarmé!"[3]

Wilson recognized the cost of change. Here is his elegy to Alfred Rolfe, his teacher at Hill School, and to his own vanished certainties:

> Suddenly, as I write this memoir, it seems to me that the stream he was following flowed out of a past that is now remote ... from the days when people went to Germany to hear Wagner and study Greek; from Matthew Arnold, from Bernard Shaw – now almost an old-fashioned classic like Arnold. And I am glad to renew my sense of Alfred Rolfe's contribution to it, as I realize that I myself have been trying to follow and feed it at a time when it has been running low. Its tradition antedates our Christian religion and has in many men's minds survived

it, as one may hope it will, also, the political creeds, with their secular evangelism, that are taking the Church's place.[4]

For half his life, Fitzgerald lived in that "lovely safe world" described by Dick Diver (*TITN* 75). The image never leaves his work: "The Ice Palace" reminds us that before our own lives "there was something, there was something! I couldn't ever make you understand, but it was there." In "Dice, Brassknuckles & Guitar" the spirit of place demonstrates that, "thank God this age is joined on to *some*thing." In "Babylon Revisited," Charlie Wales wants "to jump back a whole generation" to make sense of his life (*S* 54, 237, 619). The world of the past had its imperatives – Fitzgerald often calls them "Victorian" to let us know that they have been outmoded, replaced by new intellectual and moral authority. Yet he often tells us how much they are missed. Dick Diver's lost world reappears in disguised ways: through images of unvisited graves in "The Ice Palace" and reminders of forgotten liturgies in "The Diamond as Big as the Ritz." When Fitzgerald mentions the American "cultural background"[5] these are silently included.

Some writers admired by Fitzgerald were unambiguous about losing the past. *The Time Machine* of H.G. Wells describes a Victorian intellectual landscape in ruins, while *The Outline of History* pointedly ignores the medieval period. Shaw's *Caesar and Cleopatra* describes – gloats over, I think – the burning of the Alexandrian Library. Inferentially, a new loss of old knowledge would be a very good thing. However, the revolution bypassed many who hailed it. The great modernists revalued the past.

William James, John Dewey, Walter Lippmann, and George Santayana brought the past into the present. Public philosophers had the inestimable advantage of writing for an American audience about American issues. They knew American literature. And like novelists, they described and criticized what Lippmann called the "unseen facts" of social life.[6] Their works were published at crucial moments: *This Side of Paradise* came out in 1920 along with Santayana's *Character and Opinion in the United States*; *The Beautiful and Damned* came out in 1922, the year not only of *The Waste Land* but also of Walter Lippmann's *Public Opinion*; *The Great Gatsby* came out in 1925, accompanied by the Modern Library edition of William James and Alfred North Whitehead's *Science and the Modern World*. Literature did not answer philosophy, but it did pay attention to ideas. To take one instance, Gerald Murphy told Fitzgerald that both of them needed to read Santayana to understand their own lives, H. L. Mencken wrote that Santayana knew considerably more about America than Van Wyck Brooks, and Edmund Wilson thought that Santayana was the best example he knew of the life of the mind.

The effects of public philosophy can be seen in Fitzgerald, Mencken, and Wilson. One of them is in Mencken's satirical passage in *The American Language* about the national "self" that somehow forgot it was an adjective and decided to become a noun. From that, he implies the connection of reflexive pronouns to our national egotism.[7] But it was all in James originally:

> The individualized self, which I believe to be the only thing properly called self, is a part of the content of the world experienced ... Where the body is is "here"; when the body acts is "now"; what the body touches is "this"; all other things are "there" and "then" and "that" ... The body is the storm centre, the origin of coordinates ... Everything circles round it, and is felt from its point of view.

James adds that "my" activities are always understood to be "unique and opposed to those of outer natures,"[8] something best appreciated when we listen to Myrtle Wilson's symphony of personal pronouns at her apartment. James, like Mencken, provided a vocabulary for writers. He pointed out that "*a man's Self is the sum total of all that he* CAN *call his* ... not only his body and his psychic powers, but his clothes and his house." The idea of the material self includes (as in *The Great Gatsby*) family and even "ancestors."[9]

Santayana's "Materialism and Idealism in American Life" argues that the named quantities are not opposites. He cites the overpowering influence of "practical" attitudes on American lives. Santayana's citizen goes to college like Nick Carraway and becomes a businessman like Charlie Wales.[10] Fitzgerald's citizen in the long-forgotten story "The Rubber Check" tries "as hard as he knew how to learn the brokerage business" because it is his métier (*P* 419). Philosophers on the American scene throughout the 1920s kept a tight focus on the realities of national life. They had at least as much to convey to the authorial mind as, say, Spengler.

A breathless interviewer reported in 1923 that "F. Scott Fitzgerald, the prophet and voice of the younger American smart set, says that while Conrad's *Nostromo* is the great novel of the past fifty years, *Ulysses* by James Joyce, is the great novel of the future."[11] It was necessary to assume profundity in order to make a place in literary history – and in any case Fitzgerald's recommendations were designed to please Mencken and Wilson. But few in Fitzgerald's fiction read anything like that. The magazines bought by Myrtle Wilson speak to those who are not intellectuals. Freud had already seen the connection between modern lives and fables. In 1906, he was asked for a list of "good" books by a publisher. He explained why he was not going to include examples from Sophocles, Shakespeare, Goethe, or other "magnificent works" of world literature. A "good" book

> stands in rather the same relationship as to "good" friends, to whom one owes a part of one's knowledge of life and view of the world – books which one has enjoyed oneself and gladly commends to others, but in connection with which the element of timid reverence, the feeling of one's own smallness in the face of their greatness, is not particularly prominent.[12]

Flaubert did not make the cut, although Kipling's *The Jungle Book* was high on the list (*Freud* 540). In 1907, Freud added that he would not discuss "the writers most highly esteemed by the critics, but the less pretentious authors of novels, romances and short stories, who nevertheless have the widest and most eager circle of readers of both sexes." What mattered as the new century began was, he said, the "centre of interest" (*Freud* 440).

Fitzgerald understood that popular texts are about aspirations. Bernice reads *Little Women*[13] and for a time sees herself in it. Tom Buchanan, a literary trilobite, has the *Saturday Evening Post* read to him by Jordan Baker; Myrtle Wilson buys scandal sheets that suggest her ambitions.[14] Masscult and midcult texts in Fitzgerald's fiction serve the ends foreseen by Freud. Daisy Buchanan's identity may be suggested through the highbrow mythology of Thomas Bullfinch's *The Age of Fable* of 1913; her sense of self comes from the lowdown jazz of W. C. Handy's "Beale Street Blues" of 1916.[15]

Late in life, Fitzgerald described the hard process of knowing one's own mind in a letter to his daughter about teachers and texts: "You need, at the beginning, some enthusiast who also knows his way around – John Peale Bishop performed that office for me at Princeton. I had always dabbled in 'verse' but he made me see, in the course of a couple of months, the difference between poetry and non-poetry." He reminds Scottie of the hazards of reading criticism, especially Amy Lowell on John Keats, and of how she needs to begin the essential work of discarding the opinions of her college teachers. As for himself, after much effort he recognized in Keats the "inner mechanics" of his lines and "a scale of workmanship" that might improve his own writing (*LL* 460–61). He understood that other writers were necessary to his own writing, and he was intelligent enough to connect the usable past with modernism. The letter clearly consists of more than advice to an undergraduate, summing up the nature of "influence" on a writer's mind.[16] Fitzgerald himself had to cope with an unusual amount of literary advice. His intellectual life was a conscious attempt to see through conceptions. It showed a high degree of resistance.

Edmund Wilson, Fitzgerald's principal resource, made three main critical points, the first of them devoted to method. From the beginning, Wilson recognized Fitzgerald's talent – and also the difficulty of getting him to exert critical discipline over his own work. He uses phrases like "control" and "conscience" when he discusses Fitzgerald's work in their correspondence or in reviews. Second, was the acquisition of a new intellectual base. In a retrospective letter to Lionel Trilling after the appearance of *The Liberal Imagination,* Wilson stated that "the trouble about Scott's case, when one begins talking about Goethe, etc., is that he didn't, in the third-rate Catholic school he went to, get enough of the right kind of education to sustain him in his absolutely first-rate ambitions."[17] The "right kind" of education implied both new and old reading – in fact, Wilson dismissed Van Wyck Brooks as a critic because he did not understand the connection of the classics to modernism.[18] He demanded knowledge of the "movement" as well, that is, of those writers addressed in *Axel's Castle.* Leon Edel states in his introduction to *The Twenties* that Joyce and Eliot were not understood *even by the critics* until Wilson explained "the victories of symbolism over the naturalists."[19] The third critical area was language. Wilson insisted that the novel would have to use the new American vulgate, passing on to Fitzgerald his admiration for Mencken. With Fitzgerald particularly on his mind, Wilson wrote that all modern writers were indebted to Mencken for defining the tools of their trade:

> Looking back today, we can see that this first edition of *The American Language* marked a stage in the development of our literature. It marked the moment when the living tide of American had mounted so high along the sands of "correct English" that some formal recognition was necessary. Six years later, in 1925, the review *American Speech* was started, and Sir William Craigie, one of the compilers of the big Oxford dictionary, sailed for the United States to begin work on a dictionary of American ... we must give Mencken credit for one of the really valuable services performed in our own day by American criticism for American writing.[20]

Wilson realized that modernism would use language overheard in revues, theater and vaudeville; Mencken stated in a late edition of *The American Language* that our linguistic models for daily conversation included "movies and talkies" (vi). The pioneering sociological study *Middletown* agreed: Even in the provinces, Americans now envisioned and used the language of "a wonderful new world" created by movies, propagated by advertisements.[21] Vaudeville history reminds us that "by the teens and early twenties" the comic stage had become part of "the culture that was replacing Victorianism: sensual, expressive, individualist." Sophie Tucker wondered "Who Paid the Rent for Mrs. Rip van Winkle" when her husband was asleep, and Gracie Allen had more in mind than "Lamb Chops" in 1926 when she thought about getting "a bite tonight after the show."[22]

As to "serious" fiction, Wilson, Mencken, and Gerald Murphy had models for Fitzgerald. Wilson had Eliot and Joyce in mind; Mencken thought that Dreiser was the right choice; Murphy admired Scott's work but preferred Hemingway. All wanted him to know about modern writing. They also wanted him to embody their own political ideas, which meant that Fitzgerald's acquisition of an intellectual background was an adversarial proceeding. The Fitzgerald–Wilson relationship remained firm even though the former rejected the latter's rationalism. The Fitzgerald–Mencken friendship continued because Fitzgerald respected Mencken's mind, his editorial generosity, and his matchless knowledge of language. Yet Fitzgerald understood early on that accommodating modernism was not Mencken's only problem. His politicized view of American culture was too narrow to accommodate the expansiveness of Fitzgerald's novels. "For there exists a great chasm," Isaiah Berlin wrote, between those "who relate everything to a single central vision, one system less or more coherent or articulate," and those who, "moving on many levels, seizing upon the essence of a vast variety of experiences," find the world to be various and contradictory.[23] Mencken was a hedgehog who knew one big thing – that democracy provides satire. Fitzgerald knew many things about its social life that committed him to contradiction.

Mencken's iconoclasm can be traced in Fitzgerald's work. For example, he believed that Puritanism had become bad conscience, making hypocrisy our national virtue. Fitzgerald understood that: Even the Basil stories have tadpole moralists, "so oily and horrible," who live only to protect us from ourselves (*B&J* 136). *The Great Gatsby* has Tom Buchanan who, like that other eminent fake Warren G. Harding, is addicted to public-spiritedness. Both rely on "words that are absolutely devoid of sensible meaning … the wholesale emission of sonorous and deafening bilge." Harding was a great defender of "normalcy" or the status quo, notorious for converting other people's "ideas" into social nonsense.[24] However, Fitzgerald escaped the limits of satire. He balanced indignation with sympathy. I think that the issue is best put this way: The things that Tom Buchanan defends are worth defending – although he has deeply mistaken them.

Although Fitzgerald's individuals – notably Basil Duke Lee – display "a persistence that was more than will, that was rather a necessity of pressing its own pattern on the world, of having its way" (*B&J* 172), his characters are governed by their own ideas about remaking themselves. Wilson understood this, taking up these polarities in his review of *Notes on Democracy.* He stated that only one other conception of character in the 1920s could compare to Mencken's and it was "Scott Fitzgerald's flapper" (E. Wilson, *Literary Essays, 1920s & 30s* 245). Proof of this is in the text: Edith Bradin in "May Day" sees the social world through "the twist of her imagination" (*TJA* 81). Ardita Farnam in "The Offshore Pirate" thinks that "all the men and women she had known were but driftwood on the ripples of her temperament" (*F&P* 14). These passages are not moral accusations, but acknowledgments of reality: James reminds his readers that the "innermost center" of being is "subjective life" (132), while Freud concludes that the reactions of the id are inevitable, natural, and "totally non-moral" (*Freud* 655).

Murphy, a friend and mentor, introduced Fitzgerald to new forms of the visual arts – and also to new ideas about them. Through Murphy he met Pablo Picasso, Fernand Léger, Man Ray, and Francis Picabia. Picasso reviewed Murphy's work; Man Ray wrote about the visualization of technological objects, as did Léger, whom Murphy called his own "mentor."[25] In 1923, Murphy and Léger were observed in Paris by John Dos Passos:

> As we strolled along Fernand kept pointing out shapes and colors … Gerald's offhand comments would organize vistas of his own. Instead of the hackneyed and pasteltinted [*sic*] Tuileries and bridges and barges and bateaux mouches on the Seine, we were walking through a freshly invented world. They picked out winches, the flukes of an anchor, coils of rope, the red funnel of a rowboat … The banks of the Seine never looked banal again after that walk.[26]

We might want to think about industrial objects as Picasso and others thought about them in the 1920s. They are visually useful for they renew perception, and they do not necessarily point to a moral about capitalism.

It is worth looking over Man Ray's documentary photos, rethinking his conclusion that "the strange or surreal is not far from the real and ordinary, and the conjunction of unrelated, spontaneously chosen objects can lead to dreams, to unexpected poetic associations."[27] That suggests something about psychological relativity in *The Great Gatsby.* The story is realistic but the narrative is not. Man Ray's work on light and reflecting objects has been described in detail (Phillips 181–86) and provides a context for Fitzgerald's own allusion in *Tender Is the Night* to "refracting objects only half noticed: varnished wood, more or less polished brass, silver and ivory, and beyond these a thousand conveyors of light and shadow" (*TITN* 144). The reader is always conscious of our placement in a highly contrived social world. Léger worked in the 1920s with "machines and mass-produced things."[28] That is a capsule description of Murphy's painting. It reminds us also of Fitzgerald's practice. His stories, even in *The Price Was High,* retain cubist visualization, something Pierre Daix called Picasso's interaction "between free forms and rigid geometry."[29] "The Family Bus," one of many neglected stories, is by no means simply realist. It sees an automobile in terms of lamps, gears, fenders, running board, and tires with "a human torso underneath and a woman all veil and muff perched serene on top" (*P* 488). Throughout Fitzgerald's work, things human are offset by things mechanical. Daix observes that Picasso worked with the concept especially while with Murphy and his wife Sara at Juan-les-Pins in 1924, when Fitzgerald was also included in their lives.

Léger was one of many in Murphy's circle of friends to insist on the inclusiveness of the new arts. He wrote about "film, color photography, and popular theater and literature" becoming new modes of transmitting "narrative ... to a broad public" (Affron 127–29). Daily experience showed Fitzgerald how ideas and "material" interlocked.[30] Such debate covered a lot of ground: Wittgenstein's *Tractatus* of 1922 begins by addressing the great tradition of philosophical problems, while *Culture and Value* of 1929 discusses innovation by thinking about "a jazz dance" after seeing a movie.[31] That now seems to be a pleasant thought but meant more when first stated.

NOTES

1 E. Wilson, *Letters on Literature and Politics 1912–1972*, Elena Wilson, ed. (New York: Farrar, Straus and Giroux, 1977), 44.

2 B. F. Wilson, "F. Scott Fitzgerald Says: "All Women Over Thirty-five Should be Murdered,"" in M. J. Bruccoli and J. Baughman (eds.), *Conversations with F. Scott Fitzgerald* (Jackson, MS: University of Mississippi Press, 2004), 55–59; 55.

3 M. J. Bruccoli, *Some Sort of Epic Grandeur: The Life of F. Scott Fitzgerald*, 2nd rev. edn. (Columbia, SC: University of South Carolina Press, 2002), 344.

4 E. Wilson, *Literary Essays and Reviews of the 1930s & 1940s* (New York: Library of America, 2007), 255.

5 F. S. Fitzgerald, "In Literary New York" in M. J. Bruccoli with J. S. Baughman (eds.), *F. Scott Fitzgerald on Authorship* (Columbia, SC: University of South Carolina Press, 1996), 92.

6 W. Lippman, *Public Opinion*, 1922 (New York: Free Press, 1997), 19.

7 H. L. Mencken, *The American Language*, 1919 (New York: Alfred A. Knopf, 2000), 459. Subsequent references to this work are included in the text.

8 G. Meyers, *William James: His Life and Thought* (New Haven: Yale University Press, 1986), 351.

9 W. James, *The Philosophy of William James* (New York: The Modern Library, 1925), 125. Subsequent references to this work are included in the text.

10 G. Santayana, *Character and Opinion in the United States* (Garden City, NY: Doubleday, 1956), 115–17.

11 Anon., "Prediction is Made About James Novel," *Richmond Times-Dispatch* in M. J. Bruccoli and J. S. Baughman (eds.), *Conversations with F. Scott Fitzgerald* (Jackson, MS: University of Mississippi Press, 2004), 44–45; 44.

12 S. Freud, "Contribution to a Questionnaire on Reading," in P. Gay (ed.), *The Freud Reader* (New York: W. W. Norton & Company, 1989); 533–41; 540. Subsequent references to this volume are included in the text.

13 S. Beegel, "'Bernice Bobs Her Hair': Fitzgerald's Jazz Elegy for *Little Women*" in J. R. Bryer (ed.), *New Essays on F. Scott Fitzgerald's Neglected Stories* (Columbia, MO: University of Missouri Press, 1996), 58–73; 65.

14 S. Hamilton, "The New York Gossip Magazine in *The Great Gatsby*," *The F. Scott Fitzgerald Review* 8 (2010), 34–54; 34.

15 R. Berman, The Great Gatsby *and Modern Times* (Urbana: University of Illinois Press, 1996), 46–48.

16 L. R. Maxwell, "The Emperor's New Clothes: Keatsean Echoes and American Materialism in *The Great Gatsby*," *The F. Scott Fitzgerald Review* 8 (2010), 57–78; 62–65.

17 E. Wilson, *Edmund Wilson: The Man in Letters*, D. Castronovo and J. Groth, eds. (Athens, OH: Ohio University Press, 2001), 70.

18 E. Wilson, *Upstate* (New York: Farrar, Straus and Giroux, 1971), 185.

19 E. Wilson, *The Twenties*, L. Edel, ed. (New York: Farrar, Straus and Giroux, 1975), 6.

20 E. Wilson, *Literary Essays and Reviews of the 1920s & 1930s* (New York: Library of America, 2007), 513–14. Subsequent references to this work are included in the text.

21 R. Lynd and H. Merrell, *Middletown: A Study in American Culture* (San Diego: Harcourt Brace, 1957), 265.

22 R. Snyder, *The Voice of the City* (Chicago: Ivan R. Dee, 2000), 148–52.

23 I. Berlin, *The Hedgehog and the Fox* (New York: Simon & Schuster, 1953), 1.

24 H. L. Mencken, *A Second Mencken Chrestomathy*, T. Teachout, ed. (New York: Alfred A. Knopf, 1955), 33–34.

25 D. Rothschild, *Making It New: The Art and Style of Sara and Gerald Murphy* (Berkeley: University of California Press, 2007), 43.

26 C. Lanchner, "Fernand Léger: American Connections" in C. Lanchner (ed.), *Fernand Léger* (New York: Museum of Modern Art, 1998), 15–70; 25.

27 S. Phillips, "Themes and Variations: Man Ray's Photography in the Twenties and Thirties," in M. Foresta (ed.), *Perpetual Motif: the Art of Man Ray* (New

York: Abbeville Press, 1988), 175–231; 177. Subsequent references to this work are included in the text.

28 M. Affron, "Léger's Modernism: Subjects and Objects," in C. Lanchner (ed.), *Fernand Léger* (New York: Museum of Modern Art, 1998), 128–48; 124. Subsequent references to this work are included in the text.

29 P. Daix, *Picasso: Life and Art* (New York: HarperCollins, 1993), 186.

30 R. Overy, *The Morbid Age: Britain Between the Wars* (London: Allen Lane, 2009), 29–31.

31 L. Wittgenstein, *Culture and Value* (Chicago: University of Chicago Press, 1984), 3e.

7

Contemporary Critical Reception

Jackson R. Bryer

Because F. Scott Fitzgerald's oft-quoted declaration that "there are no second acts in American lives"[1] was so decisively disproved by the spectacular renaissance of his literary reputation in the 1940s and 1950s, far too little attention has been paid to the first act of that reputation, that is, how he fared critically during his lifetime. When mention is made of this period, emphasis has customarily been on the poor sales of his books after *This Side of Paradise* or on the fact that, at his death in 1940, those sales were virtually nonexistent. This latter statistic has fed the perception that Fitzgerald died a largely forgotten and certainly under-appreciated literary and cultural figure, an assumption belied by the more than 25 newspapers across the United States that ran eulogistic editorials in the days following his death.[2] These editorials were, in fact, merely the culmination of a robust amount of critical attention Fitzgerald and his work received during his lifetime.

The earliest assessments of Fitzgerald's writing appeared in the *Daily Princetonian*, the undergraduate newspaper of Princeton University, where, on several occasions, his contributions to the *Nassau Literary Magazine* were appraised. Two of these reviews were written by already established literary figures, and, as was to be the case with many of the notices Fitzgerald's work received during his lifetime, one was negative and the other positive. On February 24, 1917, William Rose Benét, at age 21 already the author of two books of poetry, extensively discussed Fitzgerald's story "The Spire and the Gargoyle," finding its symbolism "hardly precise enough" and "somewhat blurred." However, more positively, in the April 24, 1917, issue, short-story writer and essayist Katherine Fullerton Gerould called his story "Tarquin of Cheepside" "strikingly well written" and "as delightful as it is funny" (*Critical Reputation* [1967] 182).[3]

This earliest recognition was decidedly local and parochial, but when Fitzgerald's novel *This Side of Paradise* was published on March 26, 1920, the response was immediate, overwhelmingly positive, and came from publications throughout the United States. What captured reviewers' interest and, for the most part, their approval were the originality of Fitzgerald's approach to his material – he casually mingled prose narrative with poetry, playlets, and excerpts from letters – and his, for its day, bold and explicit descriptions of the behavior of his adolescent characters. One can virtually hear the expressions of unexpected pleasure from jaded critics as they finished this book by a hitherto unknown young writer. One such commentator, the esteemed Robert C. Benchley, exclaimed, "In these days when any one can (and does) turn out a book which has been done hundreds of times before ... I should be inclined to hail as a genius any twenty-three-old author who can think up something new and say it in a new way so that it will be interesting to a great many people." The equally prominent H. L. Mencken agreed, calling *This Side of Paradise* "[t]he best American novel that I have seen of late" and "original in structure, extremely sophisticated in manner, and adorned with a brilliancy that is as rare in American writing as honesty is in American statecraft."[4]

Adjectives such as "original," "daring," "clever," "astonishing," and "refreshing" recurred in the reviews and propelled the sales of *This Side of Paradise.* Its first printing of 3,000 copies was depleted in three days; by the end of 1920, it had gone through eight printings and more than 36,000 copies were in print. By the end of 1921, there had been twelve printings and almost 50,000 copies had been circulated.[5] Its astonishing success – none of Fitzgerald's later books sold nearly as well – was at least partially due to the fact that it appealed, perhaps for different reasons, to both younger and older readers. Reviewers for undergraduate publications at Dartmouth, Harvard, and Hamilton lauded it for the accuracy of its depiction of college life, whereas William Huse, among others, spoke for the elder generation in predicting – in a comment certain to generate sales – "beginning-to-be-middle-aged people will disapprove of its disconcerting frankness." Burton Rascoe noted, in a similarly tantalizing fashion, that Fitzgerald's novel "shows definitively that, whatever the teachings of our elders, the Victorian checks, taboos, and reticences are no longer in force among the flappers, the debutantes, and collegians of the present generation" (*Critical Reception* 16, 19–20, 31, 18, 4–5).

There were, to be sure, a few dissenting voices. Heywood Broun was "unconvinced as to the authenticity of the atmosphere which [Fitzgerald] creates"; the reviewer for the *Providence Sunday Journal* complained that the novel's protagonist, Amory Blaine, "bores us in the book just as he would have bored us in the flesh"; and the conservative Catholic magazine *America* predictably observed that "[i]f the parties to Amory's various love-affairs are faithful portraits of the modern American girl, the country is going to the dogs rapidly" (*Critical Reception* 10, 13, 25). Characteristic of these negative notices, as well as of many of the positive ones, was a focus on the novelty and sensational nature of the novel's subject matter. This focus can also be found in the numerous feature articles about Fitzgerald and his work and in the interviews with him that appeared in the first half of the 1920s. Spawned by the popularity and success of *This Side of Paradise*, many of them reflect an inability to see beyond its surface glitter and excitement. As Kirk Curnutt has astutely put it, because Fitzgerald was, for the rest of his life, associated with the "frippery" he depicted in his first novel, he was "stereotyped as a 'facile' talent."[6] Thus, Edmund Wilson, along with Mencken one of the most important critics of the day (and a contemporary of and sometime collaborator with Fitzgerald at Princeton), in the most consequential of the feature essays of the early 1920s – it appeared in March 1922 in the *Bookman*, a popular and prestigious monthly – began with a famous assertion: Fitzgerald "has been left with a jewel which he doesn't quite know what to do with"; "he has been given imagination without intellectual control of it"; "he has been given the desire for beauty without an aesthetic ideal"; and "he has been given a gift for expression without very many ideas to express."[7] In a 1925 essay, Paul Rosenfeld echoed Wilson in accusing Fitzgerald of investing his characters "with precisely the glamour with which they in pathetic assurance rather childishly invest themselves" and chastising him for having seen his material "from its own point of view ... completely from without" rather than doing "what the artist does: seen it simultaneously from within and without; and loved it and judged it, too" (*In His Own Time* 433, 435). Harvey Eagleton, writing in the *Dallas Morning News* also in 1925, sounded a similar note when he claimed that Fitzgerald "can not create beyond himself nor imagine experience very different from his own" (*In His Own Time* 438). It is ironic that Rosenfeld's and Eagleton's pieces appeared shortly after the publication of *The Great Gatsby*, a novel that is now regarded as a masterpiece of American literature precisely because of the sort of depth and resonances that they found lacking in Fitzgerald's fiction.

Curnutt points out that many of the editorial eulogies after Fitzgerald's death "focused on the social impact of *This Side of Paradise*," either positively or negatively, and singles one of them from the venerable and respected *Saturday Review of Literature* – "That [his books] are already to a great extent unread is perhaps the best testimonial to the fact that the kind of society they portrayed is even now retreating into history" – as a telling indication of the long shadow cast by *This Side of Paradise* and of the consequent limited perspective prevalent in Fitzgerald's contemporary reception. Curnutt also observes that "[n]early every review, pro or con," of *The Great Gatsby* in 1925 "compares the novel to *This Side of Paradise*, as do many commentaries on the three remaining books that Fitzgerald published in his lifetime" (*Cambridge Introduction* 118, 116), but he could have extended his remark to cover the vast majority of the reviews of *all* of Fitzgerald's books after *This Side of Paradise.* All were, to a large extent, evaluated in light of the achievement and perceived excellences and flaws of that first book, and they were largely limited by reviewers' inability to get beyond Fitzgerald's personality and experiences and the subject matter of his fiction to the sort of analysis of his style and artistry that more recent critics have increasingly come to regard as the basis of his deservedly high rank among the writers of his generation.

This was immediately apparent, a mere half-year after *This Side of Paradise* burst upon the public consciousness, when Charles Scribner's Sons inaugurated what was to be their practice during Fitzgerald's lifetime – to publish within six months or a year after each novel a collection of its author's selection of the best of his short stories published since the previous such volume. A number of the reviews of *Flappers and Philosophers* – its title, significantly, was derived from the ad Scribners had circulated for *This Side of Paradise*, "a novel about flappers for philosophers" – devoted as much space to repeating praise of the novel as they did to evaluations of the stories themselves. The reviewer for the *Nation* observed caustically that Fitzgerald "has gone from the polished literary dexterity of his first book to the manner of writing that makes 'lay' an intransitive verb and zestfully employs that indescribable particle 'onto.'" William Huse lamented that it "seems a pity" that the skills Fitzgerald displayed in *This Side of Paradise* – "[t]he artful turn of phrase, economy of material, the ability to characterize briefly yet adequately" – were, in this instance, "expended, for the most part, on themes of such slight importance," and the *New York Evening Post* proclaimed that *Flappers and Philosophers* was "largely without the native originality and unfailing inspiration that made 'This Side of Paradise' the most promising American first novel in recent years" (*Critical Reception* 35, 36, 37).

Most reviewers found the stories uneven in quality, but a few agreed with Heywood Broun, who somewhat grudgingly saw *Flappers and Philosophers* as better than *This Side of Paradise,* pointing to "The Ice Palace" as an indication "that after all F. Scott Fitzgerald did have something to say and knew how to say it." The *Catholic World* also saw it as "an advance" over the novel in its "originality and variety" and "imaginativeness," and the *San Francisco Chronicle* contended that it marked "the conversion of F. Scott Fitzgerald's undisciplined and turbid genius ... into a bridled and clarified talent" (*Critical Reception* 46, 44, 45, 51). But the most interesting reviews, especially in light of how we have increasingly come to view Fitzgerald's short fiction, are those that perceived the collection's unevenness as indicative of its author's vacillation between the demands of commercial fiction and his desire to write stories of artistic quality. H. L. Mencken described the distance between "Benediction," a "well-written story, a story with an air to it, and ... a story that rings true" and "confections" such as "The Offshore Pirate" as "like the leap from the peaks of Darien to the slums of Colon," concluding that Fitzgerald "is curiously ambidextrous" (*Critical Reception* 48).

Given the response to *This Side of Paradise*, expectations for Fitzgerald's second novel were enormous – and probably impossible to satisfy. *The Beautiful and Damned*, published on March 4, 1922, generated more reviews than any of Fitzgerald's books, and probably because it was so different in tone and subject matter from his first novel, it elicited very diverse responses. Again using *This Side of Paradise* as their point of reference, reviewers were surprised that the same author who had previously written so humorously and lightheartedly of young people in his first book could now depict them in such a serious and even tragic fashion. They responded in two essentially opposite ways: Many dismissed *The Beautiful and Damned* for what Louise Maunsell Field called its "record of lives utterly worthless and utterly futile" or for, in E. W. Osborn's view, "missing utterly the youthful zest, the buoyancy and the young impudence that gave charm to 'This Side of Paradise'" (*Critical Reception* 76, 78). More tellingly, several reviewers agreed with the claim of L. C. G. in the *Columbus* (Ohio) *Dispatch* that "The ironic touch of Mr. Fitzgerald belongs to the trivial things, in the shallow ideas to which he can give so much life," and with Gilbert Seldes's opinion that Fitzgerald's "revelations are of quite secondary importance and he has neither the critical intelligence nor the profound vision which might make him an imposing figure." The *Kansas City Star* agreed: "It is one of the pities of American letters today that F. Scott Fitzgerald spends his time on pseudo-themes and doesn't turn his hand to the eternal worthwhile" (*Critical Reception* 97, 107, 130).

A lesser, but nonetheless substantial, number of reviewers found Fitzgerald's turn toward the serious fortuitous – and they too used his first novel in comparison. Among them was Mencken, who pointed out that the author of *The Beautiful and Damned* "might have gone on rewriting the charming romance of 'This Side of Paradise' for ten or fifteen years ... Instead, he tried something much more difficult, and if the result is not a complete success, it is nevertheless near enough to success to be worthy of respect" (*Critical Reception* 107). Among those who agreed to varying degrees were such prominent reviewer/critics of the day as Henry Seidel Canby, John V. A. Weaver, John Peale Bishop, and Harry Hansen. Canby saw the novel as proof that Fitzgerald "has the artist's conscience and enough intellect to learn how to control the life that fascinates him"; Weaver called it "a huge stride forward"; Bishop viewed it "both in plan and execution an advance on" *This Side of Paradise*; and Hansen praised it as "a whale of a book – a work that definitely sets at rest the speculation whether or not Fitzgerald had the stuff of a real novelist in him" (*Critical Reception* 63, 69, 74, 90–91).

The more serious subject matter of *The Beautiful and Damned* prepared reviewers for Fitzgerald's second short-story collection, *Tales of the Jazz Age*, published in September 1922. While its title and the humorously self-deprecatory table of contents the author wrote for it might well have indicated a return to an earlier tone, inclusion of the long story "May Day," as well as other more somber, or at least more ambivalent, tales prompted a response that, in several instances, recognized the possibility that Fitzgerald's fiction was undergoing significant changes. In some cases, this simply took the form of praising the collection's diversity – "[t]here is tragedy, there is fantasy, there is whimsicality, there is sheer pure drollery, romance, and ... reality," exclaimed the *Portland* (Maine) *Evening Express* – but more perceptive commentators agreed with Hildegarde Hawthorne's observation that while *Tales of the Jazz Age* was "amusing, interesting and well done, ... it is filled besides with all sorts of hints, promise and portents that make it exciting beyond its actual content" and with the opinion of the *Philadelphia Evening Public Ledger* that "Mr. Fitzgerald has post-graduated from the naive and charming sophomorism of the younger set which was both his danger and his appeal" (*Critical Reception* 145, 151, 157).

While Fitzgerald's "graduation" was to be decisively confirmed by the publication of *The Great Gatsby* in 1925, Scribners first issued his one effort at drama, *The Vegetable*, in May 1923. Clearly designed to capitalize on its author's popularity – its rejection by Broadway producers was blithely mentioned on the dust jacket – the book received what can most charitably be described as a mixed reception. Remarkably, Edmund Wilson, certainly not one of Fitzgerald's champions, called it "in some ways, one of the best things he has done," explaining in what surely was a backhanded compliment that failed to mask his basically low opinion, "In it he has a better idea than he usually has of what theme he wants to develop, and it does not, as his novels sometimes have, carry him into regions beyond his powers of flight" (*Critical Reception* 182). Less ambivalently, Burton Rascoe called it "gorgeously funny"; Phil A. Kinsley greeted it with "a laughing welcome"; John Clair Minot felt it contained "some of the most exquisite satire that it was ever our privilege to read"; and the *New Orleans Times-Picayune* promised readers "one good chuckle – from the first page to the last" (*Critical Reception* 169, 173, 174, 181).

The negative reviews were harsher and more numerous. John F. Carter, Jr. pronounced the play "devoid of ideas and beauty" and lacking in "sincerity, simplicity, and intellectual ruggedness." Frederic Van de Water dismissed it as "just silly"; the *Wichita Beacon* asserted that "[t]here's nothing wrong with the idea, but there's any number of things wrong with the author's handling of it"; and Duncan Aikman called it "nonsense written under the guise of satire" (*Critical Reception* 184, 174, 178, 189). Ironically, in view of reviews of Fitzgerald's earlier fiction, when *The Vegetable* opened at Nixon's Apollo Theatre in Atlantic City on November 19, 1923, the reviewer for the *Philadelphia Evening Bulletin* recommended that "Mr. Fitzgerald would better stick to his modernist realism and leave fantasy to those of lighter touch and whim" (*Critical Reception* 193).[8]

Because *The Great Gatsby* is now an acknowledged classic of modern literature, it is easy to mock such reviewers of it in 1925 as the anonymous critic in the *New York World*, whose review was headed "F. Scott Fitzgerald's Latest a Dud" and who declared that it "is another one of the thousands of modern novels which must be approached with the point of view of the average tired person toward the movie-around-the-corner, a deadened intellect, a thankful resigning of the attention, and an aftermath of wonder that such things are produced." Others concurred: Ruth Hale pledged, "Find me one chemical trace of magic, life, irony, romance or mysticism in all of 'The Great Gatsby' and I will bind myself to read one Scott Fitzgerald book a week for the rest of my life"; the reviewer for *America* called it "an inferior novel, considered from any angle whatsoever"; and John M. Kenny, Jr. passed it off as "mediocre" (*Critical Reception* 195, 197, 231, 235).

As tempting as it is to dwell on these wrongheaded reviews, it is more worthwhile to note that, just as with Fitzgerald's second novel, quite a few reviewers of his third full-length work of fiction disliked it for the same reasons that others praised it, and, once again, their contradictory judgments were based on comparisons with his earlier fiction. *This Side of Paradise*, as Curnutt remarks, is mentioned in at least half of the contemporary reviews of *Gatsby*, and like parents feeling ambivalence as their children outgrow childish innocence, some reviewers lamented Fitzgerald's abandonment of his youthful style and subject matter while others praised it. Speaking for the former point of view and echoing a similar segment of the reviews of *The Beautiful and Damned*, Ralph Coghlan hoped that, someday, Fitzgerald would "return to his original and profitable theme"; the *Kansas City Star* complained about the absence of "the youthful sparkle and idealism of 'This Side of Paradise'"; and Harvey Eagleton concluded that "[t]he Roman candle which sent out a few gloriously colored balls at the first lighting seems to be ending in a fizzle of smoke and sparks" (*Critical Reception* 206, 221, 224).

An equal number of reviewers saw *Gatsby* as a major positive development in Fitzgerald's career; while most of their analyses perhaps did not penetrate much beneath the novel's surface, it is important to see that their assessments contain numerous suggestions of a focus on style and form as well as an emphasis on a sophisticated understanding of the novel's themes that foreshadow some of the most perceptive later criticism of the novel. With respect to theme, Thomas Caldecot Chubb declared that "there is something of Jay Gatsby in every man, woman or child that ever existed," and Gilbert Seldes asserted that "Fitzgerald has ceased to content himself with a satiric report on the outside of American life and has with considerable irony attacked the spirit underneath, and so has begun to report on life in its most general terms" (*Critical Reception* 238, 240). With respect to its style and design, Laurence Stallings saw in *Gatsby* "an interest in the color and sweep of prose, in the design and integrity of the novel, in the development of character, like nothing else [Fitzgerald] has attempted"; Mencken praised "the charm and beauty of the writing"; and Conrad Aiken singled out its "excellence of form" (*Critical Reception* 203, 212, 243).

What is most overlooked in the contemporary reviews of *Gatsby* is the evidence that, in 1925, some already saw what, in the 1950s, came to be called Fitzgerald's "double vision," his ability to immerse himself in the world he depicted while simultaneously observing it objectively. As noted earlier in this essay, critics such as Edmund Wilson, Paul Rosenfeld, and Harvey Eagleton, in the 1920s, specifically criticized Fitzgerald for not possessing this skill. By 1925, however, another early detractor, William

Rose Benét, the critic/poet who had so negatively reviewed Fitzgerald's apprentice fiction in 1917, eloquently praised *Gatsby* for displaying it:

> For the first time Fitzgerald surveys the Babylonian captivity of this era unblended by the bright lights. He gives you the bright lights in full measure, the affluence, the waste, but also the nakedness of the scaffolding that scrawls skeletons upon the sky when the gold and blue and red and green have faded, the ugly passion, the spiritual meagerness, the empty shell of luxury, the old irony of "fair-weather friends." (*Critical Reception* 220)

William Curtis assented, observing that Fitzgerald "has ceased to chronicle events and has begun to marshal them in perspective and to give the comment upon them which, after all, are the only excuses for the existence of literature," and the *New Yorker* commented that "[h]e still reveres and pities romantic constancy, but with detachment" (*Critical Reception* 228, 230).

Reviewers of *All the Sad Young Men*, Fitzgerald's third collection of short stories, which was published on February 26, 1926, generally saw the same evidences of artistic maturity. "Fitzgerald has acquired maturity, a happy profundity," announced the *Milwaukee Journal*, and the *Cleveland Plain Dealer* likewise recognized "a ripened art, a wistful humor, a legitimate irony that comes from a development of understanding and wisdom." Malcolm Cowley, who was to play a major role in reviving interest in Fitzgerald in the 1940s and 1950s, expressed a similar view more poetically: "With the coming of years his flappers have learned to accept responsibility, and there are tiny wrinkles round their rosebud mouths." Several reviewers picked out "Absolution" as the best story in the volume, but William Rose Benét sounded a note that was to become a familiar refrain in later Fitzgerald criticism when he observed that he felt "behind most of the writing in this book, the pressure of living conditions rather than the demand of the spirit" (*Critical Reception* 259, 261, 272, 268).

The pressure of supporting an extravagant lifestyle, combined with the onset of his wife's mental illness and Fitzgerald's realization that, after *Gatsby*, he had an obligation to continue to produce artistically significant full-length works of fiction, were the principal reasons that his next novel did not appear until 1934. The reviewers who responded to *Tender Is the Night* were doing so in a context far different from that of the 1920s. The Jazz Age had given way to the Great Depression, and a book about wealthy expatriates cavorting on the French Riviera encountered a considerable number of negative reactions. Louis Gannett spoke for many when he asked about Fitzgerald's generation, "Isn't there a young generation growing up very differently, which never had his dead faiths? Perhaps even a still younger generation of still newer faiths?" William Troy put it more directly: "It is time now for Mr. Fitzgerald, with his remarkable technical mastery of his craft, to give us a character who is not the victim of adolescent confusion, who is strong enough to turn deaf ears to the jingling cymbals of the golden girl." The most strident critique of this sort came, not surprisingly, from Philip Rahv of the Communist *Daily Worker*. Under a memorable headline drawn from the last sentence of his review, "You Can't Duck [a] Hurricane Under a Beach Umbrella," Rahv chastised Fitzgerald because, although he saw the "collapse" of his class, "he still continues to console and caress them with soft words uttered in the furry voice of a family doctor pledged to keep the fatal diagnosis from his patients" (*Critical Reception* 297, 320, 316).

Tender Is the Night did have its supporters. Gilbert Seldes dubbed it a "great novel" that signaled its author's rise "to his natural place at the head of the American writers of our time"; Cameron Rogers praised it as "a profoundly moving, beautifully written story … [that] should assure Fitzgerald's stature as an American author"; and Gordon Lewis found it "a fine, brave, tragic book, written with care and masterful grace" (*Critical Reception* 292, 293, 310, 317). But of more interest than these negative and positive reviews are two areas of disagreement among the critics in 1934 that remain subjects of debate. The first dealt with whether the disintegration of the novel's protagonist, Dick Diver, was sufficiently explained. Henry Seidel Canby spoke for those who felt it was not: "What begins as a study of a subtle relationship [between Dick and his wife/patient Nicole] ends as the accelerating decline into nothingness of Dr. Driver [*sic*] – not for no reason, but for too many reasons, no one of which is dominant." John Chamberlain disagreed so vehemently that he wrote two reviews, the second of which specifically responded to those who found Dick's collapse "insufficiently documented," contending that "Mr. Fitzgerald proceeded accurately, step by step, with just enough documentation to keep the drama from being misty, but without destroying the suggestiveness that added to the horror lurking behind the surface" (*Critical Reception* 300, 311–12).

The second area of contention that still absorbs Fitzgerald scholars and critics concerns whether Fitzgerald should have begun *Tender Is the Night* with a section told from the point of view of Rosemary Hoyt, the young movie actress who falls in love with and has an affair with Dick. Some reviewers found this opening confusing, feeling, as did H. A. MacMillan, that the novel suffered "from the introduction in the first half ... of matter which has no real and intimate connection with the main theme, and little enough interest for its own sake"; Edward Weeks and Clifton Fadiman both urged readers not to judge the novel until they got past the first section because it was only at that point that, as Fadiman explained, it "begins to move" (*Critical Reception* 313, 287, 301). Fanny Butcher, Canby, and Howard R. Walley totally disagreed, finding in the first third what Butcher described as "a dramatic premise brilliantly conceived" and Canby called "the promise of a book of first importance," while the remainder, in Walley's opinion, "explodes into sensationalism, grows incoherent, and loses itself in the sand" (*Critical Reception* 299, 300, 325).

As an indication of Fitzgerald's waning popularity in the 1930s, his fourth short-story collection and the last of his books published in his lifetime, *Taps at Reveille,* received very few reviews when it was published in March 1935. A number of the responses seemed more like premature obituaries: "[H]erein is recorded the petrification of a talent that in 1925 looked like one of the best bets in American literature," intoned Arthur Coleman; N. H. in the *New York Sun* voiced an all-too-familiar sentiment: "It is hard, in these days of the depression, to be fair to Mr. Fitzgerald. The children of all ages – from 13 to 30 – that decorate his pages seem as remote today as the neanderthal man." While there were some positive reactions – Elizabeth Hart felt that Fitzgerald had "worked an old phase thoroughly out of his system and begun to feel around for a new one" and Joan Nourse called the collection "even more readable than previous short story volumes of Scott Fitzgerald's" – the final words of William Troy's review, one of the last Fitzgerald received in his lifetime, essentially brought his contemporary reception at its end back to where it had begun: "If Mr. Fitzgerald could enlarge his vision to correspond to his interest, he would do much both for his own reputation and for the amelioration of current American fiction writing" (*Critical Reception* 338, 346, 342, 351, 349).

Of course, there was to be an almost immediate and highly ironic coda to Fitzgerald's contemporary reception when, on October 27, 1941, less than a year after his death, Scribners published the unfinished novel he had been working on, under the title *The Last Tycoon.* Not only were the reviews almost universally laudatory, with many asserting with surprising conviction that, completed, it would have been its author's greatest achievement, a great number were reappraisals of Fitzgerald's full career that often dismissed as unworthy of consideration the doubts and reservations commentators had expressed during his lifetime. Fitzgerald, Clifton

Fadiman asserted, "hardly deserves to be ticketed as the laureate of the Jazz Age and then forgotten," and Stephen Vincent Benét's famous valedictory prediction accurately set the tone for Fitzgerald's posthumous "second act": "You can take off your hats now, gentlemen, and I think perhaps you had better. This is not a legend, this is a reputation – and, seen in perspective, it may well be one of the most secure reputations of our time" (*Critical Reception* 368, 376).

NOTES

1 F. S. Fitzgerald, *The Last Tycoon Together with The Great Gatsby and Selected Stories* (New York: Charles Scribner's Sons, 1941), 163.
2 For an annotated listing of these editorials, see J. R. Bryer, *The Critical Reputation of F. Scott Fitzgerald: A Bibliographical Study* (Hamden, CT: Archon Books, 1967), 202–07.
3 For annotated listings of other reviews of Fitzgerald's *Nassau Literary Magazine* contributions, as well as of the Princeton Triangle Shows that he co-wrote, see *Critical Reputation* (1967), 180–83.
4 J. R. Bryer, ed., *F. Scott Fitzgerald: The Critical Reception* (New York: Burt Franklin, 1978), 14, 28. Subsequent references to this work are included in the text.
5 M. J. Bruccoli, *Some Sort of Epic Grandeur: The Life of F. Scott Fitzgerald*, 2nd rev. ed. (Columbia, SC: University of South Carolina Press, 2002), 133.
6 K. Curnutt, *The Cambridge Introduction to F. Scott Fitzgerald* (Cambridge, UK: Cambridge University Press, 2007), 113. Subsequent references to this work are included in the text.
7 E. Wilson, "F. Scott Fitzgerald" in M. J. Bruccoli and J. R. Bryer (eds.), *F. Scott Fitzgerald In His Own Time: A Miscellany* (Kent, OH: Kent State University Press, 1971), 404. Subsequent references to this text are included in the text as *In His Own Time.* For further discussion of Wilson's reviews and essays on Fitzgerald, see *Cambridge Introduction*, 113–14.
8 For annotated listings of other reviews of *The Vegetable* in performance, see J. R. Bryer, *The Critical Reputation of F. Scott Fitzgerald: A Bibliographical Study – Supplement One Through 1981* (Hamden, CT: Archon Books, 1984), 9–13.

8

The Fitzgerald Revival

Ruth Prigozy

Today, the phrase "The Fitzgerald Revival" can be misleading, suggesting as it may to some an awakening into an understanding of Fitzgerald's brilliance as a writer in the immediate aftermath of his death on December 22, 1940. Indeed, the word "revival" implies that there had already been a substantive discussion of Fitzgerald's reputation and of his achievements as a literary artist during his lifetime, as well as suggesting that the discourse was simply there waiting to be resurrected – his stature affirmed anew. In fact, however, only a few critics had thoughtfully considered Fitzgerald's artistic achievements while he was alive. Those serious few of the critics included Edmund Wilson, H. L. Mencken, John Peale Bishop, Paul Rosenfeld, and, perhaps most significantly, T. S. Eliot, who had said of *The Great Gatsby* that it was "the first step American fiction has taken since Henry James."[1] The debate about Fitzgerald's work and the development of his talent, however, was scattered primarily through newspaper reviews that had appeared following publication of each of the nine volumes Scribners published over the twenty years of Fitzgerald's professional career. By the late 1930s Fitzgerald had largely faded from the view of both the reading public and literary critics, and had it not been for his last short essays for *Esquire* that provided financial support, minimal as it was, until he returned for his last years to Hollywood, his writing career would have been over.

In the immediate wake of Fitzgerald's death, obituaries in major newspapers seemed patronizing, as illustrated by the one in the *New York Times*, which dismissed Fitzgerald as a writer who described "faithfully, the life and times of a certain section of our society, with the emphasis on youth," but as one whose "talent … never fully bloomed."[2] More informed tributes that appeared within the year of his death, although not in the immediate wake of it, more often took the form of apologies for and disbelief at the critical neglect that had attended Fitzgerald's career during his life. The *New Yorker*, for example, in calling down earlier newspapers (among them the *New York Times*) for their shallow assessments of Fitzgerald's life and talent characterized *The Great Gatsby* as "one of the most scrupulously observed and beautifully written of American novels" (qtd. in *Romantic Egoists* 232). After the publication of the Edmund Wilson-edited *The Last Tycoon*, appraisals of Fitzgerald's talent became even more dazzling. Stephen Vincent Benét, in a 1941 *Saturday Review of Literature* tribute to Fitzgerald and review of the novel, even concluded with these oft-repeated words: "This is not a legend, this is a reputation – and seen in perspective, it may well be one of the most secure reputations of our time" (qtd. in *Romantic Egoists* 235). By 1945, with Edmund Wilson's editing of *The Crack-Up*, containing the "crack-up" essays, letters, notebook entries, and tributes to Fitzgerald by prominent literary figures – and then with the 1945 publication of *The Portable F. Scott Fitzgerald*, edited by Dorothy Parker and with an introduction by John O'Hara[3] – the foundation for the Fitzgerald Revival, or perhaps more appropriately phrased, the Fitzgerald Resurrection that began in the early 1950s, was solidly established.

One could indeed make the case that, as it turned out and unlikely as it might seem, Budd Schulberg – a new young writer in Hollywood in the late 1930s, an admirer of Fitzgerald's work, and the son of B. P. Schulberg, a prominent Hollywood producer – would become one of the earliest central figures in this Fitzgerald resurrection of the 1950s. Producer Walter Wanger had selected Schulberg in 1939 to work with Fitzgerald on a film project related to Dartmouth's Winter Carnival because Schulberg was an alumnus of Dartmouth and closer in age to the college students about whom he and Fitzgerald would be writing. Schulberg, who maintained in retrospect that he had not realized at the time that Fitzgerald was alive and who certainly did not realize at the time of the Winter Carnival assignment that Fitzgerald was addicted to alcohol, brought with him and Fitzgerald two bottles of champagne provided by Wanger to celebrate the occasion. His account of that disastrous trip during which both Fitzgerald and Schulberg became thoroughly inebriated (*Epic Grandeur* 449–51) became the basis for Schulberg's 1950 best-selling novel *The Disenchanted*, in which the writer, Manley Halliday, is recognizable as Fitzgerald.[4] With the novel's publication, Fitzgerald was brought back posthumously into the public eye as he had been known in the last years of his life – as one associated with "the authority of failure." Schulberg's book was followed in 1951 by Arthur Mizener's *The Far Side of Paradise*, the first full-length biography of Fitzgerald.[5] Because Mizener and Schulberg remained in close touch during the composition of the biography, scholars and critics have come to see a collaboration between the two, a collaboration that produced a portrait of Fitzgerald as a writer associated with failure. Unquestionably several of the many books and articles on Fitzgerald to emerge from the 1950s and early 1960s were reactions to what was seen as the distorted picture that came from the Schulberg–Mizener collaboration. Among others, two that presented Fitzgerald from a different angle were Sheilah Graham's 1958 *Beloved Infidel*,[6] a retrospective memoir of Fitzgerald's last years with Graham, and Andrew Turnbull's sympathetic 1962 biography, *Scott Fitzgerald*.[7]

The Schulberg novel, the Mizener biography, the Graham memoir, the Turnbull biography, and additional articles on Fitzgerald such as the one published in *Esquire* in the 1950s by Frances Kroll Ring,[8] Fitzgerald's secretary for the last years of his life, established a launching pad for the extraordinarily intense academic attention that Fitzgerald's work received in the 1960s – a decade that saw some fifteen books devoted exclusively to Fitzgerald and his work, more book-length critical studies of Fitzgerald than have appeared in any single decade since. Among the most influential of the fifteen books were these three: James E. Miller's groundbreaking *F. Scott Fitzgerald: His Art and His Technique* (1964),[9] which traced Fitzgerald's development from a writer of the novel of saturation (*This Side of Paradise*) to the novel of selected incident (*The Great Gatsby* and beyond); Kenneth Ebel's 1963 *F. Scott Fitzgerald*,[10] an introductory critical study that established the direction of future Fitzgerald scholarship and that emphasized the care with which Fitgerald revised his work; and Robert Sklar's brilliant *F. Scott Fitzgerald: The Last Laocoön* (1967),[11] which argues that Fitzgerald's fiction documents his prophetic role in searching for a hero that could exist in a modern world with all faiths in God and man shaken.

By the beginning of the 1970s – thirty years after Fitzgerald's death – he had not only been resurrected, but the revival of critical interest in his work indeed had reached a high point, and critical assessments of his fiction had by that point and by virtually any standard secured for him a place in the pantheon of great American writers. One scarcely could have predicted the increased level of energy and the variety of its sources that would propel the Fitzgerald Revival into a second phase that began in the early 1970s and has shown no signs of diminished intensity now well into the twenty-first century. One important development in this phase of the revival was the increase in publication of facsimiles and the faithful transcriptions of primary Fitzgerald materials such as letters, scrapbooks, and manuscripts. Among such documents – many of them published in the

1970s largely through the efforts of Matthew J. Bruccoli, often working with the cooperation of Fitzgerald's daughter, Scottie Fitzgerald Smith – are these: *As Ever Scott Fitz –* (1972), *F. Scott Fitzgerald's Ledger* (1973), *The Great Gatsby: A Facsimile of the Manuscript* (1973),[12] *Dear Scott/Dear Max: The Fitzgerald-Perkins Correspondence* (1973), *The Romantic Egoists* (1974),[13] and *The Notebooks of F. Scott Fitzgerald* (1978). Such documents and many others published after them have provided Fitzgerald scholars and readers a treasure trove of material that arguably rivals that of any American author – material that continues to provide new insights into Fitzgerald's work and his life, now some three-quarters of a century after his death.

A second impulse that provided energy at the beginning of the 1970s phase of the revival was to use the scholarship of the 1950s and 1960s and the solid factual information it provided but to take it in new directions in order to see Fitzgerald's work from fresh perspectives. The studies that resulted from this impulse have predictably mirrored the changing perspectives of literary criticism itself from the 1970s to the present time. This new phase of the revival has filled in perceived gaps in the existing scholarship, it has applied theories from diverse disciplines to the study of Fitzgerald's art, and it has opened the canon for study of previously neglected works. There is perhaps no better example of this second impulse than Milton R. Stern's *The Golden Moment: The Novels of F. Scott Fitzgerald* (1970), which reveals the "Americanness" of Fitzgerald as shown primarily through his novels, as opposed to his biography.[14] Stern found new ways of looking at the body of Fitzgerald's work, what Stern calls a "complementary explanatory analysis that would fit the biographies" (Stern xii). Scholars such as Sarah Beebe Fryer – one of many more recent scholars who have followed Stern's lead in fashioning a coherent vision of Fitzgerald's work – have worked to build on early scholarship to construct fresh readings of Fitzgerald's work. Fryer's *Fitzgerald's New Women: Harbingers of Change* (1988), for example, uses a feminist perspective to foreground Fitzgerald's ability to hear and record the voices of the "new woman" of the Jazz Age.[15] Since Stern's *The Golden Moment* more than thirty book-length critical studies have explored theses that extend the scholarship of the Fitzgerald Revival of the 1950s and 1960s.

Perhaps the most complex area of inquiry in Fitzgerald studies that has emerged from the beginning of the 1970s, and one that has dramatically influenced the direction that the revival has taken, is the area of biography. Early biographies, particularly the Mizener and Turnbull biographies, had focused on Fitzgerald and his work, bringing in the life and work of Zelda Fitzgerald and the iconic status of the Fitzgeralds as cultural emblems of the Jazz Age only in a peripheral way. Many of the biographical studies that are now a part of the Fitzgerald Revival from 1970 forward brought Zelda to the foreground; some appropriated the Fitzgeralds as a couple and studied them to advance various agendas about the culture and about the Fitzgeralds. For example, Nancy Milford's *Zelda* (1970),[16] the first major biography of Zelda Fitzgerald, has done much to shape the public perception of the couple, and it is only in recent years that questions about Milford's interpretation of their relationship have emerged. As the Fitzgeralds, who were of course public icons during the Jazz Age, became again public icons in the 1970s phase of the revival, the perception of Zelda as a literary artist whose talents were thwarted by her husband became acceptable to general readers and to literary critics. Milford drew upon new material including interviews with the Alabama residents who remembered the Sayre family or heard stories about the couple's courtship and marriage. Their story proved fascinating to the public, but Milford's biography, as she admits in her introduction, has a clear bias in favor of Zelda: "Reading Zelda's letters to her husband moved me in a way I had never been moved before" (Milford xiii).

Another work that focuses on Zelda and one with a clear bias in Zelda's favor, Sara Mayfield's *Exiles from Paradise* (1971),[17] is a biography that recounts stories that present Scott Fitzgerald as a symbol of a patriarchal culture and maintains that he thwarted her development as a writer. The true genius in the family was Zelda, according to Mayfield. That Zelda was psychologically disturbed from her early years is ignored or unmentioned. Even Fitzgerald's daughter, Scottie, was disturbed by the direction that feminist criticism had taken: Zelda was for them the "put down" wife whose artistic efforts were thwarted by "a typically male chauvinist husband." Scottie states that it is a "script that reads well and will probably remain a part of the 'Scott and Zelda' mythology forever, but it is not, in my opinion, accurate."[18] Other books and articles that followed the Milford and Mayfield books have brought Zelda's talent as a writer and painter to the fore, and the claims of these studies have rested on the publication of Zelda's paintings and writings. These analyses have sometimes resulted in exaggerated assessments of her work, revealing an unwillingness to recognize the degree to which Fitzgerald supported her efforts and sought help for her worsening psychological condition. Clearly Zelda Fitzgerald was a talented writer, and her writing is distinguished by brilliant passages, but her work likely would not have received the attention accorded it had she not been the wife of F. Scott Fitzgerald. Their life together captured the attention of a public that up to the present day sees them as symbols of an era that will forever be remembered for its excitement, its joy in the moment, and the determination to remain forever young.

There have also been revisionist accounts of Fitzgerald's life by biographers such as Jeffrey Meyers and James Mellow, among numerous others. These biographies have often been unflattering, and their negative views have colored the portraits of Fitzgerald. In *Invented Lives* (1984), for example, Mellow uses contemporary gossip and anecdotal evidence to convey a negative portrait of Fitzgerald as an unsympathetic drunk.[19] Jeffrey Meyers's *Scott Fitzgerald: A Biography* (1994) offers similar arguments, drawing a negative portrait of Fitzgerald with psychoanalytic diagnoses.[20] Clearly, for some biographers like Mellow and Meyers, it has been important to create in the Fitzgeralds a portrait that confirms some of the most negative publicity that followed them throughout their lives – even though, it is true, Scott and Zelda were in part responsible for much of gossip that surrounded them. It is clear that the portraits of the Fitzgeralds' lives were heavily dependent upon the mythology that had arisen in popular culture. In the past three decades, F. Scott and Zelda Fitzgerald have emerged as recognizable icons of the era. For many, the images of the Fitzgeralds, and certainly of the many iconic dancing couples of the 1920s, transcend the importance of F. Scott Fitzgerald's writing. Scott and Zelda have truly entered the world of popular culture, as they had tried so indefatigably to accomplish during their years together. The story of Scott Fitzgerald's life – his early success, his struggle with his addiction, his tragic death, his "second act," the many Fitzgerald revivals, the "Gatsbys" who have become familiar to contemporary culture and the bases for fiction, for films, for images of success and failure, and the life of Scott and Zelda as a couple – all have become part of the fabric of contemporary culture.

There is no question that the Fitzgerald Revival has always been energized by the status of the Fitzgeralds as icons in the culture of the 1920s and 1930s as well as of the cultures of virtually every decade since the 1950s. From the time of Fitzgerald's death to the present, however, it has also been energized, first, by the brilliance of Fitzgerald's writing and by the rigor of the scholarship and the completeness of the record that has accompanied both the writing and Fitzgerald's life. Matthew J. Bruccoli's authoritative biography, *Some Sort of Epic Grandeur: The Life of F. Scott Fitzgerald* (1981), has provided a point of reference for assessing information in earlier biographies and is one that cannot be ignored by future biographers. Fortunately, also, Fitzgerald's secretary, Frances Kroll Ring, whose 1950s article, as mentioned earlier, was a corrective to early impressions of Fitzgerald's last years in Hollywood, has written her own firsthand account, *Against the Current: As I Remember F. Scott Fitzgerald* (1985).[21] She has also participated in many of the biannual F. Scott Fitzgerald conferences that have been held in the United States and abroad since the formation of the F. Scott Fitzgerald Society in 1992. Fitzgerald's granddaughter and Sheilah Graham's son have each written accounts of Fitzgerald's life from new and important perspectives.[22] Jackson R. Bryer's bibliographical studies – his books and essays – have appeared at regular intervals from 1967 to the present, and they provide the reader with detailed and invaluable accounts that trace his critical reputation[23]; Bryer's bibliographical essays along with those by Albert J. De Fazio III appear yearly in the *F. Scott Fitzgerald Review*, which was first published in 2002. The *F. Scott Fitzgerald Society Newsletter* has appeared annually since 1992, supported by Hofstra University, which also supports the F. Scott Fitzgerald Society and the *Review*. Also, the relationship between Fitzgerald and the worlds of art, of history and, notably, of philosophy, have finally begun to be given the kind of attention that had been lacking during the decades since the revival began. In 1997, for example, Ronald Berman published the first of several books and essays that probe the deeper meanings that have often eluded critics and readers.[24] Most recently, collections of essays such as *The Cambridge Companion to F. Scott Fitzgerald* (2002)[25] and the Kirk Curnutt-edited *A Historical Guide to F. Scott Fitzgerald* (2004) published by the Oxford University Press have opened the Fitzgerald canon to new and fresh perspectives. Another project of enormous value to Fitzgerald studies that has been ongoing since 1991 and is nearing completion is the publication by Cambridge University Press of authoritative annotated texts, with extensive textual apparatus, of virtually all of Fitzgerald's work (fourteen volumes in all). James L. W. West III has completed ten of these volumes and the final two, *Tender Is the Night* and *Taps at Reveille*, are nearing completion. Matthew J. Bruccoli edited two of the earlier volumes in the series.

One significant bit of evidence of Fitzgerald's current status is reflected in the importance of *The Great Gatsby* in the hierarchy of modern literary masterpieces. Virtually every list of great American novels places it at the top or near the top of the list, and this has been true for every year in recent memory. The prestigious Radcliffe Publishing Course, for example, listed *Gatsby* as its number one choice in its list of the century's top 100 novels prepared at the request of the Modern Library in 1998; in the 2000 *New York Times* list of the greatest fiction of the century, *Gatsby* placed second only to James Joyce's *Ulysses*. Today F. Scott Fitzgerald is one of the most recognized American writers of the modern era. Judging by the ongoing popularity of *The Great Gatsby* and Fitzgerald's continuing status during the past forty years, there will be no need for another revival, for F. Scott Fitzgerald, now resurrected for the ages, will forever remain an enduring figure in modern literature.

NOTES

1 See M. J. Bruccoli, *Some Sort of Epic Grandeur: The Life of F. Scott Fitzgerald*, 2nd rev. edn. (Columbia, SC: University of South Carolina Press, 2002), 218. Subsequent references to this work are included in the text.
2 See M. J. Bruccoli, S. F. Smith, and J. P. Kerr (eds.), *The Romantic Egoists* (New York: Charles Scribner's Sons, 1974), 230. Subsequent references to this work are included in the text.
3 F. S. Fitzgerald, *The Portable F. Scott Fitzgerald* (New York: Viking, 1945).
4 B. Schulberg, *The Disenchanted* (New York: Random House, 1950).
5 A. Mizener, *The Far Side of Paradise: A Biography of F. Scott* Fitzgerald (Boston: Houghton Mifflin, 1951).
6 S. Graham with G. Frank, *Beloved Infidel* (New York: Henry Holt, 1958). Graham was Fitzgerald's companion in Hollywood from 1938 until his death.
7 A. Turnbull, *Scott Fitzgerald* (New York: Charles Scribner's Sons, 1962).
8 F. K. Ring, "Footnotes on Fitzgerald," *Esquire* 52 (December 1959), 149–50.
9 J. E. Miller, *F. Scott Fitzgerald: His Art and Technique* (New York: New York University Press, 1964). This book, which includes discussion of *Tender Is the Night* and *The Last Tycoon*, is an expansion of Miller's earlier book *The Fictional Technique of F. Scott Fitzgerald* (The Hague: Martinus Nijhoff, 1957), which is the first book-length critical work to deal exclusively with Fitzgerald's fiction. The 1957 volume includes discussion of work up through *The Great Gatsby*.
10 K. Eble, *F. Scott Fitzgerald* (New York: Twayne, 1963).
11 R. Sklar, *The Last Laocoön* (New York: Oxford University Press, 1967).
12 M. J. Bruccoli (ed.), *The Great Gatsby: A Facsimile of the Manuscript* (Washington: Bruccoli Clark/NCR, 1973).
13 M. J. Bruccoli, S. F. Smith, and J. P. Kerr (eds.), *The Romantic Egoists* (New York: Charles Scribner's Sons, 1974).
14 M. R. Stern, *The Golden Moment: The Novels of F. Scott Fitzgerald* (Urbana: University of Illinois Press, 1970), xiii. Subsequent references to this work are included in the text.
15 S. B. Fryer, *Fitzgerald's New Women: Harbingers of Change* (Ann Arbor, MI: UMI Research Press, 1988).
16 N. Milford, *Zelda: A Biography* (New York: Harper & Row, 1970). Subsequent references to this work are included in the text.

17 S. Mayfield, *Exiles from Paradise: Scott and Zelda Fitzgerald* (New York: Delacorte Press, 1971).

18 S. F. Smith, preface in *Zelda Fitzgerald: The Collected Writings*, M. J. Bruccoli, ed. (New York: Charles Scribner's Sons, 1991), v.

19 J. R. Mellow, *Invented Lives: F. Scott and Zelda Fitzgerald* (Boston: Houghton Mifflin, 1984).

20 J. Meyers, *F. Scott Fitzgerald: A Biography* (New York: HarperCollins, 1994).

21 F. K. Ring, *Against the Current: As I Remember F. Scott Fitzgerald* (Berkeley, CA: Creative Arts, 1985).

22 E. Lanahan, *Scottie: The Daughter of ... : The Life of Frances Scott Fitzgerald Lanahan Smith* (New York: HarperCollins, 1995) and R. Westbrook, *Intimate Lies: F. Scott Fitzgerald and Sheilah Graham: Her Son's Story* (New York: HarperCollins, 1995).

23 See for example, J. R. Bryer, *The Critical Reputation of F. Scott Fitzgerald: A Bibliographical Study* (Hamden, CT: Archon, 1967) and *F. Scott Fitzgerald: The Critical Reception* (New York: Burt Franklin, 1978).

24 R. Berman, The Great Gatsby *and Fitzgerald's World of Ideas* (Tuscaloosa: University of Alabama Press, 1997).

25 R. Prigozy (ed.), *The Cambridge Companion to F. Scott Fitzgerald* (Cambridge, UK: Cambridge University Press, 2002).

PART II

An Author's Formation (1896–1920)

9

Buffalo and Syracuse, New York

Joel Kabot

When we think of F. Scott Fitzgerald and place, we think of Princeton's bucolic campus, or Paris and the French Riviera, or perhaps his native Minnesota or Zelda's Montgomery, Alabama. New York State undoubtedly comes to mind, but it is the New York of Manhattan and Great Neck, not the higher latitudes of Buffalo and Syracuse. However, Fitzgerald spent ten years of his childhood in upstate New York, first moving to Buffalo with his family in 1898 at the age of one year and seven months, not leaving the region until 1908, when he was almost twelve years old. A decade in one's youth would be considered formative for any child, but it was especially so for Fitzgerald, given his keen sense of observation and social awareness. It was in upstate New York where young Fitzgerald first encountered the social and economic elite and his first loves; where he developed interests in reading, theater, and history; where he began to write. Fitzgerald's childhood experiences in Buffalo and Syracuse laid the foundation for the themes and interests he would continue to explore the rest of his life.

At the time of Fitzgerald's birth, his father, Edward, ran a wicker-furniture factory in St. Paul, Minnesota.[1] By 1898, however, the business had failed, and in April the family moved to Buffalo, where Edward worked as a salesman for Procter & Gamble. Company transfers resulted in the Fitzgeralds' moving to Syracuse in January 1901, and then back to Buffalo in September 1903 (Bruccoli, *Epic Grandeur* 17, 19). While contemporary Buffalo and Syracuse are often considered part of the stagnant Rust Belt region, turn-of-the-century Buffalo and Syracuse were influential, fast-growing cities. In 1900, Buffalo was the eighth-largest "urban place" in the United States, well ahead of cities such as Los Angeles (ranked thirty-sixth), Atlanta (forty-third), and Houston (eighty-fifth), not to mention peer industrial cities such as Detroit (thirteenth) and Milwaukee (fourteenth). Syracuse was ranked thirtieth, the fourth-largest city in the state.[2] A decade later, two years after the Fitzgeralds returned to St. Paul, Buffalo dropped to tenth place, ceding ground to Pittsburgh and Detroit, and Syracuse slid to thirty-fourth (Gibson). However, both still experienced substantial gains in population over those ten years, 20.2 and 26.6 percent, respectively.

As befitting the eighth-largest city in the United States, Buffalo was an economic powerhouse. Situated on the eastern shore of Lake Erie, it was the "greatest grain port in the world," according to local historian Mark Goldman, with massive grain elevators constantly at the ready for Midwestern bushels.[3] Much of that grain became flour, and the prominence of Buffalo's mills rivaled those of St. Paul's neighbor, Minneapolis (*City on the Edge* 38). The second-largest city in New York, Buffalo seemed to be in competition more with the cities of the Midwest than with the Big Apple: Only Chicago bested its international standing as a livestock center, and only Chicago surpassed its importance as a U.S. railroad terminus (*City on the Edge* 39, 40). Heavy industries included not only the sprawling Lackawanna Steel plant south of downtown (*City on the Edge* 20, 32), but also the numerous factories that produced edged tools, nuts and bolts, pipes, boilers, and steam engines, among other products.[4] Out of other shops came such railroad-related items as locomotives, freight cars, and railcar wheels; the railroads themselves employed 20,000 workers, while their suppliers employed additional thousands (*City on the Edge* 40). Once again, Buffalo's geographical location aided its economic might, as many factories relied on electricity generated from nearby Niagara Falls (Larned 3, 13).

The burgeoning automotive industry had a foothold in Buffalo as well. The famous Thomas Flyer, winner of the 1908 New York to Paris Race, was produced by the E. R. Thomas Motor Company (Larned 14–15), while the prestigious Pierce-Arrow brand originated from the George N. Pierce Company (later renamed after its hyphenated model), which had outgrown its roots as a bicycle manufacturer.[5] Pierce-Arrow stood for high-class luxury and was the car of U.S. presidents and the richest Americans (Wise 147); its advertisements depicted Gatsby-like worlds of well-dressed men and women in upscale settings. Fitzgerald was, of course, familiar with the brand, mentioning it in "Winter Dreams" as Mr. Mortimer Jones's automobile and the car of young Dexter Green's dreams (*S* 218).

Pierce-Arrow was not the only bit of glamour in Buffalo at the turn of the century. All that industry created immense wealth, and those fortunate enough to possess it built lavish homes along Delaware Avenue, probably the city's most prestigious street.[6] The privileged class belonged to places like the Buffalo Club, an establishment cofounded by former president Millard Fillmore, who resettled in Buffalo after his antebellum presidency.[7] The growing city had an architectural landmark, as well: The Ellicott Square Building in downtown Buffalo was the world's largest office building at the time of its construction in 1896.[8] A *New York Times* reporter, writing about Buffalo in the midst of the 1901 Pan-American Exposition, praised the "very handsome building," believing it to be "such a building as would do honor even to the metropolis." Ellicott Square, with its ornate glass-enclosed atrium surrounded by restaurants, retail outlets, and offices, was "the heart of everything" in Buffalo, the reporter wrote.[9]

In the first year of the new century, Buffalo became more than an industrial power: Thanks to the Pan-American Exposition of 1901, it became a destination. An event designed "to promote commercial and social interests among the States and countries of the Western Hemisphere," according to its official guidebook, the Pan-American Exposition heralded Buffalo's arrival on the international stage.[10] It lasted from May to November, and some eight million visitors passed through its gates.[11] True to its titular theme, the buildings were designed primarily in the Spanish Renaissance style and were so colorful that the exposition became known as the "Rainbow City."[12] Some two-million light bulbs framed the event's structures,[13] especially the aptly named Electric Tower that, when lit, was visible even fifty miles away.[14] Buildings that held transportation, agriculture, and electricity exhibits surrounded the Electric Tower, which sat amid fountains east of the midway (*High Hopes* 6). The exposition received high praise from a visiting "gentleman" of a "city second only to New York," who, when asked why he had not accompanied family members on a summer trip abroad, explained that "'Europe is a rather shopworn old place, and this is new and fresh; so I have brought my wife and daughter here to spend six or eight weeks, believing that we can have a better time here than we should be likely to have in Europe.'"[15] As a young city, "new and fresh," Buffalo was right to be proud of the international event, the first world's fair in the new century. Sadly, all the positive feelings and press would soon be overshadowed: The Pan-American would go down in history not as a success for Buffalo, but as the site of President William McKinley's assassination in September. Buffalo was then truly on the world stage, but for all the wrong reasons.

Although much smaller than its neighbor to the west, Syracuse was also a prosperous industrial city. Long known for the salt springs that lined Onondaga Lake, the city's salt industry had given way to a more diversified economy. Turn-of-the-century Syracuse contained manufacturers of plows, specialty steel, railroad windows, pottery, coffins, and candles, among other goods.[16] In fact, a 1914 issue of Rotary International's *Rotarian* magazine partially dedicated to Syracuse boosterism proclaimed that "[i]t is impossible in the space allotted … to show more than a few plants or touch upon but a few of the largest industries," given the diversity found in Syracuse's commerce.[17] It did find the space to highlight Solvay Process Company, which it considered "the largest single industry of Syracuse" all by itself.[18] Named for the method used to produce soda ash, Solvay Process manufactured sodium carbonate and other industrial chemicals, making use of locally available limestone and salt ("Solvay Process" 43). Like Buffalo, Syracuse was also a participant in the growing automobile industry and had its own luxury rival to Pierce-Arrow: The H. H. Franklin Manufacturing Company produced the world's only "air cooled pleasure car."[19] Automobile parts were also big business, represented in Syracuse chiefly by the New Process Gear Corporation and the Brown-Lipe companies ("Automobiles and Gears" 43).

Interestingly enough for a city that was home to young Fitzgerald, who would later become one of America's greatest writers, Syracuse's most important industry was probably the manufacture of typewriters. The *Rotarian* even went so far as to proclaim Syracuse the "Typewriter City."[20] The Smith Premier Typewriter Company, headed by former gunsmith Lyman C. Smith, began in the late nineteenth century. Later, after Smith Premier was acquired by the Union Typewriter Company, Smith and his three brothers started a competing firm, L. C. Smith and Brothers Typewriter Company, which operated the biggest typewriter factory in the city by 1914. The Monarch brand, started by W. L. Smith while under Union control, brought the total to three major typewriter factories representing three distinct brands ("Typewriter Industry" 44). Such was the reputation of Syracuse's typewriter industry that when the Crown Prince of Siam visited the city in 1902 he was met at the station by Lyman C. Smith and then given a tour of the Smith Premier factory.[21]

The Buffalo and Syracuse the Fitzgeralds encountered were thus significant economically, and Fitzgerald enjoyed comfortable surroundings as a result of such civic prosperity. "Tiring of St. Paul," Fitzgerald wrote of himself in his *Ledger*, "he went east to Buffalo New York where with his parents he installed himself at the Lennox" (152), the "Lennox" being the Lenox apartment building at 140 North Street, around the corner from Delaware Avenue. At the time of the Fitzgeralds' move in April 1898, the Lenox was only two years old, its eight stories home to twenty-four apartments.[22] Although it would soon be converted to a hotel in time for the Pan-American Exposition (Linstedt), during the Fitzgeralds' stay it was an "apartment hotel" where one "rented an apartment and got hotel services," according to a local historic preservationist.[23] Edward Fitzgerald and his family did not enjoy such luxury for long, however; they moved to an apartment at Summer Street and Elmwood Avenue exactly one year later (*FSFL* 153). This relocation would be the start of a semi-transient existence in upstate New York, at least in the early years, which biographer Arthur Mizener attributes to Edward Fitzgerald's "economic insufficiency."[24] However, others suggest that the frequent moves were due to the social climbing of Fitzgerald's mother, Mollie, who "had a keen nose for the 'suitable' location,"[25] always angling for residence in "the most prestigious neighborhoods."[26] Whatever the reason, it was during the Fitzgeralds' time at Summer Street that Mollie gave birth to a daughter who lived but an hour. Here, too, the sailor-suit-wearing Fitzgerald "told enormous lies" at his fourth birthday party "about being really the owner of a real yatch," foreshadowing a career in writing fiction that would explore the lives of America's rich (*FSFL* 154–55).

Less than three years after arriving, the Fitzgeralds left Buffalo for Syracuse in January 1901, settling in "Mrs. Peck's appartment on East Genesee Street" (*FSFL* 155). Thereafter, every January while in Syracuse the Fitzgeralds moved, first to the Kasson apartment building at 622 James Street in 1902, then to an East Willow Street apartment in 1903 (*FSFL* 155–57). The Kasson, built in 1898, was one of three new apartment buildings on James Street, "considered Syracuse's most exclusive residential area," that were not intended for the city's very rich, but the "affluent middle class" (Hardin 191, 217). While the flats might not have had the square footage of neighboring James Street mansions, the emphasis was certainly on the "affluent": In the decade after its construction, the Kasson appeared in the Syracuse society pages no less than forty-nine times. (None of the appearances found referenced the Fitzgeralds.)

Syracuse was the birthplace of Fitzgerald's younger sister, Annabel, and Fitzgerald's "first certain memory" was seeing Annabel "howling on a bed" (*FSFL* 155). Another Syracuse memory recalled in his *Ledger* concerned "a filthy vacant lot, the haunt of dead cats" (157), which later found its way into *This Side of Paradise*, as Amory Blaine ponders the death of classmate Dick Humbird: "Amory was reminded of a cat that had lain horribly mangled in some alley of his childhood" (86). Fitzgerald's real-life friends of the time included "Edgar Miller the grocery man's son"; "one Dixon Green whom he has entirely forgotten"; and Jack Butler, whose father was an officer in the U.S. Army (*FSFL* 156–57). Years later, Miller would write to the successful Fitzgerald, reminding him that the young author-to-be used to "'ride in the rear of the delivery rig'" (presumably belonging to Miller's father) while "'[reciting] Friends, Romans, and Countrymen etc. at the top of your voice.'"[27] Fitzgerald's desire for attention and his theatrical impulses were evidently on display at an early age. The "Dixon Green" of Fitzgerald's *Ledger* was Grant Dickson Green, Jr., whose father was secretary of one of Syracuse's many steel companies.[28] In contrast to Miller, who lived above his father's store at the intersection of East Willow Street and Catherine Street (Turnbull 10),[29] the junior Green came from a more privileged background, and his household employed live-in help (Syracuse Census Ward 8). Green later married Hallie Stiles, a Syracuse girl who made history as the first American to obtain a contract with the Paris Opera Comique;[30] her stay in the French capital partially overlapped Fitzgerald's time in Paris.[31]

Fitzgerald's other Syracuse friend, Jack Butler, is notable for having "two or three facinating books about the civil war" (*FSFL* 156), which no doubt helped fuel Fitzgerald's interest in the historic conflict. Owing to his Maryland-born father's childhood stories about the wartime South, young Fitzgerald was a "strong Confederate sympathizer" (Bruccoli, *Epic Grandeur* 20) despite living in a Northern city that had once been a hotbed of abolitionism. In a *Ledger* entry for July 1903, Fitzgerald mentioned that "[h]e wandered off on the Fourth of July + was spanked in consequence" (157). Fitzgerald later recalled that after "'seeing in his [father's] face his regret that [the punishment] had to happen,'" he asked his father to tell him a story as a peace offering of sorts. "'[H]e had only a few,'" Fitzgerald continued, "'the story of the spy, the one about the man hung by his thumbs, the one about [Confederate Gen. Jubal] Early's march'" (qtd. in Turnbull 10). Edward Fitzgerald's tales of the Civil War were not Fitzgerald's only exposure to the South while in upstate New York, however. In August 1901, Fitzgerald briefly returned to Buffalo for the Pan-American Exposition (*FSFL* 155), home of the midway sideshow "Old Plantation" (*High Hopes* 6). Described in the event guidebook as depicting the "'South be'fo de Wah,'" it included "150 Southern darkies in their plantation songs and dances" and "a Georgia cotton field with real growing cotton" (Official Catalogue 45). As bastardized (and insensitive) as such an exhibit must have appeared, it nonetheless might have been Fitzgerald's first experience with a large-scale version of Southern culture, one live and in front of him, not relegated to paternal stories or history books. While his *Ledger* recalls a January 1899 visit to Washington,

DC, a city that borders Edward Fitzgerald's native Montgomery County, Maryland, no mention is made of visiting ancestral grounds (153); it is not until the May 1902 entry that Fitzgerald wrote of visiting "aunt Eliza Delihant's place" in Maryland (156). Fitzgerald later explored the South and Southerners in his fiction, notably in the stories of the Tarleton trilogy, and, of course, he married an Alabama belle, Zelda Sayre; the irony is that his interest in the South owes much to his childhood in upstate New York.

Friendships and Civil War stories notwithstanding, Fitzgerald's experience in Syracuse ended in disappointment. As he wrote sadly in his *Ledger*, in September 1903 "[h]e had a [seventh] birth day party to which no one came" (158). The lack of turnout was because of the rainy weather, but that was no salve to Fitzgerald's broken heart: He retreated to his home and "'thoughtfully consumed one complete birthday cake, including several candles'" (qtd. in Turnbull 11). This experience in Syracuse foreshadowed the way the Fitzgeralds would leave Buffalo – also unhappily. But that was yet a half-decade away. In September 1903, the Fitzgeralds returned to Buffalo and first lived at 29 Irving Place (*FSFL* 158), a charming brick house within eyesight of the Lenox. Compared to their hectic existence in Syracuse, where they had moved three times in less than three years, the Fitzgeralds' second attempt at Buffalo was relatively tranquil: They only switched houses once, moving to 71 Highland Avenue in October 1905 (*FSFL* 160).

Immediately upon his return to Buffalo, Fitzgerald began to interact with scions of the city's best families. Referring to that time period, Fitzgerald wrote that "[h]e remembers Ted Keating, Dodo Clifton, Jack Kimberly and Dexter Rumsey, and their facinating army" (*FSFL* 158). Theodore Barnum Keating, whose mother's family owned novelty stores in town (Dunn 273), lived at 576 Delaware Avenue but had a backyard that bordered Fitzgerald's.[32] Keating later attended The Hill School, where he was a classmate, for a time, of Edmund "Bunny" Wilson[33]; their shared prep school would appear in Fitzgerald's writing as alma mater of both Otis Ormonde in "Bernice Bobs Her Hair" (*S* 26) and an unnamed Princeton freshman-class president in *This Side of Paradise* (47). Like Wilson and Fitzgerald, Keating also matriculated at Princeton ("Author Tried His Wings"). The unfortunately nicknamed Dodo Clifton appears to have been young Gorham Clifton, who lived near the Fitzgeralds at 61 Irving Place.[34] Clifton's father, Colonel Charles Clifton, later became treasurer and president of Pierce-Arrow and played an important role in the brand's success.[35] John L. Kimberly lived between Clifton and Fitzgerald at 51 Irving Place and was also a child of means; his father was treasurer of a fertilizer company (Buffalo Census Ward 21).

Of Fitzgerald's four "army" friends, however, Dexter P. Rumsey, Jr. had the most storied lineage. Rumsey's grandfather was one of the earliest settlers of Buffalo, a native Vermonter whose tanneries later became a prosperous leather company operated by his two sons. By the turn of the century, the leather business having been sold, Rumsey's father was active in real estate and banking and resided at a palatial house on Delaware Avenue (Dunn 153–62). While not mentioned in the same *Ledger* entry as the four preceding individuals, Earl Knox was another friend, and probably the closest rival to Rumsey in terms of familial prestige. "Earl" was apparently a youthful name for Seymour H. Knox, Jr., whose father acquired a fortune through ownership of Woolworth's stores. (An "Earl R. Knox," born September 1898, son of Seymour H. and his wife, Grace, is listed in the 1900 Census[36]; Seymour H. Knox, Sr. had only one son [Dunn 374], and Knox, Jr.'s birth date was September 1, 1898.[37]) At the time of his death in 1915, the elder Knox was worth $10 million.[38] Knox, Jr., who later served as chairman of Woolworth's, became a renowned art philanthropist, lending his name to the Albright-Knox Art Gallery in Buffalo after donating many pieces of modern art (Dunn 373–77). His *New York Times* obituary recognized him as "'the dean of American art patrons,'" and noted that his "more than 700" donations included works by such artists as Willem de Kooning, Jasper Johns, Roy Lichtenstein, and Mark Rothko (Glueck). So influential and important was his presence in the art world that Andy Warhol created the colorful "Portrait of Seymour H. Knox" in 1985.[39]

Another friend not mentioned as a member of the "facinating army," but referred to later in the same *Ledger* entry, was Hamilton Wende. Out of all Fitzgerald's Buffalo friends, Wende was perhaps the most influential, as he received free tickets to Saturday shows at the Teck Theater and "always" invited Fitzgerald along (Turnbull 12), similar to how "Amory and Frog Parker went each week to the stock company" in *This Side of Paradise* (24). After the shows, Fitzgerald and Wende would hurry back to "re-enact what they had seen" (Turnbull 12). Indeed, Fitzgerald wrote that "[h]e remembers the attic where he had a red sash with which he acted Paul Revere" (*FSFL* 158). Fitzgerald would put on such early performances in his own home; Keating, a frequent guest, later recalled an admission charge of one cent and "an impromptu stage and two sheets for curtains" ("Author Tried His Wings"). After Fitzgerald's move to Highland Avenue, production relocated to the attic of a friend, James Jugham, where once again the red sash made an appearance, also in plays "based on the American Revolution" (*FSFL* 161). (In Syracuse, Edward Fitzgerald had given his son a U.S. history book that led to Fitzgerald's "[becoming] a child of the American Revolution" and which no doubt influenced his choice of subject matter as a young dramatist [*FSFL* 157].)

However, in this small amateur circle, Fitzgerald was not always the star: In one *Ledger* entry, he recalled that "Gus Shy's play put him temporarily in the shade" (*FSFL* 161). Fitzgerald could later take heart that the boy who overshadowed him became a Broadway star and sometime film actor: "Gus Shy" was the stage name for Augustus Scheu, Jr., son of Buffalo's commissioner of public works and grandson of a former mayor.[40] Shy's greatest role came as the sidekick in the Broadway musical *Good News*, a college football-themed comedy that ran for 551 performances starting in 1927; it was later made into a 1930 movie, with Shy in the same role.[41] While Shy certainly had a more successful dramatic career in the end (especially given the failure of Fitzgerald's play, *The Vegetable*), Fitzgerald could revel in the fact that in Buffalo a friend's "moving picture machine" ultimately "eclipsed" the commissioner's son (*FSFL* 161).

It was a natural transition from putting on plays to writing fiction, especially since Fitzgerald was an avid reader. Not surprisingly, given the subject matter of his theatrical creations, Fitzgerald "began a history of the U.S." at age 10 (*FSFL* 161); like Amory Blaine, whose own history "only got as far as the Colonial Wars" (*TSOP* 16), "began" is the operative word, as the *Ledger* contains no other reference to that academic pursuit. Fitzgerald was not above a foray into genre fiction, either, as he also started a detective story (*FSFL* 161). In school, Fitzgerald found success as an author, composing a "celebrated essay on George Washington + St. Ignatius" (*FSFL* 161). While his writing in Buffalo tended toward the historical, Fitzgerald's tastes in reading seemed to shift toward fiction. In the *Ledger*, he wrote of *Ivanhoe*, which he read following a nasal operation (160); his preference for *St. Nicholas*, the Scribners-produced youth magazine, over its rival *The Youth's Companion* (160); and the books of *The Young Kentuckian Series*, which included *Raiding with Morgan* (162), a romanticized young-adult novel about Confederate Gen. John H. Morgan. While on vacation in the Catskill Mountains in July 1905, Fitzgerald "ate an egg every day on the bidding of his Aunt Clara" and used his reward of 25 cents per egg to purchase books by G. A. Henty (*FSFL* 159), a British author of young-adult fiction set in exotic locales; like Amory in *This Side of Paradise*, one can assume that Fitzgerald also shared "all the Henty biasses in history" (*TSOP* 23). Perhaps the title that had the most effect upon young Fitzgerald, however, was an unnamed children's book about a fight between large and small animals in which the small animals had initial success but later met defeat (*FSFL* 158). In "The Romantic Egotist," the unpublished precursor to *This Side of Paradise*, Fitzgerald recalled that "[t]he author was prejudiced in favor of the large animals, but my sentiment was all with the small ones. I wonder if even then I had a sense of the wearing-down power of big, respectable people. I can almost weep now when I think of that poor fox, the leader" (qtd. in Bruccoli, *Epic Grandeur* 19). While he lived a life among the truly rich and elite in Buffalo, it seems that Fitzgerald may have realized at an early age that although he socialized *with* them, he was not *of* them, that no matter how valiant his efforts, he might always be an outsider.

That being said, when associating with the young members of Buffalo high society, Fitzgerald certainly played the part well. In 1905, he began attending Van Arnum's Dancing School, an institution that "provided the sine qua non cachet for small fry's entrance into higher circles" (Brady). There he set his sights on classmates of the fairer sex, falling first for Nancy Gardener. As Fitzgerald later wrote in his "Thoughtbook," a childhood proto-*Ledger*, he and Gardener "were quite infatuated with each other."[42] On one occasion, he went with a friend to the Gardeners' house, where they all took to using toboggans. However, a dust-up soon ensued between Fitzgerald and Gardener's brother, who "came along and wanted to get on" the toboggan Gardener and Fitzgerald were sharing; Fitzgerald would not allow him to do so ("Thoughtbook" VIII). Gardener soon diplomatically "smoothed it over," however, and the children went off to lunch ("Thoughtbook" VIII).

Nancy Gardener was not his only dancing-school interest, though, and Fitzgerald's affections for Gardener later gave way to feelings for Kitty Williams. Fitzgerald asked Williams to be his partner after Mr. Van Arnum picked Fitzgerald to "lead the march"; the following day, Williams "told Marie Lautz and Marie repeated it to Dorothy Knox [Earl/Seymour's sister] who in turn passed it on to Earl, that [Fitzgerald] was third in her affections" ("Thoughtbook" IX). In that particular "Thoughtbook" entry, Fitzgerald wrote that he could not remember who was number one on Williams's list, but that Earl Knox was number two. "I then and there resolved that I would gain first place," Fitzgerald recalled ("Thoughtbook" IX). His moment would come, too. At a friend's party, he and Williams "talked and talked" and then "played post office, pillow, clapp in clapp out, and other foolish but interesting games" ("Thoughtbook" IX–X). Finally, what Fitzgerald had long wished for happened: the opportunity to win young Miss Williams. "It was impossible to count the number of times I kissed Kitty that afternoon," Fitzgerald wrote in his "Thoughtbook." "At any rate when we went home I had secured the coveted 1st place" ("Thoughtbook" X). (This emphasis on ranking affection brings to mind Myra St. Claire's statement to Amory that "I like you the first twenty-five … and Froggy Parker twenty-sixth" [*TSOP* 21].) Scott Fitzgerald, the oft-moved middle-class boy, whose parents only rented in Buffalo, never owned, had vanquished an heir to one of the city's great fortunes. He had won the heart of a young lady, no matter his own economic standing.

In those last few months in Buffalo, however, Fitzgerald saw his own social success give way to familial adversity. January 1908 found him at "the Ramsdell's party in his little tuxedo," and a "charity ball where he was asked to sit in Earl Knox's box" (*FSFL* 162). In February, he saw a performance by the Princeton Glee Club – perhaps the initial source of his desire to attend Princeton – and the last words for that *Ledger* entry are the poignant "Kitty loved him" (162). They are followed, however, by the harsh opening sentence of March 1908: "His father's services were no longer required by Proctor and Gamble" (*FSFL* 162). Fitzgerald would later recall that his father "'had gone out a comparatively young man, a man full of strength, full of confidence. He came home that evening, an old man, a completely broken man … He was a failure the rest of his days.'"[43] The blow to the family finances necessitated another move, this time to St. Paul, where his mother's family waited (Bruccoli, *Epic Grandeur* 23). Fitzgerald had gone from attending black-tie affairs and kissing the sought-after Kitty Williams to praying that his family would not be sent to the "'poorhouse'" (Mok 296). He had achieved success in Buffalo, but it was fleeting; he was once again on the outside looking in. In the spring, after the end of dancing school, he even lost first place in Kitty's heart to Johnny Gowans, "a rival" ("Thoughtbook" X). It was in Buffalo where Fitzgerald first experienced substantial loss: the loss of stature that accompanied his father's dismissal; the loss of confidence in his father's ability to make things right. Throughout his career, Fitzgerald would often explore the effects of loss on his characters, and one cannot help but think of that spring day in Buffalo when Fitzgerald first realized his young world was shattered.

Given that Fitzgerald's formative years were spent in upstate New York, it is perhaps surprising that the region barely makes an appearance in his fiction. In fact, even when Fitzgerald wrote of experiences that occurred in either Buffalo or Syracuse, the setting was often changed. Fitzgerald scattered details of his upstate childhood throughout *This Side of Paradise*, but that novel takes place mainly in St. Paul, Princeton, and New York City, not Buffalo or Syracuse. In another instance, as noted by Bruccoli (*Epic Grandeur* 21), the major dramatic moment in Fitzgerald's short story "Absolution" – Rudolph Miller's lie in confession about never lying – comes from a September 1907 incident in Buffalo: "He went to Confession about this time and lied by saying in a a shocked voice to the priest 'Oh no, I never tell a lie'" (*FSFL* 162). However, "Absolution" is not set in Buffalo, but in rural Minnesota. It is the Basil Duke Lee story "That Kind of Party" – unpublished during Fitzgerald's lifetime – that appears to be that rare story in which Fitzgerald drew upon Buffalo experiences while keeping the original setting intact. In his introduction to the story's first publication in the *Princeton University Library Chronicle*, Mizener notes the story's debt to Buffalo, referencing lines about Tonawanda (a suburb of Buffalo) and the protagonist consuming a raw egg.[44] Jackson Bryer and John Kuehl state that comparing events from the *Ledger* to the story "unmistakably locates ["That Kind of Party"] as describing events of 1907,"[45] and in the introduction to the "Thoughtbook," Kuehl suggests the connection between the object of Basil's affections, Dolly Bartlett, and the real-life Kitty Williams, as both couples, fictional and real, play post office and clap-in-clap-out (105). While the Basil Duke Lee stories are often assumed to be St. Paul-based, the autobiographical details of "That Kind of Party," as well as the few geographical references given – toward the end, we learn that Basil's mother has taken a trolley to Lockport, a city north of Buffalo (*B&J* 15) – seem to suggest that at one point in time Basil was, like his creator, a Buffalonian.

Tender Is the Night is notable, then, for being one of Fitzgerald's works of fiction in which the protagonist is explicitly from upstate New York (although an expatriate for almost the entire novel). Dick Diver is originally from Buffalo, and despite many years spent at Yale, Johns Hopkins, and various places abroad, he clearly identifies himself as a western New Yorker: When asked by a dubious newspaper salesman where he is from, Dick answers simply, "[f]rom Buffalo" (*TITN* 121). In contrast to *This Side of Paradise* and "Absolution," details from Fitzgerald's upstate childhood maintain their regional setting in *Tender Is the Night*. In a Syracuse entry in his *Ledger*, dated July 1903, Fitzgerald wrote that "[o]n Sunday mornings he walked down town in his long trousers and with his little cane and had his shoes shined with his father" (157); in *Tender Is the Night*, we learn that "[i]n the summer father and son walked downtown together to have their shoes shined" (265). In a Buffalo entry, dated October 1907, Fitzgerald wrote that "[i]n church one little girl made him frightfully embarrassed when he didn't have a penny to put in the collection box" (162); in *Tender Is the Night*, we learn that young Dick "once more worried between five or ten cents for the collection plate, because of the girl who sat in the pew behind" (255).[46] At the end of the novel, we find out that Dick, now divorced, has retreated first to Buffalo and then, in succession, to smaller cities in upstate New York: Batavia, Lockport, Geneva, and Hornell. The last line assures us that "he is almost certainly in that section of the country, in one town or another" (*TITN* 408). While Dick may be viewed as a failure, having lost his wife and the life he used to have, it is telling that in the novel on which Fitzgerald worked the longest he has his protagonist leave Europe for upstate New York. Buffalo and Syracuse make rare appearances in Fitzgerald's fiction, but one can argue that in the novel "Fitzgerald may have preferred" to all his others,[47] Dick Diver's upstate identity and his eventual return may have been Fitzgerald's own attempt at coming home.

Although often overlooked in discussions of F. Scott Fitzgerald, the author's childhood in upstate New York was an important time in his life. It was during his years in Buffalo and Syracuse that Fitzgerald's interest in the arts began to blossom and his competitive desire to ascend the ladders of social hierarchy became apparent. It was a life lived among the elite and buoyed by personal success, but it was also a life ultimately darkened by his father's loss of hope. In the end, it provided Fitzgerald with many, if not most, of the trademark themes central to his fiction – themes that can be traced to his formative years in Buffalo and Syracuse. F. Scott Fitzgerald was many things: novelist, short-story writer, native Minnesotan, Princeton man, husband, father, expatriate – but he was also, indelibly, an upstate New Yorker.

NOTES

1 M. J. Bruccoli, *Some Sort of Epic Grandeur: The Life of F. Scott Fitzgerald* (New York: Harcourt Brace Jovanovich, 1981), 13. Subsequent references to this work are included in the text.

2 C. Gibson, "Population of the 100 Largest Cities and Other Urban Places in the United States: 1790 to 1990," U.S. Bureau of the Census, Population Division, June 1998. Available at: www.census.gov/population/www/documentation/twps0027/twps0027.html. Subsequent reference to this work is included in the text.

3 M. Goldman, *City on the Edge: Buffalo, New York* (Amherst, NY: Prometheus Books, 2007), 38. Subsequent references to this work are included in the text.

4 J. N. Larned, "Industrial Evolution: Metal Working and Machinery" in C. A. Conant (ed.), *The Progress of the Empire State: A Work Devoted to the Historical,*

Financial, Industrial, and Literary Development of New York, Volume III: Buffalo, Rochester and Utica (New York: The Progress of the Empire State Company, 1913), 1–17; 2, 8–9. Subsequent references to this work are included in the text.

5 D. B. Wise, "Pierce-Arrow," in *The Complete Encyclopedia of the American Automobile* (Secaucus, NJ: Chartwell Books, 1979), 147–151; 147. Subsequent reference to this work is included in the text.

6 E. T. Dunn, *Buffalo's Delaware Avenue: Mansions and Families* (Buffalo, NY: Canisius College Press, 2003), I. Subsequent references to this work are included in the text.

7 J. A. Grande, "Millard Fillmore, the Buffalo Benefactor," in *Niagara Land … The First 200 Years: Reprinted from the Series Featured in Sunday The Courier-Express Magazine* (Buffalo, NY: Courier-Express, 1976), 64–65, 65. Fillmore was not the only U.S. president with ties to Buffalo: Grover Cleveland served as mayor before becoming governor of New York and then president. Of note, he spent a large part of his childhood in Fayetteville, NY, a suburb of Syracuse.

8 R. Banham, introduction to *Buffalo Architecture: A Guide* (Cambridge, MA: The Massachusetts Institute of Technology Press, 1981), 1–3.

9 W. Drysdale, "Room for All to Eat and Sleep in Buffalo," *New York Times*, June 7, 1901, 6.

10 *Official Catalogue and Guide Book to the Pan-American Exposition, with Maps of Exposition and Illustrations, Buffalo, N.Y., U.S.A., May 1st to Nov. 1st, 1901* (Buffalo, NY: Charles Ahrhart, 1901), 5. Subsequent reference to this work is included in the text.

11 H. F. Peterson, "Buffalo Builds the 1901 Pan-American Exposition," in *Niagara Land … The First 200 Years: Reprinted from the Series Featured in Sunday The Courier-Express Magazine* (Buffalo, NY: Courier-Express, 1976), 67.

12 R. W. Rydell, *All the World's a Fair: Visions of Empire at American International Expositions, 1876–1919* (Chicago: The University of Chicago Press, 1984), 127–28.

13 M. Goldman, *High Hopes: The Rise and Decline of Buffalo, New York* (Albany, NY: State University of New York Press, 1983), 7. Subsequent references to this work are included in the text.

14 "Features at the Pan-American Show," *New York Times*, May 12, 1901, 19.

15 W. Drysdale, "At the Pan-American," *New York Times*, June 16, 1901, 7.

16 D. J. Connors, *Crossroads in Time: An Illustrated History of Syracuse* (Syracuse, NY: Syracuse University Press, 2006), 76, 79.

17 "Syracuse Industries," *Rotarian* 5.3 (September 1914), 33.

18 "The Solvay Process Co.," *Rotarian* 5.3 (September 1914), 43. Subsequent reference to this work is included in the text.

19 "Automobiles and Gears," *Rotarian* 5.3 (September 1914), 43. Subsequent reference to this work is included in the text.

20 "The Typewriter Industry," *Rotarian* 5.3 (September 1914), 44. Subsequent reference to this work is included in the text.

21 E. Hardin, *Syracuse Landmarks: An AIA Guide to Downtown and Historic Neighborhoods* (Syracuse, NY: Syracuse University Press, 1993), 132–33. Subsequent reference to this work is included in the text. See also the following: "Siam's Future King Guest in Syracuse," *Syracuse Post-Standard*, November 4, 1902, 5.

22 S. Linstedt, "Lenox Hotel Renovation Plans Call for 76 Upscale Apartments," *Buffalo News*, April 5, 2004, B1. Subsequent reference to this work is included in the text.

23 L. Haarlander, "Lenox on the Block; Apartment Hotel to be Auctioned in Foreclosure," *Buffalo News*, September 20, 2002, A10.

24 A. Mizener, *The Far Side of Paradise: A Biography of F. Scott Fitzgerald* (Cambridge, MA: The Riverside Press, 1951), 2.

25 C. A. Brady, "Tender Was the Night in Buffalo for Young Scott," *Buffalo Evening News*, June 1, 1974, C-7. Subsequent reference to this work is included in the text.

26 N. Baldwin, "Our Literati in Residence," *Sunday The Courier-Express Magazine*, September 9, 1973, 9.

27 Qtd. in A. Turnbull, *Scott Fitzgerald* (New York: Charles Scribner's Sons, 1962), 10. Subsequent references to this work are included in the text.

28 U.S. Bureau of the Census, Twelfth Census of the United States (Washington: National Archives and Records Administration, 1900), Syracuse (Onondaga County), NY, Roll 1136, Ward 8, Enumeration District 110, 4B-5A. Subsequent reference to this work is included in the text as "Syracuse Census Ward 8."

29 U.S. Bureau of the Census, Twelfth Census of the United States (Washington: National Archives and Records Administration, 1900), Syracuse (Onondaga County), NY, Roll 1136, Ward 6, Enumeration District 104, 10B.

30 "New York Welcomes Her Back," *Syracuse Herald*, April 19, 1928, 4.

31 "*Paris* Toasts a *Syracuse* Mam'selle," *Syracuse Herald*, Jan. 13, 1929, 5.

32 "Author Tried His Wings as Buffalo Boy," *Buffalo Courier-Express*, December 15, 1955. Subsequent references to this work are included in the text.

33 S. Cunningham, Jr. (ed.), *The Dial, 1910*, vol. XIV (Pottstown, PA: The Hill School, 1910), 55; E. B. Jermyn, Jr. (ed.), *The Dial, 1911*, vol. XV (Pottstown, PA: The Hill School, 1911), 59; J. K. Wood (ed.) *The Dial, 1912*, vol. XVI (Pottstown, PA: The Hill School, 1912), 57; and W. M. Russel (ed.) *The Dial, 1913*, vol. XVII (Pottstown, PA: The Hill School, 1913), 37. While Keating and Wilson were in the same fourth form (which corresponds to sophomore year, or tenth grade) initially, class of 1912, Keating apparently repeated fourth form and graduated class of 1913, one year after Wilson. Interestingly, Edward E. Paramore, Jr., who shares cowriting credit on Fitzgerald's only credited screenplay, *Three Comrades*, was class of 1914 at The Hill School (E. H. Clark, Jr. [ed.] *The Dial, 1914*, vol. XVIII [Pottstown, PA: The Hill School, 1914], 50; J. Cohen, "Three Comrades" in F. N. Magill [ed.], *Magill's Survey of Cinema: English Language Films, First Series, Volume 4: SCA-Z* [Englewood Cliffs, NJ: Salem Press, 1980], 1731–33; 1731, 1732).

34 U.S. Bureau of the Census, Twelfth Census of the United States (Washington: National Archives and Records Administration, 1900), Buffalo (Erie County), NY, Roll 1031, Ward 21, Enumeration District 172, 6A. Subsequent reference to this work is included in the text as "Buffalo Census Ward 21."

35 M. L. Bromley, *William Howard Taft and the First Motoring Presidency, 1909–1913* (Jefferson, NC: McFarland & Company, 2003), 103, 407.

36 U.S. Bureau of the Census, Twelfth Census of the United States (Washington: National Archives and Records Administration, 1900), Buffalo (Erie County), NY, Roll 1031, Ward 24, Enumeration District 202, 9A.

37 G. Glueck, "Seymour H. Knox Is Dead at 92; Buffalo Banker Was Art Patron," *New York Times*, September 28, 1990, A18. Subsequent reference to this work is included in the text.

38 "Seymour H. Knox Dead," *New York Times*, May 17, 1915, 9.

39 "Portrait of Seymour H. Knox," Albright-Knox Art Gallery. Available at: www.albrightknox.org/collection/search/piece:2017.

40 "Who's Who," *New York Times*, April 20, 1924, X2.

41 E. M. Bradley, *The First Hollywood Musicals: A Critical Filmography of 171 Features, 1927 through 1932* (Jefferson, NC: McFarland & Company, 1996), 151, 162.

42 F. S. Fitzgerald, "Scott Fitzgerald's 'Thoughtbook,'" introduction by J. Kuehl, *Princeton University Library Chronicle* 26.2 (Winter 1965). *Princeton University Library Chronicle* did not number the facsimiled pages of the "Thoughtbook." The introduction by John Kuehl runs from page 102 to 108; the "Thoughtbook" pages that follow are numbered by Fitzgerald in Roman numerals, but some pages are missing: it starts, following the cover page, at page VIII and ends at XXXX, but skips pages XVIII, XIX, and XXIV through XXVIII. When subsequent references to the "Thoughtbook" proper are cited in this chapter, the relevant Fitzgerald-supplied Roman numeral will be used. The quote to which this particular endnote refers is from page VIII.

43 M. Mok, "'A Writer Like Me Must Have an Utter Confidence, an Utter Faith in His Star,'" in M. J. Bruccoli and J. R. Bryer (eds.), *F. Scott Fitzgerald In His Own Time: A Miscellany* (Kent, OH: The Kent State University Press, 1971), 294–99; 296. Subsequent reference to this work is included in the text.

44 A. Mizener, introduction to F. S. Fitzgerald, "That Kind of Party," *Princeton University Library Chronicle* 12.4 (Summer 1951), 166–80; 167.

45 J. R. Bryer and J. Kuehl, introduction to F. S. Fitzgerald, *The Basil and Josephine Stories* (New York: Scribner Paperback Fiction, 1997), 7–8.

46 As Austin M. Fox notes, "Diver's father and Diver's relationship with him closely recall Scott's father and Scott's relationship with him," and Dick's memories of his childhood seemingly always revolve around his clergyman father. See A. M. Fox, "F. Scott Fitzgerald: His Centennial and Buffalo Folklore," *Buffalo Spree* 30.4 (Winter 1996), 64–68; 67.

47 "The Talk of the Town," *New Yorker*, January 4, 1941, 9.

10

St. Paul, Minnesota, St. Paul Academy, and the St. Paul Academy Now and Then

Deborah Davis Schlacks

St. Paul, Minnesota – the place of his birth, of his early teen years, of summers and scattered sojourns in late teens and early twenties – left an indelible mark on F. Scott Fitzgerald. St. Paul had a hierarchical social structure headed by old-stock Eastern aristocrats, yet it was known as an Irish town. In its upper-class enclave, the Summit Avenue neighborhood, Fitzgerald resided in a liminal space – among the rich, but not one of them – that ultimately became the space so many of his characters inhabit as they strive to be, understand, or criticize the elite of an unattainable world.

In the mid-nineteenth century, old-stock New Englanders came to the area for the dry air, which was good for the tubercular. Other Easterners followed for other reasons as part of the westward migration. They were Protestants, often Presbyterian. This aristocracy in the 1880s built the first big houses on the city's incipient "show street," Summit Avenue, and started the city's cultural and social institutions. In 1915, a minister at the St. Paul First Presbyterian Church called them "highly favored … the very cream of the community: the piety, the zeal, the intelligence, the wealth, and the controling [*sic*] social element."[1] In contrast, F. Scott Fitzgerald's father, Edward, though an Easterner, was not a New England Protestant, but Edward's mother was from a distinguished, largely Catholic, Maryland family. Francis Scott Key was an ancestor. However, Edward Fitzgerald was later in coming to St. Paul than the early community builders and aristocracy founders, and he did not exhibit their zeal, wealth, and control. Instead, he was a business failure, dependent on his in-laws and uninvolved in civic affairs.

Because they privileged the East, elite St. Paulites (a group eventually including more than just old-stock Americans) ensured that their children received an education that prepared them for Eastern colleges. Founded in 1900 as an offshoot of the Barnard School for Boys, Saint Paul Academy, attended by Fitzgerald from 1908 to 1911, had a curriculum designed for this purpose. Its 1910–11 catalog lists offerings in English (composition and grammar, along with spelling and penmanship, with English literature and "the essentials of rhetoric" to be introduced "as the pupils acquire facility in writing"), Latin and Greek (it was "desirable" for boys to study Latin for five years and possible for them to study Greek for three), French and German, history (of the United States, England, Greece and Rome, along with civil government and advanced American history), mathematics (arithmetic, algebra, and plane geometry for everyone, and solid geometry and plane trigonometry for prospective scientists), and chemistry and physics. The school magazine, the *St. Paul Academy Now and Then* (1909– 1969), often featured articles by alumni informing students about Eastern colleges. For example, in the same issue as Fitzgerald's first story is the article "Just a Word About Harvard" by Bronson West.[2] Meanwhile, local newspaper ads proclaimed that the school's coursework "correspond[s] with the college preparatory course of the best Eastern preparatory schools."[3]

Besides its penchant for what Fitzgerald called this "passionate imitation of Chicago imitating New York imitating London,"[4] St. Paul was known as an Irish town in which Irish-Catholics had attained considerable power. Fitzgerald was part Irish: His paternal grandfather, Michael Fitzgerald, was from a family with colonial/revolutionary roots, and his mother's parents, the McQuillans, were from potato-famine Irish immigrant families. Fitzgerald's maternal grandfather, P. F. McQuillan, became a very successful wholesale grocer in St. Paul. His daughter, Mollie Fitzgerald, and her husband were listed in the St. Paul Social Register, presumably because of the McQuillan connection.

Initially settling in large numbers in Eastern cities, Irish immigrants to the United States in the mid-nineteenth century were vilified at first and stereotyped as being ape-like, drunken, and violent. The rancor had died down by the century's turn as the Irish became established and other immigrant groups replaced them as the vilified newcomers. A new Irish stereotype emerged: the social-climbing "lace-curtain" Irish, exemplified in the nationally syndicated comic strip *Bringing Up Father* (begun in 1913), in which Irish-American Maggie and Jiggs win the lottery, resulting in Maggie's social climbing and, to her consternation, Jiggs's attempts to keep associating with his working-class buddies. Also by this time, the Irish had acquired the label "honorary Anglo Saxons," which connotes some acceptance yet smacks of condescension.[5]

Some Irish immigrants spread to the West, including to St. Paul. According to historian Mary Lethert Wingerd, in St. Paul, "a small cohort [of Irish-Americans] carved a niche of power and influence that, in time, against all odds, turned Irish identity itself into a capital asset."[6] It helped that Irish immigrants arriving in St. Paul had often already been in the United States for a while, sometimes since childhood, and had often already acquired work skills and some capital. Also, St. Paul did not have Irish wards; instead, the Irish spread throughout the city such that from one to three percent of each ward, including the upper-class ones, consisted of Irish residents. Lacking the numbers to attain power through group solidarity (there were many more German immigrants in St. Paul than Irish, for instance), they had to build, says Wingerd, "a complex web comprising both interethnic alliances and ethnic loyalty" in order to have power as a group (Wingerd 40–41). In addition, they were favored by railroad magnate James J. Hill, who had married Irish-Catholic immigrant Mary Mehegan. Uncomfortable among the old-stock elites, she preferred to spend time with her Irish-Catholic family and friends (Wingerd 43–53). Says Wingerd, "if St. Paul society hoped to lure the truculent Hill, on whom they were all dependent in some fashion, and the almost reclusive Mary to grace their soirees, then they had best keep aristocratic airs in check and shed any vestige of condescension toward either Catholic clergy or Irish-Catholics – at least those of the proper class" (Wingerd 53).

The Irish became so successful in St. Paul that twenty percent of the surnames on the 1915 Town and Country Club member roster are Irish, even though the Irish accounted for just under eight percent of the city's population (Wingerd 66). The McQuillans' presence in the Summit neighborhood, made possible by P. F. McQuillan's achievements, as well as the residency in the neighborhood of such people as the Irish-American Michael Doran,[7] who was a banker, politician, and friend of Grover Cleveland, also indicate this success. At St. Paul Academy, Fitzgerald was not the only Irish-American: Several other Irish surnames appeared on the 1909–10 student list: Fitzpatrick, Kennedy, McNair, and O'Brien. Fellow SPA student Dillon O'Brien's father was an attorney and a brother of St. Paul's first Irish-American mayor, Christopher O'Brien.

All was not rosy for the Irish in St. Paul, however. Wingerd's statement concerning condescension toward Irish-Catholics bespeaks continuing veiled negativity. And sometimes it was not veiled at all, as in 1925, when St. Paul author Grace Flandrau wrote of St. Paul's "immigrant class of soft-speaking, darling, shiftless Irish from Galway."[8] It does not get much more condescending than that. Wingerd speaks of the "mixed emotions of many ... [St. Paul] Irish Catholics, even those who had reached the upper rungs of the social ladder." They were "defensively burdened by the vestigial baggage of ethnic stereotyping" (Wingerd 64). These feelings were exacerbated as World War I ensued and President Woodrow Wilson proclaimed disparagingly that some Irish were hyphenated Americans who had not fully "come over."[9]

Being Catholic, particularly *Irish* Catholic, in St. Paul also meant having power, yet not the most power, inside and outside the local Church hierarchy. Catholicism had come early, with the arrival of French Catholic priests in the 1850s. In 1852, a priest described area Catholics as "very poor ... And what is worse very irreligious and indifferent ... They are Half breeds, Canadians, and Irish – The Yankees have all the influence, the wealth and the power."[10] In the 1860s, French dominance of the St. Paul diocese ended in favor of the Irish.[11] Well before Fitzgerald's time, then, Catholicism, with an Irish flavor, was well-entrenched in the city; some two-thirds of St. Paulites were Catholic. Yet despite Irish dominance, the French were still considered the aristocratic Catholics, even unto Fitzgerald's day. To Protestants in town, Catholics, however acceptable on some levels, were still sometimes suspect, as seen in Fitzgerald's remark that his friends, most of whom were Protestant, thought Catholics conducted drills to prepare for an insurrection.[12]

To add to the complexity, by Fitzgerald's time, St. Paul's heyday as a trading center had passed; the city had been eclipsed in Minnesota by the young mill town of Minneapolis. In the teens, in other U.S. cities the well-to-do were vacating city centers, but not in St. Paul, where the elite stayed put, perhaps because in many cases some of the oldest families among them had become the kind of "old-money" families that actually do not have very much money any more. The general decline was exacerbated by a real-estate depression in 1893. Fitzgerald's St. Paul friend Alexandra Kalman, granddaughter of Aaron Goodrich, a Minnesota Territory Supreme Court justice, was one victim of the depression: Rather than owning a home, her family lived in a row house just down the row from the Fitzgeralds.[13]

This decline produced some degree of diversity within the Summit neighborhood. Also, the city was not very large in terms of population (200,000) or geography, and only a few residents had truly large fortunes. Thus, to form a critical mass for social and civic purposes, the elite group encompassed both the rich and those with somewhat more modest finances (Wingerd 70). For example, Ramaley Dancing School in the Summit neighborhood had (within limits) a diverse clientele, as Andrew Turnbull indicates: "The wealthiest children came to Ramaley's in black limousines with monograms and coats-of-arms on the doors and liveried chauffeurs in attendance. Those less wealthy drove with their mothers in the family electric, and those not wealthy at all rode the streetcar or trudged through the snow, swinging their patent leather shoes in a slipper bag."[14]

The Summit neighborhood also contained various types of housing, indicating some range of income among residents: grand homes toward one end of Summit Avenue, more modest single-family homes toward the other end, some row houses for rental, and four apartment buildings. The streets four blocks on either side of Summit Avenue were usually considered part of the neighborhood but were a bit less fashionable, full of more decidedly middle-class dwellings, including single-family homes, row houses, and apartment buildings. Fitzgerald's family rented, always on these side streets or on the less fashionable end of Summit. But others, such as the Kalmans, also rented. Fitzgerald's family moved frequently, but so did some others in the neighborhood. For example, the family of Cecil Read, Fitzgerald's boyhood friend, had owned a home on Portland Avenue in the Summit neighborhood but gave it up two years after Read's father's death in 1909. Clifton Read, Cecil's brother, says that, "'We were gypsies ... uprooted by father's death.'"[15] Another uprooted person was Fitzgerald's Grandmother McQuillan, who, after her husband's 1877 death, moved a number of times, mostly to rentals. Perhaps the moving around stemmed from financial worry about living on a fixed income as well as psychological trauma in the face of the absence of the patriarch. Perhaps the Fitzgeralds moved for similar reasons.

Undeniably, home ownership was a status symbol. It was difficult in those times to own a home as there was no such thing as a 30-year mortgage loan; such long-term loans were illegal for banks to offer. Thus, home ownership was truly special, only for those with enough money to purchase outright. And for the Irish in St. Paul, as elsewhere, home ownership was a particularly important status symbol because Irish immigrants typically remembered keenly having been cast out of their ancestral lands and also saw home ownership as a means of their acceptance in America. Gatsby's house as a ticket to acceptance can thus be seen as a lace-curtain-Irish phenomenon.[16] Indeed, Irish-Americans had one of the highest rates of home ownership of all ethnic groups in the United States in the late nineteenth and early twentieth centuries.[17]

Conversely, renting emerged as negative – even though it was a common practice from the lowliest neighborhoods to Summit. In 1913, Thomas Frankson launched an ad campaign to sell house lots in his new Como Park development in St. Paul by using the motto "A Rented House Is Not a Home."[18] Carol Arnovici, in a 1917 study of housing conditions in St. Paul, warned against renters, speaking of "tenements, apartments or apartment hotel buildings" as "attempting to invade" residential areas where they are "out of keeping with the character of the neighborhoods."[19] To be sure, Arnovici's report emphasized poor parts of town with tenements exhibiting horrible conditions, dwellings lacking sewer service and electricity, and a dozen apartment dwellers sharing a single dingy toilet; these were far from the fashionable quarters of the Fitzgeralds and other Summit neighborhood renters. But the stigma attached to the tenement, one might speculate, may have extended a bit to even the better rentals.

That homeowners were accorded a privileged place in Summit Avenue society becomes clear in a zoning controversy that started with passage of a 1915 state law allowing for creation of restricted residential districts in large cities (Minneapolis, St. Paul, and Duluth). This law was part of a national trend. Under its provisions, fifty percent or more of the real estate owners in a proposed district had to petition for its establishment. Only single- and double-family housing – no commercial structures or apartment buildings – was allowed in a district. The Summit Avenue District (just Summit Avenue, not the surrounding blocks) was created shortly after the law was passed, having received strong support from almost all the boulevard's residents.

Trouble erupted when, as dictated by the law, the board of assessors decided on damages for real-estate owners in the new district. Those owning undeveloped lots on Summit Avenue had expected to be awarded damages because now they would not be able to build apartment buildings on their land, but to their surprise, the board of assessors awarded damages only to owners of lots next to the four existing apartment buildings. The board reasoned that these lots were undesirable locations for houses because they were adjacent to apartments. This is strange reasoning, since those who owned lots next to the apartments knew about the apartments' proximity when they bought the land. On the other hand, those who had bought lots expecting to be able to build apartments on them could not have known that the zoning ordinance would some day prohibit such use. Five uncompensated parties sued, and after several years and a court case that reached the Minnesota Supreme Court, a settlement was reached (Sandeen 30–33). This episode does show residents' displeasure with apartments on Summit Avenue and high regard for the rights of homeowners (even just potential ones), but it does not address row houses. They were apparently not regarded as a particular problem, which suggests that the issue was density, not renting in itself.

Summit neighborhood dwellers accorded a measure of acceptance to St. Paulites from other neighborhoods and of other social classes. Summit Avenue was treated like a public park of sorts by people of all classes from various corners of St. Paul; for instance, people of all classes took strolls down the boulevard. Also, the various classes frequented such concerns as the soda fountain at Frost's Drugstore, near Summit Avenue (Wingerd 72). The society page in the local newspaper did emphasize Summit neighborhood events but also listed the doings of residents of various other neighborhoods. Nonetheless, Summit Avenue emerges from the zoning controversy seeming to feel itself a bit special, the mingling at Frost's Drugstore and neighborhood strolls by the lower classes notwithstanding. In keeping with the neighborhood's special status, Fitzgerald's Basil stories, autobiographical tales of his childhood written in the late 1920s, make the city seem small, like a village, precisely because the St. Paul of the stories is most often just the Summit neighborhood.[20] The larger St. Paul and larger world are not frequently pictured, and when they are, they are often pictured as foreign, threatening, or at least unpleasant. Threats from the outside play a part in "The Scandal Detectives," when Basil, Bill, and Ripley dress up like a southerner, a Balkan, and a rabbi and are seen as "toughs" menacing the neighborhood, and when the children who play together in a neighbor's yard fight the "micks" who live below the bluff "in sordid poverty." In this case, the neighborhood becomes a refuge as the Summit children can run "into the convenient houses" if the lower-town children get the upper hand (*B&J* 20). In subsequent stories, a slightly older Basil at times seeks out the larger city. In "A Night at the Fair," at the Minnesota State Fair, located away from Summit in larger St. Paul, Basil unhappily but courteously rides the Ferris wheel with a lower-class local girl whom he feels is his inferior. And in "He Thinks He's Wonderful," Basil and Joe, whom Basil is trying to advise about life, look out from the Summit neighborhood upon the "scattered lights of the lower city," making Basil feel "the purport of his words grow thin and pale" as he sees "the mystery of unknown life coursing through the streets below" (*B&J* 85). Still, in these instances, there is clear separation between Basil's special, circumscribed world and the larger town.[21]

Having spent years of his upbringing in St. Paul, it is little wonder that Fitzgerald would come to see himself both within and without an exclusive social enclave. He exhibits this trait in even his first published stories, which appeared in *The St. Paul Academy Now and Then.* "The Mystery of the Raymond Mortgage," "Reade, Substitute Right Half," "A Debt of Honor," and "The Room with the Green Blinds" all feature in embryonic form a sense of duality. In each of these stories is an *homme manqué* ("man with something missing"). Sometimes his doppelganger (presumably with the missing element) appears. In such cases, there is doubleness.

For instance, the first story, "The Mystery of the Raymond Mortgage," opens with the narrator coming upon a second man, who is staring out a window at the lights of New York. The scene is a precursor to the scene in *The Great Gatsby* in which Nick first encounters Gatsby looking out at the stars and the green light. In both cases, one character watches a second character watching lights, and the scenes reflect the sense of a single character split in two: One breathes in the actual moment, while the other stands outside of it, forever watching.

It is tempting to imagine an F. Scott Fitzgerald who grew up in a very different place, perhaps a place where someone like him was shunned by the elite, rather than at least somewhat a part of that group as he was in St. Paul. What if he had never been allowed close enough to the elite to know them? What if, conversely, he had been a fully accepted, unassailable member of the elite somewhere? (What, in other words, if he had been "the rich boy"?) No, St. Paul, in putting him in-between, in allowing him the chance to be (in Malcolm Cowley's formulation) the boy with his nose pressed up against the window, helped make him the author he was.[22]

NOTES

1 J. G. Rice, "The Old-Stock Americans" in J. D. Holmquist (ed.), *They Chose Minnesota: A Survey of the State's Ethnic Groups* (St. Paul, MN: Minnesota Historical Society Press, 1981), 62–68.

2 St. Paul Academy advertisement, *St. Paul Pioneer Press* (September 3, 1914), 5.

3 "1910–1911 St. Paul Academy School Catalog." St. Paul Academy and Summit School Archives. The school succeeded in its goal: Many attendees and graduates went on to Eastern schools. It also produced its share of illustrious graduates. An example from Fitzgerald's era is his friend Norris Jackson ('13), who graduated from Princeton and became a pioneer in the field of labor relations. In 1987, Jackson was named a Distinguished Alumnus of the St. Paul Academy and Summit School (the name the school acquired in 1969 when it merged with the Summit School, a girls' school). While no prominent creative writer besides Fitzgerald is known to have gotten his start in the *Now and Then*, much more recently, SPA graduate Steven Levitt ('84) made the best-seller list with *Freakonomics* (2005). I am grateful to Harry Drake, archivist, and Nicholas Bancks, head librarian, of the St. Paul Academy and Summit School for their assistance with the research for this chapter.

4 F. S. Fitzgerald, "Minnesota's Capital in the Rôle of Main Street," review of *Being Respectable* by Grace Flandrau, *Literary Digest International Book Review* 1 (March 1923). Reprinted in M. J. Bruccoli and J. R. Bryer (eds.), *F. Scott Fitzgerald in His Own Time: A Miscellany* (Ohio: Kent State University Press, 1971), 142.

5 K. A. Miller, "Assimilation and Alienation: Irish Emigrants' Reponses to Industrial America, 1871–1921" in P. J. Drudy (ed.), *The Irish in America:*

Emigration, Assimilation and Impact (Cambridge, UK: Cambridge University Press, 1985), 90.

6 M. L. Wingerd, *Claiming the City: Politics, Faith, and the Power of Place in St. Paul* (Ithaca, NY: Cornell University Press, 2001), 39. Subsequent references to this work are included in the text.

7 E. R. Sandeen, *St. Paul's Historic Summit Avenue* (St. Paul: Living Historical Museum-Macalester College, 1978), 21. Subsequent references to this work are included in the text.

8 G. Flandrau, "St. Paul: The Untamable Twin" in D. Aikman (ed.), *The Taming of the Frontier* (New York: Minton, Balch, 1925), 151.

9 T. J. Rowland, "Irish-American Catholics and the Quest for Respectability in the Coming of the Great War, 1900–1917," *Journal of American Ethnic History* 15:2 (Winter 1996), 3–31.

10 A. Regan, "The Irish" in *They Chose Minnesota,* 142.

11 S. P. Rubinstein, "The French Canadians and French" in *They Chose Minnesota,* 39.

12 M. J. Bruccoli, *Some Sort of Epic Grandeur: The Life of f. Scott Fitzgerald*, 2nd rev. ed. (Columbia, SC: University of South Carolina Press, 2002), 22.

13 E. Larsen, "The Geography of Fitzgerald's St. Paul," *Carleton Miscellany* 13 (Spring–Summer 1973), 15–16.

14 A. Turnbull, *Scott Fitzgerald* (New York: Charles Scribner's Sons, 1962), 23. The significance of this passage is discussed in Wingerd, 70.

15 Quoted in J. Koblas, *A Guide to F. Scott Fitzgerald's St. Paul: A Traveler's Companion to His House & Haunts* (St. Paul: Minnesota Historical Society Press, 2004), 34.

16 See R. Ebest, *Private Histories: The Writing of Irish Americans, 1900–1935* (Notre Dame, IN: University of Notre Dame Press, 2005), 64; and Charles Fanning, *The Irish Voice in America: 250 Years of Irish-American Fiction,* 2nd ed. (Lexington, KY: University Press of Kentucky, 2000), 135.

17 K. A. Miller, D. N. Doyle, and P. Kelleher, "'For Love and Liberty': Irish Women, Migration and Domesticity in Ireland and America, 1815–1920" in P. O'Sullivan (ed.), *Irish Women and Irish Migration* (London: Leicester University Press, 1995), 53.

18 R. Bergerson, "'A Rented House Is Not a Home': Thomas Frankson: Real Estate Promoter and Unorthodox Politician," *Ramsey County History* 45.2 (Summer 2010), 14–15.

19 C. Aronovici, *Housing Conditions in the City of Saint Paul: Report Presented to the Housing Commission of the St. Paul Association* (St. Paul: Amherst Wilder Charity, 1917), 11.

20 See P. Kane, "F. Scott Fitzgerald's St. Paul: A Writer's Use of Materials," *Minnesota History* 45.4 (Winter 1976), 141–48.

21 See also A. Hook, *F. Scott Fitzgerald: A Literary Life* (Hampshire, UK: Palgrave Macmillan, 2002), 9–10.

22 M. Cowley, "Third Act and Epilogue," *New Yorker* (June 30, 1945) reprinted in A. Mizener (ed.), *F. Scott Fitzgerald: A Collection of Critical Essays* (Englewood Cliffs, NJ: Prentice-Hall, 1963), 64–69; 66.

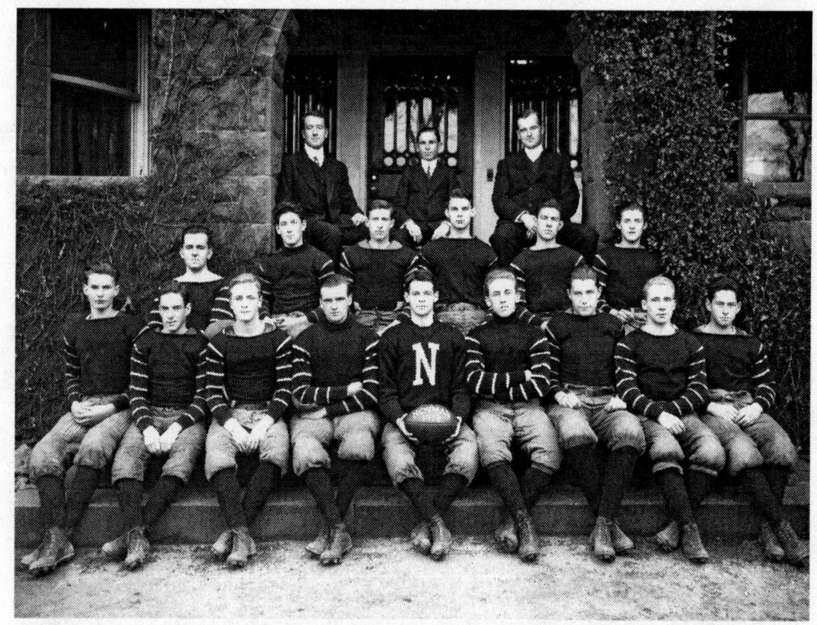

Figure 11.1. F. Scott Fitzgerald (first row, third from left) with Newman School football team, ca. 1912 (Minnesota Historical Society).

11

A Catholic Boyhood: The Newman School, the Newman News, *and Monsignor Cyril Sigourney Webster Fay*

Pearl James

F. Scott Fitzgerald attended the Newman School for Boys in Hackensack, New Jersey, for two academic years between 1911 and 1913, from age 15 to 17. During his time there, he wrote stories and poems for the school newspaper, played football (Figure 11.1.), served as an altar boy and briefly considered the priesthood, and was allowed to go to New York and travel to and from family visits by himself. Living away from his parents, he gained substantial independence. He made ties to a long-lasting friend (Charles W. "Sap" Donahoe) and an important role model, Monsignor Sigourney Webster Fay (the inspiration for Monsignor Darcy in his first novel, *This Side of Paradise*). His studies at Newman prepared him for Princeton University, where he matriculated with Donahoe in 1913. Despite those facts, Fitzgerald remembered his time at Newman as unhappy. He had been popular at his nonsectarian preparatory day school in St. Paul, St. Paul Academy, and sheltered within his family circle. Starting over by himself in a new environment was lonely, and Fitzgerald's boastful, feigned confidence irritated the other boys who, at least initially, teased and shunned him.[1] By most accounts, Fitzgerald's family sent him east in hopes that he would have to focus more on his studies and less on his writing. In that, they failed: During his time at Newman, he remained an inconsistent student, while his ambition to be a writer deepened.

The Newman School was founded in 1900 and closed in 1941. Its records seem to have been lost, and scholars interested in this period of Fitzgerald's life have principally drawn from his own scrapbooks, letters, autobiographical writings, and fictional depictions of "St. Regis" (modeled on Newman) in his novel *This Side of Paradise* and the Basil stories. Fitzgerald preserved the three stories, two articles, and one poem he wrote for the *Newman News*, all of which can be found alongside his other early writing in *Spires and Gargoyles: Early Writings, 1909–1919*.

Despite our lack of its internal records, we can learn much about Newman's mission, ethos, curriculum, and student body by situating it within its historical moment. American education went through a revolution of sorts in the late nineteenth century. Before the Civil War, one historian explains, American universities were "at best little more than good academies with a professional school or so attached."[2] As the industrial revolution expanded, so did the economy, and so did American ambitions. Leaders and educators perceived a need to modernize institutions of higher learning and equip them to prepare students in science and other professional fields. The small liberal arts college no longer seemed to offer adequate preparation. Colleges added professional schools, new facilities were built, and faculties grew. Fifty years later, several American universities "rivaled and sometimes even surpassed" the German universities upon which they had been modeled (McLachlan 189). As universities expanded, so did their budgets, and they needed more qualified and paying students. Many educators called for better secondary education, and particularly for more boarding schools. Many universities even went so far as to help endow "feeder" schools to provide them with adequate numbers of students. Ultimately, many expensive, all-male boarding schools were founded between 1880 and 1910. They offered traditional liberal arts subjects such as Latin, Greek, mathematics, and history, in addition to English and usually at least one or more of the modern sciences (physics, chemistry, and biology) (McLachlan 281–82).[3]

More important perhaps than their new curricula was the ethos of these schools. Like other institutions of its kind, the Newman School tried to instill that all-important, if nebulous, quality: "character." When Cardinal Gibbons (one of the highest-ranking Americans in the Catholic Church at the time) addressed the student body in 1914, he told them, "We want young men of character, for character differentiates the man. Show me a man with character and I'll tell you his destiny. He is bound to succeed."[4] This was an era when increased urbanization, industrialization, and immigration seemed to be putting American masculinity at risk. Elite boarding schools were founded in part to reduce such risks for those who could afford to attend. They were mostly located in suburban or rural areas with room for athletic fields. They appealed to wealthy families on the grounds that, in order to succeed, boys needed to be cloistered with others from a similar background, raised in an austere environment, supervised by men, disciplined, and spurred to physical competition. Such schools "played a critical role in socializing and unifying the national upper class."[5] Manly character and the ability to lead were more important than academic achievement or intellectual development. What made both universities (such as "the Big Three" – Harvard, Yale, and Princeton) and their feeder preparatory schools "elite" at the turn of the twentieth century was pedigree and social prominence, not intelligence. Still, the curriculum was important insofar as it "prepped" students to attend select colleges and universities. Preparatory schools, unlike most public high schools, taught subjects (such as Latin) required by the Ivies on entrance exams. Having the money and social standing to attend private schools, then, led directly to qualifying for elite universities. The student bodies of Harvard, Yale, and Princeton were "composed largely of graduates of elite private schools" and represented "the most privileged strata of society"; they were wealthy and almost exclusively white (Karabel 23). Given the continuity between them, it may not be surprising that at university, one's prep school, along with social and athletic prowess, often determined success.

The Newman School differed from more famous elite preparatory schools in one crucial respect: It was Catholic. Some elite Eastern boarding schools were nondenominational but culturally Protestant. Some had a particular Protestant affiliation, such as Presbyterian or Episcopalian. The Newman School for Boys offered Catholic families a comparable curriculum and socially exclusive environment. Just as Cardinal Newman's Oratory School in England styled itself as "the Catholic Eton," the Newman School Fitzgerald attended aimed to be a Catholic Groton or Choate. Certainly, Catholic families already had the option of sending their children away to school. However, during the nineteenth century, many of the best Catholic schools (boarding or day) were run by the Jesuits and had a different mission.

The Jesuits (Society of Jesus) used a European model for their curriculum. Jesuit schools typically offered a seven-year program of study, which did not dovetail perfectly with the evolving distinction between high school and college in the United States.[6] This, perhaps combined with anti-Catholic prejudice, led some to assert that the Jesuit colleges were inferior to their Protestant and nondenominational counterparts. Famously, the Harvard Law School decided in the 1890s to "restrict regular admission … to those men who held diplomas from a select list of colleges," none of which were Catholic. When challenged, Harvard President Charles Eliot defended the action by disputing the equivalency between diplomas from Jesuit schools and those that had more "modern" curricula.[7] This point was bitterly and publicly debated in the decade before Newman was founded. Many countered that Jesuit schools held their students to a *higher* academic standard than nondenominational or Protestant schools. Certainly, at Jesuit schools, academics and religion were privileged over athletics and social standing. "The Jesuits who taught in the United States in the nineteenth century embraced the ideals of Christian humanism. They continued to advance the concept of education as an intellectual and moral enterprise, one preparing students to contribute to the good of society and bettering their chances for success in the next life" (Mahoney 69). Thus, the culture of their schools differed from that of the preps, which emphasized success in *this* life. Jesuit schools encouraged their students to follow the vocation of the priesthood and emphasized the need for separate Catholic education (Mahoney 67). This distinction, ironically, made them less appealing to a wide section of upwardly mobile Catholics, particularly second- and third-generation children of immigrants, who wanted to assimilate more fully into upper-class American life.

This context helps explain what made the Newman School's mission and ethos distinct. Scholar Joan Allen provides certain details: that Newman was founded at the turn of the century by Jesse Albert Locke, an educator who had himself converted from the Episcopal Church to Catholicism in 1893. Locke and his wife were socially prominent and active in the Church. As their example suggests, teachers at Newman were often lay people and were allowed to marry. The Lockes advocated strong involvement among the laity in Catholic education, charity, and diocesan matters. Under Locke's superintendence, Newman provided a clear alternative to the more clerical atmosphere of Jesuit-run Catholic schools. Students were only obliged to attend mass once a week.[8] Its social life resembled that of many prep schools. For instance, as Fitzgerald reported in the *Newman News*, the school held dances. At such times, he declared, "Pandemonium reign[ed]"; "[t]he corridors and common-room [were] immediately filled with semi-graceful figures swaying rythmically" [*sic*] to modern dance-music (*S&G* 44). It was Catholic, but less ascetic, than its Jesuit equivalents. It was also expensive and allowed wealthy families to avoid the socioeconomic diversity of the parish school.

The decision to send Scott to Newman suggests how his family sought to situate themselves within the changing culture of American Catholicism. They did not choose a Jesuit school, nor would they eventually agree to send him to Jesuit Georgetown for college, as his Aunt Annabel apparently wished (Bruccoli, *Epic Grandeur* 37). Newman must have seemed both more modern and more socially elite. The school put Scott in the midst of boys whose families were "interested in having their sons educated as gentlemen," and who were "willing to pay a premium for better food, more comfortable living arrangements, and a less spartan disciplinary regime." In search of such establishments, wealthy Catholics had been advocating for "greater price differentiation among Catholic schools" (Gleason 26). The Newman School and others like it obliged; annual tuition was over $800 a year when Fitzgerald entered in 1911. But although Newman's mission to serve the needs of well-to-do Catholics suited the Fitzgeralds, they actually could not have afforded it without help from his mother's side of the family. Fitzgerald may have felt himself to be, as his narrator Nick Carraway would later put it, "both within and without" the school's economic privilege.

One of the deepest affinities between Newman and the Protestant elite preparatory schools it emulated was their shared emphasis on athletics. They competed against private and public schools from both New York and New Jersey. Before the establishment of professional football or basketball, college competitions commanded large national audiences. Indeed, American collegiate sports were already "highly commercialized and professionalized" in the late nineteenth century, and their visibility and tangible rewards explain why young men would want to enter college as skilled athletes.[9] Newman students attended games between the Ivy League teams (at that time the best in college football) and idolized their players. Fitzgerald recorded in his scrapbook that seeing the football player Sam White lead Princeton to victory over Harvard "decided" him to attend Princeton; the glamour of a star athlete was deeply appealing (Bruccoli, *Epic Grandeur* 31).[10] Even high school contests were widely followed. Results of Newman games were often reported in the *New York Times*, and the team's best players were the school celebrities. Sports, particularly football, provided an important proving ground for boys to learn and assert their manliness. Advocates, such as Walter Camp, the "Father of American Football" and a prolific writer, argued that the sport inculcated values of honesty, honor, and fair play. Sports made boys into men. In an age of social Darwinism, the football field made the contest for mastery and dominance tangible. Theodore Roosevelt defended the game and its brutality on the grounds that it played a crucial part in college life: "We cannot afford to turn out of college men who shrink from physical effort or from a little physical pain" (qtd. in Karabel 43).[11]

Football was in fact a brutal game, a much rougher game then than today. Not all agreed with Roosevelt about its value. Some critics questioned Walter Camp's "moral sensibility" and saw his power as part of the reason for football's "degradation" (qtd. in Bruccoli, Smith, and Kerr 8).[12]

Particularly dangerous were "mass" and formation plays in which players ran and tackled as a group. Players did not wear helmets or much protective padding. Every year, players died or were permanently injured. Football's brutality had led some colleges to ban it in the decade before Fitzgerald attended Newman. In the academic year 1904–05 and again in 1909–10, the number of football injuries and fatalities triggered a national dialogue. Those universities that did not ban the sport altogether adopted new rules and used more referees.

This, then, is the game that Fitzgerald played and wrote about while at Newman. It explains why the stakes – both what could be gained and lost – were so high. If he became a good player, he might earn a popularity that would endure beyond Newman and into college; if unlucky, he might be severely injured. His fate in football determined, at least to an extent, his school experience. It was a commonly held measurement of manliness. We can trace the highs and lows of Fitzgerald's time at Newman in relation to football. Certainly the nadir of his time there occurred after he ran away from an opposing player who tried to tackle him. The coach, and everyone else, thought he was a coward. But as Matthew Bruccoli describes it in his biography, Fitzgerald redeemed himself by writing a poem, his first known publication in the *Newman News*, "Football," in which an unnamed protagonist wins the game for the school. Fitzgerald recalled afterward that this experience taught him that writing could be "a back door way out of facing reality" (Bruccoli, *Epic Grandeur* 30–31; *MLC* 170). Like the football star who "straight-arm[s]" his way through the opposition "as calmly as you please" in his poem, Fitzgerald longed to prove his masculine qualities and win admiration, to be "fiercest," "fastest," "classy," and famous (*S&G* 25–26). He did get a second chance at football his senior year at Newman, and he acquitted himself well. That experience found its way into fiction in his *Newman News* story "Reade, Substitute Right Half."

Fitzgerald's other publications in the *Newman News* provide a window onto the ethos of his school. His account of "Election Night" evokes the chaos and excitement of celebrating with his schoolmates: "In the glare of a huge bonfire, merrily blazing in the crisp November night, danced sixty-five boys arrayed in sweaters, jerseys and all manner of old clothes. Some sang, some yelled, some talked, but all managed to show by some form of vocal expression that there were sixty-five of them, and that they were working off two months of pent-up energy" (*S&G* 27). Carnivalesque rituals punctuate life at many boarding schools and small colleges. Fitzgerald hints at the stifling and grinding routine of school by portraying its opposite – that fleeting exhilaration of freedom and unity the boys felt when the rules were briefly suspended.

His other contributions to the *Newman News* belong to genres of the short story and herald his future as a successful magazine writer. "The Mystery of the Raymond Mortgage" is a detective story of marital intrigue among the rich, set in the suburbs of New York. "A Debt of Honor" is a Civil War story whose plot traces the same narrative arc found in Crane's *Red Badge of Courage*: It is a masculine coming-of-age story in which a young man initially fails as a soldier and later redeems himself. "The Room with the Green Blinds" is a mystery story that brings a young man south to claim an inherited house, only to discover that it has been the hiding place of Lincoln's assassin, John Wilkes Booth. When published side by side, his writings from this time period reveal his repeated attempts to identify, portray, and master the means to success for young men. The narrator of "The Room with the Green Blinds," for instance, is "a poor young man with no outlook in life, and no money, but a paltry eight-hundred a year" who must make his way in a world still peopled by heroes and ghosts from the more glorious past (*S&G* 18). His protagonists make mistakes then struggle to make good and earn admiration. Battle and sport provide the clearest terms of success, which otherwise seems elusive.

One of the most important relationships Fitzgerald formed while at Newman was with one of the members of its board of trustees, Monsignor Cyril Sigourney Webster Fay (1875–1919). Cyril Fay lived in Baltimore, where he acted as an advisor to Cardinal Gibbons. Fay was from Philadelphia, however, where his family was both wealthy and socially prominent. Despite quite different backgrounds, in fact, both Fitzgerald's maternal family and Fay's drew their wealth from wholesale grocery and the sale of dry grains. Fay's family, however, had a longer and more prestigious history in the United States and was Episcopalian. He himself (like Jesse Albert Locke) had converted to Catholicism in 1908. As a trustee of the Newman School, he visited regularly. Indeed, a few years after Fitzgerald graduated, he replaced Locke as its headmaster.

Fay took a liking to Fitzgerald and invited him to visit him in Baltimore when Fitzgerald went south to visit his cousin. Fitzgerald must have reveled in the attention and in being selected from among other Newman students for Fay's patronage. Fay was unusual in many ways. He was a priest but did not have the pressures of leading and superintending a parish. He was wealthy and did not take a vow of poverty; once ordained a Catholic priest (later Monsignor), he continued to live a lavish lifestyle, to travel, and to pursue an active social life. His skin and hair were so pale that he appeared to be an albino. According to Mrs. Winthrop Chanler, a society woman and close friend of Fay's, he was "tall and exceedingly fat," but "very light on his feet," moving across the floor like a "toy balloon that has come down, but barely touches the earth." He giggled and played with her children. He loved to put on plays, charades, and pageants and to improvise versions of Catholic rituals. He showed off his various vestments, looking to Mrs. Chanler "like nothing so much as an enormous peony."[13] He was apparently a brilliant conversationalist, and he counted among his friends Henry Adams, the writer Shane Leslie, and others. He introduced Fitzgerald to these illustrious connections. As a result, Fitzgerald kept up a correspondence with Leslie, which proved helpful later when he was trying to publish his first novel.

Fay must have impressed Fitzgerald on many levels. He had wealth and the social assurance that came with it. He was Irish on his mother's side, like Fitzgerald, but made that heritage seem like a romantic badge of honor rather than a social demerit. Chanler recalls that Fay "was a master story-teller with a delicious sense of humor and a most convincing Irish brogue"; he spoke in "the attractive speech of the cultivated Irish" but could also "easily sli[p] into the speech of Paddy and Biddy" (Chanler 81). He was, in essence, an inveterate performer, able to make light of the same qualities that may have made Fitzgerald self-conscious. Catholicism's theatricality, its ritual, its rich settings and costumes appealed deeply to Fay. It was his chosen, not his first, religion. Despite his strange appearance, he seems by all accounts to have been exceedingly comfortable in his own skin and moved with ease between various conversations and occasions. He offered Fitzgerald a model for being in the world that was unlike anything he had seen in St. Paul, certainly within his own family circle. Fay was well-read, genteel, and fun-loving. He was irreverent and talked to Fitzgerald like a peer. Fitzgerald was undoubtedly flattered.

Like Fay, Fitzgerald loved performing. After both years at Newman, he returned home to St. Paul and while there directed and starred in plays he had written, which were put on for charity benefits. Later, while a student at Princeton, Fitzgerald would impersonate women for the Princeton Triangle Club shows, and for fun. I have argued elsewhere that in *This Side of Paradise* Fitzgerald portrays such theatricality as an impediment to manhood and a sign of not just feigned femininity.[14] Cyril Fay worried, perhaps in jest, about how Fitzgerald would portray him in the novel. He wrote to Fitzgerald and urged circumspection, telling him to keep in mind that their correspondence might later be read by others. "There are intimacies that cannot be put on paper," he writes.[15] As his own consternation in this and other letters reveals, intimate relationships between men were subject (then as now) to imputations of impropriety. In his letters, Fay characterizes Fitzgerald as one of his "children," and in *This Side of Paradise*, Monsignor Darcy is a "spiritual father" for the novel's young protagonist.[16] And yet their relationship seems different from a filial one. It was a loving relationship, full of teasing and mutual admiration, one that was chosen rather than inherited. When Fay died during the influenza pandemic of 1919, Fitzgerald's sense of loss was profound. When his novel came out the following year, he dedicated it to Fay.

Another inspiration for the summer theatricals back in St. Paul may well have been the plays Fitzgerald saw in New York while a student at Newman. Although he was sometimes confined to school grounds because of his grades, he made frequent trips to New York City (just forty minutes away). He would later put his knowledge of the musical genre to work when he authored shows for the Princeton Triangle Club.

While at Newman, Fitzgerald set his sights on attending college at Princeton. He famously admired its genteel atmosphere and compared it to a country club. His grades at Newman were uneven, and his performance on Princeton's entrance exam was below the university's admission standards. After taking it, Fitzgerald had to return to Princeton for an interview. He was admitted with "conditions" to satisfy before he could be advanced to sophomore standing. This, however, was not at all unusual. Many preparatory schools put athletics, social standing, and "character" before academics, and many of their graduates performed poorly on entrance exams. Princeton itself had a reputation for low academic expectations. In the decade before Fitzgerald attended it, Woodrow Wilson had fought to raise its standards of achievement, but the change did not happen overnight. In 1906, for instance, "only 42 percent of students were admitted without conditions" (Karabel 62). In other words, more than half of the students did not meet the stated entrance requirements and had to appeal for admission in an interview. For all his lackluster scholarship at Newman, Fitzgerald was in good company at Princeton.

The Princeton Fitzgerald entered was close to being a "WASP" (White Anglo-Saxon Protestant) "preserve; in 1910, Catholics and Jews composed just 6 percent of freshmen, and nearly two-thirds of the new entrants belonged to just two Protestant denominations: the Episcopal and Presbyterian churches" (Karabel 71). Fitzgerald left the homogeneity of his Catholic school to become part of a religious minority. In other ways, however, Fitzgerald matched the profile of the typical Princeton student. Eighty percent of the student body came from private schools. All of its students were white. Only about one in eight received any financial aid (Karabel 71). In these ways, living among the Newman student body was an excellent "prep" for Princeton. Also, in this period, a majority of Catholics were choosing not to attend Catholic schools; they were integrating themselves *en masse* into Protestant, nondenominational and public universities. Catholicism seems not to have posed much of a social impediment to Fitzgerald in college. He was admitted to the Cottage Club – one of Princeton's most prestigious eating houses. Religion probably contributed less to his sense of social limitations than did his keen awareness of his family's finances. On the other hand, despite the fact that Fitzgerald remained a practicing Catholic during college and published Catholic-themed stories in the *Nassau Literary Magazine*, it has been suggested that he increasingly became "a closet Catholic," who "successfully hid" his background from those who found it "not socially acceptable" (Allen xii–xiii).[17] Whether or not this suggestion is true, the Newman School, with its lack of emphasis on Catholic tradition, certainly prepared Fitzgerald for the larger, non-Catholic world of Princeton.

NOTES

1 See M. J. Bruccoli, *Some Sort of Epic Grandeur: The Life of F. Scott Fitzgerald*, 2nd rev. ed. (Columbia, SC: University of South Carolina Press, 2004, 30–37. Subsequent references to this work are included in the text.

2 J. McLachlan, *American Boarding Schools: A Historical Study* (New York: Charles Scribner's Sons, 1970), 189. Subsequent references to this work are included in the text.

3 McLachlan provides the example of Groton's curriculum, which offered Latin, Greek, mathematics, history, English, modern languages, and physics.

4 *New York Times*, May 5, 1914, 10.

5 J. Karabel, *The Chosen: The Hidden History of Admission and Exclusion at Harvard, Yale, and Princeton* (Boston: Houghton Mifflin, 2005), 25. Subsequent references to this work are included in the text.

6 See P. Gleason, *Contending with Modernity: Catholic Higher Education in the Twentieth Century* (New York: Oxford University Press, 1995). Subsequent references to this work are included in the text.

7 K. A. Mahoney, *Catholic Higher Education in Protestant America: The Jesuits and Harvard in the Age of the University* (Baltimore: Johns Hopkins University Press, 2003), 32–35. Subsequent references to this work are included in the text.

8 J. M. Allen, *Candles and Carnival Lights: The Catholic Sensibility of F. Scott Fitzgerald* (New York: New York University Press, 1978), 26–27, 32.

9 R. A. Smith, "Harvard and Columbia and a Reconsideration of the 1905–06 Football Crisis," *Journal of Sport History* 8.3 (Winter 1981), 5.

10 M. J. Bruccoli, S. F. Smith, and J. P. Kerr, eds., *The Romantic Egoists: A Pictorial Autobiography from the Scrapbooks and Albums of F. Scott and Zelda Fitzgerald* (New York: Charles Scribner's Sons, 1974), 16. Subsequent references to this work are included in the text.

11 This is from a speech given at Harvard in February 1907.

12 This appears in a November 3, 1905, letter from F. S. Bangs, chairman of the University Committee on Athletics, to Columbia President N. M. Butler.

13 Mrs. W. Chanler, *Autumn in the Valley* (Boston: Little, Brown, and Company, 1936), 81–84. Subsequent references to this work are included in the text.

14 See P. James, "History and Masculinity in F. Scott Fitzgerald's *This Side of Paradise*," *Modern Fiction Studies* 51.1 (2005), 1–33.

15 This is in an August 17, 1918, letter from C. Fay to F. S. Fitzgerald. In the F. Scott Fitzgerald Papers, Manuscripts Division, Department of Rare Books and Special Collections, Princeton University Library (PUL). Correspondence, Box 40A, folder 8.

16 In an undated letter from C. Fay to F. S. Fitzgerald on Newman School letterhead, C. Fay praised another boy and then included Fitzgerald by saying, "What a thing it is to have charming children!" PUL, Correspondence, Box 40A, folder 8.

17 In *Carnival Lights*, Allen identifies Fitzgerald's identity as a "closet Catholic" as the reason that so few literary studies of his work take his religious background, beliefs, and culture into account.

12

Princeton, New Jersey, Princeton University, and the Nassau Literary Magazine

Edward Gillin

Like all Ivy League institutions in the opening decades of the twentieth century, Princeton University was a bastion of wealth and privilege. Since its annual costs represented one-third of the family income, Edward and Mollie Fitzgerald had to count their pennies to send their son there. Presbyterian from its founding in 1746, the Princeton of 1913 paid implicit tribute to the nation's Protestant ascendancy by demanding daily chapel attendance; Edmund Wilson acknowledged that F. Scott Fitzgerald was the only Catholic he knew among his fellow undergraduates (Bruccoli 48, 56).[1] Fitzgerald brought with him a mediocre scholastic record and had to charm an interview committee into admitting him despite "deficiencies" in Latin, French, algebra, and physics, deficiencies that would have to be made up by passing special exams in December of his freshman year. Yet despite Fitzgerald's poor academic record and his relative lack of financial resources – and in spite of the fact that he was a Catholic in a predominantly Protestant university – Fitzgerald considered his years at Princeton among the most important of his life. As he wrote just days before his death, his good fortune at having attended Princeton was the "thing for which I am most grateful to my mother and father" (*L* 133).

Fitzgerald pointed at various times in his life to tenuous reasons for his choice of Princeton, and his accounts varied. In his scrapbook he kept a ticket stub from a 1911 Princeton–Harvard football game in which Princeton's star player had a 95-yard touchdown scamper in an 8–6 victory; Fitzgerald wrote this on the stub: "Sam White decides me for Princeton" (Bruccoli 31). Fitzgerald more frequently testified that Princeton's musical theater club, the Triangle, had played a critical role in securing his allegiance. (During high school he had been fascinated to come across the printed libretto for one of its touring shows.) In addition, a spare ledger entry from March 1913 suggests the less exotic role possibly played by a cousin's "remarks about Princeton" (*FSFL* 167). We may never know which factors were most important in painting Princeton with its "atmosphere of bright colors," as Amory Blaine phrases the fascination in *This Side of Paradise* (*TSOP* 41). Like that of his fictional alter ego, Fitzgerald's college selection seemed based on poetry rather than reason. "There was a gloss upon Yale that Princeton lacked," he would concede. Princeton "never presented itself with Yale's hard, neat, fascinating brightness. Only when you tried to tear part of your past out of your heart, as I once did, were you aware of its power of arousing a deep and imperishable love" (*MLC* 6). Intriguingly, he claimed to base his ultimate decision to attend the school on its very vulnerability, noting that Princeton regularly lost football championships to the teams from New Haven: "Yale always seemed to nose them out in the last quarter by superior 'stamina' as the newspapers called it. It was to me a repetition of the story of the foxes and the big animals in the child's book. I imagined the Princeton men as slender and keen and romantic, and the Yale men as brawny and brutal and powerful."[2] At not quite 5 feet, 8 inches tall and less than 140 pounds, Fitzgerald was dropped from football tryouts after just one day, but his image of the group he had so wished to join – romantic young men destined to suffer loss – is telling.

Princeton in the fall of 1913 may have rested in the flat heart of New Jersey amid "the ugliest country in the world," as Fitzgerald recalled it (*MLC* 7), yet he also remembered beauty in its leafy campus, in its stone collegiate gothic buildings, in the quiet town that sheltered it with a surrounding blanket of fine estates. Having witnessed a Revolutionary War battle on its grounds, the college had an appealing pedigree for the American elite. Its special attraction to the sons of old Maryland, Virginia, and other points below the Mason–Dixon line gave it a reputation as the "Southern" Ivy that enticed Fitzgerald because of the history and old grace he associated with the region.

Some of this genteel tradition had been shaken by the academic reforms of a recent college president, Woodrow Wilson, who had instituted a preceptorial system based on the Oxford–Cambridge model. Senior faculty would lecture in their special fields, while preceptors met with students in smaller groups. Little about these arrangements impressed Fitzgerald the undergraduate. Only a few professors won his approval, and he found the preceptors as a group uninspiring and dull. A net result was indifference about his studies. Hovering near the bottom of his class – 10 percent of which would not survive freshman year (Bruccoli 51–52) – Fitzgerald appeared utterly careless about academics, openly daydreaming during lectures or using class time to scribble verse. A declaration for the 1917 yearbook that he intended to pursue graduate studies in English at

Harvard was sheer bravado. He took the maximum allowance of absences and for two years barely limped by, under continual obligations to make up failed courses.

For all his laxity as a student, he ardently endorsed Princeton's honor system. The individual's pledge not to tolerate academic dishonesty in any form was "handed over as something humanly precious" to the freshmen within their first week: "I can think of a dozen times when a page of notes glanced at in a wash room would have made the difference between failure and success for me," Fitzgerald wrote, "but I can't recall any moral struggles in the matter" (*MLC* 11). In later years he would plead with college representatives to retain the "sacred tradition" lest something crucial disappear "out of the life and pride of every Princeton man" (*L* 383). Given these feelings, it seems unsurprising that the slender plot of Fitzgerald's autobiographical college novel, *This Side of Paradise*, climaxes when Amory Blaine sacrifices his reputation on behalf of a classmate too weak to do the right thing under morally trying circumstances. Princeton officials who condemned the novel for its portrayal of their institution as an effete "country club" failed to recognize Fitzgerald's implicit tribute to the character instilled in its faithful sons. (Similar themes continued to mark his important fiction. Jay Gatsby, Dick Diver, and Monroe Stahr possess faults in abundance as well as abundant promise. But each surrenders opportunities for selfish advancement when called to act within an internalized framework of what might be styled "schoolboy honor.")

If becoming academically acceptable at Princeton proved problematic for Fitzgerald, the college's social demands presented their own challenge. Although Fitzgerald was delighted that a fellow graduate of the Newman School, Sap Donahoe, had also chosen Princeton, the two soon found themselves greatly outnumbered by those who had attended more prestigious preparatory schools. Lacking the social cachet that wealth and connections provided so many classmates – and having to abruptly surrender the hope that football would be a means to acclaim – Fitzgerald relied on the brashness and bravado that had served him unevenly in the past. Inserting himself into the Triangle Club, perhaps the outstanding social force on campus after the football team, the eager freshman was soon writing the plot and lyrics for *Fie! Fie! Fi-Fi!* – destined to become the Triangle's 1914–15 show. In following years Fitzgerald would entertain audiences with witty lyrics in two more Triangle productions, *The Evil Eye* and *Safety First!* Even amid his successes, Fitzgerald revealed some awareness that he was involved in a show-within-a-show. The opening chorus of *Fie! Fie! Fi-Fi!*, for example, asks the spectator to contemplate a social order of "millionaires, / Nouveau riche, pedigreed, of a high or petty breed" (*S&G* 47). Thus, the first "public" words he wrote at Princeton subtly mocked the people who generally made up his classmates' families. Fitzgerald recollected that "Goulds, Rockefellers, Harrimans, Morgans, Fricks, Firestones, Perkinses, Pynes, McCormicks, Wanamakers, Cudahys and DuPonts" had made Princeton their choice, while the names "Pell, Biddle, Van Rensselaer, Stuyvesant, Schuyler and Cooke titillate second generation mammas and papas with a social row to hoe in Philadelphia or New York" (*MLC* 8). Edmund Wilson, the literary upperclassman who befriended both Fitzgerald and the campus poet John Peale Bishop, described each as a "victim" of "too much respect for money and country house social prestige."[3] Yet Wilson misled himself about the background of his St. Paul classmate, who had apparently convinced Wilson that he represented "the standards of the wealthy West."[4] However skilled his pose, Fitzgerald recognized the truth that he was in fact "a poor man in a rich man's club at Princeton" (*AE* 357). His sense of essential *difference* from his classmates afforded him a stance from which to observe and criticize, even as he desperately participated in, the intense struggle for social standing at his alma mater.

No aspect of Princeton life highlighted this struggle more keenly than the competition surrounding the university's eating clubs, which held the place typically occupied by fraternities on other campuses. Three-quarters of the sophomore class were tapped each year for membership in one of the eighteen clubs, which were housed in impressive buildings along Prospect Street. Everyone hoped to entertain offers from one of the "big four": Ivy, Tiger Inn, Cottage, or Cap and Gown. Not to be chosen by any club condemned one to the social exile of meals in the university dining halls for the remainder of one's time at Princeton. On the day bids went out for his class, Fitzgerald had to nervously ponder how much credit he'd earned through work for the Triangle and on various college publications, how much he'd squandered by his brash posture, and the eccentricities he'd cultivated to make himself stand out in the world of Princeton gentlemen. With satisfaction Fitzgerald received bids from Cap and Gown, Quadrangle, Cannon, and Cottage. In selecting the last, a larger club housed in a splendid mansion, Fitzgerald enjoyed what was one of the few unmitigated triumphs of his career at Princeton. Cottage bestowed not only prestige but the social benefit of weekend parties where, in fine weather, debutantes from New York or Philadelphia motored in to fill the lovely patio gardens. (Fitzgerald may later have reconstituted such memories into the riotous parties on Gatsby's back lawn. The upper floor of Cottage even contained an elaborate, wood-paneled reproduction of the Merton College Library, a clear model for the one where Owl Eyes admired Gatsby's splendid collection of unread books.)

Scott Fitzgerald's first published presence at Princeton was on the pages of the college's humor magazine, the *Princeton Tiger*. Many of his contributions were short and disarming comments on newspaper items. After a *New York Sun* headline that "Yale's swimming team will take its maiden plunge tonight" he editorialized, "How perfectly darling!"; lost amid the confusing negatives when the *New York Evening Post* commented that "It is assumed that the absence of submarines from the Pacific will not necessitate American naval activities in that ocean," he queried: "Will it not not?" (*S&G* 186). His longer *Tiger* pieces also tended to play with forms and language, extending his "show-within-a-show" sensibility to something akin to literary postmodernism. In "Little Minnie McCloskey," the "school drudge" at Miss Pickswinger's Select Seminary for Young Ladies begins each day at 3:00 A.M. when she "made the beds, washed the dishes, branded the cattle, cut the grass," and generally makes Cinderella look like a piker. In "Cedric the Stoker," as a ship's captain imparts some terrible news, his "voice changed." "He would change it now and then," Fitzgerald's narrator adds helpfully (*S&G* 137, 237). Such exaggerations and self-conscious literary extravagances would be a signature of later professional humor in "The Offshore Pirate" and "The Cruise of the Rolling Junk." But the young writer's feel for the absurd would also find expression in the prose surrealisms of *The Great Gatsby*, where sidewalks transform into scaling ladders and dead men ride by in automobiles.

Fitzgerald occasionally submitted elaborate humorous parodies such as "The Usual Thing" and "Jemina" to the *Nassau Literary Magazine*, but generally he made the college's undergraduate literary magazine, then under Wilson's capable control, the destination for more serious efforts such as "Shadow Laurels" and "The Ordeal." For a time Fitzgerald determined to make his mark as a poet, as testified by samples intercalated into *This Side of Paradise*. The wistful, Millay-like cynicism of the sonnet "On a Play Seen Twice" expresses his most successful note in this genre, but the *Nassau Lit* poetry generally suffers from its derivative quality. What is singularly disappointing, in light of Fitzgerald's skill for striking expression in prose, is his reliance on outmoded poetic diction in verse: "the burden of the heavy air / Is strewn upon me where my tired soul cowers" (*S&G* 170). His poems rarely display the value of the sharp and brilliant word as a primary tool, and no image emerges from them with the vividness of Gatsby's grotesque rose or Diver's prayer-rug beach.

In several *Nassau Lit* fictions ("The Debutante," "Babes in the Woods," "Sentiment – And the Use of Rouge") Fitzgerald found a sturdier voice. One hallmark became his way of avoiding conventional romantic sentiment to express how his own generation approached the modern dating scene. Fitzgerald's literary interest in the subject was doubtlessly influenced by developments in his personal life.

During Christmas vacation of his sophomore year, while he was at home in St. Paul Fitzgerald met Ginevra King. Sixteen-year-old Ginevra had the polish and romantic glamour that bespoke her privileged upbringing among suburban Chicago's social elite. Fitzgerald threw himself into the pursuit of this Lake Forest beauty with all the passion of a first intense romance. Over the next two years there would be several dates and visits, but above all countless letters exchanged between Princeton or St. Paul and Westover, Connecticut (where King attended a finishing school). Fitzgerald invested boundless stores of imagination in this one person who was becoming the first "golden girl" who promised not just love but a form of transcendent self-affirmation. Gaining her affection was somehow to conquer life, to prove worthy. Until the end of his life Fitzgerald kept every letter he received from Ginevra King, and he had them recopied and bound into a 227-page volume. For her part, Ginevra gradually tired of Scott's scrutinizing attention and jealousy. In an August 1916 ledger entry, amid details of a final disappointing visit to Ginevra's hometown, Fitzgerald summarized the romantic tragedy the experience embodied in one searing comment from that time: "Poor boys shouldn't think of marrying rich girls" (*FSFL* 170).

Whether or not the distracting disintegration of the two-year involvement was a crucial cause or merely synecdoche, as the romance with Ginevra King lurched toward disaster so did Fitzgerald's academic career. By the fall of 1915 he seemed to be failing everything. Finally, his health failed, too. Admitted to the college infirmary with malaria-like symptoms, Fitzgerald found an advantageous excuse to temporarily withdraw from Princeton and its associated trials. After rusticating in St. Paul from late 1915 through the summer of 1916, he was unprepared for the shocks of his return to college the subsequent fall. No longer officially part of the Princeton class of 1917 (although he identified himself with it for the rest of his life), Fitzgerald had to retake his junior year. Moreover, due to his accumulated academic failures he was deemed ineligible to participate in extracurricular activities or to hold club offices. Gone was the expected ascension from secretary to president of the Triangle Club; gone was a titled position on the *Nassau Lit* editorial board.

Fitzgerald never got over these losses. His ledger entry labels 1916 "A year of terrible disappointments & the end of all college dreams," adding: "Everything bad in it was my own fault" (*FSFL* 170). Twenty years later he looked through some of the wreckage of his personal life in the essay "Handle with Care" to recall the period: "To me college would never be the same. There were to be no badges of pride, no medals after all. It seemed on one March afternoon that I had lost every single thing I wanted" (*CU* 76).

Yet if Fitzgerald's "old desire for personal dominance was broken and gone," something came out of the experience. Neither buckling down to studies nor giving up in the face of the "irrecoverable 'jolts'" of 1916, Fitzgerald instead "set about learning how to write" (*CU* 76). What this meant, specifically, is that he used his personal experience of glories withdrawn to inform much of the writing to appear in the *Nassau Lit* after January 1917: "The Spire and the Gargoyle," "Tarquin of Cheepside," "Babes in the Woods," "Sentiment – And the Use of Rouge," and "The Pierian Springs and the Last Straw." Strains of failure, disgrace, or loss thematically unite most of these tales. Perhaps the clearest way to perceive the unmistakable "Fitzgerald" quality in each is to compare the set of fictions to "Basil and Cleopatra," the climactic short story of the series he would write a decade later to capture the essential autobiography of his youth. In this fiction Basil Lee enters his Ivy League college with a couple of deficiencies, including a failed trigonometry exam that prevents him from trying out for the freshman football team; meanwhile, his personal life crumbles when a much-exalted girlfriend from a Connecticut academy throws him over. "Basil and Cleopatra" is unique in the way it addresses these issues. Basil studies hard enough to pass a retaken trig exam; he unexpectedly makes the team as a late roster addition, displays sufficient talent and skill to earn his way into the quarterback slot, and dramatically wins the big game with a touchdown pass. He even finds some realistic perspective about the fickle beauty he has lost. At the end Basil is poised beneath the stars "of ambition, struggle and glory," which he views with "the practiced eye of the commander" (*B&J* 184). To decode this fiction, a reader only need note that all of this has transpired in young Basil's opening weeks at *Yale* University. "Basil and Cleopatra" is anti-autobiography, its artifice reflecting the alternate universe of a college career that absolutely inverts Fitzgerald's Princeton experience.

Contrasting sharply is the emotional truth found in the undergraduate fiction. The young Princetonian in "The Spire and the Gargoyle" also needs to pass make-up exams to remain in good institutional standing, but he fails to do so, and he flunks out. When he returns to campus on a misty night five years later, this Fitzgerald-like figure realizes that he can never climb to the heights of achievement the campus spires represent to his imagination. He utters agonized cries "from a complete overwhelming sense of failure. He realized how outside of it all he was" (*S&G* 169). These striking words in the 1917 story bring into focus a remark the author made to his wife just months before he died in 1940. "It is the last two years in college that count," he wrote Zelda, "I got nothing out of my first two years – in the last I got my passionate love for poetry and historical perspective and ideas in general (however superficially); it carried me full swing into my career" (*L* 124). The revelation here is fundamental. Nearing the end of his life, Fitzgerald summarized the first two years of his Princeton experience – when he gained admission to the great institution, when his Triangle efforts met with acclaim, when he was elected to prestigious offices and to one of the big clubs that then mattered so much – as worth precisely "nothing." The period after, with its medical leave and academic failures, the fall from grace with his clubs and with his special girl – the time when he produced "The Spire and the Gargoyle" – he saw as the year of special insights, "the foundation of my literary life" (*FSFL* 171). Princeton had become aligned with the worldly comprehension that poor boys shouldn't dream of marrying rich girls. One seriously doubts that Basil Lee could have described Yale as anything more than a pedestal for his achievements. But like the Princeton washout of "Spire" who realizes "how outside of it all he was," Fitzgerald's sense of being "a poor man in a rich man's club" was a special condition of his literary gift. By the time he composed "The Pierian Springs and the Last Straw," he implied that becoming a success might well destroy a writer of like sensibilities.

On the personal level the experience of Princeton never left Fitzgerald. Occasionally he remembered the college with disdain for its country-club snobbishness and for its stultifying classrooms. When Princeton President John Grier Hibben chided the author by letter for putting such peeves on evident display in *This Side of Paradise*, Fitzgerald admitted that many of its uncritical sons doubtlessly found college "the happiest time in [their] lives": "I simply say it wasn't the happiest time in mine" (*L* 462). Yet even in that 1920 letter to Hibben, Fitzgerald displayed his capacity for retaining multiple ideas in his mind, for among his next words he allowed that "I love it now better than any place on earth" (*LL* 37, 40). That regard registered itself over the years by solicitous attention to the careers of classmates and the alumni newsletter's accounts of club elections, and to a passionate interest in the fortunes of the football team. The devotion was largely unrequited during his lifetime, and even beyond. When Zelda attempted to sell her recently dead husband's papers to the university for $3,750, the offer was declined (Donaldson 40). In the early 1940s the college could confidently disdain an author who seemed destined for diminished repute, an alumnus who hadn't even obtained his degree from the institution.

Yet the most consequential fallout from Fitzgerald's rocky relationship with Princeton occurred during Fitzgerald's own lifetime. Trying to react constructively in a period of personal stress, in 1934 Fitzgerald contacted Dean Christian Gauss, one of the few Princeton academics he'd admired since his days of studying French literature in Gauss's classes. Fitzgerald proposed giving a series of approximately eight lectures at the university on the "actual business of creating fiction." If granted a lecture hall he pledged to do no inordinate drinking at Princeton, and he asked no payment. He would take the task seriously, his remarks "written out rather than spoken from notes, straight lectures rather than preceptorials," about the writing temperament, the choice and organization of creative material, and so forth (*L* 387, 386). As the surviving evidence of Fitzgerald's editorial work on the opening of Ernest Hemingway's *The Sun Also Rises* indicates, the St. Paul writer could be a first-rate critic of the writing craft. His "crack-up" essays reveal his brilliance for mingling self-reflection with stunning insight and memorable expression. How many readers and scholars today wish Princeton's administrators of 1934 had not begrudged the author of *The Great Gatsby* and *Tender Is the Night* the use of a classroom to lecture their community about his art? Yet perhaps such regrets belong with the false triumphs of Basil Lee at Yale. Instead, we retain Princeton's real legacy as the place where Fitzgerald suffered loss and the sense of being "outside" life's glamorous possibilities. Here he acquired his unique perspective as an authority of failure, discerning in the college's gothic spires the extraordinary distance between the capacity for hope and the general human tragedy of its frustration.

NOTES

1 M. J. Bruccoli, *Some Sort of Epic Grandeur: The Life of F. Scott Fitzgerald*, 2nd rev. ed. (Columbia, SC: University of South Carolina Press, 2004), 48, 56. Subsequent references to this work are included in the text.

2 A. Turnbull, *Scott Fitzgerald* (New York: Charles Scribner's Sons, 1962), 42.

3 S. Donaldson, *Fool for Love: A Biography of F. Scott Fitzgerald* (New York: Congdon & Weed, 1983), 33. Subsequent references to this work are included in the text.

4 E. Wilson, "F. Scott Fitzgerald" in M. J. Bruccoli and J. R. Bryer (eds.), *F. Scott Fitzgerald In His Own Time: A Miscellany* (Kent, OH: Kent State University Press, 1971), 404–9; 406.

13

World War I

James H. Meredith

When America entered World War I in April 1917, Fitzgerald waited only a month to enlist, as many of his Princeton classmates had already enlisted. In fact, America's entering the war was in some ways a godsend for Fitzgerald, since he would quite likely have failed out of Princeton had he stayed to finish the academic year; instead, he was allowed to enlist as a second lieutenant, to receive full credit for his "dropped" academic courses, and to bask at least for a time in the glow of his willingness to give up his life for a romantic cause, a fate he seemed heroically ready to accept in a letter to his mother in which he asked her to "pray for my soul and not that I won't be killed – the last doesn't seem to matter particularly and if you are a good Catholic the first ought to" (*LL* 14). Ironically, Fitzgerald never saw combat during the war, and in fact he was never shipped overseas, although as a lieutenant in the United States Army, Fitzgerald was practically waiting to go "over there" when the guns fell silent on the eleventh hour of the eleventh day of the eleventh month, 1918, Armistice Day. World War I had finally ended, and so did Fitzgerald's romantic hopes for gaining heroic glory on a European battlefield.

World War I was the most significant event of Fitzgerald's generation of writers, and Fitzgerald wanted desperately to be on the front lines to experience combat. When that opportunity was lost to him, this loss formed another sense of personal failure among others that plagued him throughout his life. Fitzgerald has until recently not been acknowledged as a war writer like his one-time close friend Ernest Hemingway. Yet Fitzgerald's personal sense of loss and his profound understanding of what was also culturally lost for a generation because of the war combine to make him one of the age's great writers. Therefore, understanding the historical context of how the war began as an anachronistic, old-world event and evolved into a modern, global nightmare is crucial to comprehending how profoundly Fitzgerald wrote so well about this time in history.

The old-world, opulent veneer of the Belle Epoch period, around the time of Fitzgerald's birth in 1896, disguised many of the deepening new-world cultural and political cracks that were forming across Europe. In the beginning of the twentieth century, Europe was roughly divided by two major rivalries for the world's economic resources, rivalries that intensified the cultural and political differences even more. Basically, Germany and the Austrian Empire were on one side of this divide, and Great Britain, France, and Russia were on the other. As a consequence, Europe had been smoldering in a cultural, economic, and political cauldron several years before any guns were fired in anger. At this time, most of the countries in Europe were bound together by two complex alliances. The actual war between these alliances would ignite in Europe during the summer of 1914 following the assassination by a Serbian radical of Archduke Ferdinand, the presumptive successor to Emperor Franz Joseph of Austria.[1] In response to this assassination, Austria and its ally, Germany, were forced to declare war against Serbia. Russia, an ally of Serbia, was then forced to declare war against Germany and Austria. France, an ally of Russia, soon joined the confrontation as well. One of the basic tenets of these alliances and treaties was that war on an allied country by another country eventually meant war against the whole alliance. While the intent of these alliances was to deter war, the eventual result was to embroil the whole continent of Europe in the most destructive war the world had ever known.

Unable or unwilling to resolve the situation diplomatically, both alliances ignorantly plunged toward war. Germany, which had become under Kaiser Wilhelm II a major military force, grew restive that it would have to fight a two-front war against Russia in the east and France in the west. Thus, Germany implemented the Schlieffen Plan (Gilbert 29). This plan set the German invasion of France through neutral Belgium on a strict timetable so that Germany could defeat the French before concentrating on Russia. German General Alfred von Schlieffen, the originator of the plan, had calculated that it would take antiquated Russia much longer to mobilize for war than the more modern France, so the French had to be defeated first. The ultimate goal of the Schlieffen Plan was to take Paris. For its part, France, which had lost territory to Germany in the Franco-Prussian War of 1870, thirsted for revenge against its archenemy and set into motion their Plan XVII. This plan called for a quick mobilization of France's civilian reserves. Both countries, having turned the apparatus of government completely over to the military, were on a collision course for war.

Open warfare exploded between these alliances throughout the month of August. On August 2, the German army, poised on the Belgian frontier, issued an ultimatum for free passage through the neutral country, which was summarily rejected, so the German army marched across the border and into war. Germany then declared war against France on August 3. Great Britain, an ally of France and Russia, felt compelled to declare war against Germany on August 4 because of the violation of Belgium's neutrality (Gilbert 32). Despite these political considerations, however, there were no British troops stationed on the European continent, but that would soon change as the British government scrambled to field an army for battle in Belgium. On August 22, with finally enough troops to engage the advancing German army, the British fought their first battle in the war at Mons, Belgium. This marked the first time British troops fought an enemy on foreign soil to defend another country's sovereignty. In the Old World, Britain fought for power and in response to immediate threats to its own sovereignty; such had been the case in the battle against Napoleon at Waterloo.

The remainder of the month of August 1914 witnessed some of the bloodiest and most desperate battles ever held on European soil. The battle strategy primarily followed the old Napoleonic ways of maneuvering: positioning to end the war with a heroic cavalry charge against an enemy's unsuspecting flank. The lumbering German army advanced headlong into northern France until the Allies could combine all their scattered forces against the enemy at the Marne on September 5. The Battle of Marne ended with the defeat of the German advance and ended the old ways of fighting. Instead of retreating back to their homeland, as would have been customary in traditional warfare, the Germans dug in and built defensive entrenchments in order to consolidate their gains. For their part, the French dug their own entrenchments against the German army as well. After a series of engagements, commonly known as the "Battle to the Seas," the British army likewise dug in against the Germans in Belgium. This formation of defensive entrenchments that cut across Europe soon became known as the Western Front. In the meantime, the German army defeated the Russian army at the Battle of Tannenberg, which created a similar, entrenched stalemate along the Eastern Front.

As this first phase of the war ended, another more infamous phase soon began, a period of the most violent and destructive warfare hitherto known to the world. During the romantic old-world military days, it would have never occurred to Napoleon, or any other military leader for that matter, to dig entrenchments. They would either have retreated or sued for peace. Yet, in this new, modern period, both sides dug trenches, gambling that each country's perceived industrial or technological superiority would eventually win the war. August 1914 truly marked an end of the old world and the beginning of the new. As a consequence of the major battles that followed, such places as the Somme, Verdun, and Ypres now would become known on the global map as locations of abject horror and ruin, rather than quaint places of beauty. During August and the first phase of the war, most casualties occurred from the traditional form of combat, with soldiers still dressed in old-world, decorative uniforms, heroically standing face-to-face with the enemy. During the second phase, however, which lasted until the end of the war, the use of toxic gas, long-range, high-explosive artillery shells, and rapid-firing, high-caliber machine guns became common. Trench warfare, which has become synonymous with combat conditions during World War I, created a radically new, dehumanized battlefield environment. The effect on the human spirit was not only devastating but also so pervasive that it greatly altered civilian society as well.

While all of this transformative carnage was occurring in Europe, the United States had been standing by, participating in a cynical form of neutrality. Woodrow Wilson had been elected president in 1914, campaigning on the promise to keep the United States out of this ghastly foreign war, a promise that he was able to maintain until April 6, 1917. Wilson was finally forced to declare war against Germany after the Zimmerman Telegram became public, and along with it Germany's plan to have Mexico invade the sovereign United States. Before April 1917, the United States had attempted to remain neutral, but long-standing national and commercial ties that favored Great Britain and France over Germany eventually drew the United States into the war effort anyway. When the enormity of this modern war had quickly exhausted the military resources of Great Britain and France, the United States was more than willing to ship them additional supplies, and Wall Street was eager to finance the exchange as well. Recognizing that the United States was already a de facto enemy early in the war, Germany in 1915 unleashed a submarine campaign against all shipping in the Atlantic. As a result, Germany sank the *Lusitania* on May 7, 1915, which had 159 Americans onboard (Gilbert 157). It is important to note that also onboard this ship was a large cargo of American-made ammunition bound for British weaponry. While this particular incident did not actually provoke the United States to officially engage in the fray, the sinking had moved the shocked

U.S. citizenry closer into a war footing; therefore, it came as no surprise when America finally entered the war.

Fitzgerald, as a student at Princeton, which was a hotbed of war sentiment against Imperial Germany, and as a romantic under the influence of Rupert Brooke, whose poetry proclaimed his own feelings about the nobility of dying young on the battlefield, quickly joined the Army in solidarity with many of his classmates and in keeping with his chivalric ideals. In 1917 he was commissioned a second lieutenant and trained for combat overseas in several stateside locations that included Fort Sheridan near Montgomery, Alabama, where he met his future wife, Zelda Sayre. Despite the rigors of military training and the grim realities of modern combat being reported everywhere, Fitzgerald seemingly never got over his romantic old-world notions of armed combat, and although he did not make it to the battlefield, he made certain that some of his major fictional characters did.[2] Jay Gatsby and Nick Carraway in *The Great Gatsby* are two of the most notable. Of all of Fitzgerald's novels, *Gatsby* best conveys the sociological impact of the war on American culture. The United States had not been physically touched by the war, but America's wounds were spiritual and deeply psychological. The war had spawned a cultural wasteland in America.

As a sensitive chronicler of these times, Fitzgerald wrote about this American wasteland most strikingly in *Gatsby*. As Sidney H. Bremer notes:

> Fitzgerald explicitly identified the war as a dividing point and elaborated his sense of disjunction in terms of contrasting urban images in *The Great Gatsby*. The past that Jay Gatsby "can't repeat" is literally his wartime past of whirlwind courtship. And it is the war – though only vaguely romantically experienced – that marks Nick Carraway's alienation from the family based urban community of his childhood. After the war, Nick feels the traditional, moral orderliness and communal cohesion of the old mid-western cities recede.[3]

Representative of these sociological changes are the personal post-war situations of Gatsby and Carraway, both veterans of the war, having served in the same U.S. Army division. Carraway is a bond salesman, a lucrative occupation after the Allied war debt made America the wealthiest country in the world. Gatsby, a wealthy "entrepreneur," is making his fortune by skimming as much money as he can illegally from America's expansive financial capital.

A significant but often overlooked aspect of *The Great Gatsby* is Carraway's retelling of Gatsby's wartime exploits, which actually mirrors in many ways that of famous war hero Alvin York. York, who was born in backwoods Pall Mall, Tennessee, was given the U.S. Congressional Medal of Honor for his heroic exploits during the battle for the Argonne Forest, which was at the time the largest military engagement ever fought by the U.S. Army. Acting alone, York "was credited with the killing of 25 Germans and capturing 132, and with putting 35 machine guns out of action while armed only with a rifle and a pistol."[4] For his incredible heroism, York was given virtually every conceivable decoration for valor, including a medal by the small country of Montenegro, a decoration reminiscent of the Montenegrin medal Gatsby had received and that he tells Nick about in some detail during their trip into the city. This contextual allusion is just one example of how Fitzgerald infused his romantic fiction with the facts of the war.

Although Fitzgerald is perhaps best known as a writer of romance infused with a nineteenth-century idealist sensibility, his short stories involving war are incongruously grounded in the stark realities of the war's social impact, a fact which gives the "war stories" a realistic or even a naturalistic tinge. The story perhaps most representative of Fitzgerald's social realism inserted in a romantic wartime setting is "The Last of the Belles." In the story, first published in 1929 and later collected in the short-story volume *Taps at Reveille* (1935), Andy, the narrator, reminisces about his experiences during his wartime army training near the town of Tarleton, Georgia, a fictional representation of Montgomery, Alabama. The focus of this story is on debutante Ailie Calhoun, who represents the old-world manners of a lost romantic age as she is forced to contend with men who represent the crassness of new-world America. The war alone had brought the old- and new-world Americas together. The army men who were in Tarleton as temporary officers in service to their country typically did not have the slightest notion of what constituted a chivalric code. Chivalry, which had for centuries brought profound meaning to the value of heroic death in battle, now had no meaning in the modern context. Andy, unlike many of these soldiers, but like Fitzgerald himself, believed in the sanctity of chivalry, and he saw its loss as powerful indicator of the spiritual and cultural depravity of the modern age that the war had created.

The lasting effects of the war remained a major impulse in Fitzgerald's fiction throughout his career as well, particularly in his 1934 novel *Tender Is the Night*, which is one of the finest novels about the aftermath of World War I – a novel that is concerned primarily with the broad and enduring effects of the war rather than with the immediate effects of combat on individual soldiers. Hemingway, who experienced combat conditions in

World War I, wrote primarily about the effect of war on the individual soldier as he re-entered post-war society. Fitzgerald, on the other hand, who did not experience combat conditions, wrote more about the effect of change on the culture. In this novel, published two decades after the war ended, Fitzgerald addresses the lingering damage of the war, especially the psychological effects of shell shock, more commonly known now as post-traumatic stress, which affected many more than merely those who experienced the war directly. While all war throughout the ages has traumatized the individual soldier, what rendered World War I a distinctive turning point in human history is not only the advancement of technology that made the battlefield so highly destructive and dehumanizing, but also the involvement of huge numbers of individuals involved in the overall war effort, from the girls with toxic yellow hands who made the high-explosive artillery shells that decimated the European countryside to the sensitive psychiatrists like Dick Diver who were attempting to understand the complexity of war-shattered nerves that now plagued modern culture.[5]

World War I exacted an enormous cost on American culture and on the world overall. The cultural cost is reflected powerfully in the works of many post–World War I American writers, who, like Fitzgerald, also remembered an age before the war and before modern times, when a romantic, ideal old world full of artistic and spiritual achievement once existed – a world not yet seen through the eyes of a generation "grown up" in Amory Blaine's words in *This Side of Paradise*, "to find all Gods dead, all wars fought, all faiths in man shaken" (*TSOP* 260). There is a pervasive sense of loss in Fitzgerald's work, as there is in so much modernist fiction, and the single most important event that caused that sense of loss was World War I. Yet, there is also deeply embedded in Fitzgerald's fiction an abiding hope and faith that the idyllic old world could once again be possible if only the modern times, brought on by a terrible modern war, could somehow cease to cast a deep and darkening shadow upon the everlasting light of the modern day.

NOTES

1 M. Gilbert, *The First World War: A Complete History* (New York: Henry Holt, 1994), 16. Subsequent references to this work are included in the text.

2 For a full discussion of Fitzgerald and World War I, see J. H. Meredith, "Fitzgerald and War" in K. Curnutt (ed.), *The Oxford Historical Guide to F. Scott* Fitzgerald (Oxford, UK: Oxford University Press, 2004), 163–213.

3 S. H. Bremer, "American Dreams and American Cities in Three Post-World War I Novels," *South Atlantic Quarterly* 79 (1980), 274–85; 278.

4 D. D. Lee, *Sergeant York: An American Hero* (Lexington, KY: University of Kentucky Press, 1985), 39.

5 For a full discussion of this subject, see J. H. Meredith, "*Tender Is the Night* and the Calculus of Modern War," in D. Noble (ed.), *Critical Insights: F. Scott Fitzgerald* (Pasadena, CA: Salem Press, 2010), 192–202.

Figure 14.1. Zelda Sayre Fitzgerald, study by Gordon Bryant (*Metropolitan Magazine*, June 1922).

14

Zelda in the Shadows

Linda Wagner-Martin

One of the reasons twentieth-century literary culture remains fascinated with F. Scott Fitzgerald is his chameleon-like figuration on the modernist scene. During a twenty-year period crowded with writerly invention, when the much-acclaimed "new" was bombarded by stylistic and thematic innovation, no American fiction writer was more visible than Scott Fitzgerald. A key part of Fitzgerald's life from the moment Scribners decided to consider his first novel, *This Side of Paradise*, was his courtship of the talented young Southern belle Zelda Sayre (Figure 14.1.). In an age of aggressive experimentation, Zelda's writings themselves cut to the quick of accepted literary form in many ways, most notably in her attempts to create a female *Bildungsroman*.

Readers of the 1920s knew Zelda Sayre Fitzgerald as the sexy, if hoydenish, young wife of the writer (usually identified with Ivy League living and with the elite of Princeton) whose ascent to celebrity had been truly meteoric. As a couple, the handsome Scott and winsome (and always fashionable) Zelda became New York's sweethearts. After their marriage in early April 1920 in the vestry of St. Patrick's Cathedral[1] and a honeymoon at the Biltmore Hotel, the Fitzgeralds moved upstate. During their three weeks in the city, journalists and photographers had discovered their celebrity charm, and the images of their splashing in fountains, riding on the hood of a yellow cab, and making a riotous game out of the hotel's revolving doors became a part of New York City lore. The "talk of the town" columns that fueled readers' interest in these beautiful people marked them indelibly, without doing justice to their symbiotic balancing of individual against couple. As Scott wrote later to Zelda, "I have often thought that those long conversations we used to have late at night, that began at midnight + lasted till we could see the first light dawn that scared us into sleep, were something essential in our relations, a sort of closeness" (Bruccoli, *Epic Grandeur* 128–29). The Fitzgeralds were a couple known not only for their high jinks, but also in the literary world.

Even as they were targeted for commentary by calling attention to sexuality, drinking, and "flapper" culture (in Zelda's case), they were also considered a couple who wrote.

The Fitzgeralds were given much attention by the media, which, at the time, focused on how Fitzgerald supported himself and Zelda with his writing. While Scott was considered the consummate professional, Zelda came to be seen as his partner, in some ways his cowriter, because he consistently credited her with being his sounding board and creative helpmeet. Several of his early famous stories, such as "Head and Shoulders," "The Ice Palace," "The Offshore Pirate," and "The Jelly-Bean," support these descriptions, because they contain characters clearly inspired by Zelda. The fact that Zelda was charmingly, traditionally "Southern" was set against the somewhat austere – if always dapper – Eastern mien of her husband. In many ways, the Fitzgeralds represented a marriage of opposites, but each was talented, and their verbal abilities, in part, created their unusual celebrity power.

During those first few years, within the Fitzgeralds' marriage, glamour was eclipsed by sheer hard work: Scott knew he had to keep writing at what had become his expected speedy pace, and he relied on Zelda to be his best – and often his most critical – reader. They worked well together, and they worked steadily. This compatibility may have been sexual as well, but it most assuredly was imaginative. As Scott implied, Zelda gave him details, language, characters, emotions, and plots. As she had written in 1919, "I love to feel that maybe I can help just a little – I want to so much" (*S&Z* 38). This remark, however, follows her recognition that she does, indeed, know a little something about writing herself; she notes to Scott the falsity of O. Henry, who "never *created* people – just things to happen to the same old kind of folks and unexpected ends " (*S&Z* 40). Zelda's intellect and her passion were often the sources of his fiction, and if Zelda was contributing to the origin and completion of his fiction, Scott and his ready lectures were giving her some formal orientation in what the role of modernist fiction was to be. John Dos Passos remembers that, although Scott drank exhaustively in the early years of their marriage, he also was "a born professional. Everything he said was worth listening to."[2]

As early as April 2, 1922, Zelda saw her name in print – and in the *New York Tribune*. Asked to "review" her spouse's second novel, *The Beautiful and Damned*, she wrote a complacently ironic piece about Scott's having stolen some of his material from her. That was the first of several essays that were published in this first phase of Zelda's writing on her own. The stories that she treasured came later, and were, in her mind, always headed for collection into a book – her book. Living with a novelist, Zelda quickly adopted much of Scott's interest in not only the writing itself but the professionalism involved in being a successful, serious novelist. For Michael Nowlin, even as Scott was writing *The Beautiful and Damned*, he was drawing on some decidedly fashionable aesthetics (about "professionalism," along with the techniques of modernist fiction). According to Nowlin, Fitzgerald conceptualized the ways in which modernism differed from the Victorianism of thirty years before. Nowlin suggests that Fitzgerald's interest in irony was at the heart of his concept, and he emphasizes that *The Beautiful and Damned* was titled in draft "The Diary of a Literary Failure," a novel in which scrutiny falls on the differences between Richard Caramel and Anthony Patch, especially in their understandings of both aesthetics and modernism. As Patch grew in significance, Nowlin suggests, Fitzgerald was also growing into a cynical acceptance that his own success – in both short fiction and long – was based on his popular (i.e., commonplace) appeal to readers. Having read Willa Cather's 1920 essay "On the Art of Fiction," in which she divided writers into artists and popularizers, Fitzgerald began to wean himself from the easy patois of his college-day characters and to create a structure that would allow the reader to see how ironic his view of those characters was.[3] Drawing from the criticism of H. L. Mencken and George Jean Nathan, as well as Edmund Wilson and other of his Princeton literary friends, Fitzgerald knew that his next book needed to reflect the tendencies of full-blown modernist styles, but he was naively disappointed when sales of *The Great Gatsby* – a title that would vex any reader who didn't understand irony – fell far short of his expectations. Max Perkins repeatedly explained that once again Fitzgerald's "double-edged irony" kept readers from identifying with the novel (although Perkins found the use of Nick Carraway "exactly" right, providing the vantage point of ironic voice), and he also lamented that many of Fitzgerald's readers were impervious to the power of irony (Nowlin 65–67).

Immersing himself in the uses and roles of irony as he wrote and then revised *Gatsby* and, earlier, *The Beautiful and Damned* showed that Fitzgerald was thoroughly conscious of the gospel of H. L. Mencken, long a champion of the irony of the upper classes, those elite readers who peopled his literary consciousness. It may also have shown that Zelda's achievement in that 1922 review, "Mrs. F. Scott Fitzgerald Reviews 'The Beautiful and Damned,' Friend Husband's Latest" brought him a laugh that was more anguished than amused. In paragraph after paragraph of the review, Zelda relied on self-deprecation, cultural references that smack of the upper-class snobbery reflected in Fitzgerald's novels, and cheap uses of such literary references as those to Henry James (who would not know which kind of mink coat Gloria should have purchased) and Thomas Hardy, master of tragedy far lighter than that resulting from Gloria's error.[4] Somewhat later in 1922, however, Zelda wrote a more controlled essay for *Metropolitan Magazine*. "Eulogy on the Flapper" makes good sense in treating the figure of the "flapper," with whom Zelda was often compared, with irony – but not in the joke-littered mode of her review. Zelda writes, convincingly, "I see no logical reasons for keeping the young illusioned. Certainly disillusionment comes easier at twenty than at forty – the fundamental and inevitable disillusionments, I mean" (Z. Fitzgerald 392). Never solipsistic or revealingly autobiographical, Zelda crafts a prose that seems to be self-revelatory. It is this voice that she adopts for her series of short stories to come, most of them written closer to the end of the decade.

Once the Fitzgeralds realized that they needed a greater income in order to support their lifestyle, even Scott seemed amenable to Zelda's trying to sell some of her writing to the "slicks" and women's magazines. In 1923, for example, while living in Great Neck, Zelda wrote "Our Own Movie Queen," a story that used to good effect her natural voice with its educated colloquialism and Southern idiom, which Scott admired. Zelda draws loosely on the experience of her Montgomery friend, Tallulah Bankhead, who became a star after submitting a photograph to a *Photoplay* contest, and the story is filled with details germane to teenagers' lives in Montgomery, Alabama. Scott marketed the story as his, and in the summer of 1924 it appeared in the *Chicago Sunday Tribune*; his payment was $1,000. He noted in his *Ledger* that he split the money with Zelda, but that two-thirds of the story was hers (Wagner-Martin 79–80).[5]

Because contemporary critics have necessarily remained much more interested in Scott Fitzgerald's work than with Zelda Fitzgerald's output, it is difficult to chart her literary reputation. Since Scott kept the records that detailed the writing and marketing of their work, the facts about Zelda's work have had to come from his sources, and his antipathy toward any recognition of his wife as a truly professional writer is well known. Zelda's efforts to write are combined with her consistent efforts to paint and, somewhat later, to return to her adolescent prowess in the ballet. Many of these efforts are shadowed by the first of her psychological and physical breakdowns, as Bruccoli points out in his preface to *The Collected Writings*: "She started serious work late and under terrible strains; most of the work in this volume was written after her 1930 breakdown." Later in that brief essay, he announces that the fragments that remain of her last novel, *Caesar's Things*, are "incoherent" (Bruccoli, preface, xi, xii).[6]

The Fitzgeralds' marriage provided a mirror of their aesthetic partnership; as their personal relationship worsened, Zelda's health deteriorated and Scott drank increasingly more. After *The Great Gatsby* appeared in 1925, Scott was marked as being at the apex of modernist fiction, and the nine long years until *Tender Is the Night* saw publication in 1934 constituted a plethora of painful narratives – both his versions and Zelda's. When the Fitzgerald family returned to Ellerslie (Wilmington, Delaware) in 1928, after more than two years abroad, Zelda spent time with her Montgomery friend Sara Haardt (later, Sara Haardt Mencken), who was a professional writer; through Sara, Zelda had already published in *College Humor*. The stories she began now, with Harold Ober serving as agent, all appeared there. Although she shared a byline with Scott, they were Zelda's stories about young American women, some based on her Montgomery friends, some showing the difficulties of ambition, others showing the sheer love of both place (Montgomery) and work (dance).[7]

The dating of these substantial fictions, which could easily have been collected and published as a book, shows a clear progression toward Zelda's first novel, *Save Me the Waltz*, which was published by Scribners in 1932. Zelda began the novel when she was living alone in a rental house in Montgomery, helping her mother and an older sister care for her dying father, and Scott was living in Hollywood doing screenwriting. She finished it while she was institutionalized at the Phipps Clinic at Johns Hopkins. The novel's setting is again Montgomery; the ostensible plotline is her father's stern control over his family of daughters, jostled as it is by their various courtships, leading to the romance of David and Alabama (and David's condescending carving on the doorpost: "David, David, Knight, Knight, Knight, and Miss Alabama Nobody") (Z. Fitzgerald 39).[8] Ultimately, *Save Me the Waltz* is a *Bildungsroman* of an unusual kind – that of a girl growing into a woman. The "waltz" of the romantic-sounding title, representative of the way young Montgomery teens lived their lives during wartime, is also representative of the grueling work of becoming a professional dancer – in Alabama's case, a ballerina. Suffused with nostalgia, the novel becomes a hard-driven testament to the difficulties, and the losses, of a person, regardless of gender, driven by ambition.

Zelda submitted the novel to Max Perkins, and Scott was angry over the fact that Perkins (his editor, after all) accepted Zelda's novel in its first-draft state. He believed that Perkins had betrayed him, and that

Zelda had betrayed him, too, in that she had planned to submit the manuscript to Perkins, or that she had sent the manuscript without telling him she had finished it. The frighteningly vociferous storm of emotions that ensued began with Scott's letters to Dr. Squires, a representative of Phipps, and Max Perkins – Scott did not communicate with Zelda at all. His anger at Squires was rooted in the fact that he was paying them to care for Zelda, and not to foster her writing, which, he implied, embarrassed him (Wagner-Martin 156–62; Bruccoli, *Epic Grandeur* 317–24). The fallout from Zelda's defiance of Scott in writing and publishing *Save Me the Waltz* was an utter emotional imbroglio, and present-day critique of the couple's relationship hinges largely on the 114-page transcription of their joint interview with Dr. Rennie, their Phipps therapist, on May 8, 1933.[9]

Much of the Rennie transcription replays material from Scott's original letters to Perkins, Squires, and, eventually, Zelda. In order to justify his anger, he claimed that Zelda had used "his material." She carefully replied, in Bruccoli's words, that "the things that had happened to them were community literary property" (Bruccoli, *Epic Grandeur* 322). Zelda continued, "I would like you to thoroughly understand that my revision will be made on an aesthetic basis: that the other material which I will elect is nevertheless legitimate stuff which has cost me a pretty emotional penny to amass and which I intend to use when I can get the tranquility of spirit necessary to write the story of myself versus myself. That is the book I really want to write" (Bruccoli, *Epic Grandeur* 323).[10] Much of Scott's argument was defensive as well: He loved Zelda and tried to make her into the artist she wanted to become; his abilities were always at her service. By the time of the May interview, the cautionary tale Scott had put forth had given way to harsh criticism of what he saw as Zelda's attacks on him and his motivations and a fully expressed need to defend himself. Several interchanges from the May 1933 transcripts focus on the issue of ownership of experience. Scott explained to Zelda that he was "a professional writer, with a huge following. I am the highest paid short story writer in the world ... one in ten million," and he therefore owned their lives. "Everything we have done is mine ... I am the professional novelist, and I am supporting you. That is all my material. None of it is your material." To his accusation that Zelda is "a third rate writer and a third rate ballet dancer," she replied quietly, "You have told me that before" and that she thought he was making "a rather violent attack on a third rate talent." As the discussion continued, Zelda said she would rather be in an institution than trying to live with Scott: "One reason I have to do things behind your back is because you are so absolutely unjust and abusive and unfair, that to go to you and ask you anything would be like pulling a thunderbolt down on my head." To his accusation that she is "a useless society woman, brought up to be that," she asks what he would like her to be, and his answer is, "I want you to do what I say." Toward the end of the interview, Zelda comes to a self-affirming point: "I don't want to live with you, because I want to live some place that I can be my own self" (qtd. in *Zelda* 166–77; Bruccoli, *Epic Grandeur* 345–52). Again, the search for self – a woman's self – repeats earlier themes in her letters. When Zelda read the first installment of Scott's *Tender Is the Night*, serialized in *Scribner's Magazine* early in 1934, however, she of course recognized not only Nicole's symptoms of mental instability but also language from her letters to Scott about her own instability. The question of whose material belonged to whom had been answered definitively. Zelda first went to bed, and then she asked to go back into the Phipps Clinic.

The painful arguments between the Fitzgeralds have drawn much attention to what seemed to be their incompatibility. Much of their behavior seems to be inexplicable, complicated as it was throughout their lives by excessive drinking, frantic activity (especially moves from place to place), and general lack of focus. Beyond biography, Greg Forter places the Fitzgeralds' angry assaults on each other, and on each other's role as writer, into a gendered context. Forter takes Scott back into his identification with the feminine (as with his mother, bereft from the sisters' deaths) and notes that such identification might be "pleasurable or dangerous … what's key is that Zelda's own gender ambiguity intensified his contradictory impulses toward virile manhood, on one hand, and a more passive, emotionally expressive and receptive masculinity, on the other. This contradiction was no doubt disquieting; to satisfy one aspiration within it would be to thwart the others, at least in the binarized gender university to whose dictates Fitzgerald was subject" (Forter 164). Whether Scott's contradictory impulses led to what seemed to be defensiveness about his masculinity or to just plain destructive behavior in various friendships, Forter seems accurate in his suggestion that Zelda's very toughness – her unwillingness to change her writing simply to please her spouse – may have intensified his reactions. In the end, the professionalism that seemed to draw them together may have driven them further apart, and they seldom lived together during the last stages of Scott's life.

Despite the assessment of Jackson Bryer and Cathy Barks that "[t]he most important relationship that either Scott or Zelda Sayre Fitzgerald had was with each other; it was the catalyst for and foremost theme of most of their fiction" (*S&Z* xiii), the fact of impermeable gender remains. Although their claim may be true of Scott's fiction, it is much less accurate where Zelda's fiction is concerned. Arguably, the foremost subject found in the body of Zelda's work, and in *Save Me the Waltz* in particular, is the development of a young woman protagonist. To write her *Bildungsroman* in a female voice was to break sharply with a tradition dominated by men: From Goethe to Dickens, and with few exceptions, this kind of novel was based on the life of a male character. But in Zelda's repeatedly bleak stories, as well as in her novel, the character learning to be an adult – with all the coercion and disillusion that education entails – was female, and the novel itself, like the first novel of her husband, was thoroughly modern.

NOTES

1 M. J. Bruccoli, *Some Sort of Epic Grandeur*, 2nd rev. ed. (Columbia, SC: University of South Carolina Press, 2002), 128. Subsequent references to this work are included in the text. See also L. Wagner-Martin, *Zelda Sayre Fitzgerald: An American Woman's Life* (New York: Palgrave McMillan, 2004). Subsequent references to this work are included in the text.

2 J. Dos Passos, "The Best Times" in *On Books and Writers, Selected Essays*, M. J. Bruccoli and J. C. Unrue, eds. (Columbia, SC: University of South Carolina Press, 2010), 3–14; 12.

3 M. Nowlin, *F. Scott Fitzgerald's Racial Angles and the Business of Literary Greatness* (New York: Palgrave MacMillan, 2007), 36–39. Subsequent references to this work are included in the text. Greg Forter gives this concern with artistry and professionalism a psychosexual underpinning. He traces much of Fitzgerald's melancholy tendencies not to his "black Irish" heritage but to his mother's grief over the deaths of his two young sisters. Because they died before Scott's birth, Forter describes the psychopathy as linked "creativity, unmournable loss, and an internalized femininity." Scott's desire for the feminine modified the role of his father, whose own professional history was that of recurring business failures. Scott thus identified more usually – albeit uneasily – with the power and money of his mother and her family. See G. Forter and P. A. Miller, eds., *Desire of the Analysts: Psychoanalysis and Cultural Criticism* (Albany, NY: State University of New York Press, 2008), 154–55. Subsequent references to this volume are included in the text.

4 Z. Fitzgerald, "Friend Husband's Latest" in *The Collected Writings of Zelda Fitzgerald*, M. J. Bruccoli, ed. (Tuscaloosa: University of Alabama Press, 1991), 387–89. Subsequent references to this volume are included in the text.

5 In his preface to *The Collected Writings*, Matthew J. Bruccoli summarizes inaccurately: He notes that Zelda wrote ten stories or sketches (including this one), and that at least eight others are lost. But he groups all ten of her published stories as being from 1930 to 1932, but this one originates in 1923. He

also suggests that Scott and Zelda collaborated on her fiction (271; this story, 273–92). See M. J. Bruccoli, preface to Z. Fitzgerald's *The Collected Writings of Zelda Fitzgerald*.

6 Essays by W. R. Anderson ("Rivalry and Partnership," 1977), Alice Hall Petry ("Woman's Work," 1979), and Jacqueline Tavernier-Courbin ("Art as Woman's Response and Search," 1979) present a more balanced view of Zelda's own professionalism, but the scattered effect of essays has had a more ephemeral impact.

7 Bruccoli recounts, correctly, Zelda's anger at Scott's outright usurpation of one of the last of these stories, "A Millionaire's Girl," which Ober sold to the *Saturday Evening Post*, without asking Zelda's permission, as a story by Scott – and was paid $4,000 (preface, xii).

8 Clearly a reflection of the usurpation of authorship, this carving is followed by the line "angry about the names. David had told her about how famous he was going to be many times before" (Z. Fitzgerald 39).

9 Caught by surprise at Scott's anger, Dr. Squires had recommended that Scott and Zelda separate; she could see no way out of his terrible anger. In return, Scott wrote to her what he thought was a complete history of the Sayre family; unfortunately, much of what he wrote, as well as much of what he said, had little basis in truth. His refusal to consider divorce – because of the great love he and Zelda shared – meant that the Phipps Clinic had to resort to other strategies in order to preserve both Zelda and Scott.

10 If Zelda realized how much of her letters Scott was using in his drafts of *Tender Is the Night*, she would have been chagrined to think that her second novel – about psychiatric problems – would overlap his fiction to an even greater extent.

15

Fitzgerald's Southern Narrative: The Tarleton, Georgia, Stories

Bryant Mangum

In a 1922 feature article pasted in the Fitzgeralds' scrapbooks and subtitled "Novelist Says Southern Type of Flapper Best," Fitzgerald "classifies American flappers according to their locality." Accompanying the article is a quarter-page map of the United States containing cartoon renditions of flappers from every geographical area and depicting Fitzgerald with a pointer singling out the Southern flapper.[1] This Southern flapper is, in many ways, a hybrid of the flapper and the Southern belle types, and, importantly, she is the embodiment of Fitzgerald's complex relationship with the South. Fitzgerald's fascination with the South had begun at an early age, associating it as he did with the legacy of his Maryland-born father: "Fitzgerald ... developed an early tug toward the country of his father's youth, sympathizing with the cause of the Confederacy and admiring the impeccable manners of the Old South."[2] When he was stationed at Camp Sheridan, near Montgomery, Alabama, and after he met Zelda Sayre at a country club dance in July 1918, Fitzgerald's fascination with the South was reawakened. He explores his complex and changing ideas about the South in the characters of Sally Carrol Happer, Nancy Lamar, Ailie Calhoun, and the males that surround them as they appear in what has come to be known as the Tarleton Trilogy, three stories set in the fictional town of Tarleton, Georgia. And yet, in the tangentially related story "Dice, Brassknuckles & Guitar" (1923), a story that serves as a bridge between the first and second Tarleton stories, "The Ice Palace" (1920) and "The Jelly-Bean" (1920), and the last, "The Last of the Belles" (1929), he arguably signals his move away from a romanticizing of his fictional characters based on type – here the Southern type – and toward an embracing of characters who embody human complexity and universal ideals not tied to geographical location.

Although the serious critical discourse on Fitzgerald's deep connections to the South and the recurrence of Southern settings and Southern characters in his fiction began more than thirty-five years ago, there has been little agreement as to his final stance regarding Southern manners and morals associated with the chivalric code. In his 1973 foundational study "Scott Fitzgerald's Romance with the South," Scott Donaldson traces the origins of Fitzgerald's fascination with the South, first, to his admiration of his father's Maryland family heritage, his genteel manners, and his belief in "the romance of the lost Southern cause"; and, second, to his enchantment with the quaint Old-South origins and ways of his Alabama wife, Zelda Sayre. Ultimately Donaldson concludes that the magic of the Old South became "mingled in Fitzgerald's mind with the golden girl" and that when she failed him, his "illusions [about the romantic appeal of the South] are shattered" (3). Donaldson sees in Andy's loss of Ailie Calhoun in "The Last of the Belles" what he calls "Fitzgerald's ultimate rejection of the Southern belle," a rejection that brought about his loss of illusions and resulted from Fitzgerald's "confusion of place and person" (3).

In 1982, C. Hugh Holman extended Donaldson's idea to include symbolic associations that became part of Fitzgerald's dialectic construction of the contrast between South and North. The South to Fitzgerald, as Holman sees it, was "a land of beauty and romance, of lost order, of tradition and dignity, and of a glorious past … [something] to be dreamed of and to be loved in youth, but it must be abandoned in maturity." The North, by contrast, was the "home of accomplishment, effort, and hard work, the bedrock of reality [although also] a killer, or at the very least a duller, of the romantic dreams of youth, which the South represents."[3] These romantic dreams, according to Holman, were so seductive to Fitzgerald that he adopted a view of the South that was characterized by a savoring of "the backward glance" (56) and a privileging of nostalgia that Fitzgerald and his narrators eventually outgrew as time passed and youthful dreams faded. Holman disagrees with Donaldson that Ailie Calhoun is Fitzgerald's rejection of the Southern belle. She is, rather, "wistful nostalgia made flesh" (64) and, as Fitzgerald understands, it is time itself, rather than Ailie, that can be seen as the villain who makes the South empty for Andy forever.

John Kuehl, in his 1992 "Psychic Geography in 'The Ice Palace,'" sees many of the same dichotomies that Holman points out, but he argues that within the story's structure of "Geographical antithesis"[4] the North represents death in life, whereas the South is a form of life in death (178). Sally Carrol Happer, whose story this essentially is, opts in the end for the latter, and Kuehl leaves open the possibility that this may imply a preference in "The Ice Palace" for South over North in Fitzgerald's mind, although he reminds the reader that in the second story of the Tarleton

Trilogy, "The Jelly-Bean," Fitzgerald is critical of things Southern. Kuehl is particularly interested in the degree to which the Tarleton stories indicate that the civil war in Fitzgerald's psyche may have resulted from conflicts within the Southern half of the dichotomy stemming from tensions within his relationship with Zelda, tensions that ultimately brought him to reject the part of the South associated with Zelda's willful "indolence," while believing still in his "Southern" father's "historical American values of 'honor, courtesy, and courage'" (179) – a point that proves over and over to be true in Fitzgerald's fiction.

Building on Donaldson's central point regarding the Southern belle, Alice Hall Petry in her 1989 study of Fitzgerald's stories observes that by the time of his final Tarleton story "The Last of the Belles," Fitzgerald had become more judgmental in his short fiction and thus had come to appreciate more fully the mode of satire. Extending Donaldson's earlier suggestion that Ailie Calhoun in "The Last of the Belles" was "all artifice" and represented Fitzgerald's ultimate rejection of the Southern belle, Petry argues that Andy's portrait of Ailie is satirical and aimed at stripping away Ailie's mask to reveal "the chill-minded flapper under the alluring Southern belle."[5]

Heidi Bullock in her 1996 essay "The Southern and the Satirical in 'The Last of the Belles'" takes Petry's idea and turns it away from Ailie and onto Andy. She maintains that virtually all who have read the story have been drawn in by Andy's seemingly reliable narrative voice when, in effect, Andy is the one who has failed to question his stereotypical assumptions about Ailie and about the South. In the process he has assumed a "universally apprehended South" that is "relentlessly trite."[6] In the end the object of Fitzgerald's satire, Bullock argues, is Andy, through whom Fitzgerald is revealing the underlying problem of the characters in the story, of general readers, and also of critics, most of whom neglect to consider the source of their information. The popular imagination, according to Bullock, insists solipsistically that all characters in the story "represent" something, rather than that they are unique individuals with stories of their own.

Perhaps the most interesting thing about these major critical treatments of various aspects of Fitzgerald's Southern narrative is that all, with the exception of Bullock's, move in the end toward definitive conclusions regarding Fitzgerald's final "stance" in relation to the South, or at least to some aspect of Southern values and customs. Donaldson sees Fitzgerald as having ultimately rejected the South on the basis of his rejection of the Southern belle; Holman believes that Fitzgerald saw his romanticizing of the South and its belles for what it was – a phase of the worship of "wistful nostalgia" that had to be given up as youth faded; Kuehl understands that Fitzgerald, though he balances praise and criticism of both North and South, ultimately solves the either/or conflict in his own psyche by rejecting the willful indolence of the South's Zeldas and accepting the American values of his Southern father: honor, courtesy, and courage. Petry argues that Fitzgerald finally strips away from his belle the mask of seductive charm that conceals a dark flapper-like manipulativeness, presumably generalizing outward to a rejection of the South itself. Of the five, only Bullock concludes that Fitzgerald could, through his satirical stance toward Andy in "The Last of the Belles," be urging the reader to examine her/his own solipsistic tendency to generalize without verifiable evidence about any person or region on the basis of preconceived notions and stereotypes. It is also interesting to note that the critical views, again with the exception of Bullock's, have tended to draw conclusions based on the creation of binary structures: North (masculine)/South (feminine); North (death in life)/South (life in death); North (future)/South (past); Southern belle (surreptitiously charming)/flapper (chill-minded), for example. In defense of all who have critically engaged Fitzgerald's Southern narrative, particularly that part of it contained in his Tarleton stories, it must be said that Fitzgerald has invited – even seemingly required, especially in the first two stories, "The Ice Palace" and "The Jelly-Bean" – the kind of dialectical reasoning that critics have engaged in by having his narrators and characters create the dichotomies themselves, as Sally Carrol Happer does, for example, when she characterizes Northern men as canine and Southern men as feline (*S* 59), or as Nancy Lamar does in "The Jelly-Bean" when she maintains that all people in England have "style," whereas Americans, especially all Southern Americans, lack "style" (*S* 151).

It is also of particular interest that all of the critics mentioned above, except Holman, fail even to mention "Dice, Brassknuckles & Guitar" in their assessment of Fitzgerald's Southern narrative, an understandable omission since, although Jim Powell is from Tarleton, technically the story is set in the North. Holman mentions "Dice" only in passing to suggest that the story and its central male character, Jim Powell, are tangentially related to the Tarleton trilogy. In a footnote, Holman makes this observation: "Jim Powell is the protagonist in Fitzgerald's 1923 short story 'Dice, Brass Knuckles & Guitar [*sic*].' In this story he goes North to make an improved living by running a school to teach rich youths social grace and self-defense. When he learns that the rich regard him as 'just a servant,' he heads bitterly back to the South and to being a jelly-bean" (Holman 59). The brevity of Holman's analysis of "Dice, Brassknuckles & Guitar" coupled with the absence of any other thorough examination of the story and its relationship to the other Tarleton stories underline the need for a study of the intertextual connections between "Dice" and the other Tarleton stories, particularly a study of the ways in which the story sets up what well might be Fitzgerald's later satirical portrait of Andy in "The Last of the Belles," finally shedding light on Fitzgerald's ideas about the South.

Although Fitzgerald included allusions to the South and focused on North/South contrasts in many of his works, a fact that Scott Donaldson has carefully documented, the clearest picture of Fitzgerald's characterization of the mythic South and the Southern belle can, indeed, be found in those three stories mentioned above and referred to as the Tarleton Trilogy: "The Ice Palace," "The Jelly-Bean," and "The Last of the Belles." These stories are set in Tarleton, Georgia, which is a thinly disguised Montgomery, Alabama, described in "The Jelly-Bean" as "a little city of forty thousand that has dozed sleepily for forty thousand years in southern Georgia, stirring in its slumbers and muttering something about a war that took place sometime, somewhere, and that everyone else has forgotten long ago" (*S* 143). In addition to the romantic moonlight-and-magnolias atmosphere of Tarleton, Fitzgerald or his narrators are drawn to the three Southern belles who live there. As Andy, the narrator of "The Last of the Belles" is told by his friend who is about to leave Tarleton, "You see, there're really only three girls here –," a fact that intrigues the narrator, who says that "there was something mystical about there being three girls" (*S* 449–50).

The three girls are characterized as being highly individual, distinctly different from each other, but at least on the surface and in varying degrees they possess characteristics that qualify them as both flapper and belle. Sally Carrol, on the one hand, has the flapper's bobbed hair, two spots of rouge dabbed on her lips, and a grain of powder on her nose. On the other, she is one of those "gracious soft-voiced girls, who were brought up on memories instead of money" (*S* 50), one who can eloquently describe her Southern legacy to her Northern fiancé in a Confederate cemetery: "people have these dreams they fasten onto things, and I've always grown up with that dream … I've tried in a way to live up to those past standards of noblesse oblige – there's just the last remnants of it, you know, like the roses of an old garden dying all round us – streaks of strange courtliness and chivalry in some of these boys " (*S* 54).

Sally Carrol is quite aware of the conflicting needs within her, one related to the independent, flapper spirit that pulls her toward the larger world outside Tarleton and what she thinks will be freedom, and the other, the Southern side, that keeps her attached to Tarleton. "There's two sides to me, you see," she tells her Tarleton friend Clark. "There's the sleepy old side you love; an' there's a sort of energy – the feelin' that makes me do wild things. That's the part of me that may be useful somewhere, that'll last when I'm not beautiful any more" (*S* 51). After being trapped in an ice palace during a winter carnival that she attends when she goes North to visit her fiancé's family, she realizes that she must return, presumably forever, to the South, her ancestral home. Similarly, Ailie, "the Southern type in all its beauty" in "The Last of the Belles" (*S* 450), whose eyes have been drawn North after a winter in school in New York and a Yale prom, turns down the men who could take her there to marry a man from Savannah. "You know I couldn't ever marry a Northern man," she tells Andy, who proclaims of her that "Beneath her mask of an instinctive thoroughbred she had always been on to herself" (*S* 462).

The case of the third belle of Tarleton, Nancy Lamar from "The Jelly-Bean," is more complicated than that of Sally Carrol Happer and Ailie Calhoun. She is clearly the wildest of the three, frequently gambling away more money than she has, and without a trace of *noblesse oblige*, urging Jim Powell to drain the gas from a stranger's car so she can use it to remove chewing gum from her shoe and return to the dance floor. Nancy has no apparent loyalty to the chivalric code of the Old South, and she, more vehemently than Sally Carrol or Ailie, professes a profound regret that she cannot escape Tarleton. In her case she regrets "that I wasn't born in England" (*S* 151). When she gives a farewell kiss to Jim, she tells him, "I'm a wild part of the world, Jelly-bean" (*S* 155). Nancy is more flapper than belle, and she, perhaps more than Ailie, is that chill-minded flapper hiding beneath the "alluring Southern belle." In a clear reference to her in "The Last of the Belles," the narrator Andy refers to her as "a lady I promptly detested" (*S* 450) – a judgment that points, among other things, to Andy's inclination to draw conclusions about people based on slight objective evidence.

As Holman has noted, the Southern belle is the central image of the three stories. In his description of the Tarleton belles and the types from which they descend, they are "the embodiments of a tradition that stretched back before the Confederacy and that enchanted and hypnotized men for a century, permanent embodiments of the dream of beauty and youth and the romantic aspiration of the aggressive male" (Holman

61). It is important to note, however, that Sally Carrol, Ailie, and Nancy are quite different manifestations of the Southern belle, possessing as they do varying degrees of allegiance to the genteel tradition associated with the belle and to the ethos of freedom from tradition associated with the flapper. Sally Carrol's defense of the chivalric tradition is inspired, and she returns to the South after quite consciously rejecting the larger theater in which her ambitions might have been realized. Ailie takes longer, but she finally acknowledges she could never have married a Northern man, although she has felt the sincerity of two of her Northern suitors, who would have perhaps freed her from the constraints of her legacy. Both Sally Carrol and Ailie opt consciously not to reject the legacy of the chivalric tradition and choose consciously to remain Southern belles, a decision that Nancy, however, makes quite unconsciously when she marries her Savannah suitor while she is intoxicated.

One might assume that with Sally Carrol back in Tarleton, apparently for good, at the end of "The Ice Palace," with Nancy already married to a man from Savannah in "The Jelly-Bean," and with Ailie about to become comfortably established in marriage to a man from Savannah at the end of "The Last of the Belles," Fitzgerald's ideas about the Southern belle have been brought to closure. And perhaps in a limited sense they have. Clearly, his rendition of the belle represents a movement forward of the stereotype in that it reflects changing times, particularly the revolution of manners and morals that came with World War I and its aftermath. The Fitzgerald belle has become a wilder part of the world from her contact with the flapper creed. And her destiny is similar to that of the flapper, which in Zelda's words was to go "where all good flappers [one could here substitute "belles"] go – into the young married set, into boredom and gathering conventions and the pleasure of having children, having lent a while a splendor and courageousness and brightness to life, as all good flappers should."[7] The differences of opinion noted above among those who have examined Fitzgerald's attitudes toward the Southern belle point to the open-endedness of the Tarleton stories and toward the ambivalence on Fitzgerald's part as to how he finally viewed Sally Carrol, Nancy, and Ailie.

A window, however, that might well provide additional insight into Fitzgerald's attitudes toward Tarleton's women, and ultimately toward the South itself, is the neglected Tarleton-related story "Dice, Brassknuckles & Guitar," which serves as a sequel to "The Jelly-Bean" and a prequel to "The Last of the Belles." When Jim Powell, a resident of Tarleton, first appears on the scene in front of the New Jersey house of Amanthis

Powell in his dilapidated jalopy, accompanied by his African American body servant, in "Dice, Brassknuckles & Guitar," readers of the story when it first appeared in *Hearst's International* in May 1923 would not likely have known what a rich "fictional" history he has brought with him – and what insights his story might provide into the Tarleton stories. There is a hint of Jim's origins in the "mangy pennant bearing the legend 'Tarleton, Ga.'" (*S* 238) attached to the rear of his car, and he immediately introduces himself to Amanthis by the name "Powell" – a name that connects them even as it softens barriers of gender and geography – and reveals to her that he is "a resident of Tarleton, Georgia" (239). He further tells her that he comes "from mighty good people ... Pore though. I got some money because my aunt she was using it to keep her in a sanitarium and she died" (*S* 240). He explains to Amanthis that he has inherited his aunt's money, left the principal of his inheritance back in Tarleton, and come "north for the summer" on the interest he has recently collected. Only those readers who had read "The Jelly-Bean" when it first appeared in the October 1920 issue of *Metropolitan* would have recognized him as the title character from that story, a "type" of Southern character: the corner loafer who "spends his life conjugating the verb to idle in the first person singular – I am idling, I have idled, I will idle" (*S* 143). In "The Jelly-Bean," Jim has succumbed to the charms of Nancy Lamar and resolved to reclaim the aristocratic heritage that had once been his family's when they owned land and a big white house in Tarleton. But that had been long ago, and as it turns out he had waited too long to reclaim his legacy and the Southern belle in the form of Nancy who would have accompanied this reclamation. Nancy, shortly after consuming too much corn liquor, elopes with a man from Savannah whom she would not have married sober, leaving Jim "feelin' right sick" and without purpose at the end of the story (*S* 158). During the interval between the end of "The Jelly-Bean" and the beginning of "Dice, Brassknuckles & Guitar" Jim has apparently decided to acquire a body servant and the jalopy that brings him to the threshold of Amanthis's house in New Jersey, hoping, it seems, to earn a living in the land of opportunity, the North. Six years after the publication of "Dice, Brassknuckles & Guitar" popular magazine readers would learn that Nancy, although not mentioned by name, was likely one of "only three girls" in Tarleton whom Andy's friend Bill Knowles considered worth meeting. The other two are Ailie Calhoun, the Southern "belle" of "The Last of the Belles (*Saturday Evening Post* March 2, 1929), and Sally Carrol, the nineteen-year-old belle from "The Ice Palace" (*Saturday Evening Post*, May 20, 1920) who had spoken so eloquently in a Confederate graveyard to her Northern boyfriend about "the most beautiful thing in the world – the dead South" (*S* 53–4). Clearly, Jim Powell's story is an intricately woven thread in Fitzgerald's Tarleton series. It is noteworthy that when we first encounter him in "The Jelly-Bean" he is characterized as a "type" – a "bred-in-the-bone, dyed-in-the-wool, ninety-nine three-quarters per cent Jelly bean" (*S* 142) – that Fitzgerald moves within the circle of other "types," most notably Southern belles. By the end of "Dice, Brassknuckles & Guitar," however, it has become clear that Fitzgerald is developing in the story complex ideas that he intends forcefully to communicate with regard to characterization by type.

Fitzgerald begins his 1926 story "The Rich Boy" with the following lines: "Begin with an individual, and before you know it you find that you have created a type; begin with a type, and you will find that you have created – nothing" (*S* 317). With these lines Fitzgerald may on some level be delineating the process of character development in any given story; he may also, perhaps, on another level, be admonishing not only himself but also his popular audience about the tendency to reduce characters to generalized types. At least as early as 1923, with the composition of "Dice, Brassknuckles & Guitar," he had begun to counter what had been a tendency at least in the first two Tarleton stories to rely heavily on stereotypes in the development of character. From the moment the reader encounters Jim Powell in "Dice" (and this is especially true if the reader has been acquainted with him in "The Jelly-Bean") it is clear that whatever preconceptions the reader has brought into the story are quite possibly suspect. Granted, Jim is described early in the story as "a southern gentleman" (*S* 238) and he does, in fact, have the manners associated in the popular imagination with that type, properly introducing himself and his body servant Hugo to Amanthis and referring to her throughout their exchanges by the title "mamm." However, the Jim Powell presented in "Dice" is not the Jim Powell of "The Jelly-Bean," the character whom Fitzgerald had described in that story as an idler, one who "might have been known in the indiscriminating North as a corner loafer" (*S* 143). The Jim Powell of "Dice" is energetic and entrepreneurial. He has planned to take his body servant into New York and earn money as a taxi driver. When this enterprise fails, largely due to the inadequacy of his car rather than lack of effort, he initiates another plan in which he establishes a school to instruct the young people of Southampton, New York, how to throw dice, use brass knuckles, and play the guitar. To this endeavor – granted, the idea of it, and even the story itself, is outrageous and absurd – he devotes a boundless energy that would be out of type and out of character for the old jelly-bean Jim Powell. In line with his "Southern" values, however, he does demonstrate great courage in forcibly ejecting Martin Van Vleck from of his jazz school when Van Vleck violates the rules against drinking on the premises, an act that results in Jim's having to close his school and in his being honor-bound to return the tuition he had collected, even though an injustice had been done to him. By the end of the story, it is true that Jim has become disenchanted with the members of Southampton society who have treated him badly, and at this point Fitzgerald regresses into stereotype, calling him "a child of the South – brooding was alien to his nature" (*S* 253). However, the reader would be right to question Holman's observation that Jim is finally heading "bitterly back to the South and to being a jelly-bean" (*S* 59). In any case, Fitzgerald brings into high relief Jim's paternalistic treatment of Hugo, having him in conversation with Amanthis refer to him, among other patronizing and demeaning terms, as "my boy Hugo" (239), a move that undercuts the honorable traits Jim displays by refunding the tuition for the jazz school. Here, perhaps, Fitzgerald is satirizing the blatant racism of privileged Southern whites toward African Americans. Certainly by the time of *The Great Gatsby* (1925) Fitzgerald was calling attention through Tom Buchanan to the "'Nordicist' and Anglo-Saxonist narrative of American history and … the racism it legitimized" – a narrative with which he was clearly familiar and seems to have begun increasingly to show discomfort.[8] Ultimately, throughout "Dice" Jim has shown himself to be too complex to be entirely predictable. Only two things seem certain at the end of the story: the Jim of "The Jelly-Bean" and "Dice" cannot be known through a simple stock phrase based on geographical stereotype, and at the heart of Jim the individual, regardless of where he is located at a given moment, there is a foundation of his morality that is built on honor, courtesy, and courage, those values that, to Fitzgerald, transcend place.

Fitzgerald addresses the idea of character delineation by "type" even more dramatically and intricately in his characterization of Amanthis Powell. Despite being geographically located in the North, Amanthis Powell may be associated with what Holman has suggested to be Fitzgerald's construction of the South – "a land of beauty and romance, of lost order, of tradition and dignity, and of a glorious past … [something] to be dreamed of and loved in youth, but … abandoned in maturity" – as delineated in the first of the two Tarleton stories, and yet she also defies this construction by performing actions that stand in direct contradiction to this construction. As Ronald Berman points out, "the color gold often appears in [Fitzgerald's] southern stories, suggesting a haunting beauty that deserves to be remembered."[9] Just as the color gold imbues Fitzgerald's Tarleton stories (as Berman suggests, most notably in "The Ice Palace"), so the color yellow is everywhere in evidence in "Dice." Early in the story the narrator remarks how "There was something enormously yellow about the whole scene – there was the sunlight, for instance, that was yellow, and the hammock was of the particularly hideous yellow peculiar to hammocks, and the girl's yellow hair was spread out upon the hammock in a sort of invidious comparison" (*S* 238). While in the earlier Tarleton stories the color gold suggests "a haunting beauty," here another, less burnished, shade of that same color appears to suggest that, in the North at least, such beauty is only surface; it is, in fact, a more "hideous" version of the color he had heretofore associated with the South. And yet, on another level, Fitzgerald may have been at least tacitly acknowledging that his *construction* of the South was losing its luster, for Amanthis is ultimately a character who shares the traits of Fitzgerald's most obvious female representation of the South, Sally Carrol Happer. Like Sally Carrol, Amanthis is first depicted in an indolent pose: While Sally Carrol "gazed out down sleepily" from an upper-story window (*S* 48), Amanthis "slept with her lips closed and her hands clasped behind her head" in a hammock (*S* 230). And just as Sally Carrol leads an impassive life in the South, so Amanthis "opened her left eye slightly to see June come in and then closed it and retired contentedly back into her dreams" (*S* 242). Both Sally Carrol and Amanthis suggest the indolence that Fitzgerald associated with the South, an indolence characteristic of a "life in death," of a "golden [or yellow] past."

Amanthis is a character capable of distinguishing human virtue, and Fitzgerald further associates her with his construction of the South with regard to the values of "tradition and dignity" that are part of the concept of *noblesse oblige*. In her assessment of Jim Powell as compared to her high-society compatriots, Amanthis finds him "better than all of them put together" (*S* 252) – a judgment that situates her morally in the camp of Nick Carraway. Her words reflect her ability to see outside the boundaries of social and economic status in order to judge Jim on his character, and his character is one driven by the intent to improve another's condition (albeit socially and, perhaps, economically). And yet, Amanthis defies Fitzgerald's construction of the South in her deceitful actions: She allows Jim to persist in the erroneous notion that she is not part of high society, but rather a woman from a lower social and economic class whose suitors are "promising young barbers from the neighboring village with somebody's late hair still clinging to their coat-sleeves" (*S* 241). She observes his actions with regard to his jazz school – actions he has taken in order to afford her entrance into high society – with baffled and detached amusement, and she abandons him for sub-debutante dances during much of their time in Southampton. In her prolonged deceit she is shown to be a character who is not the embodiment of Fitzgerald's construction of the South; in effect, she both is and is not: She is the construction and the antithesis of that construction, a complex character that defies easy categorization on a geographical level.

Ultimately, Fitzgerald's complex portraits of Amanthis and Jim, but particularly of Amanthis, suggest that neither can be typed in relation to geography, which in turn indicates Fitzgerald's growing realization that his symbolic structure of the South was breaking down. This realization is echoed in the opening lines of "The Rich Boy" and ultimately plays itself out in Fitzgerald's abandonment of the Southern symbolic structure in his satirical portrait of Andy in "The Last of the Belles." When Andy in "The Last of the Belles" realizes that Ailie will not marry him – as she says, "Oh, no, I couldn't marry you" (*S* 461) – Andy comes to this realization about the South: "All I could be sure of was this place that had once been so full of life and effort was gone, as if it had never existed, and that in another month Ailie would be gone, and the South would be empty for me forever" (*S* 663). This flash of insight appears to say more about Fitzgerald's understanding of his early romantic construction of the South and of southern "types" than it does about Andy's romantic inclinations toward Ailie.

What, then, is one to conclude about the importance of a Fitzgerald story that deconstructs regional stereotypes, particularly those closely related to his Southern stories, as does "Dice, Brassknuckles & Guitar," which clearly serves as a link between the other three stories in the Tarleton Trilogy? With regard to his Southern narrative the story marks the point at which Fitzgerald begins to abandon his previous construction of the South that is rooted in regional types to write stories that are more firmly grounded in individualized characters. By analogy, just as Fitzgerald needed to play out his indictment of the excesses of capitalism in the dress-rehearsal fantasy "The Diamond as Big as the Ritz" before treating its themes in a more subtle manner in "Winter Dreams" and *The Great Gatsby*, so he had to work in the mode of the absurd romantic comedy in a bridge story such as "Dice, Brassknuckles & Guitar" before settling into his more nuanced treatment of the reductive nature of regional stereotyping in "The Last of the Belles." As for those qualities that he will carry from his Southern narrative into his larger American narrative, he arguably leaves behind all types and calls out as negative such qualities as hypocrisy and inhumanity, while embracing, as John Kuehl has noted, certain universal values such as honor, courtesy, and courage – values that play well far beyond the bounds of Dixie.

NOTES

1 M. J. Bruccoli, S. F. Smith, and J. P. Kerr (eds.) *The Romantic Egoists* (New York: Charles Scribner's Sons, 1974), 97.
2 S. Donaldson, "Fitzgerald's Romance with the South," *Southern Literary Journal* 5 (Spring 1973), 3–17; 3. Subsequent references to this work are included in the text.
3 C. H. Holman, "Fitzgerald's Changes in the Southern Belle: The Tarleton Trilogy" in J. R. Bryer (ed.) *The Short Stories of F. Scott Fitzgerald: New Approaches in Criticism* (Madison, WI: University of Wisconsin Press, 1982), 53–64; 56. Subsequent references to this work are included in the text.
4 J. Kuehl, "Psychic Geography in 'The Ice Palace,'" in J. R. Bryer (ed.) *The Short Stories of F. Scott Fitzgerald: New Approaches in Criticism* (Madison: University of Wisconsin Press, 1982), 169–79; 174. Subsequent references to this work are included in the text.
5 A. H. Petry, *Fitzgerald's Craft of Short Fiction: The Collected Stories* (Ann Arbor, MI: UMI Research Press, 1989), 156.
6 H. K. Bullock, "The Southern and the Satirical in 'The Last of Belles'" in J. R. Bryer (ed.) *New Essays on F. Scott Fitzgerald's Neglected Stories* (Columbia, MO: University of Missouri Press, 1996), 130–37; 131.
7 Zelda Fitzgerald, "What Became of Our Flappers and Sheiks?" reprinted in M. J. Bruccoli, S. F. Smith, and J. P. Kerr (eds.) *The Romantic Egoists* (New York: Charles Scribner's Sons, 1974), 133.
8 See M. Nowlin (ed.), "Appendix E: Race and the National Culture, 1920–1925" in F. S. Fitzgerald, *The Great Gatsby* (Peterborough, Ontario: Broadview Press, 2007), 237.
9 R. Berman, "Fitzgerald's Intellectual Context" in K. Curnutt (ed.), *A Historical Guide to F. Scott Fitzgerald* (Oxford, UK: Oxford University Press, 2004), 69–84; 82.

PART III

Jazz Age Literary and Artistic Movements (1918–1929)

16

American Literary Realism

James Nagel

When F. Scott Fitzgerald sat down to begin the novel that would later be entitled *The Great Gatsby*, he was writing in the wake of the most powerful literary movement ever to invest the world of American letters. No coalescence of ideas, no set of artistic principles, had ever so energized national writers across a broader range of races and nationalities and religions. Underscoring the indigenous tendencies, the literary traditions of European immigrant groups emphasized a new fiction that dealt with everyday actualities, the conflicts and struggles at the center of the common lives of familiar human beings. The focus of this form of art was on social and ethical problems, and the literature that emerged from it was unabashedly anthropocentric, featuring ordinary characters in often mundane circumstances, struggling with the racial, economic, and moral issues of American life.

The term *realism* had its origins in the world of art and literature. It was first used in 1853 as part of a review of Honoré de Balzac published in the *Westminster Review* in England, and it was frequently used in Paris to describe paintings. Gustave Courbet established his Pavillon du Réalisme in 1855, and the following year Edmond Duranty established a review with the title *Réalisme*. Important novels soon appeared that embraced the aesthetic of mimeticism, of portraying life as it is commonly experienced, including Ivan Turgenev's *A Sportsman's Sketches* in 1852, followed by Leo Tolstoy's *Sevastopol* and Gustave Flaubert's *Madame Bovary* in 1856. What was so remarkable about this new trend in representation is that it seemed true to life, and the verisimilitude of fictional characters in these novels revealed something of the social norms of the age, the working-class taverns, dance halls, and tenements of the day. That kind of subject for literature quickly caught on in America. In 1867, for example, John William DeForest published *Miss Ravenel's Conversion from Secession to Loyalty*, which contained brilliantly graphic depictions of Civil War scenes, including images of mutilation and death. The following year, he published "The Great American Novel" in the *Nation*, an essay calling for works that captured life faithfully and showed the immense diversity of America, a true portrait of national life that presented accurate descriptions, regional dialects, and the varied conflicts that confronted ordinary characters in the course of their everyday lives.[1]

Such humble objectives originally involved a simple journalistic mimeticism, a slice of American middle-class life as it appeared in the light of common day, as William Dean Howells described it. But even such basic assumptions rested on more complex ideas. The physical world was available for empirical scrutiny, and the conclusions drawn from such investigation could be made the basis for art. The social and political situation confronting Americans during Reconstruction and its aftermath provided a rich context for depicting conflict and resolution, the standard plot line for stories and novels. The characters portrayed in such fiction normally understand the world they inhabit, and their works evolved to focus on a climatic decision point at which an ethical choice must be made about a course of action. Mark Twain's Huck Finn arrives at a moment in which he must decide either to turn Jim in to the authorities as a runaway slave, thus violating the human bond that has developed between them, or to contravene everything he has been taught about race relations by lying for Jim, even though he believes, given his religious training, that he will surely go to hell as a result. In William Dean Howells's *The Rise of Silas Lapham*, the climax presents the protagonist with an agonizing choice between going bankrupt by revealing the truth about the value of his paint factory or becoming wealthy by consummating the sale of what he knows is a worthless company. His choice involves not only his personal wealth but the stature of his family in society, the kinds of suitors his daughters can attract, and the future of the family in Boston. Realism often featured such dramatic moral choices. A more subtle development of this idea dealt with personal growth, with new realizations, acceptance of responsibility, a deepened compassion, or psychological change, a matter frequently at the center of stories and novels at the end of the nineteenth century.

Such personal subjects required a refined narrative method congruent with subtle themes, a humane point of view limited to the range of information that an individual could conceivably possess. Although some Realistic novels employed omniscience – Twain's *Pudd'nhead Wilson: A Tale* is an example – in general Realistic fiction tended to be told in first person or in third-person limited, tightly restricted to the speaker's personal experience, what was said to the narrator, or summary formulations putting together information from multiple sources, unified into a coherent pattern by the speaker's reflections and presented not as certain information but as the most sensible explanation of what happened. Realistic narration is thus unreliable, and it often conveys more about the narrator than it does about the events described; even when rendered with utmost sincerity, it can no more be relied upon for exact "truth" than can the everyday comments of friends describing their own experiences. Memory shapes experience into meaningful patterns, sorting out meaningless details, and it emphasizes those things that contribute to the central point of the recollection. Realistic narration must be interpreted in that vein, including Nick Carraway's summaries of events he did not personally witness but that were related to him by others, often with gaps that Nick fills in with conjecture, assumptions about character, or guesses. None of it can be taken as absolute truth; indeed, there are no omniscient passages in *The Great Gatsby*.

One other aspect of first-person narration is that the mode is nearly always retrospective, a person looking back on events and relating them in some meaningful pattern. This method thus necessarily presents a dual temporal scheme, the time of the telling distinct from that of the events. At the moment of narration, the speaker has had time to reflect on the meaning of things, to sort out conflicting emotions, to clarify the degree of personal responsibility or individual celebration for what happened. Thus, the emotions of the telling can be quite different from those of the action. The events related could be those of a joyous and intriguing courtship, for example, but the time of narration could be many years later, when the loved one has been dead for many years, and thus it contains deep veins of pain and nostalgia in addition to the pleasure of remembering happy moments. The time of telling is always more complex than the sequence of action, and the artistry of these matters is handled with subtlety and consummate skill in *The Great Gatsby*.

These two aspects of realism – a limited, humanistic method of narration and a central theme of personal growth and ethical maturity – are perhaps the most important contributions the movement made to the artistry and meaning of *The Great Gatsby*, one of the great first-person novels in American literature. Among works written in the mode, two previous books stand out: Twain's *Adventures of Huckleberry Finn* and Willa Cather's *My Ántonia*, both of which are told from a first-person retrospective stance by a narrator who is also a character in the action. *Huck Finn* is a marvel of artistic integrity, a *tour de force* of language and a tightly controlled monologue of things Huck did or said or thought about at the time of the action. However, the distance between the action and the relation of it is short, no more than roughly a month, since Tom is shot near the end of the novel and Huck comments that his friend's leg is almost healed at the time of the narration.[2] There is thus little time for reflection or the reassessment of things, and what Huck relates constitutes essentially what he was thinking at the time of the events, not his subsequent, more mature, appraisal of things. Although he grows morally through his affirmation of Jim's humanity, Huck as speaker seems very much the same person as Huck the character.

Not so Willa Cather's *My Ántonia*, much of which is told more than two decades after the events have taken place and which thus contains important reflections and implications derived from Jim Burden's life as a married lawyer in New York. He is a very different person at the time of the telling than he was in the early years in Nebraska. He begins as a young boy, orphaned by the death of his parents, on his way from Virginia to a farm he has never seen. He never fully embraces rural life, for unlike other boys his age, he does not work in the fields, tend animals, or mention the excruciating labor of harvest time, and he generally keeps to the house and his recreations, leaving his aging grandfather and the hired hands to do the work. When they move to town, he experiences the normal life of the community: going to school, learning to dance, spending time with friends. By the time he tells the story in the novel many years later, it is clear that although Jim succeeded in the halls of academe, studying at the University of Nebraska and earning a Harvard degree before going to law school, his personal life is essentially empty. His wife, an urban socialite, seems to mean little to him; what gives his emotional inner-being sustenance is his memory of the simple life he enjoyed growing up in Nebraska and his deep affection for the Bohemian girl on a neighboring farm, Ántonia Shimerda. He relates his personal experiences with her and fills in the gaps with what he has learned from other people, as when the Widow Douglas tells him what Ántonia revealed to her about the betrayal by Larry Donovan.[3]

These sections are not omniscient, but rather are summations by a narrator attempting to round out the story he is telling, precisely what Nick does in *The Great Gatsby*. Jim Burden's memories are shaped by his emotions, and he selects for the telling those scenes that advanced their relationship, those things that relate to his intellectual and personal growth, and those things that proved transitional in Ántonia's life. At the time of the telling, he has learned that economic rewards are ultimately unfulfilling, precisely the lesson Nick Carraway derives from his observation of

Jay Gatsby. Similar to Jim Burden's narrative stance, by the time Nick tells his story in the novel, he has relinquished his dream of becoming rich in the bond market, rejected the idea that his future was somehow to be found in the East rather than in the Midwest, and has quite obviously devoted a great deal of psychic energy to reflections on the meaning of what happened to Gatsby and the implications for his own life. In both *My Ántonia* and *The Great Gatsby*, the narrator is ultimately the most important character in the novel, the one who experiences internal growth, wrestles with ethical issues, and changes as a result of the action.

In comparison to Nick Carraway, Jay Gatsby is a static entity, frozen in his adolescent dream of Daisy as the fulfillment of his romantic longings, and he is unable to grow or change. He is precisely the same from his first appearance in the novel to his last, an idealist who concentrates on the appearances of life rather than on its substance. It is perfect that the pages in the books in his library have not been cut, and Gatsby has apparently read none of them. His attempt to win Daisy has not involved internal improvement, further education, or intellectual, moral, or social transformations. He sustains the program he embraced as a child reading about Hopalong Cassidy, and he has devoted his life to the quixotic quest to secure Daisy and a place in cultivated society all in one grand gesture. He is oblivious to her superficiality, her callous emphasis on money, and her lack of genuine commitment to either him or her husband. Ultimately, she is unworthy of his profound devotion.

The basics of the novel are simple; the subtleties are much more complex. Nick is narrating in 1923 and, perhaps 1924, back in the Midwest, probably in his hometown of St. Paul, and the core of what he can relate takes place in a period of three months in 1922, from his dinner with the Buchanans in East Egg in early June to Gatsby's funeral in early September and Nick's departure from the East in October. Everything he speaks of prior to that he has learned from someone else, often different versions from two or more people. Jordan Baker, Gatsby, and Daisy all tell him parts of the romance in 1917, for example, and his reflections on the meaning of that courtship over the last two years allow him to present a coherent version of it. It is not the truth; it is not omniscient, as many critics have assumed. It is Nick's attempt to make sense of the most remarkable series of events he has ever encountered. Time is thus a central issue in several senses, in the acquisition of information, in the course of events, in the opportunity to understand and order the meaning of things. Nick has learned that the passage of time brings change, the inexorable mutability of life, and with transformation comes bewilderment and a sense of loss, feelings that Nick attempts to sort out in the course of the telling.

From the very beginning Nick makes it clear that his primary subject is himself. He does not start his narrative with Gatsby, who, after all, has been dead for two years. It is Nick who matters at the time of the telling, and his assessment of Gatsby's character apparently means a great deal to him, even though they were quite different people. Gatsby was an impoverished child who struggled through a hardscrabble early life to find financial success after his rejection by Daisy. Nick was born to privilege, to a father with a Yale education who could afford to send his son to the finest prep schools in the East and to Yale for his undergraduate years and to bankroll Nick's foray into the bond market. He emerges, as Scott Donaldson has demonstrated, as something of a snob, highly judgmental of the people around him, condescending to social inferiors, and oblivious to his father's admonition that not everyone has had his advantages.[4] The opening chapter is essentially a definition of self, and much of Nick's consideration of Gatsby's life is an attempt to clarify what he has become as a person. It is significant that he has little to say about his adventures in World War I or in Europe, despite the fact that millions of people would look back on that period as the most dramatic and meaningful experience of their lives. Rather, the implication is that his brief exposure to Gatsby is what changed him, what informs him as a human being. Only now, at the time of the telling, can he appreciate that he abhorred Gatsby's pretenses and garish display of wealth but admired the fact that he had "some heightened sensitivity to the promises of life," an awareness Nick did not possess upon their first meeting (*GG* 6).

Nick often refers to "now," the time of the telling, differentiating it from "then," the time of the action. In chapter 4, for example, he reflects on the list of visitors to Gatsby's house he maintained in 1922 on an old train schedule: "It is an old time-table now, disintegrating at its folds and headed 'This schedule in effect July 5th, 1922'" (*GG* 49). He is self-consciously writing his narrative, for he reflects at one point that "reading over what I have written so far" he fears he has given a false impression that only the parties occupied his time (*GG* 46). His memory is good but uncertain: "Clarence Endive was from East Egg, as I remember" (*GG* 49), and there was a man who was "a prince of something whom we called Duke and whose name, if I ever knew it, I have forgotten" (*GG* 51). Epistemological uncertainty is a hallmark of realism, which fundamentally limits access to reliable information. Thus, in chapter 6, when Nick presents his overview of Gatsby's early life with Dan Cody, his summation must be read not as a shift to an omniscient frame of reference but as a generalization of things Nick has been told. He makes clear, in a later passage, that this is the case, that Gatsby "told me all this very much later" (*GG* 79). In chapter 8, just after Myrtle was killed, Gatsby again shared this information with Nick: "It was this night that he told me the strange story of his youth with Dan Cody" (*GG* 115). After Gatsby is killed, Wolfsheim reminisces about the young Gatsby with Nick, as does Mr. Gatz, when he arrives for his son's funeral. All of those details, in reflection, merge with other accounts to form Nick's sense of his friend's life. Similarly, when Nick relates what seems to be privileged knowledge about what happened in Wilson's garage after the accident, he is synthesizing what he learned from the testimony of Michaelis at the inquest, what George Wilson shared with him later, what Myrtle's sister, Catherine, said when she was questioned, and what Gatsby told him about the accident itself (*GG* 127). His comments in the conclusion about Gatsby's death are formulated as speculation, as Nick's imaginative reconstruction of what "probably" happened, not as the unquestionable utterings of an omniscient mind. He thinks of Gatsby waiting for a phone call from Daisy assuring him that she arrived home safely the night of the accident. Nick conjectures that "I have an idea that Gatsby himself didn't believe it would come and perhaps he no longer cared. If that was true he must have felt that he had lost the old warm world, paid a high price for living too long with a single dream" (*GG* 126). It is a rather poetic formulation for a bond salesman.

Some of what he knows he learned from the chauffeur; the rest is constructed from bits and pieces of information and from conjecture. None of the narration is spoken with authority. Nick tells his novel in the same way Jim Burden tells his, recalling experience and synthesizing what was told to him and reformulating it into his own narrative, complete with imaginative elements. Thus, in the tradition of the best of Realistic fiction, *The Great Gatsby* has narrative integrity, consistency, and unity. All of it is limited, unreliable, and profoundly human recollection, speculation, and summation by Nick. To tell the story of Gatsby, he needs to create a coherent pattern in the events, a plot with a dramatic beginning, intriguing development, and a tragic ending, but all of it is shaped by his attempt to tell a compelling narrative.

The central issues in the novel resonate with themes from the tradition of American realism, which was built on the assumption that people are free moral entities who are influenced to some extent by environment, genetics, and socioeconomic circumstances but who nevertheless retain ethical agency. They are thus able to shape themselves, and they must take responsibility for the decisions they make, unlike Naturalistic characters, who are driven by external forces beyond their control or comprehension. Realistic characters are free to engage the world as they wish, and in this regard Jay Gatsby is one of the most intriguing characters in literary history. He was born on a farm in North Dakota, and early on he constructed a program for self-improvement based on Benjamin Franklin's scheme in his autobiography. Gatsby, largely uneducated despite his brief sojourn at Oxford, seems to understand only the surface of the American Dream and Franklin's plan to achieve it. As Kirk Curnutt has perceptively pointed out, Franklin's plan focused on the development of inner character, including humility, discipline, and the world of ideas. Gatsby, on the other hand, stresses only appearances: clothing, speech, and ostentatious wealth. In Curnutt's words, "His ultimate goal is to have his existence validated by the recognition of others. What he fails to comprehend is that the attention that the mystique of personality generates is transitory ... His real desire – to be accepted by the wealthy world that Daisy represents – cannot be achieved through personality."[5] Had Gatsby actually understood the American Dream, he would have embarked on a very different program.

The concept that John Winthrop envisioned in 1630 in establishing a society in New England was a land of economic opportunity, to be sure, for worldly success was perceived as an expression of God's approval, but he also called upon his flock to live humbly, to contribute to the welfare of the community, and to emphasize justice and mercy.[6] As he made clear in his "A Model of Christian Charity," those were to be the central elements of his "city upon a hill." The corruption of the objectives of the American Dream to material acquisition grasps only the most superficial aspects of the concept. Gatsby is guilty of this simplification. He gains wealth without acquiring knowledge or wisdom. He has a large library, but he has an extremely limited frame of reference, unlike Nick Carraway, and his thinking is limited almost exclusively to current events, the bond market, and his romance with Daisy. Within the tradition of American realism, he is an abject failure. He has not learned what Silas Lapham did in his novel: that moral stature is ultimately more important than economic and social standing. He does not grow in his grasp of ethical issues, as does Huck. He wishes to return to the past and change events, rather than reflecting on the meaning of the past, as does Jim Burden. Gatsby commits his life to an idealistic vision of a romance with Daisy, through which he could enter the privileged social class at the same time as he realized emotional fulfillment, but he never grasps that Daisy is not worthy of his idealism, something she demonstrates when she runs away after the accident, leaving Gatsby to take responsibility. Her emotional commitments are as superficial as the other areas of her life. Tragically, Gatsby dies with his romantic dreams intact.

From a Realistic perspective, Gatsby is responsible for what he made of himself, an issue at the center of Nick Carraway's contemplation of the meaning of the summer of 1922. Nick is also chasing the American Dream, although he has a far more profound response to the quest. For Gatsby, the only objective is Daisy, and his obsession with money is as a means rather than an end. For his part, Nick seems little interested in the bond business that employs him: he says almost nothing about it in the entire novel. Instead, he is more concerned with the inner lives of the other characters, with their values, emotional commitments, and personal dilemmas. Gatsby's life was built on external appearances; Nick's is focused on personal psychology, those needs that drive the action.[7] One of his first observations about Tom Buchanan is that he "would drift on forever seeking a little wistfully for the dramatic turbulence of some irrecoverable football game" (*GG* 9). It is an unusually perceptive awareness for a bond salesman, and Nick does not remain one very long. Throughout the parties at the center of the first three chapters, Nick stresses the behavior and motivation of the people around him, assessing their character, and he seems to be the only person in the novel with what Richard Lehan calls "an interiority of self, the only character who internalizes this strange and fascinating world."[8] Part of the motivation for this stance is that Nick is fundamentally inchoate, still forming himself, and thus is acutely aware of what guides the lives of others. The other reason is that this summer was transformative for him: After his months in the East, he reverses course and returns to a quiet life in the Midwest, where he is when, over the last year or more, he has synthesized enough of the meaning of the events to tell his story in a coherent fashion.

Always somehow at the center of the action, Nick is the only one who knows about Tom and Myrtle, discovers that Daisy was driving the "death car," hears about Gatsby's early life, knows Catherine lied at the inquest about Myrtle's marriage, and can implicate Tom in the chain of events that led to Gatsby's murder and Wilson's suicide. He carries a heavy moral burden by the end of the novel, one with enough specific gravity to draw his mind to it persistently. He is the only one who understands Gatsby, his idealistic longing, his optimism, his dreams. Nick seems to admire Gatsby's commitment to "the orgastic future that year by year recedes before us" (*GG* 141), but Nick's cynicism makes it difficult for him to share in it. Rather, he knows life will be difficult, offering a daunting quest with disappointment and disillusionment, something he faces with resignation. That is the meaning of the nautical metaphor he offers as a conclusion: "So we beat on, boats against the current, borne back ceaselessly into the past" (*GG* 141). To "beat" is to sail into the wind at an angle, and in this case there is also a current holding back progress, so much so that instead of moving forward the boat is swept ever backward, just as Nick's mind is brought back to the events of 1922. He needs to get on with his life, and his telling of the story would seem to be a means to clear away what has preoccupied him for so many months to allow him to do so. He needs to move forward into his future, into a richer and more humanistic appreciation of life than what he brought with him on his sojourn East, and that larger existence will constitute Gatsby's final gift to him, the real meaning of his fragile greatness.

NOTES

1 J. W. DeForest, "The Great American Novel," *Nation* 6 (January 9, 1868), 27–29.
2 M. Twain, *Adventures of Huckleberry Finn* (Berkeley, CA: University of California Press, 1988), 362.
3 W. Cather, *My Ántonia* (New York: Penguin, 1994), 233.
4 S. Donaldson, "The Trouble with Nick" in S. Donaldson (ed.), *Critical Essays on F. Scott Fitzgerald's* The Great Gatsby (Boston: G. K. Hall, 1984), 131–39.
5 K. Curnutt, "All That Jazz: Defining Modernity and Milieu" in J. R. Bryer and N. P. VanArsdale (eds.), *Approaches to Teaching Fitzgerald's* The Great Gatsby (New York: The Modern Language Association, 2009), 40–49; 42–43.
6 J. Winthrop, "A Model of Christian Charity," *Old South Leaflet No. 207*, S. E. Morrison, ed. (Boston: Old South Meetinghouse, 1916).
7 I am indebted here to J. B. Chambers, *The Novels of F. Scott Fitzgerald* (New York: St. Martin's Press, 1989), 111.
8 R. Lehan, The Great Gatsby: *The Limits of Wonder* (Boston: Twayne, 1990), 111.

17

Naturalism and High Modernism

Michael Nowlin

F. Scott Fitzgerald's fiction was infused with the spirit of modernism from the outset. It documented a cultural revolution of sorts from the point of view of a "new generation grown up to find all Gods dead, all wars fought, all faiths in man shaken," in the view of its putative representative, the hero of Fitzgerald's autobiographical first novel *This Side of Paradise* (*TSOP* 260). And it did so in a relatively *au courant*, even formally experimental manner. Witness the mélange of forms and styles in that novel and *The Beautiful and Damned*: echoes of *fin de siècle* aestheticism and decadence; the intrusion of dramatic form, poetry, satire, and symbolic motifs into a predominately realistic framework. But there is a showy novelty about Fitzgerald's play with novelistic convention in his first two novels. After reading *This Side of Paradise*, his friend and intellectual mentor, Edmund Wilson, advised Fitzgerald to "tighten up [his] artistic conscience" and "pay a little more attention to form"; otherwise, he was on track to "become a very popular trashy novelist without much difficulty."[1] That he took Wilson's advice to heart accounts in good part for the immense qualitative difference between *This Side of Paradise* and *The Great Gatsby*. Before doing so, however, he came under the spell of the critic H. L. Mencken, who also spurred him on toward greater artistic seriousness, but by the different route that led to *The Beautiful and Damned*. That "false lead," as he came to call it, which brought his work closer to literary naturalism, promised to confine him to the ranks of provincial literary luminaries (*C* 139). Recognizing his error and resuming the course pointed out to him by Wilson, he left the United States for the more cosmopolitan milieu of France and managed to write what he thought "about the best American novel ever written" (*S&M* 76), one, in the telling praise of William Curtis's review, that "can be put on the same book shelf with the best of London, Vienna, Paris, or Rome."[2]

F. Scott Fitzgerald became the great writer he is because he followed an artistic trajectory toward what we have come to call high modernism, and his flirtation with and repudiation of naturalism looks in hindsight to have been a crucial step along the way. These terms must be used with due reserve for a number of reasons: First and foremost, Fitzgerald himself rarely used them (in a 1923 review he referred, somewhat oxymoronically, to Sherwood Anderson's "transcendental naturalism"[3]); second, the term *naturalism* was often used interchangeably with *realism* in popular American criticism; third, naturalism, like realism, is an early and persistent mode of modernism that inadvertently paved the way for its displacement by more radical, anti-mimetic modes; and finally, high modernism is a canon-making term that confers distinction on the select body of writings it purports to classify, which would explain why some "high modernist" writing aligns neatly with a certain strand of realism and some with various esoteric tendencies launched by French symbolism.[4] Nonetheless, because the high modernist canon has been in good part defined by the devaluation of naturalism, the terms help us discern and describe crucial aesthetic choices Fitzgerald made in the interest of achieving what he took to be the highest form of success the literary field affords: variously put, "to be endorsed by the intellectually élite," as he would have it; to have crossed over "into the artist class" (*S&M* 47), as his friend John Peale Bishop wrote him; and to have made it "into the cool cloisters of the literary elect," in the words of Curtis's review (Curtis 68). Fitzgerald's 1925 triumph, in this respect, derived in good part from the way he positioned himself from roughly mid-1922 onward in relation to what he took to be the dominant tendencies of homegrown American fiction, on the one hand, and what he took to be the dominant tendencies on the international literary stage, on the other.

The national literature at its most promising came to be represented by Mencken, under whose sway Fitzgerald fell soon after placing his first story in the *Smart Set* in 1919. He quickly paid tribute to him in a passage inserted into the proofs of *This Side of Paradise* detailing Amory Blaine's developing literary tastes: he was "rather surprised by his discovery through a critic named Mencken of several excellent American novels: [Frank Norris's] 'Vandover and the Brute,' [Harold Frederic's] 'The Damnation of Theron Ware,' and [Theodore Dreiser's] 'Jennie Gerhardt.'" (*TSOP* 195). This snapshot of Mencken making his impact would seem to justify the assumption that Mencken spoke for a naturalist "school" and that Fitzgerald discovered in it the most promising direction for contemporary American fiction. Naturalism became influentially identified with the notorious novels of Dreiser in a 1915 essay by Stuart P. Sherman, who decried both, and Mencken quickly became Dreiser's most prominent champion.[5] Mencken thought him the leading light of a still destitute American literature; alongside the likes of Charles G. Norris and Sherwood Anderson he was treading in the same path earlier founded by Frank Norris – the path most literary historians identify with naturalism.[6]

Mencken's tastes were in fact far more catholic than the popular association of him with naturalism would suggest, and his impact on *The Beautiful and Damned* is far more manifest in its irreverent, satirical attitude toward contemporary American pieties. Neither he nor Fitzgerald was committed to literary naturalism's first article of faith, that human behavior was radically determined by the forces of heredity and environment, nor to its social Darwinist premise that civilized human beings were but thinly veiled beasts (Cowley 429–32). Naturalism, more broadly construed, was but a grittier, more aggressively pessimistic mode of realism. Novels in this vein tended to be long and sprawling (*The Beautiful and Damned* is Fitzgerald's longest, over twice the length of *Gatsby*) and pretend via the traditional omniscient narrator to a systematic grasp of contemporary social reality, as in this heavy-handed passage toward the end of *The Beautiful and Damned*:

> It was November, Indian summer rather, and a warm, warm night – which was unnecessary, for the work of the summer was done. Babe Ruth had smashed the home-run record for the first time and Jack Dempsey had broken Jess Willard's cheek-bone out in Ohio. Over in Europe the usual number of children had swollen stomachs from starvation, and the diplomats were at their customary business of making the world safe for new wars. In New York City the proletariat were being "disciplined," and the odds on Harvard were generally quoted at five to three. Peace had come down in earnest, the beginning of new days. (*B&D* 323)

Naturalistic fiction above all stood out for its shock value – perfect for offending the sensibilities of latter-day puritans – due to its sordid subject matter, sexual frankness, and general interest in human degradation. Fitzgerald's fiancée, Zelda Sayre, to whom he sent a copy of Frank Norris's *McTeague* just before *This Side of Paradise* came out, was notably unimpressed by it: "All authors who want to make things true to life make them *smell bad* – like McTeague's room – and that's my most sensitive sense. I do hope you'll never be a realist – one of those kind that thinks being ugly is being forceful – " (*C* 52). In retrospect, Fitzgerald's tastes were always more in harmony with his most important female reader's than they were with Mencken's. And to the extent that Zelda helped him gauge the sensibility of his popular, "feminine" readership, he tended to excuse himself before such readers when he became too much the realist: hence his description of "May Day" in the table of contents for *Tales of the Jazz Age* as "a somewhat unpleasant tale" (*TJA* 6). The naturalistic tropes somewhat forcefully incorporated into his early work might be recognized by the almost visceral sensual revulsion they would most likely arouse in the female reader, an effect he risked in order to impress a predominately masculine literary elite.

The influence of naturalism makes itself felt most obviously in Fitzgerald's ruthless depiction of the decline of the preciously self-absorbed Anthony and Gloria Patch in the final third of the novel. Fitzgerald had clearly embraced Mencken's dictum that "character in decay is … the theme of the great bulk of superior fiction,"[7] which is why, as Wilson damningly put it in his 1922 profile of Fitzgerald, he "ruined his characters wholesale with a set of catastrophes so arbitrary that beside them, the worst perversities of Hardy were like the working of natural laws."[8] But literary naturalism pervades *The Beautiful and Damned* more subtly through one of its most recognizable tropes – the city as slum, and the slum as jungle or zoo – which is used to distinguish Anthony and his wife from the masses beneath them.

In a section aptly subtitled "Breath of the Cave," Anthony's initially romantic sense of New York City's sounds is jarred by "a new note," "the noise of a woman's laughter," a woman he assumes must be a "servant-maid with her fellow": "Try as he might to strangle his reaction, some animal quality in that unrestrained laughter had grasped at his imagination, and for the first time in four months aroused his old aversion and horror toward all the business of life." Recoiling, he yearns to be "miles above the cities, and to live serene and detached back in the corners of his mind" (*B&D* 129–30). He will later enjoy a modest version of this condition while riding on the elevated from the Bronx,

> above and past half a hundred cheerful sweating streets of the upper East Side, each one passing the car-window like the space between the spokes of a gigantic wheel, each one with its vigorous colorful revelation of poor children swarming in feverish activity like vivid ants in alleys of red sand. From the tenement windows leaned rotund, moon-shaped mothers, as constellations of this sordid heaven; women like dark imperfect jewels, women like vegetables, women like great bags of abominable laundry. (*B&D* 237)

Safe above this world, Anthony can "feel as though it's a performance being staged for me," but it becomes more threatening when he associates it with the "slow, upward creep" of Jewish immigrants, with their "hawk's eyes and a bee's attention to detail" (*B&D* 237). For Gloria, the world of naturalism beckons through the reproductive instinct, which, as a "practicing Nietzschean," she repudiates: "The reality, the earthiness, the intolerable sentiment of child-bearing, the menace to her beauty – had appalled her ... her ironic soul whispered that motherhood was also the privilege of the female baboon" (*B&D* 324). Her refusal to be but an animal correlates with her refusal to be part of that common herd of humanity "swarming like rats, chattering like apes, smelling all like hell ... monkeys! Or lice, I suppose" (*B&D* 326).

The ironic thrust of the novel more often than not justifies her revulsion, even as Fitzgerald also wants to treat ironically Gloria and Anthony's snobbish, fruitless, and ultimately self-destructive detachment from both "nature" and the contemporary American scene. He seems to share their disdain for the fictional novelist Richard Caramel's "The Demon Lover," which exploits the prurient vogue for gritty realism by dealing with "a Don Juan of the New York slums," and gets duly praised for its descriptions of "the atavistic and unsubtle reactions of that section of society" (*B&D* 123). *The Beautiful and Damned*, by contrast, is about the effort of its characters to keep "that section of society" at bay. It is as though Anthony and Gloria are resisting as best they can the universe of the naturalist novel; in the end, after being dragged through the gutter, they triumph – but in the grimly pyrrhic way proper to it. The "Holy Ghost of this later day," as Fitzgerald calls "irony" in the first sentence of his novel (*B&D* 11), their irony remains the uncertainly handled content of *The Beautiful and Damned*, undercut finally by a heavy-handedly ironic event. Fitzgerald had not yet found a way to make his irony a more rigorously impersonal matter of form.

In the summer of 1922, Fitzgerald gave Perkins an early hint of artistic ambitions that would take him far beyond the achievement of his first two novels: "I want to write something *new* – something extraordinary and beautiful and simple + intricately patterned" (*C* 112). The emphasis on that word "new" suggests he had caught the spirit of a more international modernism being guided by American expatriates such as Ezra Pound and Gertrude Stein, and the desire to create something "intricately patterned" suggests a newfound inclination toward formal abstraction. Fitzgerald's reading of James Joyce's *Ulysses* and Stein's *Three Lives* under the tutelage of Wilson during that summer likely lay behind this announcement.[9] His declaration to Thomas Boyd in the spring of 1923 that he would "never write another document-novel" but had "decided to be a pure artist + experiment in form and emotion" followed consistently from this (*C* 126). In repudiating the "document-novel," as good a term as any for covering the common tendency of contemporary American realism and naturalism, he was signaling his critical grasp of two problematic assumptions behind it: that the novelist's task is but to document a self-evidently available "reality," and that the documentation of American "reality" will of itself produce good American literature.

His work in progress, he wrote Moran Tudury a year later, was to be "a new thinking out of the idea of illusion" (*C* 139), which entailed finding the right form for representing the ways in which desire, sensual perception, belief, and, of course, language constitute the "real." By the time he was writing *The Great Gatsby*, he was deeply conversant with what made for the rarest achievements of modern fiction: the rendering of reality as a discipline of style that, in Conrad's words, "should carry its justification in every line."[10] Responding to Mencken's lukewarm review of the novel in the spring of 1925, he underscored the extent to which he had left formally careless realism – and along with this, his deference to Mencken's critical authority. "Despite your admiration for Conrad," he wrote his former hero, "you have lately – perhaps in reaction against the merely well-made novels of James' imitators – become used to the formless. It is in protest against my own formless two novels, and Lewis' and Dos Passos' that this was written" (*LL* 110). His break from the "school" of Mencken was sealed with the 1926 essay "How to Waste Material: A Note on My Generation," in which he criticized his former hero for having "begotten a family of hammer and tongs men – insensitive, suspicious of glamour, preoccupied exclusively with the external, the contemptible, the 'national' and the drab ... men who manufactured enthusiasm when each new mass of raw data was dumped on the literary platform – mistaking incoherence for vitality, chaos for vitality."[11]

Fitzgerald's departure from this family – signaled most obviously by his decision to join his fellow expatriates in France – enabled him to rediscover the virtues of a higher realist vein going back to Gustave Flaubert, running through Henry James and Joseph Conrad, and finding its "modernist" manifestation in the experimental work of Stein and Joyce. Wilson wrote of *Ulysses* that its pages were "probably the most completely 'written' ... to be seen in any novel since Flaubert,"[12] and nothing more readily justifies putting *The Great Gatsby* on the same shelf with modernist landmarks like *Three Lives* and *Ulysses*, as well as antecedents like *Madame Bovary*, *Nostromo*, and *The Ambassadors*, than its meticulous composition and rigorous commitment to *le mot juste*. Wilson repeatedly noted Flaubert's influence on Joyce in his review of *Ulysses* (though the Flaubert of *Madame Bovary*, not of *Bouvard et Pécuchet*; he thought Joyce's stylistic parodies and departures from novelistic convention willfully perverse). He also undoubtedly recognized Stein's debt to *Trois Contes*. He probably helped Fitzgerald see that his Mencken-influenced enthusiasm for Conrad should logically entail an enthusiasm for Flaubert and James. When in a 1923 public letter Fitzgerald declared Conrad's *Nostromo* the novel he would most like to have written, he insisted it was "the greatest novel since 'Vanity Fair' (possibly excluding 'Madame Bovary')" (Bruccoli and Bryer 168). His estimate of James's importance seems to have risen steadily between 1921 and 1925. Both Carl Van Vechten and Gilbert Seldes affiliated Fitzgerald with James in their favorable reviews of *The Great Gatsby*, and Fitzgerald was clearly elated when T. S. Eliot wrote him saying it represented "the first step that American fiction has taken since Henry James" (*CU* 310). But Flaubert remained more of a touchstone for him. Late in his career he tried to mentor Thomas Wolfe into becoming a more "conscious artist" by recalling him to "the novel of selected incidents," which artfully depends on judicious omissions and understatement: so "Mme Bovary becomes eternal while Zola already rocks with age" (*LL* 332). Near the end of his life he described his work-in-progress, *The Love of the Last Tycoon* as "a novel a la Flaubert without 'ideas' but only people moved singly and in mass through what I hope are authentic moods" (*LL* 470).

The "sustained imagination of a sincere and yet radiant world" (*S&M* 70) that he aimed for with *The Great Gatsby* depended heavily on the invention of Nick Carraway as a solution to problems with point of view and ironic distance that dog his earlier work. After reading the manuscript, Max Perkins congratulated him for having "adopted exactly the right method of telling it, that of employing a narrator who is more of a spectator than an actor: this puts the reader upon a point of observation on a higher level than that on which the characters stand and at a distance that gives perspective. In no other way could your irony have been so immensely effective" (*S&M* 82). Like many a subsequent reader, Perkins was content to overlook what might otherwise strike one as a flaw in the method, the fact of Nick's having literally written the novel before us ("Reading over what I have written so far," writes Nick toward the end of chapter 3, interrupting his narrative about Gatsby to tell us more about himself) (*GG* 46). What this means is that we must attribute *The Great Gatsby*'s literary virtuosity to this rather staid, provincial narrator, writing from his father's home rather than from the expatriate's world elsewhere. The perennial argument that Fitzgerald stands at an ironic distance from Nick is difficult to square with the fact that it is precisely through him that Fitzgerald came closest to achieving the stylistic impersonality that was one of modernism's aesthetic imperatives. If we readily forget that Nick the character is supposed to have written such magnificent passages as the novel's visionary conclusion about the Dutch sailors encountering the "fresh, green breast of the new world" (*GG* 140), it is because at such moments his prosaic actuality gets refined away by the force of Fitzgerald's poetry.

What aligns *The Great Gatsby* with the best modernist fiction is the formal pressure it brings to bear on the illusions, the narratives, and indeed the very language of the nineteenth century, or a whole bygone era displaced by a spectacular modernity in which, as Nick thinks after witnessing African Americans being driven by a white chauffeur across Blackwell's Island, "anything can happen ... Even Gatsby could happen, without any particular wonder" (*GG* 55). Gatsby's story is in many respects the simplest: A poor boy from the provinces sets out to make his fortune and win the girl of his dreams, only to be thwarted by entrenched social forces and his own moral innocence. It is inspired by such homegrown products as the autobiography of Benjamin Franklin and the novels of Horatio Alger, but it owes its deeper shape and tenor to the European *Bildungsroman*, as Lionel Trilling pointed out some time ago.[13] It is predicated on those increasingly bankrupt myths of the New World, the frontier, the Puritan work ethic, romantic self-fashioning, romantic love, material progress, and historical emancipation, all of which nonetheless retain their power to issue in facts – at once banal, grotesque, and gorgeous. Its complexity stems almost exclusively from Fitzgerald's masterful treatment, in which the problem of perspective is paramount.

If Nick's higher point of observation "gives perspective," as Perkins admiringly noted, it also orchestrates a play of discordant perspectives and makes the opposition between blindness and insight the novel's leading leitmotif. Nick not only constructs his story in impressionistic fashion, à la Conrad, revealing his titular hero more or less as he came to know him, with the help of fragmentary contributions from Jordan Baker, Meyer Wolfsheim, Gatsby's father, and, of course, Gatsby himself; he allows for dissonances within his own perspective. How else can we account for the spell cast upon him by a man "who represented everything for which I have an unaffected scorn"? Nick affects a certain skeptical aloofness through much of the novel, but "two finger bowls of champagne" are enough to transform Gatsby's gaudy summer parties "into something significant, elemental, and profound." Gatsby's "sentimentality" appalls him, but it also reminds him of "something – an elusive rhythm, a fragment of lost words ... heard somewhere a long time ago," leaving this apparent wordsmith hauntingly speechless. Gatsby's seduction of Daisy is figured as the descent of a godlike hero to impregnate with "unutterable visions" a "perishable" flower-like woman; but it is later more realistically recalled as a moment of carnal opportunism, with the "penniless young man without a past" taking the Southern belle "ravenously and unscrupulously ... because he had no real right to touch her hand." Toward the end of the novel, Nick confesses the extent to which the East he had set out to make it in "had always for me a quality of distortion," visiting him in his dreams as "a night scene by El Greco," Picasso's favorite old master.[14] Nick's testimony to the instability, ambiguity, and vulnerability to distortion inherent in even so "honest" a perspective as his own is reinforced throughout by the novel's contrapuntal recurrence to the theme: in the discrepant views of West and East Egg suggested by gulls flying overhead and "wingless" denizens; in the eyes of T. J. Eckleburg, which suggest both divine judgment and the two-dimensional illusions of a billboard; in Owl Eyes's amazement at a fraud so transparent it seems genuine; in Gatsby's disillusioned discovery of a "new world, material without being real"; in the very different "new world" that "flowered once for Dutch sailors' eyes."[15]

Such details but hint at the extent to which *The Great Gatsby* meets Fitzgerald's goal of writing something "intricately patterned." His metaphor supports Joseph Frank's characterization of modernist literature in terms of its "spatial form," "the continual reference and cross reference of images and symbols that must be referred to each other spatially throughout the time-act of reading."[16] In a novel about the impossibility of recapturing life's glorious moments, such patterning puts pressure on the reader to remember, to slow down and savor verbal harmonies and counterpoints, above all to re-read and thereby repeat the experience of Gatsby's triumph and downfall. *The Great Gatsby*'s design may be more readily accessible to readers than those of *Ulysses* or Eliot's *The Waste Land*, but it is arguably as capacious relative to its scale. Fitzgerald's prose shifts seamlessly between registers, dryly connotative for the most part, but suddenly lyrical as occasion demands: "The lights grow brighter as the earth lurches away from the sun, and now the orchestra is playing yellow cocktail music, and the opera of voices pitches a key higher." It discovers the mythological in the actual: a Siren's voice in a voice that "sounds like money"; a "valley of ashes" in the outskirts of Queens; a Christ-like mission run aground against the ambiguities of the "Father's business, the service of a vast, vulgar and meretricious beauty." In the catalogue of Gatsby's guests, we get a deadpan performance worthy of Flaubert. And with his remarkably fine ear, Nick gives considerable rein to the uncanny poetry in the American vernacular: "It's all scientific stuff; it's been proved" (Tom); "The only *crazy* I was was when I married him" (Myrtle); "He went to Oggsford College in England. You know Oggsford College?" (Wolfsheim); "you see, I carry on a little business on the side, a sort of side line, you understand" (Gatsby); "Jimmy always liked it better down East" (Mr. Gatz).[17] Finally, the novel incorporates and pays a backhanded homage throughout to the language of popular, expressive forms: photography, advertising, popular song, cinema, and, of course, jazz. Fitzgerald clearly had gained a far steadier handle than he held in *The Beautiful and Damned* on a cultural landscape that challenged the novel's representational capacities and artistic supremacy, although in both novels that landscape was notably marked by the creative and entrepreneurial energies of African Americans and Jewish immigrants.

The Great Gatsby brought Fitzgerald the confidence to imagine himself not just the leading American novelist of his time, but one of the great novelists on the international stage. This entailed conceiving his subsequent work in distinctly "modernist" terms. "The happiest thought I have is of my new novel," he wrote Perkins from Paris in May 1925: "it is something really NEW in form, idea, structure – the model for the age that Joyce and Stien are looking for, that Conrad didn't find" (*LL* 108). Fitzgerald's arrival at the center of modernist cultural production perhaps unfortunately brought with it expectations he would prove unable to meet. The novel that finally appeared as *Tender Is the Night* in 1934, for all its brilliance, hardly fits the bill of a "really NEW ... model for the age," and indeed partly harks back to naturalism in its harrowing portrait of alcoholism and its ominous description of Dick Diver as a civilized man "swayed and driven as an animal" (*TITN* 119). Notwithstanding Fitzgerald's devotion to Stein, whom he befriended in the spring of 1925, he found himself aghast at the direction of her magnum opus *The Making of Americans*, which he initially tried to interest Perkins in before conceding that it was unintelligible (*LL* 85, 132). And for all his tributes to Joyce, there is no record of any enthusiasm for the "Work in Progress" that became *Finnegans Wake*. He would shy away from Stein and Joyce's extreme experimentation, however drawn he might be to the rhetoric justifying such work and the prestige attached to it. With his eye acutely focused on his contemporary moment, Fitzgerald nonetheless kept formally close to Conrad, James, and Flaubert, keeping his foothold in the stylized, carefully focalized novel of selection – the highest manner of realism, in the end, that the nineteenth century produced, and with which the modernist novel for the most part remained continuous.

NOTES

1 Cited in W. Goldhurst, *F. Scott Fitzgerald and His Contemporaries* (Cleveland: World Publishing Company, 1963), 54.

2 W. Curtis, "Some Recent Books," *Town & Country* 81 (15 March 1925), 68. Subsequent references to this work are included in the text.

3 See F. S. Fitzgerald, "Sherwood Anderson and the Marriage Question" in M. J. Bruccoli and J. S. Baughman (eds.), *F. Scott Fitzgerald on Authorship* (Columbia, SC: University of South Carolina Press, 1996), 84.

4 Edmund Wilson still remains a relatively trustworthy guide to these distinctions. "The literary history of our time," he wrote in 1931, "is to a great extent that of the development of Symbolism and its fusion or conflict with Naturalism" (*Axel's Castle* [New York: Charles Scribner's Sons, 1931], 25). *Axel's Castle*, for all Wilson's critical reservations, helped make possible later definitions of a "high modernism" tied to a narrow canon of esoteric writing (by Yeats, Joyce, Stein, Proust, Valery, and Eliot). For a broader, more scholarly overview of naturalism's relation to modernism in general, see M. Bradbury and J. McFarlane, "Movements, Magazines and Manifestos: The Succession from Naturalism," in M. Bradbury and J. McFarlane (eds.), *Modernism: A Guide to European Literature, 1890–1930*, 1976 (reprinted New York: Penguin, 1991), 192–205.

5 See S. P. Sherman, "The Naturalism of Mr. Dreiser" in G. J. Becker (ed.), *Documents of Modern Literary Realism* (Princeton, NJ: Princeton University Press, 1963), 452–64; for Mencken's criticism of Sherman, see *A Book of Prefaces*, 5th ed. (Garden City: Garden City Publishing, 1924), 135–36.

6 See M. Cowley, "A Natural History of American Naturalism," *Documents of Modern Literary Realism*, 429–51, for a still excellent and insightful overview. Cowley does not count Anderson among the naturalists but does identify Mencken alongside Joseph Wood Krutch as the movement's most notable critical voices. Subsequent references to this work are included in the text.

7 H. L. Mencken, *Prejudices: Second Series* (New York: Knopf, 1920), 41.

8 E. Wilson, "The Literary Spotlight – VI: F. Scott Fitzgerald," *Bookman* 55 (March 1922), 24. Subsequent references to this work are included in the text.

9 The letter to Perkins is dated mid-July 1922 by Bruccoli. In a letter dated June 25, 1922, Fitzgerald let Wilson know that he had bought *Ulysses* and had started reading it. He also let him know that he found the book depressing, in large part because of his identification with the world of middle- to lower-class Dubliners (see *LL* 61). He presumably gained a greater appreciation of the novel's innovations and its "intricate pattern" from reading Wilson's essay on it in the *New Republic*, "the only criticism yet I could make head or tail of" (*L* 337). The next year he was publicly proclaiming that in newspapers that "*Ulysses* is the great novel of the future" (see *F. Scott Fitzgerald on Authorship*

81, 86). Stein's *Three Lives*, however, seems to have had the bigger stylistic impact on Fitzgerald. He championed her work throughout the period of *Gatsby*'s composition, publication and reception, and, despite his resistance for her more wildly avant-garde work, spoke fondly of *Melanctha*, the volume's experimental second story, for the rest of his life. He wrote Mencken in 1935, in response to the latter's criticisms of Stein in general and *Melanctha* in particular, that "you would have felt the book more remarkable had you read it in 1922 as Wilson + I did. She has been so imitated + thru Ernest her very rythm has gone into the styles of so many people … I still believe Gertrude Stien is some sort of a punctuation mark in literary history" (*C* 412).

10 J. Conrad, "Preface to *The Nigger of the Narcissus*" in "*The Nigger of the Narcissus*," "*Typhoon*," *and Other Stories* (New York: Penguin, 1963),11,12.

11 M. J. Bruccoli and J. R. Bryer, *F. Scott Fitzgerald in His Own Time: A Miscellany* (Kent State University Press, 1971), 146–47. Subsequent references to this work are included in the text.

12 E. Wilson, review of *Ulysses* by James Joyce, *New Republic* 26 (July 5, 1922), 164.

13 See L. Trilling, *The Liberal Imagination*, 1950 (New York: Harcourt Brace Jovanovich, 1978), 234–37.

14 *GG*, 6, 39, 87, 86, 116, 137.

15 *GG*, 48, 8, 124–25, 38, 126, 140.

16 J. Frank, *The Widening Gyre: Crisis and Mastery in Modern Literature* (New Brunswick: Rutgers University Press, 1963), 32.

17 *GG*, 34; 11, 94; 21; 77; 49–51; 14; 30; 57; 65; 131.

18

Avant-garde Trends

Linda Patterson Miller

Artists tend to be classified as avant-garde when they seek forms and themes that will capture what modernist poet Ezra Pound called "the shock of the new." Many of the most transformative art movements, often grouped under the heading of modernist art, began in Europe at the turn of the twentieth century. Such initiatives as Dada, Surrealism, and Cubism defy easy labels, emerging as they did out of the collaborative and also reactionary artistic spirit of the day. As art historians Erika Langmuir and Norbert Lynton describe it, "movements promising radical innovation followed hard upon each other's heels from the 1890s on and rarely lasted long after their launching and initial propaganda."[1] The modernist art of Europe with its skewed perspectives had begun to make its way to America early in the century, yet many American painters and writers, including Fitzgerald, had little direct contact with it and scant understanding of what specifically it meant to make things new artistically. Fitzgerald had an intuitive awareness of the evolving forms of early-twentieth-century art, particularly Surrealism and Cubism, as reflected in some of his earliest writing that captured the emotional temper of the day. Works such as his first novel, *This Side of Paradise* (1920), or his short story (some might call it a novella) "May Day," published in that same year, incorporated juxtaposition, contrast, and collage as structural elements to render a sense of motion on the page. Although these structural elements comprise the scaffolding of modernist art, Fitzgerald was not, in the truest sense, an avant-garde artist until after he had left America to live in France in 1924. There he encountered modernist art head on as he mingled with other artists on the forefront of change. This led to his reshaping of the novel that in 1925 would become his modernist masterpiece *The Great Gatsby*.

The Armory Show in New York City in 1913 famously shocked the American art world with what critics considered its "ugly" paintings brought over from Europe, and many viewers singled out Marcel

Duchamp's "Nude Descending the Stairs" as representative of just how far this new art had gone in violation of academic tradition. When Fitzgerald began his freshman year at Princeton in the fall of 1913, the Armory Show had already left town, and Fitzgerald would not have seen the show, but he might have heard of Duchamp when the artist came to stay in New York during the years of World War I. Fitzgerald did, in fact, frequent New York with classmates during his Princeton years to participate in city life, mainly by attending the musical comedies popular on Broadway. His writing for Princeton's Triangle Club mimicked Broadway's whimsical fare through a collage of satiric verse and sketches that parodied the frivolity and excess of the new age, and Fitzgerald dreamed of a future in the theater. Ten years after the Armory Show, however, the colossal flop of his play *The Vegetable*, to which he devoted his creative energy during 1923, convinced him to focus more on his novel in process, *The Great Gatsby*. Although *The Vegetable* folded almost overnight in the fall of 1923 in Atlantic City, New Jersey, primarily because it lacked unity as either political satire or burlesque, the play did pay ironic tribute ten years later to the artistic significance of Duchamp's "Nude Descending the Stairs." As one of the characters, named Dada, mindlessly moves up and down the stairs throughout Act One, and then drifts amorphously in and out of swinging doors (similar to the unifying pattern of Mr. In and Mr. Out in "May Day"), Fitzgerald seems to mock but also utilize Duchamp's painting, which cubistically fractured the human form to convey not so much the form but the motion – the nude in actual descent of the stairs. Fitzgerald demonstrated here his awareness of the avant-garde art movements of the day, including that of Dada (as referenced in the naming of his character) and also Cubism, arguably the most significant art movement of the twentieth century.

Fitzgerald and his wife, Zelda, had made an initial trip to Europe during the spring of 1921, but their two-month whirlwind tour succeeded in exhausting rather than inspiring them by the time they returned to America. Three years later, however, Fitzgerald decided to settle in France, where he hoped to find the stability to restructure his novel within a more cohesive artistic mindset. He had told Thomas Boyd as early as 1923 that he would "never write another document-novel. I have decided to be a pure artist + experiment in form and emotion" (*C* 126). The Fitzgeralds spent several weeks in Paris before settling on the French Riviera, where Scott worked intensively on reconfiguring the novel from a stance and outlook that increasingly profited from the cubist milieu, which in 1920s France pervaded the streets, galleries, and cafes. When

Fitzgerald's soon-to-be friend and artistic guide Gerald Murphy walked the streets of Paris in 1921, he saw for the first time – like a modernist pilgrim – "Paintings by Braque, Picasso, and Juan Gris," and he felt a "shock of discovery." He told his wife, Sara, "If that's painting, it's what I want to do."[2] Murphy had set out to be a landscape architect but instead began to execute a small but noteworthy body of work (of the approximately fourteen paintings he completed during the 1920s, only seven survive). That this modern art informed by cubist principles created such a seismic shift in Murphy's orientation well illustrates its transformative power and the great degree to which it reconfigured the world for the Murphys and their growing circle of American artist friends during the 1920s and thereafter.

By 1924, when the Murphys met the Fitzgeralds, Cubism had already reinvented artistic realism for a new age. As scientific and technological advancements challenged traditional notions of space and time, artists sought an artistic integrity that had less to do with physical verisimilitude and more to do with emotional ambiguity. To accomplish this, they created a malleable language out of geometric forms and multiple perspectives that competed for authority on the canvas and on the page (for Cubism shook up the world of writing in equal measure). As imagery and angular lines and shapes worked both sequentially and on different planes simultaneously, cubist art evoked in unsettling ways an invisible emotional space and the sense of life in motion. Art historian Herbert Read rightly argues that Cubism's revisionist imperative called for "a new vision to express a new dimension of consciousness – not only harmony, but the truth which is, alas, fragmentary and unconsoling." He illustrates this by quoting Fernand Léger, one of the early cubist painters and among the first to join the Murphys' circle of friends. Léger articulated well how quickly and permanently this new vision, characterized by oddly skewed and overlapping planes and angular juxtapositions and layers of shadow and light, would usurp the way they saw and experienced the world. "Days and nights, dark or brightly lit, seated at some garish bar," wrote Léger, the "epic figure who is variously called inventor, artist or poet" would literally see and enter the surrounding world on cubist terms. He would experience "renewed visions of forms and objects bathed in artificial light. Trees cease to be trees, a shadow cuts across the hand placed on the counter, an eye deformed by the light, the changing silhouettes of the passers-by." What emerges is "the life of fragments: a red finger-nail, an eye, a mouth. The elastic effects produced by complementary colours ... in the whole of this vital instantaneity which cuts through him in every direction. He is a sponge: sensation of being a sponge, transparency, acuteness, new realism."[3]

Because Fitzgerald seemed more acutely attuned to an emotional than a physical reality, the sensory milieu of the City of Light, as Léger defined Paris, quickened Fitzgerald's working vision to give him a new cubist slant. Whether it was "something that happened twenty years ago or only yesterday," Fitzgerald stated in 1933, "I must start out with an emotion – one that's close to me and that I can understand" (*MLC* 87). Thinking about his new novel when he was back in America in 1922, he told Maxwell Perkins that he wanted "to write something *new*" and something "intricately patterned," but he did not appreciate what he saw as his "new angle" until he was about to leave for France in early 1924.[4] And even then, the shape of his novel did not crystalize until after he had arrived in Paris, where he absorbed (like a sponge) the discordancy and angularity of cubist art and where he met Gerald Murphy, who was already seen as an original among the avant-garde circles. When the Fitzgeralds met Gerald and Sara Murphy, they were immediately thrust into the Dadaist swirl that characterized the artistic life of Paris. The Murphys had forged relationships with the international community of avant-garde artists through Serge Diaghilev's Ballets Russes, which galvanized musicians, painters, and writers as they collaborated on such modernist productions as Stravinsky's *Les Noces*. The Ballets Russes became a meeting ground for both European and American artists, and the Murphys helped to introduce their new American artist friends to this collective reminiscent of the earliest Dadaist gatherings that sought "absolute freedom from preconceptions" through an "interplay of different arts."[5]

Before settling in to the French Riviera, the Fitzgeralds stayed near the Murphys' Paris apartment and close to Gerald's studio at 69, rue de Froidevaux, a high-ceilinged warehouse that allowed Murphy the freedom to execute huge canvases, including "Boatdeck," which measured 18 feet high by 12 feet wide. This monumental work renders the smokestacks of an American ocean liner as they slant upward against a disinterested sky and then are sheared off by the top edge of the painting. Even the size of Murphy's painting seems inadequate to contain the disembodied machinery representative of a new age. Murphy had just exhibited "Boatdeck" at the 1924 Salon des Independants show in Paris, and he had begun work on "Razor," a canvas smaller than "Boatdeck" yet equally bold in its conception, when he met Fitzgerald. "Razor" depicts three objects cubistically, such that a Gillette safety razor, a Parker Big Red fountain pen, and a box of Three Stars safety matches overlap each other from three different angles to create a sense of fractured space and caught motion. Both of these paintings portray recognizable objects both flatly and multidimensionally, and they reflect the new commercialism and cubism of the day in a kind of oversized poster-board format. Art curator Deborah Rothschild summarizes well the avant-garde nature of Murphy's painting: He "did not mimic the work of other artists," she asserts, but rather he "assimilated not only Cubism and Purism, but also Dada and Surrealism, as well as American folk art, advertising, and graphic design, to create works that were entirely original."[6]

Murphy's "Boatdeck," not unlike Duchamp's "Nude Descending the Stairs" ten years earlier, was the talk of the 1924 Salon exhibit to the degree that Murphy's painting diminished the other paintings with its bold assertions. Initially the president of the Societé des Artistes Independants "tried to keep it out of the Salon, claiming that it was 'architectural drawing' rather than fine art," but Murphy gained entrance nonetheless and "'Boatdeck' drew large crowds and a great deal of press." To commentators who questioned the size of his painting, Murphy responded in this way: "If they think my picture is too big, I think the other pictures are too small." As he came to say of his style, "I seemed to see in miniature detail, but in giant scale" (Rothschild, 37–38, 60). Still flush with the success of his latest exhibition, Murphy was at work on "Razor" when he met Fitzgerald, who was no doubt struck by the originality of Murphy's work (although no direct comments that Fitzgerald made on Murphy's work have survived). Fitzgerald's revision of *Gatsby*'s chapter 2 might well have been influenced by Murphy's "Boatdeck." This chapter (previously positioned as chapter 4) recounts Nick Carraway's train ride with Tom Buchanan into New York City, and it highlights the novel's darker ruminations on the loss of the American Dream (*Gatsby Literary Reference* 62). As Nick and Tom go from Long Island to Manhattan, they see through the train window passing snatches of the Valley of Ashes, surrealistically rendered as a place "where ashes grow like wheat into ridges and hills and grotesque gardens; where ashes take the forms of houses and chimneys and rising smoke and, finally, with a transcendent effort, of men who move dimly and already crumbling through the powdery air." Looming over this futuristic wasteland is the outsize billboard of Doctor T. J. Eckleburg, whose eyes "are blue and gigantic – their retinas are one yard high. They look out of no face, but, instead, from a pair of enormous yellow spectacles which pass over a non-existent nose." The eyes, "dimmed a little by many paintless days under sun and rain, brood on over the solemn dumping grounds" (*GG* 21).

Much has been made of the Francis Cugat dust jacket cover created for the original publication of *Gatsby*, which some argue caused Fitzgerald to devise and then embellish his billboard image of Doctor T. J. Eckleburg as a defining symbol of the spiritual malaise of the novel's setting. Charles Scribner III has discussed the evolution of that cover based on different Cugat sketches that have survived, most of which portray variations of an "ethereal and mystical" image of large, outsized eyes on a disembodied face, the nose effaced, that look down on the world from above.[7] While Fitzgerald might have seen an initial sketch for this cover prior to leaving for France, the timing makes this unlikely, and it remains uncertain when, or even if, Fitzgerald saw any of the sketches prior to the novel's publication in April 1925. Nonetheless, he seemed to have a strong enough sense of the gist of the sketch to write Max Perkins in late August that he must save that jacket for him and not give it away to someone else's book. "I've written it into the book," Fitzgerald stated (*S&M* 76). Fitzgerald's creation of Doctor T. J. Eckleburg might well have been inspired by Cugat, and yet Murphy's art, as Fitzgerald first saw it in Paris, provided a more concrete influence. Murphy's outsize paintings in particular, reminiscent of billboard art, embodied the cubistic and surreal treatment that increasingly defined the new shape and scope of Fitzgerald's novel as he discovered it with new eyes and from a foreign land.

The brilliance of Fitzgerald's *The Great Gatsby* as a cubist narrative cannot be overplayed. Fitzgerald had told Max Perkins that he wanted to write a "structured" novel, and he arrived at that new structure while under the direct influence of cubist art with its sustained interplay, through contrast and juxtaposition, of opposing elements. Nick Carraway as narrator embodies the contrast of voice that defines the novel's artistic credo. When Carraway thinks about escaping from the escalating violence of the party in Myrtle Wilson's New York apartment, he realizes that entanglements hold him in suspension, and he imagines that the "casual watcher in the darkening streets" might be looking up to "our line of yellow windows." "I was him too," Carraway reflects, "looking up and wondering. I was within and without, simultaneously enchanted and repelled by the inexhaustible variety of life" (*GG* 30). Throughout Nick's telling of Gatsby's story, his fluctuations between objectivity and subjectivity build a point/counterpoint tension that is both palpable and elusive in the "unquiet darkness." Nick's articulation of his own creative stance defines the poise embodied in the best cubist art that upholds in stasis an interior and an exterior reality along with multiple points of view. As Carraway yanks the reader back and forth between his own involvement and detachment, the reader experiences the emotional yo-yoing that Nick describes as being perpetually pulled back "with ropes." As an historian who aims to understand Gatsby, Nick is forced to get "the facts" by piecing together various versions of Gatsby's story as told by Jordan Baker and by Gatsby himself at different points in time. Rather than telling Gatsby's story chronologically, Fitzgerald fractures the telling by moving both forward and backward simultaneously, recreating layers of time and providing increasingly varied and contradictory renditions of the "true" story. Within this perfectly balanced structure that continues to provide checks and balances and counterbalances, *Gatsby* becomes the quintessential cubist narrative that evokes the "fragmentary and unconsoling" feel of lived life. André Le Vot articulates most eloquently the provocative reverberations of Fitzgerald's cubist text, suggesting that it arrives at what Le Vot calls "the symbolic truth of a global vision." He goes on to explain that "[t]his vision relies for its effectiveness on a coexistence of contrasts, on their simultaneous operation." He further argues that Fitzgerald with this work went beyond anything he had done previously. With *Gatsby*, "he built an intricate palace of echoes and mirrors, a meticulous architectonic complex, all in trompe l'oeil that traps, refracts, fragments, reconstructs a reality in which he is invisible, but which reflects better than all his autobiographical writing the heart of the problems he and his generation faced."[8]

As Fitzgerald was working to shape his novel cubistically, both he and Perkins questioned his characterization of Gatsby. Perkins saw Gatsby as too unrealized because he seemed "older" than he was and the source of his wealth remained too mysterious. Fitzgerald admitted that initially he was uncertain about Gatsby also: "*I myself didn't know what Gatsby looked like or was engaged in* & you felt it." He goes on to say, though, in this letter of late December 1924 that "I know now." He explains that "the man I had in mind, half unconsciously, *was* older (a specific individual)" (*S&M* 89). Fitzgerald does not name this individual, and critics have argued that Gatsby can be aligned with various Long Island figures such as Edward M. Fuller (See Le Vot 130–31). However, a stronger and more direct influence on both the emotional and physical configuration of Gatsby would seem to be Gerald Murphy, who was almost a decade older than Fitzgerald. Most scholars have noted Fitzgerald's use of Gerald Murphy in the characterization of Dick Diver in *Tender Is the Night* while failing to recognize the stronger parallels in *The Great Gatsby*. Both the physical and psychological dimensions of Gatsby reflect Murphy as Fitzgerald came to know him in Paris and on the Riviera during 1924. Fitzgerald told Perkins that "after having had Zelda draw pictures until her fingers ache I know Gatsby better than I know my own child," which implies that Zelda's conceptions, more than Scott's, determined the configurations of Gatsby physically (*S&M* 89). Nonetheless, whether unconsciously or consciously influenced by Fitzgerald's close observation of Gerald during the few crucial months of his writing in France, Gatsby began to emerge in Fitzgerald's own mind, and by the time of his December letter, he did know Gatsby "now."

Gerald Murphy emerged as his own walking self-portrait as described by friends who knew him in Paris. Deborah Rothschild argues that "the modern, mechanically precise style that marked his paintings also characterized the man" such that even before he had taken up painting, he "had developed a contemporary, meticulously honed aesthetic that he applied to the ephemeral business of living." This carried over even to the way he dressed: "he used his body as an armature for severe Constructivist assemblages comparable to works by Léger, El Lissitzky, or Sonia Delaunay." Murphy's "clothing would be entirely monochrome, with just a dash of color at the pocket, and he would carry his belongings in a square of brightly colored fabric, so as not to disturb the strict line of his suit" (Rothschild 39). Art historian Wanda Corn aptly describes Murphy as "a walking machine age abstraction."[9]

The calculated arrangement of Murphy's clothing and his demeanor echoed the trompe l'oeil art of Gatsby's character. In photos of the Murphys and their friends cavorting in Paris or on the French Riviera, Gerald often stands posed, seeming to organize events from a point of detachment. In one particular photo, he stands rigidly in front of a beach changing house, and one feels unsettled by his immaculately pressed linen pants and spotless white shirt as he stares off into the Mediterranean Sea. In another photo, not unlike repeated images of Gatsby, he stands in isolation on the terrace of his newly renovated Villa America in Cap d'Antibes, seeming to greet guests even as he holds them off at arms' length.[10] Fitzgerald came to feel that Gerald, not unlike himself, could keep people away with charm. He also recognized Murphy's posturing and conveyed that through Gatsby, as both Gatsby and Murphy adhered to the American tradition of becoming self-created men. "Not for one waking hour of my life since I was fifteen have I been entirely free of the feeling of these [personal] defects," Murphy would tell Archibald MacLeish at the end of the decade. He felt that his life was "ersatz" to the degree that he kept people from knowing his real self: "Eight years of school and college, after my too willing distortion of myself into the likeness of popularity and success, I was left with little confidence in the shell that I had inhabited as another person ... My subsequent life has been a process of concealment of the personal realities, – at which I have been all too adept," he concluded."[11] Murphy, like Gatsby, created a shadow self even as he used the business world for his own purposes while also rejecting what he saw as the crass materialism of 1920s America. Ultimately, in going to France, he would renounce his father's lucrative Mark Cross Company in New York in favor of searching for the things that mattered most. It was a spiritual quest, really, not unlike Gatsby's desire to be about his Father's business (which in the novel ironically alludes to all of the corruptions enacted under the name of God). Fitzgerald, along with Murphy's other friends, came to recognize Murphy's self-inventions and his emotional inaccessibility. Murphy himself would finally tell Fitzgerald in 1935 that Fitzgerald was right: "I know now that what you said in 'Tender is the Night' is true. Only the invented part of our life, – the unreal part – has had any scheme any beauty. Life itself has stepped in now and blundered, scarred and destroyed" (Miller, *Letters* 150–51).

In the spring of 1925 when *Gatsby* was published, Fitzgerald was already at work on *Tender Is the Night*, his novel that would be nine years in the making and that was based in early versions on the lives of Gerald and Sara Murphy at their Villa America and in Paris. He and Zelda planned to stay in Paris for much of the year as he began his "new novel." As he told Perkins in May, just shy of the April publication of *Gatsby*, this novel would be "something really NEW in form, idea, structure – the model for the age that Joyce and Stien are searching for, that Conrad didn't find" (*S&M* 104). He clearly now aligned himself with the avante-garde after having absorbed modernist art while he was at work on *Gatsby*. He had read Joyce's *Ulysses*, and he had begun to read Hemingway's *in our time* (the early version published in Paris in 1924). Struck by its artistic innovations, Fitzgerald immediately recommended Hemingway's work to Perkins, who agreed that the cubistic power of Hemingway's vignettes functioned through accumulation (*S&M* 95). Fitzgerald had also been reading Gertrude Stein's *The Making of Americans* (just then being published sequentially through the assistance of Hemingway), and he urged Perkins to read it. Perkins thanked Fitzgerald "for the tip" and added, "I am reading the Gertrude Stein as it comes out, and it fascinates me." Perkins expressed his doubt, however, that "the reader who had no *literary* interest, or not much, would have patience with her method, effective as it does become" (*S&M* 79). Fitzgerald seemed surprised by Perkins' editorial resistance to experimental art that would unduly challenge the average reader, and he responded around November 7, 1924: "I am confused at what you say about Gertrude Stien I thought it was one purpose of critics & publishers to educate the public up to original work. The first people who risked Conrad certainly didn't do it as a commercial venture. Did the evolution of startling work into accepted work cease twenty years ago?" (*S&M* 81–82).

Fitzgerald came to see *The Great Gatsby* as a canvas that built its vision through distortion, the defining feature of all modernist art. When Carraway returned home to the Midwest to piece together the interlocking components of Gatsby's story, he realized that the East, for him, was "haunted" and "distorted." "[I]t had always for me a quality of distortion," Carraway writes. He goes on to write,

> West Egg, especially, still figures in my more fantastic dreams. I see it as a night scene by El Greco: a hundred houses, at once conventional and grotesque, crouching under a sullen, overhanging sky and a lustreless moon. In the foreground four solemn men in dress suits are walking along the sidewalk with a stretcher on which lies a drunken woman in a white evening dress. Her hand, which dangles over the side, sparkles cold with jewels. Gravely the men turn in at a house – the wrong house. But no one knows the woman's name, and no one cares. (*GG* 137)

The El Greco painting Fitzgerald alludes to seems to be that of "View of Toledo," painted c. 1604–10 and owned by the New York Metropolitan Museum of Art. Fitzgerald might well have seen it firsthand in New York and been struck by its ghostly vision of disembodied houses that both tumble and slide down the mountainside. El Greco's work, like that of any avant-garde artist, cannot be classified with its times. Indeed, it anticipated the slanted perspectives and jagged edges, and the unconventional spatial relationships, of modernist art. The surrealistic dimensions of El Greco's paintings become vehicles "for intensely expressive spirituality" (Langmuir and Lynton 296), the predominant quality that defines the essence of Fitzgerald's expressionist novel. It is interesting to note that Fitzgerald added in the El Greco passage at the very end of his revision process, after he had already absorbed the cubist milieu of life in France during 1924 (*A Literary Reference* 71). As such, Fitzgerald seems to have put the stamp on this novel as a work he had arrived at through a painterly artistic lens.

Although Fitzgerald was aglow with excitement over his new avant-garde work in process in 1925, *Tender Is the Night* never realized the creative tension and unity of *Gatsby,* primarily because Fitzgerald tried to work on it over too many years as his own life had begun to fray. He utilized such modernist devices as flashback so as both to fragment and layer time, yet the novel ultimately feels more disjointed than suspended in time, and reviewers by and large dismissed it as dated. Part of the problem was that the novel appeared during the Depression in America, and critics felt that Fitzgerald, ironically, no longer spoke to his times. As the *Newsweek* review stated, "It is a long time since the decay of American expatriates on the Riviera was hot news." Or, as the *Daily Worker* put it even more succinctly, "Dear Mr. Fitzgerald, you can't hide from a hurricane under a beach umbrella."[12]

Even as Fitzgerald struggled to write stories that might earn him money during the 1930s, he most often knew that he was working to formula rather than from the forefront of innovation. Following the 1934 publication of *Tender Is the Night*, Fitzgerald crafted three essays (now referred to collectively as Fitzgerald's "The Crack-Up") that analyzed his personal and artistic disintegration. Published in three successive monthly issues of *Esquire* beginning in February 1936, these essays have earned accolades from many who regard them as Fitzgerald's most controlled and innovative work. Fitzgerald's contemporaries castigated him for shamelessly exposing his personal woes ("when you get the damned hurt use it [for your art] – don't cheat with it," Hemingway had chided earlier), and yet Fitzgerald anticipated and inaugurated the confessional memoir writing that has become increasingly popular on into the twenty-first century.[13] Le Vot recognizes that when Fitzgerald "was convinced he could no longer write," "he no longer wrote to please" and thus "developed a new style, sober and effective" (Le Vot 293). This new style upheld the autobiographical thrust that characterized much of Fitzgerald's writing while finding a way yet again to build its tension through contrast, what Fitzgerald defined in "The Crack-Up" as that "ability to hold two opposed ideas in the mind at the same time, and still retain the ability to function." He also references the need to place in counterpoise the "outside" world and the stuff "that comes from within," what Nick Carraway had understood as standing both inside and outside simultaneously so as to achieve artistic truth (*CU* 69). This recognition – really an artistic stance – pays tribute to the essence of cubist art that could successfully present multiple points of view simultaneously as it also integrates the three-part structure of "The Crack-Up" into a unified whole, what some, including Le Vot, now aptly refer to in painterly terms as Fitzgerald's "Trip-Tych," each "panel" depicting "a stage in the descent into hell by which he strove stubbornly to exorcise his despair" (Le Vot 294). Even to the end, Fitzgerald arrived at his vision through the artistic lens of his times.

NOTES

1 E. Langmuir and N. Lynton, *The Yale Dictionary of Art and Artists* (New Haven: Yale University Press, 2000), 34. Subsequent references to this work are included in the text.
2 C. Tomkins, *Living Well Is the Best Revenge* (New York: Viking Press, 1971), 25.
3 H. Read, *A Concise History of Modern Painting* (New York: Frederick A. Praeger, 1959), 81, 88.
4 Quoted in M. J. Bruccoli, "Writing the Great Gatsby" in M. J. Bruccoli (ed), *F. Scott Fitzgerald's The Great Gatsby: A Literary Reference* (New York: Carroll & Graf Publishers, 2000), 53–174; 53. Subsequent references to this work are included in the text.
5 H. Richter, *Dada: Art and Anti-Art* (New York: Oxford University Press, 1965), 34–35.
6 D. Rothschild, "Masters of the Art of Living" in D. Rothschild (ed.), *Making It New: The Art and Style of Sara & Gerald Murphy* (Berkeley, CA: University of California Press, 2007), 11–87; 35. Subsequent references to this work are included in the text.
7 C. Scribner III, "The Dust Jacket" in M. J. Bruccoli (ed.), *F. Scott Fitzgerald's The Great Gatsby: A Literary Reference,* 160–68; 161.
8 A. Le Vot, *F. Scott Fitzgerald: A Biography* (New York: Doubleday & Company, 1983), 142–43. Subsequent references to this work are included in the text.
9 W. M. Corn, *The Great American Thing: Modern Art and National Identity, 1915–1935* (Berkeley, CA: University of California Press, 1999), 117.
10 See Rothschild, 39. *Making It New* compiles the best collection of vintage photos of Gerald and Sara Murphy and their artist friends together in France.
11 Gerald Murphy to Archibald MacLeish, January 22, 1931 in L. P. Miller (ed.), *Letters from the Lost Generation: Gerald and Sara Murphy and Friends* (New Brunswick, FL: University Press of Florida, 2002), 53–58.
12 M. J. Bruccoli with J. S. Baughman (eds.), *Reader's Companion to F. Scott Fitzgerald's Tender Is the Night* (Columbia, SC: University of South Carolina Press, 1996), 33.
13 Letter to Fitzgerald of May 28, 1934, in Carlos Baker (ed), *Ernest Hemingway Selected Letters: 1917–1961* (New York: Charles Scribner's Sons, 1981), 407–9, 408.

PART IV

Historical and Social Contexts in the Jazz Age (1918–1929)

19

Prohibition in the Age of Jazz

Linda De Roche

The iconography of America's "noble experiment," National Prohibition, has for decades encapsulated the 1920s in the popular imagination. To the accompaniment of songs such as Irving Berlin's "You Cannot Make Your Shimmy Shake on Tea," speakeasies and flappers, bathtub gin and moonshiners, Al Capone and Eliot Ness, hot jazz and hotter cabarets put the roar in the "Roaring Twenties," obscuring the fact that for nearly fourteen years, from 1920 to 1933, America was by statute a "dry" nation. Just seconds after midnight on January 16, 1920, the Eighteenth Amendment to the U.S. Constitution, ratified by the states in less than two years, prohibited "the manufacture, sale, or transportation of intoxicating liquors within, the importation thereof into, or the exportation thereof from the United States ... for beverage purposes." The law enabling it, the National Prohibition Act, more commonly known as the Volstead Act (for its sponsor, Andrew Volstead, a Republican senator from Minnesota), defined "intoxicating liquors" as any beverage containing .05 percent alcohol, established a schedule of fines and prison terms for violations, outlined exemptions for religious and medicinal uses of alcohol, and charged the federal Bureau of Internal Revenue with enforcing its provisions. As the clock chimed the new decade, few could have anticipated the political, social, and cultural changes that the law would usher forth. By 1933, however, with the ratification of the Twenty-first Amendment repealing Prohibition, few would have denied that for all its nobility of motive the experiment had failed. Yet, despite that failure, the lasting impact of National Prohibition is undeniable. Indeed, stereotypes and myths about the era testify to the ways in which Prohibition shaped almost every aspect of American culture in the 1920s and thus provide a lens through which to view the contradictions inherent in the nation's first modern decade.

Despite the speed with which the Eighteenth Amendment became law, National Prohibition was in fact the culmination of decades of struggle by religious leaders and social reformers, with the support of captains of industry, to rid the nation of an evil that prevented it from achieving its destiny. Drink led inevitably to excess, to lack of control, to vice and disorder. It undermined the work ethic upon which the prosperity of the nation depended, and it was especially damaging to women and children, who were often left impoverished by the husband and father who drank away his weekly wages or vented his anger, frustration, or guilt in physical violence upon them. Evangelical Christians had begun agitation for temperance in the early nineteenth century, firm in the belief that individual reform would spark the spiritual renewal that would lead to the creation of the virtuous society their forebears had envisaged in their "errand in the wilderness."[1] By the end of the century, however, the evangelical and millenarian focus of the movement had been largely supplanted by an emphasis on progressive reform and a shift toward legislative coercion of change.

Although the name of one of the most important of the voluntary associations leading the fight for prohibition, the Women's Christian Temperance Union (WCTU), established in 1873, revealed the persistence of religion and the moral imperative in the movement, an equally important, and perhaps more effective, association, the Anti-Saloon League, established in 1895, was increasingly secular and political. Its leaders built a coalition of Protestant congregations and leading citizens and mounted a sophisticated campaign in middle-class newspapers and magazines against the saloon, the locus of vice, prostitution, crime, and political corruption. In urban centers especially, the saloon was, after all, the place where party bosses met to choose candidates, plot strategy, and consolidate their constituencies, in seeming contradiction to the democratic process. The saloon, moreover, represented monopolistic business interests that threatened to undermine the ideal of democratic capitalism. In the years prior to World War I, when public drunkenness was a serious problem throughout the country, the League's strategies had begun to work. Between 1906 and 1917, dry laws were enacted in hundreds of communities and twenty-six states. By 1919 and the ratification of the Eighteenth Amendment, thirty-three of the forty-eight states were already dry.

Reform spirit was not the only force driving the temperance movement. Almost from its inception a strong nativist impulse, the effect of rapid and seemingly uncontrollable changes that were transforming the American landscape and threatening its traditional foundations, garnered support for the initiative from an increasingly anxious middle class. The years following the Civil War had been characterized by an expansion of urban America, an industrial revolution, a "Great Migration" of African

Americans from the South to the North, and a surge in immigration. For the sober middle class, who were largely descended from the nation's Protestant forebears, these new waves of immigrants, especially those arriving in record numbers from southern and eastern Europe, were creating cultural chaos. Not only was their Catholic faith, with its parochial schools, a challenge to mainstream beliefs, but so, too, were their views of sexual morality, leisure, and drink. While those in the middle class were not opposed to a glass of wine or an after-dinner drink in the privacy of their homes or a convivial whiskey in their gentlemen's clubs, they deplored the excesses of the saloon, where the ethnic working class congregated, and gradually lent their support to Prohibition, as Lynn Dumenil claims, in "an attempt to promote Protestant middle-class culture as a means of imposing order on a disorderly world" (Dumenil 226). Prohibition, in other words, would coerce unruly, unassimilated immigrants into conformity with the "American" values of sobriety, industry, and restraint that were generally conflated with Protestantism.

While the temperance movement was slowly achieving its goal of a dry nation, World War I provided the compelling occasion for the swift enactment of National Prohibition. America's young men were sacrificing their lives on European battlefields. It was the patriotic duty of all its citizens to contribute to the effort to make the world safe for democracy. In May 1917, Congress enacted wartime prohibition to conserve valuable resources for the war effort. During a time of voluntary food rationing, and what historian William E. Leuchtenberg terms federally imposed "heatless Thursdays"[2] and daylight savings time, Americans could surely sacrifice intoxicating drink, with its waste of valuable grain that could provide meals to soldiers at the front. The nation's breweries, moreover, were generally owned by German Americans, who came under increasing suspicion of being in alliance with the Kaiser as war progressed. Indeed, as anti-German sentiment escalated, brewing and drinking beer were viewed as unpatriotic. In the aftermath of "the ultimate U. S. triumph overseas, many patriotic citizens," according to Kathleen Drowne, "were eager to face their grand destiny as leaders of the free world and were therefore amenable to legislation that appeared to position America as the world's moral leader."[3] So the nation's fighting men returned from the front to find that patriotic fervor had transformed their homeland into a place where they could take a celebratory drink, if only they could find one.

It was this curious provision of the Eighteenth Amendment that from the beginning doomed its success. Prohibition outlawed the manufacture, transport, and sale of alcoholic beverages, but it did not criminalize purchasing or drinking them. Advocates of Prohibition had seriously underestimated the drinking habits of Americans of all classes, for many Americans had been under the impression that beer and wine would not be included in the definition of intoxicating liquors and had wrongly assumed that virtually everyone would obediently comply with the law. Yet, as the example of Sinclair Lewis's Midwestern middle-class Everyman, George Babbitt, the hero of his 1922 novel *Babbitt*, indicates, many otherwise law-abiding citizens believed that Prohibition was "a mighty beneficial thing for the poor zob that hasn't got any will-power," but for them and their fellow upstanding friends and associates, it was an "infringement of personal liberty."[4] While the law initially curtailed drinking, reducing alcohol consumption by as much as 30 percent, primarily because the cost of bootleg liquor skyrocketed as much as 600 percent (Dumenil 232–33), drinkers like Babbitt, and even President Warren G. Harding, who had voted for the legislation as a senator and been elected to the presidency in 1920 as a dry candidate and who enjoyed a glass of whiskey with a good cigar, were soon flouting its provisions. The sources of illegal alcohol were simply too numerous to be contained.

In advance of Prohibition, many people had stockpiled wine and spirits, a practice that was not illegal. By 1920, for example, the cellars of New York City's Yale Club held a fourteen-year liquor supply for its privileged clientele. Many drinkers also developed medical conditions, colloquially known as "thirstitis," and sought from sympathetic physicians prescriptions for medicinal liquor, which had not been prohibited. Home stills multiplied, providing a boon not only to rural moonshiners, who had a long tradition of flouting liquor laws, but also to the California grape industry. Others doctored everything from industrial to rubbing alcohol to make it potable, but not necessarily safe. Indeed, the legacy of Prohibition-era drinks was serious health problems and sometimes even death: "Panther whiskey," for example, contained dangerous levels of fusel oil, a toxin that was thought to trigger paranoia and hallucinations; "jackass brandy," distilled from peaches, destroyed the intestines; and "jake," a Jamaican ginger extract, permanently paralyzed thousands, leaving them with what was known as "jake walk" or "jake leg" (Drowne 28–29). Those with resources could always purchase "the real McCoy," premium spirits smuggled into the country by rumrunner Bill McCoy or whiskey transported on sleds across a frozen Lake Erie from Canada into Detroit by Samuel Bronfman, who eventually became head of Seagram's distillery. Prohibition, in other words, did not end the consumption of alcohol. It merely created a new drinking culture.

In private homes, for instance, where people could drink legally so long as their alcohol had been purchased prior to Prohibition, the accoutrements of the mixed drink, especially the cocktail shaker, became standard household items – indeed, Anthony and Gloria Patch receive an "elaborate 'drinking set'" (*B&D* 124) as a wedding gift in F. Scott Fitzgerald's 1922 novel *The Beautiful and Damned* – and the house party flourished. Ranging from intimate dinners with friends of the sort that Babbitt hosts in his quiet Zenith home to the raucous parties that Anthony and Gloria Patch make infamous to the opulent entertainments in Jay Gatsby's West Egg mansion in Fitzgerald's 1925 novel *The Great Gatsby*, where "floating rounds of cocktails permeate the gardens" (*GG* 34) and "champagne was served in glasses bigger than finger bowls" (*GG* 39), the house party provided an opportunity for the social drinking that Prohibition had outlawed, and at little risk. Even if guests were drinking bootleg liquor, which was highly likely, law enforcement generally ignored these private gatherings of the white middle and moneyed classes. They were less forgiving, however, of the "rent parties" that became fixtures of Harlem's African American community. Because exorbitant rents and low wages squeezed the local residents, they organized private parties in their apartments, charging admission for the food, drink, and entertainment they provided their guests. A form of welfare, for guests knew that they were providing financial support to their host, rent parties were popular venues in Harlem, and along with house parties, provide an indication of the degree to which Americans of all classes and races subverted Prohibition.

The bolting shut of the saloon doors not only gave rise to private parties but also created an underground landscape of illicit commercial venues for the consumption of alcohol. In rural communities, where voluntary prohibition had often preceded passage of the Eighteenth Amendment, roadhouses and "jook joints," situated in old barns and other seemingly abandoned buildings on the outskirts of town, where detection by revenuers was less likely, came to riotous life at night, offering welcome escape from the drudgeries of daily existence in music, dance, and moonshine. Speakeasies, already fixtures in dry communities, opened almost overnight in the basements and back rooms of legitimate businesses throughout the entire "dry" nation. Behind their locked doors, patrons, who were admitted only if they could convince the establishments' bouncers that they were trustworthy, could join others, including women, who had seldom crossed the saloon's threshold, for a sociable drink in a communal environment. Cabarets, or nightclubs, whose wealthy clientele could afford to pay their exorbitant prices (which generally purchased protection for the establishment) for the privilege of live entertainment such as chorus girls and jazz performers, also continued to flourish in urban centers. Although patrons of these drinking venues risked arrest and fines if they were captured during a raid, that fact may have contributed to their mystique. They were sites of opposition to a law that made criminals of otherwise law-abiding citizens, and those citizens were determined to resist government attempts to define morality and to impinge on personal freedoms.

The unabated demand for intoxicating liquors prompted many enterprising citizens to go into business to meet the needs of a new, and thirsty, clientele. Despite the risk of fines and imprisonment, moonshiners, who tended to be rural producers of illegal alcohol, and bootleggers, who were generally its urban distributors, could not resist the potential fortunes to be made in the liquor trade, and they soon became well-known figures in their communities. On one occasion, for instance, Babbitt, Lewis's model citizen, makes his way to a local speakeasy to purchase a quart of bootleg gin to serve to dinner party guests, and everyone who attends Gatsby's lavish house parties is aware, at least subconsciously, that their host is a bootlegger. Indeed, it is one of the persistent rumors about him.

Because they engaged in illegitimate business, the moonshiner and bootlegger operated on the margins of society. Like the gentleman gambler, however, the bootlegger frequently used his wealth to cultivate an image of gentility and sophistication that, as the example of Gatsby suggests, permitted entry to or at least association with the upper class. The bootlegger George Remus, for instance, who made a fortune in medicinal liquor distribution and may have been a model for Fitzgerald's hero, hosted extravagant parties at his Cincinnati, Ohio, mansion to court favor with the city's elite, and the gangland bootlegger Salvatore "Lucky" Luciano boasted of his association with New York's elite (Drowne 56). Yet the bootlegger, as Fitzgerald's fiction reveals, was always and ever only an outlaw figure. Late in the tale of Anthony Patch, for instance, the dissolute scion of one of America's most elite families reassures his wife that he has no reason to worry about the underfunded check that he had written in payment for his most recent purchase of illegal alcohol, boldly asserting, "Bootlegging's too risky a business" (*B&D* 350). The bootlegger who lives outside the law, in other words, cannot expect the protection of the law. Nor can he expect the regard of those who enjoyed his hospitality. For instance, with the exception of Nick, none of Gatsby's friends and associates, not even his mentor, Meyer Wolfsheim, attends his funeral. Their absence, presumably and in part, is to avoid association with the bootlegger. More damning, however, is Tom Buchanan's gloating denunciation of Gatsby to an increasingly appalled Daisy: "I picked him for a bootlegger the first time I saw him" (*GG* 104). The East Egg arbiters of the social hierarchy clearly would never have included among their ranks a man who runs a chain of "drug-stores" (*GG* 104), even if they have purchased his drugs.

Given their notoriety, Prohibition's outlaw entrepreneurs had to be adept at eluding law enforcement and quickly developed strategies and perfected tactics to ensure their continued economic success. Moonshiners, who had long catered to a local trade from home stills at secret locations and were thus well-practiced in subterfuge, periodically relocated their contraptions to avoid detection. Bootleggers, who tended to have substantial resources because they frequently owned the speakeasies and cabarets in which their illegal liquor was illegally sold, could afford to pay to protect their businesses, bribing agents to look the other way during delivery of their contraband liquor or paying the police not to raid their premises. The Volstead Act had charged the Bureau of Internal Revenue with enforcement of Prohibition, but government officials had seriously underestimated the number of agents such enforcement would require, increasing its force by less than half, from 1,520 to 2,836, during the 1920s (Drowne 35). Those agents, moreover, were poorly paid and therefore easily corrupted by the bootleggers' bounty.

Stories of agents who were chauffeured to work in limousines or whose wives were wrapped in expensive furs abounded, but according to Frederick Lewis Allen, who documented the decade in his 1931 history *Only Yesterday*, it should have been obvious to anyone that "men employable at thirty-five or forty or fifty dollars a week" were unlikely to have "the force of character to resist corruption by men whose pockets were bulging with money."[5] Eliot Ness, the Chicago G-man famed for his relentless pursuit of the city's criminal elements during Prohibition, may have been the era's icon of incorruptibility, but the fate of another scrupulous agent, Isadore "Izzy" Einstein, and his partner, Moe Smith, is perhaps more indicative of the difficult task of enforcing the law. The flamboyant Izzy, according to historian Lucy Moore, spoke nine languages, had a talent for disguise as well as "self-promotion," and "reckoned that in most cities it took just half an hour to get a drink." He and Moe had "smashed hundreds of home-stills, raided 3,000 bars, arrested over 4,300 people … confiscated five million bottles of bootleg liquor," and posted a "staggering 95 percent conviction rate." Yet in 1925, they were dismissed from the force, victims, perhaps, of their own success, which made some agents resentful and embarrassed by their "vaudevillian antics," and others, deprived of their bribe money, angry.[6] There was money to be made in Prohibition, and everyone, including those charged with upholding the law, wanted a cut.

Despite their toleration of the bootlegger, and their own unslaked thirst for illegal liquor, Americans became increasingly alarmed throughout the decade by the rise of organized crime, with its accompanying violence, which threatened the nation's safety and security. Prohibition did not, of course, lead to the invention of criminal gangs and crime syndicates, but the fortunes to be made in the illicit liquor trade certainly helped them to flourish. In Chicago, for instance, where rival gangs vying for control of the trade were fighting the city's Beer Wars in 1927, Al "Scarface" Capone had become the less-acceptable face of bootlegging. When threat and intimidation were ineffective in achieving control, Capone knew, beatings and assassination always achieved their ends. Indeed, in 1929, when a group of gangsters disguised as policemen gunned down seven members of a rival gang, the notorious St. Valentine's Day Massacre revealed the audacity of his ruthless power. Capone's conviction for tax evasion in 1931 was cause for relief among the public. It was one thing for the bootlegger to ply his trade but another thing entirely for mob bosses such as Capone and Charlie "Lucky" Luciano in New York to control the trade and reign with terror.

The common thread in this and other elements of Prohibition culture was hypocrisy, especially in the eyes of America's youth. Prohibition was good for the nation, but not for fine, upstanding citizens like themselves. Bootleggers with the entrepreneurial spirit to give their customers what they wanted were outlaw heroes, but gangsters who organized the trade were criminals. Those sworn to enforce the law and protect the nation were easily corrupted and turned their eyes from the roadhouses and jook joints, the speakeasies and cabarets, the house and rent parties where drinkers congregated for a good time. According to Fitzgerald in his 1931 essay "Echoes of the Jazz Age," the elder generation, grown "tired of watching the carnival with ill-concealed envy, had discovered that young liquor will take the place of young blood" (*CU* 15). These "honest citizens of every class, who believed in strict public morality and were powerful enough to enforce the necessary legislation," then preferred not to acknowledge the effects of their behavior or to admit that "they had contributed to it" (*CU* 16). In the face of their elders' obvious double standards and blatant disregard for the law, it was inevitable that American youth in the 1920s became equally disdainful of it, and that they, too, embraced the cultural changes of Prohibition with all the gay abandon generally ascribed to the younger generation.

The 1920s youth culture, according to Paula S. Fass, after some debate of the issue, initially made an effort to comply with Prohibition because it was the law of the land, just as their elders had done.[7] On college campuses, however, where drinking enlivened sporting events, homecoming weekends, fraternity parties, and other social occasions, bootleggers quickly established their presence. "By the spring of 1920," according to historian Herbert Asbury, "campuses swarmed with bootleggers, and most college towns supported a larger number of speakeasies than they ever had saloons."[8] For youths in the 1920s, Prohibition had become law at a time of social and cultural change: women were embracing new freedoms, Hollywood and the movie industry were redefining popular entertainment, and consumer culture was on the rise. In addition, these young men and women would have been eager to push boundaries, to experiment with new fashions and fads, to consider new ideas, to embrace the modern, and they were fulfilling those expectations. Although much of the action of Fitzgerald's first two novels occurs just prior to 1920, Amory Blaine of *This Side of Paradise* (1920) and *The Beautiful and Damned*'s Anthony and Gloria Patch epitomized 1920s youth (much to the horror of their elders), and drinking was part of their lives. A sign of liberation from convention, it was "an unofficially sanctioned peer activity" (Fass 314). Not surprisingly, then, by the end of the decade, the polls of the Congressional Hearing on the Repeal of the Prohibition Amendment revealed that young adults were drinking in significant numbers (Fass 311) and that college "students overwhelmingly opposed the law" (Fass 321). Like their elders, young adults believed that National Prohibition was a failed experiment. Many even claimed that criminalizing alcohol had fostered their drinking culture (Fass 321).

Those congressional hearings clearly signaled the end of Prohibition. In 1929, Congress had attempted to reinforce the Volstead Act by increasing fines and prison terms, even for first offenses, but that law, too, the Jones Act, was evidence that Americans had never fully accepted the limits on their freedoms and that when it came to drinking they were unwilling to conform to others' ideas of moral behavior. It took the Depression, however, to make the country "wet" again. Just as it had been patriotic to support Prohibition during World War I, so, too, did it become patriotic to accept its repeal in 1933, when the promise of increased tax receipts and economic expansion and job creation offered hope in the midst of financial collapse. On December 5, 1933, President Franklin D. Roosevelt signed the Twenty-first Amendment to the Constitution, repealing Prohibition. America's noble experiment was over.

National Prohibition, however, had largely defined an era. It had created bootleggers and speakeasies, booze barons and gangsters, corrupt officials and a climate of violence, and, above all, a seemingly insatiable thirst for alcohol. By making drinking fashionable across every age and gender and race, it had also done irreparable harm to the temperance movement, which effectively presided over an increase in alcohol consumption and a shift from beer to spirits. Perhaps most significant, it had undermined Americans' belief in their government. By criminalizing an activity that most citizens did not consider a crime because they engaged in it themselves, the government lost much of its credibility among Americans convinced that they knew as well as, if not better than, their representatives what constituted right behavior. In 1920, at the beginning of the modern moment, many of these and other phenomena associated with Prohibition may have developed on their own, but the link between jazz and the cabaret, for instance, the cabaret and the cocktail, and the cocktail and the bootlegger makes it clear that Prohibition helped to drive the changes of the era and left its indelible mark on it.

NOTES

1 L. Dumenil, *The Modern Temper: American Culture and Society in the 1920s* (New York: Hill and Wang, 1995), 226. Subsequent references to this work are included in the text.

2 W. E. Leuchtenberg, *Perils of Prosperity, 1914–1932*, 1958 (Chicago and London: University of Chicago Press, 1993), 34.

3 K. Drowne, *Spirits of Defiance: National Prohibition and Jazz Age Literature, 1920–1933* (Columbus, OH: The Ohio State University Press, 2005), 18. Subsequent references to this work are included in the text.

4 S. Lewis, *Babbitt*, 1922 (New York: Penguin Books, 1996), 125.

5 F. L. Allen, *Only Yesterday: An Informal History of the 1920's*, 1931 (New York: Harper & Row, 1964), 208.

6 L. Moore, *Anything Goes: A Biography of the Roaring Twenties* (New York: The Overlook Press, 2010), 28–29.

7 P. S. Fass, *The Damned and the Beautiful: American Youth in the 1920's*, 1977 (Oxford: Oxford University Press, 1979), 311–12. Subsequent references to this work are included in the text.

8 H. Asbury, *The Great Illusion: An Informal History of Prohibition* (Garden City, NY: Doubleday and Company, 1950), 162.

20

Class Differences in Fitzgerald's Works

Peter L. Hays

F. Scott Fitzgerald was the son of a failed Procter and Gamble salesman who had descended from Maryland landed gentry, what Dickens would have called shabby gentility; the author's full first and middle names are Francis Scott Key, for the cousin who wrote the lyrics to "The Star-Spangled Banner." His mother was a first-generation American descendent of Irish immigrants who built a wholesale grocery business in St. Paul, Minnesota; they had the money to send him to Newman School in New Jersey and then Princeton, but not enough to give him the best clothes, a car, or a lavish allowance, as many of his classmates at Princeton had. He always felt like an outsider because of his relative poverty, writing that his experience had been that "of a poor boy in a rich boy's school, a poor boy in a rich man's club at Princeton ... I have never been able to forgive the rich for being rich" (*LL* 233–34, 352). While courting his first love, Ginevra King, Fitzgerald was told that "poor boys shouldn't think of marrying rich girls" (*FSFL* 170). Fitzgerald himself said that he "would always cherish an abiding distrust, an animosity, toward the leisure class – not the conviction of a revolutionary, but the smoldering hatred of a peasant ... I have never been able to stop ... thinking that at one time a sort of *droit de seigneur* might have been exercised to give one of them [the wealthy] my girl" (*CU* 77). Despite all myths of equality to the contrary, there were and are class distinctions in America, and here Fitzgerald names a major distinction, that of money, that divides the "leisure class" from the "peasants." Or, as he quoted from the lyrics to "Ain't We Got Fun" by Raymond B. Egan and Gus Kahn in *The Great Gatsby*, "One thing's sure and nothing's surer/The rich get richer and the poor get – children" (*GG* 75). The rhyme, of course, demands "poorer," but the begetting of children primarily by the poor implied their lack of access to birth control or knowledge about it, as well, perhaps, as the implication that American Protestants had fewer children than recent immigrants from Ireland and Europe, many of whom were Catholic and therefore did not practice birth control.

Fitzgerald's well-to-do characters are snobs who look down on those they perceive as beneath them; perhaps that had happened to him at school. Anson Hunter of "The Rich Boy" had a "sense of superiority," which he accepted "as the natural state of things," and "he expected it to be given him freely" (*S* 319). He will not compete, because he assumes preeminence; thus, he lets the love of his life, Paula Legendre, marry another because he assumes she is his. When she expects his proposal of marriage, he defers: "He need say no more … Why should he, when he might hold her so, biding his own time, for another year – forever? … He hesitated, thinking, first, 'This is the moment, after all,' and then, 'No, let it wait – she is mine'" (*S* 327). He humiliates another woman, Dolly Karger, who expects him to marry her, and he drives his aunt's lover to suicide, all without remorse. He is of the elite, in his own mind, and therefore beyond reproach, and Anthony Patch and Tom Buchanan feel much the same way. Even Nick Carraway, with whom we are supposed to identify, is a snob, as he says on the first page of the novel, and he shows no sympathy whatsoever for lower-middle-class, hard-working, cuckolded George Wilson.

Fitzgerald did not write about the poor. There are no manual laborers or shopgirls among his main characters, few farmers or truck drivers. There is James Gatz's farmer father in *The Great Gatsby,* but he is only a background figure, and his lower-class status is established when he informs Nick that his son "told me I et like a hog once and I beat him for it" (*GG* 135). There is middle-class garage owner George Wilson, whose passion for his wife in another novel might be heroic, but Fitzgerald undercuts his devotion to his wife by his obtuseness to his wife's affair, and by Myrtle's declaring that she had thought George was a gentleman, someone who "knew something about breeding" (*GG* 30), but was disabused of that notion of his class status when she discovers that the suit he married her in was borrowed from another man. His religious belief is also undercut when Fitzgerald juxtaposes George's "God sees everything" with Michaelis's "That's an advertisement" (*GG* 125). Even the lower-middle class has its pretensions, as Myrtle denounces the "shiftlessness of the lower orders" (*GG* 27). Members of the working classes are minor, secondary characters, such as the discharged soldiers and socialist press editor in "May Day," or Earl Schoen, the streetcar conductor in "The Last of the Belles." We see very little of Anthony Patch's soldiering and more of his drinking and affair with Dorothy Raycroft; that Dexter Green of "Winter Dreams" is a caddy is just a way for him to meet Judy Jones, and soon he becomes the owner of many laundries.[1] Fitzgerald wrote about the very rich – the Patches, Buchanans, and Warrens – and an upper-middle class striving to be like them, like them less in obvious wealth than in manners, dress, and confidence, as Nick Carraway does, ignoring the fact that old money looked down on arrivistes, and as Fitzgerald also did, buying a second-hand Rolls-Royce while he lived in Great Neck, New York. Nick, the grandson of a hardware wholesaler, comes to New York to sell bonds. At Gatsby's parties, young men "were all selling something: bonds or insurance or automobiles" (*GG* 35). Yet the class structure remains, "the staid nobility of the country-side – East Egg condescending to West Egg" (*GG* 37), "the less fashionable of the two" (*GG* 8).

Eric Schocket writes, "A conservative discourse . . . has always maintained (the facts notwithstanding) that class simply does not describe the experience of people in this country, that our lives are mobile, self-fashioned, and free of determinations."[2] He continues, explaining that "the terms *rank, order,* and *station* all preexisted [class] and served quite adequately to demarcate a system of feudal distinctions organized around bloodlines . . . The concept of class arose only with the ascendant bourgeoisie and [quoting Raymond Williams[3]] 'their increasing consciousness that social position is made rather than merely inherited'" (Schocket 12–13; Williams 61–62). Yet standard books of sociology of the time surveyed Americans who made the distinction clear between inherited wealth and position and those who were newly rich: "The upper class can be subdivided into two categories – the self-made men who have climbed from middle-class origins to the very top positions in business and the professions, and the men who have inherited wealth and position from the efforts of a previous generation." Further, standard charts of class structure in these texts, as determined by people who were interviewed, separated upper class into "old aristocracy," and "aristocracy but not old"[4] – that is, the newly rich. Anthony Patch scorns Bloeckman in part because he is a Jew and therefore not of Anthony's social circle; Anthony's grandfather, Adam Patch, married a woman whose $100,000 allowed him to enter Wall Street, and Anthony at college had an allowance that "was more than liberal. He . . . purchas[ed] first editions of Swinburne, Meredith and Hardy . . . He became an exquisite dandy, amassed a rather pathetic collection of silk pajamas, brocaded dressing gowns, and neckties too flamboyant to wear" (*B&D* 14–15) – much more of an allowance than Fitzgerald had at Princeton. But Anthony also looks down on Bloeckman because he works for his money. Part of Gatsby's tragedy – besides his idealization of Daisy – is his belief in the American myth of a classless society, that his newly acquired wealth has made him the equal of Tom Buchanan; no one told him that "poor boys shouldn't think of marrying rich girls" or that there is a distinction between inherited and recently earned wealth. But another part of his reason for wanting to marry Daisy is for confirmation of his social acceptance, much as Faulkner's Sutpen in *Absalom, Absalom!* seeks social respectability in marrying Ellen Coldfield.

As the sociological surveys above indicate, Americans distinguished between old money and new, between fine manners (however conservative, racist, and stifling) and those crudely imitating them. Edith Wharton had made a career of documenting that gap; Fitzgerald did so, too. His characters act as they presume their social betters act, as Myrtle Wilson does, putting on airs in her New York City apartment, trying to behave as the regal hostess as she believes that Daisy would do, imitating, in Ronald Berman's belief, wide-gesturing actresses of the silent screen.[5] Helping the social-climbing aspirants was Emily Post, whose 1923 book *Etiquette,* while providing proper deportment, used demeaning names to help the Unsuitables, Mr Richan Vulgar, and "pathetic Miss Nobackground" behave like the Oldnames and Miss Wellborn (Berman 73); among the unsuitables we could place *Gatsby*'s McKees and *Tender*'s Mrs. Abrams and the McKiscos. Yet the upper-middle classes could easily detect the lower classes. Ailie Calhoun of "The Last of the Belles" says that if her mother "ever saw anybody like" former streetcar conductor Earl Schoen "come in the house, she'd just lie down and die" (*S* 455). Earl had "about everything wrong with him that could be imagined. His hat was green, with a radical feather; his suit was slashed and braided … It wasn't as though he had been shiny and poor, but the background of mill-town dance halls and outing clubs flamed out at Ailie" (459). Poor whites did not have the necessary wardrobe acumen, apparent in Gatsby's flamboyant shirts, "shirts with stripes and scrolls and plaids in coral and apple green and lavender and faint orange with monograms of Indian blue" (72). Businessmen dressed in black or dark gray with white shirts, and Tom Buchanan's scorn for Gatsby's pink suit is obvious (95). Nor did the poor or nouveau riche have the social graces of those to the manor born, and therefore they were snubbed by those who did, as Gatsby is snubbed by Mr. Sloane for not recognizing that the invitation he has received to dinner is at best social courtesy by a drunken woman and not at all an invitation between social equals (80). Gatsby simply does not realize that his new wealth, even if it were not criminally earned, does not make him Tom Buchanan's social equal.

Women, often second-class citizens in terms of financial and social power, receive different treatment from Fitzgerald based on their class status. Poor women – Dot Raycroft, Myrtle Wilson – are used by those more wealthy or with greater social standing – Anthony Patch and Tom Buchanan, respectively – even as they try to raise their own status by their relationships with these men (much as Gatsby tries to do with Daisy). Wealthy women, or sexually attractive upper-class women, have power. Judy Jones of "Winter Dreams" is a female Anson Hunter, using her beauty and social position to toy with the men who desire her: "She was entertained only by the gratification of her desires and by the direct exercise of her own charm" (*S* 227). Baby Warren in *Tender Is the Night* regards middle-class Dick Diver as a doctor to be purchased for her sister, and even Nicole, infused with Dick's vitality, ultimately discards him as worn-out, as she might any other no-longer-working appliance or article of clothing. Daisy can choose between her repulsive but socially acceptable husband or loving but lower-class Gatsby, and she chooses to stay with "her own kind." Nick, sexist snob that he is, dismisses Jordan's incurable dishonesty, saying that "Dishonesty in a woman is a thing you never blame deeply" (*GG* 48), ignoring his own dishonesties throughout the novel.[6] But Nick also states that Jordan "felt safer on a plane where any divergence from a code would be impossible" (*GG* 47) and so limits her associations, something her social status allows, something not within a poor woman's scope. Jordan (named for a flashy roadster of the era), from a socially prominent family, commands middle-class Nick's respect: "Almost any exhibition of complete self-sufficiency draws a stunned tribute from me" (*GG* 11). Of course, it is her social station that grants her self-sufficiency. In *Gatsby*, the privileged girlhoods of Daisy and Jordan in Louisville have to be seen as products of white privilege: Fitzgerald repeats "white" four times during Jordan's description of Daisy and Gatsby in Louisville (*GG* 59), in contrast to segregated African Americans restricted by Jim Crow laws and considered in the South as socially inferior.

Fitzgerald recognized that women of his time had been freed from the restricting corsets their mothers wore and were entering sports, but sports such as golf and tennis were for the well-to-do like English Joyce Wethered, Lady Heathcoat-Amory, who tied for the British Open in 1921; American Helen Mills, who won two Olympic gold medals in Paris in 1924 and played in the finals at Wimbledon in 1926; or Jordan's actual model, Edith Cummings, who won the 1923 U.S. Women's Amateur championship. Cummings was a Chicago debutante and friend and classmate of Ginevra King. Poor men like Jack Dempsey or Babe Ruth could advance financially through sports, as did players on the Chicago White Sox, the team Wolfsheim purportedly bribed to throw the 1919 World

Series, but such avenues of advancement were denied women. Professional boxing, baseball, and football did not allow women; their only sports were ones that demanded wealth and access to country clubs. Poor girls, like the accounting clerk with whom Nick has a brief affair (*GG* 46) and then discards for Jordan, has no time for sports: she must work to support herself, and probably her family. Myrtle expects Tom to divorce Daisy and marry her; Dot dreams that Anthony will marry her (*B&D* 278). As Anthony reflects, "Gloria and he had been equals … To this girl his very caresses were an inestimable boon" (277), but when his company moves north, Dot is abandoned, with no apparent word from Anthony, just as Nick abandons the girl in accounting from New Jersey, again, presumably with no word from him (*GG* 46).

Ethnic and racial minorities in the period of the 1920s and 1930s are presented in Fitzgerald's fiction as groups that were demeaned because they were deemed, by white Anglo-Saxon Protestants, the Nordics of eugenicist texts, and Tom Buchanan's racist rant in *Gatsby* (14), as socially inferior. The nouveaux riches saw themselves under assault by hordes of immigrants and ethnic minorities, and so the privileged class held tightly to its prominence. To maintain their prestige, the well-to-do employed exclusive clubs, fine but understated clothes, and snobbish manners. Thus, Tom derides Gatsby's garish clothes and his opulent "circus wagon" of a car (*GG* 94), whereas he drives a more discreet blue coupe. Tom fears that his position of social supremacy will be eroded by the Mister Nobodies from Nowhere (101); he cannot understand how Gatsby could have approached Daisy unless he was delivering groceries to her back door (102). Nick, lower in social standing than Tom, can still mock "three modish Negroes, two bucks and a girl" (*GG* 55). Anthony looks down on Bloeckman, whose behavior toward Gloria is irreproachable, while Anthony dallies with Dot. Fifi Schwartz, in "The Hotel Child," is considered declassé both because she is Jewish and because of "[s]uch ghastly taste … The stage, the shop window, the manikins' parade"; the social elite consider Fifi "was as much of a gratuitous outrage as a new stripe in the flag" (*S* 599–600). After she scratches the face of the Marquis Kinkallow in response to his unwelcome advances (Fitzgerald's pun in his name no doubt intended), the marquis tells her that she is "a common little person" and "a laughingstock of the hotel" (*S* 604). In *Tender,* death and a breakdown for Nicole occur because Abe North goes drinking in a bar with those beneath his social class and, perhaps, gets robbed of a thousand-franc note. The man who, along with Abe, misidentifies the thief, a Swede named Jules Peterson, is killed in Rosemary's hotel bedroom by friends of a restaurateur named Freeman, also arrested in the incident. No one in the novel mourns for Peterson. When a friend of Freeman's contacts Nicole at her hotel, she "disclaim[s] with a vehement clap of the [telephone] receiver" (*TITN* 126) the whole sordid business of these inferiors and goes out to buy "artificial flowers and all-colored strings of colored beads," and for her son, "Greek and Roman soldiers, a whole army of them, costing over a thousand francs" (*TITN* 126–27). Jules Peterson is killed, while Abe North, who created the situation, desires his next drink, and Dick's immediate concern is only for Rosemary. That Peterson, Freeman, and the thief are black is irrelevant to what happens, even though Dick calls the event a "nigger scrap" (145). There is little sympathy for Peterson from Abe, none from Rosemary or Dick, or from Fitzgerald either, except for his description of Peterson as "ill nourished" (145). Fitzgerald complicates our feelings for Peterson by resorting to stereotypical descriptions of blacks – "his insincere eyes, that from time to time, rolled white circles of panic into view" (140) – and by Peterson's incorrect English: "I was drove away" (140). Peterson's problems are an irritant in their lives, and his death causes Nicole to break down. He is a social inferior, and Fitzgerald, identifying with Dick, wants our sympathies to lie with Dick and Nicole, not with the murdered, penniless man.

Along with the influx of immigrants to America the landscape was changing. Gatsby commiserates with Mr. Sloane on how paved roads have changed riding paths (*GG* 79). Automobiles changed America as Fitzgerald grew up. Fitzgerald documents "new red gas-pumps" in front of wayside garages (*GG* 20). People had greater mobility; they could more easily move from city to city seeking jobs or leave behind unpaid debts. Dating habits changed. A young man could take a woman for a ride into the country or to a club for dinner and dancing – hence the rapid development of roadhouses – rather than sit with her in her parents' parlor, as George O'Kelly has to do in "'The Sensible Thing.'" Industries developed, making cars, supplying them with fuel, providing appropriate clothing for motoring, and catering to them at roadsides. John D. Rockefeller, the robber baron purposefully named in *Gatsby* with regard to acquiring wealth (*GG* 24), made his fortune through Standard Oil. George Wilson seeks to make his modest fortune with a garage and the sale of cars, such as Tom Buchanan's. Fitzgerald notes the effect of the automobile by naming his narrator of *Gatsby* "Car-away," by having a car kill Myrtle Wilson, after Tom has exchanged cars with Gatsby, automobile for wife. Poor driving is a sign of irresponsibility. Nick accuses Jordan of being a bad driver (*GG* 48), and she returns the criticism (138). The prime example in *Gatsby* occurs when a drunk drives a car into a wall, shears a wheel off, and tries to back up (*GG* 44–46). For the well-to-do, cars could be replaced, and so could wives and mistresses. The increasingly rapid motion of the era was the opposite of staid moral solidity. As Fitzgerald notes in "Dice, Brassknuckles & Guitar," "When tourists come to … last-century landmarks, they stop their cars and gaze for a while … The tourist doesn't stay long. He drives to his Elizabethan villa of pressed cardboard or his early Norman meat-market or his medieval Italian pigeon-coop" (*S* 237). In contrast is Nick's hometown, reached by train, "where dwellings are still called through decades by a family's name" (*GG* 137), houses inhabited by middle-class and upper-class families generation after generation, such as the house lived in by James J. Hill, that other robber baron mentioned in the novel (*GG* 131), just up Summit Avenue from the Fitzgeralds' rented apartment in St. Paul.

Fitzgerald, that spoiled priest, as he called himself,[7] had mixed feelings about the progress of the automobile and the increasing fluidity of social classes, much as Edith Wharton had. Change was inevitable, and women in the 1920s were liberated in many ways. However, the changes also brought increasing commercialism, an eroding of the values of honor and family tradition instilled by his Confederate father (Mizener 11), and an influx of lower-class individuals – immigrants, Jews, blacks – seeking middle-class respectability, and newly wealthy members of the middle class aping the behavior of the social elite. Instead of going back from Great Neck to St. Paul to finish *Gatsby,* as he had gone from New York to finish *This Side of Paradise,* Fitzgerald went to the French Riviera. In the end, Fitzgerald could not dismiss his own desire to rise above the background of his maternal immigrant forebears and paternal line that had fallen onto hard times and blend seamlessly into the stratum of the rich, the cultured, the well-mannered – the class he had been educated in, dreamed of, and aspired to.

NOTES

1 As Veronica Makowsky notes, Fitzgerald "avoid[s] the middle class in his works." See V. Makowsky, "'Among Ash-Heaps and Millionaires': Teaching *The Great Gatsby* through the Lens of Class" in J. R. Bryer and N. VanArsdale (eds.), *Approaches to Teaching Fitzgerald's* The Great Gatsby (New York: The Modern Language Association, 2009) 75–83; 76.

2 E. Schocket, *Vanishing Moments: Class and Literature in American Literature* (Ann Arbor: University of Michigan Press, 2006), 12. Subsequent references to this work are included in the text.

3 See R. Williams, *Keywords: A Vocabulary of Culture and Society* (New York: Oxford University Press, 1983). Subsequent references to this work are included in the text.

4 J. A. Kahl, *The American Class Structure* (New York: Rinehart, 1957), 188. The charts are reprinted in D. Gilbert and J. A. Kahl, *The American Class Structure: A New Synthesis* (Belmont, CA: Wadsworth, 1987), 28, 32.

5 R. Berman, The Great Gatsby *and Modern Times* (Urbana: University of Illinois Press, 1994), 64. Subsequent references to this work are included in the text.

6 See P. L. Hays, "Enough Guild to Go Around: Teaching Fitzgerald's Lesson in Morality," in J. R. Bryer and N. VanArsdale (eds.), *Approaches to Teaching Fitzgerald's* The Great Gatsby (New York: The Modern Language Association, 2009), 169–74; 172–73.

7 A. Mizener, *The Far Side of Paradise: A Biography of F. Scott Fitzgerald* (Boston: Houghton Mifflin, 1951), 60. Subsequent references to this work are included in the text.

21

Ethnic Stereotyping

Suzanne del Gizzo

F. Scott Fitzgerald's vivid depictions of Ivy League youths, daring flappers, and sinister bootleggers have long been celebrated as a valuable entry point into American society in the 1920s (or at least a particular slice of it). But Fitzgerald's ability to capture his cultural moment also encompasses some of its less glamorous and savory aspects, including the period's obsessive fascination with ethnic and racial distinctions. In fact, Fitzgerald's frequent and uncritical use of racial and ethnic stereotypes – from clownish, obsequious African Americans to arrogant, hostile Jews – in his writing prompted Robert Forrey to observe in 1967 that "On the question of race [and ethnicity], Fitzgerald does not belong to the liberal tradition of American letters."[1]

Scholars have attempted to explain Fitzgerald's ubiquitous and persistent use of stereotyping in his writing in a variety of ways. Many critics observe that his use of racial and ethnic stereotypes reflects the attitudes of the period and is thus an extension of his interest in faithfully representing the world around him. Alan Margolies notes that "the United States during [Fitzgerald's] lifetime was racist and anti-Semitic in many respects"[2] and explains that Fitzgerald's use of words like "coon" and "pickaninny" may be understood as an attempt to depict contemporary speech accurately (77). Forrey and Margolies also suggest that Fitzgerald's stereotypes frequently serve artistic or dramatic purposes within his works. Forrey observes that Fitzgerald generally uses black characters (especially in his early fiction) for comic effect, pointing out that "Fitzgerald ... had a weakness for cheap jokes" (294). Margolies adds that Fitzgerald often deployed stereotypes with some thematic purpose in mind. For example, he contends that in *The Great Gatsby* the stereotypical Jewish gangster Meyer Wolfsheim is linked to the equally stereotyped Nordic, Tom Buchanan, to highlight Tom's disagreeable qualities, and that in *Tender Is the Night* Dick Diver's decline is in part demonstrated through his increasing use of racial and ethnic slurs.

Mimetic and artistic reasons aside, critics have also probed the extent to which Fitzgerald's use of racial and ethnic stereotypes may have reflected his personal views. Such efforts are necessarily speculative and perhaps ultimately irrelevant to assessments of an author's literary work, but Fitzgerald's iconic status and his use of biographical details in his fiction have made such speculations irresistible. Michael Nowlin has suggested that Fitzgerald's reliance on ethnic and racial types may have been linked to his personal anxieties and preoccupations about his social, racial, and artistic status. As any reader of Fitzgerald knows, the author and his characters are obsessed with extraordinarily fine distinctions between people by physical type, manners, class, or even club membership. Throughout his life Fitzgerald was plagued by feelings of inadequacy. He memorably lamented that he felt like "a poor boy in a rich man's club" (*LL* 352), and he was self-conscious about his "half black Irish" background (*L* 503), since the Irish were among the immigrant groups excluded from contemporary definitions of whiteness. In addition, he agonized over the nature of his literary output, feeling torn between the financial necessity of publishing commercially viable short stories and his desire to write less profitable but artistically ambitious novels. From this perspective, Fitzgerald's readiness to deploy exclusionary stereotypical images of racial and ethnic others may be seen as a means of securing his insider, elite status.

Regardless of the reason behind it, most scholars agree that Fitzgerald's attitude toward and use of racial and ethnic others in his writing became more sensitive and nuanced over the course of his career. A brief survey of his writing bears this out. Monroe Stahr, the multi-faceted Jewish, movie-producer protagonist of Fitzgerald's unfinished final novel, *The Love of the Last Tycoon*, cuts a more realistic, sympathetic, and compelling figure than the shady Meyer Wolfsheim, with his "gonnegion[s]" in *The Great Gatsby* (*GG* 55–56). And there is a notable difference between the ignorant African-American characters in early short stories like Jumbo in "The Camel's Back" and the thoughtful black man who reads Ralph Waldo Emerson and rocks an industry when he tells Stahr that he won't let his children go to the movies in *The Love of the Last Tycoon*. Fitzgerald's increasing sensitivity, however, is tempered by his persistent reliance on racial and ethnic stereotypes in essays and personal correspondence late into his life.

The America of Fitzgerald's formative years was characterized by a stunning amount of energy and anxiety around the issues of race and ethnicity. While Fitzgerald's flappers and their beaux were smoking on country club verandahs and "petting" in automobiles, the Ku Klux Klan was experiencing a resurgence, the United States Congress was passing legislation severely restricting immigration, and that mainstay of middle-class culture, the *Saturday Evening Post,* was publishing articles that espoused the pseudo-scientific racist theories of prominent eugenicists. Much of this energy was sparked by changes in the economic and social landscape owing to industrialization and the attendant influx of immigrant and African American labor into Northern cities. Between 1880 and 1924, 24 million European immigrants (2.5 million were Jews) entered the United States,[3] and between 1915 and 1920, half a million African Americans moved North, followed by a million more during the 1920s as part of the Great Migration.[4] These mass migrations not only made immigrant and African-American populations increasingly visible in American cities, but they also highlighted the rapid economic, social, and cultural changes that self-christened "native" Americans perceived as a threat to their power and control.

These nativists, a group largely comprised of white Americans, usually of a particular ethnic background and social class, desperately tried to control the definition of American identity. According to John Higham, the nativist movement defined itself through "intense opposition to [internal minorities] on the grounds of [their] foreign (i.e. 'un-American') connections."[5] Walter Benn Michaels further explains that by the 1920s the rhetoric of nativism was grafted onto discourses of blood and family in an attempt to make American identity "the sort of thing that had to be inherited (from one's parents)" and not "the sort of thing that could be acquired (through naturalization)."[6] In this way, nativism intersected with the pseudo-scientific field of eugenics. Although "scientific" ideas about race began to circulate in America during the eighteenth century, such thinking gained legitimacy during the first quarter of the twentieth century through publications such as Madison Grant's *The Passing of the Great Race* (1916), C. B. Davenport's "The Effects of Race Intermingling" (1917), and Lothrop Stoddard's *The Rising Tide of Color Against White Supremacy* (1920).[7] These authors and many others like them created a hierarchy of racial types that attempted not only to draw a firm line between whites and obvious "others," but also to delineate gradations of whiteness and thus of moral, cultural, intellectual, and spiritual superiority. Grant, for example, argued that white people from Western Europe were a "race" superior to other white people, and of course, to non-whites everywhere,[8] while Stoddard constructed a racial hierarchy with the Nordic at the top followed by the Alpines and Mediterraneans (Rohrkemper 23). Such schemas encouraged separation between "races" and enabled arguments that the perceived loss of white cultural and social dominance was to some extent due to the degenerative effects of racial "contamination."

As archaic, artificial, and marginal as such gradations and concerns may seem to most twenty-first century readers, they were widely accepted as part of mainstream discourse in the America of the 1920s. Such thinking infiltrated nearly all spheres of American life. Respected public officials such as Theodore Roosevelt expressed concerns about "race suicide" (Gidley 173), and Vice President Coolidge explained in the pages of *Good Housekeeping* that "Biological law tells us that certain divergent people will not mix or blend. The Nordics propagate themselves successfully. With other races, the outcome shows deterioration on both sides."[9] These attitudes motivated political initiatives such as the Johnson-Reed Act of 1924, which not only severely restricted immigration, but also established immigration quotas based on a principle of national origins; immigration from a given country could not exceed 2–3 percent of the current population from that country in the United States. Michaels explains that "eligibility for American citizenship was now dependent upon ethnic identity" (30). Such thinking was present in cultural institutions as well. Fitzgerald's highly respected publisher, Scribners, also published Grant's *The Passing of the Great Race*. While Scribners editors were fastidious about tempering or editing out "sexual or blasphemous passages" in works by their authors, they clearly did not object to the inclusion of racial and ethnic stereotypes (Margolies 75). Even popular magazines that catered to a large middle-class audience published articles that validated eugenics and condoned racial purity. The *Saturday Evening Post*, which according to John Higham was "the most widely read magazine in the United States" in the 1920s and one of the major publishers of Fitzgerald's early short stories, not only "began to quote and urgently commend [Grant's] doctrines" (265), but also published a series of alarmist and xenophobic articles by Kenneth Roberts with titles such as "Guests from Italy," "Shutting the Sea Gates," and "Slow Poison" about the inferiority of immigrant populations and the dangers of race mixing.[10]

The exclusionary ethos of Fitzgerald's country clubs and dinner clubs may thus be seen as microcosmic versions of the hierarchical structures and discriminatory practices that dominated American public life at this time. In particular, his writings from the 1920s capture – and to some extent critique – the discourses of nativism and eugenics. Amory Blaine, the protagonist of Fitzgerald's first novel, *This Side of Paradise* (1920), obsesses over different dinner clubs and activities that will secure his status at Princeton. At one point, he takes refuge in a kind of primitive (almost parodic) eugenics. After careful study of the last ten years of Princeton yearbooks, the fair Amory finds comfort in the fact that there are a preponderance of blonds on the senior council, a marker of collegiate success, even though only "thirty-five per cent of every class are blonds, are really light" (*TSOP* 122). His friend Burne Holiday agrees: "The light-haired man is a higher type. I worked the thing out with the Presidents of the United States once and found that over half of them were light-haired" (122–23). Although the tone here is arguably ironic, such reasoning echoes two serious studies from the *Journal of Heredity* in 1920 that "attempted to correlate nose shape, and hair and eye color of Nordic families with worldly achievement and power" (Nies 85). In addition, Amory's elitist sentiments co-exist with feelings of "repulsion" when he is thrown in a train car across from "stinking aliens – Greeks, he guessed, or Russians" (139). As he considers his pending service in World War I, "[h]e thought how much easier patriotism had been to a homogenous race, how much easier it would have been to fight as the Colonies fought, or as Confederacy fought" (139). Despite Amory's feelings – some of which, like admiration for the "'racial purity' of the Confederacy" (Gidley 175), reflect Fitzgerald's opinions – there is evidence that Fitzgerald was not wholly certain of the validity of eugenics, or at least that he believed it was already too late to secure Nordic dominance. Amory falls from grace. He is not invited back to Princeton and is flirting with socialism, a political affiliation associated with immigrant groups, at the end of the novel, suggesting that his genetic endowments and privileged memberships have not been guarantors of success.

Amory is in many ways an autobiographical character, and Fitzgerald appears to have shared at least some of his character's views on race and eugenics at this point in his life. In a 1921 letter to Edmund Wilson, written shortly after a trip to Europe, Fitzgerald complained: "The negroid streak creeps northward to defile the Nordic race ... Raise the bars of immigration and permit only Scandinavians, Teutons, Anglo-Saxons and Celts to enter" (*L* 326). Although Fitzgerald acknowledges these "reactions" are "philistine, anti-social, provincial and racially snobbish," he continues that "I believe at last in the white man's burden" (*L* 326).

The Beautiful and Damned (1922) also demonstrates anxieties about ethnic others and the loss of white power and control, but this novel targets Jews specifically as "initiator[s] of undesirable social change."[11] Set in New York, a city known for its diversity, Fitzgerald's protagonist, Anthony Patch, rehearses the sentiments about immigrants espoused by Amory in *This Side of Paradise* and Fitzgerald in his 1921 letter to Wilson. Walking with his wife, Gloria, down a street in New York, Anthony observes "a dozen Jewish names on the line of stores; in the door of each stood a dark little man watching the passers from intent eyes – eyes gleaming with suspicion, with pride, with clarity, with cupidity, with comprehension" (*B&D* 237). Anthony sees these stores as evidence of "the slow, *upward creep* of this people" (237; my italics). The "upward creep of this people" almost directly repeats Fitzgerald's concern about the "negroid streak [that] *creeps* upward to defile the Nordic race" (my italics). Immigrants, and particularly Jewish immigrants, present a menace to white dominance in this novel.

Fitzgerald explores this menace primarily through the intersecting storylines of the privileged Anthony Patch, descendant of "old stock" Northern European settlers, and the Jewish immigrant Joseph Bloeckman. Early in the novel, Anthony is described as possessing Nordic features – a "sharp" nose and "blue eyes" (*B&D* 16) – and as "very clean in appearance and reality, with that special cleanliness borrowed from beauty" (16), a description that evokes the link between physical features and cleanliness that marks eugenic discourse (Nies 90); his wife, Gloria, is described as a classical beauty, a "Nordic Ganymede" (94). Bloeckman, on the other hand, is described as "boiled looking" (84), a "stoutening, ruddy Jew of about thirty-five" (84), who is associated with the carnival (he got his start as a peanut vendor). By the end of the novel, Anthony and Gloria have been reduced to squalor – Gloria is described as "unclean" (368) and Anthony's once fine physique is "stooped and flabby" (365) and his blue eyes are "blood-shot" and "weak" (325) – while Bloeckman, who has changed his name to Black and obscured his ethnicity, has become "a dark, suave gentleman, gracefully engaged in the middle forties" (328). Anthony and Gloria's descent coupled with Bloeckman's rise suggests that Fitzgerald may have considered white dominance as something already lost, particularly in metropolises such as New York.

While Fitzgerald's first two novels take the threat posed by new immigrants, particularly Jews, seriously, his early short stories contain less defensive but equally stereotypical portrayals of African Americans. As Forrey points out, African Americans in Fitzgerald's early fiction are nearly always hapless, menial characters who serve as a kind of comic relief based on the notion that "[w]hat is tragic for whites is comic for Negroes" (294). African Americans do not represent the direct threat that immigrants do, probably because their "otherness" was at least in theory more readily discernable through their dark skin color. Moreover, there was a tradition of their intimate service to whites in the Confederate

South, which established them in a benign and comfortable relation to white superiority. Although Fitzgerald would later explore more threatening and enigmatic black characters in novels such as *Tender Is the Night* (1934), early in his career blacks were familiar, and the idea of their social success was generally laughable.

Fitzgerald's complex attitudes toward issues of race and ethnicity are perhaps most clearly visible in his third and best-known novel, *The Great Gatsby* (1925). The novel not only contains some of his most memorable racial and ethnic stereotypes, but it also explicitly and implicitly critiques eugenics through the language of breeding. Fitzgerald locates eugenic theories in the strained, feeble musings of the unsympathetic, hypocritical, Nordic Tom Buchanan, a man who "breeds" horses as a pastime. Early in the novel, Tom explains with "pathetic" concentration how "[c]ivilization's going to pieces" and how "the white race will be – will be utterly submerged," "scientific stuff" gleaned from a book called "'The Rise of the Coloured Empires' by this man Goddard" (*GG* 14).[12] Although not explicitly linked, the implied association between animal and human breeding was a common theme in eugenic literature and would have been familiar to Fitzgerald's readers. In a 1922 issue of the *Saturday Evening Post*, Kenneth Roberts writes the following: "[T]here are certain biological laws which govern the crossing of different breeds, whether the breeds be dogs or horses or men" (qtd. in Nies 101). Tom's ideas are further satirized through the bumptious pronouncements of his lower-class mistress, Myrtle, who opines about "breeding" in both dogs and men, although her lack of discrimination is made evident when she has Tom buy her an "Airedale" puppy that clearly has a mixed pedigree and by her marriage to the anemic George Wilson.

Most significantly, Nick Carraway's overall sympathy for the parvenu Jay Gatsby, a man with mysterious antecedents who is closely associated with the Jewish gangster Wolfsheim, also suggests a critique of bloodlines as a marker of meaningful distinction. Gatsby, whose ethnic and racial background is left tantalizingly unclear,[13] represents the social threat posed by "outsiders" who "by the bluff and bravado of their self-transformation have been made into the forceful levers of wealth that will, they believe, propel them into society."[14] Fitzgerald here explores anxieties about competing modes of establishing distinction – money and ancestry – with the understanding that ancestry is the ultimate requirement. Arguably, Gatsby longs to acquire Daisy Fay Buchanan because she gives him access to the right names and bloodlines, which will allow him to secure his position in a way that money alone cannot. Tom reveals the eugenic twist when, discovering Daisy's affair with Gatsby, he retorts, "I suppose the latest thing is to sit back and let Mr. Nobody from Nowhere make love to your wife ... Next they'll throw everything overboard and have intermarriage between black and white" (*GG* 101).

The parodic tone toward eugenics in the novel, however, is undermined by Nick's nostalgia for a simpler (romanticized) American past, which frames the narrative and informs the narrative's hypersensitivity to distinctions between people. After his tumultuous summer out East, Nick returns to the stable predictability of the Midwest and his hometown where "dwellings are still called through the decades by a family's name," a "white" landscape that he likes to think of as covered in "our snow" (*GG* 137). In addition, Fitzgerald's insensitive use of stereotypes (albeit from Nick's point of view) complicates the novel's tone. In particular, two moments are singled out repeatedly by critics for their unfortunate use of stereotype: the haughty but harmless "three modish negroes, two bucks and a girl" in a limousine driven by a white chauffeur and the "small, flat-nosed Jew" with a "large head," "tiny eyes," and "an expressive nose," Meyer Wolfsheim (55). The stereotyping, however, helps to safely contain these characters through the obvious markers of difference on their bodies and in their mannerisms. In this way, they highlight the danger posed by Gatsby, who is less clearly "other" and who has encroached upon the Long Island retreat of the established classes.

Fitzgerald was sensitive to criticism about his use of stereotypes. His secretary, Frances Kroll Ring, recalls his denial that the portrayal of Wolfsheim was anti-Semitic; his defense was that "Wolfsheim was a character whose behavior fulfilled a function in the story and had nothing to do with race or religion. He was a gangster who happened to be Jewish" (qtd. in Abramson 125). Despite his defensiveness and justifications, Fitzgerald exhibited personal bias toward Jews and ethnic others in letters and essays into the 1930s. In a 1931 essay, "Echoes of the Jazz Age," Fitzgerald scathingly presents a "fat Jewess, inlaid with diamonds" who sat behind him at a ballet making superficial observations in a grating dialect as a representative of the uncouth Americans with money ("fantastic Neatherals") who travelled abroad in the late 1920s. In a 1935 letter to Tony Buttitta, Fitzgerald feels at liberty to speculate about his friend's name and proffer a kind of confession: "Sounds Italian. I hated Italians once. Jews too. Most foreigners. Mostly my fault like everything else. Now I only hate myself" (qtd. in Margolies 86). Such a statement reveals Fitzgerald's changing attitude toward ethnic and racial others and suggests that it may have been rooted in a sense of personal culpability and vulnerability.

Fitzgerald did become more nuanced in his portrayals of racial and ethnic others in his fiction from the 1930s. He maligns people who are prejudiced against Jews in "Crazy Sunday" (1932) and creates positive and multidimensional Jewish characters, particularly in "The Hotel Child" (1932) and his final, unfinished novel *The Love of the Last Tycoon*, which also includes a minor but important black character. "The Hotel Child" features Fifi Schwartz, a beautiful, young, American Jewish woman, who overcomes a corrupt European social scene and bravely faces the prejudices of her American compatriots who "considered Fifi ... as much of a gratuitous outrage as a new stripe in the flag" (*S* 600). Significantly, however, Fitzgerald presents Fifi as a classical beauty with only a fleeting reference to her slightly large nose. His insistence on her beauty, however, to some extent continues the logic of eugenics, which located morality and intelligence in physical appearance (Nies 107). In *The Love of the Last Tycoon*, Fitzgerald's hero is a charismatic, ambitious, and handsome Jewish movie producer, Monroe Stahr, based on Irving Thalberg, and the antagonist, Pat Brady, is a gentile.

Fitzgerald's increased sensitivity, particularly in his representation of Jews, may be attributed to the significant shift in cultural attitudes about race and ethnicity as World War II had begun to expose how truly dangerous racist thinking and eugenics could be. But Fitzgerald's compassion may have had a personal component as well. As Fitzgerald aged and experienced setbacks and failures throughout the 1930s, he became more introspective and self-aware, often criticizing his youthful bravado and toughness toward others. Through these personal experiences, he became less strident and more sympathetic to ethnic and racial others, arguably even identifying with their outsider status.

NOTES

1 R. Forrey, "Negroes in the Fiction of F. Scott Fitzgerald," *Phylon* 28.3 (1967), 293–298; 295. Subsequent references to this work are included in the text.

2 A. Margolies, "The Maturing of F. Scott Fitzgerald," *Twentieth-Century Literature* 43.1 (1997), 75–93; 75. Subsequent references to this work are included in the text.

3 B. Gross and E. Fretz, "What Fitzgerald Thought of Jews: Resisting Type in 'The Hotel Child'" in J. Bryer (ed.), *New Essays on F. Scott Fitzgerald's Neglected Short Stories* (Columbia, MO: University of Missouri Press, 1996), 189–205; 190.

4 C. Lester, "Racial Awareness and Arrested Development: *The Sound and the Fury* and the Great Migration (1905–1928)" in P. Weinstein (ed.), *The Cambridge Companion to William Faulkner* (Cambridge, UK: Cambridge University Press, 1994), 123–45; 130.

5 J. Higham, *Strangers in the Land: Patterns of American Nativism, 1860–1925* (New Brunswick, NJ: Rutgers University Press, 1988), 4. Subsequent references to this work are included in the text.

6 W. B. Michaels, *Our America: Nativism, Modernism, and Pluralism* (Durham, NC: Duke University Press, 1995), 8. Subsequent references to this work are included in the text.

7 J. Rohrkemper, "Becoming White: Race and Ethnicity in *The Great Gatsby*," *Midwestern Miscellany* 31 (2003), 22–31; 25–6. Subsequent references to this work are included in the text.

8 M. Gidley, "Notes on F. Scott Fitzgerald and the Passing of the Great Race," *Journal of American Studies* 7.2 (1973), 171–81; 174. Subsequent references to this work are included in the text.

9 S.T. Joshi (ed.), *Documents of American Prejudice: An Anthology of Writings on Race from Thomas Jefferson to David Duke* (New York: Basic Books, 1999), 535.

10 B. Nies, *Eugenic Fantasies: Racial Ideology in the Literature and Popular Culture of the 1920's* (New York: Routledge, 2002), 97–8; 101. Subsequent references to this work are included in the text.

11 E. A. Abramson, "Aliens, Stereotypes, and Social Change: The Jews and Hollywood in F. Scott Fitzgerald's Fiction," *Studies in American Jewish Literature* 24 (2005), 116–36; 116. Subsequent references to this work are included in the text.

12 Gidley explains that according to Lewis A. Turlish, "'The Rise of the Coloured Empires'" by "Goddard" is a playful reference to Theodore Lothrop Stoddard's *The Rising Tide of Color* (172).

13 In fact, some critics have speculated that Gatsby is black or Jewish and only passing as white. For the argument that Gatsby is black see C. V. Thompson, *The Tragic Black Buck: Racial Masquerading in the American Literary Imagination* (New York: Peter Lang, 2004). Various critics have made the argument that Gatsby is Jewish or at least closely connected to Jews.

14 M. Baumgarten, "Seeing Double in the Fiction of F. Scott Fitzgerald, Charles Dickens, Anthony Trollope, and George Eliot" in C. Bryan (ed.), *Between 'Race' and Culture: Representations of 'the Jew' in English and American Literature* (Stanford, CA: Stanford University Press, 1996), 44–45.

22

Gender in the Jazz Age

Heidi M. Kunz

Dividing history into eras suggests a tidiness that belies reality. To speak of the 1920s is to denote a particular span of time, and yet not necessarily a coherent set of cultural signifiers. In the United States, the decade that began with the May Day riots of 1919 and ended with the stock market crash of October 29, 1929 – the dates F. Scott Fitzgerald specified as the bookends of the Jazz Age – witnessed events such as the signing of the Treaty of Paris and the ratification of the Eighteenth and Nineteenth Amendments, as well as circumstances such as a rapidly expanding economy and the rise of Hollywood. Important as these events and unprecedented as these circumstances may be, however, they transpired at a time when, as Lisa Rado notes, "science, art, psychology, technology, sociology, anthropology, and philosophy" were already well along into "a period of revolutionary change"[1] that dates to the waning years of the previous century. Indeed, in 1896 Fitzgerald was born into an America where a multifaceted revolution in culture was already underway. The Jazz Age that coincided with his first decade as a professional writer may be understood best as a temporal slice of the "modern" period of U.S. history that Rado and other scholars protract through 1940. Not surprisingly, the gender constructions of the "Roaring Twenties" are complex, sometimes contradictory, and plastic. Accordingly, Fitzgerald writes them just so.

Fitzgerald's characteristic focus was racially white and socioeconomically privileged. His writing of the period tacitly asserts the normativity of his own race and class identifications, which in turn frame his constructions of gender. The issues of the manhood that Fitzgerald apprehended in the Jazz Age were long-standing and legion, according to political and academic commentators of the turn of the twentieth century such as Theodore Roosevelt and G. Stanley Hall. Since before the Civil War, the conventional wisdom reasoned, the social imperative of "separate spheres" had accorded women domain in the "private sphere" of the household, including corollary responsibility for the rearing and education of children. Processes of urbanization and industrialization operated to relocate the traditional authority of the father figure away from his household for most of the waking hours of the day (the five-day, forty-hour standard workweek would not be established nationwide until 1938). Families who observed Victorian gender practices consequently relegated male children to the potentially emasculating "petticoat rule" in homes and schools. The much-discussed "boy problem" of the *fin de siècle* was an alleged crisis in the bringing up of sons: How would boys learn true manhood from fathers who were not there? Phenomena from the combative gangs of major cities to the spread of venereal diseases might be attributed to the dearth of proper men available to participate meaningfully in the "molding of character" of male children otherwise left to some combination of the anarchy of the streets and the feminizing influence of doting mothers and teachers likely to be female, even in Sunday school. The adult males, many in factories or offices, frequently worked at spatially restrictive or sedentary employments far removed from the comparative autonomy of the "Self-Made Man"[2] or the "Heroic Artisan" (Kimmel 18) of historical ideal. At a time when Darwinism figured prominently in public discourse, it seemed to many observers that time-hallowed distinctions of American masculinity – individuality, aspiration, self-determination – were threatened by home and work environments evolving in manhood-adverse directions. As the old century drew to a close, steady improvements in educational opportunity for girls and young women, regional migrations of African-Americans seeking release from the sharecropping system and escape from Jim Crow, as well as surges of immigration from southern and eastern Europe both changed the demographic of the potential workforce and intensified competition in men's "public sphere." In order to maintain what seemed to him his rightful position in this unprecedented version of the United States, Fitzgerald's type of American man sensed new kinds of social pressure to validate his presumptive identity in a rapidly changing cultural context where manhood was undergoing uncertain and often unwelcome redefinition. Roosevelt's exaltation of "the strenuous life" and bodybuilder Bernarr Macfadden's promulgation of "physical culture" found eager audiences and catalyzed new institutions – the national park system, the reorientation of the Young Men's Christian Association into an Americanized *Turnverein* – and inspired popular new images of self-reliant, environment-conquering, naturally hegemonic manhood embodied in hypermasculine Caucasian physiques, for example, the eponymous heroes of Owen Wister's *The Virginian, a Horseman of the Plains* (1902) and Edgar Rice Burroughs's *Tarzan of the Apes* (1912) that reinscribed essentialist boundaries of race, class, and heterosexuality. U.S. participation in the dehumanizing Great War from 1917 through its bitter end exploded the pulp-fiction fantasy of romantic heroism in the modern world, however, as the legend of the Western frontier gave way to the brutal reality of the Western front. To more sophisticated observers of U.S. culture, "the war did not significantly shift the terms of masculinity, largely because of the continuity of social developments through the second decade of the twentieth century."[3] The "boy problem" had persisted until in the third decade of the twentieth century it became a man problem, too, and early translations of Freudian theory that assigned shocking significance to nuances of mothering seemed to find women primarily to blame. Fitzgerald would later recall conversing about the predicament of bourgeois white masculinity in the Jazz Age: "And what is a 'He-man?'" demanded Gertrude Stein one day. "Isn't it a large enough order to fill out to the dimensions of all that 'a man' has meant in the past? A '*He*-man!'" (*MLC* 134).

That an icon of the avant-garde would express a preference for a gender construction of the past indicates the complicated pass to which manhood in the United States had come by the 1920s. According to sociologist Michael Kimmel, as it developed through the first two decades of the twentieth century, "masculinity was increasingly an act, a form of public display; ... men felt themselves on display at virtually all times; and ... the intensity of the need for such display was increasing" (100). At the same historical moment, the recently invented motion picture offered a medium of display that presented larger-than-life images of manhood to a mass public and developed rapidly into a major industrial enterprise with major implications for U.S. culture. Film scholar Gaylyn Studlar believes that male movie stars of the 1920s represent "the circulation of meaning around [the concept of] masculinity," at that time a "transformative masculinity" best understood as "a process, a liminal construction, and ... a performance."[4] In this view, stardom is an assertion of popular acclaim: the star serves at once as a projection of mass culture and as an influence upon it; the male star, specifically, embodies contemporaneous notions of masculinity and participates in developing them further. Four leading men of the decade – the energetic gymnast Douglas Fairbanks, the matinee idol John Barrymore, the eroticized exotic Rudolph Valentino, and the grotesque contrarian Lon Chaney – constitute a spectrum of male bodies that simultaneously incarnate and advance more or less incompatible constructions of Jazz Age manhood. Was the all-American man the game athlete, whom Roosevelt applauded for his vitality and in whom Macfadden saw "the virile powers of superb manhood?"[5] Was he the suave cosmopolite capable of profound feeling? Was it possible for him so to lack control of his body that he commits brutal rape, yet so to discipline his body that he masters the art of the dance? Could a single person manifest several masculinities? If so, would he reduce himself to what Nick Carraway of *The Great Gatsby* (1925) derides as "that most limited of all specialists, the well-rounded man" (7) and, effacing his uniqueness through sheer reach, render himself indistinguishable from other men trying to do the same, committed to a manhood where "standing out was a matter of fitting in" (Kimmel 103)? If not, at what point does mindful individuality become monstrous alterity? Who decides? That is, should the spectacle of manhood suppose an audience male, female, or both? Fitzgerald formulated no expository answer to Stein's question. Instead, he explores, tests, and measures various combinative and liminal masculinities, including homosexuality, in his fiction.[6] As if to summarize the results of his literary investigation, he causes his character Dick Diver of *Tender Is the Night* (1934) to reminisce about the "heroic period" of his medical residency, when, with "assurance chuckling inside him" thanks to "his body that had done the flying rings at New Haven, and now swam in the winter Danube"(116), he aspires, in a way that his friend Franz Gregorovius recognizes as "'very American,'" to become the greatest psychologist "that ever lived" (*TITN* 132). Dick recalls that, as a more reflective young man in the 1920s, "he wanted to be good, he wanted to be kind, he wanted to be brave and wise, but it was all pretty difficult. He wanted to be loved, too, if he could fit it all in" (*TITN* 133). And he must not appear too much to care for any audience's response to his efforts; Malcolm Cowley would recall that in the 1920s men worthy of the label were expected to live "in the moment with what they liked to call 'an utter disregard of consequences.'"[7] One early working title of *Tender Is the Night* was "The Boy Who Killed His Mother." Another was "Our Type."

Fitzgerald's gender sensibilities extended to the similarly fraught condition of Jazz Age womanhood. *This Side of Paradise* (1920) affirms one of his authorial gifts, "a quality that very few writers are able to acquire: a sense of living in history," with especial relevance to the evolution of American constructions of femininity.[8] "None of the Victorian mothers – and most of the mothers were Victorian – had any idea of how casually their daughters were accustomed to be kissed," the *Paradise* narrator muses (61). "The 'belle' had become the 'flirt,' the 'flirt' had become the 'baby vamp'" (*TSOP* 62). He measures the social distance the young American woman, the "Popular Daughter," had travelled from her historical antecedents: "The 'belle' was surrounded by a dozen men in the intermissions between dances. Try to find the P. D. between dances, just *try* to find her" (*TSOP* 62). Like his apprehension of manhood, Fitzgerald's sense of womanhood posits unacknowledged parameters of race, class, and sexual orientation and understands gender as a plastic concept subject to modification by cultural circumstances. Late-twentieth-century specialists in U.S. women's history such Ann Douglas and Ellen Wiley Todd corroborate Fitzgerald's view, using the New Woman, rather than Fitzgerald's belle, as the template. The very term *New Woman* accumulated multiple, sometimes contradictory meanings to successive generations toward the end of the nineteenth century and into the first decades of the twentieth that complicate its use. At first a title of honor embraced by female participants in reform initiatives of the early Progressive Era, by the 1890s it became a label that carried both positive and pejorative connotations for college-educated, independent-minded young women more likely to pursue bohemian inclinations than Victorian domesticity or social work. Eventual variations of New Womanhood included the Gibson girl, a dramatically emotional beauty portrayed by illustrator Charles Dana Gibson, whose corseted vitality was matched by the vigorous stamina with which she maintained her opinions, and the flapper, whose rejection of movement-restrictive clothing and long hair that required elaborate coiffuring suggested corporeal liberation and revised sexual and gender coding. Todd explains, "New [W]omanhood is ... one site of the continuous production, definition, and redefinition of women's roles and women's behavior. Neither the 'new' nor the 'woman' of this construct is a fixed term"[9] at any moment, much less over a span of many years. Congress's passage in 1920 of the federal mandate for woman suffrage instituted in legal form the equality to which New Women of various sorts long had been aspiring. Yet the New Woman phenomenon fell short of effecting economic parity or social equality, partly because of pervasive resistance in the greater culture, but also because of the unresolved discrepancies between different factions within the women's movement itself that clouded its coherence and consequently hindered its further effectiveness. The first draft of the Equal Rights Amendment, presented to Congress in 1923, failed for want of sufficiently widespread support. Broadly speaking, after 1920 one sort of New Woman advocated thoroughgoing equality of the sexes, while another attributed the female of the species with unique sociobiological capacities that comprehensive notions of equality threatened to obscure. As a collective, postfranchise feminists offered a self-contradictory message, seeming to contend that women were both the same as and different from men. New Women of the decade wrestled with this paradox on a personal level. In *Save Me the Waltz* (1931), Zelda Fitzgerald causes her 1920s fictional counterpart Alabama Beggs to declare, "'it's very difficult to be two simple people at once, one who wants to have a law to itself and the other who wants to keep all the nice old things and be loved and safe and protected.'"[10] F. Scott Fitzgerald critic Sarah Beebe Fryer credits contemporary history with shaping the heroines of his novels, for example the erratic femme fatale of *The Beautiful and Damned* (1922): "Shifting attitudes toward women and cross-gender relationships leave Gloria [Patch] in a precarious position ... with the inevitable result that her words and behavior often strike others – including her husband – as irrational."[11] Fryer judges that the reverse is also true, that Fitzgerald's "women characters – in all their confusion and imperfection – are among his finest monuments to his era" (17). The female figures of Fitzgerald's 1920s fiction attest his astute historianship of the conundrum of bourgeois womanhood in the Jazz Age.

In chronicling the evolution of American womanhood from the late nineteenth through the early twentieth centuries Fitzgerald contributed to a lively discourse already in progress. Caroline Ticknor had measured changes in female gender norms in her fanciful sketch "The Steel-Engraving Lady and the Gibson Girl" (1901), where stereotypifications of the True Woman and the New Woman engage one another directly in a contest of feminine values. "'I can do everything my brothers can do ... I am an athlete and a college graduate, with a wide, universal outlook,'" declares the Gibson girl.[12] "'The theory of my education is utterly opposed to yours, I fear,' the [Steel-Engraving Lady] answered. 'Mine was designed to fit me for my home; yours is calculated to unfit you for yours'" (Ticknor 107). By the mid-1920s, the descendants of the Gibson girl and the flapper – the latter of which Fitzgerald declared dead by 1922 – largely had abandoned political activism. The term *feminism* took on a negative charge even among its most fortunate beneficiaries. Writer Dorothy Dunbar Bromley believed that the "modern young woman" admired the "pioneering feminists," but "does not want to wear their mantle (indeed, she thinks they should have been buried in it)."[13] "Second-generation feminists" who are "still throwing hand grenades" when "the worst of the fight is over" – women having won the right to vote – "antagonize men with their constant clamor" about a sexism, which other, by implication, more modern young women (and obviously, the writer herself) do not credit (Bromley 552). She strove to reconcile the discordant strains of contemporary womanhood with certain legacies of True Womanhood in a ten-tenet manifesto of the "Feminist – New Style" (1927). Bromley's essay depicts an "honest, spirited young woman" who eagerly capitalizes upon expanding educational and business opportunities, defines independence as financial self-sufficiency, and desires companionate marriage as well as gratifying occupation beyond obligatory duties to home and children that she expects a husband to share willingly, even cheerfully (552). The Feminist – New Style has little interest in other women in the collective abstract, unlike the old-style feminists, but prefers to choose her loyalties idiosyncratically, although physical grace and fashionable tastes will probably denote for her womanly worthiness. To the twenty-first-century reader, she is distressingly classist – she learns to cook for her family or to mend their clothing only "so that she can direct a servant intelligently and economically" – and fatuous, especially when she disregards the structural and social barriers that would hinder her selectively egalitarian vision (Bromley 558). However, in her own time and frame of reference, Bromley seems quite unaware of the ironies of her race- and class-inflected formulation. The Feminist – New Style conducts her performance of gender on a tenuous line between transgression and reification, clutching her precious liberty in one hand and her attractiveness to men in the other (her sexual orientation is never in question). Fitzgerald, who called her the "contemporary girl" at the end of the decade, attributed her confusions and imperfections to the indetermination of American manhood. "With the general confusion as to what men want – 'Shall I be fast or shall I be straight? Shall I help him succeed or join him only after he has? Shall I settle down or keep young?' ... [young women] have begun to turn for approval not to men but to each other" (*MLC* 101–2).

The gender nexus of the 1920s inevitably ties the difficult questions of transformational masculinity to the nonlinear evolution of New Womanhood. Fitzgerald wrote about this cultural knot, as one would expect, with more than historianship. Indeed, his understanding of the gender dynamics of the era underwent an evolution of its own. His early story "Head and Shoulders" (1920) and the story he published scant days before the stock market crash, "The Swimmers" (1929), serve to demonstrate the growing sophistication of his insight into the changing terms of masculinity and femininity – and their dynamic interrelation – in the Jazz Age United States. The contrived tale "Head and Shoulders" turns on a primary, Porteresque reversal of roles that warrants the consistent disdain of critics: The hero, Horace Tarbox, an academic prodigy, opts for a lucrative career as a stunt gymnast in order to support financially his pregnant wife, Marcia, a former musical-comedy shimmy dancer, who pens a first novel to celebrity as a literary prodigy. Details of device and narrative color the plot ironic, and Horace's own attitude – he reacts in red-faced exasperation when his intellectual idol pays homage to his wife – indicates that he feels she has bested him even without meaning to do so, that his reward for making a chivalrous sacrifice of head for shoulders is wholly unanticipated humiliation. Beneath the surface of its hammy plot and characterizations, however, the historically authentic gender coding of "Head and Shoulders" resists the superficial tendency of the text. Fitzgerald writes Jazz Age manhood and womanhood as coreferential constructions that, when negotiated between a young man and a young woman acting in love with the best of intentions, potentiate unexpected, even painful, results. That the story presents episodes of physicality both male and female, moments of disembodiment both male and female, elements of performance both male and female, and code-scrambled versions of success for a male and for a female as tradeoffs indicates that Fitzgerald in the early 1920s conceived gender as a closed system, where the ascendancy of American womanhood necessarily levies correspondent costs on American manhood. Henry Clay Marston, the hero of the similarly unimaginative tale "The Swimmers," ponders this very idea as he gazes upon the accomplished young athlete on the *plage* at St. Jean de Luz: "In her grace, at once exquisite and hardy, she was that perfect type of American girl that makes one wonder if the male is not being sacrificed to it" (*S* 499). Like that of "Head and Shoulders," the trite plot of "The Swimmers" – nice guy Marston, betrayed by his unpleasant wife and his unprepossessing business associate, wins nicely – serves as an expedient for a far more interesting study of late-Jazz Age gender negotiations than its ostensible action would suggest. Fitzgerald characterizes Marston as a culturally flexible sort of man and sets him to find his place in a gallery of bourgeois Southern masculinities engaged in various male-coded competitions. In spite of what feminist critics would call his "male dread," Marston finds the swimmer's authentic, nonperformative femininity – she "was obviously acting like nothing but herself" (*S* 499) – attractive, and discovers that allowing himself to learn from her unexpectedly revives the best qualities of his hereditary manhood. Fitzgerald writes him as an agent as well as a site of construction: Marston brings his sons to swimming lessons, too. Marston dismantles the historical conventions of home by divorcing the mother of his children, and, insisting on full custody of their boys, opts for a newly gendered family configuration where the father is both the breadwinner and the more morally suited to the rearing of children. Fate in the guise of coincidence restores the instructress to the creaky plot. More significantly, the New Henry, clearly named to underscore the growth of his open-mindedness out of U.S. history, finds his worthy match in the New Woman. Far from being sacrificed for the excellences of the New Woman, he becomes a true believer: "Americans, he liked to say, should be born with fins, and perhaps they were" (506). Far from forcing a zero-sum game, the ascendancy of the New Woman, thoughtfully embraced, can make for a mutual positive. This is not to say that the happy result of "The Swimmers" derives from a definitive compromise, with all due respect to Henry Clay. Rather, say that Fitzgerald, to borrow the words of scholar of American masculinity Peter Lehman, asserted that "rigid notions of male-female difference are oversimplified," and that we should understand gender better by "conceiving of multiple, fluid, and contradictory positions."[14] Fitzgerald the insightful historian could not restrict himself to writing artificial binaries of gender in the Jazz Age. Fitzgerald the visionary artist could not help but join the revolution.

NOTES

1 L. Rado, *Modernism, Gender, and Culture: A Cultural Studies Approach* (New York and London: Garland, 1997), 8.

2 M. Kimmel, *Manhood in America: A Cultural History* (New York: Simon & Schuster, 1996), 16. Subsequent references to this work are included in the text.

3 E. J. Segal, "Norman Rockwell and the Fashioning of American Masculinity," *Art Bulletin* 78.4 (December 1996), 633–46; 633 n 4).

4 G. Studlar, *This Mad Masquerade: Stardom and Masculinity in the Jazz Age* (New York: Columbia University Press, 1996), 4.

5 B. A. Macfadden, *The Virile Powers of Superb Manhood: How Developed, How Lost: How Regained* (New York: Physical Culture Publishing Company, 1900).

6 See, respectively, F. Kerr, "Feeling 'Half Feminine': Modernism and the Politics of Emotion in *The Great Gatsby*," *American Literature* 68.2 (June 1996), 405–431; H. M. Kunz, "'Love in the Night,' Without Polish Eyes to See It," *F. Scott Fitzgerald Review* 7 (2009), 37–51; and A. C. Jones, "Fitzgerald's 'Wet Space Between Worlds': Geography and Modern Masculinity in 'The Rich Boy'" (unpublished essay presented to the 11th International F. Scott Fitzgerald Conference, Lyon, France, July 2011).

7 M. Cowley, "Introduction" in F. S. Fitzgerald, *The Stories of F. Scott Fitzgerald: A Selection of Twenty-Eight Stories* (New York: Charles Scribner's Sons, 1951), vii–xxv; xi.

8 M. Cowley, *A Second Flowering: Works and Days of the Lost Generation* (New York: Viking Press, 1973), 30.

9 E. W. Todd, *The "New Woman" Revised: Painting and Gender Politics on Fourteenth Street* (Berkeley, CA: University of California Press, 1993), xxviii.

10 Z. Fitzgerald, *Save Me the Waltz* in M. J. Bruccoli (ed.), *The Collected Writings of Zelda Fitzgerald* (Tuscaloosa: University of Alabama Press, 1991), 1–196; 56.

11 S. B. Fryer, *Fitzgerald's New Women: Harbingers of Change* (Ann Arbor, MI: University of Michigan Research Press, 1988), 31. Subsequent references to this work are included in the text.

12 C. Ticknor, "The Steel-Engraving Lady and the Gibson Girl," *Atlantic Monthly* 88 (July 1901), 105–8. Subsequent references to this work are included in the text.

13 D. D. Bromley, "Feminist – New Style," *Harpers Magazine* 155 (October 1927), 552–60; 552. Subsequent references to this work are included in the text.

14 P. Lehman, *Running Scared: Masculinity and the Representation of the Male Body* (Detroit, MI: Wayne State University Press, 2007), 9.

Figure 23.1. "Flapper" by Ellen Bernard Thompson Pyle (*Saturday Evening Post*, February 4, 1922).

23

Postwar Flappers

Kathleen Drowne

In 1923, an enthusiastic journalist for the *Des Moines Capital* claimed, perhaps somewhat hyperbolically, "When F. Scott Fitzgerald, the twenty-five year old author, wrote 'The Beautiful and Damned,' he did more than merely write one of the cleverest stories ever done by an American; he immortalized the flapper (Figure 23.1.). As a result, when you think of a flapper your mind travels instinctively to 'The Beautiful and Damned,' either in its novel or screen adaptation form; and when you think of the novel or picture of this name, your thoughts revert to the much-discussed flapper." Fitzgerald himself seemed pleased to embrace the role of the flapper spokesman as the interview continued. "'I sometimes wonder,' says Mr. Fitzgerald, 'whether the flapper made me or whether I made her. At any rate, we both should be grateful to one another. My story has helped her to understand herself, and it has made the world of non-flappers more appreciative and tolerant.'"[1] Of course, Fitzgerald's comments were disingenuous; he certainly did not "make" the flapper (though one might argue that she made him, or at least started him off). But by the time *The Beautiful and Damned* came out in 1922, Fitzgerald, riding the wave of popular flapper fiction, was already widely regarded as an expert in the area of young modern women and their various behaviors, strategies, and goals. Indeed, Fitzgerald's *This Side of Paradise* (1920) was the first major novel to feature the rebellious and brazen flapper, and his first two collections of short stories, *Flappers and Philosophers* (1920) and *Tales of the Jazz Age* (1922), also included memorable flapper characters, including Marjorie Harvey in "Bernice Bobs Her Hair," Ardita Farnam in "The Offshore Pirate," and Nancy Lamar in "The Jelly-Bean." By the mid-1920s, Fitzgerald had become permanently associated in the popular imagination with the daring young flappers of post-World War I America.

The beautiful young flapper has come to symbolize the flamboyant Jazz Age, but the term itself predates the 1920s by at least a century. In *The American Language*, H. L. Mencken traces *flapper* to early nineteenth-century England, where it denoted "a very immoral young girl in her early teens"; by the early twentieth century the label had migrated to America and had come to be used as "one of a long series of jocular terms for a young and somewhat foolish girl, full of wild surmises and inclined to revolt against the precepts and admonitions of her elders."[2] In the June 1922 issue of the *Atlantic Monthly*, G. Stanley Hall recounts searching for a definition of *flapper*: "[T]he dictionary set me right by defining the word as a fledgling, yet in the nest, and vainly attempting to fly while its wings have only pinfeathers; and I recognized that the genius of 'slanguage' had made the squab the symbol of budding girlhood."[3] During the 1920s the term also became associated in multiple ways with fashion, first with the loose "flapper dresses" that younger teenage girls wore, allegedly to cover their awkwardness, and then later "flapper heels," the low, wide heels suitable for dancing. The term also applied to the literal flapping of the unlaced galoshes that fashionable young women took to wearing in all sorts of weather.

Regardless of the provenance of the label, though, the flapper quickly became an identifiable category of postwar womanhood. Historian Elizabeth Stevenson admiringly describes the flapper as "a new American girl, a new woman, a new arrangement of the elements of sex and love. She no longer exists; she existed for only a few years in the mid- and late twenties, but during that short epoch she was a completely defined and recognizable type."[4] The passage of time has indeed demonstrated that the flapper was an ephemeral, inadaptable creature, and the Jazz Age was her only natural environment. But while she existed, she became a vessel into which every sort of social and cultural anxiety was poured, and thus it is no wonder that her image – part idol, part vixen – dominated American popular culture during the 1920s. The flapper's ubiquitous presence in Hollywood films, Tin Pan Alley songs, best-selling novels, magazine illustrations, and even advertisements elevated her to the status of a powerful and sometimes paradoxical icon.

The flapper may have achieved unparalleled visibility in the 1920s, but she did not appear out of nowhere. The flapper image replaced an older ideal of American femininity from the late nineteenth and early twentieth centuries: the so-called Gibson girl. Originally based on pen-and-ink magazine illustrations by artist Charles Dana Gibson, this representation of the pre–World War I American woman emphasized her curvaceous, tightly corseted figure (creating an unnaturally tiny "wasp waist"), her long, thin neck, and her full hair piled gracefully on her head. The Gibson girl was elegant and sophisticated, and her stylish clothing, complete with full sweeping skirts and mutton-chop sleeves, provided a model of beauty and refinement for young girls from the 1890s until the mid-1910s. But the Gibson girl had mostly faded from the American popular scene by the mid-1910s, and in her place rose the flapper, who quickly became known for her controversial fashion sense and self-centered behavior.

The most important detail to remember when examining and assessing the flapper's role in the literature and culture of the Jazz Age, and the easiest to forget, is that she amounts to nothing more than a collection of stereotypes that coalesced around young women during the great social and cultural turbulence that followed World War I. In other words, the term *flapper* functions as a kind of cultural shorthand for the sorts of behaviors and values that many women found attractive during this era of increasing social permissiveness. The label itself became an identity marker not unlike the term *hippie chick* in the 1960s or *Valley girl* in the 1980s; it can reveal some important information about a large group of women, but nothing very specific about the individuals who comprise this group.

A flapper in the 1920s could be identified by her appearance, her behavior, or both. Women looked the part of the flapper by bobbing their hair, wearing makeup, and adopting the latest fashions (including a dropped waistline and a hemline that rose steadily from 1920 until it nearly reached the knee in 1927). To achieve the boyish silhouette that epitomized the flapper look, women discarded old-fashioned corsets and flattened their breasts with brassiere-like undergarments or by wrapping strips of cloth around their torsos. They exposed their limbs by wearing short sleeves or sleeveless tops and donned nude-colored silk or rayon stockings rolled below their knees or discarded altogether in hot weather. The small felt cloche hats that they tugged down over their foreheads contrasted dramatically with the enormous and elaborate millinery favored by the Gibson girl. Women acted the part of the flapper by dancing, drinking, smoking, driving, swearing, "petting" with young men, and generally engaging in activities that emphasized both their freedom from traditional notions of respectability and their flamboyant – even aggressive – sexuality. Most importantly, perhaps, flappers adopted the attitude that life was primarily for having fun, and that few limits should be imposed on the all-important quest for a good time.

Of course, few women could possibly have enacted every element associated with this stereotype. Indeed, the flapper identity was fraught with conflicting connotations, and some women who adopted the look rejected the label, equating *flapper* with flighty, narcissistic, or even promiscuous behavior. Other women may not have looked or acted the part but otherwise sympathized with the flapper's agenda of defying widely held notions of the "proper" or the "respectable." Ultimately, the flapper identity was malleable, and individual women adapted it to suit their needs. For example, women's studies scholar Angela Latham describes a rural schoolteacher in the 1920s whose job contract forbade her to cut her hair into a fashionable bob. She cut it anyway, but then pinned the long severed braid to her remaining hair before school each morning in order to appear a "traditional," respectable woman and thus to retain her job.[5] Her students and their parents surely perceived her as a modest, conservative young schoolmarm, while she herself embraced the identity of a stylish modern flapper, at least in her private life.

Although twenty-first-century readers tend to harbor relatively one-dimensional ideas of the flapper as simply the epitome of the fashionable 1920s party girl, she actually evolved significantly from the late 1910s to the early 1930s. During World War I, the flapper was truly a radical figure. Media coverage of early flappers, who deliberately challenged long-standing models of decency and propriety, was unsurprisingly harsh. Preachers, politicians, and other self-proclaimed guardians of morality excoriated the flapper, claiming (among other things), "she is intoxicated with her new freedom, dabbles in dangerous heresies, religious and personal, and expects to shirk the responsibilities of home-making and motherhood."[6] Dress-reform advocates promoted legislation specifically targeting flappers that would require dress hems to be no more than seven inches off the floor, since "the skirt that flaps around the knees is pretty much of a menace to the modesty of the woman who wears it ... [and] a back to normalcy drive on the too short dress will do a lot to protect the morals of the rising generation." School boards banned cheek-to-cheek dancing on school property, and bathing suit censors stationed on public beaches expelled women for bare legs, short skirts, and general "neglect to surround themselves with sufficient bathing raiment."[7] But despite all the backlash, the model of the daring flapper increasingly took hold, and when Fitzgerald commented in *This Side of Paradise* that "None of the Victorian mothers ... had any idea how casually their daughters were accustomed to be kissed," he was likely correct (*TSOP* 61). Soon, flapperism and all its associated fashions and behaviors became the norm rather than the exception.

As flapper fashions became mainstream and flapper behavior became widespread, the flapper lost most of the radical associations that had defined her earlier incarnations. As early as 1922, Zelda Fitzgerald pronounced, "The Flapper is deceased," and went on to delineate the important differences between the first wave of flappers, who were inspired by a philosophy of genuine independence and liberation, and the second wave of flappers, who simply followed the fashions with no aspirations to become trendsetters themselves. She describes the first generation as privileging pleasure over adherence to old standards of behavior: "She flirted because it was fun to flirt and wore a one-piece bathing suit because she had a good figure; she covered her face with powder and paint because she didn't need it and she refused to be bored simply because she wasn't boring. She was conscious that the things she did were the things that she had always wanted to do." In contrast, the second generation of flappers, "galumphing along in unfastened galoshes are striving to do not what is pleasant and what they please, but simply to outdo the founders of the Honorable Order of Flappers: to outdo *everything*. Flapperdom has become a game; it is no longer a philosophy."[8] A year later, in a 1923 interview published in the *Louisville Courier-Journal*, Zelda echoed this notion: "Three or four years ago, girls [like Rosalind in *This Side of Paradise*] were pioneers. They did what they wanted to, were unconventional, perhaps, just because they wanted to for self-expression. Now they do it because it's the thing everyone does."[9]

During the 1920s, flappers in particular, and youth culture in general, garnered so much attention that from our vantage point it appears that nearly all of America during that decade must have been white, well-off, and college-aged, full of confidence, lacking inhibitions, spouting the latest slang phrases, craving liquor and cigarettes. Of course, this was far from the case. But the American media's obsession with the daring flapper and her beau, the dapper "sheik," led to wildly exaggerated depictions of outrageous young people that often functioned as symbolic repositories for the anxieties of an older generation. Whatever fears and insecurities the newly emerging modern life engendered, from the danger of automobiles to the immorality of contraception, it seemed that they all could be blamed on the irreverent, decadent, ill-mannered flapper. In "Eulogy on the Flapper," Zelda Fitzgerald writes, "I came upon an amazing editorial a short time ago. It fixed the blame for all divorces, crime waves, high prices, unjust taxes, violations of the Volstead Act and crimes in Hollywood upon the head of the Flapper. The paper wanted back the dear old fireside of long ago, wanted to resuscitate 'Hearts and Flowers' and have it instituted as the sole tune played at dances from now on and forever, wanted prayers before breakfast on Sunday morning – and to bring things back to this superb state it advocated restraining the Flapper" (Zelda Fitzgerald 392). But by 1922, the flapper's virtual monopoly on pop culture femininity already seemed permanent, and she refused to be restrained.

Although the flapper was routinely derided for being shallow, selfish, and vain, and she became the punch line for innumerable jokes, the American public seemed to possess an unquenchable thirst for all things related to her. Editorial pages regularly addressed what came to be called "the flapper question" – essentially, what was to be done about these unconventional young women who defiantly flouted traditional values? Newspaper advice columns were flooded with letters allegedly written by flappers seeking advice about how to manage their many boyfriends, or by resentful old-fashioned girls whose boyfriend had been lured away by a racy flapper in a short dress. Illustrators, most famously John Held, Jr., got endless mileage from the flapper, casting her as flighty, flirty, and a constant challenge to the older generation. Images of the flapper were everywhere, sometimes portrayed as the savior of modern womanhood, and other times as the harbinger of cultural decline.

The flapper image was pursued not just by young people but, remarkably, by adults two and three times their age, who doggedly imitated their clothing, hairstyles, slang phrases, and dance steps in an effort to recapture the elusive qualities of youth. As a result, the flapper helped to fuel the rise of an entire consumer mass market composed of products designed to capture and retain youthfulness. Madison Avenue advertising agencies bombarded consumers with ads for cosmetics, dieting regimens, health "supplements," and other products, including soaps that allegedly washed fat away, intended to help women transform themselves into flappers. Stories abound of middle-aged and even elderly women who bobbed their hair and shortened their skirts in obeisance to the flapper style; popular Tin Pan Alley songs such as "Mama's Gone Young, Papa's Gone Old" (1929) promoted the notion that youth could – and should – be purchased by everyone. Even more specifically, films such as *The Flapper* (1920), starring Olive Thomas; *Flaming Youth* (1923) and *The Perfect Flapper* (1924), starring Colleen Moore; *The Plastic Age* (1925), *Mantrap* (1926), *It* (1927), starring Clara Bow; and *Our Dancing Daughters* (1928), starring Joan Crawford, all educated audiences about the latest trends in fashion, dancing, and courtship rituals. Young Americans serve as both the nation's cultural trendsetters and its social scapegoats for a single reason: They embodied all that was new, radical, and "modern."

Thus, it is perhaps not surprising that dozens of American writers of the 1920s seized upon the flapper as an icon of both immorality and virtue. The prevalence of flapper characters in Jazz Age literature was highlighted, for example, in a November 29, 1925, literary review in the *Oakland*

Tribune. The author points out the alarming and widespread influence that rebellious flapper characters were exerting on readers, noting that these characters "jazz their way, fearfully and wonderfully adorned as to face enamel, all too unadorned as to petticoats and flounces, through the pages of the popular novels, where their slang adds to the vocabulary of most of the readers, and the thrills are nearly as scarlet as the author dares to make them." Sensational novels about flappers and college life, the author adds, have "become one of the most remunerative sports of fiction."[10] And while young readers certainly devoured flapper stories, older readers also enjoyed such fare. One published review of a forgettable 1925 flapper novel titled *Babbie* noted that while the book will "appeal to the literary taste of the John Held generation," it will also "furnish plenty of entertainment for those who renew their youth vicariously via the printed page ... while pretending to be scandalized at modern ways."[11]

Indeed, flapper stories found eager, paying audiences at magazine counters and bookstores across the nation. F. Scott Fitzgerald is so frequently associated with this outpouring of flapper literature that it is easy to believe that he cornered the market on her adventures and foibles. But Fitzgerald was only one of dozens of American writers who hitched his wagon to the flapper's star, and the early 1920s witnessed the publication of a spate of flapper novels and stories in the popular press. In fact, the flapper quickly became a stock character in fiction and drama, often appearing as a foil for a virtuous, old-fashioned girl. For example, Ellen Glasgow's 1923 story "The Artless Age," first published in the *Saturday Evening Post,* follows a common plotline: An old-fashioned girl and an impudent flapper vie for the attention of an attractive young man. In this case the flapper triumphs, and Glasgow's story repeats a familiar refrain in popular literature of the 1920s: The whole flapper persona is merely an act that nice girls are forced to perform in order to keep pace with the changing times and to keep men interested. Glasgow's flapper candidly admits, "Why, there's scarcely one of us [flappers] who doesn't hate the smell of cigarettes on her fingers, and who wouldn't rather have the taste of rose water in her mouth any day than whisky. We get so tired of it sometimes that we'd like to have a vacation in an old ladies' home as a change; but it's as much as our popularity is worth to drop out of the rush."[12]

Like Glasgow, many other writers (and filmmakers, too) chose to adopt the reassuring position that, deep down, young women were just as refined and delicate as their mothers and grandmothers had been, but that modern times and changing courtship rituals demanded that they play the part of the wild, fast girl who will stop at nothing to attract her man. In her 1925 article "What Became of the Flappers?," Zelda Fitzgerald concurs with this domestic conclusion to the flapper's adventures: "The flapper! She is growing old … She has come to none of the predicted 'bad ends,' but has gone at last, where all good flappers go – into the young married set, into boredom and gathering conventions and the pleasure of having children, having lent a while a splendor and courageousness and brightness to life, as all good flappers should."[13] Numerous flapper novels and stories of the 1920s end with a reinforcement of traditional moral values symbolized by a wedding and the promise of motherhood and a predictable life to come. But dozens of others indicate that the reading public was deeply fascinated with the transition – sometimes awkward and sometimes graceful – from flapper to wife.

The question of whether a flapper would happily trade her dancing slippers and whiskey flask for a kitchen apron and bassinet fueled a spate of "flapper wife" novels and short stories in the mid-1920s. For example, the prolific popular writer Beatrice Burton's 1925 novel, aptly titled *The Flapper Wife*, chronicles the fate of Gloria, a beautiful, selfish flapper who, after her marriage, slowly learns to love the domestic life of a conventional housewife. The novel gleefully concludes, "And so the story of Gloria, the Flapper Wife, ends. And the modern chronicle of Gloria, the Wife and Mother, begins. We say to-day that we have a New Woman, who votes and drives her own car, who plays golf and … sometimes … smokes a cigarette. But she's not a New Woman, at all!"[14] Many "flapper wife" novels reinforced this notion – just as Zelda Fitzgerald claimed – that flappers are flappers for a few short years, but they are good wives and mothers for the rest of their lives. Other stories challenged the notion that this transition was either smooth or inevitable; F. Scott Fitzgerald's *The Beautiful and Damned* (1922), for example, fits into the larger category of "flapper wife" stories, but instead of offering a comforting domestic tale, it portrays young wife Gloria Patch struggling to maintain her self-absorbed flapper ways and unrealistically longing for a marriage that is a perpetual "live, lovely, glamorous performance" (*B&D* 127).

Regardless of whether members of the older generation approved or disapproved of the flapper, they had no choice but to deal with her. In fact, the youthful "revolution in manners and morals," as it was commonly called, was far too widespread and influential to be ignored. The uninhibited flapper found herself at the forefront of this social and cultural revolution, functioning as a lightning rod for controversies related to everything from hairstyles and makeup to sex and marriage. Through it all, she never failed to fascinate, to entertain, to bewilder, and to outrage. For a brief moment she reigned as the quintessential

American woman of the Roaring Twenties, but with the onset of the Great Depression, she rapidly disappeared from American novels and short stories, motion pictures, fashion magazines, and editorial pages. America found new heroes to idolize and new scapegoats to vilify, and the flapper – the object of so much attention and the source of so much anxiety – quietly faded away.

NOTES

1 Anon., "F. Scott Fitzgerald and His Popular Novel," *Des Moines Capital*, February 18, 1923, 33.
2 H. L. Mencken, *The American Language: An Inquiry Into the Development of English in the United States, Supplement I*, 1945 (New York: Alfred A. Knopf, 1962), 314–15.
3 G. S. Hall, "Flapper Americana Novissima," *The Atlantic Monthly* 129 (June 1922), 771.
4 E. Stevenson, *Babbitts and Bohemians: From the Great War to the Great Depression*, 1967 (New York: Macmillan, 1998), 139.
5 A. J. Latham, *Posing a Threat: Flappers, Chorus Girls, and Other Brazen Performers of the American 1920s* (Hanover, NH: Wesleyan University Press, 2000), 3.
6 "Where is the Girl of Today Bound? 200 at Vassar Tell," *New York Times*, June 3, 1921, xxi.
7 Anon., "Fixes Length of Skirts," *New York Times*, January 31, 1922, 14; H. B. Lowry "Mrs. Grundy on the Job of Reforming the Flapper," *New York Times*, March 27, 1921; Anon., "Coney Censors Busy," *New York Times*, July 6, 1920, 11.
8 Z. Fitzgerald, "Eulogy on the Flapper" (1922) in M. J. Bruccoli (ed.), *The Collected Writings of Zelda Fitzgerald* (Tuscaloosa, AL: University of Alabama Press, 1991), 391–93. Subsequent references to this work are included in the text.
9 Anon.,"What a 'Flapper Novelist' Thinks of His Wife," [Louisville] *Courier-Journal*, September 30, 1923, 112. In *Conversations with F. Scott Fitzgerald*, eds. Matthew Bruccoli and Judith Baughman (Jackson: University Press of Mississippi, 2004), 47.
10 N. B. Mavity, "The College Flapper – Is She a Sign, a Portent, or an Imaginary Animal?" *Oakland Tribune*, November 29, 1925, 90–91.
11 Anon., "'Babbie' Tale to Delight 'Flappers,'" *Oakland Tribune*, November 29, 1925, 69.
12 E. Glasgow, "The Artless Age" in R. K. Meeker (ed.), *Collected Stories of Ellen Glasgow* (Baton Rouge, LA: Louisiana State University Press, 1963), 200.
13 Z. Fitzgerald, "What Became of the Flapper?" (1925) in M. J. Bruccoli (ed.), *The Collected Writings of Zelda Fitzgerald* (Tuscaloosa, AL: University of Alabama Press, 1991), 397–99.
14 B. Burton, *The Flapper Wife* (New York: Grosset & Dunlap, 1925), 344.

24

Youth Culture

Jarom Lyle McDonald

In her 1920 commentary on Fitzgerald's first novel, *This Side of Paradise*, Margaret Emerson Bailey called it "a convincing chronicle of youth by youth,"[1] an appraisal that soon became the essence of subsequent reviews of the novel. Begun when Fitzgerald was 21 and published when he was 25, *This Side of Paradise* was heralded as a book written by someone "still in the thick of the fight" (Bailey 471), and after the novel appeared Fitzgerald quickly found himself a celebrity, both as an author and as an icon. He was, according to the contemporary critical reception, the representative of and the interpreter for an ever-incomprehensible generation.

The composition of this generation, however, is far more difficult to characterize than is Fitzgerald's role in chronicling it. Historical commentators on the era often see youth in the 1910s and 1920s as more a collection of stereotypes than anything else: the flappers and sheiks, the bobbed hair and petting parties, the hordes of youth flocking to new media technologies of radio and film. Such caricatures of modern American youth culture, material not only for *This Side of Paradise* but also for much of Fitzgerald's early short fiction, relied on both self-identification and on definitions from outside representation, creating a complex relationship where individuals aspired to these stereotypes, yet at the same time shunned the notion of conformity and definition. Societal commentary of the time often put forth the argument that the social and economic choices of the rising generation were irreconcilable with those of the established generations. While every generation seems to embrace the frustration (and often nostalgic misremembering) embodied in the complaint that "we were nothing like that when we were young," history looks back at the first few decades of the twentieth century as an era when this really was true. The rapid urbanization, expansion of education, explosion of new industries and technologies, and emergence of a popular culture constructed from materialism, consumption, and leisure fostered a lifestyle where, perhaps for the first time in American culture, large populations of youth were leading starkly different lives than their parents had led. Young Americans found themselves living and associating with peers far more than with family, and they gradually coalesced into a demonstrable culture where being young "mattered."

One of the best-known covers of *Life* magazine appeared on February 2, 1922 – an illustration by Frank X. Leyendecker entitled "The Flapper." This painting prominently displayed a set of butterfly wings set on the back of a youthful, exuberant woman garbed in clothing and donning a hairstyle fairly typical of the common "flapper girl" of the Jazz Age. The butterfly wings are an obvious symbol of metamorphosis, underscoring the sense of liberation and rebirth often sought after by women striving to live as they thought youth should. The cover functions as more than just a cultural "snapshot," however; it is as much a commentary on the degree to which different forms of media influenced young Americans (and influenced the perception of youth by older generations). In fact, perhaps nothing contributed more to the image of modern American youth culture than the exploding culture machine of mass media. The growing prominence of magazines, with their ever-increasing amount of advertising, relied on visual images of young men and women dancing, drinking, and reveling in social nightlife as a way to attract their desired readership. Magazine artists such as John Held, Jr.[2] became well known for their sketches of youthful indulgence, and they were in high demand at *Vanity Fair* and the *New Yorker*. Other magazines quickly followed the trend, even when the publications were not directly marketed to youth culture; the May 1927 issue of *Science and Invention*, for example, depicted a slick young man passionately kissing a flapper girl, with the caption "40,000 germs in every kiss." Consumer marketing campaigns also appropriated the popular youthful ideals to sell everything from men's and women's clothing to automobiles, Campbell's soup, and toothpaste. Such magazines also gravitated toward publishing stories and poems that celebrated in text the same images portrayed in the cover art. Fitzgerald himself parlayed his popularity and acclaim as the chronicler of youth to emerge as the creator of the flapper in fiction, and stories such as "Head and Shoulders" and "Bernice Bobs Her Hair" are widely thought of as archetypal "flapper stories." Yet other authors promulgated the conception of youth culture as the sort of flapper culture that advertising agencies were selling. For example, Anita Loos's series of sketches she wrote for *Harper's Bazaar* depicted Lorelei Lee, a young woman caught up in material culture and ever-changing morals, and her popular magazine sketches were later brought together in Loos's best-selling 1925 novel *Gentlemen*

Prefer Blondes. In 1922, the *Flapper*, a magazine dedicated to young flappers, appeared. It contained stories, pictures, advice, and original work by readers, illustrating everything from commentary on dress and fashion to poems about "the new fashioned girl."

Even more powerful than print culture, though, was the rapidly growing world of motion pictures.[3] Movies provided an entertainment outlet for groups of youth to attend together; this sense of shared viewership and spectacle often separated older generations from the youth who, again in a pattern common to youth today, naturally gravitated both to new technologies and to multimedia forms of storytelling. Youth with money to spend flocked to matinees to absorb stories and pictures that reflected Hollywood's view of youth culture and then reflected those images back in their own dress and manners as a way to demonstrate their familiarity with their on-screen idols. This was particularly true for teenage boys: A modernized, Hollywood romanticism inundated young men with a desire to live up to big-screen heroism. Douglas Fairbanks, Hollywood's most popular actor by 1918, gave audiences of young men such swashbuckling (and often exotic) role models as Zorro, Robin Hood, and the Thief of Baghdad. It is certainly appropriate to read Fitzgerald's narrative of the young man winning a woman's love through an extraordinary deed (such as young Moreland's courting of Ardita in "The Offshore Pirate") in terms of its literary resemblance to the epic adventures of a Douglas Fairbanks hero. Ironically, while trying to act like Fairbanks, most young men sought instead to physically model themselves after Rudolph Valentino, whose on-screen image was best described by Fitzgerald (when penning a young Basil in "The Scandal Detectives") as a young man in "white duck knickerbockers, pepper-and-salt Norfolk jacket, a Belmont collar and a gray knitted tie … and his black hair wet and shining" (*B&J* 22). Valentino was the first teen sex object – his Hollywood image generated hysteria among younger girls and mimicry among boys who wanted to impress those girls. Of course, these girls had female icons, too: Clara Bow and Joan Crawford, among others, offered a flapper image more vibrant and enthusiastic for young women than anything they would see in a magazine. Crawford, especially, understood both the power of movies and the power of cultivating the image she portrayed, building her own celebrity through self-promotion. The photograph of a newlywed Crawford vivaciously embracing her new husband (Fairbanks's son, Douglas Fairbanks, Jr.) in 1929 solidified her place as the princess of youth culture, the happy ending that mass media promised to American youth who strove to follow suit.

While mass media tended to portray the visual extremes of youth culture and often created some of the simplified and clichéd (yet nevertheless extremely powerful) images still associated with the 1920s, not all facets of youth culture revolved around the sort of wild, youthful socializing that the publishing or movie industries sold to America. As business and industry became more a way of life than a revolution, a growing demand for a more educated workforce led ever-larger numbers of youth to attend school, especially secondary school. The baby boom that followed World War I also contributed to a more widespread need for education. American education in the 1910s and 1920s was marked by changes in curriculum and demographics, with reforms fueled by John Dewey's progressivism and with classrooms populated in large part by immigrant youth pressured to assimilate into American culture. And while the content and curriculum of the changing educational system was a notable (if not particularly strong) contextual force on American youth culture, the accompanying social "reformation" among American students was of particular importance. Youth lived among their peers and lived for their peers' acceptance, whether within the male's world, which revolved around athletics or heroics, or the female's world, which revolved around competition for beaus.

The changing educational mores also brought an increased awareness of the importance of social status within the youth culture, particularly in relation to attendance at institutions of higher education. For youth with the proper social status (or the proper amount of money and the desire to attain proper social status), four years at Princeton, Harvard, or Yale were "concentrated on matters of popularity" (*TSOP* 32). Many established university alliances, notably those that today comprise the Ivy League, actively marketed themselves as cultivators of an elite body of youth. These institutions and those running them held to the theory of training youth in a sort of refigured American feudalism, one where graduates of elite universities were charged to take their place among the American economic royalty with a duty to "fight in the name of honor and of chivalry."[4] Young students attending these universities were deeply immersed in a recapitulation of the stark social status lines of American society, evidenced in Amory's perception of "the intricacies of a university social system and American Society as represented by Biltmore Teas and Hot Springs golf-links" (*TSOP* 32). Outside the ranks of the select Ivies, the emerging state colleges and state universities came to emphasize college life as a life of socialization rather than education. In the May 19, 1922, issue of the *Daily Illini*, a publication of the University of Illinois, an editor illustrated the typical attitude regarding the purpose of college, maintaining that "The man who has taken no part in the social side of college life usually comes a very long way from having all the characteristics that the world implies in the use of the term 'a college man.'"[5] Higher education was characteristically an upper-middle- to upper-class pursuit[6] of American youth culture that solidified notions of status into the cultural psyche. And whether it was Ivy League eating clubs, like Fitzgerald's Cottage Club at Princeton, or state-supported dormitories, college and university life, in providing opportunities for social interaction, reinforced a class consciousness within youth culture that led toward social climbing.

College social life also provided something else essential to the evolution of modern American youth culture: leisure time. Fraternities and sororities spread nationally, becoming an intricate part of college campus life as the "Greek organizations" and similar social institutions offered an outlet for spending leisure time engaged in dancing and drinking (even throughout Prohibition). Specialized periodicals such as *College Humor* appeared. College athletics also grew exponentially in popularity, first in the East (growing out of the Ivy League tradition of football at Harvard, Yale, and Princeton) and then spreading throughout the Midwest. College football, especially, acquired a "tenacious hold upon players and spectators,"[7] and offered yet another locus of gathering youth in the form of pep rallies and tailgate parties and added yet another component to the cultural discourse that emphasized the desirability of being young. Athletic prowess on the field led to status and prominence not only among peers but nationwide, and youth and adults alike idolized players such as Red Grange, Jim Thorpe, and the four horsemen of Notre Dame. Just as advertising harnessed youthful trends in fashion and celebrity, it also gravitated toward images of college culture. Youthful exuberance, health, and athleticism became something that could be bought and sold and emerged in the form of strength-gaining products for men or rejuvenating cosmetics for women. Youth culture itself became the commodity, and a nation of college students graduated and grew up in age but not in attitude. From the guests at Gatsby's parties to Tom Buchanan "forever seeking a little wistfully for the dramatic turbulence of some irrecoverable football game" (*GG* 9), upper-class America was inextricably linked with the depiction of the well-educated, well-socialized youth with money to spend and time to waste.

As the rising generation (and members of their parents' generation) embraced the images of youth presented by mass media, a pervasive undertone of disapproval often manifested itself in the national discourse. "What, then, really is this that has happened, or is happening, to our young people?" wrote George Albert Coe, a professor of education at Columbia.[8] Coe's book was a self-proclaimed attempt to understand why modern youth were "getting on the nerves of many members of the older generation" (Coe vi). Many of the commentaries on the new generation criticized the youth culture, especially when it came to young people's attitudes toward sex and gender roles. Popular music, magazines, and movies convinced many adults of a widespread epidemic of extramarital sex among youth, and while there is little to indicate that there was a marked increase in casual sexual intercourse during the 1920s, the young people who constituted the youth culture did nothing to dissuade their parents from believing their perception. Yet there was certainly a change in attitude toward other forms of physical intimacy; in the 1920s, for example, kissing became both a common courtship exercise and a social one. The core of the sexual revolution among modern youth was one in which, as Fitzgerald maintains, none of the Victorian mothers "had any idea how casually their daughters were accustomed to be kissed" (*TSOP* 61).[9] The movies, once again, heavily influenced this softening of the moral code. When young men and women saw their on-screen idols, again and again, involved in exciting, romantic love affairs in which the lovers often lived happily ever after, they constructed rules of courtship for their own generation and abandoned those of their parents' generation. The dark settings of the movie theaters themselves also reinforced these new courting habits, as did other advances in technology; automobiles, for example, offered a freedom of mobility that encouraged youth to practice courting rituals away from the watchful eyes of parents. With these radical changes, intimacy for youth became more about experience than about standards, and the morality of this new generation came to be grounded in the following maxim: "What is moral is what you feel good after, and what is immoral is what you feel bad after."[10]

The sexual revolution of Fitzgerald's Jazz Age extended far beyond simply the attitudes toward physical intimacy described above. Young women of the 1920s were the inheritors of the first wave of American feminism, which led to freedoms for women that had never before existed in American culture. The cynicism brought on by World War I led masses of upper-middle- and upper-class young women to enroll in college; by 1930, females made up almost 40 percent of the student body nationwide. Women were just as likely to use the time at college for socialization and "having fun" as men were; a *Life* cover illustration in 1926 (drawn by

Held) depicted a young female graduate with a short skirt and bobbed hair lighting a cigarette with her burning diploma. But the increasingly educated Jazz Age woman was also poised to enter the workforce, and while many who worked during the war were displaced by returning veterans, the number of women moving from (or attempting to move from) youth to adulthood through involvement in the American workplace continued to expand throughout the 1920s. As Kirk Curnutt notes, this liberation of youth was often accomplished by, paradoxically, an "ability to blur the distinction between the child and adult"[11]: The dress, style, and body image of the flapper were both prepubescent and sexually charged. The young, modern woman blurred traditional gender lines as she migrated into the urban workforce environment. Many social commentators of the time saw this trend as dangerous to traditionally held notions of domesticity, motherhood, and family structure. This challenge to traditional gender roles was often perceived (especially by removed generations) as adding to the moral depravity of youth culture. As the well-known literary sketch of "Flapper Jane" describes it, "Do the morals go with the clothes? Or the clothes with the morals? … If they want to wear their heads shaven, as a symbol of defiance against the former fate which for three millenia forced them to dress their heavy locks according to male decrees, they will have their way."[12]

Fitzgerald always viewed his position as the chronicler of the Jazz Age youth with a certain amount of ambivalence. As he looked back on a time that "leaped to a spectacular death in October 1929" (*CU* 13), Fitzgerald described in retrospect his view of the generation that came of age in the 1920s in this way:

> The wildest of all generations, the generation which had been adolescent during the confusion of the War, brusquely shouldered my contemporaries out of the way and danced into the limelight. This was the generation whose girls dramatized themselves as flappers, the generation that corrupted its elders and eventually overreached itself less through lack of morals than through lack of taste. (*CU* 15)

It is clearly difficult to separate the content of Fitzgerald's fiction of the early 1920s from the cultural context of the Jazz Age, given that his writings did so much to influence the popular images of early-twentieth-century American youth culture. For Fitzgerald, and for the nation, youth culture was, more than anything, "a succession of quick, unrelated scenes" (*TSOP* 215). Yet, ultimately, his writings came to underlie many of the historical perspectives on just what American youth were like in the period that he himself named the Jazz Age.

NOTES

1 M. E. Bailey, "A Chronicle of Youth by Youth," *Bookman* 51 (June 1920), 471–72; 472. Subsequent references to this work are included in the text.
2 Held also illustrated covers for several of Fitzgerald's publications, notably the short story collection *Tales of the Jazz Age.*
3 Although Fitzgerald claimed the contrary in "Echoes of the Jazz Age," where he said that movies were far too conservative and behind the times, it is clear that movies, in reflecting attitudes and actions of American youth, recapitulated these ideologies as new children continually entered young adulthood.
4 J. Hibben, Commencement address to the Princeton class of 1913. Quoted in D. Brooks, "The Organization Kid," *Atlantic Monthly* (April 2001), 40–54; 50.
5 Anon., "Nothing Gained by Being a Hermit," *Daily Illini*, May 19, 1922, 4.
6 Implicit (and perhaps detrimentally so) in many historical analyses of modern American youth culture is the notion that, for the most part, youth culture of the first few decades of the twentieth century was very much a white, middle- and upper-class pursuit. The lack of educational and economic opportunities (due to poverty, the prevalence of Jim Crow laws, and a number of other complex social factors) shaped the lives of immigrant, African-American, and lower-class youth, who inhabited a "Jazz Age" youth culture far different from the one that Fitzgerald was part of and about which he wrote.
7 W. Camp, *The Book of Football* (New York: The Century, 1910), 96.
8 G. A. Coe, *What Ails Our Youth?* (New York: Charles Scribner's Sons, 1927), 1. Subsequent references to this work are included in the text.
9 Fitzgerald always seemed stung, however, that Heywood Broun doubted this notion when he reviewed *This Side of Paradise* and claimed that "not a few undergraduates are given to the sin of not kissing and then telling anyway."
10 E. Hemingway, *Death in the Afternoon* (New York: Simon & Schuster, 1999), 13.
11 K. Curnutt, "Age Consciousness and the Rise of American Youth Culture" in R. Prigozy (ed.), *The Cambridge Companion to F. Scott Fitzgerald* (New York: Cambridge University Press, 2002), 39.
12 B. Bliven, "Flapper Jane," *The New Republic* (September 9, 1925), 65–67; 66.

25

American Expatriates in France

Elisabeth Bouzonviller

During the nineteenth century, clinging to their Baedekers, young Americans went to Europe for the Grand Tour, which was supposed to provide them with a cultural background that would prepare them for their future life at home. Following World War I, some Americans perceived Europe as the only escape from an America that no longer met their expectations. In 1940, Gertrude Stein declared that "Paris was where the twentieth century was" and concluded that "Paris was the place to be."[1] Valérie Bougault estimates that during the 1920s between 25,000 and 50,000 Americans lived in France,[2] and to Fitzgerald, it seemed that "[e]very morning a new boat-load of Americans poured into the boulevards and every afternoon our room at the hotel was filled with familiar faces until, except that there was no faint taste of wood-alcohol in the refreshments, we might have been in New York" (*MLC* 43–44). The attraction seemed to be mutual:"[t]he French ... were fascinated by anything American."[3] While Stein points out the postwar "Americanisation of France" (52), Christine Bard reports that in 1921, "favorite movies were American, fashionable tobacco was American, cocktails were American, dances were American, the ideal feminine face was American, interest in sports was American, the money that people earned seemed American, ambition itself had an American turn."[4]

Along with many other anonymous compatriots, a great number of American writers chose France as a place to profit from a fruitful artistic environment that would nourish their works, even if the French scene was rarely their main literary focus. They reacted to expatriation in various ways, but they were all artistically influenced by their stay and in turn contributed to a certain flavor of the Roaring Twenties there. New habits in terms of culture and entertainment were part of the legacy of this American presence, in particular jazz music and the developing fashion of the Riviera as a summer vacation place. Sharing their time between Paris and the Riviera, artists met, created, and gave birth to what was to be termed modernism before the world economy and personal tragedies caught up with them and sent most of them back home at the end of the decade.

From the *fin de siècle* until the early 1930s, Paris functioned as a magnet for all those fascinated by modernity. In 1889 the city held the Universal Exhibition, in 1925 the Decorative Art Exhibition, and, finally, in 1931, the Colonial Exhibition. And although Paris had been an artistic center for years, an incredible number of talents in various fields ranging from painting to sculpture, dancing, music, literature, fashion, and the decorative arts gathered there in the 1920s. Gerald Murphy, who settled in France in 1921, declared:

There was a tension and an excitement in the air that was almost physical. Always a new exhibition, or a recital of the new music of *Les Six*, or a Dadaist manifestation, or a costume ball in Montparnasse, or a première of a new play or ballet, or one of Etienne de Beaumont's fantastic "Soirées de Paris" in Montmartre – and you'd go to each one and find everybody else there, too. There was such a passionate interest in everything that was going on, and it seemed to engender activity. (Tomkins 33)

Painters from abroad had been attracted to Paris in the early 1900s, but whereas they had typically lived in Montmartre, as Picasso did at the Bateau-Lavoir, they now moved to Montparnasse, a new, modern neighborhood nicknamed "The Quarter" by Americans, who tended to be concentrated in the area. If Mount Parnassus had been the residence of Apollo and his muses, Montparnasse was now the modern center of the arts: "Any artist who has contributed to the birth of modern painting has been in Montparnasse" (Bougault 8). In 1913, Americans had discovered modern art at the Armory Show in New York; subsequently, many American artists aimed for Montparnasse and its various painting academies. Actually, Paris had launched the century with its Universal Exhibition; it then hosted the 1925 Decorative Art Exhibition and closed this revolutionary decade with its 1931 Colonial Exhibition, working all along as a magnet for all those fascinated by modernity.

In 1909, the itinerant Ballets Russes, under the directorship of Sergei Diaghilev, adopted Paris as their home base. On May 29, 1913, Stein attended the first performance of *The Rites of Spring*. She claimed that the music could not be heard due to the outraged reactions of audience members, yet the scandal established the Ballets Russes as an innovating challenger to tradition (Bougault 96). Soon after their arrival in Paris, the Murphys helped repaint the company's scenery under the regular supervision of Picasso, Braque, Derain, and Bakst. Murphy called the troupe "the focal center of the whole modern movement in the arts" (Tomkins 15). In 1923, he collaborated with Cole Porter on *Within the Quota*, a burlesque representation of American culture for the Ballets Suédois. Given the cultural creativity in Paris at the time, it is no wonder that American expatriates had the feeling, like Fitzgerald's narrator in "A Penny Spent," of being in "one of the predestined centers of the world" (*ASYM* 205).

Expatriation to France was also a matter of finance, as Fitzgerald demonstrated in "How to Live on Practically Nothing a Year," since, over the decade, a dollar bought between fifteen and thirty-six francs. Fitzgerald's essay opens with a letter that urges expatriation on financial grounds: "I don't see why everybody doesn't come over here … It costs about one-tenth as much to live over here" (*MLC* 40). In addition, France provided an escape from the Eighteenth Amendment and a desperate attempt to flee from prigs like Tom Buchanan or the narrow-minded Babbitts of middle-class America. As Gerald Murphy put it: "You had the feeling that the bluenoses were in the saddle over here, and that a government which could pass the Eighteenth Amendment could, and probably would, do a lot of other things to make life in the States as stuffy and bigoted as possible" (Tomkins 25–26). According to Frederick Lewis Allen, "[American intellectuals] were united in a scorn of the great bourgeois majority which they held responsible for prohibition, censorship, Fundamentalism, and other repressions."[5] Harold Stearns confirmed this sentiment: "What should a young man do? … A young man had no future in this country of hypocrisy and repression. He should take ship for Europe, where people know how to live."[6] Paris, and Bohemian Montparnasse in particular, offered a personal and intellectual freedom unknown to the America of the Roaring Twenties, one that was reflected in a generation that gathered at Parisian cafés, dances, and parties in search of new modes of expression that would relate to the social and moral changes brought about by modernity.[7]

In a 1927 interview, Fitzgerald declared that "[t]he best of America drifts to Paris. The American in Paris is the best American. It is more fun for an intelligent person to live in an intelligent country. France has the only two things toward which we drift as we grow older – intelligence and good manners."[8] In the same enthusiastic mood, Stein, whose salon attracted both painters and writers, claimed that France "was the proper background for the art and literature of the twentieth century" (22–23). Like Edith Wharton in 1907, Stein had been a pioneer expatriate who had discovered France as a child. The younger generation would follow, like "leaves in the autumn," Ezra Pound wrote,[9] and if they were a "lost generation," as Stein, according to Hemingway, claimed,[10] they nevertheless found their way to 27 rue de Fleurus, where she discussed and encouraged their talents while her companion, Alice B. Toklas, entertained their wives (Hemingway, *A Moveable Feast* 31). The Steins were at the heart of creative modernity and, in the wake of Juliette Récamier or Madame de Staël, other women became key figures in Parisian intellectual life. An early expatriate like Stein and Wharton, Nathalie Barney welcomed the intellectual and artistic elite to her salon. As bookstore owners, librarians, and publishers, Sylvia Beach and Adrienne Monnier, respectively, provided American expatriates with two other exceptional places for fruitful artistic meetings, bold literary ventures, and resources. Hemingway recalled: "In those days there was no money to buy books. I borrowed books from the rental library of Shakespeare and Company, which was the library and bookstore of Sylvia Beach at 12 rue de l'Odéon" (Hemingway, *A Moveable Feast* 29). In 1922 Beach published Joyce's *Ulysses*, which had been censored in Britain and the United States; her friend Monnier, at "La Maison des Amis du Livre," 7 rue de l'Odéon, published its first French translation in 1929. In addition, both stores were constantly patronized by the leading French- and English-speaking writers of the period. With regard to the vitality of the English-speaking literary community in Paris, Bougault notices there were about ten English-language literary journals and five English-language publishing companies in Paris at the time (76). Many of the most notable American books of the period were written and sometimes even published in Paris, including Hemingway's *In Our Time*, Stein's *The Making of Americans*, and William Carlos Williams's *The Great American Novel*. Malcolm Bradbury concludes that "[t]he Modern movement that laid its imprint right across the most daring arts of the century owes nearly everything to Montparnasse" (177).

Whether American artists remained in France after the war, as did John Dos Passos, or arrived in the early 1920s, they recreated an expatriate America with an atmosphere of their own making that corresponded to their artistic tastes and thirst for freedom. Murphy communicated the gestalt as follows: "Even though it happened in France, it was all somehow an American experience" (Tomkins 11). Despite the fact that they could barely speak French, the Fitzgeralds went to France four times between 1921 and 1931.[11] Never as acclimated to France as Hemingway, who first arrived in Paris in 1922, or Henry Miller, who arrived at the end of the decade, Fitzgerald was always caught between attraction and repulsion and, in the end, primarily remained a tourist, making few contacts with local people and adopting few of their habits. However, France provided an opportunity for Fitzgerald to meet Hemingway and recommend him to Scribners,[12] to engage in a friendship with French novelist André Chamson and arrange to have him published in the United States,[13] to dream of catching a glimpse of Anatole France, to discover Radiguet's *Count Orgel's Ball*,[14] to be praised by Stein,[15] and to meet Joyce and Wharton. Despite his visits to Stein or Beach, his "dangerous friendship" with Hemingway, and the parties at the Murphys, Fitzgerald was rather aloof from the American expatriates' circles. As he confessed to Hemingway: "You were the first American I wanted to meet in Europe – and the last."[16]

Hemingway considered "Paris poisonous for" Fitzgerald (Bruccoli, *Fitzgerald and Hemingway* 42), and Fitzgerald himself called the city "a mad-house" (*L* 358) and summarized his 1925 summer as "1000 parties and no work" (*FSFL* 179). However, France provided him with a place to write and with material to use as background for *Tender Is the Night*, as well many short stories partially or completely set in France. In 1924, Fitzgerald rented the Villa Marie at Valescure, where he managed to complete *The Great Gatsby*, a novel that represented a radical departure in style from his two earlier novels. His new narrative technique, his use of colors and visual elements, and his distorted chronology were, no doubt, partly the result of his growing artistic maturity, yet his new style was also influenced by the challenging artistic environment he encountered in France, in particular through the Murphys, with whom he became close friends that summer. The Murphys introduced the Fitzgeralds to a busy artistic world quite different from the provincial one they had come from in America. Fitzgerald concluded this about the Riviera: "One could get away with more on the summer Riviera, and whatever happened seemed to have something to do with art" (*CU* 19). In September 1925, he wrote ironically that

> There was no one at Antibes this summer except me, Zelda, the Valentinos, the Murphys, Mistinguet, Rex Ingram, Dos Passos, Alice Terry, the MacLeishes, Charlie Brackett, Maud Kahn, Esther Murphy, Marguerite Namara, E. Phillips Oppenheim, Mannes the violinist, Floyd Dell, Max and Crystal Eastman, ex-Premier Orlando, Etienne de Beaumont – just a real place to rough it, an escape from all the world. (*L* 359)

The Murphys' visitors included American artists but also avant-guard creators like Léger, Picasso, and Stravinsky, who dealt in raw colors and sounds, distortion, juxtaposition, and the debunking of traditional harmony. The stimulating atmosphere of the Riviera no doubt influenced Fitzgerald in his writing, as it did Zelda in her later paintings of landscapes and dancers.

In *The Sun Also Rises*, Jake Barnes exclaims that "going to another country doesn't make any difference. I've tried all that. You can't get away from yourself by moving from one place to another."[17] Yet, in this novel, as in *Tender Is the Night*, characters move frantically and make certain to stay away from America. In both novels, France is not so much presented as a new home, but rather as a temporary stop-over en route to elsewhere. Both novelists depict in vague terms the French setting, for they are not concerned with exotic Europe, but with native origins and attachments. Their fictional French map is a palimpsest for an American one. In "Early Success," the narrator remembers the scenery of the Riviera and reflects on it in this way: "It was not Monte Carlo I was looking at. It was back into the mind of the young man with cardboard soles who had walked the streets of New York. I was him again – " (*CU* 90). As the self and America lie at the heart of expatriate writing, the French scene is not what matters, but rather the happenings that occur in bars, taxis, hotels, and, most importantly, the mind. Paris acquires a labyrinthine, Kafkaesque quality as the characters rush through it without paying much attention to its specificity. Their "dissipation," as Fitzgerald terms it in "Babylon Revisited" (*TAR* 388), makes it hard for them to escape and go back home, but in the long run, their French expatriation works as a catalyst that reveals their hidden selves: The fictional French trips are actually mental expeditions that tell of man's inner fears and disenchantments and of his efforts to overcome these impediments to his fulfillment. Ultimately, France does little to ameliorate the difficulties faced by the novels' characters. By the end of *The Sun Also Rises*, Jake and Brett are still lost in a traffic they do not master, as it is ruled by "a policeman in khaki" (247), and Dick Diver, who knew that he was "just passing through" Paris (*TITN* 121), returns home, only to dilute himself within the American landscape.

In "The Swimmers," Henry Marston believes that he has settled permanently in Paris; however, a typical French vaudeville scene puts an end to his illusions so that he is able to detect a pastoral, primeval America beneath contemporary corruption. Marston's revelation recalls that of Nick Carraway as he intuits the "fresh, green breast of the new world" (*GG* 140): "Far out past the breakers he could survey the green-and-brown line of the Old Dominion with the pleasant impersonality of a porpoise" (*S* 505). Although the story closes on a return to Europe, Marston's sons will be brought up in America, and in the liminal territory of the Atlantic liner, he meets again the Virginia girl and begins something new with her as he waits for another America to emerge: "under the ugly débris of industry the rich land still pushed up, incorrigibly lavish and fertile" (*S* 512). "The Swimmers" ends on a maternal simile regarding America: "He had come as to a generous mother and had been profusely given more than he asked" (*S* 511–12). As the ship departs one more time for Europe, sight blurs but attachment remains stronger than ever: "Watching the fading city, the fading shore, from the deck of the Majestic, he had a sense of overwhelming gratitude and of gladness that America was there" (*S* 512). The homeland remains a mooring point to which the traveler and the expatriate writer always returns.

In 1929, the "great fair" was over and "at the most gorgeous paradise for swimmers on the Mediterranean no one swam any more, save for a short hang-over dip at noon" (*MLC* 135). In October, the American economy had been brutally shattered, and economic depression would soon spread to the rest of the world. Curiously, the fate of those who had led the "Carnival by the Sea" (*CU* 90) paralleled the one of the nation they had earlier fled. Switzerland became a temporary refuge for the Murphys, whose youngest son was afflicted with tuberculosis, as well as for Zelda, diagnosed with schizophrenia. All would eventually go home to America by the early 1930s in search of comfort and security, but there the Murphys experienced the deaths of both their sons and the Fitzgeralds would live with Zelda's incurable condition. Moore concludes the following about American expatriates in Paris:

> The more insightful among them recognized that, paradoxically, living abroad made it possible to look more clearly at the United States, to better judge and comment on what they had left behind. Their time away actually intensified their Americanness, rather than diluting it, and this became a powerful inspiration for many. Then, too, returning Americans found that they liked being back home – that the familiar had charms more potent than they remembered. (240–41)

The French experience had provided them with a vantage point from which to view America, but in the end, most expatriates rushed home for personal or financial reasons. Their lives in France would be remembered as youthful, heedless, transient ones, for as Hemingway suggests in *A Moveable Feast*,

> [t]here is never any ending to Paris and the memory of each person who has lived in it differs from that of any other. We always returned to it no matter who we were or how it was changed or with what difficulties, or ease, it could be reached. Paris was always worth it and you received return for whatever you brought to it. But this is how Paris was in the early days when we were very poor and very happy. (211)

NOTES

1 G. Stein, *Paris France*, 1940 (London: Peter Owen, 2003), 13. Subsequent references to this work are included in the text.
2 V. Bougault, *Paris Montparnasse. A l'heure de l'art moderne 1910–1940* (Paris: Terrail, 1996), 76. Subsequent references to this work are included in the text.
3 C. Tomkins, *Living Well Is the Best Revenge*, 1962 (New York: New American Library, 1972), 32. Subsequent references to this work are included in the text.
4 Bard, Christine, *Les Garçonnes* (Paris: Flammarion, 1998), 85–86.
5 F. L. Allen, *Only Yesterday: An Informal History of the Nineteen-Twenties*, 1931 (New York: Harper Perennial, 1992), 194, 196.
6 L. Moore, *Anything Goes: A Biography of the Roaring Twenties* (London: Atlantic Books, 2008), 238. Subsequent references to this work are included in the text.
7 American expatriates gathered at La Closerie des Lilas, Le Dôme, La Coupole, La Rotonde, and Le Dingo in Montparnasse or at the Ritz and Harry's bars on the Right Bank.
8 M. J. Bruccoli, *Some Sort of Epic Grander: The Life of F. Scott Fitzgerald*. 2nd rev. edn. (Columbia, SC: University of South Carolina Press, 2004), 255.
9 M. Bradbury (ed.), *The Atlas of Literature* (London: De Agostini, 1996), 176. Subsequent references to this work are included in the text.
10 E. Hemingway, *A Moveable Feast*, 1964 (New York: Charles Scribner's Sons, 1970), 29. Subsequent references to this work are included in the text.
11 They first sailed to Europe on May 3, 1921, to be back home in July. Their second crossing was in May 1924 with a return in December 1926. They were in Paris again in April 1928 and back in the United States on October 7. Eventually, they left a last time for Europe in March 1929 with a return on September 15, 1931.
12 On October 10, 1924, Fitzgerald wrote the following to his editor, Maxwell Perkins: "This is to tell you about a young man named Ernest Hemingway, who lives in Paris, (an American) writes for the transatlantic Review & has a brilliant future" (*S&M* 78).
13 Eventually, Scribners published *Les Hommes de la route* as *The Road* in 1929.
14 On July 8, 1925, he wrote to Perkins: "I still think *Count Orgel's Ball* by Radiguet would sell like wildfire"(*S&M* 117).
15 Fitzgerald was considered very favorably by this severe critic: "Here we are and have read your book [*The Great Gatsby*] and it is a good book" (Bruccoli, *Epic Grandeur* 232).
16 M. J. Bruccoli, *Fitzgerald and Hemingway: A Dangerous Friendship* (London: André Deutsch, 1995), 66. Subsequent references to this work are included in the text.
17 E. Hemingway, *The Sun Also Rises*. 1926 (New York: Charles Scribner's Sons, 1970), 11. Subsequent references to this work are included in the text.

PART V

Popular and Material Culture in the Jazz Age (1918–1929)

26

Popular Literary Tastes

Philip McGowan

In 1945, Alice Payne Hackett produced her first compilation of the nation's bestselling works since 1895, *50 Years of Best Sellers*, which was followed at almost ten-year intervals by *60 Years of Best Sellers* (1956), *70 Years of Best Sellers* (1967), and *80 Years of Bestsellers* (1977). Such lists first appeared as a cultural barometer in the *Bookman* monthly magazine, founded in New York in 1895, under the editorship of Harry Thurston Peck. By its 1977 edition, Hackett's combined fiction and nonfiction list of bestsellers contained only three titles from the 1920s in its top 100, and a paltry ten in the top 350, testifying to the fluctuating social and economic forces in the United States during that decade. Hackett's indispensable survey lists the biggest-selling 1920s text, within the time frame of her statistical research, as *Roget's Pocket Thesaurus* (1923); slightly more than seven million were sold. The bestselling fictional work by 1975 from the same decade was *The Great Gatsby*, ranked fortieth on her overall list, with 6,036,000 sales.[1] Such success and popularity, however, came late to Fitzgerald. Fitzgerald's novels received somewhat varied critical acclaim at the time of their release but sales were somewhat promising. His novels did not become commercially successful, however, until after his death. Sales of *Gatsby*, for instance, initially struggled to match those of his two previous novels, *This Side of Paradise* and *The Beautiful and Damned*; roughly half the number of copies of *Gatsby* were sold compared to the other two in their release years.[2]

Taste, popularity, and how they are accounted for are elusive variables. If literary taste is reflected either in the fluctuations of the book-buying habits of a particular class or the bestseller lists of a country, then the 1920s was a decade in which the now-notable authors from that time were notably absent from the frontline of America's reading choices. With one or two exceptions (Edith Wharton appeared twice on the bestseller lists in the 1920s), the now-canonical figures are subsumed within the contemporary and transient demand-and-supply pressures of a period when readers chose romance fiction at least as often as they chose to read work by such authors as Hemingway, Faulkner, or Dos Passos. The variability of the authors who populate the bestseller lists across the 1920s might suggest a similarly volatile or discordant reading audience, with different class or cultural interests producing spikes of popularity across the decade. Yet, in a 1928 article on "British and American Taste" for the *English Journal*, Montgomery Belgion, a former sub-editor of the *Daily Mail*, who at that time was working for Harcourt, Brace in New York, noted that "American novel-readers all belong to the same class" and that in America "it is common for a novelist to turn famous in a night."[3] Indeed, mapping the different approaches to book reading and popular tastes on both sides of the Atlantic, Belgion makes this assertion: "England is a country in which there are traditions, America is a country in which one makes money" (Belgion 188).

Just glancing at the bestseller book lists in the United States for the 1920s makes obvious one key fact: F. Scott Fitzgerald, a writer obsessed with how much money he earned, his public success, and his fame, is absent from every one of the annual lists of top ten bestsellers. The author synonymous with the Jazz Age, the man most associated with its articulation and definition in his three novels and multiple stories from that decade, may seem now a surprising absentee from the records of book sales from almost a century ago. However successful Fitzgerald may appear in retrospect, his self-vaunted early success was balanced on a tide of mutable critical acclaim and changing literary fashion. His short stories published in the *Saturday Evening Post* were undoubtedly his most successful commercial venture in the 1920s. Indeed, as Fitzgerald's *Ledger* notes for 1929, royalties for his three novels in print that year amounted to a paltry $13.84: $4.80 for *This Side of Paradise* (1920), $3.60 for *The Beautiful and Damned* (1922), and $5.10 for *The Great Gatsby* (1925). He received a further $0.34 from English sales of *Gatsby*.[4] The writer whose debut novel opened the decade declaring "all gods dead, all wars fought, all faiths in man shaken" (*TSOP* 260) would end it overshadowed, in terms of sales at any rate, each year of that decade by other authors. Sinclair Lewis, Edith Wharton, Thornton Wilder, and Booth Tarkington (an author whom Fitzgerald had admired in his youth) number among those that eclipsed him, as did more populist writers such as Zane Grey, who featured in the top ten bestselling fiction list each year between 1920 and 1924. If such lists are taken to be useful indicators of a nation's reading habits at any particular moment, this period was one in which Americans who bought books were still influenced by the pull of the sentimental fictions or stories of western adventure more usually identified with the last decades of the nineteenth century. In a 1944 article, also for the *English Journal*, Harrison Smith, then president of Smith & Durrell publishers, reflecting back on the previous twenty-five years of bestsellers, bemoaned the fact that "no distinguished novel entered the top ten sellers until 1925," citing Margaret Kennedy's *The Constant Nymph*, Michael Arlen's *The Green Hat*, and Anne Douglas Sedgwick's *The Little French Girl* as the first glimmers of hope amid the deluge of "historical romances and other soporifics"[5] that had characterized the first half of the decade. Kennedy, Arlen,[6] and Smith were ranked second, fifth, and sixth, respectively, in that year's bestselling fiction list, pushing Sinclair Lewis's *Arrowsmith*, a tale of medical ethics intercut with aspirational materialism, for which Lewis declined the Pulitzer Prize, down to seventh.

However, to conclude that the early-decade American appetite for romance accorded to a wider sociocultural pattern would be to make too many assumptions about the literary marketplace in the 1920s. Indeed, the role of the publishing houses, which sought to capitalize on the potential for new readership constituencies while simultaneously maximizing the contemporary shelf life of certain authors and texts, needs careful examination. Fitzgerald's attachment to Scribners, while granting him a certain status and literary caché, limited his opportunities of appearing on the decade's bestseller lists. Add to this the success of popular magazines such as the *Reader's Digest* (founded 1922, providing among other attractions summaries of contemporary literary works) or *Time* (1923) and the developing variety at the heart of American reading habits in the period becomes evident. In 1926, the launches of Captain Joseph T. Shaw's *Black Mask* (detective) and Hugo Gernsback's *Amazing Stories* (science fiction) magazines supplemented an already diverse monthly magazine fiction market. Smith's retrospective glance in 1944 over the fictional trends of the previous twenty-five years concludes that America's more literary writers "looked at our world with suspicious eyes and did not like what they saw" during the 1920s; "they had to tear down our literary traditions before new ones could be created, and so they were busy during the twenties and early thirties with the monumental task of altering our literary scenery" (Smith 402–3). Bowing out of the formula-fiction arena around them, they retreated either to the more intellectual purlieus of their modernist interests or, like Fitzgerald and Hemingway, removed themselves from the American scene altogether, journeying to the Prohibition-free environments of Paris, the Riviera, and wider continental Europe.

Popular literary tastes in the 1920s reflected and responded to a series of interconnecting concerns: the changes in American society as it emerged from wartime into a period of new economic affluence; the development of a consumerist ethos in a nation in which for the first time the majority, recorded by the 1920 Census, lived in cities;[7] and the production of a new set of literary interests and concerns that would shift the focus of a previous generation forward to that of an altogether different one that was coming of age as war ended and the Jazz Age began. A newly urban populace was beginning to cut the link with a prevailing nineteenth-century ethos (marked most particularly by the Prohibition amendment) within the United States, an ethos that had dominated American social, political, and cultural life for the first two decades of the century. The 1920s in America's expanding cities was a time of consumptive excess: Fitzgerald, like Nick Carraway, was drawn to New York as the symbol of this new sense of freedom and American independence. Within the fluid spaces of the Jazz Age that his fictions so capably represented, Fitzgerald carefully, indeed obsessively, charts his progress against the fluctuating habits of America's book-buying public. Indeed, he readily offered the magazine and commercial market examples of the new brand of popular fiction that readers were buying and for which publishing companies and fashionable periodicals were willing to pay. While royalties from novels may have been drying up as the decade ended, Fitzgerald was still able to command strong four-figure fees for his short fiction: The *Saturday Evening Post* paid $3,150 for each of his first four stories ("Forging Ahead," "Basil and Cleopatra," "The Rough Crossing," and "Majesty") published in 1929, and this amount rose to $3,600 per story for "At Your Age," "The Swimmers," "Two Wrongs," and "First Blood" (Bruccoli 636). Publishing was a lucrative business in this period for both authors and publishers alike, as new readerships were developed on the back of modern methods of publication and nationwide dissemination that ensured America's book buyers and magazine readers could access the kinds of materials they wished to read.

In a brief "Letter of Transmittal" that serves as a foreword to the 1917 U.S. Bureau of Education study *A Graphic Survey of Book Production, 1890–1916*, the Southern educator Philander Priestly Claxton noted that "[a]ny comprehensive understanding of the … intellectual and cultural tendencies of a country must include some knowledge of the numbers and kinds of books produced and the relative demands for books of the several classes."[8] The study that follows this observation, mostly bar charts of dry statistics, indicates that the percentage of fiction titles as an element of overall book sales in the United States had been falling year to year, from 24 percent in 1890 to 8.91 percent in 1916 (Woodward 6), in part due to an expansion in subject areas (a proliferation of geography, poetry, travel, religion, history, and reference books), but also due to the impact of the October 1907 Wall Street panic, as well as that of the Great War. The near-invisibility of 1920s novels in Hackett's survey becomes all the more understandable. Claxton's desire to distinguish between the reading habits of low-, middle-, and high-brow readers suggests that not only do such distinctive groupings exist but that they are serviced by particular branches of the publishing industry that either respond to or anticipate the specific requirements of each subset. While this may be true, Megan Benton's analysis of book ownership in the 1920s in the United States cautions against simply accepting at face value such generalized statistical evidence given that, in 1927 for example, book sales of 200 million translated into a per capita purchase rate of fewer than two books per citizen. Indeed, "[b]y comparison, weekly movie attendance grew from 40 million in 1922 to 95 million in 1929, and continued to rise to some 115 million the following year."[9] The picture produced of America's popular literary tastes in the Jazz Age is somewhat skewed by reference to statistics alone, which do not account for the myriad forces affecting a class's, or indeed an individual's, choices about not just which books to buy, but whether to buy them at all. Figures of how many units an individual title sold can be revelatory, however: Sinclair Lewis's *Main Street* (1920) sold 295,000 copies to top the 1921 bestseller lists (Hackett 91), while, in the nonfiction category, sales of H. G. Wells's *The Outline of History* in the 1920s totaled more than a million copies, arguably on account of Macmillan's reissuing of it in three formats, first as a $10.50 two-volume set, then a $5.00 one-volume edition, and finally a $1.00 abridged version of half a million units (Hackett 92). That said, its sales would take a sharp downturn, arguably because the historical events of the 1930s and 1940s bypassed its linear outline of a future based in and "designed by the present";[10] by Hackett's cut-off date of 1975, Wells's text had sold a total of 2,070,170 copies, qualifying it as the tenth bestselling title from the 1920s, and 345th in the combined bestseller lists of the period from 1895 to 1975.

To account for the diversity of taste and the popularity of both fictional and nonfictional forms in the period, it is clear that in America "there were three or four publics all of which could develop simultaneously best sellers in the million class."[11] Add to this the impact that the Literary Guild Book Club, founded by Frank Doubleday in 1926, or the Book-of-the-Month Club, started in 1927, had: Both outlets provided the public with discounted access to the latest hardback fiction titles on a month-to-month basis, anticipating similar developments in Britain in the 1930s. Within two years, the Book-of-the-Month Club had enlisted approximately 50,000 members (Hackett 108). Other pressures and trends also combined to help explain the nation's developing reading patterns. Following the war, America became a nation of consumers due in part to advances in marketing techniques as well as in technology that aided a turn to mass production. The 1920s also saw "the advent of installment buying and consumer credit industries,"[12] and increased emphasis on and availability of leisure time fed into a new sense of individualism, one couched in terms of consumption. It was in 1921 that the economist Sidney Reeve coined the phrase "consumerism," anticipating the Fordism that would define the decade, at least among America's urban and aspiring middle-class populations. The days of Wilson's idealistic policies were at an end, and while his successors Harding and Coolidge can be rightly accused of being "masters of inaction"[13] with regard to resolving the Prohibition question, they oversaw a cultural turn toward permissiveness and excess somewhat at odds with more conservative and reactionary elements still operating within U.S. society.[14]

In 1920, 1922, and 1925, the years when Fitzgerald's novels of the decade were published, the fiction bestseller lists were topped by Zane Grey's *The Man of the Forest*, Arthur Hutchinson's *If Winter Comes*, and A. Hamilton Gibbs's *Soundings*, respectively. Grey's preeminence in the first half of the decade, with five novels registering in the top ten rankings of *Publishers Weekly* between 1920 and 1924, signals a rather obvious supply-and-demand publishing phenomenon: cheap copies of his work, "packaged in garish covers and emblazoned with vulgar buy-me blurbs" (Benton 289), were produced to satisfy a seemingly insatiable demand for frontier tales of heroic males, redeemed females, and justified violence. Hutchinson, by contrast, was a British writer, and this two-dollar novel was partly a wartime tale of love and misadventure; it was reprinted eleven times in 1922 alone. Indeed, the early to mid-1920s was a fruitful time for Hutchinson and his work: *This Freedom* also secured seventh place on the 1922 list, rising the next year to sixth. His *One Increasing Purpose* (1925) ranked as the nation's tenth bestseller the same year another British author, Gibbs, topped the lists with nearly 100,000 sales (Hackett 99), the two men forming part of a resurgence of British writing in the United States in the immediate postwar period. John Sutherland notes that twenty-eight percent of the bestsellers of the 1920s came from Britain (71 percent were homegrown[15]), a transatlantic connection fostered during the war. Indeed, the recent international situation, combined with longer-term studies of history, took precedence in the early-decade nonfiction bestseller lists: H. G. Wells's *The Outline of History* outsold all other nonfiction titles in 1921 and 1922 and still ranked fifth in 1923. Political biographies of American (Theodore Roosevelt) as well as international figures (Queen Victoria, Napoleon, Disraeli) vied with a rising tide of books dedicated to social etiquette, personal health, and cooking. For example, American nonfiction tastes intermeshed strong sales for Giovanni Papini's *Life of Christ* (first published in Italy in 1921) in 1923 (it ranked second to Emily Post's *Etiquette*), 1924 (second again, this time to Lulu Hunt Peters's *Diet and Health*), and 1925 (falls to fifth in the nonfiction list, just behind Barton Bruce's *The Man Nobody Knows*, a depiction of Christ as a businessman by a businessman) with the revised edition of Fannie Farmer's *The Boston Cooking School Cook Book* (ranked third in 1924, second in 1925, and fifth in 1926) and a mid-decade rage for crossword puzzles (*The Cross Word Puzzle Books* by Prosper Buranelli and others was the nation's tenth bestselling nonfiction title in 1925).

In comparison, Fitzgerald's sales, while notable, kept him outside the bestseller lists. Although *This Side of Paradise* sold its first 3,000 copies within three days at a price of $1.75, it was, according to James L. W. West III, "a hard book to find on publication day."[16] Indeed, looking more closely at its early publication history and retail figures, "*This Side of Paradise* sold a little over 49,000 copies in its initial trade run … There were twelve impressions of the novel between March 1920 and October 1921, all of them small" (West 648). Andrew Hook notes that the initial sales of *The Beautiful and Damned* in 1922 were promising: three printings of the novel, totaling 50,000 copies, resulted in Fitzgerald's appearance on the March, April, and May bestseller lists that year (Hook 43). Compared to the print runs of a bestseller such as Grey (published by Harper), it is clear that Scribners adopted a cautious and conservative approach to Fitzgerald's work. The 1920s would not turn out to be the period of prolific book sales that Fitzgerald may have anticipated. Lewis's *Main Street* was "the best-selling American novel of the first quarter of the century."[17] His tale of rebellion amid the enclosed surroundings of Gopher Prairie, Minnesota was nominated for the Pulitzer Prize in 1921, only to be defeated by that year's fourth-bestselling work, Edith Wharton's *The Age of Innocence*. Indeed, it is interesting to compare Lewis and Wharton to Fitzgerald during the Jazz Age. Lewis enjoyed both the sales figures and the fame that went with them during the 1920s; five of his novels appeared on the bestseller lists. After the breakthrough success of *Main Street*, his seventh novel, came *Babbitt* (tenth best seller of 1922, fourth in 1923), *Arrowsmith* (seventh on the 1925 bestselling fiction list), *Elmer Gantry* (which topped the 1927 fiction list, selling 200,000 in its first week alone [Sutherland 53]), and *Dodsworth* (runner-up in the 1929 bestseller list to Erich Maria Remarque's *All Quiet on the Western Front*). In Wharton's case, Fitzgerald may have located a useful precedent with regard to his relationship with Scribners: As West notes, Wharton had once been a Scribners author but left "in frustration over its failure to promote her books as vigorously as she would have liked" (West 650). Wharton had last made the bestseller list in 1906 with *The House of Mirth*; the success of *The Age of Innocence*, followed by her 1927 novel *Twilight Sleep*, which became the seventh best selling fictional work of that year, may have persuaded Fitzgerald that popular success, however short-lived, could have been possible with a different publisher.

Fitzgerald capitalized to a certain degree on his exposure in publications such as the *Smart Set*, "a magazine known for its ability to spot talent, its willingness to promote material that took risks in style and subject matter, and its appeal to American youth."[18] *This Side of Paradise* had sold almost 50,000 copies by the end of 1921, a "respectable," if not bestseller, showing.[19] Maxwell Perkins's cautious letter of September 16, 1919, informing Fitzgerald that Scribners "are all for taking a chance and supporting [*Paradise*] with vigor" (*S&M* 21) arguably marked the tentative entry of "one of the most staid, conservative, and prestigious of American publishing houses" (West 644) into the contemporary bestseller market otherwise dominated by Harper, Harcourt, Brace, Macmillan, and Doubleday. Indeed, between 1920 and 1929, Scribners would register a mere four times on the bestselling fiction lists: It placed second in 1923 with Arthur Train's *His Children's Children*; sixth for John Galsworthy's *The Silver Spoon* in 1926; third, again with Galsworthy, for *Swan Song* in 1928; and fourth in 1929 for S. S. Van Dine's *The Bishop Murder Case*.

Against a backdrop of seismic cultural change, Fitzgerald's career stands as a key register of the reading habits of the United States in this period, not just because of the commercial success of his short fiction, which, allied to the critical acclaim that would later follow in the wake of his longer works, positions him as central to the definitions of the age. As the voice of an emergent youth culture, Fitzgerald mapped the changing economic face of the nation within texts that challenged or, in some cases, overthrew previous definitions of social and sexual propriety. As Andrew Hook's literary biography of Fitzgerald notes, he was a man divided, and this sense of fracture is readily apparent in his fictional output. Where the money-making short fiction may at times have the frivolous appeal of more sentimental bestsellers of the time, Fitzgerald's longer fictional meditations on a generation maturing into adulthood, marriage, and intrigue provide a link back to more typically nineteenth-century notions of social responsibility: Carraway is repelled by the gaudy and amoral eastern seaboard for more reasons than just the murder of Jay Gatsby. As Kirk Curnutt makes perceptively clear, Fitzgerald's fictions, whether the short stories that he produced for lucrative financial reward or his longer works, were released into a United States that was highly conscious of age issues as the Great War ended. This "age consciousness"[20] operated both in terms of the youth of a coming generation as well as an awareness of the spirit of the divided times. This "distinct subculture, replete with its own slang, styles, and rites of passage" (Curnutt 30) produced a new set of demands on the nation's authors, to which Fitzgerald, for one, responded. American youth was now on the publishing agenda, whatever the surviving traces of the old Protestant orthodoxies of the previous century. This dichotomy within Fitzgerald's writing traces where the new urban, metropolitan, and sexualized youth of the nation came from as much as it vocalized what they wished to believe in. This division is similarly evident in the publishing history of the 1920s; the reading habits of the nation displayed a notably bifurcated accommodation of older fictional motifs combined with now-forgotten authors who flared briefly in the excitement of the period, sharing the nation's bookstore shelves with histories of the recent war, or a growing repertoire of self-help books on health and etiquette for a particularly aspirational generation.

NOTES

1 A. P. Hackett and J. H, Burke, *80 Years of Bestsellers 1895–1975* (New York: R.R. Bowker Company, 1977), 10, 11. Subsequent references to this work are included in the text.

2 A. Hook, *F. Scott Fitzgerald: A Literary Life* (Basingstoke, UK: Palgrave Macmillan, 2002), 71. Subsequent references to this work are included in the text.

3 M. Belgion, "British and American Taste," *English Journal* 17.3 (March 1928), 185–193; 185. Subsequent references to this work are included in the text.

4 M. J. Bruccoli, *Some Sort of Epic Grandeur: The Life of F. Scott Fitzgerald* (New York: Harcourt Brace Jovanovich, 1981), 637. Subsequent references to this work are included in the text.

5 H. Smith, "Twenty-Five Years of Best-Sellers," *English Journal* 33.8 (October 1944), 401–8; 403–4. Subsequent references to this work are included in the text.

6 Arlen achieved notoriety in other ways, too: Armenian (Dikran Kouyoumdjian) by birth, his bestseller resulted in his "[having] his trouser-buttons torn off by mobs of fans on the quay at New York." Cited in C. Cockburn, *Bestseller: The Books that Everyone Read 1900–1939* (London: Sidgwick & Jackson, 1972), 171.

7 B. Noggle, *Into the Twenties: The United States from Armistice to Normalcy* (Urbana: University of Illinois Press, 1974), 153.

8 F. E. Woodward, *A Graphic Survey of Book Production, 1890–1916* (Washington: Bureau of Education, 1917), 3. Subsequent references to this work are included in the text.

9 M. Benton, "'Too Many Books': Book Ownership and Cultural Identity in the 1920s," *American Quarterly* 49.2 (1997) 268–97; 273. Subsequent references to this work are included in the text.

10 R. Berman, "Fitzgerald: Time, Continuity, Relativity," *F. Scott Fitzgerald Review* 2 (2003) 33–50; 36.

11 F. L. Mott, *Golden Multitudes: The Story of Best Sellers in the United States* (New York: R.R. Bowker Company, 1947), 243. Subsequent references to this work are included in the text.

12 L. B. Glickman, "Rethinking Politics: Consumers and the Public Good During the 'Jazz Age,'" *Magazine of History* 21.3 (July 2007), 16–20; 16.

13 A. Sinclair, *Prohibition: The Era of Excess* (London: Faber and Faber, 1967), 271.

14 In the August 1921 edition of the *Ladies Home Journal*, A. S. Faulkner, head of the Music Department of the General Federation of Women's Clubs, but no relation to William Faulkner, claimed that jazz was a force for evil and could intoxicate a dancer just as much as alcohol could in her article "Does Jazz Put the Sin in Syncopation?" (16–34).

15 J. Sutherland, *Bestsellers: A Very Short Introduction* (Oxford: Oxford University Press, 2007), 11.

16 J. L. W. West III, "Did F. Scott Fitzgerald Have the Right Publisher?" *Sewanee Review* 100. 4 (Fall 1992), 644–56; 648. Subsequent references to this work are included in the text.

17 C. MacGowan, *The Twentieth-Century American Fiction Handbook* (Oxford: Wiley Blackwell, 2011), 218.

18 S. Hamilton, "Mencken and Nathan's *Smart Set* and the Story Behind Fitzgerald's Early Success," *F. Scott Fitzgerald Review* 4 (2005), 20–48; 21.

19 R. Prigozy, *F. Scott Fitzgerald* (Woodstock and New York: Overlook Press, 2001), 46.

20 K. Curnutt, "F. Scott Fitzgerald, Age Consciousness, and the Rise of American Youth Culture" in R. Prigozy (ed.), *The Cambridge Companion to F. Scott Fitzgerald* (Cambridge: Cambridge University Press, 2002), 28–47; 29.

27

Magazines

Robert Beuka

At the end of a long, advice-filled 1938 letter to his daughter, Scottie, F. Scott Fitzgerald tacked on this sardonic postscript: "P.S. At the *Saturday Evening Post* rate this letter is worth $4000. Since it is for you only and there are so many points, won't you read it twice?" (*LTD* 57). While offered in a humorous spirit, this closing remark offhandedly provides a telling glimpse of Fitzgerald's relationship to the world of popular magazines that was so influential in his career. Written at a time when he was working as a screenwriter in Hollywood, well past his heyday as a top writer of short fiction for the mass magazine market, this funny little postscript seems to contain both a hint of wistfulness (he could no longer place anything with the *Post* by 1938, let alone get paid thousands of dollars for a story) and sarcasm, as if in his prime it was merely a matter of word count, rather than quality, that could assure him of regular big paydays from popular magazines such as the *Post*. This was not the only time Fitzgerald engaged in a little biting of the hand that fed him: Nearly a decade earlier, at the height of his earning power as a short-story writer, he had noted wryly in an otherwise depressing, self-pitying letter to his friend Ernest Hemingway his new fee from the *Post*: "Here's a last flicker of the old cheap pride: – the Post now pay the old whore $4000 a screw. But now its because she's mastered the 40 positions – in her youth one was enough" (*LL* 169). This idea of himself as whoring his talents for the popular magazines suggests just how conflicted Fitzgerald was toward a publishing market that sustained him throughout his writing career. Though he is remembered primarily as a novelist, author of perhaps the definitive "great American novel," *The Great Gatsby* (1925), Fitzgerald's career as a writer of short stories for magazines deserves attention, not only because of the number of highly successful stories he wrote, including several established classics, but also because of the impact the magazine market in the 1920s and 1930s had on Fitzgerald as a writer. No assessment of Fitzgerald's writing career is complete without an understanding of the primary outlet for his work, the magazines.

During Fitzgerald's roughly twenty-year career, which spanned the 1920s and 1930s, the magazine market was an important outlet for fiction writers, as there was a wide range of magazines that published fiction. To the reader of today, an era when fiction has been largely superseded by any number of digital entertainment forms, the possibilities open to writers of Fitzgerald's time might seem surprising. At one end of the magazine market spectrum were the haute-literary "little magazines," specialty publications with circulations only in the hundreds, which published the fiction and poetry of modernists and others in the literary avant-garde. At the other extreme were the "pulps," magazines printed on paper made from cheap wood pulp that tended to publish sensationalistic action stories. The vast middle ground between these two extremes was the territory of popular weeklies and monthlies that garnered high circulations by featuring a blend of popular fiction and general-interest stories. This middle ground, which provided Fitzgerald's market, can be divided further into two main camps. On the one hand were the "slicks," mass-market, advertising-driven magazines so named because they were printed on high-quality, glossy paper; among the slicks that published Fitzgerald's writing were *Collier's*, *Cosmopolitan*, *Red Book*, *Liberty*, *Metropolitan*, and the most successful and influential of them all, the *Saturday Evening Post*. On the other side of the middle ground was a group of somewhat lower-circulation but still popular magazines with reputations for publishing more highbrow literary fiction – magazines such as *Scribner's Magazine*, *Vanity Fair*, the *Smart Set*, and the *American Mercury*. Fitzgerald published stories in each of these as well. These two realms of the popular magazine market, best exemplified by the middlebrow *Saturday Evening Post* – the magazine to which Fitzgerald would be most often linked – and the more adventurous *Smart Set*, which gave him his start as a writer of commercial magazine fiction, provided his main source of income throughout his professional life while also exerting an important influence on his novel writing.[1]

Fitzgerald was well aware of the power of the popular magazines in shaping public taste and opinion, in the literary realm and beyond. And although he tended to deride his own magazine fiction as a sort of necessary evil – at times going so far as to refer to his stories as "trash" – he understood that regular magazine publication, particularly in the slicks, brought him not only ever-growing paychecks, but also notoriety among readers across the country. Editors like George Horace Lorimer, of the

Post, and H. L. Mencken and George Jean Nathan, who co-edited the *Smart Set* were, at their peak of influence in the 1920s, cultural authorities with the ability to shape the reading public's interests, purchases, and political ideas, in addition to their literary tastes. Nowhere was this more true than in the case of the *Saturday Evening Post*, a publication that has been described as "the veritable bible of bourgeois mores … the arbiter of middlebrow refinement."[2] The contemporary writer and critic Leon Whipple memorably assessed the power and influence of the 1920s *Post* in an article from 1928: "This is a magic mirror; it not only reflects, it creates us. What the SatEvePost is we are. Its advertising helps standardize our physical life; its text stencils patterns on our minds. It is a main factor in raising the luxury-level by teaching us new wants … This bulky nickel's worth of print and pictures is a kind of social and emotional common denominator of American life."[3] With a weekly circulation of 2,750,000 at its peak in the 1920s,[4] the *Post* reached and had an impact on readers from all social strata and was "unrivaled in codifying the ground rules that explained and defined Americanism."[5] Given the *Post*'s incredible popularity in the first third of the twentieth century, it is difficult to overstate the importance of Lorimer, a man gushingly but accurately described by his biographer as "the articulate voice of millions, the purveyor of entertainment, advice and political sentiment to a considerable body of Americans."[6] Fitzgerald would come to see Lorimer's middlebrow bible as both a blessing and a curse, the venue that provided him wealth and fame, even as it all the while drew his attention away from the work that he considered his artistic vocation, his novel writing.

As Matthew J. Bruccoli notes, Fitzgerald felt the lure of potential profit from magazine fiction from the outset of his writing career. In early 1919, after his discharge from the army and his move to New York City, the young would-be author worked furiously composing magazine fiction, his submissions earning a steady stream of rejection slips, which covered the walls of his room at 200 Claremont Avenue near Columbia University: "During the spring of 1919 he wrote 19 stories and accumulated 122 rejections" (*Epic Grandeur* 93). His first sale was to Mencken and Nathan's adventurous, iconoclastic *Smart Set*, where he was paid $30 for the story "Babes in the Woods," which appeared in the September 1919 issue. Further acceptances by the *Smart Set* followed in the coming months, but the prestige of appearing in this magazine came at a price, as the *Smart Set* paid even a returning author such as Fitzgerald at that time "only $35 or $40 for a story" (*Epic Grandeur* 107). By 1920 Fitzgerald had found the magazine to which he would become most closely connected, the king of the slicks, the *Saturday Evening Post.* As its circulation climbed in the 1920s, Bruccoli notes, "advertising revenues permitted the *Post* to pay top prices and thereby attract the best commercial literary talent" (*Epic Grandeur* 109). For Fitzgerald, his first publication in the *Post*, the February 1920 story "Head and Shoulders," introduced the American reading public to the character that would become something of a national obsession – the Fitzgerald flapper. His depiction of the new breed of liberated, fast-living young woman caught on instantly with readers. As Kirk Curnutt notes, Fitzgerald found a way in his flapper stories to "package personality"[7] for a consumer market eager to identify with images projected in both the fiction and advertising of popular magazines. Demand among the reading public for more flapper stories led Fitzgerald to turn out a series of such tales between 1920 and 1924, an output that would prove immensely profitable, even if it threatened to pigeonhole his writing and damage his reputation among critics.[8] And the threat of imperiling his reputation by turning out too many predictable commercial stories was real. James L. W. West III notes the immense popularity of and demand for the flapper stories: "It seemed no matter how hackneyed the plot or how flat the male protagonist – Fitzgerald's famous heroine could carry almost any story into print."[9]

With his early success in magazine fiction came the beginnings in Fitzgerald of a conflicted sense of himself as a writer, the worry that somehow his frothy commercial magazine work might undercut the merit of his novels. As Bruccoli puts it, "he developed the pattern of regarding his career as double or divided – separated into commercial short stories and serious novels. The problem would be to keep his two careers separated" (*Epic Grandeur* 107–108). Fitzgerald disdained the commercialism of the magazine market, even as he relied on it to support his lifestyle. This paradox that he "was writing stories that were supposed to free him from the necessity of writing more stories"[10] plays out in his conflicted attitude toward the slicks and highbrow magazines. In a 1922 letter to his agent, Harold Ober, in which he discussed where to place what he seemed to know would be thought of as one of his great stories, "The Diamond as Big as the Ritz" (then circulating under the working title "The Diamond in the Sky"), Fitzgerald lamented the fact that the ambitiousness of the story – its interweaving of fantasy and scathing social commentary – had rendered it ineligible for publication in the high-paying slicks. His solution to the dilemma of placing such a story was to offer it to Mencken's *Smart Set.* While this decision to return to the pages of the *Smart Set* could be seen as one made "out of loyalty"[11] to those who had put him on the map a couple of years earlier, in effect Fitzgerald's acceptance of the *Smart Set*'s far lower fee amounted to trading a material payoff for an artistic one: "In short I realize I can't get a real good price for the three weeks work that story represents – so I'd much rather get no price but reap the subtle, and nowadays oh-so-valuable dividend that comes from Mencken's good graces" (*LL* 54). Fitzgerald goes on to note his frustration at what he sees as an inverse relationship between the quality of his short story efforts and the fees they would fetch on the magazine market: "I am rather discouraged that a cheap story like *The Popular Girl* written in one week while the baby was being born brings $1500.00 + a genuinely imaginative thing into which I put three weeks of real enthusiasm like *The Diamond in the Sky* brings not a thing. But, by God + Lorimer, I'm going to make a fortune yet" (*LL* 54). This strategizing letter to Ober, with its direct references to Mencken and Lorimer as contrasting, near-omnipotent figureheads in the world of popular culture and taste, suggests the extent to which Fitzgerald's writing career was shaped by tension between art and commerce represented in the magazine market.

Indeed, Fitzgerald's two writerly identities – lightweight commercial entertainer and "serious" novelist – may not have been as entirely separated as he himself wished them to be or thought they were. Ample evidence, both biographical and textual, suggests the extent to which Fitzgerald's relationship to the world of popular magazines influenced his more serious writing in the novels. On the most literal level, there is the occasional textual overlap between the two realms, as Fitzgerald at times borrowed material from previously published magazine stories to incorporate – directly or nearly so – into the novels. Stylistically, commercial story work helped to shape his better writing as well; Alice Hall Petry notes that the concision demanded by the magazine story form helped Fitzgerald learn to reduce the "chattiness to which [he] was temperamentally inclined."[12] More subtly, the novels can be seen as indebted to the story writing in other ways. Susan Hamilton has argued convincingly that Fitzgerald's relationship with the *Smart Set* at the outset of his writing career was central to the success of his first novel, *This Side of Paradise*, in 1920. Hamilton points out that the *Smart Set*, where Fitzgerald published six stories in late 1919 and early 1920, the months leading up to the publication of his novel, "attracted the audience that mattered, particularly to Fitzgerald – America's youth."[13] Mencken's glowing review of the novel in the August 1920 *Smart Set*, in which he called it the "best American novel I've seen of late," and hailed its "highly civilized and rather waggish"[14] young author, provided Fitzgerald with much-needed cultural cachet.

Mencken's influence on Fitzgerald would grow in the coming years, and Fitzgerald would continue his association with Mencken and Nathan after they left the *Smart Set* in 1923 to found the *American Mercury*. They would, for example, publish two of Fitzgerald's best stories in *American Mercury*, "Absolution" in 1924 and "Crazy Sunday" in 1932. The shadow of Mencken's influence also hangs over Fitzgerald's second novel, *The Beautiful and Damned* (1922), although not necessarily for the better. Mencken was a champion of writers from the school of literary naturalism, particularly Frank Norris and Theodore Dreiser, and for his second novel, presumably in an attempt to distance himself from the reputation of his own light commercial fiction, Fitzgerald adopted the bleak, deterministic tone of the naturalists. Fitzgerald admitted picking up on this philosophical and aesthetic thread for *The Beautiful and Damned*, writing to fellow novelist James Branch Cabell that it contains "much of Mencken" (*L* 464), and three years later again noting the connection, albeit in a different key, when he characterized the novel as "a false lead . . . a concession to Mencken" (*C* 139). Although a strictly naturalistic mode works counter to Fitzgerald's romantic lyricism, this "concession to Mencken" did lead to a stronger focus on narrative form, paving the way for the great step forward in *Gatsby*.

That novel, as well, can be seen as connected to Fitzgerald's popular magazine fiction. Fitzgerald scholars have identified a cluster of *Gatsby*-related stories, appearing in the years leading up to the novel's publication, in which he was working through thematic and stylistic ideas that would come to fruition in the 1925 masterpiece. Two oft-noted *Gatsby* cluster stories are the 1922 classic "Winter Dreams," which appeared in *Metropolitan*, and the lower-profile but similarly themed "'The Sensible Thing,'" which appeared in *Liberty* in July 1924. With its intense focus on time, ticking clocks, houses of the past, and the attempt to recreate a lost love, "'The Sensible Thing'" may be in some ways the most direct precursor story to *Gatsby*. This story is relevant to *Gatsby* in another way as well: It is one of eleven stories Fitzgerald composed over a frenetically productive period of writing, the winter of 1923 to 1924, from his home at the time in Great Neck, New York, the Long Island town that would provide the setting of *The Great Gatsby*. Left in precarious financial straits by the unexpected, and total, failure of his play *The Vegetable* in the fall of 1923, Fitzgerald confined himself to his writing desk in a small room above the garage, pounding out commercial stories that would eventually pay his debts and raise enough money to finance the family's time on the French Rivera, where he would write *The Great Gatsby*. Fitzgerald's reaction to these stories, in an April 1924 letter to his friend Edmund Wilson, expresses his characteristic attitude toward the magazine fiction: "I really worked hard as hell last winter – but it was all trash and it nearly broke my heart and my iron constitution" (*LL* 77). While there are unquestionably some lightweight pieces among those eleven Great Neck stories, there are also important explorations of setting, theme, and character types that would figure prominently in *Gatsby* – a novel that may not have materialized were it not for the "trash" that underwrote its composition. The direct link here between the commercial stories and the artistic novel is further evidence that, as Bryant Mangum concludes, "The two Fitzgeralds, the short story writer and the novelist, may finally have been in much closer touch with each other than conventional wisdom has thus far placed them."[15]

While the remainder of the 1920s and the early 1930s would be strong years, both artistically and commercially, for Fitzgerald's short stories, ultimately the Great Depression hurt not only Fitzgerald's reception with the reading public, but also key parts of his market itself. The somber mood of the Depression years spelled the end to Mencken's power and influence, as his bitingly satirical stance on American foolishness no longer appealed to a hurting nation. In the first three years of the decade, the *American Mercury* lost half of its readership (Mott 17), and Mencken stepped down as editor in 1933. Although the *Post* continued to purchase Fitzgerald stories into the middle 1930s, publishing his classic "Babylon Revisited" in 1931 and other solid works such as "Family in the Wind" in 1932, even the once all-powerful magazine fell on some hard times in the 1930s. With sales hurt by the general economic devastation and advertising dollars lost to radio networks, it was inevitable that the *Post* would suffer financially. In addition, Lorimer's increasingly strident political tone, highlighted by his strong editorial stance in opposition to the New Deal, and a growing sense among the public of the magazine as a stuffy, stale leftover from a previous era led to declining readership and cultural influence. Curtis Publishing, the parent company of the *Post*, saw its net income drop to one-third of its previous highs in the first two years of the decade.[16] In 1935, Fitzgerald's professional relationship with the *Post* would essentially come to an end.[17] After Lorimer's retirement in that year, the magazine showed little interest in paying top fees for Fitzgerald's stories; for his part, Fitzgerald was well enough aware that he had lost the *Post* touch. As Bruccoli explains, "His commercial stories became forced and padded as he struggled to simulate emotions that he no longer felt" (*P* xviii). With the commercial *Post* story no longer a viable option, these years would be "a time of trial and error"[18] in which Fitzgerald moved away from his earlier light romance and sought to find fictional forms that would be at once commercially successful and appropriate to his maturing vision.

While Fitzgerald forged a solid relationship with newcomer *Esquire* magazine, which would publish more than two dozen stories from the mid-1930s onward, as well as essays that included the famous "Crack-Up" series published in 1936, the association with *Esquire* was not nearly as lucrative as had been the connection to the *Post.* But times had changed, and the stories for which Fitzgerald had first become famous, redolent with images of rich boys and rich girls negotiating high-society life, fell out of favor with critics of the 1930s who were concerned with the plight of the suffering masses, as well as the ascent of a more proletarian strain in the national literature. Again, magazines played a crucial role in shaping Fitzgerald's career, but this time at his expense. Leftist journals such as *New Masses,* which rose to prominence under the editorship of Mike Gold in the late 1920s and 1930s, championed a brand of socially engaged writing about the plight of the common man, rejecting what they saw as increasingly irrelevant "bourgeois" literature. Gold's 1929 *New Masses* editorial "Go Left, Young Writers!" is often credited as starting in earnest the proletarian literature movement in the United States. In it, Gold bemoans the "lacquer of cynicism, smartness and Ritzy sophistication with which popular American writing is now coated," as well as the fact that the culture is "dominated by a hard, successful, ignorant jazzy bourgeois of about thirty-five, and his leech-like young wife."[19] It is not difficult to detect the target of Gold's critique, and indeed, though Gold's vision would require a few years to come to fruition, in the end the landscape of popular fiction would never be quite the same for Fitzgerald: As Azar Nafisi succinctly puts it in her recent, popular memoir, *Reading Lolita in Tehran,* Gold and his followers "took over ... In the thirties people like Fitzgerald were pushed out by this new breed."[20]

Perhaps it is fitting that Fitzgerald's career as a magazine writer would come to something of a sad end. As he himself once noted, even his early popular stories, filled though they were with youthful romance, "had a touch of disaster in them" (*CU* 87), as if he sensed in advance the inevitable demise of the good times. Moreover, Fitzgerald never did seem comfortable with his role as a writer of popular fiction. For a time, though, when he was nearing his peak as a writer, Fitzgerald's commercial sensibility and artistry (never as opposed to one another as he thought) were shaped by an American magazine market similarly at the peak of its power, capable of influencing popular writers while at the same time generating the market that would sustain them.

NOTES

1 For a discussion of the differences, often misunderstood, regarding the quality of Fitzgerald's fiction published in more literary magazines as opposed to "the slicks," see K. Eble, *F. Scott Fitzgerald* (Boston: G. K. Hall & Co., 1977), 61. See also F. L. Mott, *A History of American Magazines, Volume V: Sketches of 21 Magazines 1905–1930* (Cambridge, MA: Belknap Press, 1968), 264.

2 K. Curnutt, "All that Jazz: Defining Modernity and Milieu in *The Great Gatsby*" in J. R. Bryer and N. P VanArsdale (eds.), *Approaches to Teaching Fitzgerald's* The Great Gatsby (New York: Modern Language Association of America, 2009), 40–49.

3 Qtd. in J. P. Wood, *Magazines in the United States*, 3rd edn. (New York: Ronald Press, 1971), 156.

4 M. J. Bruccoli, *Some Sort of Epic Grandeur: The Life of F. Scott Fitzgerald*, 2nd rev. edn. (Columbia, SC: University of South Carolina Press, 2002), 109. Subsequent references to this work are included in the text.

5 J. Cohn, *Creating America: George Horace Lorimer and* The Saturday Evening Post (Pittsburgh: University of Pittsburgh Press, 1989), 5.

6 J. Tebbel, *George Horace Lorimer and* The Saturday Evening Post (Garden City, NY: Doubleday & Co., 1948), 1.

7 K. Curnutt, "Fitzgerald's Consumer World" in K. Curnutt (ed.), *A Historical Guide to F. Scott Fitzgerald* (New York: Oxford University Press, 2004), 85, 128; 123.

8 Bryant Mangum explains that Fitzgerald produced somewhere between ten and thirteen flapper stories altogether, depending on how you do the math: "Fitzgerald would write only ten of these stories – twelve if the boundaries of the genre are loosened slightly; and thirteen if one includes his resurrection of the Southern belle variation of the flapper-grown-older in his 1929 story 'The Last of the Belles.'" See his introduction to *The Best Early Stories of F. Scott Fitzgerald* (New York: Modern Library, 2005), xvii–xxv; xxi.

9 J. L. W. West III, "F. Scott Fitzgerald, Professional Author" in K. Curnutt (ed.), *A Historical Guide to F. Scott Fitzgerald* (New York: Oxford University Press, 2004), 49–68; 57.

10 M. J. Bruccoli (ed.), *The Price Was High: The Last Uncollected Stories of F. Scott Fitzgerald* (New York: Harcourt Brace Jovanovich, 1979), xi–xv; xv.

11 T. Q. Curtiss, *The Smart Set: George Jean Nathan and H. L. Mencken* (New York: Applause, 1998), 218.

12 A. H. Petry, *Fitzgerald's Craft of Short Fiction: The Collected Stories 1920–1935* (Ann Arbor: UMI Research Press, 1989), 6.

13 S. Hamilton, "Mencken and Nathan's *Smart Set* and the Story Behind Fitzgerald's Early Success," *F. Scott Fitzgerald Review* 4 (2005), 20–48; 39.

14 H. L. Mencken, "Review," reprinted in J. R. Bryer (ed.), *F. Scott Fitzgerald: The Critical Reception* (New York: Burt Franklin & Co., 1978), 28.
15 B. Mangum, "The Short Stories of F. Scott Fitzgerald" in R. Prigozy (ed.), *The Cambridge Companion to F. Scott Fitzgerald* (Cambridge: Cambridge University Press, 2002), 57–78; 60.
16 T. Peterson, *Magazines of the Twentieth Century* (Urbana, IL: University of Illinois Press, 1964), 184.
17 The *Post* would publish three more Fitzgerald stories over the span of 1936–37, finishing with "'Trouble'" in March 1937, but this total contrasts sharply with the more than two dozen they published in the first half of the decade.
18 R. Prigozy, "Fitzgerald's Short Stories and the Depression: An Artistic Crisis" in J. R. Bryer (ed.), *The Short Stories of F. Scott Fitzgerald: New Approaches in Criticism* (Madison, WI: University of Wisconsin Press, 1982), 111–26; 112.
19 M. Gold, "Go Left, Young Writers!" *New Masses* 4 (January 1929), 3–4; 3.
20 A. Nafisi, *Reading Lolita in Tehran: A Memoir in Books* (New York: Random House, 2008), 88.

28

Broadway Melodies

Anthony J. Berret, S. J.

F. Scott Fitzgerald arrived in Hackensack, New Jersey in 1911 to attend Newman School, where his family hoped that he would apply himself seriously to studies in preparation for college. With New York City just forty minutes away, however, Fitzgerald took advantage of this center of popular culture by making frequent trips to Broadway to see the latest musical comedies. He even wrote plays of his own in which he attempted to imitate work by Gilbert and Sullivan.[1] When he entered Princeton two years later, he continued to live near enough to New York to attend plays, and during his Princeton years he wrote the complete lyrics for three of the school's annual Triangle Club shows. Like his contemporaries Cole Porter, Ira Gershwin, and Oscar Hammerstein, he might have proceeded from college to Broadway as a distinguished lyricist. Although he chose a literary career instead, he filled his novels and stories with popular songs, many of which were taken from musical comedies, and he developed plots and themes that reflected those found in Broadway shows of the time.

In *This Side of Paradise* (1920), Fitzgerald incorporated not only the song "Oh, You Wonderful Girl"[2] from George M. Cohan's *The Little Millionaire*,[3] but also created scenes in which the subject of the play, the intermingling of characters from different social classes in romantic interplay, was reflected in the novel. In *Steppin' Out*, Lewis Erenberg documents the rise of the newly rich in the early 1900s and their choice of public spaces for recreation and entertainment. Rather than holding dinners and dances at their homes or in private clubs, they wanted to mingle and compete with others of their class in public restaurants and cabarets. New restaurants hired orchestras for dancing during meals and provided dance instructors for afternoon teas. Cabarets ran floor shows in which performers invited patrons to join them on the floor for dance contests and demonstrations, or patrons welcomed performers to their tables for refreshments. In addition, actors from Broadway theater might attend a cabaret for a late supper and mix with patrons from the upper social classes.[4] Class-crossing situations such as these appeared in the plots of a number of musical plays of the period, and some plots even culminated in the engagement and marriage of socially incompatible characters, as in *The Little Millionaire.*

In a study of songs in *This Side of Paradise*, T. Austin Graham points out the variety of perspectives and responses occasioned by the songs and their presence in a novel. While their lyrics, of course, may be trivial and their melodies monotonous, or their singers melodramatic or posturing, the songs may still evoke profound responses from an audience or character, including a choice or mixture of responses.[5] While seeing this variety and openness of response as typical of popular art, Graham also finds it fundamental to the structure of Fitzgerald's novel and to modernist literature in general. To carry this idea a step further, variety in response to a song arguably increases when the song comes from a show. Amory, for example, may freely relate to the singer-actress or to the character that she plays, to a song either by itself or by its function in the plot of a play. To enjoy this choice or mixture of responses, the reader should know both the song and the play. The plot of *The Little Millionaire*, which concerns marriage to a stage dancer, invites such a variety of responses, as do Amory's other emotional scenes accompanied by songs and shows.

The story of *The Little Millionaire* begins at a casino on Long Island and then moves to a private home and later to a luxury hotel roof garden in Manhattan, and one of the musical numbers, the song "New Yorkers," celebrates the city's residents as international party people: In whatever place of the world you find them, "They'll help you paint the town red, white, and blue," the song suggests. Cohan's use of patriotic colors and the lyrics of this song, as well as the song "Any Place the Old Flag Flies," establishes America's legitimacy as a setting for musical drama. The male lead of the show, "Little Millionaire" Robert Spooner, matches Beau Brummel in style and Vanderbilt, Morgan, and Rockefeller in riches. Boasting in the title song that riches always attract women, Robert reserves a bayside casino on Long Island for a 100-guest dinner to celebrate his engagement to Goldie Gray, who dances in a chorus line for the Zig Zag Folly Company, an obvious allusion to the Ziegfeld Follies. As a dancer, Goldie would be considered underclass by Robert's moneyed set, and Robert fears that his father will not consent to the wedding. For Robert, paternal consent is crucial, because Robert's deceased mother stipulated in her will that both father and son had to marry and consent to each other's marriage in order to inherit the family fortune. The class-crossing romance of

Robert and Goldie is reflected in Amory Blaine's desire for romance with an actress in *This Side of Paradise.*

In the novel, Amory escapes one day from prep school with a classmate to see *The Little Millionaire* in New York. Amory is dazzled by the electric lights of Broadway and the sparkling eyes of women in the Astor dining room. Later, at the show, he is thrown into ecstasy by the actress who dances while the actor playing her lover sings "Oh, You Wonderful Girl" (*TSOP* 35). In the show, the song "Oh, You Wonderful Girl" is performed by Roscoe Handover and Bertha Burnham, who pose as newspaper reporters but plan to blackmail little millionaire Robert by threatening to inform his father of the engagement to dancer Goldie Gray. The only clue to possible villainy in the song is the ragtime melody underlying the ideal and sentimental lyrics. For example, "I never knew why the roses grew … 'til I met you" has syncopated notes on *why* and the second syllable of *roses:*

Because of its origins in saloons, gambling halls, and houses of prostitution, ragtime music suggested disreputable activity no matter what words accompanied it. After the show, Amory's friend claims that he would "marry that girl tonight," meaning apparently the actress, rather than the character that she plays, for he says that, "I'd be proud to take her home and introduce her to my people" (*TSOP* 36). Amory, however, questions his friend: "I wonder about actresses; are they all pretty bad?" (*TSOP* 36). Unlike his more "worldly" friend, Amory intuits his social superiority to the actress (*TSOP* 36). Still, other than his distrust of actresses, there is no sign that Amory or his friend realize that the woman who draws their attraction is a villain in the play. They identify with the actress instead of the character, the song instead of the show.[6]

Although *The Great Gatsby* does not have an overt collage structure as does *This Side of Paradise,* it contains musical pieces almost equally distributed among its chapters, making it resemble a Broadway show with songs used to dramatize certain scenes. One song contained within the novel, Otto Harbach and Frank Mandel's "The Love Nest,"[7] comes from Louis A. Hirsch's 1920 musical, *Mary,*[8] and both the song and the show reflect concerns of the novel. Set at the Keene mansion on Long Island, the story begins when Jack enters singing "The Love Nest" song and carrying a model of the small prefabricated homes, or "love nests," that he intends to build for people with modest incomes. Rich party guests mock the model house as a place in which one would have to sleep standing up, but Mary, the title character and Jack's mother's secretary, likes the house because it reminds her of the one that she lived in back in Kansas and that Jack used to visit. Mary's father was a college president and Jack's father a benefactor of the college, so Jack often stayed at Mary's house. Later in the show, Mary and Jack sing "The Love Nest" together, but when the Keenes learn that they have lost their fortune, Mary and Jack will have to seek wealthier spouses. Jack proceeds with his plan to build the small houses in Kansas, and while there he accidentally discovers oil. He returns to Long Island a rich man and finds Mary singing to a lone pigeon in the model house, which is now set on a pole like a dovecote. Jack adds another pigeon, and then he decides to let the pigeons go so that he and Mary can figuratively move into the nest. With its Long Island setting, its renewal of a relationship begun earlier in the Midwest, its mixing of business and money with romance, its successful turning of a dream into reality, and its class-crossing romances, *Mary* could serve as a model and source for *Gatsby*. The popular show touches on financial loss, practical effort, and real success, and two songs add realism to the romance: "Deeper" – on the hazards of drilling for oil – and the socially critical "Money! Money! Money!" In the novel, Gatsby may dream of love, but he uses extravagant and pragmatic means to fulfill his dream. Both this show and the song cited from it furnish the reader with additional images and attitudes for understanding Fitzgerald's novel and identifying with its characters and action.

Just as the plot of the play is reflected in the plot of the novel, so the song "The Love Nest" resonates with the thematic concerns of the scene in which it appears. In chapter 5 Gatsby and Daisy meet again for the first time in almost five years in Nick's bungalow. Then Nick accompanies them on a tour of Gatsby's mansion, where eventually they relax in a music room, listening to houseguest Klipspringer play the piano (*GG* 74). He plays two songs, making it the only chapter in *Gatsby* with more than one titled musical piece. Other than Klipspringer's dissatisfaction with his own playing, there is no response to the songs by the other characters, although in an earlier draft Gatsby objects to the second song, "Ain't We Got Fun," and requests "something a little more serious," suggesting "un peu d'amour," or "A Little Love a Little Kiss."[9] Of the two songs cited in the novel, one appears with just its title, "The Love Nest," while the second has selected lyrics. The presentation of the lyrics of "Ain't We Got Fun" suggests that Nick and/or Fitzgerald wants the reader to recall the lyrics to the song, perhaps to suggest some larger thematic undertone to the scene. Although the lyrics of the first song, "The Love Nest," are not rendered in the text, they too resonate since they reflect the subtext of the scene as well as voice a mild judgment on Gatsby's strained efforts to impress Daisy. They contrast different types of houses – palaces, mansions, and cottages – and prefer the smaller, simpler ones: "Better than a palace with a gilded dome, / Is a love nest / You can call home." A more appropriate setting for these lyrics would have been the tea held earlier at Nick's place: "Then a small room, tea set of blue, / Best of all room, dream room for two." True, the song describes a dream house, but the house should resemble "a dove nest / down on a farm," a place, unlike Gatsby's, or even Tom's, mansion, built more for love and warmth than for pride. To support this dreamy yet simple farm setting, the song mentions the nursery rhymes "Jack and Jill" and "The House That Jack Built," both farm stories. Although in the tales themselves the lovers fall down the hill and the maiden marries a "man all tattered and torn," the mood of the song is rustic, nostalgic, and moral rather than tragic. In the melody of the chorus, the octave leaps on *Just a* and its parallel phrases, and the notes, mostly on the chord, describe a reaching but still comfortable dream:

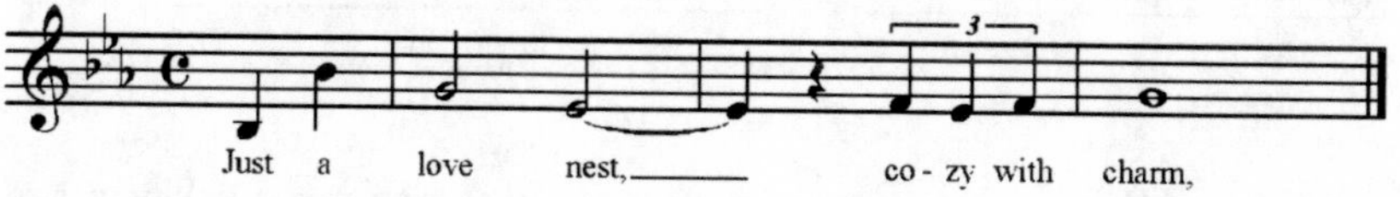

The major-scale descents in the later phrases bring the dream to earth in a gentle, realizable way. The music and lyrics of this song might guide the reader to a kinder and more hopeful judgment of Gatsby than do Nick's comments on his colossal illusion.

Just as the musical comedies and the songs that appear within them resonate within the texts of *This Side of Paradise* and *The Great Gatsby*, so do both the song "Tea for Two"[10] and the musical comedy in which it appears, *No, No, Nanette*,[11] figure prominently in *Tender Is the Night*.[12] In the show, Tom Trainer, a straight-laced young man who works for a lawyer, sings the song to Nanette, his intended fiancée, but she does not want to settle down too soon. As a woman of the 1920s she wants to "raise a little Cain" before she raises children, which is why her elders constantly say "no" to her. In a song that she sings with Tom, "I'll Be

Waiting For You," she insists that living for the present moment "Is not throwing Heaven away, / It's simply saving it up for a rainy day." When Tom invites her to a concert of sacred music at Carnegie Hall, she prefers a trip to Atlantic City instead. It is in Atlantic City, under morally suspicious circumstances, that they sing "Tea for Two." Tom heard that she spent the night there with a man, but she claims falsely that she spent it with her grandmother in Trenton. He believes her, and they dreamily sing the song.

In *Tender Is the Night*, Dick Diver interprets his relationship with Rosemary Hoyt through music when during a visit to Paris he calls her hotel room and hears the song "Tea for Two" playing over the phone (*TITN* 94). Although the telephone here provides the only contact between Dick and Rosemary, the couple in the song imagines an intimacy that will not be interrupted by phone calls: "We won't have it known, dear, that we own a telephone, dear." Despite added notes and different levels of the scale, the repeated four-note phrases that accompany the words "Just me for you and you for me" maintain their identity in the notes on *No friends, re- la-, on week, va- ca-* just like the two persons want to keep their "aloneness" despite the interferences of other company:

Dick and Rosemary reflect the sentiments of this couple. Dick wants to be more than her mentor or guide. When he returns home to the Riviera with Nicole and reminisces about Rosemary by fingering the notes of the same song on a piano, he stops suddenly for fear that Nicole might notice his thoughts about the younger woman (*TITN* 170). He could be concerned about more than just jealousy. As the couple in the song plan ahead for marriage and family, the phrases "A boy for you, / a girl for me," meaning a boy for the wife and a girl for the husband, could apply dangerously to Nicole's traumatic experience with her father. Twice shortly before this, Nicole had erupted into hysterical acts probably induced by her unconsciously relating the experience with her father to Dick's flirtations with Rosemary. Rosemary's openness and daring to love and Dick's reluctance and fear of infidelity may reflect the situation of Nanette and Tom, but a more oblique yet extensive relation between the novel and the show is also possible.

In addition, Dick relates to another character in the show, Jimmy Smith, a married man, who publishes Bibles and religious books, gives money to young women to "make them happy," and is raising Nanette as his ward. When he offers her money, she hugs and kisses him, but he protests that he should kiss only his wife. Although Jimmy plays the role of guardian to Nanette, their relationship is marked by romantic innuendo. Jimmy considers taking her to his Atlantic City cottage, fears that it would not look right, then tells her to pack. In Atlantic City, when Nanette plans to go swimming with her friends, Jimmy asks her to go with him, and she embraces him for this. He warns her, "Don't do that; I'm beginning to like it." She notices that he "feels funny about letting people know we're here," so when detectives show up he asks her to leave: "We're ruined if this gets out." Still, she sits on his lap and pets him. She admits that "a girl's heart grows soft when a man lays the whole world at her feet." The relationship of Jimmy to Nanette clearly reflects that of Dick to Rosemary. Both Jimmy and Dick are married but open to other possibilities. Dick also publishes books, but on psychology rather than religion, and he collects and espouses talented people, especially women. He represents the world to Rosemary, and as her substitute parent and mentor he will show her the world. This dependent relationship quickly develops into a romance, with a mixture of reluctance and consent on Dick's part. Unlike the show, however, which portrays the romance in a comic way, the novel makes it serious and tragic by its psychological effects on Nicole.

The song "Tea for Two," therefore, is first used by Dick to imagine a romance with Rosemary, but playing the song later in the presence of Nicole, Dick fears that it might apply in disturbing ways to her as well. Similarly, knowing the song's place in *No, No, Nanette*, Dick might identify with either the younger and straight-laced romantic lead Tom, or the older parental and professional Jimmy, who mixes romance with his other roles. The reader, of course, would have the same choices. Various perspectives and identifications become possible in the popular and the modern arts.

In *Reading* The Waste Land, Jewel Spears Brooker and Joseph Bentley describe the cultural field or context from which T. S. Eliot's poem emerged. A principal characteristic of this field and its products is "multiperspectivism," the need and use of several mirrors or reflectors to present an action, character, or idea.[13] The authors locate this phenomenon in the philosophy, science, and arts of the time, linking it to relativity and Cubism. They claim that its influence reached all levels of culture and may perhaps have remained unconscious to persons affected by it. Like Eliot, Fitzgerald perceived and re-presented his own time. Fitzgerald was, of course, aware of subtle differences between genres, and he was aware as well of conventions that were in his time associated with high art as opposed to popular entertainment. However, a study of his novels – those works including *The Great Gatsby* and *Tender Is the Night* that he considered prime exhibits of his legacy as a literary artist – shows him integrating into them in both general and specific ways many of the components of popular art forms. He used popular songs in his fiction to carry thematic strains through his narratives, and he underscored complexities related to class conflict in America through his use of resonant story lines found in Broadway shows and popular tunes often associated with them and familiar to most of his readers. Indeed, one might argue that Fitzgerald's enduring fascination with and knowledge of Broadway – its melodies, its rhythms, its tropes – contributed to his ability to create works that appealed across the social spectrum.

NOTES

1 M. J. Bruccoli, *Some Sort of Epic Grandeur: The Life of F. Scott Fitzgerald*, 2nd rev. edn. (Columbia, SC: University of South Carolina Press, 2002), 31.
2 G. M. Cohan, "Oh, You Wonderful Girl" (New York: Cohan and Harris, 1911).
3 G. M. Cohan, *The Little Millionaire* (New York: Billy Rose Theater Collection, 1911).
4 L. A. Erenberg, *Steppin' Out: New York Night Life and the Transformation of American Culture, 1890–1930* (Chicago: University of Chicago Press, 1984).
5 A. T. Graham, "Fitzgerald's 'Riotous Mystery': *This Side of Paradise* as Musical Theater," *F. Scott Fitzgerald Review* 6 (2001–2008), 21–53.
6 The song did stand on its own apart from the show by sheet music publication in 1911, the year of the show's opening, and by a phonograph recording a year later. Since Amory attends the whole show, however, both he, and perhaps the reader, might be expected to respond to the song also in the context of the show.
7 O. Harbach and F. Mandel, "The Love Nest" (New York: Victoria, 1920).
8 L. A. Hirsch, *Mary* (New York: Billy Rose Theater Collection, 1920).
9 *The Great Gatsby: A Facsimile of the Manuscript*, ed. M. J. Bruccoli (Washington: Bruccoli Clark/NCR, 1973), 141–42.
10 I. Caesar and V. Youmans, "Tea for Two" (New York: Harms, 1924). I. Caesar and V. Youmans, "Tea for Two" (New York: Harms, 1924). "Tea for Two," copyright 1929 (Renewed) Warner Brothers Corp. and Irving Caesar Music Corp., is used by permission.
11 O. Harbach. *No, No, Nanette* (New York: Billy Rose Theater Collection, 1925).

12 The song was interpolated into the musical comedy during road tryouts in 1924, although it appeared in sheet music and a phonograph recording, and even in a different show, *Big Boy* (1925), before *Nanette* opened in New York in the fall of 1926. Thus, there is ample reason to consider the song by itself rather than as part of a show. However, interesting plot links between *Nanette* and *Tender Is the Night* make the song serve also as a bridge between the novel and the show. Beginning in the spring of 1924, *Nanette* played in Detroit, Chicago, Boston, Philadelphia, and even London before its New York opening. It would not be anachronistic, therefore, for the show to apply to events in the summer of 1925, when the first part of the novel occurs. In earlier drafts of the novel, Dick and Nicole, with other names, sing "several things from *No, No, Nanette*," including "Where Has My Hubby Gone Blues," at a dinner party on the Riviera. (See *F. Scott Fitzgerald Manuscripts Iva*, Tender Is the Night II: *The Melarky and Kelly Versions* Part 2, introduced and arranged by M. J. Bruccoli [New York: Garland, 1990]), 71, 21.

13 J. S. Brooker and J. Bentley, *Reading* The Waste Land: *Modernism and the Limits of Interpretation* (Amherst: University of Massachusetts Press, 1990), 31–32.

29

Stage and Screen Entertainment

Walter Raubicheck and Steven Goldleaf

In 1939 F. Scott Fitzgerald wrote a letter to his daughter, Scottie, in which he contrasted his own work with that of the popular songwriters and showmen of the 1920s: "Again let me repeat that if you start any kind of career following the footsteps of Cole Porter and Rodgers and Hart, it might be an excellent try. Sometimes I wish I had gone along with that gang, but I guess I am too much a moralist at heart and really want to preach at people in some acceptable form rather than to entertain them" (*L* 63). Knowing as we do that Fitzgerald spent much of his time at Princeton writing lyrics for musical comedies, such a comparison is not so far-fetched. It is certainly a possibility that he could have become a successful lyricist during the boom in popular song that took place in the 1920s, whose most accomplished representatives were the songwriters he mentions, along with Irving Berlin, the Gershwin brothers, and Oscar Hammerstein II, who was writing lyrics for varsity shows at Columbia at the same time Fitzgerald was doing the same at Princeton (and whose renown Fitzgerald acknowledged in "Head and Shoulders," a story he published when he and Hammerstein were not yet 25). Fascinated by vaudeville, musical comedy, popular song, and the movies, Fitzgerald held a profoundly ambivalent attitude toward them, applauding their energy but deploring their vulgarity. Although he intuited that the new popular culture possessed a potential for artistic achievement, he also failed to recognize many such achievements already in the multifaceted world of American entertainment that thrived on new technology and the economic postwar boom.

American popular entertainment reached a fertile crossroads in the 1920s: Older forms, such as vaudeville, were reaching their commercial peaks before imploding by the end of the decade; other older forms, such as musical comedy, were being reinvigorated by a new talented generation of composers, lyricists, and performers; and whole new forms, such as cinema, were reaching their first decade of creative and commercial maturity. F. Scott Fitzgerald incorporated representations of all these forms of popular culture and more in his novels and stories of the 1920s; indeed, the short story, which became the major source of his income as the decade progressed, was one of the newer forms as the slick and pulp magazines created a new market for short fiction.

Ronald Berman has analyzed the significance of the word "energy" for Fitzgerald's early work, tracing it to William James's identification of energy as a psychic state undergirding the activity of the moral will;[1] it also has a Bergsonian derivation in that Fitzgerald was among early twentieth-century authors such as T. S. Eliot, James Joyce, and Gertrude Stein who understood Henri Bergson's "*élan vital*" as a spiritual impulse, irreducible to chemistry, that is the most powerful dynamic factor in both nature and art. Eliot found this energy in music-hall performers such as Marie Lloyd, and Fitzgerald acknowledged it in the epic films of D. W. Griffith, the comic films of Charles Chaplin, and the songs of Irving Berlin; both hoped to integrate this energy into their modernist art, Eliot in his verse dramas and Fitzgerald in his novels and more ambitious stories.

We know that in the summer of 1917 Fitzgerald read Bergson, William James, and Arthur Schopenhauer.[2] Although he mocks the craze of Bergsonism in *The Beautiful and Damned* (1922), classifying it along with Bilphism (his own parody of theosophy) as a popular pseudo-intellectual current of 1913,[3] he found in some of Bergson's ideas an explanation for the charm of the flappers who embodied the new popular culture, as opposed to their Victorian counterparts of the highbrow and staid culture inherited from the nineteenth century. *The Beautiful and Damned* uses the word "energy" nine times, the word "intensity" eight times, and the word "vitality" eight times, as, for example, in this line: "Gloria appeared, fresh in starched yellow, bringing atmosphere and an increase of vitality" (*B&D* 180). The number of instances slackened by the time of *The Great Gatsby* (1925), but vitality is still a key concept, as illustrated by Nick's observation that Myrtle Wilson's "intense vitality that had been so remarkable in the garage was converted into impressive hauteur" (*GG* 26). In "Winter Dreams" (1923), Judy Jones is described in terms that resonate with Bergson's vocabulary: "This color and the mobility of her mouth gave a continual impression of flux, of intense life, of passionate vitality – balanced only partially by the sad luxury of her eyes" (*ASYM* 49).

Fitzgerald throughout the 1920s used the new popular arts for the subject matter of many of his stories and novels, but he usually treated them with an irony appropriate for a view that simultaneously recognizes them as dynamic entertainment but inherently limited as genuine art. The brief preface to the 1920 *Vanity Fair* story "Jemina, the Mountain Girl" advertises the story as follows: "This don't pretend to be 'Literature.' This is just a tale for red-blooded folks who want a *story* and not just a lot of 'psychological' stuff or 'analysis.' Boy, you'll love it! Read it here, see it in the movies, play it on the phonograph, run it through the sewing-machine" (*TJA* 269). Fitzgerald's comical apology for the story to follow equates his commercial fiction with commodification, on par with that sort of light entertainment that the movies (and records and sewing machines) might offer a modern audience. But his serious short stories and his novels neither require nor receive such apologies.

Because phonograph records, movies, and slick fiction rarely require the kind of close analysis required by traditional art, the strengths of the former lie in their immediacy and the vitality that goes with their spontaneity. The kind of undisciplined spontaneity that popular culture requires can be seen in the early boy-meets-girl *Saturday Evening Post* story "Head and Shoulders" (1920), in which the male character's role is to assist the showgirl in achieving success in the entertainment field and to witness it as it occurs. Marcia Meadow, the vulgar showgirl heroine, displays her intellectual shortcomings, mistaking "Bergsonian trimmings" for "Brazilian" ones throughout, and "rationality" for "nationality"(*S* 8). Fitzgerald portrays his successful performers as people who succeed in the entertainment field by such vital traits as luck, or charisma, or sex appeal. Horace Tarbox, Marcia's cultured, discerning, priggish, and cautious mate, in contrast, falls so far for the vulgar world that he transforms himself into an entertainer with his body while she transforms herself into an intellectual of sorts – a fantastic quality in that those fabulous transformations allow Fitzgerald to posit that contemporary success (in either the physical or mental sphere) is a matter of luck or will rather than training and discipline, that what is needed for success is a healthy disregard for particular talents, or at least a suspension of judgment of one's own talent or lack of it.

"Head and Shoulders," in fact, encapsulates Fitzgerald's attitude toward ironic treatment of popular art, in this case vaudeville. Horace's transformation from an inert, virtually bodiless bookworm into a celebrated acrobat is not shown as a particularly difficult transformation: He simply spends a summer working out in a gym, and he gets an offer to perform his acrobatics at the Hippodrome. He goes from a scholar who nicknames his reading chairs after philosophers to an athlete who routinely bounds up stairs "five steps at a time" (*S* 21). Meanwhile his wife has written a popular book, without any technical training either, a book with "constant mistakes in spelling and grammar, and … weird punctuation" (*S* 22). Both husband and wife in this story achieve popular success without any significant training or dedication, just the luck of having some innate ability.

Certainly the most important new art form for Fitzgerald was the movies. In his first published stories and in his stories and novels throughout the Jazz Age, the art of film, and particularly of Hollywood film, becomes a major concern of Fitzgerald's own art, and at times serves as a trope for it. As early as 1922, he told his friend Thomas Boyd that movies were a kind of necessary evil, which no writer could afford to ignore: "You might as well protest against a Cunarder or the income tax as protest against the movies," which he claimed were "here to stay."[4] Their appeal, as Ruth Prigozy notes, was the opportunity they gave "to escape from the mundane and to live, albeit vicariously, in a world illuminated by wealth and beauty" (Prigozy 130). Fitzgerald's work sometimes featured the movies as the ultimate in grotesque luxury: In "The Diamond as Big as the Ritz," Hollywood intersects with the fabulous world of the unimaginably wealthy. John Unger asks his host, Percy Washington, who planned all of his "wonderful reception rooms and halls, and approaches and bathrooms," and he is informed by his friend, "I blush to tell you, but it was a moving-picture fella. He was the only man we found who was used to playing with an unlimited amount of money, though he did tuck his napkin in his collar and couldn't read or write" (*S* 203). Again, education, training, and simple literacy, in Fitzgerald's fantasy world of popular fiction, are meaningless compared to the advantages garnered by talent and money.

Fitzgerald's attitude toward the film industry in the early 1920s is most clearly identified in *The Beautiful and Damned* through his integration of the pretentiously titled movie company Films Par Excellence into the rise and fall of Anthony and Gloria's hopes (*B&D* 118). It is run by Joseph Bloeckman, a Jew who does "a lot of business" with Gloria's father and is one of her suitors, along with Anthony himself. A former peanut vendor, sideshow manager, and vaudeville promoter, Bloeckman had now taken the next logical step in trying to make money from America's popular entertainment: "Just when the moving picture had passed out of the stage of a curiosity and become a promising industry he was an ambitious young man of twenty-six with some money to invest, nagging financial ambitions, and a good working knowledge of the popular-show business" (86). It is interesting here to note that the emphasis in this phrase in 1922 would be on "popular-show" as denoting the kind of business Bloeckman had begun to conquer: "show-business" as an entity in itself had not yet entered the demotic language. When Bloeckman is out for the evening with Gloria, Anthony, and their friends, Gloria mocks him because he does not dance, and instead acts like a much older, patronizing chaperone. Indeed, she takes to calling him "Blockhead." Yet she continues to let him take her out, and he emerges as one of Anthony's most hated rivals despite his lack of formal education and sophistication – attributes that Anthony and his friends pride themselves on. Bloeckman has money, he is in love with her, and he has already asked her to marry him. For Gloria at this point such attributes are enough to keep her interested: "To the time of Anthony's arrival in the arena he had been making steady progress" (118). But when she finally decides to submit to her feelings for Anthony, Bloeckman temporarily disappears from their lives and the story. He reappears when Anthony encounters him in a train about a year after his marriage to Gloria, and Anthony and is taken aback by the man's improvements in taste and social graces: "The last aura of the successful travelling-man had faded from him, that deliberate ingratiation of which the lowest form is the bawdy joke in the Pullman smoker … Anthony no longer felt a correct superiority in his presence" (176). He then visits them at their summer home in Connecticut to offer Gloria a screen test, "infinitesimally improved, of subtler intonation, of more convincing ease" (180). Gloria decides to turn down the invitation at this time, but she agrees to go for an automobile ride alone with him one afternoon, which almost destroys Anthony, who is jealous and insecure about what he really has to offer his wife. Indeed, it is now clear to the reader that Bloeckman's increasing success in the film industry and its accompanying enhancement of his own self-presentation will serve as an index to Anthony's decline.

When the loss of his uncle's inheritance has reduced Anthony and Gloria to desperate financial worry back in New York, Bloeckman makes another appearance in their lives: "The process of general refinement was still in progress – always he dressed a little better, his intonation was mellower, and in his manner there was perceptibly more assurance that the fine things of the world were his by a natural and inalienable right" (*B&D* 255). While Anthony's desire to write fiction has been thwarted by his own frailties, his counterpart has triumphed in a world of entertainment that Anthony considers beneath him in every respect. When Bloeckman last enters the story three years later, the couple has nearly hit bottom financially and spiritually. A few days before her twenty-ninth birthday Gloria calls him out of desperation, since he had always wanted to put her in the movies. By now the social climber has changed his name to the less ethnic Black; he himself is now a "dark suave gentleman, gracefully engaged in the middle forties," and his studio is equally impressive: "a great hall, as large as an armory with busy sets and blinding rows of unfamiliar light" (328). He arranges a screen test for Gloria, which she finds confusing, intimidating, and somewhat humiliating – especially when Black tells her that the director who ran the test concludes that "*for the part he had in mind he needed a younger woman*" (333). All that might be available for Gloria is a "*small character part supposed to be a very haughty rich widow*" (333). Immediately she is overcome by the painful awareness that her youth and beauty have faded: "'Oh, my pretty face! Oh, I don't want to live without my pretty face'" (333).

The parallel between Bloeckman's rise and Anthony's fall reaches its apogee when Anthony confronts the older man at a nightclub shortly after Gloria has finally told him about her abortive attempt to become a movie actress. Pathetically drunk, Anthony angrily reprimands Bloeckman for dashing his wife's aspiring theatrical hopes: "'Un'erstand you kep' my wife out of the movies.'" Bloeckman tries to get past this belligerent drunk, but Anthony finally unleashes all his hatred and condescension when he exclaims, "'Not so fas,' you Goddam Jew,'" upon which the producer punches Anthony "squarely in the mouth" and sends him to the carpet, ultimately ordering the waiters to have him thrown out: "The 'bum' was propelled violently to the sidewalk, where he landed on his hands and knees with a grotesque slapping sound and rolled over slowly onto his side" (359–60).

When, shortly thereafter, Anthony and Gloria finally inherit the millions they have so desired and so feared would never be theirs, Anthony's degradation has irreparably damaged his mental stability, and the reader understands that the riches have truly come too late to save his marriage and save him from foolish self-justification. Fitzgerald's point in making the final scene with Bloeckman at the nightclub represent the low point in Anthony's loss of dignity and self-respect is that the movie industry – this nascent, raw, crude form of popular entertainment – has no place for the refined likes of Anthony and Gloria Patch, neither for his intelligence and talent nor for her charm and beauty. The genteel culture they represent lacks the initiative and the vigor to compete with the superficial commercialism of the movies, which thrive on their appeal to mass culture.

That contrast between genteel culture and mass culture also appears in his next novel, *The Great Gatsby*, in which popular entertainment, particularly that of the movie industry, helps attract the hordes of partygoers swarming to Gatsby's mansion. His fabulous parties draw on the vulgar nouveau-riche entertainers from West Egg who are gazed upon by admirers from other parts of Long Island and New York City. It is particularly amusing to note that one of the West Egg guests, the absurdly named Newton Orchid, runs the same film company associated with Bloeckman in the previous novel, Films Par Excellence, its supposed French origins revealing the grasping for middlebrow acceptance by this upstart, unsophisticated American industry. Gatsby is presented through the two parties described at length in the novel as a young impresario determined to integrate into his parties the major types of Broadway entertainment then current: vaudeville through the stage "twins" who perform a "baby act in costume" (*GG* 39) and the comedian "getting off some funny stuff" whose company Tom Buchanan prefers to his wife's (82); jazz and its recent pretensions as high culture through the orchestra's playing Vladimir Tostoff's "Jazz History of the World," which "had attracted so much attention at Carnegie Hall" (41), presumably a nod to the Paul Whiteman concert at Aeolian Hall in 1924 at which Gershwin premiered *Rhapsody in Blue*; and movies through the director and his "star" sitting under the white plum tree.

The parties come to a sudden end as soon as Gatsby has attracted the presence of the one person he has sought, Daisy Buchanan. As it turns out, Daisy – almost alone of all of Gatsby's party guests – ultimately does not care for his parties and the show business celebrities who populate them: She is offended and "appalled by West Egg, this unprecedented 'place' that Broadway had begotten upon a Long Island fishing village – appalled by its raw vigor" (*Gatsby* 84), and Gatsby immediately perceives her distaste. "She didn't like it" (85), he repeats after his final party. The following chapter of the novel begins by noting that the lights in Gatsby's mansion failed to come on again, and his career as Long Island's greatest purveyor of popular entertainment was suddenly over. Now that Gatsby has what he wants, Daisy herself, he has no further need for the superficial attractions that Broadway and the movie industry provide. A mere means to his end, rather than a defining part of Gatsby's character, the entertainment world gets shut off as easily and quickly as he might shut off a light switch.

By comparing certain passages in *Trimalchio*, the early version of the novel, to the same passages as they appeared in the published text of *The Great Gatsby*, one can trace some of Fitzgerald's evolving thoughts about West Egg celebrities. Surprisingly, in the early version of the famous catalog of party guests from West Egg, the only difference from the later *Gatsby* text is that "all [of the party guests] connected with the movie industry in some way" are specified as coming from East Egg, rather than West Egg, and vice versa. During the revision process, the two catalogs are otherwise identical, but Fitzgerald's conception obviously shifted because of the contrast he wanted between West Egg (based on Great Neck, where he had lived alongside other successful but socially suspect people from the entertainment world) and East Egg (based on Port Washington, where more established people from more respectable backgrounds, such as the Buchanans, lived). In the immediately preceding paragraph, the two Eggs are also switched around: it begins "Clarence Endive was from West Egg" in *Trimalchio* (*T* 51), but after revision, he "was from East Egg" (*GG* 49).

And nowhere is the notion of West Eggers as "artists" emphasized. Instead, what Fitzgerald focuses on is their celebrity and the financial power that they wielded: "I've never met so many celebrities," Daisy exclaims at what would be Gatsby's final party, noting their fame rather than their talents as their mark of distinction, and that is also how Gatsby thinks of his party guests (*GG* 82). He informs the Buchanans that they "must see the faces of many people [they've] heard about." When Tom Buchanan refuses to play along with Gatsby's game, Gatsby points out one famous guest in particular:

> "Perhaps you know that lady," Gatsby indicated a gorgeous scarcely human orchid of a woman who sat in state under a white-plum tree. Tom and Daisy stared, with that particularly unreal feeling that accompanies the recognition of hitherto ghostly celebrity of the movies.
>
> "She's lovely," said Daisy.
>
> "The man bending over her is her director [Gatsby explains]." (82)

In *Trimalchio*, this passage is rendered during the first party that Nick Carraway attends, not the last, and the description of the show-business celebrities is extended. Instead of Gatsby's explaining to the Buchanans the fame of his party guests, in the *Trimalchio* version this speech is attributed to Jordan Baker, who explains this fame to Nick. He is the one who stares at the "elaborate orchid of a woman," who turns out to be a famous film actress. Meanwhile, in *Trimalchio* her director is the subject of gossip that Jordan passes on to Nick: "He's just been married. It's in all the movie magazines" *(T* 36.) The function of these famous movie people, then as now, is to be celebrated in the "movie magazines" almost more than to be regarded as artistic performers. When transposed into the *Gatsby* text, this famous couple appears as Nick is "standing with Daisy and watching the moving-picture director and his Star [capitalization Fitzgerald's]" *(GG* 83). Nick and Daisy observe them kissing, and it is this easy access to the celebrities' private lives that Gatsby's parties, like the gossip magazines, can give.

Other than the commodification of public figures' private lives, the movie industry also serves Gatsby's parties as the source of wealth for his West Egg guests. In the novel, Nick notices the presence at Gatsby's first party of a "number of young Englishmen," trying to sell something to wealthy Americans, "agonizingly aware of the easy money in the vicinity and convinced that it was theirs" (*GG* 35). In the earlier version, Fitzgerald includes a brief list of the potential buyers of these "somethings": *Gatsby*'s "solid and prosperous Americans" (*GG* 35) are identified in *Trimalchio* as "moving picture magnates and bankers," again emphasizing the financial quality of the movies rather than an artistic one (*T* 36).

Throughout the rest of his career after *The Great Gatsby*, Fitzgerald was drawn to this same dichotomy between the current state of popular culture and its potentialities. After his 1927 visit to Hollywood, the conflict is played out principally in relation to the film industry. His relationship with Lois Moran gave him the material to use in the *Tender Is the Night* cluster story "Jacob's Ladder," as well as in the novel itself, for both the "Daddy's Girl" motif and for his exploration of subjects related to illusion and reality. His 1931 visit led him to create "Crazy Sunday," in which the genuine artist is the director Miles Calman, while the mere craftsman is the writer Joel Coles. And, of course, during his last years, 1939 to 1940, he worked simultaneously on the stories featuring the hack writer Pat Hobby and the novel that featured his one real artist-hero, the film producer Monroe Stahr. Clearly, Fitzgerald's ambivalence concerning the artistic quality of popular art provided the tension in Fitzgerald's own art from the beginning of his professional career to the end.

NOTES

1 R. Berman, *Fitzgerald, Hemingway, and the Twenties* (Tuscaloosa, AL: University of Alabama Press, 2001), 3.

2 M. J. Bruccoli, *Some Sort of Epic Grandeur: The Life of F. Scott Fitzgerald*, 2nd rev. edn. (Columbia, SC: University of South Carolina Press, 2004), 75. Subsequent references to this work are included in the text.

3 T. Quirk, *Bergson and American Culture: The Worlds of Willa Cather and Wallace Stevens* (Chapel Hill, NC: University of North Carolina Press, 1990), 81. Subsequent references to this work are included in the text.

4 R. Prigozy, "Fitzgerald's Flappers and Flapper Films of the Jazz Age: Behind the Morality" in K. Curnutt (ed.), *A Historical Guide to F. Scott Fitzgerald* (New York: Oxford University Press, 2004), 129–61; 130. Subsequent references to this work are included in the text.

30

Consumer Culture and Advertising

Lauren Rule Maxwell

In "Early Success" (1937), F. Scott Fitzgerald muses about his Jazz Age popularity, suggesting that his success derived from his ability to project "a fresh picture of life in America" as it gave rise to a new consumer culture (*CU* 87). He explains that "there seemed little doubt about what was going to happen – America was going to be the greatest, gaudiest spree in history and there was going to be plenty to tell about it." In his short stories and novels, Fitzgerald told the tale of this spending spree, depicting "the whole golden boom ... in the air." His telling of it made such an impression that he became the spokesman of the era, which "bore him up, flattered him and gave him more money than he ever dreamed of" (*CU* 13). Fitzgerald came to personify the age because he understood what the potential benefits and risks of this boom were, as well as the how advertising fueled new patterns of consumption. Fitzgerald, in fact, had experience in the advertising business: He worked for four months in 1919 for New York's Barron Collier agency while trying to woo Zelda. Although Fitzgerald later claimed that he was "mediocre at advertising work," he was able to apply his knowledge of the business of advertising within his fiction and even used it to cultivate his own image and public celebrity (*CU* 26). Fitzgerald's "picture of life in America" itself became iconic and began to symbolize the boom of the Jazz Age, both capitalizing on and contributing to the consumerism that was sweeping the country.

Fitzgerald points out in "Early Success" that his representations of the consumer boom were not all "golden," that, in addition to "splendid generosities," they included "outrageous corruptions" and foreshadowed impending doom (*CU* 87). "All the stories that came into my head had a touch of disaster in them," he insists; "the lovely young creatures in my novels went to ruin, the diamond mountains of my short stories blew up, my millionaires were as beautiful and damned as Thomas Hardy's peasants" (*CU* 87). Although the fallout of the stock market crash was still years away when he wrote most of these pieces, Fitzgerald incorporated these foreboding elements because "I was pretty sure living wasn't the reckless, careless business these people thought." With outrageous antics like frolicking in the Plaza Hotel fountain and lighthearted articles such as "How to Live on $36,000 a Year," Fitzgerald might have seemed to personify the very reckless abandon and spendthrift mindset he attributes to others. But a closer look at Fitzgerald's writing reveals a more complex relationship to consumer culture that involves his glamorizing this spending spree while at the same time critiquing it. He describes America during the Jazz Age as both "the greatest nation [where] there was a gala in the air" and "bloated, gutted, stupid with cake and circuses" (*CU* 25, 31). These statements are representative of the "double vision" of Fitzgerald's fiction that reflects the glittery glory and unwise excess of the time without attempting to reconcile them. Ultimately, though, in his writings Fitzgerald recognizes the social and economic costs of the spree that fueled the boom, which made it, in his words, "the most expensive orgy in history" (*CU* 21).

Fitzgerald is not alone in claiming that the American marketplace was forever transformed by the Jazz Age: Historians and economists agree that consumer culture as we now know it developed during that time. As Liette Gidlow asserts, "Consumer culture was a defining element of public life in the 1920s, and the 1920s were a defining moment in the development of consumer culture. Though consumer goods and advertising, of course, predated the 1920s, a mature consumer society did not."[1] There are several reasons why modern consumer culture emerged during the 1920s. Lawrence B. Glickman describes the convergence of factors that made the 1920s the "takeoff period for consumer society":

> During the decade, pundits, scholars, and many ordinary Americans claimed to be observing an epochal and multifaceted transformation whose key feature was a shift from production to consumption. While a robust consumer economy had been developing since at least the market revolution of the early nineteenth-century, several elements converged in the 1920s to create a fully mature consumer society. Those elements included a much-expanded advertising industry, the advent of installment buying and consumer credit industries, the mass production on Henry Ford's assembly lines, and the mass consumption at Woolworth's chain stores. Increasingly, American life, not just economically but culturally, centered on mass consumption.[2]

Glickman's discussion highlights the importance of the confluence of cultural and economic elements such as advertising, consumer credit, and mass production for creating modern American consumers, who increasingly began to realize their purchasing power and to identify with the things they bought rather than what they produced.

Consumer data from the era reflected this shift in the Jazz Age from production to consumption. Economist Martha L. Olney has documented what she terms the "consumer durables revolution" of the 1920s. She demonstrates that the purchases of durable goods rose in the 1920s and that Americans were buying more big-ticket items – such as cars, household appliances, and radios – while using a greater proportion of their disposable income to do so at the expense of saving, which fell from a rate of 7.1 to 4.4 percent between 1898 to 1916 and 1922 to 1929.[3] In the 1920s people were not only more likely to spend what money they had, with installment buying and consumer credit, they were also more likely to purchase luxury goods, such as automobiles, they could not afford. The number of cars sold in the United States rose from 6.8 million in 1919 to more than 23 million in 1929 as working-class people, like George Wilson from Fitzgerald's *The Great Gatsby* (1925), sought to own cars (Gidlow 163; *GG* 22, 96). While in 1919 only 5 percent of cars were purchased on installment, over a decade that percentage also tripled, rising to 15 percent by 1929.[4] That same year, overall consumer debt in the United States topped $7 billion.[5]

The impulse for people to buy things they did not really need or could not afford was driven in part by a cultural shift that devalued thriftiness. Glickman explains that "[r]ecognizing that consumption is what drove the economy, many Americans … redefined thrift not as saving (which was redefined by some as 'hoarding') but as what a business group called 'wise spending.' In this sense, thrift meant purchasing quality merchandise" (17). The redefinition of thrift as a form of consumption can be seen even in government rhetoric: In 1924, the U.S. Department of Commerce concluded: "Production cannot be possible unless it produces, first of all, consumers" (Glickman 18). This leveraging of purchasing power for political capital helped legitimize the widespread use of credit and installment buying and made traditional American values of saving seem outdated. The Muncie, Indiana, Chamber of Commerce went so far as to say that "the American citizen's first importance to this country is no longer that of citizen, but that of consumer" (Glickman 18). The conflation of citizenship and consumerism might have influenced Fitzgerald's decision to wire Maxwell Perkins, his editor at Scribners, three weeks before the publication of *The Great Gatsby* with this message: "CRAZY ABOUT THE TITLE UNDER THE RED WHITE AND BLUE STOP WHART WOULD THE DELAY BE."[6] Although it was too late for the change to take effect, this message suggests that Fitzgerald saw Jay Gatsby – who went from following a Benjamin Franklin-like schedule for self-improvement in his youth to later in life spending a fortune at whim – as representative of a pervasive shift in American life.

In many of his fictional works, Fitzgerald highlights and shows the downfalls of the new consumer culture. *The Beautiful and Damned* (1922), for example, depicts the personal crash of Anthony and Gloria Patch, who squander Anthony's Wall Street allowance on luxuries and parties that lead them into debt, force them to write bad checks, and result in their being disinherited. More subtly, Fitzgerald parodies the burgeoning industry of consumer finance in *The Great Gatsby* through the naiveté of Nick, the novel's narrator, who has moved to New York to pursue a career in business. After Nick has escaped the rat race for a slower-paced life in the Midwest, he recalls his preparations to pursue wealth in the banking industry:

> I had that familiar conviction that life was beginning over again with the summer. There was so much to read for one thing and so much fine health to be pulled down out of the young breath-giving air. I bought a dozen volumes on banking and credit and investment securities and they stood on my shelf in red and gold like new money from the mint, promising to unfold the shining secrets that only Midas and Morgan and Mæcenas knew. (7)

Nick's certainty about his life and life in general experiencing a fresh start was representative of the way that many people felt during the Jazz Age. To pursue the opportunity he foresees in the world of finance, he takes on the role of the consumer and buys things, in this case books "on banking and credit and investment securities." Parodying the sentiment that wise spending is the new saving, Fitzgerald describes volumes that "stood on [his] shelf in red and gold like new money from the mint, promising to unfold the shining secrets" of wealth. By associating these secrets with three very different figures – Midas, the mythical king who was cursed to turn everything he touched to gold; J. P. Morgan, the American financier; and Mæcenas, Roman statesman for Caesar Augustus and patron of the arts – Fitzgerald emphasizes Nick's lack of real understanding about the business world while contrasting the new reliance on credit with the lessons history teaches us about sound personal finances and fiscal policy.

Similar critiques that focus on out-of-control spending can be found throughout Fitzgerald's fiction, even in his early works. In the opening passages of the short story "May Day" (1920), for example, Fitzgerald satirizes the demand for luxury items by "more and more spenders" in the wake of World War I:

> All through the long spring days the returning soldiers marched up the chief highway ... while merchants and clerks left their bickerings and figurings and,

crowding to the windows, turned their white-bunched faces gravely upon the passing battalions.

Never had there been such splendor in the great city, for the victorious war had brought plenty in its train, and the merchants had flocked thither ... to taste of all the luscious feasts and witness the lavish entertainments prepared – and to buy for their women furs against the next winter and bags of golden mesh and varicolored slippers of silk and silver and rose satin and cloth of gold.

So gaily and noisily were the peace and prosperity impending hymned ... that more and more spenders had gathered from the provinces to drink the wine of excitement, and faster and faster did the merchants dispose of their trinkets and slippers until they sent up a mighty cry for more trinkets and more slippers in order that they might give in barter what was demanded of them. Some even of them flung up their hands helplessly, shouting:

"Alas! I have no more slippers! and alas! I have no more trinkets! May heaven help me, for I know not what I shall do!" (*TJA* 61)

Fitzgerald brings the pitfalls of conspicuous consumption to the foreground by starting the story with a preface laced with biting satire. Now that "the victorious war had brought plenty in its train," the lack of slippers and trinkets became a cause of grave concern, and the "mighty cry," fueled by the "wine of excitement," is for "more trinkets and more slippers." While images such as the merchants and clerks cramming "their white-bunched faces" against storefront windows to see the passing spectacle might seem humorous, they provide American readers with an unflattering glimpse of themselves losing sight of what is important. This loss of values is at the heart of Fitzgerald's famous lampoon "The Diamond as Big as the Ritz" (1922), which, as Kirk Curnutt has noted, offered such a resounding critique that it "depreciated its own market worth." Curnutt explains that in the "probusiness environment of 1922, few periodical editors were prepared to question the reality of the new prosperity" in the way Fitzgerald clearly was (112).

Fitzgerald's most famous characterization of spending for displays of wealth – the personification of conspicuous consumption – is found in *The Great Gatsby*'s Jay Gatsby. From his trademark Rolls-Royce to his parties with "a corps of caterers [who] came down with several hundred feet of canvas and enough colored lights to make a Christmas tree," Gatsby becomes known for his ostentatious spending for the sake of excess (33). Generations of readers have been struck by the ridiculousness of Daisy Buchanan's sobbing over Gatsby's "soft rich heap" of shirts because she's "never seen such – such beautiful shirts before" (72, 73). Several critics have read Daisy's reaction to Gatsby's shirts as a parody of the ways in which luxury items operate as objects of eroticized desire, which Fitzgerald presents in all of their beauty. Gatsby's eventual fate, however, represents Fitzgerald's thoughts on the emptiness of accumulating possessions: The notoriety of Gatsby's excessive luxury is fleeting, and his shirts – with the rest of his showy possessions – ultimately "vanished," "leaving Gatsby – nothing" (117).

Readers might wonder how to reconcile Fitzgerald's reputation as a "careless spendthrift" with the critiques of conspicuous consumption in his fiction. But William J. Quirk, who has analyzed Fitzgerald's tax returns and finances, says that this reputation is "untrue."[7] "Fitzgerald was always trying to follow conservative financial principles," Quirk explains, "[u]ntil 1937 he kept a ledger – as if he were a grocer – a meticulous record of his earnings from each short story, play, and novel he sold." While he admits that "[n]o one could call Fitzgerald frugal," Quirk suggests that Fitzgerald "was always trying to save money" until he started incurring steep expenses related to Zelda's illness. Fitzgerald undoubtedly worked hard to earn money – first, to win Zelda, and later, to give her and Scottie, his daughter, a comfortable life. "For sixteen years," Fitzgerald reveals, "I pretty much lived ... distrusting the rich, yet working for money with which to share their mobility and the grace that some of them brought into their lives" (*CU* 77). Despite his success as an author, Fitzgerald was always in a financial position where he had to write to pay his expenses; he reveals that "[t]he man with the jingle of money in his pocket who married the girl a year later would always cherish an abiding distrust, an animosity, towards the leisure class – not the conviction of a revolutionist but the smouldering hatred of a peasant" (*CU* 77).

Fitzgerald's "smouldering hatred" for the leisure class is evident in his harshest critique of the wider implications of conspicuous consumption, which appears in his novel *Tender Is the Night* (1934). Many critics have deemed one scene in particular, Nicole Diver's Paris shopping spree, as Fitzgerald's most damning portrait of commodity culture and capitalism more generally. In this scene, Nicole takes Rosemary Hoyt shopping; while Rosemary purchased only "two dresses and two hats and four pairs of shoes with her money," Nicole "bought from a great list that ran two pages, and bought the things in the windows besides" (*TITN* 71). From the excessive – "a travelling chess set of gold and ivory" – to the ridiculous – "a rubber alligator" – Nicole seems to buy just about everything (71). Even things "she couldn't possibly use, she bought as a present for a friend" (71). Fitzgerald's discussion of Nicole's adherence to "simple principles" in buying all of these things reveals that she doesn't care about the larger costs associated with the production for her consumption:

Nicole was the product of much ingenuity and toil. For her sake trains began their run in Chicago and traversed the round belly of the continent to California; chicle factories fumed and link belts grew link by link in factories; men mixed toothpaste in vats and drew mouthwash out of copper hogsheads; girls canned tomatoes quickly in August or worked rudely at the Five-and-Tens on Christmas Eve; half-breed Indians toiled on Brazilian coffee plantations and dreamers were muscled out of patent rights in new tractors – these were some of the people who gave a tithe to Nicole, and as the whole system swayed and thundered onward it lent a feverish bloom to such processes of hers as wholesale buying, like the flush of a fireman's face holding his post before a spreading blaze. (71–72)

The ramifications of Nicole's mindless "wholesale buying" seem to justify the animosity Fitzgerald has for the leisure class, which does not account for the people who toil as the "system ... thunder[s] onward." The parting image of the fireman trying to control the "spreading blaze" represents the incendiary risk of such consumption patterns, reflecting the widespread devastation of the middle class in the wake of Jazz Age consumption.

In addition to providing members of the leisure class with more disposable income for excessive spending sprees, Jazz Age prosperity also resulted in leisure itself becoming a commodity, one that furthered consumer culture through advertising. People paid their hard-earned money to relax at movie theaters and baseball stadiums, to read magazines and tabloids, and to listen to the radio. While enjoying these media, they were also surrounded by ads. The growth of the radio industry in particular coincides with the boom in advertising during the Jazz Age; in 1920 there were only a few radio stations in the United States, but by 1922 there were almost 600, many of which were commercial and some of which were even owned by department stores.[8]

Having worked for an advertising agency, Fitzgerald understood very well the possibilities for marketing media. His 1923 essay entitled "How I Would Sell My Book If I Were a Bookseller" shows that he knew how to sell not only books, in this case copies of *The Beautiful and Damned*, but also himself: "'This is a novel by Fitzgerald,' booksellers might say to customers, 'the fella that started all that business about flappers. I understand that his new one is terribly sensational (the word 'damn' is in the title). Let me put you down for one.'"[9] Although Fitzgerald did not intend on creating that "business about flappers" with *This Side of Paradise*, he capitalizes on it to create a name for himself. Later, he wrote that "[f]or just a moment, before it was demonstrated that I was unable to play the role, I … was pushed into the position not only of spokesman for the time but of the typical product of that same moment" (*CU* 27). As Curnutt observes, Fitzgerald was haunted by a "remorseful recognition that he never escaped the advertising business … the commodity he has sold has merely been himself" (87).

"Advertising is a racket like the movies and the brokerage business," Fitzgerald revealed to Scottie in a 1940 letter: "You cannot be honest without admitting that its constructive contribution to humanity is exactly minus zero. It is simply a means of making dubious promises to a credulous public" (*CU* 300). Fitzgerald's skepticism about advertising reflects a shift in admen during the 1920s – instead of focusing on the product itself, ads focused on what the consumer lacked. Roland Marchand explains that "[w]hat made advertising 'modern' was the advertisers' discovery of techniques for both responding to and exploiting the public's insecurities."[10] Marchand discusses the rousing success of Listerine's legendary campaign, which raised profits from $100,000 in 1921 to more than $4,000,000 in 1927, as inspiring "a whole new school of advertising practice" (76). Instead of marketing Listerine as a general antiseptic, copywriters "exhumed [a word] from an old medical dictionary" to "induce the public to discover a new need" – combating halitosis. A series of print ads, including "He Never Knew Why" and "You Wouldn't Care to Meet Marvin," suggested that even those who seem to have everything going for them might be repulsive if they did not wash their mouths with Listerine, reinforcing the admen's "parable of the first impression" (84).

Advertisements for a wide variety of goods followed this formula, suggesting that a certain product was necessary because it made you more seem more desirable (attractive, successful, younger, healthier) or set you apart as having class and distinction. Although Fitzgerald depicts this phenomenon in several of his works, his most prominent examination of advertisements and their effects on consumer culture appears in *The Great Gatsby*. Importantly, all of the novel's characters – no matter their class – take notice of and respond to advertising. Myrtle Wilson, for example, says that she "had to pretend to be looking at the advertisement" over Tom Buchanan's head, when she cannot "keep [her] eyes off" of his "dress suit and patent leather shoes" (31). Daisy, though of a higher class, similarly equates Gatsby with the Arrow Collar man, whose "predominant characteristic was *class*," insisting to Gatsby that "'you resemble the advertisement of the man' … 'You know the advertisement of the man'"

(93). In addition to referencing advertisements, the characters show signs of internalizing the advertisements' messages. Myrtle, for example, "let four taxi cabs drive away before she selected a new one, lavender-colored with grey upholstery" (24), seeming to parody the Paige Company ad that floated models of cars of various colors through a woman's imagination to represent "motor cars that match milady's mode – yes, her every mood" (Marchand 75).

The faded billboard advertisement for oculist T. J. Eckleburg appears throughout *The Great Gatsby* and can be seen to represent Fitzgerald's ambivalence about both the advertising industry and consumer culture. The sign consists of gigantic blue eyes peering out from "a pair of enormous yellow spectacles" that "brood over the solemn dumping ground" of the valley of ashes and its "waste land" of consumption (21, 22). Although some, like George Wilson, think the billboard represents the eyes of God judging the world below, ultimately the sign is just that – a sign. But nevertheless it continues to make an impression on the physical and psychological landscape. Fitzgerald is able to appropriate the eyes of Dr. Eckleburg for his critique precisely because of the pervasiveness of advertising in modern society; it is a "picture of life in America" that remains as true today as it was during the Jazz Age.

NOTES

1 L. Gidlow, *The Big Vote: Gender, Consumer Culture, and the Politics of Exclusion* (Baltimore: Johns Hopkins University Press, 2004), 163. Subsequent references to this work are included in the text.

2 L. B. Glickman, "Rethinking Politics: Consumers and the Public Good in the 'Jazz Age,'" *OAH Magazine of History* 21.3 (2007), 16–20; 16. Subsequent references to this work are included in the text.

3 M. L. Olney, "Advertising, Consumer Credit, and the 'Consumer Durables Revolution' of the 1920s," *Journal of Economic History* 47.2 (1987), 489–91; 489–90.

4 R. J. Samuelson, "What We Learn from the 1920s," *Newsweek* 37.7 (2001, 33.

5 K. Curnutt, "Fitzgerald's Consumer World" in K. Curnutt (ed.), *A Historical Guide to F. Scott Fitzgerald* (Oxford, UK: Oxford University Press, 2004), 85–128; 107. Subsequent references to this work are included in the text.

6 M. J. Bruccoli, *Apparatus for F. Scott Fitzgerald's* The Great Gatsby (Columbia, SC: University of South Carolina Press, 1974), 31.

7 W. J. Quirk, "Living on $500,000 a Year," *American Scholar* 78.4 (2009), 96–101; 96.

8 N. Arceneaux, "A Sales Floor in the Sky: Philadelphia Department Stores and the Radio Boom of the 1920s," *Journal of Broadcasting & Electronic Media* 53.1 (2009), 76–89; 76.

9 S. Donaldson, "Fitzgerald's Nonfiction" in R. Prigozy (ed.), *The Cambridge Companion to F. Scott Fitzgerald* (New York: Cambridge University Press, 2002), 164–88; 167.

10 R. Marchand, *Advertising the American Dream: Making Way for Modernity, 1920–1940* (Berkeley, CA: University of California Press, 1985), 74.

31

Fashion

Doni M. Wilson

In 1915, F. Scott Fitzgerald showed an early interest in the importance of fashion and appearance when he wrote a didactic letter to his sister, Annabel, instructing her on such subjects as "The General Subject of Conversation," "Poise: Carriage: Dancing: Expression," and, most strikingly, "Dress and Personality." Emphasizing Fitzgerald's awareness of the social importance of fashion, this letter would later serve as part of the basis for his 1920 short story "Bernice Bobs Her Hair," which appeared in the *Saturday Evening Post.* Fitzgerald's epistolary advice to his sister included the observations that "No two people look alike in the same thing, but very few realize it" and "Shop keepers make money on the fact that the fat Mrs. Jones will buy the hat that looked well on the thin Mrs. Smith," both of which indicate the connection between advertising, fashion, and social success that appears frequently in his writing. With the admonishment to his sister that she "Never buy so much as a sash without the most careful consideration," Fitzgerald underscored the role of fashion in terms of social identity, and in the process of offering specific opinions concerning outward appearance (such as, "Almost all neatness is gained in a man or a woman by the arrangement of the hair" and "slimness is a fashion you can cultivate it by exercise") also pointed to a general consciousness of the importance of fashion in contemporary American life (*LL* 7–9).

Fitzgerald was not alone. As Kathleen Drowne and Patrick Huber explain in *The 1920s: American Popular Culture Through History*:

> During the 1920s, the notion of keeping up with fashion trends and expressing oneself through material goods seized middle-class Americans as never before. Purchasing new clothes, new furniture, new appliances, new automobiles, new *anything* indicated one's level of prosperity, and the ability to consume represented an important social marker in the 1920s. Being considered old-fashioned, out-of-date, or – worse yet – unable to afford stylish new products was a fate many Americans went to great lengths to avoid during this decade of unprecedented consumerism. More than anything else, fashionable clothes served as the principal marker of social respectability.[1]

In order to keep up with clothing that was in style, young women spent substantial amounts of money on shoes, hats, hosiery, dresses, and a variety of accessories. Some considered this spending part of the recklessness attributed to youth and the modern New Woman, while others saw it as an enabling factor in creation of one's identity, and a necessary expense for social acceptance. Women tried a variety of expressions of fashion that could simultaneously be considered as liberating and immoral, depending on one's views.[2] In any case, fashion was revolutionary and permeated everyday American life.

While the major fashion statements of the time were seen in women's wear, fashion for men and children also carried notable, if less radical, new characteristics. The fashions of Fitzgerald's age were significantly shaped by a rampant consumerism fueled by an increasingly aggressive advertising industry, the rise of motion pictures and their cultural influence, and a virtual worship of youth. Fashion channeled all of these cultural phenomena, which often intersected and informed one another, into a concrete manifestation in everyday life of some of the significant beliefs held by Americans at the time.

Women's fashion of the late 1910s and 1920s followed two broad trajectories: an ultra-feminine romantic look favored and influenced by such French designers as Jeanne Lanvin and Jean Patou and the less feminine, more angular and modern "garconne" or "flapper" look that dominated the decade in terms of redefining the possibilities for female identity and expression through dress. The more traditional ultra-feminine look still had a place, especially for high-end social attire, but it was somewhat eclipsed by a fascination with bolder, more modern clothes.[3] While the ruffles and flourishes of the romantic look seemed more in line with the aesthetic of the Victorian Age, the "flapper" look rebelled against these conventions and, in the process, created new ones that became extremely popular in American advertising and popular culture. According to Joshua Zeitz, after World War I, "flappers" referred to "young women in their teens and twenties who subscribed to the libertine principles that writers like F. Scott Fitzgerald and actresses like Clara Bow popularized in print and on the silver screen."[4] Furthermore, Zeitz explains that the flapper was "the notorious character type who bobbed her hair, smoked cigarettes, drank gin, sported short skirts, and passed her evenings in steamy jazz clubs, where she danced in a shockingly immodest fashion with a revolving cast of male suitors" (5–6). Thus, long before Ralph Lauren made country-leisure clothes hallmarks of a highly coveted lifestyle for many American consumers in the later decades of the twentieth century, the shorter dresses with straight and long silhouettes that women wore in the late 1910s and 1920s were not merely shorter dresses, but signifiers for the entire range of behaviors that constituted the flapper lifestyle. And many Americans feared the flapper lifestyle, believing that the young women who were influenced by it or adhered to it had lapsed morally.

Leaving behind the fashion trends and constructions of beauty of the 1890s, such as those popularized by Charles Dana Gibson in his illustrations of the "Gibson girl," the late 1910s and 1920s saw hemlines rise and tight lacing dispensed with in favor of a new silhouette. The flapper, "with her slim, boyish body, short hair, and insouciant manner, became the new model of beauty, embodying the personal independence and social rebelliousness of the decade."[5] As with any codified construction of beauty, the new convention had its price: The aesthetic called for its adherents to wear striking makeup and to maintain a strict diet in an effort to be thin, and the trend "also dictated a bosomless body line best achieved by binding the breasts, often destroying muscular structure" (Banner 384). Yet for some, flapper attire was liberating, and fashionable young women pulled from the trend to create to create an overall, and sometimes paradoxical, look. As Betsy Israel notes of flapper culture, "Now all hair was short, and often covered by a cloche [hat] modeled on a World War I GI helmet; dresses, tubular sheaths set off by long strands of beads, hung from the shoulders. The eyes were kohl-lined and the lipstick so dark it almost looked purple" and "above the regiment of pointed shoes, the flapper wore sheer hose that she often rolled down several inches along the thigh, suggesting socks and school girls while at the same time alluding to a stripper."[6] Such contradictory messages were part of the allure of the unpredictable flapper.

F. Scott Fitzgerald's writings on America youth earned him the designation of the "flapper king." In a Wellesley College student newspaper, a poem appeared in which the New Woman about whom Fitzgerald wrote is characterized primarily through her sense of fashion: "Her fortune went in purchases – /Cosmetics, clothes and such," and "They ask her where she got her pep,/Her snappy Frenchy air/And where she learnt to wear her clothes/And henna rinse her hair." The answer, of course, is that the girl who knows all the "tricks" to fashion and social success does so through reading Fitzgerald's book, *This Side of Paradise* (Zeitz 41). Fitzgerald's flappers wore clothes, such as sleeveless shirts or short skirts, which gave prospective partners easier access to the body, and therefore suggested sexual availability. In addition, "Scott's female characters smoked, rouged their cheeks and lips, cut their hair short, and took swigs from the hip flasks of their world-weary boyfriends" (Zeitz 44); in short, they flouted the acceptable constructions of femininity and conventions of social acceptability of the previous generation. However, Fitzgerald's flappers were flirtatious, but not promiscuous, a theme that would be echoed in many representations of the New Woman throughout the 1920s, and which perhaps justified the huge interest in flapper-like attire in the era, even for more conservative women. Professional women, too, followed the flapper aesthetic: "[B]y the end of the 1920s, almost four of every ten working women qualified as white-collar. Their jobs demanded that they dress fashionably, groom themselves carefully, and stay abreast of aesthetic cultural trends" (Zeitz 93). These women incorporated popular trends into their own aesthetic in order to rise professionally, economically, and socially.

Along with other manifestations of modernization, simpler and less constrictive clothing served as symbols of newfound independence for women of the 1920s. Paris couturiers such as Paul Poiret, who designed the restrictive hobble skirt, were to be overshadowed by other French designers, the most important being Coco Chanel. Chanel was able to incorporate less restrictive elements into her clothing: She embedded design elements found in menswear and was influenced by clothing related to sports and athleticism. In her designs she often erased the formerly strong demarcations between feminine and masculine clothes. Her innovations ushered an element of androgyny into modern fashion and also acknowledged the widening array of activities that marked women's lifestyles. Chanel even claimed that she had discovered the flapper silhouette by wrapping a sash around the waist of a man's sweater that she was wearing – instantaneously creating a particular look on which she was able to capitalize with a wide consumer audience (Zeitz 153). Chanel had the talent for making it new, and making it chic, and used beadwork and the echoes of modern art in her designs.[7] Her "garconne look" was roughly synonymous with the "flapper look" and would "dominate women's fashions for the better part of the decade" (Zeitz 156). In this look, the waistline was dropped or eradicated, and hemlines were short. Chanel, like other fashion designers, "regularly incorporated 'Oriental' or 'primitive' themes drawn from sub-Saharan and Asian civilizations, like skull-caps adorned with Egyptian textiles," and "to borrow 'Oriental' themes was to suffuse one's designs with raw sexual power" (Zeitz 157). While Chanel had rivals, such as Madeline Vionnet, who invented the technique of cutting against the bias of material in order for the body to dominate the shape of the attire, she still held the most influence over the look of female fashion consumers in the 1920s. Creator of "the little black dress" and pioneer in the mass merchandising of perfume, her contributions to fashion were without peer. Mail-order catalogs, such as Sears, Roebuck and others, made the Chanel look available even to Americans who lived in small towns or rural locales and aided in the shift from homemade clothes, which dominated the nineteenth century, to a ready-to-wear revolution that is still in effect today.

The increased popularity of sports in the late nineteenth and early twentieth centuries had a profound impact on the reforms in fashions. Before the 1920s, swimwear was often made of uncomfortable wools and, for women, covered so much of the body in the service of modesty as to make swimming rather difficult. As Drowne and Huber note, when swimmer Annette Kellerman in 1908 introduced the "one-piece bathing suit, which came to be known as the controversial 'Kellerman suit'" (103), she began the change in trend from "bulky, unathletic swimming dresses to form-fitting modern bathing suits" (103). Some suits were unisex, and some, particularly those worn by women, were considered too immodest (usually because of the lack of coverage in relation to the legs or back) for some of the dress codes imposed by club and beach proprietors who attempted to regulate the direction taken by bathing-suit designers. In a 1922 article she wrote for *Metropolitan Magazine* called "Eulogy on the Flapper," Zelda Fitzgerald proclaimed that "Now audacity and earrings and one-piece bathing suits have become fashionable," and in so doing implied how quick the more modern, more form-fitting swimwear had become normative.[8] Just as bathing attire radically changed, underwear, too, became more lightweight and less restrictive, as embodied in the new "cami-knickers" (lightweight camisoles attached to panties that covered the thighs) and "step-ins." In addition, brassieres often were purchased to flatten the chest for women in order to accommodate the newer, straighter dress styles (Drowne and Huber 103–106; Latham 69–97).

Just as women of the 1920s adopted less cumbersome clothes, they also adopted shorter hair styles; in addition, the use of cosmetics and accessories became more fashionable. Although some women continued to wear their hair long, they usually wore it in a knot at the nape of the neck or in buns held behind the ears "earphones" style. As Frederick Lewis Allen recounts in his popular history of the 1920s, during "the early years of the decade, the bobbed head – which in 1918 ... had been regarded by the proprietor of the Palm Garden in New York as a sign of radicalism – became increasingly frequent among young girls, chiefly on the ground of convenience."[9] Introduced before World War I and later popularized by such celebrities as Louise Brooks and Coco Chanel, part of the initial shock of the bob was that it dared to expose the ears and the flesh on the back of the neck. Although women wore the bob with various lengths and at times with bangs, not to mention under hats so that only a curl was revealed, what is notable about the bob is that by the end of the 1920s it was popular with women of all ages, rather than just the young. Some women wore their bobs in "Marcel Waves," which were horizontal waves made possible through crimping and curling irons, among other waving techniques. At the same time, women of nonwhite ethnicities often straightened their hair with a variety of products, including pomades and hot combs. Along with new hairstyles came new trends in hats and headwear, such as "flapper beads" (Drowne and Huber 107–111). In addition, women, particularly those who were flappers, wore face makeup and lipstick and often lined the eyes with dark pencil for a dramatic effect. Over the course of the decade, the cosmetics industry grew, and it catered to all ranks of American life. Other fashion accoutrements were popular as well. The late 1910s and 1920s offered consumers a startling array of choices in terms of women's accessories, including jewelry and handbags. Innovations in the plastics industry resulted in the manufacture of inexpensive imitation jewelry that was accessible and affordable, and made even more popular by Chanel and her merchandising of costume jewelry. The flapper look also included handbags, as most flapper dresses lacked pockets. The mass marketing of these items also made social distinctions between classes less obvious, as more women could follow similar fashion trends as they became increasingly affordable and more widely available.

For men, a growing national interest in sports culture resulted in specialized clothing for athletic endeavors such as tennis, golf, and swimming, and more casual dressing in general manifested itself in such men's fashions as plus-fours (so-called because that was the measurement of the fabric over the knee) and outfits that had Scottish patterns, made popular by the Prince of Wales (Mendes and De La Haye 68–9). Celebrities influenced men's casual wear in a myriad of ways: Golf and tennis professionals popularized sweaters and V-neck sweater vests, and Charles Lindbergh ushered in the aviation-attire craze. Young men were influenced by film stars, such as Rudolph Valentino, to shave their facial hair and to part and slick their hair. In imitation of the fashion trends at British universities, young men of the early 1920s also wore more wide-legged trousers, the fabric creased and the hems cuffed. Collegiate wear also often included blazers or sports jackets with a decorated front pocket. Shirts, such as

Arrow shirts, were branded for and marketed to the type of person who would buy such an item: a handsome young man accompanied by a beautiful woman headed for an evening out on the town.[10] Thus, activities that brought pleasure and happiness were key marketing elements in the sale of men's clothing and accessories. Jay Gatsby's London-tailored silk shirts signify a larger world of luxury in his attempts to impress Daisy Fay Buchanan and point to the truth that London acted as the arbiter of tastes for men's fashions in the 1920s, even though his choice of pink suits is a less-successful fashion risk. Ultimately, fashion for men, just as for women, was an emblem of social success, and the prevailing wisdom that fashion could influence the impression one made in the world was a notion underscored often in Fitzgerald's writings.

New advertising campaigns greatly influenced the rise of the fashion industry, often with kaleidoscopic effect. Women, in particular, were targeted in these campaigns, and were responsible for "at least 80 percent of all consumer purchases."[11] In addition, the figure of women in advertisements of the 1920s is not only "striking in its complexity," but is also notable in that "no other figure in the tableaux shifted roles and appearances so frequently" (Marchand 167). Such representations underscored the presence of fads and trends in fashion, also indicative of the fast-paced lifestyle of Fitzgerald's era. Women were seen as the principal consumers of "style," and this view operated under two fundamental assumptions the advertising industry held about women: first, that women "were the preservers of beauty and culture in an industrial society," and second, that as consumers, women were "emotional, irrational, and lacking in self-control" (Marchand 131). In addition to specific fashion trends related to dress and accessories, the "crowning achievement of advertising's emphasis on color, beauty, and style in the 1920s was its popularization of the idea of the ensemble" (Marchand 132), with women's wear acting as the dominant manifestation of this phenomenon. In other words, hats and bags were no longer individually purchased objects, but part of a "consumer response to the idea of matching ensembles, suggesting a broader, more sustained trend" (Marchand 132). The flapper reigned queen in the forces of advertising, particularly in selling sex appeal and in providing direction for consumer purchases: "She promoted a range of consumer products and services, but her main work was selling fashion. So closely was her fashion style associated with John Held, Jr.'s magazine art that F. Scott Fitzgerald called the flapper's clothing 'John Held Clothes.'"[12]

Glamour magazines, fashion shows, beauty contests, and celebrities influenced many American consumers' choices, as did the burgeoning youth culture and moving-picture industry. Whether their covers were graced by illustrations of the stylish New Woman as represented by the fashion artist Gordon Conway, or by the quasi-satirical depiction of flappers as represented by John Held (who drew the cover art for Fitzgerald's *Flappers and Philosophers*), magazines held significant cultural sway over much of the population. Celebrity endorsements and slick advertisements dictated purchases as well as physical and fashion ideals, and they made a fashionable aesthetic appear to be a necessity rather than a luxury. A cultural shift in relation to fashion took place:

> As advertisers encouraged the American consumer to take greater stock of his or her appearance – to ratchet up standards of cleanliness, grooming, and artificial enhancement … to sculpt one's features in the never-ending quest for eternal youth and perfection – old taboos against lipstick, mascara, rouge, and face powder gave way to a new imperative: self-improvement. (Zeitz 203)

In addition, the fashionable aesthetic was also closely associated with youth and its accompanying pleasures and betrayed a cultural obsession with youth that arguably has never ended. In her discussion of the changes in youth culture during the 1920s, Paula Fass argues that "campus peer groups and peer society as a whole were able to carve out a sphere of social control and direction within the universities and colleges of the twenties."[13] Furthermore, youth culture ascended in prominence even among younger Americans as the "high school peer network set very clear standards of acceptability and served to increase conformity in consumer tastes in line with the effect of fads and rapid fashion changes" (Fass 219). Working hand in hand with the worlds of advertising and youth culture, Hollywood and the motion-picture industry served as a formidable force in fashion. Readers devoured fan magazines, and film stars such as Colleen Moore, Clara Bow, and Louise Brooks endorsed products and inspired imitation. Many people, however, did not think that the Hollywood influence was conducive to a strong moral foundation. In fact, "a study of delinquent girls in the late 1920s revealed that three-quarters of them tried to boost their sex appeal by mimicking the way on-screen stars dressed, applied make-up, and fixed their hair" (Zeitz 261). Although the behavior of the girls in this study cannot necessarily be proven corollary to a lapsed sense of morality, many people of the older generation continued to be skeptical of Hollywood and its influence on fashion and subsequent behavior.

Fashion changes during Fitzgerald's lifetime were both rapid and radical, particularly during the 1920s. The era saw the rise of the fashion critic, as exemplified by the commentary of Lois Long, who wrote for the *New Yorker* through the 1920s until 1970. The relationship between fashion and social success was emphasized in many popular cultural arenas, including advertisements, department stores, cinema, fiction, and radio. Images of a constructed fashionable aesthetic were widely distributed, and affordable ready-to-wear clothes made owning fashionable clothes more possible for American consumers than ever before and signaled a new era of personal choice and freedom in terms of dress. If the House of Chanel could inaugurate fashions for a moneyed leisure class, it did not take long for those styles to trickle down to a mass audience. Through the magic of mass-produced ready-to-wear clothes, the ideals promoted in magazine advertisements become possible for more consumers. Just as Fitzgerald's character Bernice, in "Bernice Bobs Her Hair," must negotiate with changing fashions in a way that mirrors larger cultural changes, fashion often produced a level of cultural anxiety, particularly regarding the morality and manners of the New Woman. Ironically, some of the Jazz Age innovations in fashion that signaled newfound personal freedom were suspect: Feminists despaired that women, obsessed with being fashionable, would turn to shopping rather than working for social equality. Just as two of Fitzgerald's most famous characters, Jay Gatsby and Myrtle Wilson, attempt to form their identities and rise socially by being fashionable, many Americans of the 1920s, too, viewed the adoption of a fashionable aesthetic as a way to defy limiting social scripts.

NOTES

1 K. Drowne and P. Huber, *The 1920s: American Popular Culture Through History* (Westport, CT: Greenwood Press, 2004), 95. Subsequent references to this work are included in the text.

2 K. Drowne and P. Huber, 95–141. See also A. J. Latham's *Posing a Threat: Flappers, Chorus Girls, and Other Brazen Performers of the 1920s* (Middleton, CT: Wesleyan University Press, 2000), 18–63.

3 For a fascinating discussion of the intricacies of these directions, see V. Mendes and A. De La Haye's *20th Century Fashion* (London: Thames & Hudson, 1999), chapter 2, "1914–1929: La Garconne and the New Simplicity," 48–75.

4 J. Zeitz, *Flapper: A Madcap Story of Sex, Style, Celebrity, and the Women Who Made America Modern* (New York: Three Rivers Press, 2006), 5. Subsequent references to this work are included in the text.

5 L. Banner, qtd. in E. Foner and J. A. Garraty (eds.), *The Reader's Companion to American History* (Boston: Houghton Mifflin Company, 1991), 385. See also V. Steele, *Fashion and Eroticism: Ideals of Beauty from the Victorian Era to the Jazz Age* (New York: Oxford University Press, 1985), 213–48.

6 B. Israel, *Bachelor Girl: The Secret History of Single Women in the Twentieth Century* (New York: Harper Collins, 2002), 127. Subsequent references to this work are included in the text.

7 For the biographical outlines of Chanel's rise to fashion fame, see J. Picardie, *Coco Chanel: The Legend and the Life* (New York: Harper Collins, 2011). See also the chapter entitled "Chanel: The Order of Things," in C. Driscoll, *Modernist Cultural Studies* (Gainesville: University Press of Florida, 2010), 113–139 for a full discussion of "The Chanel Look."

8 Z. Fitzgerald, *The Collected Writings*, M. J. Bruccoli and M. Gordon, eds. (New York: Collier Books, 1991), 391–93.

9 F. L. Allen, *Only Yesterday: An Informal History on the 1920's*, 1931 (New York: Harper & Row, 1959), 87.

10 For an interesting application of the influence of Arrow on Fitzgerald's writings, see T. Dilworth, "*The Great Gatsby* and the Arrow Collar Man," *F. Scott Fitzgerald Review* 7 (2009), 80–93.

11 R. Marchand, *Advertising the American Dream: Making the Way for Modernity, 1920–1940* (Berkeley: University of California Press, 1985), 167. Subsequent references to this work are included in the text.

12 C. Kitch, *The Girl on the Magazine Cover: The Origins of Visual Stereotypes in American Mass Media* (Chapel Hill: University of North Carolina Press, 2001), 133.

13 P. S. Fass, *The Damned and the Beautiful: American Youth in the 1920's* (Oxford and New York: Oxford University Press, 1977), 208. Subsequent references to this work are included in the text. In addition, the best discussion of the intersections between youth culture, advertising, and fashion is in K. Curnutt, "Fitzgerald's Consumer World" in K. Curnutt (ed.), *A Historical Guide to F. Scott Fitzgerald* (New York: Oxford University Press, 2004), 85–128.

32

Transportation

Deborah Clarke

When F. Scott Fitzgerald died of heart failure in 1940, author John O'Hara remarked, "Scott should have been killed in a Bugatti in the south of France, and not to have died of neglect in Hollywood, a prematurely old little man haunting bookstores unrecognized."[1] The comment very astutely captures Fitzgerald's status not only as chronicler of the Jazz Age but also of the golden age of automobility. Forever linked with Gatsby's "circus wagon" car, Fitzgerald was one of the first American writers to acknowledge the role of transportation in shaping twentieth-century American culture. Trains, planes, ships, and, most frequently, cars traverse the pages of his fiction, reflecting the excitement of an ever speedier transportation system as well as its dangers, and providing an excellent lens for considering issues of mobility, consumerism, nationalism, gender, and class in his work.

Fitzgerald's close attention to transportation reflects a society that was increasingly on the move. Exploring the details of what enabled this motion exposes the intricate logistical and financial implications of such movement; one of the first things to note is that not all transportation was created equal. It is highly significant that a Bugatti, not a Ford, is imagined as the appropriate vehicle of his demise. Henry Ford may have envisioned the automobile as a democratizing tool, but one finds few Model Ts in Fitzgerald's work, where cars with varying degrees of luxury – some bordering on the absurd such as the "Rolls-Pierce" in "The Diamond as Big as the Ritz," an apparent merging of a Rolls-Royce and a Pierce-Arrow – reflect a highly stratified society. The various forms of transportation not only expose different kinds of transit but also remind us of the varying implications behind specific means of movement. Cars provide independent passage, while trains impose time and order; planes function largely to enable aviators to impress women, ships confer transient citizenship, and subways and trolleys are uncomfortable reminders that the underpaid masses cannot afford most of the preceding forms of transit. The means by which one moves is as significant as the movement itself.

All of this travel pushes the boundaries of region and nation. Southerners come North, Northerners go South, Americans go abroad, all with greater ease and speed. In questioning the continuing significance of place, Fitzgerald uses transportation to extend the limits of American identity. The Ritz Bar in Paris, for example, briefly becomes American, at least in the eyes of Americans such as Charlie Wales in "Babylon Revisited." Transportation, however, means more than literal movement, as Fitzgerald was well aware. Vehicles of transportation muddy the boundaries between public and private; now, what takes place in a Pullman car, for example, becomes almost a public display as Dick Diver obsessively imagines Rosemary's amorous interactions on a train in *Tender Is the Night* (*TITN* 116). Transportation is also intricately bound up with economic concerns, both in terms of paying for it and seeing it as an investment opportunity. Following the money uncovers the extent to which transportation affects class. Finally, transportation is inextricably linked to gender; while Fitzgerald does not seem to place the same degree of emphasis on the car as an emblem of masculinity as his fellow modernists Faulkner and Hemingway, he does associate women drivers with disaster, in marked contrast to the actual statistics regarding women drivers. Regardless of the facts, Fitzgerald is uneasy with the idea of women being in control of transit.

Given the rapid growth of systems of transit in the first half of the twentieth century, remarkably little work has been done on the intersection of transportation and American literature. Unremarkable, however, is that a significant amount of what does exist focuses either partially or exclusively on Fitzgerald and *The Great Gatsby*. Certainly Gatsby's extravagant, self-aggrandizing "death car," with its numerous mirrors reflecting the sun, links him to Icarus, flying too high and crashing down. Daisy may weep over Gatsby's abundant and colorful shirts, but readers and critics have identified the car, which "everyone" has seen, as paramount in determining his identity (*GG* 51). Yet for all his attention to the automobile, Fitzgerald recognized that other forms of transportation played significant roles in the 1920s and 1930s.

Ships, probably the most comfortable mode of transportation, find scant mention in Fitzgerald's fiction. While yachts regularly turn up, they function more as luxury space than as a form of transportation. It is somewhat surprising, given the extent to which ships functioned as social spaces, that Fitzgerald rarely capitalizes on this possibility, particularly given the opportunity to explore the elaborate class structure that ships provide. When Fitzgerald and Zelda traveled to Europe in 1921 they sailed in first class on the best available ship, the *Aquitania*, at precisely the time when Americans were eschewing so-called one-cabin ships for the luxuries of lavishly decorated suites and saloons.[2] He may have resisted extensive treatment of ship life, given his suggestion in "The Rough Crossing" that the ship constitutes "a ghostly country that is no longer Here and not yet There" where one "is a citizen of a commonwealth smaller than Andorra."[3] Represented as an in-between space where one is denationalized, the ship imposes an uncomfortable intimacy. If transportation is about movement, ships do not allow for the right kind of movement: escape from those around you.

Fitzgerald appears much more drawn to trains, although they were already beginning their decline as he began his writing career. In 1916, American railroads carried 98 percent of intercity travelers and reached their peak in terms of miles of rail in operation in the country. Nearly the whole population of the nation lived within 25 miles of a railway line.[4] The golden age of the railroad, of course, was in the nineteenth century, as it played a major role in the Civil War and then linked the country with the completion of the transcontinental railroad in 1869. By the first decades of the twentieth century, however, its dominance began to be eclipsed – in hauling both freight and passengers – by the burgeoning automobile industry. Even the promise of the railroad seemed unfulfilled: "Railways, it was supposed, would be a means of uniting the nations, of spreading a progressive gospel of democracy and modernization the world over" (Faith 59). However, by 1865, George Pullman had designed a luxury sleeping car, which enabled those of means to travel in greater comfort.[5] Restricted to whites and serviced largely by African American porters, such cars, though relatively modest in price,[6] created a more privileged space, although that privilege was limited, as Amory Blaine discovers to his consternation. Resenting the "stinking aliens" in a Pullman car to Washington, D.C. during wartime, he "thought how much easier patriotism had been to a homogeneous race, how much easier it would have been to fight as the Colonies fought, or as the Confederacy fought. And he did no sleeping that night, but listened to the aliens guffaw and snore while they filled the car with the heavy scent of latest America" (*TSOP* 139). The fact that anyone, as long as he or she was white and had the cost of a Pullman ticket, could experience the comforts of Pullman travel, simultaneously standardizes American identity and emphasizes its heterogeneity, its ability to accommodate difference. Trains, with their ability to provide links between disparate places, acknowledge that the future of America, the "scent of latest America," is no longer segregated, although, ironically, the railway system of the South remained so. Emblems of both equality and racial hierarchy, trains encapsulated the contradictions of American culture and identity.

Even more importantly, trains standardized time. The railroad industry established a uniform standard of time in 1883, although it was not officially adopted by Congress until 1918 (Faith 146). Experimental modernist literature challenged such uniformity with its emphasis on achronological order; thus we see a resistance to linear time in both *The Great Gatsby* and *Tender Is the Night*. With standardized time came standardized order (also anathema to the modernists), as people adjusted their days to the railway schedule. Amory Blaine and his fellow Princetonians organize their outings to New York based on train times. This standardization suggests a kind of normalcy, something that Fitzgerald's fiction constantly undermines – in both plot and character. Even on the train itself, as represented in "A Short Trip Home," the normative gives way to the fabulous. It may be precisely owing to the imposed order the train represents that few scenes in Fitzgerald's work actually take place on trains. Rosemary Hoyt's alleged dalliance on the train is presented through Dick's imagination. Murder occurs at the train station in *Tender Is the Night* – a vibrant area, teeming with action – but trains themselves function primarily to get people from one location to another. At a time when the railroad industry was losing vast sums of money, the excitement of transit is largely relegated to cars.[7]

If trains were slowly declining, aviation was only beginning to function as something more than a vehicle of war or a show of daring exploits. The U.S. Postal Service instituted limited airmail service in 1918, and while commercial aviation was launched in the 1920s, it was not until after the World War II that air travel began to pick up significant shares of the transportation market.[8] By 1940, airplanes carried fewer than three percent of intercity commercial travelers.[9] But despite its limited use as a means of travel, the airplane captured the American imagination, inspiring belief in its messianic possibilities.[10] Certainly Lindbergh's 1927 transatlantic flight generated tremendous excitement. However, Fitzgerald, unlike Faulkner, does not appear to have been drawn to the romance of the air. He enlisted in the infantry, not the aviation corps. World War I pilots do pop up frequently throughout Fitzgerald's fiction, and Amory Blaine finds himself drawn to aviation, apparently agreeing with his friend Tom that "aviation sounds like the romantic side of the war, of course – like cavalry used to be" (*TSOP* 142). The association of aviation with cavalry indicates that Fitzgerald links aviation with romance rather than technology; he appears more interested in the image of the pilot than in the plane itself.

The most striking example of aviation appears in the fantastical story "The Diamond as Big as the Ritz." Rather than subscribing to the notion of the airplane as what Laurence Goldstein calls "humanity's preferred emblem of uplifting hope, higher consciousness, and ecstatic revelation,"[11] Fitzgerald's playful use of it deflates its divine status. Not only is it instrumental in destroying a billionaire's paradise, it also functions, like the train, to challenge the privacy of the American home – even if that home sits on a heavily fortified diamond mountain. In an ironic twist, the airplane helps to obliterate wealth rather than serving as an emblem of it as the anti-aircraft guns employed by the Washington family ultimately fail to stem the tide of technological progress. It is no accident that young Percy Washington identifies airplanes as the "only thing" (*TJA* 133) that could both discover and destroy the realm so carefully hidden. Both avenging angel and technological marvel, the plane reminds us that private space is no longer inviolate, even for the fabulously wealthy. Transportation has fulfilled its promise to unite America, eliminating any pockets of other sovereignty. John Unger may travel to the Washington enclave via the Transcontinental Express, a buggy, and a jewel-encrusted car (assisted by a crane), but all modes of transportation are eclipsed by the miracle of the airplane. It rarely functions as a mode of travel for Fitzgerald, but the plane does remind us of the complexity of its being: It seems to bring one up to God and to remind one that Heaven is now a place filled with technology.

If Fitzgerald recognized the complexity of the relationship among speed, technology, and wealth – that planes did not always reinforce the power of the rich – he was also well aware of the transportation options open to most Americans. Early in his career, he worked writing advertisements for trolley cars, an experience that may have colored what appears to be a marked antipathy to urban mass transit. Amory Blaine chafes while riding in "the ghastly, stinking crush of the subway" (*TSOP* 236), and Anthony and Gloria find the bus crowded with "unprosperous" people in *The Beautiful and Damned* (*B&D* 142). While Samuel Meredith in "The Four Fists" ultimately finds sympathy for the exhaustion of a workingman on the streetcar, it is clear that urban transit plays a minimal role in Fitzgerald's fictional world, an omission that reflects the ultimate narrowness of that world in terms of class and economics. As opposed to the geographical breadth enabled by massive advances in means of transportation evident throughout his work, his characters generally inhabit the world of the wealthy, either as central or peripheral members.

The majority of urban Americans, however, were riding mass transit. Streetcars, interurban train lines, electric trolleys, and subways all peaked in the first quarter of the twentieth century.[12] In 1926, Americans averaged 162 annual trips per capita on some form of mass transit. By 1940, the number had dropped to 99 (Cudahy 250). There are numerous reasons for mass transit's precipitate fall from grace. Fares, regulated by the government, remained a nickel for nearly half a century, even though production costs continued to rise; the cost of a subway car skyrocketed from $14,000 in 1914 to $40,000 by 1920 (Cudahy 154). Railways and urban mass transit thus ran significant deficits, partly explaining why Amory Blaine's inheritance, largely invested by his mother in streetcars, disappears.[13] In the meantime, car prices dropped. The Model T debuted in 1909 for $650; by 1927, the last year of production, it priced out at $290.[14] But mass transit remained cheaper; it would cost roughly $25 to $30 a year to take mass transit twice a day, five or six days a week, considerably less than even the Tin Lizzy's 1927 sticker price. Despite the ease and economy of mass transit, however, nothing appealed to the American public like the motorcar.[15] As a 1919 article in *Harper's Weekly* gushed, cars bring "freedom from timetables, from fixed and inflexible routes, from the proximity of other human beings than one's chosen companions."[16] In other words, the car is the perfect vehicle for the modernist writer. Fitzgerald, regardless of his awareness of all forms of transportation, is ultimately a chronicler of automobility.

This is hardly surprising. The Jazz Age, now synonymous with Fitzgerald, marked the ascendency of the automobile. American car ownership nearly tripled during the 1920s. In 1920, there was one car for every thirteen people; by 1929, that proportion had dropped to one car for every five Americans (Foster 58). The auto industry was the largest industry in the nation, and by 1927 the United States housed 80 percent of the world's automobiles.[17] The 1920s also saw General Motors, with its emphasis on style, overtake Ford, which focused on cost. As GM president Alfred Sloan and his style guru, Harley Earl, understood, cars were about much more than transportation; cars were about image (see Gartman 73–99).[18] Further, just as trains extended regional boundaries, cars pushed urban borders. American cities, in the 1920s, expanded more rapidly around their edges than in their urban cores, largely due to the availability of better transit (see Foster 46–64). The ability to open up land beyond train lines provided a boon for those looking for more rural- or suburban-style housing. Anthony and Gloria, in *The Beautiful and Damned*, move to the country and buy a car, though it appears largely to give them something else to fight about as well as added expense. As automobile historian James J. Flink has observed, Americans spent 18 percent of their take-home pay on car payments in 1926 (*Car* 146). Regardless of his fascination with the car, Fitzgerald was by no means blind to the trials and tribulations of automobility.

He was, however, very attuned to the Sloan/Earl philosophy that the car you drove defined the person you saw yourself to be. The first car he bought was a used Marmon, and in his sardonic report of the drive he and Zelda made to Alabama in "The Cruise of the Rolling Junk," he both insists on its status and mocks it by its irreverent moniker, the Rolling Junk.[19] A descendent of the Marmon Wasp, winner of the first Indianapolis 500 in 1911, Fitzgerald's car had a distinguished name and pedigree but had been largely stripped of its accompanying tools as well as having suffered what Fitzgerald referred to as a "broken backbone" ("Junk" 25). It is a mystery why they purchased this vehicle, and Fitzgerald represented himself as a victim of unscrupulous salesmen: "About once every five years some of the manufacturers put out a Rolling Junk, and their salesmen come immediately to us because they know we are the sort of people to whom Rolling Junks should be sold" ("Junk" 24–5). Yet a new 1918 Marmon, as Fitzgerald admits, sold for roughly $3,500. To identify the Marmon manufacturers as producing "junk" is grossly unfair; it is Fitzgerald's apparent desire to own a luxury car – however damaged – that causes his automotive difficulties. This 1924 account of their 1920 journey anticipates his understanding of the trouble and notoriety luxury cars can instigate, developed to epic grandeur in *The Great Gatsby.*

What constitutes farce in "Rolling Junk" becomes tragedy in *Gatsby.* Gatsby's car, of course, reflects his belief that bigger and better positions indicate bigger and better people. But the extravagant car, of "monstrous length," only serves to reinscribe his position as an outsider (*GG* 68). If Sinclair Lewis's Babbitt is correct that a family's car "indicates its social rank as precisely as the grades of the peerage determined the rank of an English family," then Gatsby situates himself firmly as new money, insecure, and showy.[20] This becomes even clearer when we compare Gatsby's car to Tom's blue coupé, a term that simply indicates a two-door model, not a specific make or brand. Tom's wealth is measured not by his car but by his horses, aligning him with a more long-standing form of wealth, one not announced by the latest and most flamboyant gadgets and machines.

Nick's old Dodge, roughly a mid-level car, situates him as simpler, more moderate, aligned with old values – as opposed to his creator, who foolishly succumbed to the charms of the Rolling Junk. The dual taste in automobiles reflects the dual narrative perspective in which Gatsby's pretensions invite both condemnation and sympathy.

But cars also remind us of the darker side of modernity. George Wilson's garage is situated on the boundary of the infamous valley of ashes. It is one thing to own expensive cars; it is quite another to be struggling to make a living in the auto business. Wilson's decrepit garage contains only a "dust-covered wreck of a Ford" (*GG* 29), revealing both his monetary position – low, given the price of Fords – and his failure in his chosen enterprise: Fords, with their interchangeable parts, were among the easiest cars to repair and rebuild, a task apparently beyond him. He seems to envision himself as a middleman, buying and selling, but lacks the personality and charisma necessary to succeed at such a position. In fact, this scene with the Ford wreck in the valley of ashes conjures images of Henry Ford's assembly line, an experience that some former workers likened to "a form of hell on earth that turned human beings into driven robots."[21] As opposed to Gatsby's car, which may be custom-made, the vast majority of automobiles came off assembly lines with interchangeable parts, made by men who were themselves defined by their employer as pieces of machinery. "There is every reason to believe," wrote Henry Ford, "that we should be able to renew our human bodies in the same manner as we renew a defect in a boiler" (Lacey 12).[22] Cars may have freed one from standard times and routes, but at the cost of individual human identity. Built on the backs of men like George Wilson, the glamour and glitz of the 1920s turned out to have a very precarious foundation. By allowing George to gun down Gatsby, however, Fitzgerald challenges Fordist automation by reminding us that the robots of the underbelly of the automotive world are equally capable of grand gestures. Ultimately, the visibility of the showy car betrays its owner as he pays the ultimate price for its luxury.

Automobility is tied to gender as well as class. *Gatsby*, of course, is well known for its problematic representation of women drivers (as well as its racist description of African Americans in cars). Jordan Baker, named for two cars specifically marketed to women, the Jordan Playboy and the Baker Electric, is a "rotten driver" who airily believes that others are obliged to keep out of her way (*GG* 63). Daisy's reckless driving has fatal results, and her disregard for human life is mirrored in Nicole Diver's apparent attempt to force Dick to drive over the side of a mountain, with her children in the car (*TITN* 250–51).[23] Gloria Patch drives recklessly in *The Beautiful and the Damned*, ripping the transmission from a newly purchased car (*B&D* 152). These accidents resonate as a far greater threat than the comically portrayed scene in *Gatsby*, where a drunk Owl Eyes refuses to acknowledge that cars need wheels to function (*GG* 45). The myth of women as poor drivers has been around as long as the automobile. "Someday a man with a head for statistics is going to show us just how many deaths and disablements women drivers are responsible for," grumbles a writer in *Literary Digest* in 1924.[24] Those statistics, however, establish that women are responsible for far fewer fatalities, and while they may have more frequent accidents than men drivers, such accidents tend to be minor.[25] Fitzgerald is certainly not the only one to perpetuate these stereotypes, but his association of women drivers with utter calamity is striking. Even in less dramatic situations, women are warned against claiming the car. Bernice, of "Bernice Bobs Her Hair," learns that the way to attract men is not to talk about cars (*F&P* 124).

There are numerous reasons for the general discomfort with women drivers; Virginia Scharff's path-breaking study, *Taking the Wheel*, offers an astute analysis of the situation. In particular, the idea that the car served as a place for sexual activity caused considerable concern, a concern borne out by Robert and Helen Lynds in their 1929 Middletown study.[26] The Mann Act of 1910, ostensibly targeting white slavery, reflects the fear of trafficking women, a practice further enabled, many felt, by the automobile. Yet what we see in *Gatsby* is not so much the car as site of sexual action but the car doling out terrible punishment for the expression of sexuality, reflected in Myrtle's brutal death, her breast "swinging loose like a flap" (*GG* 107). Myrtle's vitality and its expression in unlawful sexuality meet a devastating fate at the hands of the machine, driven by a woman. The dual and linked threat of female sexuality and female drivers is both contained and released in this horrific event, its imagery seared into the reader's brain as a constant reminder that an integral element of modern America is women behind the wheel. Fitzgerald's portrayal of women and cars both reflects and shapes the concerns of the age. As Ray W. Sherman wrote in *Motor* in 1927, "Every time a woman learns to drive … it is a threat at yesterday's order of things" (qtd. in Scharff 117). As much as Fitzgerald was interested in change and movement, he was also wary of its implications, especially for gender.

Fitzgerald's fascination with transportation helps to remind his readers of a rapidly changing and moving world. Over the course of his writing career he witnessed the triumph of the automobile over mass transit, the beginnings of the aviation industry, and a growing ease of movement within and beyond national borders. Few modern writers portray a greater geographical breadth – Hemingway being an obvious exception – or express greater awareness of the complications and contradictions that modern transportation has brought to modern life. Modernism is at least partially constructed in response to questions surrounding the impact of technology, mobility, consumerism, and standardization, all of which find expression through transportation. Fitzgerald's understanding of these complex phenomena enabled him to change the shape of American identity and American fiction.

NOTES

1 Qtd. in M. J. Bruccoli, *Some Sort of Epic Grandeur: The Life of F. Scott Fitzgerald*, 2nd rev. edn. (Columbia, SC: University of South Carolina Press, 2002), 486.

2 J. M. Brinnin, *The Sway of the Grand Saloon: A Social History of the North Atlantic* (New York: Delacorte Press, 1971), 434. Brinnin describes both the luxurious quarters and the social etiquette needed to negotiate the intricacies of life at sea. See 338 ff. and 434 ff.

3 F. S. Fitzgerald, "The Rough Crossing" in M. Cowley (ed.), *The Stories of F. Scott Fitzgerald* (New York: Charles Scribner's Sons, 1951), 263.

4 N. Faith, *The World the Railways Made* (London: Bodley Head, 1990), 59. Subsequent references to this work are included in the text.

5 L. E. Leyendecker, *Palace Car Prince: A Biography of George Mortimer Pullman* (Niwot, CO: University Press of Colorado, 1992), 79.

6 T. Hultgren, *American Transportation in Prosperity and Depression* (New York: National Bureau of Economic Research, Inc., 1948), 70. Hultgren's chart indicates that there was often little to no difference in fares.

7 J. F. Stover, *The Life and Decline of the American Railroad* (New York: Oxford University Press, 1970), 172–73. Subsequent references to this work are included in the text.

8 R. E. Bilstein, *Flight in America: From the Wrights to the Astronauts*, 3rd ed. (Baltimore: Johns Hopkins University Press, 2001), 53, 55.

9 J. F. Stover, *American Railroads*, 2nd ed. (Chicago: University of Chicago Press, 1997), 196.

10 J. J. Corn, *The Winged Gospel: America's Romance with Aviation, 1900–1950* (New York: Oxford University Press, 1983), xiii.

11 L. Goldstein, "The Airplane and American Literature" in D. A. Pisano (ed.), *The Airplane in American Culture* (Ann Arbor: University of Michigan Press, 2003), 219–49; 220.

12 B. J. Cudahy, *Cash, Tokens, and Transfers: A History of Urban Mass Transit in North America* (New York: Fordham University Press, 1990), 152. Subsequent references to this work are included in the text.

13 M. S. Foster, *From Streetcar to Superhighway: American City Planners and Urban Transportation, 1900–1940* (Philadelphia: Temple University Press, 1981). Foster cites an investment broker's remarking in 1919 that only "anonymous losers" would invest in the trolley industry (qtd. in Foster 51). Subsequent references to this work are included in the text.

14 J. J. Rubenstein, *Making and Selling Cars: Innovation and Change in the U.S. Automotive Industry* (Baltimore: Johns Hopkins University Press, 2001), 10.

15 The partial failure of mass transit, however, was not entirely due to the greater popularity of the automobile and the hardships of government regulation. The auto industry helped it along. In particular, General Motors launched a move to buy up and close down streetcar and trolley lines, replacing them with motor buses and often tearing out the electric cables at their own expense to guard against a potential return of electric transit.

16 Qtd. in D. Gartman, *Auto Opium: A Social History of American Automobile Design* (New York: Routledge, 1994), 35.

17 J. J. Flink, *The Car Culture* (Cambridge, MA: Massachusetts Institute of Technology Press, 1975), 70. Subsequent references to this work are included in the text.

18 Also see J. J Flink, *The Automobile Age* (Cambridge, MA: Massachusetts Institute of Technology Press, 1988), 229–50.

19 F. S. Fitzgerald, "The Cruise of the Rolling Junk" (1924), reprinted in [M. J.] Bruccoli and [C. E. F.] Clark, eds. (Bloomfield Hills, MI: Bruccoli Clark, 1976). While Fitzgerald claims the model to be an "Expenso," no accounts relating to Marmon cars note such a name. The model he bought would have been rather simply referred to as Model 34, which debuted in 1916. Thus, his playful evocation of the expense of the car reinforces his urge to claim its status as a luxury item as well as his resigned realization that he had succumbed to image by buying a junked up luxury car rather than a functional, if lesser, car. Subsequent references to this work are included in the text.

20 S. Lewis, *Babbitt* (1922) (New York: New American Library, 1980), 63.

21 Qtd. in R. Lacey, *Ford: The Men and the Machine* (Boston: Little, Brown, 1986), 128. Subsequent references to this work are included in the text.

22 H. Ford, *My Philosophy of Industry*, authorized interview by F. L. Faurote (New York: Coward-McCann, Inc., 1929), 12.

23 Fitzgerald's inspiration for Nicole's action may stem from an apparent attempt by Zelda to drive off a cliff in 1929 (Bruccoli, *Epic Grandeur* 282).

24 Qtd. in J. Boneseal, "Women and the Automobile," *From Horses to Horsepower: One Hundredth Anniversary of the Automobile Industry, Volume 1: The First Fifty Years* (Flint, MI: McVey Marketing, 1996), 21–7; 23.

25 See A. W. Whitney, *Man and the Motor* Car (New York: National Bureau of Casualty and Surety Underwriters, 1936), 65.

26 See V. Scharff, *Taking the Wheel: Women and the Coming of the Motor Age* (New York: The Free Press, 1991), 138. Subsequent references to this work are included in the text. Also see R. S. Lynd and H. M. Lynd, *Middletown: A Study in Modern American Culture* (New York: Harcourt Brace, 1957), 258.

Figure 33.1. Dust Jacket for *Tales of the Jazz Age* by John Held, Jr. (*Tales of the Jazz Age*, 1922).

33

Parties

Christopher Ames

In 1922, Fitzgerald's second novel, *The Beautiful and Damned*, was published, as was the first edition of the twentieth century's most widely known guide to social etiquette, Emily Post's *Etiquette in Society, in Business, in Politics, and at Home* (Figure 33.1.). To read *Etiquette* alongside *The Beautiful and Damned* is to see a social world split dramatically between generations. Indeed, any codification of manners tends to be a rearguard action, and Emily Post's guide is no exception. *Etiquette* is explicit about how the shifting social sands are precisely what make such a guidebook necessary. The book is dotted with phrases such as the following: "Notwithstanding the present flagrant disregard of old-fashioned convention" and "Big and lavish entertainments are dwindling, and small informal ones increasing."[1] Post frequently cites New York City, the location of much of *The Beautiful and Damned*, as a specific exception to her carefully crafted rules for social behavior. As previously mentioned, the gap between the social events depicted in *Etiquette* and those depicted in *The Beautiful and Damned* is fundamentally generational, and it is no surprise that such different values and modes of behavior coexist, just as different generations coexist. Edith Wharton and Scott Fitzgerald were a generation apart but were contemporaries: The wild parties that inspired scenes in *The Beautiful and Damned* and *The Great Gatsby* happened alongside the seated dinner parties reflected in Wharton's *Glimpses of the Moon* (1922), in which one had to remember that "Dukes ranked higher than Princes."[2] Nevertheless, the change that occurred in the 1920s in the ways in which people socialized was unusually profound.

The period in which Fitzgerald wrote saw the development of the modern party as an important social occasion. The social gatherings called *parties* in the American 1920s were more similar to the parties of today than they were to the social events of the immediately preceding generation. Although the social activities catalogued by Post – teas, luncheons, receiving guests at home, and formal balls – served the same celebratory desires that are expressed in every culture, they differed from contemporary parties in many respects. In particular, young single people were always under the supervision of a chaperone and polite decorum was rarely breached.[3] The elaborate balls of the previous generation to which an entire social set was invited did include many forms of festive excess: rich spreads of food, fine champagne, music, dancing, and socializing to late hours. But they were highly regulated affairs planned weeks in advance, accessible by formal invitation only, and carefully arranged to avoid opportunities for impropriety. The parties of the 1920s that are reflected throughout the works of Fitzgerald and his contemporaries were often quickly organized, permitted acquaintances to join without invitations, mingled the married and unmarried, featured excessive drinking of liquor, and became the sites of gossip about premarital and extramarital sex.

The development of the modern party parallels the development of dating as a form of social interaction between men and women, for it developed in response to less supervised and less formal modes of social gathering. Fitzgerald is widely credited with being the most influential chronicler of changing modes of courtship and sexual behavior in the 1920s, especially in *This Side of Paradise*. Dating was a recent enough phenomenon that the term still appears in quotation marks in *The Beautiful and Damned*. As Paula Fass makes clear in her analysis of youth culture in the 1920s, dating was part of a larger social change: "Dating emerged in response to a modern environment in which people met casually and irregularly, and in response to new kinds of recreations like movies, dance halls, and restaurants … Moreover, it developed as youths were increasingly freed from the direct supervision of family and community."[4] Fitzgerald's fiction from *The Beautiful and Damned* forward underscored the social significance of the informal, private party in much the same way that *This Side of Paradise* famously revealed the dynamics of the new unchaperoned sexuality of young people in the 1910s and 1920s. Parties form crucial scenes in all of Fitzgerald's novels and in many of his short stories. They appear not just as a telling part of the social milieu, but as the primary site for exploring the interaction of individual and society and for understanding the nature of celebration and festivity in modern life.

A shorthand way of expressing the change in modes of socialization in the 1920s is to assert simply that the afternoon tea gave way to the cocktail party. This change is wryly inscribed in *The Beautiful and Damned*: "Even Rachel, whom she had grown to dislike, was a relief from ennui, and together they went to the Ritz for tea. After a second cocktail they became enthusiastic" (*B&D* 302). This same joke occurs pointedly in

Carl Van Vechten's *Parties* (1930): "Hamish had been to a tea, as cocktail parties are still occasionally called in New York."[5] Though mixed drinks or cocktails have a history that dates back to the seventeenth century, the codification of the cocktail party as a late afternoon or early evening gathering offering drinks (but no formal meal) dates from the 1920s. The rise of social occasions held in the home with men and women drinking hard alcohol (as opposed to wine) is widely cited as an effect of Prohibition. Prior to ratification of the Eighteenth Amendment, drinking behavior was associated with men and took place largely in taverns or bars. But with Prohibition, formalized events, organized around alcohol consumption, became the norm, and these events were attended by men and women. Fitzgerald uses the cocktail party as a metaphor to characterize the 1920s in "Echoes of the Jazz Age," in which he writes that the era started with a "general decision to be amused that began with the cocktail parties of 1921" (*CU* 3). Writing in 1925, Benjamin de Casseres describes middle-class dinners in which guests would "assemble at four o'clock for a seven o'clock dinner ... and for three hours they sosh up on cocktails."[6] Cocktail parties were a phenomenon both risqué and widespread, and a modest scandal was created when a sitting judge, presiding over a high-profile divorce case in the midst of Prohibition, stated that his daughter both attended and hosted cocktail parties and that "cocktail drinking and cigarette smoking by women are questions of manners not of morality."[7]

The fact that the cocktail party replaced the afternoon tea symbolizes a larger alteration in social interaction and entertainment. All cultures develop modes and rituals of celebration, and the modern private party is a descendant of ancient traditions of feasts, banquets, communal drinking, and community festivals. Modern parties derive most directly from the private social entertainments that became popular in the eighteenth century as genuine folk festivals waned. As the growth of towns and cities contributed to the decline of rural communal festivals, the importance of drawing-room gatherings, salons, dances, masquerades, and balls increased. The rise of "parties of pleasure" follows the growth of the middle class and the urbanization of Europe and America. Parties thus not only bring together individuals who are acquainted, but they serve the functions that festivity has traditionally served: celebrating human community through heightened activity in an environment that licenses activities that are ordinarily strictly regulated or suppressed during non-festive times. People eat more, drink more, dress more ostentatiously, and stay awake for longer hours during parties and festivities than they do in normal everyday circumstances. Parties reflect one side of the archetypal binary opposition of release followed by control, disorder followed by the reimposition of order, carnival followed by Lent, Saturday night followed by Sunday morning.

As any party host or guest knows, parties can succeed or fail. If we consider the party as a form of festive behavior that can be characterized as a controlled transgression of everyday norms of behavior, we can see a paradigm of how parties can fail: through an excess of control or an excess of transgression.[8] To the younger generation of the 1920s, the teas and formal dinners of the older set were examples of excessive control, parties in which social decorum was maintained so strenuously that the magic of true celebration was lost. As a "post-debutante" explained in the *New Yorker* in 1925: "Our elders … drop into a plaintively reminiscent vein and gently deplore the present decay of society. They speak of the grandeur of the balls that used to be. They describe gay and glamorous parties. (It seems, incidentally, that these Elders of ours managed to amuse themselves very thoroughly in spite of the masses of dowagers who sat on gold chairs to observe the proceedings)."[9] To the critics who bemoaned the immorality of 1920s youth, the new unchaperoned informal party represented the dangers of excessive transgression, and stories of parties that end in intoxicated disaster became popular cautionary tales. When party-going became so frequent that it represented everyday activity rather than a specially designated festive time set apart from the everyday, critics characterized such excessive party-going as evidence of decadence and social decline.

Fitzgerald's work illustrates both extremes and reveals what is at stake culturally in parties. In *The Beautiful and Damned*, Fitzgerald connects excessive and frequent parties with Anthony's financial and psychological deterioration. In his descriptions of parties, he explicitly chronicles decadence: "They filled the house with guests every week-end, and often on through the week. The week-end parties were much the same. When the three or four men invited had arrived, drinking was more or less in order, followed by a hilarious dinner" (*B&D* 198). In *The Great Gatsby*, Fitzgerald depicts parties as sites of social climbing: Myrtle Wilson aspires to the middle class amid the party in her apartment, and Gatsby aspires to court Daisy by throwing enormous and notorious parties in hopes she will attend. When Daisy finally does attend and appears unimpressed with the extravagance on display before her, Gatsby puts a halt to his regular parties and tells Nick Carraway, "Old sport, the dance is unimportant" (*GG* 85). In *Tender Is the Night*, Fitzgerald depicts the Divers' parties, at their best, as a site where true social communion is possible. Fitzgerald's best description of what is really possible at parties appears in the opening of the novel as the Villa Diana party reaches its magical moment: "There were fireflies riding on the dark air and a dog baying on some low and far-away edge of the cliff. The table seemed to have risen a little toward the sky like a mechanical dancing platform, giving the people around it a sense of being alone with each other in the dark universe, nourished by its only food, warmed by its only lights" (*TITN* 44). Fitzgerald captures the heart of what is celebrated at a party: "a sense of being alone with each other in the dark universe, nourished by its food, warmed by its only lights" (*TITN* 44). Indeed, we are alone in the dark universe, and such inevitable solitude can be broken by our communities when we celebrate food, light, and life together – the festive communion. This sense of both connection and transcendence is what humans seek in celebration, what Gloria and Anthony seek and fail to find in *The Beautiful and Damned*, what Dick and Nicole are unable to recapture in *Tender Is the Night*.

Although some might be tempted to see the literary treatment of parties as simply a satire of a youthful shallowness, the transcendent festive moments in *Tender Is the Night* offer a useful corrective to this view. The drive that sends Gloria and Anthony out each evening in search of company and diversion expresses crucial human needs at a time when the social means for meeting those needs was in flux. The best literary example of the use of parties as a means of social satire, however, is Carl Van Vechten's novel *Parties*, a book whose lead characters, David and Rilda Westlake, are obviously modeled on Scott and Zelda Fitzgerald. Van Vechten was a music, literary, and drama critic who wrote six novels, four of which depict New York social life in detail. Van Vechten also was known for introducing many white intellectuals to the Harlem nightclub world.

The novel *Parties* comically describes the occurrence of daily party-going and nightclub or speakeasy attendance that was famously reflected in the columns written by "Lipstick," a pseudonym for Lois Long, in the first years of the *New Yorker*. Lois Long created a sensation by writing weekly under this pseudonym in the column "Tables for Two" of her escapades at parties, nightclubs, and speakeasies.[10] She cheerfully celebrated heavy drinking and late-night partying in the midst of Prohibition, and her column provides some of the best evidence that although Prohibition reduced consumption of alcohol overall it lent a sophisticated allure to drinking that attracted many of the urban young. Long approvingly asserted that "[t]he most ribald of my Vassar classmates are doing social work between parties."[11] Her journalistic presentation of the ubiquity of drunken celebration in New York City seems no more exaggerated than Van Vechten's fictional treatment. She wrote, as a "cross my heart and hope to die" true story, an anecdote about a young man looking for an apartment of a friend of a colleague's somewhere in the West Forties or Fifties. He begins to randomly buzz apartments, identifying himself as a "Friend of Mr. Miller's" and gains admittance to over a dozen speakeasies in the process, "where Bacardi flows like water."[12]

Van Vechten's novel seems to take that joke as a starting point. He follows a handful of main characters, including the constantly drunken and feuding David and Rilda, through dozens of parties and nightclubs, with their favorite bootlegger in tow. Rilda complains to David, "[i]t doesn't seem as if I'd seen you alone in years. We meet at parties and speakeasies. We love and eat and live at parties. Probably we'll die at a party too" (40). People even flock to the parties known for being poorly done: "Rosalie Keith was celebrated for giving the worst parties in New York, but despite this undesirable reputation she never ceased giving them and people continued to go to them. It is impossible to persuade people not to go to a party in New York, particularly if they are uninvited and English" (63). Van Vechten and Long also suggest that the social climate regarding parties and drinking in the 1920s is distinctly different in New York City than elsewhere, and this observation is borne out in the detailed study of Prohibition in New York, *Dry Manhattan*. Michael Lerner discusses the political efforts in which Prohibitionists saw New York City as the most difficult territory in their temperance campaign: "Nowhere in the United States were the clashes over Prohibition more visible or the questions about its wisdom more pressing than in New York" (3). He concludes, "[m]ost of all, New Yorkers drank during Prohibition despite knowing that it was illegal and bad for them (especially given the often abysmal quality of bootleg liquor) because drinking was a form of cultural rebellion against the heavy-handed moralism of the dry lobby and its insistence that all Americans adhere to the same social mores" (130). Fitzgerald's most party-filled novels – *The Beautiful and Damned* and *The Great Gatsby* – take place in greater New York. Following Fitzgerald's life and writings, it might also seem that he and other expatriates exported their fondness for liquor-fueled social occasions to the Continent. And, indeed, precisely this concern was raised in the press, as in the 1929 article in the *New York Times* headlined "Cocktail Menace Is Seen in France." The concern was that the American cocktail party, itself partly a response to Prohibition, was gaining popularity in France and augmenting the habit of moderate wine consumption at meals: "the cocktail party, between 5 and 7 o'clock, has begun to attain something of the status of a social institution, especially in circles where French, English and Americans mingle."[13]

Van Vechten's *Parties* introduces us to one use of the word "party" that is less familiar today: the idea of a party as a traveling group of acquaintances seeking entertainment together at nightclubs. The early hour of the cocktail party often left guests without clear plans for dinner and after-dinner entertainment. In *Parties,* the impulse is often to head to Harlem, even if it is still too early in the evening: "Harlem at eight P.M.!" exclaims the bootlegger Donald, "That's like Hollywood in 1840" (32). Eventually, the Harlem music clubs and dance halls, where fashionable new dances such as the Charleston and the Lindy Hop debuted, become the late-night destinations for the characters in *Parties* and for columnists like Long from the *New Yorker.* Thus, the typical evening begins at an afternoon cocktail party, follows with people cadging invitations to dinner parties, and then closes at the uptown clubs.

In the midst of this bacchanalia, there occurs an exhausted apostrophe to parties, one related to an era marked by a pervasive sense of malaise. In *Parties*, this sentiment is echoed by David and ratified by Rilda:

> We're swine, filthy swine, and we are Japanese mice, and we are polar bears walking from one end of our cage to the other, to and fro, to and fro, all day, all week, all month, for ever to eternity. We'll be drunk pretty soon and then I'll be off to Donald's to get drunker and you'll be off with Siegfried and get drunker and we'll go to a lot of cocktail parties and then we'll all turn up at Rosalie's where you are never invited ... And we'll get drunker and drunker and drift about night clubs so drunk that we won't know where we are, and then we'll go to Harlem and stay up all night and go to bed late tomorrow morning and wake up and begin it all over again.
>
> Parties, sighed Rilda. Parties! (87)

This expression of ennui, capturing how the repetition of festivity robs celebration of its holiday distinctiveness, is echoed elsewhere in the literature of the time, including passages already cited from *The Beautiful and Damned.* In *The Great Gatsby,* Fitzgerald describes two of Gatsby's parties in detail, but he makes it clear that those are events in a repetitive series: "On week-ends his Rolls-Royce became an omnibus, bearing parties to and from the city ... And on Mondays eight servants, including an extra gardener, toiled all day with mops and scrubbing brushes and hammers and garden shears, repairing the ravages of the night before" (*GG* 33). This sense of boredom also appears in Evelyn Waugh's *Vile Bodies.* Adam's pronouncement, "Oh, Nina, *what a lot of parties,*" is followed by this passage, set off by powerful parentheses:

(Masked parties, Savage parties, Victorian parties, Greek parties, Wild West parties, Russian parties, Circus parties, parties where one had to dress as somebody else, almost naked parties in St. John's Wood, parties in flats and studios and houses and ships and hotels and night clubs, in windmills and swimming baths, tea parties at school where one ate muffins and meringues and tinned crab, parties at Oxford where one drank brown sherry and smoked Turkish cigarettes, dull dances in London and comic dances in Scotland and disgusting dances in Paris – all that succession and repetition of massed humanity. … Those vile bodies).[14]

These similar scenes evidence a common theme in the literature of the 1920s and 1930s. Youth culture was defined by the party and the excessive behavior licensed by it. As a target for social satire of superficiality, it is an easy one. But in Waugh and Fitzgerald, and even in Van Vechten's lighter novel, the characters' behavior is not criticized from a traditional moralistic perspective. Condemnation of intoxication does not seem to be the point of these cautionary tales. Rather, the authors suggest that the social behavior epitomized in these wild parties represents a response to emptiness and meaninglessness, what Fitzgerald characterizes through Daisy Buchanan's eyes as "the too abtrusive fate that herded its inhabitants along a short-cut from nothing to nothing" (*GG* 84).

Ultimately, festivity is the celebration of life in the midst of death or the awareness of mortality. Thus, we can understand the resonance of the skull described in the climactic party in *The Beautiful and Damned,* which prefigures the entrance of Adam Patch as a literal death's head, or the figure of Gatsby floating dead in the swimming pool before the last "party" at his house, the ill-attended funeral. In Van Vechten's *Parties,* David and Rilda joke about death throughout the book, but then a murder actually occurs at the height of a celebration. The problem posed by the party as contemporary celebration is whether or not the vibrancy of human society highlighted at a party can sustain the affirmation for which the celebrants long. Dick Diver asserts: "I want to give a really *bad* party. I mean it. I want to give a party where there's a brawl and seductions and people going home with their feelings hurt and women passed out in the cabinet de toilette. You wait and see" (*TITN* 35). Against the risks of throwing the lifeless party, or the debauched orgy, or the party in which festive difference is dulled by repetition into the everyday, Dick

Diver attempts to create the communal magic of the night on the Riviera with which Fitzgerald opens the novel.

The host is not unlike the author: He or she brings people together, creates a multiplicity of voices and interactions, and promotes a world bounded by the party's dimensions or the covers of a novel. The impulse is creative and celebratory, but it is unconvincing if the party or the novel glosses over the forces that threaten celebration and affirmation. Mortality, infidelity, cruelty, and excess are all guests at the party, parts of the difficult world being celebrated. It has to be "a really *bad* party" to have the potential for success. The parties of the 1920s and 1930s reflected in the literature of the time should remind us of the long association between literature and festivity, from the festivals out of which ancient drama grew to the green worlds of Shakespeare's festive comedy to the balls of Jane Austen and the parties of Scott Fitzgerald.

NOTES

1 E. Post, *Etiquette in Society, in Business, in Politics, and at Home* (New York: Funk and Wagnalls, 1922), 98, 280.

2 E. Wharton, *The Glimpses of the Moon* (New York: D. Appleton, 1922), 284.

3 See Post: "Young girls always go to private parties of every sort without their own chaperon, but the fact that a lady issues an invitation means that either she or another suitable chaperon will be present" (289).

4 P. Fass, *The Damned and the Beautiful: American Youth in the 1920s* (New York: Oxford University Press, 1977), 263.

5 C. Van Vechten, *Parties: Scenes from Contemporary New York Life*, 1930 (Los Angeles: Sun and Moon Press, 1993), 154. Subsequent references to this work are included in the text.

6 M. A. Lerner, *Dry Manhattan: Prohibition in New York City* (Cambridge, MA: Harvard University Press, 2007), 145. Subsequent references to this work are included in the text. Lerner quotes from B. de Casseres, *Mirrors of New York* (New York: Joseph Lawren, 1925), 167–68.

7 "Jurist's Daughter Backs Modern Girl," *New York Times*, June 25, 1925, 23.

8 For a full discussion of controlled transgression as a paradigm for analyzing festivity, see C. Ames, *The Life of the Party: Festive Vision in Modern Fiction* (Athens, GA: University of Georgia Press, 1991).

9 E. MacKay, "Why We Go To Cabarets," *New Yorker* (November 28, 1925), 7–8; 7.

10 For a good discussion of Lois Long as a paradigmatic "flapper," see J. Zeitz, *Flapper: A Madcap Story of Sex, Style, Celebrity, and the Women Who Made America Modern* (New York: Three Rivers Press, 2006).

11 Lipstick, "Tables for Two," *New Yorker* (January 9, 1926), 28.

12 Lipstick, "Tables for Two," *New Yorker* (January 23, 1926), 40.

13 H. Callender, "Cocktail Menace Is Seen in France: Vogue of Drink Considered Typically American Has Spread Until the Academy of Medicine Asked to Take Account of Its Effects," *New York Times*, June 16, 1929, XX2.

14 E. Waugh, *Vile Bodies* (Boston: Little, Brown, 1930), 170–71.

34

Architecture and Design

Bonnie Shannon McMullen

Fitzgerald was born into a world of eclectic, traditional buildings but died when the ideas of modernist architects and designers were ascendant. His writings reflect these changes, from his early stories to his last, unfinished novel. From the nineteenth-century American domestic and commercial buildings of St. Paul to the traditions and innovations of Europe to the sometimes surreal atmosphere of Hollywood, Fitzgerald registered and recorded the settings of his age.

Near the end of *The Great Gatsby,* Nick reflects on his upbringing "in the Carraway house in a city where dwellings are still called through decades by a family's name" (*GG* 137). The idea is dramatized in a story from 1920, "Dalyrimple Goes Wrong," in which the war hero turned cat burglar passes "the red-brick Sterner residence," "the Everetts', colonial and ornate; the little cottage where lived the Watts old maids between the imposing fronts of the Macys' and the Krupstadts'" and several others known to him by name (*F&P* 161). This was Fitzgerald's St. Paul, where his own family lived modestly, surrounded by grand houses of the very rich. Dalyrimple, however, is overcome by the need to enter these houses, to make some of their contents his own, just as Nick explores Gatsby's house and, in a different way, makes it his. Dalyrimple's and Nick's trespasses are not dissimilar to the trespasses of the author, who imaginatively entered and appropriated buildings, grand and ordinary, in his fiction.

The traditional houses of numerous early stories – detached, spacious, built for comfort and entertaining, set back from the street, with lawns and shade trees designating a blurred line between public and private space – are familiar in residential neighborhoods throughout the United States. Most were variations on popular styles adapted from Europe, such as American Queen Anne, Colonial Revival, Gothic, Dutch Colonial, or Arts and Crafts. They were often statements of social status and political leaning. Where most houses were of timber-frame construction, a brick house was a statement of solidity, like the house of the prudent third little pig. A colonial house, especially in the North after the Civil War, suggested an agrarian background probably never experienced by mercantile or professional owners, a misleading historical reference. None offer the security or solidity they seem to signal.

Many had porches, sometimes wrapping around the house. These porches were a liminal space between the interior and the outside, a place to shelter from the sun in summer and meet with friends or passersby, especially in days before car use became ubiquitous. Gatsby recalls meeting Daisy on her porch "bright with the bought luxury of star-shine," where "the wicker of the settee squeaked fashionably" (*GG* 117). Here is a space public enough for courting couples to avoid suspicion, but private enough for a degree of intimacy. In "Bernice Bobs Her Hair," however, Warren McIntyre's front porch becomes the semi-public scene of Marjorie's humiliation when Bernice flings her cousin's severed braids at the foot of her former boyfriend's door. This common architectural feature served Fitzgerald in many ways as a symbol of the threshold between private and public, inner and outer worlds.

Lawns were also social and economic statements. As these grasses were not native to North America, the lawn was a reference to the stately homes of England. Lawns were difficult and, in hot areas, expensive to maintain, so the size and condition of a lawn was a measure of relative wealth. Nick Carraway, who comes from "a country of wide lawns and friendly trees" (*GG* 6–7), represents the flight from the city to the suburbs and chooses to live in Long Island, where he can enjoy a familiar ambience. His first impression of the Buchanans' house is its vast lawn, a quarter of a mile from the beach to the front door. It seems to have a life of its own, appearing to continue up the house "as though from the momentum of its run" (*GG* 9). Gatsby's vast lawn is the outdoor room for his lavish parties, and, in preparation for his reunion with Daisy, Gatsby sends a man to mow Nick's modest lawn. Jordan Baker spends her days on golf courses, the most high-maintenance stretches of grass of all.

In *This Side of Paradise,* lawns feature in Amory Blaine's first impression of Princeton, where he notes "the wealth of sunshine creeping across the long, green swards" at the university he has chosen for its "alluring reputation as the pleasantest country club in America" (*TSOP* 42, 41). Lawns were an important part of the collegiate Gothic plan for Princeton promoted by Professor Andrew Fleming West, who admired the Gothic buildings of Oxford and Cambridge. He had seen this style successfully adapted by Philadelphia architectural firm Cope and Stewardson for the campus of Bryn Mawr College, and the firm was engaged to design several buildings in Princeton in the late nineteenth century. Further Gothic buildings were designed by the firm Cram, Goodhue, and Ferguson in the early twentieth century. West, Woodrow Wilson, and others believed that the Gothic style of the old English universities directly contributed to the educational and social values they wished to promote in Princeton. Princeton had only become a university under that name in 1896, the year of Fitzgerald's birth, and its early leaders intended the campus to be a physical embodiment of their educational philosophy.

Although Fitzgerald seems to have accepted the Princeton campus, and the ideas of a liberal education that lay behind it, without question, his own reaction, as recorded in *This Side of Paradise,* was romantic rather than scholarly. Amory notices "leaded window-panes ... spires and towers and battlemented walls" (*TSOP* 42). He loves it for "its lazy beauty, its half-grasped significance" (*TSOP* 47), rather than its architectural detail. Part of its magic was its reference to its English prototypes, and in *Gatsby,* the protagonist would try to clinch his social and academic credentials and trump Nick's alma mater, Yale, by producing a photograph of himself at Trinity College, Oxford, spires towering in the distance.

Princeton was a rural campus, conceived as a better place for the intellect to thrive. It was dangerously close to New York, however, an environment that both fascinated and repelled the midwestern author. The city is the backdrop for much of Fitzgerald's second novel, *The Beautiful and Damned,* but, as in his descriptions of Princeton, the setting is more impressionistic than specific. Like Dalyrimple's incursions into private houses, however, Fitzgerald becomes much more detailed when describing interiors. For example, in the exceptionally precise scene which is Anthony Patch's Manhattan apartment, we are told that "it escaped by a safe margin being of any particular period" (*B&D* 17). The narrator moves from the sitting room with "a deep lounge of the softest brown leather" and a Chinese lacquer screen to the canopied bed and crimson velvet rug of the bedroom to the "habitable" and "facetious" bathroom, with its enormous wardrobe and large bathtub, equipped with a bookholder (*B&D* 17). A stage or film set could be constructed from the description with no further help. The glorious inner sanctum, the bathroom, is an example of the importance of modern, luxurious plumbing to the lives of the rich in the twentieth century. Here they could wallow in "soothing steamings" like Eastern sultans (*B&D* 18).

In "My Lost City," Fitzgerald recalls the spell that New York cast over him as a young man. He sees it as a "show," and "the designers of the Woolworth Building ... could ask for no more appreciative spectator"

(*MLC* 107). This Broadway building, by the European-trained architect Cass Gilbert, finished in 1913, was, in its day, the tallest in the world. Its Gothic style would have been familiar to Fitzgerald from Princeton, but, unlike those buildings, it was steel-framed, with non-load-bearing walls clad in terra cotta. Office space was accessible by high-speed elevators. Mosaic decoration covered the vaulted ceiling of the lobby. It was called the "Cathedral of Commerce," and Fitzgerald must have mused on the irony of the religious references in this monument to a five-and-ten-cent-store fortune.

The verticality of buildings in New York and Chicago contrasted with another movement toward horizontal lines, best exemplified by the suburban and rural houses of Frank Lloyd Wright. Most Americans, who neither lived nor worked in skyscrapers, saw them only as spectacles, and, in the end, they became too commonplace to evoke much of a response. "Oh yeah?" (*MLC* 113) summed up the enthusiasm for a new one, Fitzgerald reports. At the conclusion of the essay, he describes climbing to the top of the Empire State Building, which rose "lonely and inexplicable as the Sphinx" (*MLC* 114). This building, by architects Shreve, Lamb, and Harmon, completed in 1931, was again the tallest in the world, until it, too, was superseded in the skyscraper race. In the 1930s, when Fitzgerald was writing, demand for office space had fallen, and it contained much unused space. From its vast height, Fitzgerald contemplated, not the grandeur of New York, but its limits.

For Fitzgerald, however, the urban buildings that featured most in his writing were the grand hotels – The Ritz, The Plaza, The Biltmore, and others – palaces for those who could not afford to live in palaces, or even for those who could, places to go when you did not want to stay at home. In his day, they were of relatively recent construction, the last word in luxury. They were spaces for balls, weddings, or casual encounters. The Fitzgeralds started their honeymoon in 1920 in the Biltmore, erected in 1913 over the Grand Central Terminal. Anson Hunter encounters his former love, Paula, in the lobby of the Plaza in "The Rich Boy." The Plaza is also the setting for the pivotal scene between the five main characters in *The Great Gatsby*. Built in 1907, this hotel was intended to reproduce the atmosphere of a French chateau, with 1,650 chandeliers and other extravagances.

In Long Island, where much of *The Great Gatsby* is set, the same copying of European precedents, the same drive to impress with the biggest and most dramatic effects, can be seen in domestic architecture. All-American Tom Buchanan lives in a brick Georgian Colonial mansion, announcing his old money and conservatism, although the architectural references are to eighteenth-century England and, before that, Greece. Nick describes his own modest dwelling as "a weather beaten cardboard bungalow" (*GG* 7). The house that causes astonishment to all that see it, however, is the mansion of hisneighbor, Gatsby. As America is said to be a melting pot, Gatsby's house is a container for many European styles and periods, making it, paradoxically and perhaps arguably, the most representative and most egregious house in American literature. The building itself, with arched doorways and square towers, is a copy of some Hotel de Ville in France, and consequently a structure never intended by design to be a residence. A tour of the inside is a journey through a museum of the history of interior design. Rooms are variously in the Adams style of eighteenth-century England, Restoration style of the seventeenth century, French eighteenth century from the period of Marie Antoinette, and, crowning all, including anything Princeton can boast, the Merton College Library. Nevertheless, the house is quintessentially of its time and place, with electric lights that illumine the night, and plumbing that leaves nothing to be desired in comfort or convenience.

Corresponding to Gatsby's eclectic taste in interiors is Myrtle Wilson's New York apartment, with its over-large furniture with a tapestry pattern of ladies on swings in the Versailles gardens, an unsophisticated imitation of the supposed furnishings of the rich. This small apartment is described in hideous particularity, but the evocations of the Buchanan house and Gatsby's house rely more on suggestions of the general effect. The stage-set attention to detail that characterized the description of Anthony Patch's apartment has given way to more impressionistic backdrops, vividly characterized but still vague settings for the characters who inhabit them.

Separating Manhattan from Long Island, an emanation from both, is the Valley of Ashes, presided over by a billboard with the eyes of T. J. Eckleburg. Here, Fitzgerald evokes what was to become an increasingly pervasive feature of the American landscape, outdoor advertising. André Le Vot identifies the linearity, flatness, and contrast of primary colors in this billboard as "a product of contemporary commercial civilization," the "frontal gaze" identical to the depiction of holiness in Byzantine art. Eckleburg's eyes are "a pop version of the eyes of the Byzantine God."[1] In the godless world it presides over, the image of Eckleburg is the nearest thing that the benighted inhabitants have to design, but it is a design on their pockets and their souls.

Between 1921 and 1931 Fitzgerald encountered, in Paris and on the French Riviera, a group of artists who challenged his earlier perspectives. As part of the vital circle of writers and artists who were drawn to Gerald and Sara Murphy, Gerald himself a talented Cubist painter, Fitzgerald experienced the excitement of new aesthetic ideas. For him, Europe, with a few exceptions such as Oxford, was more about learning to be part of the new than discovering the old. In 1925, a movement that had been gathering momentum for some time – a movement that drew inspiration from numerous sources including the English Arts and Crafts movement, Art Nouveau, Cubism, the Far East, Ancient Greece, and, after Carter's discovery of Tutankhamen's tomb in 1922, Pharaonic Egypt, to name only some of its various sources – held, in Paris, the Exposition des Arts Decoratifs et Industriels. Although its center of energy was France, Art Deco was a truly international revolution in the arts, which, in spite of its varied progenitors, had its own unity and integrity. Le Corbusier was to write, "Right now one thing is sure: 1925 marks the decisive turning point in the quarrel between the old and the new. After 1925, the antique lovers will have virtually ended their lives, and productive industrial effort will be based on the 'new.' Progress is achieved through experimentation: the decision will be awarded on the field of battle of the 'new.'"[2]

Fitzgerald's reaction to these innovations was complex. He was excited by the energy of innovation but repelled by some of its results. The effect is registered by Rosemary in *Tender Is the Night* in a house she visits with Dick. The building is a former palace, but "the outer shell, the masonry, seemed rather to enclose the future so that it was an electric-like shock, a definite nervous experience" (*TITN* 94). It feels "perverted," like "a break-fast of oatmeal and hashish" (*TITN* 94). Although the design elements, "blue steel, silver-gilt" and "many oddly bevelled mirrors" were similar to the Decorative Arts Exhibition, this was not a spectacle to look at but a place to be in (*TITN* 94). Rosemary, an actress, feels as if she is on a set and guesses that everyone else has the same feeling. It is an alienating, literally shocking, environment, where the would-be spectator involuntarily becomes part of the spectacle. The room is impossible to interpret because it is "evolving into something else," and functioning in its surroundings is like "walking on a highly polished moving stairway" (*TITN* 95). Caution is required, as for "a hand moving among broken glass" (*TITN* 95). The room is inimical to human needs and comfort. Dehumanized, the occupants become "posters" (*TITN* 96), flat and one-dimensional, or, like the three young women "with small heads groomed like manikins' heads" waving about "like cobras' hoods," exotic and dangerous animals (*TITN* 95–6). Outside, beyond "the brief threshold of the future," Rosemary and Dick encounter "the sudden past" (*TITN* 97), Rosemary so shaken by the effect of the room that she bursts into tears.

Like the Divers, Fitzgerald had little interest in fashions in architecture and art for themselves, but he was intensely concerned with the effect on people of the changing environments of his time. Just as the Divers moved to a "contemporaneous rhythm and beat" (*TITN* 101), so Fitzgerald noted these effects on a psychological and emotional level. He shared the idea, common in the 1920s,[3] that the principles of one art could be transferred to others, so he always reacted to these innovations from the vantage point of his own art of writing, rejecting the merely flashy or shocking, but looking for underlying structural principles that might reflect the essence of this postwar world.

While Fitzgerald was making final revisions to *Tender Is the Night* in 1933, one of his most original stories was published by the *Saturday Evening Post.* "More Than Just a House" traces, over eight years, the attitude of a man to a house and the family that inhabits it. Lew Lowrie, whose name suggests "low place," is "starved for a home" (*S* 723) and enters, not as a cat burglar, like Dalyrimple, but as one who would steal a daughter. The Gunther house, built around 1880, is surrounded by vine-covered verandas and a wild garden. The gingerbread the family serves for tea suggests also the external architectural detail. In addition there are "decorative balconies," "fickle gables" (*S* 716), while inside are open bookshelves and portraits. Upstairs, Lew imagines a plethora of old photos, miscellaneous books, trunks full of old clothes, dolls' houses left over from several generations of settled family life. The daughters call it a "barn," a "shack," a "tomb," a "mouse trap" (*S* 719–20). No architect would give it a glance, except to advise radical alterations. Yet, in Lew's mind, its structure stands for "something humanly valuable" (*S* 720). Four years later, he finds the house neglected, smaller than he remembered, and the father lost in senile dementia. He decides there is something "degenerate" (*S* 728) in the reduced family's continued occupancy of the house. Another four years, and he is not so sure, realizing "that life was not always a progress, nor a search for new horizons, nor a going away" (*S* 728). He finds the house in advanced dilapidation, stripped of its contents by creditors, its only resident the youngest sister, Bess, "a home girl" (*S* 730). Acknowledging the importance of the house, "an effort towards some commonweal," Lew concludes that its "purpose … was achieved" (*S* 733). Taking Bess, who embodies the values the house had formerly nourished, Lew leaves it behind.

The story was written when the long-gestated *Tender Is the Night* was in its final stages of revision. It is hard not to see "More Than Just a House" as a backward glance toward Fitzgerald's problems with that novel, whose rootless characters struggle to adjust to a restless world of new design and innovation on multiple levels, while, like their creator, inhabiting hotels and rented properties in various places. The story's time span, 1925 to 1933, is exactly the period between *Gatsby* and the completion of *Tender Is the Night.* Like those recreating the built environment around him, Fitzgerald wanted to reflect the spirit of his own age in the form of his own chosen art, and not just in its contemporary subject matter. The monumental Victorian novel, to which the Gunther house is an architectural counterpart, would no longer do. Fitzgerald was already thinking about where to go next, what kind of house to build for the characters of his next novel.

In an *Esquire* article, written by Zelda and revised by Scott, "Show Mr. and Mrs. F. to Number –," the Colonial Exposition of 1931 is described as "an immutable story of work and death. The juxtaposition of so many replicas of so many civilizations was confusing and depressing" (*CU* 54). One is reminded of the impossibly eclectic mix of period and style in Gatsby's house, an incoherence that ultimately has a lowering effect on Nick. This carnival-like spectacle, prefiguring Disneyland, is seen at its most intense in Hollywood, where Fitzgerald mapped out his last novel. In the scene at the back lot of Monroe Stahr's studio in *The Love of the Last Tycoon,* Cecilia describes the locations of "African jungles and French châteaus and schooners at anchor and Broadway by night," looking, not like what they were supposed to represent, but "like the torn picture books of childhood, like fragments of stories dancing in an open fire" (*LT* 25). The man who must turn this chaos into coherence is Stahr.

For the house that he is building, Stahr chooses the starkest modernism, a radical break with the past. Eschewing ideas that a building should blend in with its natural surroundings, the site of Stahr's coastal house is "an open wound in the sea-scape" (*LT* 81). In a commanding position on a promontory, the house appears to offer no historical references, and Kathleen and Stahr feel no more at home there than "people on the shiny surface of a moon" (*LT* 84). What stands is a "fuselage" (*LT* 81), owing its concept in part to the pre-War Italian Futurists, who emphasized speed and movement in their designs and left their mark on Art Deco. Still under construction, it has no protecting roof, but the only finished room is equipped with modern technological conveniences, such as a trap door for a film projector. It suggests the ultimate expression, in America, of the Rationalist Modernist style developed in Europe after the war and practiced by architects such as Richard Neutra in his famous Phillip Lovell House of 1928, built against a hillside outside Los Angeles. Like Gatsby on the opposite coast, Stahr will have a swimming pool, but in every other respect his house is the antithesis of Gatsby's historically referential but stylistically confused dwelling.

Stahr's house is still under construction; anyone can enter. Fitzgerald's last novel presents a pregnable structure, open to the elements and every reader's imagination. In fact, throughout Fitzgerald's work, there can be found a mistrust of apparent completeness, limitation, whatever the style or context. This theme is a continuation of his theory of character, as illustrated by Dick Diver's youthful reflection that "the price of his intactness was incompleteness," even "though it'd be nice to build out some broken side till it was better than the original structure" (*TITN* 153).

Stahr's "fuselage" of a house, given what we know of Fitzgerald's plans for Stahr's death in a plane crash, hints at the author's misgivings about this degree of innovation. Just as in his writing Fitzgerald straddled the modern and the traditional, not from any inability to adopt an avant-garde approach, but from genuinely recognizing the value of many features of the stylistic legacy he inherited, so he withholds his wholehearted endorsement from Stahr's house, or, indeed, any other. Structures are only valuable for the life they hold, and when what they hold outgrows them, they lose their purpose and reality. When Stahr and Kathleen return to his house in the fog, it has "dissolved a little back into its elements" (*LT* 87), reminiscent of Nick's sense of the melting away of "the inessential houses" (*GG* 140) of West Egg.

It should be remembered, in terms of the built environment that surrounded most Americans in this period, that the modernist approach, or, more accurately, approaches, as modernism was in reality as eclectic as much of what it sought to replace, had never completely routed older styles, even in new structures. True, modernism's sun continued to rise after World War II, but Fitzgerald, at least, is unlikely to have been surprised by how soon the traditional building surfaced again in the postmodernism of the later twentieth century, a revival of taste and values that roughly parallels the resurrection of his own reputation as a writer. The revolutionary experimentalism hailed by Le Corbusier in 1925 would prove to be one phase, among many others, in the history of architecture and design.

NOTES

1 A. Le Vot, *F. Scott Fitzgerald: A Biography*, trans. W. Byron (Garden City, NY: Doubleday, 1983), 157–58.

2 Qtd. in V. Arwas, *Art Deco* (London: Academy Editions, 1980), 49.

3 R. Berman, "F. Scott Fitzgerald, Gerald Murphy, and the New Arts," *F. Scott Fitzgerald Review* 7 (2009), 127–41; 127.

PART VI

The Depression Era (1929–1940)

35

The Crash and the Aftermath

Richard Godden

The premise of Fitzgerald's very short *Esquire* story "The Lost Decade" (December 1939) is simple, but its implications are not. Louis Trimble, architect of the Armistead Building (1928), arrives early for an appointment at a New York newsweekly editorial office. The editor delegates a subeditor, Orrison Brown, to take the visitor to lunch. Brown, "puzzle[d]" by "some vague memory" attaching to "[t]he name on [the visitor's] card," does so (*LD* 65–68; 65). As the pair walk, Brown "wonder[s]," "guess[es]," puts out a "feeler" and considers one "clue" and another "that led nowhere" as to Trimble's identity (66). The reader, like Orrison, in ignorance of the architect's past and profession (disclosed only on the penultimate page), and prompted by the editor's enigmatic observation that Trimble "*feels*" himself "to've missed the last decade" (65), does likewise. The two names, or their conjunction, operate as a key clue. Indeed, in making the introduction, the chief editor builds the names toward a titular chiasmus, "'Mr. Trimble – Mr. Brown,' said the Source of all luncheon money. 'Orrison – Mr. Trimble's been away a long time'" (65).

Orrison's primary tasks, despite his claim to be "one of the editors," amount, we are told in the initial paragraph, to "straightening out illegible copy" and "playing call-boy without the title" (65). Readers, operating from within Orrison's purview throughout the story, and faced with the names "Orrison" and "Trimble," engage in versions of his editorial duties: "straighten[ed] out," the proffered "title[s]," each with seven letters, inter-inflect. Trimble, "taken drunk" (68) in 1928, and sober again only in 1939, "trembles"; "Orrison" follows suit in the matter of a single letter, becoming "orison" or "prayer," and most famously, therefore, Ophelia's "prayers" ("Nymph in thy orisons/be all my sins remembered").[1] To hear Ophelia within "Orrison" might seem a stretch, were it not that Orrison Brown has already puzzled over memories latent in a name. Furthermore, Orrison, an editorial "call-boy," wonders as he wanders whether "his duties" might not "include introducing Mr. Trimble to complaisant girls"

(66): "call-boy," care of "call-girl" – a usage available by 1939 – solicits the lexicon of prostitution, enabling "compliant" to hang antonymically above "complaisant," although the chosen term infuses the former with "lassitude." The precision of Fitzgerald's intertextually triggered associative network elicits the recognition that Orrison's services are analogous to those of Ophelia, as defined by Claudius and Polonius. Led by "Orrison" to Act 3, scene I of *Hamlet*, readers may recall that the king and his advisor propose to "loose" Ophelia to Hamlet, in the hope that the couple's exchange will reveal Hamlet's purposes to the hidden Polonius. Pimping forms the subtext of their, as of Orrison's, imagined purposes. Gertrude, less venal, trusts that Ophelia may draw Hamlet from his "wildness" (or madness) "to his wonted way again."[2] Faced with Trimble's request to eat in "some place with young people to look at" (66), Orrison, "glancing" at his companion, "thought of bars and gray walls ... and simultaneously wondered if he could possibly have spent the thirties ... in an insane asylum" (66). As the intertext between story and play extends, so "Trimble" and "Orrison" are drawn together and toward a transposition in which "illegible copy" will become "legible double," an editorial switch whose motivation has yet to be, "straighten[ed] out." Meanwhile, readers between the texts may recall that Ophelia famously dies damply in a "glassy stream," which briefly "bore her up."[3] For the brief duration of "The Lost Decade," Orrison, Ophelia-like, will find himself immersed in Trimble, who, for that decade and after the manner of Abe North before him, has been "entirely liquid" (*TITN* 96), which is to say, not a "glassy stream," but a "stream of glasses. " It will be the contention of this essay that, during the 1930s, when Fitzgerald writes of alcohol he engages with notions of liquidity that extend far beyond liquor.

Some might object that I have constructed a textual edifice on the basis of one modified word, an edifice whose elaboration skirts the silly. I would counter that "Orrison" is a strange word whose strangeness invites exegesis, for which Orrison's transformation by Trimble provides grounds. Orrison Brown does not record Trimble's "sins"; indeed, he notes emphatically that "there was nothing about him that suggested or ever had suggested drink" (68); rather, he records instances of Trimble's "absolute and deepseated curiosity" (66), a curiosity whose structure, akin to trembling, derives from a liquidity understood to be nonalcoholic.

To revert to the premise of the story: Trimble, architect of the Armistead Building, for Brown "the daddy" of the Rockefeller Center, the Chrysler Building, and the recently "begun" Empire State Building (66, 67), cannot remember the building that he designed. He confesses that though he has been "in it – lots of times" he has "never seen it" (68), being "every-which-way drunk" since the design's inception. Moreover, although sober, he neither "want[s]" nor "would … ever be able to see it now" (68). Kindleberger and Aliber, in their history of financial crises, note usefully that the tallest office buildings in the world rise typically from "asset price bubbles … during periods of economic euphoria"; they cite the Empire State Building, started in 1929, as their first instance.[4] But structures built from bubbles do not crash when bubbles burst. Nor, accordingly, does the Armistead Building, in the eye of its designer, fall; it simply is and is not, being seen and not seen.

So, to perceive is to perceive metaphorically. In effect, Trimble presents Orrison with a metaphor in the form of a riddle: "How may one look at a building and not see it?" Answer: by submitting that building to the liquidity that constitutes its "cornerstone." Paul Ricoeur, in his work on metaphor, comments that "to see the *like* is to see the same in spite of, and through, the different." He adds, "[t]his tension between the sameness and difference characterizes the logical structure of likeness."[5] Insofar as the "compatibility" (or resemblance) of the terms drawn together by the metaphor retains their "incompatibility" (or difference), the metaphor – *figure* of speech inviting sight as a prelude to insight – requires that its recipient see double. "Stereoscopic vision," in Ricoeur's words (154), or "seeing relationally" (150), yields a "split referent" whose innovative referentiality (marked by aporia and ellipsis) proves inextricable from the metaphor's initial and tense conjunction of terms (here, "concrete" … "liquid"). The Armistead Building is leveled by Trimble's perception of it (invisible) and yet reconceived through his perception (visibly altered by its submission to invisibility). Ricoeur again proves useful in the matter of split reference:

> I suggest that we take the expression "split reference" as our leading line in our discussion of the referential function of the metaphoric statement. The expression, as well as the wonderful "it was and it was not," contains *in nunce* all that can be said about metaphoric reference. To summarize, poetic language is no less *about* reality than any other use of language but refers to it by means of a complex strategy which implies, as an essential component, a suspension and seeming abolition of the ordinary reference attached to descriptive language. This suspension, however is only the negative condition of a second-order reference, of an indirect reference built on the ruins of the direct reference. (153)

By "second-order reference" Ricoeur does not seek to downplay the perceptual seriousness of metaphor's referential effect; rather, he adds that "split reference," the progeny or metaphor, "constitutes the primordial reference to the extent that it suggests, reveals, unconceals … the deep structures of reality" (153).

To return, via my formal detour, to Trimble and Orrison: Fitzgerald, so glossed, allows Trimble to "unconceal … deep structures" – in economic terms, the deeply liquid structures – that produce the reality of New York. The city, accordingly, trembles. More is involved, for Trimble, than his own "design." During their walk, Orrison inquires what Trimble would most like to see; "Trimble considered":

"Well – the back of people's heads," he suggested. "Their necks – how their heads are joined to their bodies. I'd like to hear what those two little girls are saying to their father. Not exactly what they're saying but whether the words float or submerge, how their mouths shut when they've finished speaking. Just a matter of rhythm – Cole Porter came back to the States in 1928 because he felt that there were new rhythms around … "
"The weight of spoons,' said Trimble, "so light. A little bowl with a stick attached. The cast in that waiter's eye." (67)

The list proves lengthy, amounting, at first glance, to a fairly random set of items, paratactically set down. Adorno defines *parataxis* as a conjunction that "eludes subsumption under ideas" (or, perhaps, as metaphor waiting to happen).[6] Yet Trimble "considered" his list, and more generally, to Orrison's ear, "spoke in a measured way" (66). Moreover, he is not averse, as we shall soon learn, to riddles. What, then, may necks, mouths, Cole Porter's rhythms, spoons, and a waiter's eye have in common? To advance, as I believe Trimble advances, by stealth and the slow aggregation of resemblances: necks join heads to bodies and seen from behind may be thought to share something of that declivity that links the "bowl" of a spoon to its "stick." Said spoon, "weight[ed]" and tapped, sticklike, may keep tune with "new rhythms" or old (the acoustic of "spoon" after all contains "tune"), and "spoons" go to "mouths," which they dampen. But prior to the "mouths" and their singular capacities, according to Trimble's "absolute … curiosity," what of the "waiter's eye"? "Wait" and "weigh": to track associative skid across textual items takes time. The eye, liquid and lodged in a bone bowl of sorts, allows Trimble to "cast" across, and to "[re]cast" liquidity, since he requires that sight be impaired in order that it may not miss the mediation (liquid) within the immediacy of (architectural) surfaces.

Liquid tacitly links Trimble's preferred sights, in ways that prove prevalently speculative and textual. To return, in explication, to the presence of Cole Porter, repatriated from Paris to New York in pursuit of "rhythm," a spoon-fed and liquid sound. By 1928, according to Fitzgerald in "Echoes of the Jazz Age" (1931), "something subtle [had] passed to America" from Europe, "the style of man" (*MLC* 130–38; 131). While Fitzgerald cites as evidence "the American long-waisted figure and loose-fitting taste" in suits tailored during the 1920s on Bond Street, rather more was involved than a preference in "gentlemen's clothes," though it should be noted (in anticipation) that a long waist and a loose fit accentuate the flow of cloth (MLC 131). As Fitzgerald wrote to Edmund Wilson in 1921, "[c]ulture follows money" (*L* 326). The cut of suits did likewise. During the fifty years preceding the First World War, seeking to develop the infrastructure of its domestic economy, the United States borrowed massively, in large part from Britain. Consequently, U.S. foreign debt (or European claims on incomes and assets produced in the United States), which had stood at $200 million in 1843, by 1914 had risen to $3,700 million. The Great War saw a striking reversal in the flow of currency across the Atlantic; Britain's need for armaments, machines, and raw materials allowed the United States as provider to accumulate huge war credits ($9 billion [U.S. billion]). By the end of the war, therefore, the United States controlled a substantial share of global liquidity, and "joined … Britain in the production and regulation of world money."[7] Furthermore, during the 1920s, manufacturing grew faster in the United States than among debtor nations, even as the dependency of the world's payment system on the dollar increased. Since yesterday's surplus value needs must seek tomorrow's profitable investment, U.S. purchase of foreign assets grew "with a rapidity … unparalleled in the experience of any major creditor nation in modern times."[8]

But liquidity flows flooding toward America carried the risk of over-accumulation. As David Harvey argues, capital's enigma and crisis tendency lies in the imperative that "the continuity of flow … be sustained at all times" in a quest for "endless compound growth," an imperative that engineers a perpetually present "surplus disposal problem."[9] Put reductively: too much flow, not enough fixity, begging the question, where in terms of boom might such flows go? As the Regulation School economist Michel Aglietta points out, "*the financial crisis begins with a business euphoria*" whereby in the expectation of an upward curve in consumption, and seeking to speed and expand its own reproduction accordingly, business turns for investment to the creation of credit; this credit takes the form of corporate stocks issued against work not yet done on product not yet sold. All well and good, except that during the 1920s, while incomes from profits, interest, and rent rose by 45 percent, wages increased by only 13 percent.[10] The figures capture a distortion of income that eventually (after

1926) resulted in a declining demand for consumer durables, or the collapse of what Fitzgerald calls "the first burst of luxury manufacture after the war" (*TITN* 23).[11] With surplus increasingly difficult to achieve in the "real economy,"[12] excess liquidity takes to speculative means, understood as money that makes money from money, without pausing to fix and risk itself in the laborious creation of networks of production, distribution, and consumption. Such monies, for Marx, amount to "fictitious capital," a fiction that "mystifies" to the degree that, "pregnant" with itself, it announces "a capacity … to expand its own value independently of reproduction."[13] Expressed as equations, the "dematerialization"[14] or "vaporization"[15] of financial monies might be written as a transition from $M\text{-}C\text{-}M^1$ (where M equals money and C equals commodity or capital invested in commodity production), to $M\text{-}M^1\text{-}M^2$ (where M^1, variously compounded, equals money, plus some). In the second equation, money, as interest-bearing capital, becomes the tradeable good from which more money is created.[16]

For instance, during the Florida real-estate boom of 1925, investors who purchased lots did not in any real sense buy land, many of the lots being marginal, unusable, or nonexistent. Rather, in an expectation of rapidly rising prices, they bought to resell, thereby gaining profit that involved neither labor nor capital investment in the underlying asset.[17] Monies, so made, seemingly exhibit "self-expanding value" (Marx, vol. 3, 394). Strictly speaking, purchasers purchased their own euphoria, which, added to the euphoria of others, drove the ascendant price curve. "Irrational exuberance"[18] made land from price volatility, where there was no land. Such lands amount to lands made from language, or, more accurately, from exorbitant paper and tape, issuing in celebration of price and its expansion. Likewise, when the bubble burst, what investors sold (if they had time) was not land but panic, adding to the panic of others, and realized through the paper on which it was not worth printing the falling prices. Liquidity and text, in their jointly materializing passage through mood, prove inextricable from financialization. As J. K. Galbraith puts it, in his study on 1929, "by the summer … the market not only dominated the news. It also dominated the culture," in the form of market talk involving "abstraction associated not with the fact or reality, but with the man who asserts it and the manner of its assertion" (*The Great Crash* 99). One might have expected Galbraith to deploy the personal pronoun "his" in reference to "assertion" ("*he* who asserts … *his* assertion"); his preference for the impersonal ("its assertion") catches exactly the degree to which finance, as a cultural dominant, appears "self-expanding," not least in the matter of its own vocal assertions.

Money made nominally in Florida (though actually "in money" and talk of it), after 1925, most typically went in search of "compound growth" to the stock market, where it might engage in selling short. I take shorting as a second instance of "fictitious capital," and of the concreteness specific to speculative reality. I would note, in passing, that Charlie Campbell, at the center of "Babylon Revisited" (1931), acknowledges losing "everything I wanted," not in the crash but "in the boom," by the moral equivalent of "selling short" (*TAR* 406). The short sell involves an investor (or his broker) borrowing a security (for a fee to its lender) in the expectation that its price will fall. Prior to that fall, the borrower sells the security. When the market drops (as anticipated) he rebuys that which he sold, handing it back to the lender. He gains the difference between the high sale price and the low buy-back price (minus the fee). His risk can, however, be unlimited, since he is obliged to return that which he has borrowed (at a designated date), whatever the price of the borrowed security. Should the price rise rather than fall (no matter what its elevation) he must rebuy that which he has borrowed; since he may well have borrowed additionally to cover the anticipated buy-back price his losses will compound. He who shorts, whether successfully or unsuccessfully, trades in an asset that is no more than a locus of price variation, or of money made through volatility from borrowed money. The referent of the short trade might be figured as M-M', where the dash equates with risk; this risk amounts to a conjunction of anxiety and exuberance, mediated through stock price and small print. The trader trades less in a "substance" than in the peculiar materialization of affect through the textualized rhythm of market movements.[19] To return, perhaps better equipped, to "The Lost Decade": Trimble imagines words forming in the damp mouths of "two little girls" as they speak to their father. Fitzgerald's story contains one further reference to paternity: Orrison characterizes the Armistead Building as "the daddy of all the new ones" (67) as they follow it upward. His phrase ("the new ones") reaches for "new rhythms" (just seventeen lines earlier) as the latter generates a severally split referent, referring simultaneously to spoken and musical rhythms, and by associative extension to architecture; in this framework of "semantic impertinences," care of shared liquidity, elements "float" and "submerge." One might add that Trimble's associative transitions enact syntactically the very rhythm that he seeks to see, drawing sound toward notation by way of marks of punctuation. "[…] speaking. Just a matter of rhythm – Cole Porter […]": the period, after the children's speech, confirms that their "mouths shut," only for "rhythm" to recall, across the end note, the curtailed vocal that the period cut short, so that " –," carrying "rhythm" toward "Porter," may seem too hasty in its singular direction. Moreover, Trimble's musical predilections prove intertextually percussive, being full of the urban "sounds of horns and motors, which shall bring/Sweeney to Mrs. Porter in the spring."[20] Fitzgerald, throughout his career, used *The Waste Land* as a source of reference and allusion. Since he knew the poem intimately, one cannot doubt that he heard, in the liquid sounds of Trimble's "little girls," the voices of other children "singing in the copula":

> O the moon shone bright on Mrs. Porter
> And on her daughter
> They wash their feet in soda water
> *Et O ces voix d'enfants, chantant dans la coupole!*
> Twit twit twit
> Jug jug jug jug jug jug
> So rudely forc'd.
> Tereu
> Unreal City

Mrs. Porter (Porter), "daughter," "*enfants,*" ("little girls"); "soda water" ("every-which-way drunk"); "*chantant*" ("new rhythms"); "*coupole*" (the dome of the mouth): the links across the texts are systematic and inescapable, particularly since Eliot's lines recast the "*chantant,*" Mrs. Porter may or may not have heard, as the song of a nightingale (Tereu),[21] itself recast, in multiples of "jug" and "twit," as a problem of rhythm and text. How may reiterative and announcedly graphemic matter become, care of punctuation, famously liquid sound, or so much "matter" made from "rhythm"?

Where the economic rhythm of liquidity proves to be the "matter" of those buildings through which a city is iconicized, that city may indeed "tremble," becoming, if not "Unreal," then "too real." Note Orrison's final reaction to his time spent with Trimble: As the architect prepares to depart along the avenue, saying that he "simply wants to see how people walk and what their clothes and shoes and hats are made of. And their eyes and hands" (68), Orrison "felt suddenly of the texture of his own coat and then reached out and pressed his thumb against the granite of the building by his side" (68). Alerted to "new rhythms" and their performance by syntax (". [. . .] – " [67]), one hears rhythmic variables whisper first through Trimble's and then through Fitzgerald's phrasing. Take ". And their hands and eyes": a capitalized conjunction allows Trimble to poise between sartorial and corporeal enquiry. We might expect him to wish to see new kinds and cuts of clothing, and to consider that from which they are made, but ". And" threatens to extend his wish into matters of the flesh. If the term breaches backward, lowering its case ("a") to unstop the stop, then the architect's "curiosity" breaks ontological bounds, submitting "eyes and hands," like "shoes and hats," to constitutive question. The meaning of his desire depends upon its extent, and the extent of his desire depends upon the rhythm of its phrasing; this rhythm derives from ".", "A" and "a," textual marks made musical by their "float[ing] or submerge[ing]" in Trimble's mouth, in conjunction with his eye for the deliquescence of urban assets.

Exposed, "Orrison felt suddenly of the texture of his own coat": His reaction may simply mean that the touched cloth, although that might more normally have been phrased "he suddenly felt the texture of the cloth." Equally, "to feel of a texture" could submit the subject who feels to the object felt – that object, care of Trimble's way with objects (be they buildings or eyes), may tremble toward liquidity. To linger, briefly, over the problematic term "of," as a preposition, sets up relations; relations require distinctions between which they may be drawn. Contra distinction, Orrison's "of" dissolves the separation of subject from object. At this point, the tremulous subject, lapsing into the objects that surround him, seeks reassurance as to his "own" solidity. (Does Orrison's coat "own" Orrison, or does Orrison "own" it?) For Orrison Brown to recover his skin by thumbing stone recalls an earlier reference to the "brownstone" of "the famous 21" (*LD* 66). The subeditor's recourse to nominal palpability alludes to building materials synonymous with Victorian New York. Archaism[22] proves but briefly reassuring, given that the transposition of "granite," via "brownstone" and "Brown," toward figuration as "21" involves a redistribution of textual elements that renders any referent, beyond the ductility of its textualization, questionable.

In his study of speculative capital, Christian Marazzi speaks of the "linguification" of the "real" within the financial (Marazzi 40). J. K. Galbraith, less given to neologism, observes that during the months prior to the crash, "incantation" materialized as ascendant value on the New York stock exchange (*The Great Crash* 111). By both accounts, "[financial] facts are created by speaking them" (Marazzi 33). I, in accordance, have read "The Lost Decade" with an ear to risky utterance and an eye to textual volatility, doing so because persuaded by Fitzgerald's extraordinary acuteness regarding the financialization of facts. To read in the above manner is to experience neither an absenting of the referent nor a recession of referential concreteness. Rather, it is to feel that any usage (whether Trimble's "spoons" or Orrison's "of," or, indeed, each of their names) may spiral through "split" and "impertinence" toward semantic liquidity – the locus of an alternate concreteness, apt to the "strange stuff"[23] of financial monies. For Fitzgerald, an alcoholic case, "liquor" means more than either alcohol or "loss."

NOTES

1 W. Shakespeare, *Hamlet*, Act 3, Sc. 1, lines 88–89 (Harmondsworth, UK: Penguin, 1980), 125.

2 *Hamlet*, "loose," Act 2, Sc. 2, line 163 (108); "wonted way," Act 3, Sc. 1, lines 40–41 (123).

3 *Hamlet*, Act 4, Ac. 7, lines 117 and 176 (177–78).

4 C. P. Kindleberger and R. Z. Aliber, *Manias, Panics and Crashes: History of Financial Crises* (London: Palgrave Macmillan, 2005), 97.

5 P. Ricoeur, "The Metaphoric Process as Cognition, Imagination, and Feeling," *Critical Inquiry*, Vol. 5, No. 1 (Autumn, 1978), 148. "Likeness," so understood, can never be without "impertinence." Ricoeur adds, "All new rapprochement runs against a previous categorization which resists, or rather which yields while resisting, as Nelson Goodman says. This is what the idea of semantic impertinence or in congruence preserves. In order that a metaphor obtains one must continue to identify the previous incompatibility through the new compatibility" (148). Subsequent references to this work are included in the text.

6 T. Adorno, "Parataxis: On Hölderlin's Late Poetry," in *Notes to Literature*, Vol. 2, ed. R. Tiedermann, trans. S. W. Nicholsen (New York: Columbia University Press, 1992), 134.

7 G. Arrighi, *The Long Twentieth Century: Money, Power and the Origins of Our Times* (London: Verso, 2002), 271. My figures for the transatlantic flow of credits are drawn from Arrighi, 269–75.

8 M. Dobb, *Studies in the Development of Capitalism* (London: Routledge and Kegan Paul, 1963), 377. For details and the specific pattern of U.S. outward investment see also E. S. Rosenberg, *Spreading the American Dream: American Economics and the Cultural Expansion, 1890–1945* (New York: Hill and Wang, 1982), 63–86 and G. Feiss, *The Diplomacy of the Dollar* (Baltimore: Johns Hopkins Press, 1950).

9 D. Harvey, *The Enigma of Capital and the Crises of Capitalism* (London: Profile Books, 2010), 117, 192, 214.

10 M. Aglietta, *A Theory of Capitalist Regulation: The US Experience*, trans. D. Ferbach (London: Verso, 1987), 358. The figures are taken from Aglietta.

11 Fitzgerald's listed examples include "a pneumatic rubber horse" and "a portable bath house," items that enable swimming and flotation.

12 The phrase is R. Brenner's, for whom the "real economy" retains links to manufacture. See Brenner, "What Is Good for Goldman Sachs Is Good for America: The Origins of the Current Crisis," Center for Social Theory and Comparative History, University of California, Los Angeles (18 April, 2009).

In his study *The Violence of Finance Capital*, trans. K. Lebedeva (Los Angeles: Semiotext(e), 2010), C. Marazzi notes that, "[t]he typical twentieth century financialization … represented an attempt, in certain ways 'parasitic' and 'desperate,' to recuperate on the financial markets that which capital could no longer get in the real economy" (27). He adds that crises, accordingly, stem from "a contradiction between real and financial economies" (28). Subsequent references to this work are included in the text.

13 K. Marx, *Capital*, Vol. 3 (London: Lawrence and Wishart, 1959), 400, 393, 392.

14 D. Harvey, *The New Imperialism* (Oxford: Oxford University Press, 2003), 62.

15 J. R. Saul, *The Collapse of Globalism and the Reinvention of the World* (London: Atlantic Books, 2005), 25.

16 The equations borrow from Marx; see particularly *Capital*, Vol. 1 (Penguin: London, 1990), 247–57, and *Capital*, Vol. 3, 391.

17 J. K. Galbraith comments, "at some point in the growth of a boom all aspects of property ownership become irrelevant except the prospect of an early rise in price. Income from the property, or enjoyment of its use, or even its long-run worth, are now academic. As in the case of the more repulsive Florida lots … [w]hat is important is that tomorrow or next week market values will rise – as they did yesterday and last week - and a profit can be realized." See *The Great Crash* (London: Penguin, 2009), 46. Subsequent references to this are included in the text.

18 Alan Greenspan (chair of the Federal Reserve Board) used this phrase in 1996, immediately prior to a precipitous drop in stock market prices. R. J. Shiller took Greenspan's words as the title for his study in market activity, *Irrational Exuberance* (Princeton: Princeton University Press, 2005), emphasising the degree to which "information cascades" (159) and "unsubstantial whispers" (xiii) produce market volatility.

19 The economic theorist C. Marazzi sets what he calls "the bodiless self-referentiality of financial language" at the very center of financial dealing. For Marazzi, J. L. Austin's account of what we *do* with words proves particularly apt to what is *done* with language in the financial sector. The language of "the financial performative … does not describe a state of things," rather "taking as its institutional ballast, the serial behaviour of others," the financial contract "becomes an instrument [for the] … production of real facts." Ergo, in finance, "facts are created by speaking of them." The process is both linguistic and performative. See Marazzi, *Capital and Language*, trans. Gregory Conti (Los Angeles: Semiotext(e), 2002), 33–35.

20 T. S. Eliot, "The Waste Land," in his *Collected Poems, 1909–1962* (London: Faber, 1963), 70.

21 "Tereu"/Tereus: Eliot alludes to Philomel pursued by Tereus and translated into a nightingale as the source of the "Jug jug" song, whose transcription he owes to John Lyle ("Alexander and Campaspe"). Fitzgerald had reason to be alert to the singing of the nightingale, which, care of Keats ("Ode to a

Nightingale") provided him with his title, *Tender Is the Night*. More pertinently, in *The Great Gatsby,* he proved capable (Sweeney-like) of discerning the notes through the "sounds of horns and motors"; indeed, he transposes them into the vehicular noise ("jug-jug-*spat*!") of a speeding police motorcycle, pursuing Gatsby and Carraway as they approach the Queensboro Bridge (*GG* 54).

22 Old Specker, an architect in J. Dos Passos' *Manhattan Transfer* (published in 1925; set in 1915) has "got an idea that the skyscraper of the future'll be built of steel and glass ... He's got a great sayin about some Roman emperor who found Rome in brick and left it in marble. Well he says he's found New York of brick an that he's goin to leave it of steel ... steel an glass." See *Manhattan Transfer* London: Penguin, 1986), 76.

23 N. Kiyotaki and J. Moore, "Evil Is the Root of All Money," *American Economic Review,* 92, 2 (2002), 62.

36

Fitzgerald and the Great Depression

Michael K. Glenday

"Nine mocking years with the golden calf and three long years of the scourge! Nine crazy years at the ticker and three long years in the breadlines! Nine mad years of mirage and three long years of despair!"[1] The lurid contrasts between America's boom and bust years, as drawn here by President Franklin D. Roosevelt in 1936, are a stark reminder of the national calamity that afflicted most of its citizens living through the period of the Great Depression, a time when many, including F. Scott Fitzgerald, had to exchange the "mad years of mirage" of the 1920s for the "long years of despair" of the 1930s. "The Crash! Zelda + America" was the dramatic headline entry in his ledger for 1929 (*L* 184). The contrasts were of course painful in their results, although the 1920s had themselves been a time of hardship and fiscal uncertainty for many. While low taxes had permitted standards of living to rise, the economic system was fat, and overproduction by labor in farms and factories had not been matched by any commensurate increase in wages. The result was more of everything than was wanted, and therefore the labor that produced it was no longer needed; unemployment and impoverishment followed for many, and wages continued to be minimal for those only somewhat less unfortunate. The industrial magnates and plutocrats of the Hoover administration (1928–32) had presided over an economic system that had run out of control. Writing in 1934, Bertrand Russell expressed the views of many when he concluded that "it is incontrovertible that to intrust power to the very rich is to court widespread ruin and starvation."[2] These words were written in the same year that F. Scott Fitzgerald published *Tender Is the Night*, and they certainly explain his fears that its focus upon a wealthy and privileged milieu was hardly to be welcomed in the midst of New Deal regulation and austerity.

The concluding chapter of Malcolm Cowley's memoir *Exile's Return: A Literary Odyssey of the 1920s* (also published first in 1934) is a personal, authoritative and still affecting account of that transition between "the ticker … and the breadlines" as it affected the literary community of those years. Taking 1930 as his marker, Cowley remembers there "the signs that an age was ending."[3] The 1920s, which "had on the whole been an era of good feeling among writers," passed into one of "violent discussion" and attacks (303), a view supported by Alfred Kazin in his own memoir *Writing Was Everything* (1995). As the 1930s began, Kazin, politically unaligned but working for the liberal, left-leaning *New Republic* as a book editor and reviewer, also testified to the prevailing mood of intolerance: "violence of feeling marked the thirties in every sphere, not least among the righteous."[4] An example of this righteous stance is found in Michael Gold's *New Republic* review of Thornton Wilder, which Cowley offers as a significant case in point. The kind of language that Gold used to lambast Wilder's books might, in fact, also have been used to attack Fitzgerald: "Where are the cotton mills … the child slaves of the beet fields? Where are the stockbroker suicides, the labor racketeers or the passion and death of the coal miners?" (Cowley 303). Looking away from contemporary American crisis, Thornton Wilder's readers are led "into castles, palaces and far-off Greek islands, where they may study the human heart when it is nourished by blue blood." There, they will never be reminded "of Pittsburgh and the breadlines" (304), which by autumn of that year had begun to spread "from back streets into the business section" (306) of New York.

Such was the grim *zeitgeist* the Fitzgeralds returned to as they left France for the last time, arriving in America in September 1931. That return was at least partly provoked by the Depression and had been preceded in January of the same year by Fitzgerald's solo voyage home for his father's funeral. Matthew J. Bruccoli notes in his *The Price Was High* headnote to "Between Three and Four" that during that brief visit Fitzgerald "had observed the effects of the Depression" (*P* 339) for the first time. As he told a Baltimore reporter in 1934, in the shadow of American decline, French residency had come to seem more and more like exile and isolation: "Off there in a little village we had such a horrible feeling of insecurity … We had so little information from home, and we kept hearing these reports about business conditions until we didn't know but that any moment the United States would go smash and we'd be cut adrift."[5] Fitzgerald's authorship signature, so long a witness to wealth and its lures, risks, and contagions, was being challenged by these currents of change, both in terms of subject matter and approach. Although returning homeward, he yet defended the American novelist's right to remain aesthetically and politically independent:

No, I can't see that there's been any pronounced political or economic swing in the novel recently … A few have shown a tendency in that direction, inspired by the depression, but the majority retain their highly individualistic attitude. I think it's a good thing that we're getting over our boom-years period when we pictured life and success as easy, but I think it's a mistake for the novelist to sacrifice his detached viewpoint. (*Conversations* 104)

Like many American writers of the time, such as Theodore Dreiser, Ernest Hemingway, and Henry Roth, Fitzgerald also regarded himself as left-leaning. At the same time as he was writing *Tender Is the Night*, he was also "telling his daughter at Vassar to read 'the terrible chapter on the working day in *Das Kapital*'" (Kazin 33). But if Fitzgerald was reading Marx in these years, he was hardly a fellow-traveller, and his communism was never systematically ideological or programmatic.[6] In one of the Crack-Up essays, "Handle with Care," for instance, he was unequivocal in characterizing his politics as being defined by "an abiding distrust, an animosity, towards the leisure class – not the conviction of a revolutionist but the smouldering hatred of a peasant" (*CU* 47). As Bruccoli notes in his headnote to "Six of One –," Fitzgerald had described himself as a socialist in his first *Who's Who* listing (*P* 369), although his skepticism about the effects of any wholehearted Communist subscription are clear in his letter of January 2, 1933, to Max Perkins, in which he commented upon Edmund Wilson's turn toward communism, connecting Wilson's "rather gloomy" mood of the time with the latter's "decision to adopt Communism definitely." This, "no matter how good for the soul, must of necessity be a saddening process for anyone who has ever tasted the intellectual pleasures of the world we live in" (*LL* 226).

As noted by Robert Sklar, "Fitzgerald is rarely mentioned among the radical writers of the thirties: the incongruity with his reputation would be too great."[7] The first dedicated study of the fiction of that period was Maxwell Geismar's *Writers in Crisis: The American Novel 1925–1940* (1947). The "writers in crisis" that his book focused on did not include Fitzgerald as one of the literary spokesmen of the selected period, and he is reduced to a single reference in the book's index. This perhaps confirms Sklar's perception, although Geismar's study also preceded the full onset of the so-called Fitzgerald Revival that commenced at midcentury. Geismar's preface to the book's later edition (1961), however, echoed Fitzgerald's terms in finding that the "even and peaceful" culture of the 1920s had its downside in that "the dazzling materialism of 1929 led only to spiritual frustration on the part of the American writer" and that "the social and cultural crisis of the new decade brought to our writers a set of spiritual positives based, as it were, on the actual collapse of their own society." American writers were the beneficiaries of challenges presented by the era; their gains included "moral stature, a sense of [their] own cultural connection, a series of new meanings and new values for [their] work."[8] Fitzgerald's self-critical belief that he was "too much of a moralist at heart" (*L* 63) may thus have found in the culture of the 1930s a more enabling context.

Writing in 1982, Ruth Prigozy also found that "the problems facing the nation in the Depression stimulated Fitzgerald's use of communal social problems as subjects for fiction … A number of the stories touch on the spectre of poverty, on class differences, on social snobbery, on the lust for money and power, and on the myth of success which took on greater significance than ever as the economic basis of the nation was being tested."[9] By 1934, Fitzgerald had already shown his readiness to engage in his fiction with the results of economic privation for Americans, and for a writer so finely tuned to the national mood it would have been odd had this not been the case. After a three-day visit in 1933, he "[f]ound New York in a high state of neurosis … and met no one who didn't convey the fact to me" (*LL* 226). This mood of neurosis is something we catch in much of the short fiction he wrote then, one could say almost in response to its palpable presence (Prigozy's term "spectre" is very apt in this regard) in the atmosphere of those years. It was already manifest in, for instance, his *Saturday Evening Post* story of September 1931, "Between Three and Four," in which Depression-era paranoia leads to New York businessman Howard Butler's suicide. As Bruccoli notes, this story, "the first in which Fitzgerald treated the Depression scene in response to the *Post*'s request for stories with American settings" (*P* 339), has been criticized for its apparently implausible plot contrivances, but these can easily be read as intended manifestations of Butler's complete ingestion of the toxic Depression atmosphere. In the story's opening paragraph, written approximately five years before the Crack-Up essays, Fitzgerald used the image "cracking" or "cracking up" for the first time in his fiction, setting it alongside "neurosis" as companion terms common in the Depression. Whereas "[a]lmost everyone cracked a little" in those years, and neurosis is presented as a disease of the wealthy, "a privilege of people with a lot of extra money" (339), the crack-up itself arrives only "when money troubles came to be added to all the nervous troubles accumulated in the prosperity" (339).

The stock market crash of 1929 caused an immediate and dramatic spike in suicide; indeed, the Great Depression saw the biggest rise in suicides in American history, when the national suicide rate jumped from 18 per 100,000 adults in 1928 to more than 22 per 100,000 people in 1932, a rise of 22.8 percent over four years. Fitzgerald was most certainly aware of this baleful phenomenon, and much more than anecdotally. If he found that *Tender Is the Night* "completes my story of the boom years" (qtd. in Sklar 299), their aftermath was largely explained in "Pasting it Together." There, he remembered that from his own generation "one famous contemporary of mine played with the idea of the Big Out for half a year ... while another, equally eminent, spent months in an asylum ... [a]nd of those who had given up and passed on I could list a score" (52). Among those he knew were Jules Pascin, "the Prince of Montparnasse," who was at the heart of Bohemian Paris in the 1920s;[10] Manhattan socialite Emily Vanderbilt Thayer Whitfield, whose life "finally ended by her own hand in Montana in 1934 [actually 1935] in a lonely ranch house" as Fitzgerald told his daughter in a letter penned a week before his own death in 1940 (*LL* 475); the great poet Hart Crane, who in 1932 jumped to his death from the USS *Orizaba* ten miles off the Florida coast; and, much closer to home, Fitzgerald's brother-in-law, Anthony Sayre, who, suffering from what his doctors called "nervous prostration," took his own life in 1933 by leaping from his hospital window in Mobile, Alabama, a further casualty of the times: "depressed about the loss of his job and his inability to meet his expenses ... he told his doctor that he knew he should destroy himself."[11]

The Depression was not, of course, responsible directly for every suicide that happened during its season, but it did provoke widespread self-destructive despair. It is little wonder that Fitzgerald responded to this in his fiction of the time. In a story such as "Between Three and Four" he dramatized the literal fallout as Howard Butler "stepped out into the dark air" (*P* 350–51) of suicide, burgeoning neurosis easily finding its plot and personification. The further text of Fitzgerald's quote above gives this story's rationale quite explicitly: "Found New York in a high state of neurosis, as does everybody else ... it possibly proves that the neurosis is in me" (*LL* 226). In "Between Three and Four" we find Fitzgerald's narrator using very similar terms, in a signal link with unemployment, emasculation, fear, and guilt:

> Sometimes, when he read the newspapers a lot, he felt that he was almost the only man left with enough money to get along with; and it frightened him, because he knew pretty well that he was not much of a man and they might find it out and take his position away from him. Since he was not all right with himself in his private life, he had fallen helplessly into the clutches of the neurosis that gripped the nation, trying to lose sight of his own insufficiencies in the universal depression. (*P* 344)

The story's apparent implausibility is informed by this local context of immanent breakdown contaminating Wall Street and the national psyche. For Howard Butler, this folds him into a darker narrative,[12] in which the logic of action and reason is undermined. His guilty conscience may derive explicitly from his refusal to offer Sarah Summer (a supplicant former employee and partner, now fallen on hard times as a result of the Depression) any work, but his responses are out of any proportion to reality yet also indicative of the harried culture of the time. Butler is presented as a hapless victim of that, with a futile subconscious awareness of such illogic just before his dying fall:

> Simultaneously he knew, with a last fragment of himself, that there was something wrong in the very nature of the logic that had brought him to this point, but it was too late now. He ran across the office like a frightened cat, and with a sort of welcome apprehension of nothingness, stepped out into the dark air beyond his window ... already too much engrossed in death to connect it with anything ... (350)

The link to feline fright here may be intentionally suggestive of distemper, a viral disease that affects animals, especially cats. Certainly Butler's distempered mental state allows no escape from the guilt that has unhinged his mind, and the illogic that informs his thinking (very similar to that cited above regarding Anthony Sayre – "he told his doctor that he knew he should destroy himself") provides a perverse rationale for self-destruction that is nevertheless expressed in chillingly logical terms: "He began making a systematic effort to pull himself together ... he astonished himself at the coolness with which he deliberated this – if the matter reached an intolerable point, one could always take one's own life, thus automatically destroying whatever horror had come into it" (347).

With "A Change of Class" (1931), we have what Ruth Prigozy has called "the clearest example of Fitzgerald's attempt to treat the Depression fictionally" (119), a story whose main character, Earl Johnson, a barber working in Wilmington, Delaware, is in motion from 1926 through 1931 in a revolving-door narrative of boom to bust. Johnson is presented as fulfilled by his work, at first immune to the snares of wealth and the lure of the wealthy financiers who recognize his skills, "a fine barber" who unlike his colleagues "kept his dignity" (*P* 352) when wealth walked into the barbershop of the Jadwin Hotel. Knowing his place and liking his work are Johnson's virtues; prior to transgressing the boundaries he is safe: "he worked silently and well, with deft tranquillizing hands" (353). A stock tip from one of his wealthiest and best-connected customers, Philip Jadwin, nets him a fortune, and Johnson "blundered into the golden age" (355). As

Bruccoli's headnote reminds us, "the plot is not far-fetched: fortunes were made during the boom on stock-market tips, and reports about rich bartenders or wealthy bootblacks were commonplace" (*P* 352). In "My Lost City," Fitzgerald uses his own barber as personification of both boom – "my barber retired on a half million bet in the market" (*CU* 31) and bust – "my barber was back at work in his shop" (*CU* 32).

Fitzgerald's story plays off mundane and grounded referents to barbering and the service economy against the unlikely class makeovers and equally sudden annihilations of the imminent stock market frenzy. So, for Jadwin, "a simple man with simple tastes" (*P* 359–60), there was "the fine razor respecting its sensibility, or the comb, which seemed proud in the last fillip with which it finished him. Earl's chair was a place to rest, a sanctuary" (359), while for Johnson himself, newly rich and no longer in need of his job, there would be many returns to the same "sanctuary," as though to "touch base," to absorb again its codes, signs, and practices that seem invested with non-negotiable value: "He came often ... he liked the gleaming nickel of the chairs, the sight of a case of clean razors, the joking abuse of the colored porter that made the hours pass. Sometimes he just sat around and read a paper" (355). While the subtext here is nowhere near as harrowing as that of Hemingway's "A Clean Well-Lighted Place," published just two years after Fitzgerald's story, there are similar masculinities involved, and both stories stress objects and environments and the comfort they provide to the displaced male. In Fitzgerald's story we see aesthetic formalizations such as Johnson's pleasure in "the gleaming nickel of the chairs" while inside the "clean and pleasant café" with its "shining steam pressure coffee machine,"[13] but the lonely old man and the older waiter in Hemingway's story are given a minimal assurance in the midst of existential drift.

The emphasis upon a masculine ethos here (the barbershop as "sanctuary") is further consolidated when the reader learns that Johnson, despite his considerable wealth, "had worked in the barber shop two years after he needed to, taking ten-cent tips from men he could have bought out a dozen times over" (*P* 355), and that "he quit because Violet [his wife] insisted upon it" (355). This suggests that the apparatus of bourgeois respectability afforded by his new wealth is explicitly associated with his wife's upwardly mobile aspirations, an impression buttressed when we hear that "his trade didn't go with the colored servant and the police dog, the big machine for outdoors and the many small noisy machines for the house" (355). Indeed, it had been on Violet's promptings that Johnson had asked Philip Jadwin for the stock tip, and Fitzgerald's narrative conveys a heavily gendered vision of domestic and bourgeois fulfillment: wealth brings happiness of a kind for Violet but is quite at variance with Earl Johnson's simpler understanding of pleasure. He had been happy before the advent of material uplift, "content with his prospects, liking his work in the cheerful, gossipy shop, loving his wife and his new existence with her in a new little apartment" (380). The labor-saving domestic machinery creates not harmony but noise, making us wonder little at Johnson's frequent returns to the "sanctuary" of the barber salon.

In "A Change of Class," the simple American dream of success is readily deconstructed to reveal its internal contradictions: that material increase is no guarantee of happiness, and that, at least in this story, it may result in breakdown along gender and class lines. So much is made explicit by Fitzgerald's narrator: Earl "was worth more than a hundred thousand dollars. In his front yard he paused, thinking to himself that it was like a dream. That was as near as he could analyze his feelings; he was not even sure whether the dream was happy or unhappy – Violet was sure for both of them that it was happy" (*P* 356). The story goes further than this, however, in its suggestion that sudden exaltation through the class divisions will in itself prove transgressive, unstable, and hence socially destructive to those who experience such displacement. The language used reflects the politics of the time, mobilized in a critique of the unassimilable flux of class, while any effort to find affiliation within the bourgeois status system leads to other losses, as individualism and reactive integrity are undermined and emasculated, made "sterile and devitalized":

> From the day when they moved into the new house, Violet adopted the manner of one following a code, a social rite, plain to herself but impossible for Earl to understand. She herself failed to understand that from their position in mid-air they were constrained merely to observe myopically and from a distance, and then try to imitate. Their friends were in the same position. They all tried to bolster up one another's lack of individuality … but they were all made sterile and devitalized by their new environments, paying the price exacted for a passage into the middle-class. (356)

Inasmuch as the discourse above is mediated through the narrator's consciousness of class struggle, the presence of such a passage as this indicates that in these years of Depression Fitzgerald was willing on occasion to produce fictions capable of dramatizing the context within a discourse that offers an interrogation of Marxist concepts liberally understood.

The story's title, "A Change of Class," indicates its concerns. The stock boom has upset traditional class barriers and inaugurated a new social flux. In the immediate aftermath, "It's all awfully mixed up" (*P* 361), as

Philip Jadwin ruefully ponders. Transitioning from one class to another is thus figured as confusing and potentially disabling, as is clear from Earl Johnson's newly moneyed misery as he tries to assess his place within the society he and Violet now have access to. He finds himself attending parties thrown by successful bootleggers: "He didn't like it. He felt he was in Mr. Jadwin's class – not Mr. Jadwin's equal but a part of the structure to which Mr. Jadwin belonged ... Not the most bored captive of society had any more sense of being in a cage than had Earl as he walked into that house to have fun" (357–58). Jadwin himself also regrets the cage of class, although in his case it prevented the downward mobility that would have allowed love to flourish: "three years ago he should have married that girl in his office ... He had been afraid. Now ... a cousin of his had since married his stenographer and had not been very strongly persecuted" (358).

While Ruth Prigozy is right to note that the story invokes "a sub-plot that incorporates nearly every worn-out trick imaginable" (119), this story of a financier and a barber is important because it shows clearly Fitzgerald's core politics at the time of writing. The very explicit intervention of the involved narrator in the final sentence of the story's coda may strike some readers as odd, but it is unique in Fitzgerald's fiction and does have the resonance of an intervention by Fitzgerald himself. The stock market crash and subsequent Depression have rid Johnson of both his wife and his fortune (she takes his last dollars to elope with the bootlegger, who has defaulted on his own debts to the mob), but his modest resumed existence as a contented servant of the community is appreciated locally, not least by Philip Jadwin, who, having bankrolled Johnson's new barber business, also eventually resumes his place in Earl's barber chair, so leading to the narrator's final judgment upon Earl Johnson: "The soul of a slave, says the Marxian. Anyhow that's the sort of soul that Earl has, and he's pretty happy with it. I like Earl" (368). Political rhetoric is here put in its place as a kind of surface marking that cannot revise the perfectly grounded, unapologetic, and embodied reality of a life lived in tune with its instincts.

National values were under stress in the Depression years, and we find in Fitzgerald's short fiction of the time what Cowley found in *Tender Is the Night*, an effort "to discover and even create values in a society where they had seemed to be lacking."[14] In a letter of 1931 Fitzgerald wrote to Max Perkins, "The Jazz Age is over ... I claim credit for naming it ... it extended from the suppression of the riots on May Day 1919 to the crash of the stock market in 1929 – almost exactly one decade" (*L* 225). It is likely that Fitzgerald was well aware of "the distorted popular impression of him as the totemic figure who embodied" or was even somehow responsible for the excesses of the boom and the punitive depression.[15] If he did feel such responsibility, the stories considered here present him as a writer who was willing to engage determinedly with what his *Ledger* refers to as "Recession and procession" (*FSFL* 186).

NOTES

1 F. D. Roosevelt, "Organized Money" (1936) in A. Breidlid et al. (eds.), *American Culture: An Anthology of Civilization Texts* (London: Routledge, 1996), 204–6; 204–5.

2 B. Russell, "Can the President Succeed?" in B. Feinberg and R. Kasrils (eds.), *Bertrand Russell's America: His Transatlantic Travels and Writings Volume One 1896–1945 A Documented Account* (London: Allen and Unwin, 1973), 276–7; 276.

3 M. Cowley, *Exile's Return: A Literary Odyssey of the 1920s* (London: The Bodley Head, 1961), 302. Subsequent references to this work are included in the text.

4 A. Kazin, *Writing Was Everything* (Cambridge, MA: Harvard University Press, 1995), 36. Subsequent references to this work are included in the text.

5 M. J. Bruccoli and J. S. Baughman (eds.), "Scott Fitzgerald Seeking Home Here" in *Conversations with F. Scott Fitzgerald* (Jackson, MS: University Press of Mississippi, 2004), 103–5; 105. Subsequent references to this work are included in the text.

6 See R. J. Gervais, "The Socialist and the Silk Stockings: Fitzgerald's Double Allegiance" in H. Bloom (ed.) *Modern Critical Views: F. Scott Fitzgerald* (New York: Chelsea House, 1985), 167–80. This is an excellent study of what Gervais terms Fitzgerald's "idiosyncratic and highly personal Marxism" (180).

7 R. Sklar, *F. Scott Fitzgerald: The Last Laocoön* (New York: Oxford University Press, 1967), 305. Subsequent references to this work are included in the text.

8 M. Geismar, *Writers in Crisis: The American Novel 1925–1940* (New York: Hill and Wang, 1961), vii.

9 R. Prigozy, "Fitzgerald's Short Stories and the Depression: An Artistic Crisis" in J. R. Bryer (ed.) *The Short Stories of F. Scott Fitzgerald: New Approaches in Criticism* (Madison, WI: University of Wisconsin Press, 1982), 111–26; 118. Subsequent references to this work are included in the text.

10 In chapter 11 of *A Moveable Feast* (London: Cape, 1964), "With Pascin at the Dôme," Hemingway gives a fondly etched recall of "the lovely painter that [Pascin] was, and afterwards, when he hanged himself, I liked to remember him as he was that night at the Dôme."

11 N. Milford, *Zelda Fitzgerald: A Biography* (New York: Harper & Row, 1970), 280.

12 In this context Bruccoli's judgment that the story, like "all of these Depression stories" written at the time by Fitzgerald, has a "happy ending" is very wide of the mark (*P* 365).

13 E. Hemingway, "A Clean, Well-Lighted Place" in *The First Forty-Nine Stories* (London: Cape, 1964), 313.

14 Qtd. in D. Welland, "The Language of American Fiction Between the Wars" in M. Cunliffe (ed.) *American Literature Since 1900* (London: Barrie and Jenkins, 1975), 48–70; 69.

15 M. J. Bruccoli, *Some Sort of Epic Grandeur: The Life of F. Scott Fitzgerald*, 2nd rev. ed. (Columbia, SC: University of South Carolina Press, 2002), 286.

37

The Writer in Hollywood

Richard Fine

F. Scott Fitzgerald returned to Hollywood in 1937 after an absence of nearly a decade, determined to make a success of his third attempt at screenwriting. Other than one five-week stint in 1931, he had not worked in a film studio since First National Pictures had paid him $3,500 to write a modern romance for its young star Constance Talmadge in 1927. Fitzgerald and Zelda had spent several months circulating in Hollywood society, but they left after First National shelved the project, disappointed in his script. Fitzgerald ruefully calculated that he had spent more than he had earned from First National in this brief period of extravagant living.[1]

Ten years later, and possessing little of the original luster that had made him attractive to Hollywood earlier, Fitzgerald arrived in Los Angeles in hopes of rebuilding his shattered professional career. He had been hired by Metro-Goldwyn-Mayer on a six-month contract, based on his reputation as a chronicler of youth and campus life. Fitzgerald, at forty, proved an aging chronicler of youth, but the story editor at MGM believed he could contribute to the studio's profitable run of campus-based musicals and romances. The studio paid him $1,000 per week, and MGM had the option to extend his contract for another year at a slightly higher salary (Bruccoli 416). "I feel a certain excitement," Fitzgerald wrote to his daughter from the train headed west. "Given a break, I can make them double this contract in less [than] two years," he predicted with newfound confidence, verging on bravado (*L* 16–17). Once in Los Angeles, Fitzgerald earnestly schooled himself in scriptwriting and the visual language of film. "He liked pictures," Budd Schulberg, his screenwriting collaborator and friend, later recalled, "and felt his talent was well suited to the medium."[2]

While much in Hollywood was familiar, Fitzgerald was alert enough in 1937 to understand that much else in the film industry had changed dramatically. For one thing, in 1927 the talkies had been a novelty; a decade later, the conversion to sound production was complete. For another, and more crucially, these changes in the moviemaking process as practiced in

Los Angeles, known collectively as "the studio system," meant that the writer's role in the film production process was moving toward the center, even as his or her actual status within the studios and authority in that process remained marginal.

Hollywood's shift to sound production was not quite as seismic in fact as legend would have it. "The motion picture industry did not turn topsy-turvy because of the talkies," according to film historian Donald Crafton, who claims that "[n]o studios closed on account of the coming of sound; most increased their profits."[3] That said, technical hurdles to sound recording were taken on and rapidly overcome. Cameras became quieter and easier to isolate during recording. Film acquired the ability to capture faithfully all types of ambient sound, to record asynchronous sound (musical soundtracks, sound effects, and such), and to combine them through sound editing. The conversion to sound also created an obvious need for more actual speech on screen and thus for more written dialogue. Suddenly, movies were filled with "talk, talk, talk," as silent movie star Norma Desmond bemoaned in *Sunset Boulevard*.

Hollywood at first had looked to its own cadre of contract writers from the silent era, of whom there were too few, and of those, even fewer who could write credible dialogue. The writer's experience to date in the film industry had not been a particularly happy one. In the early silent days, directors were able to do without writers entirely by sketching out their own stories and scripts, often little more than an elaborated list of scenes. Well into the 1920s, there were few screenwriters of any real prominence, with the notable exceptions of Anita Loos and Roy McCardell. The studios had tended to hire ex-journalists or public relations agents for their contract writers, who did little more than construct serviceable plots. What dialogue they did write was severely limited to that printed on a few title cards. Given the growing demand for writers in the wake of sound conversion, the studios quickly turned to the theatrical and literary demi-monde in New York. The literary marketplace in New York was hit hard by the Depression, as publishers retrenched, magazines and newspapers shrank with their advertising revenues, and fewer opening nights occurred on Broadway each year. By 1933, as sources of income dried up in Manhattan, scores of such writers – novelists, playwrights, newspaper reporters, and columnists – were accepting Hollywood's offers.

Just as *Hollywood* serves as a metonym for the entire film industry spread beyond its geographic boundaries, so the *studio system* exists as shorthand for the means of film production that Hollywood adopted in the late 1920s and then refined into the 1940s. Some crucial elements of that system had not changed since Fitzgerald's previous visits. The studios still relied on the creation and promotion of stars among actors as their basic marketing strategy, for example. Producers also still relied on a handful of audience-tested genres – comedy, romance, western, gangster, horror, and such – for the bulk of their annual catalog. However, the massive capital costs incurred in shifting sound just at a time of national financial crisis had forced the studios to rationalize what had been desultory production practices throughout the silent era.

The movies as a business organization also looked profoundly different in the 1930s. For one thing, the industry had changed ownership. "The thirties transformed the American film industry into a modern business enterprise," film historian Tino Balio notes, elaborating with this observation: "No longer run by the founders as family businesses, motion-picture companies were managed by hierarchies of salaried executives who rationalized operations to ensure long-term stability and profits."[4] In the 1920s, dozens of smaller independent studios, often still under the control of their founders, had each made a modest number of films each year and frequently in haphazard fashion. Many consolidated into a smaller number of larger, more cost-effective companies, so that by the mid-1930s only eight companies controlled the manufacture of virtually all theatrical film production: the "Big Five" (MGM, Paramount, Universal, Twentieth Century Fox, and RKO) and the "Little Three" (Columbia, Warner Brothers, and United Artists). The Big Five studios themselves were but subsidiaries of larger corporations that also distributed and exhibited the films through theater chains they also owned, so that collectively they formed what business historians refer to as a vertically integrated oligopoly, a handful of companies controlling an entire industry from top to bottom – in this case, the production, distribution, and exhibition of feature-length films.

The film studios had also appropriated and customized the industrial assembly line as their basic mode of operation, and the process of moviemaking was broken down into its component parts, each now organized to use all workers more efficiently, from acting to editing, screenwriting to set construction. The major studios had to meet enormous payrolls for their skilled and unskilled labor pools, to the point where Mae D. Huettig, in her classic study of the film industry at just this time, wryly observes that "the production of films, essentially fluid and experimental as a process, is harnessed to a form of organization which can rarely afford to be either experimental or speculative."[5] To manage this assembly line, from locating a story or script through actual production to a film's final editing and release, the studios had developed a class of executives at first called supervisors but by the 1930s more often termed "producers." Making films in the studio system of the 1930s, then, was far less a collaborative endeavor than "a group effort involving a strict division of labor with the producer at the helm," as Tino Balio points out (10).

Writers reported directly to the unit or line producer responsible for some portion of the studio's output. The producer was the face of filmmaking for writers, and this key producer–writer relationship, although often workmanlike and occasionally quite cordial, could be and often was quite fraught. Such producers thought of themselves as managers, and some also considered themselves showmen, but few cared much about literature or the aesthetics of film. Most, in fact, knew little about the technical aspects of filmmaking and could not exert much influence over production through, for example, supervising camerawork or lighting. However, the one crucial part of that entire process that they could control was the story itself, which required no technical knowledge and which they sought to shape through their handling of the writers in their employ.

Few writers were hired to write original scripts, and fewer still adapted their own novels or plays. Most took on projects already begun – to adapt books and plays, or to revise scripts written by others in the studio. The larger studios often had writers who specialized in polishing existing scripts by adding humor, romance, dialogue, or another distinctive element to an existing script without overhauling its basic structure. Virtually all scripts passed through several hands. In *The Last Tycoon* (1941), Fitzgerald attributed this assembly-line method of using writers to the dynamic studio head Monroe Stahr, and thus by inference to Irving Thalberg, the successful chief of production at MGM through the mid-1930s, but variants of the practice of using multiple writers in collaboration or succession emerged in several studios in the early 1930s. At all of the major studios, more scripts were developed than films produced, in some studios far more. Once finished with a script, writers would either go off contract or be assigned to begin again with other projects; in either case, their involvement with the first film had ended. From a writer's perspective, assignments typically ranged from a "length of picture" contract of a few weeks for work on a specific script to the standard seven-year option contract, with the studios offering a steady salary for six months or more while holding an option to extend the contract or cancel it at any time. The pay was stunningly high by New York standards – $1,000 per week on average in the early 1930s.

Nonetheless, whatever its attractions and rewards, and they were considerable, those writers who had been involved professionally in the literary marketplace in New York often found working in this studio system a frustrating and at times deeply unsatisfying experience. In midtown Manhattan, writers were valued for their individual voices, for their originality, and were vested with large degrees of creative autonomy and control over their work. Such was hardly the case in Los Angeles, where the enticements offered to writers to head west often proved chimerical. In the first place, while weekly salaries could be extremely high, few writers worked even a fair portion of the year. In addition, the seven-year option contract placed all options in the hands of the studios and the writer in a kind of indenture. Moreover, the workday for contract writers often involved unreasonable deadlines, interminable story conferences, and uncongenial writing partners. After 1934, they butted heads with the censors in the Production Code Administration, which enforced Hollywood's guidelines regarding screen content, especially profanity, sexuality, criminality, and other objectionable material, this in an attempt to co-opt calls for state or federal censorship laws.

Finally, writers had to defer creatively to producers, most of whom they thought their inferiors. Fitzgerald himself famously complained to producer Joseph L. Mankiewicz, who had hired Fitzgerald to adapt Erich Maria Remarque's *Three Comrades*. Mankiewicz had first teamed him with another screenwriter whom Fitzgerald considered a hack, and then Mankiewicz had rewritten Fitzgerald's script himself. "Oh, Joe, can't producers ever be wrong?" Fitzgerald pleaded with his boss: "I'm a good writer – honest. I thought you were going to play fair" (*L* 564).

Another way that producers did not play fair concerned screen credits, the lifeblood of screenwriters then as now. Instances abound of producers in the 1930s who took for themselves undeserved writing credits, who denied writers deserved story or script credit, and who pitted writers against each other for what credit was granted. Fitzgerald himself, in nearly four years of work in Hollywood, managed only one screen credit, ironically for *Three Comrades*, a fact used as evidence of his struggles in Hollywood and mistreatment by the studios. Writers fought unsuccessfully through the 1930s to form an effective union to combat the option contract, screen credit, and other employment abuses, but not until 1941 did the Screen Writers Guild win recognition as the legitimate representative of Hollywood's writers. Only then did the worst of the writer's grievances get resolved.

Beyond that of the writer as exploited employee, a second and more potent myth surrounds writers in Hollywood during the 1930s. Within the larger American writing, and especially among the literary demimonde in New York, "going Hollywood" became code for selling out, for a kind of literary prostitution. This notion, promoted by theater and literary critics in the East as writers migrated west, quickly grew into the accepted belief that serious writers were lured to Hollywood, where they cashed handsome paychecks, lounged poolside in the Mediterranean climate, and basked in the reflected glow of Hollywood glamour. While there, they wrote beneath their dignity, working on unworthy material, and thus risked dulling their real gifts. Screenwriting, then, was essentially hack work, and Hollywood was dangerous ground for writers whatever its allures. In the immediate wake of the deaths days apart of Fitzgerald himself and of Nathanael West, Edmund Wilson distilled what he termed "Hollywood's already appalling record of talent depraved and wasted" into these sardonic couplets:

> What shining phantom folds its wings before us?
> What apparition, smiling, yet remote?
> Is this – so portly yet so highly porous –
> The old friend who went west and never wrote?[6]

Thus arose the myth of Hollywood as destroyer of writers. The 1930s were in fact bookended by two such writers, Herman Mankiewicz and Clifford Odets. Mankiewicz had moved west in 1926, leaving behind a successful career as both theater critic and playwright in Manhattan. He urged his friends back East to follow, wiring Ben Hecht that "MILLIONS ARE TO BE GRABBED OUT HERE AND YOUR ONLY COMPETITION IS IDIOTS STOP DON'T LET THIS GET AROUND."[7] However, by the end of the 1930s Mankiewicz was very much a lost man, drinking heavily and considered unreliable by the studios. His career was only salvaged when Orson Welles hired him to draft a script for *Citizen Kane*. The second writer, Clifford Odets, arrived in Hollywood straight from a series of successes with the politically engaged Group Theater, including *Waiting for Lefty* (1935) and *Golden Boy* (1937). He married a glamorous starlet, Luise Rainer, purchased the requisite mansion with swimming pool, and joined the Hollywood social whirl. Although he enjoyed some success as a screenwriter through the 1940s and 1950s, his promising career as a playwright had ended for good. There were many other "old friends," in Wilson's words, "who went west and never wrote" among the hundreds of writers who migrated to Los Angeles at some point in the 1930s.

That said, like all such myths, the Hollywood-as-destroyer narrative distorts by reduction, and the actual historical experience of writers in the studios during the 1930s proves more nuanced. In particular, the assertion of Hollywood's ill-treatment of writers is largely just that: myth; many writers found the studios civilized and the work congenial. "I loved it," playwright George Oppenheimer recalled of his years working for Samuel Goldwyn. He added, "I was employed, free of debts, and moving in an ambience of glamor. Small wonder that I too was beglamored."[8] Veteran screenwriter Ben Hecht recalled of this time, "For many years Hollywood held this double lure for me, tremendous sums of money, for work that required no more effort than a game of pinochle" (516).

Those writers who hoped to establish themselves in Hollywood or yearned for more control over their scripts pursued a number of strategies to cope with the reality that, as writers, they were essentially powerless in the studios. Many formed partnerships with established directors or producers they respected, as Dudley Nichols did with John Ford or as William Faulkner did with Howard Hawks. Others became producers or directors themselves, most successfully the writing partners Billy Wilder and Charles Brackett. In short, a sufficient number of Eastern writers enjoyed productive and happy careers in Los Angeles. Yet, for all that, the notion that Hollywood is dangerous territory for writers has persisted, and Fitzgerald, it turns out, is often presented as Exhibit A in the indictment of the film industry's treatment of writers. In the three and a half years he lived in Los Angeles before his death, this indictment reads, the studios employed Fitzgerald only intermittently. Ultimately, he was reduced to taking lesser work at much less pay, and then only when he could find it. When he did work in the studios, it was with a series of unsympathetic collaborators and interfering producers. Hollywood's abuse of Fitzgerald surfaces most vividly in Budd Schulberg's novel *The Disenchanted* (1950), based on the disastrous trip the two took from Hollywood to Dartmouth College (Schulberg's alma mater) while working on the script for a campus musical called *Winter Carnival*. In New Hampshire in midwinter and annoyed at being paraded in front of the literature faculty by both Schulberg and the film's producer, Walter Wanger, a tired and sick Fitzgerald publicly fell off the wagon. An embarrassed Wanger fired him on the spot and sent him packing back to Los Angeles. Fitzgerald's screenwriting career never quite recovered.

Thus, Fitzgerald's experience in Hollywood very much involved a third kind of mythmaking, this at the personal level given that his final Hollywood years complete the dramatic arc of Fitzgerald's rise, fall, and rebirth. *The Last Tycoon* was "Fitzgerald's most mature piece of work," insisted Edmund Wilson when the manuscript was first published in

1941. It was "far and away the best novel we have had about Hollywood."[9] A decade after Fitzgerald's death, biographer Arthur Mizener and Budd Schulberg, in both fiction and memoir, picked up Wilson's claim to argue that even if Fitzgerald had failed as a screenwriter, he had still risen phoenix-like from the ashes of his wrecked career. Fitzgerald the novelist had not lost his talent and should be judged not by his failures in Hollywood but rather by his undiminished skills as evidenced in *The Last Tycoon*. Moreover, in the process, Fitzgerald had also helped create a distinct genre of twentieth-century American fiction, the Hollywood novel.

Indeed, Hollywood as setting and the film industry as subject provided any number of writers a means to engage larger issues swirling through American culture in the late 1930s, among them the seeming failure of the American industrial economy, and the rise of fascism and communism as viable alternatives to democratic capitalism. Eastern writers from James M. Cain to Nathanael West also understood that California generally had long gripped the American imagination – as the site of the fabled gold rush and as the new American Eden, a veritable paradise regained at the farthest reaches of the continent, the last frontier. The word "Hollywood" itself connoted for writers far more than the stereotypes of glamour and celebrity. Indeed, it was one of the most resonant words in the twentieth-century writer's vocabulary. Nowhere else but in Hollywood were the paradoxes of American life and cultural values – success and failure, wealth and poverty, art and commerce – so starkly opposed. Norman Mailer's *The Deer Park* (1955), Joan Didion's *Play It as It Lays* (1970), David Mamet's *Speed-the-Plow* (1988), and Michael Tolkin's *The Player* (1988) attest to the persistence of the genre, but at the end of the Depression and as world war loomed, three books written at essentially the same time established its defining features.

Hollywood novels, according to cultural historian Morris Dickstein, "looked to the wider world of Southern California that enclosed the movies and matched their fantastic culture. The novels focused more on those who made the films – producers, writers, studio heads – than on those that appeared in them. Power, not stardom, was their subject; naked ambition, not the hunger for celebrity."[10] Thus Budd Schulberg's *What Makes Sammy Run?* (1940) dissected Hollywood from the inside, skewering the producer class. In Sammy Glick, his shamelessly dishonest but wildly successful Hollywood producer, Schulberg saw the "blueprint of a way of life that was paying dividends in America in the first half of the twentieth century."[11] In *The Day of the Locust* (1939), Nathanael West saw in the shattered dreams of Hollywood dress extras and naïve retirees, their desires first stimulated then thwarted by the movies, nothing less than the American dream reduced to a monstrous nightmare.

In telling the story of Monroe Stahr in *The Last Tycoon* (1941), Fitzgerald also connected to the broader sweep of American history. Stahr was not only the powerful and assured head of a major studio, but he was also squeezed between, and ultimately defeated by, the forces of organized labor and capital. Stahr was fading, literally the last of an era of individualists who could dominate whole industries. In this sense, *The Last Tycoon* expands and completes Fitzgerald's sharp critique of America in cultural decline begun in *The Great Gatsby* (1925). In writing about Hollywood, then, Schulberg, West, and Fitzgerald each found they could write about America as a whole, and this became a defining characteristic of the genre.

F. Scott Fitzgerald may not have had a knack for screenwriting (and there is some debate about this), but he observed the studios with his sharp eye. He understood well the writer's peculiar status and role in that domain. In a crucial scene in *The Last Tycoon*, Monroe Stahr meets with Arthur Brimmer, the communist labor leader in Los Angeles, to help organize the Screen Writers Guild. "It looks to me like a try for power," Stahr tells Brimmer of the effort to form the Guild, "and all I am going to give the writers is money" (*LT* 122). Money but no power: that was the writer's bargain with the studios in Fitzgerald's time. Much the same remains true to this day.

NOTES

1 M. J. Bruccoli, *Some Sort of Epic Grandeur: The Life of F. Scott Fitzgerald*, 2nd rev. ed. (Columbia, SC: University of South Carolina Press, 2002), 257. Subsequent references to this work are included in the text.
2 B. Schulberg, *The Four Seasons of Success* (Garden City: Doubleday, 1972), 97.
3 D. Crafton, *The Talkies: American Cinema's Transition to Sound, 1926–1931*, vol. 4 of *History of the American Cinema* (New York: Charles Scribner's Sons, 1997), 4.
4 T. Balio (ed), *Grand Design: Hollywood as a Modern Business Enterprise, 1930–1939*, vol. 5 of *History of the American Cinema* (Berkeley: University of California Press, 1993), 8. Subsequent references to this work are included in the text.
5 M.D. Huettig, *Economic Control of the Motion Picture Industry* (Philadelphia: University of Pennsylvania Press, 1944), 69.
6 E. Wilson, *The Boys in the Back Room* (San Francisco: Colt Press, 1941), 5.
7 B. Hecht, *Child of the Century* (New York: Simon and Schuster, 1954), 272. Subsequent references to this work are included in the text.

8 G. Oppenheimer, *The View from the Sixties: Memoirs of a Life Spent* (New York: David McKay, 1966), 123.

9 E. Wilson, foreword to *The Last Tycoon: An Unfinished Novel* by F. Scott Fitzgerald (New York: Charles Scribner's Sons, 1941), x.

10 M. Dickstein, *Dancing in the Dark: A Cultural History of the Great Depression* (New York: W. W. Norton, 2009), 323.

11 B. Schulberg, *What Makes Sammy Run?* (New York: Random House, 1941), 303.

Figure 38.1. Irving Thalberg and Norma Shearer, ca. 1936 (Courtesy of Mark A. Vieira and the Starlight Studio).

38

The Golden Age of Hollywood

Laura Rattray

F. Scott Fitzgerald's delight in visual adventures guaranteed from the outset that Hollywood and its movies would hold for him a genuine, if at times tarnished, allure. While a number of his contemporaries responded with unadulterated bile, targeting the industry that had offered them financial salvation with Hollywood novels dipped in venom, Fitzgerald – whose own relationship with Hollywood was complex, often exasperated, and troubled – remained a writer who recognized the transformative possibilities of the Hollywood factory of dreams. During the author's protracted, final period in Hollywood, *Stars and Films of 1937* effusively proclaimed this of cinema: "As an industry it ranks in the first half dozen; as an art it is the most virile and progressive of our time; as an entertainment of the peoples of the world it has no rival. It is one of the crucibles in which the analysis of our times will be formed."[1] Acutely aware of the potency of the image, Fitzgerald – who as a young man had worked in advertising – could never quite promote himself to best advantage in the film industry, yet for all his misgivings he remained attuned to the glamour and power of cinema, and in three periods of his career he experienced Hollywood's inner workings firsthand (Figure 38.1.).

Fitzgerald's timing almost always proved prescient, and signature events in his personal life were often uncannily linked to the wider social scene. In the 1920s, he would brand popular culture, an emerging youth culture, consumerism, and the Jazz Age into the American literary consciousness; his third novel prophetically warned an overindulgent, frenetic country of the hangover to come; and the unraveling of the Fitzgeralds' personal lives almost perfectly coincided with national collapse at the onset of the new decade. Similarly, the magic and excitement of film entered Fitzgerald's imagination at approximately the same moment it entered the popular imagination of America. (He was born one year after the Lumière brothers first projected moving pictures onto a screen.) While defining the writer's lifelong connection with movies as "shifting and frequently ambivalent," Ruth Prigozy observes that "no other author of his time was as enraptured with the medium as Fitzgerald," charting the early trajectory from childhood matinees of westerns in Buffalo through frequent visits to Broadway movie houses during prep school and at Princeton, and his "worship" of silent-film director maestro D. W. Griffith.[2] In a 1922 interview, Fitzgerald matter-of-factly asserted that "[t]he movies are here to stay."[3]

While commentators continue to question the exact dates of the era's inception and duration, the appearance of Warner Brothers' *The Jazz Singer* in 1927 stands as a pivotal moment in ushering in Hollywood's "Golden Age." "Wait a minute, wait a minute, you ain't heard nothing yet," promises Jakie Rabinowitz/Jack Robin (Al Jolson) to his nightclub audience on the silver screen. Though by no means the first production to use sound, *The Jazz Singer* takes its historic place as the first feature film with synchronized speech as well as music – Jolson's songs were synchronously recorded, alongside brief sequences in which he speaks, using the Vitaphone, sound-on-disc system. Whereas Donald Crafton's painstaking research has established that the film was not quite "the monumental success of its journalistic legend," it was, he records, "by any estimation … a hit." By March 24, 1928, the studio claimed the film was "playing in 235 theatres, a 'day and date' record for any film," ensuring a combination of *The Jazz Singer*'s "popularity and the augmented revenue from Warners' expanding theater chain … propelled the company's earnings 500 percent ahead of 1927," with the studio's stock rising from $21 to $132 per share.[4] Meanwhile, William Fox had been investing heavily in a rival sound-on-film system, Movietone, showcasing dialogue shorts and newsreels that captivated audiences with their vocal coverage of iconic events such as Charles Lindbergh's solo transatlantic flight in May 1927. Whereas other movie moguls had initially proved reluctant, continued resistance was futile. For better or worse, sound was here to stay.

As all of the major studios belatedly followed suit, title writing was swiftly consigned to history: talking pictures, "the talkies," took over cinema screens, and theaters across the country were wired for sound. Yet the era-defining transition was not without its casualties. Among them, many of the technical innovations of the silent screen were mothballed, as focus centered on the often-clumsy demands of the microphone hidden within each scene – a situation later immortalized in Gene Kelly and Stanley Donen's loving 1952 parody-homage, *Singin' in the Rain*, with the ear-piercing lament of its phonetically challenged silent-screen star Lina Lamont (Jean Hagen): "I can't make love to a bush!" As Kenneth

Macgowan terms it, "During the first three years of the talkies, from 1928 through 1930, Hollywood all but took the motion out of motion pictures."[5] A number of silent screen stars struggled to make the transition; sound decimated live musical accompaniment; and vaudeville reached its death throes – although the "new" Hollywood offered redeployment, and Jolson himself had been one of vaudeville's biggest stars. (Tellingly, Nathanael West's movie-straggler creation Harry Greener in his 1939 Hollywood novel *The Day of the Locust* is an old-time vaudevillian, in demand only when a director requires his maniacal signature laugh for an asylum or haunted castle scene.) Yet sound brought extraordinary benefits, too: The novelty of the "talkies" allowed Hollywood to stave off the initial impact of the Depression as audiences continued to flock to the movies, generating record profits. For a short time, indeed, film was considered Depression-proof. Benjamin B. Hampton notes that "[t]hrough the final quarter of 1929 and the first four months of 1930, while all other industries were fighting to keep above the floods of disaster, screen theaters rolled up new records of earnings and profits that astonished Wall Street." Hampton adds these details: "Paramount's balance-sheet for that year [1929] showed total assets of $230,000,000, and net income of $15,500,000. Fox's profits amounted to $13,500,000 and Loew's [MGM] to about $12,000,000. Warner Brothers' net income (including First National) was $17,000,000, and RKO's $2,000,000."[6]

As the nation's health continued to deteriorate, however, Hollywood could not remain Depression-proof. In 1932, U.S. unemployment stood at 23.6 percent. The following year, nearly 14 million people were out of work.[7] While moviegoers remained keen to forget their troubles for a few hours in the world of celluloid make-believe, many Americans could no longer spare a dime – the price of admission at some local movie theaters (Thompson and Bordwell 213). Robert Sklar calculates that the total deficit in 1932 for studios and exhibition companies was more than $85 million. In 1933, records Sklar, "the movies reached the nadir of their economic fortunes. Nearly a third of all theaters were shut down," with "[f]our of the eight major motion-picture companies … in financial disarray: Paramount, the industry's leader during the silent period, in bankruptcy; RKO and Universal in receivership; Fox in the process of reorganization and within two years to be taken over by a much smaller company, Twentieth Century."[8] Although the following year the industry revived and theaters reopened, attendance figures increased, and many studios returned to profit, confidence had been knocked: The business of dreams had not proved immune. Even so, timing was crucial. As film historians have observed, it was fortunate that studios had embraced sound before the Depression in a climate in which exhibitors could borrow the money required for sound equipment. If the producers had waited until late October 1929, Macgowan speculates, "sound would have been impossible for ten more years, and receiverships would have come quite some time before 1932" (287).

Against the backdrop of the Depression, however, Hollywood's Golden Age produced its own modern industrial revolution, one dominated by the studio system. The "Big Five," or the "majors," were Paramount, Metro-Goldwyn-Mayer (MGM), 20th Century-Fox (so named following a studio amalgamation in 1935), Warner Brothers, and RKO. Each of the big studios endeavored to maximize its profits by tightly overseeing every stage of the process. Indeed, producing films was only the first part of that process: The majors also controlled distribution and exhibition through their ownership of vast cinema circuits in which to block-book their own products. The biggest studios owned vast acreage of real estate on which to construct sets and from which to order their fantasy world, while directors, cameramen, actors, writers, editors, and composers usually served under contract. The "little three" or "major-minors" – Universal, Columbia, and United Artists – could not compete on the same scale, often either supplying films to fill vacant slots in the Big Five's cinemas or catering to independent theaters outside the majors' control, while the so-called "Poverty Row" studios such as Republic and Monogram specialized in B pictures. In the "hothouse atmosphere" of the studio system, writes John Baxter, "were bred the worst excesses of Hollywood and its greatest glories." The industry results may have been mixed, but the system was phenomenally productive, illustrated by Baxter's directorial tally: "Michael Curtiz made 44 films between 1930 and 1939, Mervyn LeRoy 36, John Ford 26."[9]

In such a hothouse, each studio had a distinctive brand – although never one followed to the exclusion of all others. At Warner Brothers, Darryl Zanuck – head of production between 1929 and 1933 – focused on realism; the early gritty, violent, tightly edited gangster movies *The Public Enemy* and *Little Caesar* in 1931 showcased the talents of James Cagney and Edward G. Robinson, respectively. Even Warners' musicals focused on Depression-born backstage stories, as seen in *42nd Street* (1933) and *Gold Diggers of 1933* (1933) – both films "built round hard work, with attendant sourness and disillusion," notes David Shipman in a chapter memorably titled "Sex, Crime and Booze: Warner Bros. in the Thirties."[10] At the outset of the sound decade, Universal relied on its profitable horror films, casting Bela Lugosi in *Dracula* and Boris Karloff in *Frankenstein*, both released in 1931. At MGM, meanwhile, emphasis fell on classy star-vehicles with larger-than-average budgets, in a program overseen by the "boy wonder" and inspiration for *The Last Tycoon*'s Monroe Stahr, Irving Thalberg, until his premature death in 1936 at the age of 37.

Underpinning the studio system of the Golden Age was the star system. Although not every studio could claim "more stars than there are in heaven," each of the majors boasted its own roster of leading names. Between 1935 and 1938, the number-one box-office star was the ringleted, dimpled cherub, Shirley Temple, with whom America would fall out of love as she committed the cardinal sin of growing up. Often forgotten is that MGM's biggest box-office draw in the early 1930s was the robust Marie Dressler, before her death in 1934; Clark Gable, Greta Garbo, Joan Crawford, Jean Harlow, and Judy Garland were among the studio's brightest and most bankable stars. Deanna Durbin's popularity offered a financial lifeline for beleaguered Universal, while censors' itch Mae West ultimately saved Paramount from bankruptcy with controversial successes such as the 1933 release *She Done Him Wrong.* RKO's most profitable stars during the 1930s were Fred Astaire and Ginger Rogers, whose dance and musical partnership at the studio ran from 1934 to 1939. Warner Brothers' hardworking leading lights included James Cagney, Bette Davis, Humphrey Bogart, and Errol Flynn. (In the summer of 1937, Fitzgerald listed with relish his social meetings with the stars [*LL* 334] and gleefully impressed his daughter by arranging for her to meet her favorite performers, notably "hero" Fred Astaire – an encounter duly reported by Sheilah Graham in "Hollywood Today: A Gadabout's Notebook."[11]) For a star-struck nation, studio publicity was engineered. Inconvenient sexualities, relationships, and pasts were airbrushed from existence; back-stories, names, and identities were often reinvented à la Gatsby's. Fan magazines both fed and fostered the public's seemingly insatiable desire for stories of films and their affluent stars. (The Hollywood novels of Fitzgerald's contemporary Horace McCoy present fan magazines as criminally culpable, most dramatically when Dorothy Trotter commits suicide in *I Should Have Stayed Home* [1938] and a ghoulish request by press photographers to view the "Instrument of Death" prompts her grieving friend to surround the lifeless body with movie magazines.[12])

Fitzgerald himself had been attuned to the publicity, fictional, and commercial possibilities of Hollywood long before his first visit. Indeed, he wrote film treatments and scripts from the outset of his career – unsuccessfully submitting a number of these before the publication even of his first novel. Film rights to his early work would establish an important income stream, while his second novel, *The Beautiful and Damned* (1922) – in many respects Fitzgerald's prescient dress rehearsal for a Hollywood novel – offered the author's first major film protagonist in the figure of "Films Par Excellence" studio tycoon Joseph Bloeckman. In an April 1925 letter to Perkins, Fitzgerald concluded that if he could support himself "with no more intervals of trash" he would "go on as a novelist"; "[i]f not he would quit, come home, go to Hollywood and learn the movie business" (*LL* 107). Though he would later label them "failures" (*LL* 330), the author's first two visits to Hollywood served their purpose. Returning from Europe to an offer of a $3,500 advance to write a screenplay for a flapper film, *Lipstick*, which would never be produced, Fitzgerald made the trip to Hollywood with his wife in January 1927. His second Hollywood adventure also resulted in a check, but no realized film: In the autumn of 1931 he accepted an offer of $1,200 per week from MGM to work on a Jean Harlow vehicle, *Red-Headed Woman* – only to be replaced by Anita Loos.

By the time of Fitzgerald's final, thirty-month residency, however, Hollywood's Golden Age was at its most dazzling. Between July 1937 and his death in December 1940, the studios produced an unrivaled roll call of screen triumphs: *The Wizard of Oz*, *Gone With the Wind* (on which he fleetingly worked), *The Adventures of Robin Hood*, *Stagecoach*, *Mr. Smith Goes to Washington*, *Jezebel*, *Dark Victory*, *The Roaring Twenties*, and *Ninotchka*, to name a few. Fitzgerald's own reputation by this point, however, was much less alluring. Anthony Powell recalled in "Hollywood Canteen" that "one could not fail to notice the way people in Hollywood spoke of Fitzgerald. It was almost as if he were already dead; at best risen from the dead, and of somewhat doubtful survival value."[13] It was a mythology to which Fitzgerald himself contributed. Morris Dickstein notes that "[t]he legend of his decline, which he helped broadcast – everyone who met him during his last years in Hollywood heard it – continues to haunt his reputation today."[14] Fitzgerald's letters often prove the most faithful barometer of his fluctuating responses to Hollywood and his work in this period: "I feel a certain excitement. The third Hollywood venture" (*LL* 330); "You don't realize that what I am doing here is the last tired effort of a man who once did something finer and better"(*LL* 363); "To say I'm disillusioned is putting it mildly" (*LL* 343); "I love it here. It's nice work if you can get it and you can get it if you try about three years" (*LL* 341); "am I glad to get out! Ive hated the place" (*LL* 375). It was in 1936 – a period in which Fitzgerald was away from Hollywood – that he made his strongest criticism, in the often-quoted passage about the novel "becoming subordinated to a mechanical and communal art that, whether in the hands of Hollywood merchants or Russian idealists, was capable of only the tritest thought, the most obvious emotion" (*CU* 78). Yet Fitzgerald was no literary Lazarus: 1937 to 1940 were typically productive years for the writer – through economic necessity as much as through virtue – resulting in a mix of full-time studio work, in excess of thirty articles and stories (among them the Pat Hobby series), and seventeen of the projected thirty episodes of the novel *The Last Tycoon*.

From July 1937 to the end of 1938 Fitzgerald wrote under contract for MGM, earning $1,000 per week for the first six months and $1,250 per week in 1938. During this tenure, he worked on scripts for *A Yank at Oxford*, *Three Comrades*, *Infidelity*, *Marie Antoinette*, *The Women*, and *Madame Curie*. Hollywood screenwriting in the Golden Age was typically a collaborative, communal process – and hard work. Writers were assigned projects; they often worked in teams; they could be moved from one project to another without notice; and – a particular bête noir – unless a writer had contributed at least 25 percent of the screenplay, he or she was not entitled to a screen credit. Fitzgerald both experienced and captured this collaborative process of screenwriting. In *The Last Tycoon*, George Boxley, a novelist employed to work on a screenplay, complains to Monroe Stahr about the working practices and the "hacks" with which he is teamed: "'I can't get what I write on paper,' broke out Boxley. 'You've all been very decent but it's a sort of conspiracy. Those two hacks you've teamed me with listen to what I say but they spoil it – they seem to have a vocabulary of about a hundred words'" (*LT* 31). Stahr informs another writer, Wylie White, that it is a "question of merchandise," that he is a "merchant" and wants to "buy" what is in his mind (*LT* 17). Fitzgerald's own frustrations would memorably boil over when Joseph Mankiewicz rewrote part of his script for *Three Comrades* (the only film for which the author received a screen credit, a co-credit with E. E. Paramore, Jr.). "I feel somewhat outraged," he protested (*LL* 344) – to no avail, petulantly renaming Mankiewicz "Monkeybitch" thereafter. Yet the system about which many writers complained brought results, seemingly at times against the odds. "Seventeen writers and tinkerers" worked on the script of *Gone with the Wind* before the film was done,[15] and while on paper the "Selznick process" may have suggested a recipe for disaster, on screen it translated into cinematic magic. Although writers often felt aggrieved, they were not alone in their working conditions. Even the star actors of the Golden Age were luxuriously indentured: Warner sisters Bette Davis and Olivia de Havilland were notable luminaries who would take their studio brothers to court in protest at the films they were being forced to make and/or at the practice of adding suspension time to an already long (seven-year) contract.

In January 1939 MGM did not renew Fitzgerald's option, obliging him to seek short-term, insecure freelance opportunities with Columbia, Paramount, Universal, Samuel Goldwyn, and Twentieth Century-Fox. The sale to *Esquire* at $250 apiece of seventeen Hollywood stories about fictional studio hack, Pat Hobby – stories often mistakenly read as autobiographical portraits – bought time for Fitzgerald's projected new novel, *The Last Tycoon*, on which he worked between August 1939 and December 1940. "[I]t is not the story of deterioration," he wrote; "it is not depressing and not morbid in spite of the tragic ending ... I hope it will be something new, arouse new emotions perhaps even a new way of looking at certain phenomena" (*LL* 412). While most Hollywood novels focused on the aspirants, the extras, the soon-despairing young hopefuls, Fitzgerald takes his readers through the studio gates to the heart of the business, to its working practices and production processes. His Hollywood can be dark, duplicitous, even murderous, but in its illumination of the visionary figure of Monroe Stahr – a studio producer who aspires to great art while mastering the machinations of the movie-making process – the novel also acknowledges the potential of Hollywood's Golden Age. Sketching the figure of Stahr in September 1939, Fitzgerald suggested that "[s]uccess came to him young, at twenty-three, and left certain idealisms of his youth unscarred. Moreover, he is a worker. Figuratively he takes off his coat and pitches in" (*LL* 410). The "great literary invention of the thirties," according to Leslie Fiedler, was the Hollywood book, or, "more properly," he suggests, "the anti-Hollywood book."[16] *The Last Tycoon* gestated at the end of this period and was published posthumously in its unfinished form in 1941. Despite the work's "tragic ending," however, Fitzgerald would not compose a poison-pen letter to the industry, leaving instead a nuanced literary bequest to Hollywood's Golden Age.

Ultimately, MGM's motto – *Ars Gratia Artis* – was a luxury neither the studios nor Fitzgerald could afford. For both studio magnate and professional author, financial realities ensured that artistic choices were rarely made without considering the marketplace. In a telling 1937 article, "The Task of Trying to Please You," producer Samuel Goldwyn concluded with this observation: "I grant that there are things wrong with the motion-picture industry. After all, it is still only 25 years old. When you consider that the stage has 3,000 years of experience and background on its side, then we have done pretty well in only a quarter of a century" (Watts 8). At times brutal and unforgiving in its processes, the Golden Age did not always guarantee gold standard, yet it would prove overall a phenomenal era of American filmmaking, its collective achievements unmatched. The Golden Age outlived Fitzgerald: Further studio triumphs were to be realized in the decade beyond. In a letter to his daughter, Scottie, the year before he died, Fitzgerald wrote, "Sorry you got the impression that I'm quitting the movies – they are always there."[17] In the final frame, F. Scott Fitzgerald undoubtedly did not produce anything like his best work *for* Hollywood. *The Last Tycoon*, however, suggests some of his finest writing would have been *about* Hollywood and its Golden Age: Hollywood, that is, via the novelist's page.

NOTES

1 S. Watts, foreword in S. Watts (ed.), *Stars and Films of 1937* (London: Daily Express Publications, 1937), 5. Subsequent references to this work are included in the text.

2 R. Prigozy, "Fitzgerald's Flapper and Flapper Films of the Jazz Age" in K. Curnutt (ed.), *A Historical Guide to F. Scott Fitzgerald* (New York: Oxford University Press, 2004), 129–61; 129–30.

3 F. S. Fitzgerald quoted in M. J. Bruccoli and J. R. Bryer (eds.), *F. Scott Fitzgerald in His Own Time: A Miscellany* (Kent, OH: Kent State University Press, 1971), 249.

4 D. Crafton, *The Talkies: American Cinema's Transition to Sound, 1926–1931* (Berkeley: University of California Press, 1999), 521, 111.

5 K. Macgowan, *Behind the Screen: The History and Techniques of the Motion Picture* (New York: Delacorte Press, 1965), 289. Subsequent references to this work are included in the text.

6 B. B. Hampton, *History of the American Film Industry* (New York: Dover Publications Inc., 1970), 408–9.

7 K. Thompson and D. Bordwell, *Film History: An Introduction*, 2nd edn. (New York: McGraw-Hill, 2003), 213. Subsequent references to this work are included in the text.

8 R. Sklar, *Movie-Made America: A Social History of American Movies* (New York: Random House, 1975), 162.

9 J. Baxter, *Hollywood in the Thirties* (London: Tantivy Press, 1968), 9–10.

10 D. Shipman, *The Story of Cinema* (New York: St. Martin's Press, 1982), 241.

11 Undated clipping in M. J. Bruccoli, S. F. Smith, J. P. Kerr (eds.), *The Romantic Egoists* (New York: Charles Scribner's Sons, 1974), 218.

12 H. McCoy, *I Should Have Stayed Home* (London: Serpent's Tail, 1996), 128. For a discussion of McCoy's Hollywood novels and the impact of the studio experience on his writing style and approach to fiction, see L. Rattray, "Cinematic License: Editorial Imprints on the Hollywood Novels of Horace

McCoy," *Papers of the Bibliographical Society of America* 102:1 (March 2008), 77–94.

13 A. Powell, "Hollywood Canteen: A Memoir of F. Scott Fitzgerald in 1937," *Fitzgerald/Hemingway Annual* (1971), 71–78; 75.

14 M. Dickstein, "Fitzgerald: The Authority of Failure" in J. R. Bryer, R. Prigozy, and M. R. Stern (eds.), *F. Scott Fitzgerald in the Twenty-first Century* (Tuscaloosa: University of Alabama Press, 2003), 301–16; 304.

15 R. Harwell (ed.), Gone With the Wind *as Book and Film* (Columbia, SC: University of South Carolina Press, 1983), 30.

16 L. Fiedler, *Waiting for the End* (London: Cape, 1965), 51.

17 Letter cited by R. A. Martin, "Hollywood in Fitzgerald: After Paradise" in J. R. Bryer (ed.), *The Short Stories of F. Scott Fitzgerald: New Approaches in Criticism* (Madison: University of Wisconsin Press, 1982), 127–48; 148.

Figure 39.1. F. Scott Fitzgerald and Sheilah Graham in Encino, California in 1939 at the Horton estate (Courtesy of the Sheilah Graham Westbrook estate).

39

Hollywood and the Gossip Columnists

Gail D. Sinclair

The popularity of American films increased steadily during the 1920s but suffered a blow with the financial crash at decade's end and the onslaught of subsequent Depression-era economics. Going to the "moving picture show" became a luxury and ticket sales faltered accordingly, but a need for escapism kept the public turning to entertainment nonetheless, and Hollywood was happy to oblige by providing a temporary balm in the darkened theaters on Main Street. The best-known writers of the day, including F. Scott Fitzgerald, signed with major studios to churn out scripts, and technical advances such as sound and color, in tandem with the growing influence of the studio system and its burgeoning stable of actors, helped define the 1930s as the "Golden Age" of Hollywood, where stars were born, or, put more aptly, where powerful movie moguls and studios manufactured them. An insatiable appetite for details about those glamorous figures whose larger-than-life images beamed in the darkness sparked a new form of pseudo-journalist: the gossip columnist. While many viewed these reporters with shades of disdain for the unsavory aspects of voyeurism, negative innuendo, and gossip-mongering in which they dealt, they became stars of a sort in their own right, wielding enormous power in at least two camps: the court of public opinion, which clamored to hear the latest about the professional lives and private steps and missteps of the stars, and the studios, where executives jockeyed to garner favorable publicity that would promote their actors. Thus began the dance between the purveyors of Hollywood's inside scoop, influential forces shaping tinsel town's "star system," and the mass consumer.

Three columnists forging the way in this relatively new genre – Louella Parsons, Hedda Hopper, and Sheilah Graham – were aptly dubbed Hollywood's "Unholy Trio" as they carved out a delicate balance between befriending and advancing the notoriety of those in the limelight while also holding the potential to destroy or at least disparage stars' reputations in the public eye (Figure 39.1.). Each woman had begun her career elsewhere and gravitated to the rapidly developing movie capital of the West hoping to boost her own fame by riding on the coattails of the rich and famous and reporting news related to them. A fiercely competitive rivalry developed by the mid-1930s as all three vied to win coveted syndicated newspaper columns and popular radio programs. These mass media outlets provided collective audiences eventually numbering in the millions, and as Parsons, Hopper, and Graham competed to become the most revered or feared voice making or breaking the stars, they sometimes generated as much interest in the purveyors of gossip as did the gossip itself.[1]

The first and arguably most influential member of the triumvirate of tattle was Louella Parsons, who reigned as undisputed "First Lady of Hollywood" gossip from 1925 until 1937, when serious competition emerged. Unlike Hopper and Graham, Parsons had an initial advantage because she came to California with a background in the print industry and with the support of newspaper magnate William Randolph Hearst. Parsons got her journalistic start as a small-town news reporter in Dixon, Illinois in the first decade of the twentieth century and by 1910 was employed as a reporter for the *Chicago Tribune*. In addition, she worked as a script reader and writer for Essanay Studios, eventually selling to the company one of her own screenplays in 1912. In 1915 she also published *How to Write for the Movies*, a guide for would-be film writers, in which she admonishes them with these words: "When we consider that many of the greatest minds in the literary world today have given and are now giving their work to be ground in the studio mill into big feature productions it will be realized how essential it is to master the detail and to learn scenario construction."[2] Parsons eventually broke with Essanay over demands for a larger salary but continued cultivating her path toward the industry at large.

Parsons's next career step was to convince the *Chicago Herald* to adopt her proposed movie column, and she took advantage of the fact that stars traveling by train from New York to Los Angeles had a two-hour layover in the Windy City and time to kill before resuming their westward journey. Eventually, she moved east and took a job at the *New York Morning Telegraph,* and while there she caught the eye of Hearst. He hired her for his *New York American* publication in 1922 and, after Parsons's 1925 bout with tuberculosis and a move to the west for health reasons, Hearst engaged her again. They continued a professional relationship in various forms throughout her career. Although few would deny the long-standing and independent power Parsons had in Hollywood, the success of her professional relationship with Hearst likely had much to do with her highly favorable support of his mistress, Marion Davies, and of her acting career. Generally considered to have comedic talent, Davies was perhaps unwisely pushed by Hearst to star in serious roles he often bankrolled or over which he exerted influence, and these parts tended to provide the actress more critical detractors than supporters. Showing her loyalty to Davies, Parsons championed the actress with a plea in her column to "give the girl a chance."

Even with backing by the powerful newspaper czar, Parsons's early years in Hollywood in the mid-1920s did not bring immediate success as she struggled to find a niche. After two successive failed radio shows, the failures of which she blamed for the most part on inarticulate stars whose careers had been anchored in the silent films and had not successfully translated to the "talkies," she established in 1934 a radio interview program, *Hollywood Hotel.* An outgrowth of the earlier *45 Minutes in Hollywood*, Parsons found in this latest rendition a successful format, financial backing, an eager audience, and the interest of major studios in supplying stars for the programs. Where Warner Brothers, Metro-Goldwyn-Mayer (MGM), Paramount, United Artists, Twentieth-Century Fox, Universal, Columbia, and other production companies had previously shied away from participating in movie-related radio programs because of the damage that potentially negative press could pose, they now came to appreciate the flip side of such power. Parsons introduced an early version of movie trailers, the "sneak preview," which became a vehicle for stars to read dramatically from scripts of soon-to-be released films. With large and interested audiences ready-made and eagerly buying subscriptions or tuning in to the radio to learn the latest on the "glam set," studios could generate interest in their actors and boost ticket sales through promotion of upcoming films, and, better still, they were able to do so without investing capital that might instead be spent on production.

By the mid-1930s Parsons's reputation was solidified, and the fact that rivals entering the scene openly competed with her only served to strengthen her notoriety and competitive spirit. Hollywood insider Luke Sader notes, "The truth is that, throughout her more than forty-year career, Parsons was always looking over her shoulder. She constantly had to fight to stay on top, and to make her way not merely in a man's world, but in the labyrinth of show business."[3] Her career became the paradigm that others would follow and try, mostly unsuccessfully, to eclipse.

Parsons had wisely learned to straddle the divide between appealing to small-town mores and the average American's desire to peer into the complicated and sometimes sordid lives of those whose daily regimen was anything but ordinary. She championed the stars as "just folks" living the normal lives of homemakers and breadwinners even as they challenged the boundaries of convention with the overlay of glamorous social soirées and flirtations with infidelity – in short, living their lives as they coped with the traps and trappings of wealth and fame. Biographer Samantha Barbas writes that in order to assure readers of her own Midwestern grounding, although she had abandoned the heartland for the glitz of Hollywood, "Parsons played up her rural roots and referred frequently to her friends back in Dixon." Barbas characterized this as "a shrewd strategy in a nation that was still largely rural and that associated rural imagery with honesty and tradition."[4] Unlike Graham, who would hide her humble beginnings spent in an English orphanage, and Hopper, who enhanced her almost caricaturized persona as a purveyor of glamour sporting an endless array of exaggerated hats and over-the-top fashion, Parsons presented a rather plain figure by Hollywood standards and magnified her role as one of the common disenfranchised masses.

Arriving on Hollywood's journalistic scene in midcentury and nearly a decade behind Parsons, Hedda Hopper and Sheilah Graham had both begun their careers as actors, not as writers: the English-born Graham had performed on stage, and Hopper initially acted on the stage and then in modest film roles. Each could boast only mediocre success as entertainers, and both were shrewd enough to recognize they would be lost in the ranks of aspiring starlets if they continued to pursue acting as a career. Like Parsons, Hopper and Graham saw a rising opportunity with tangential but significant connections to the world of entertainment-industry fame to which they aspired, and the growing use of mass media for information dissemination provided the career break each sought.

Hedda Hopper's occupational description, "actress turned gossip columnist," succinctly encapsulates her years in Hollywood. With an active career of more than two decades – one that was active but lackluster – to her credit and appearances in over 100 films in mostly supporting roles, Hopper was at a crossroads by the mid-1930s. Aging in Hollywood was, and is, not conducive to landing good parts, and she approached her career's death knell, a fiftieth birthday, with a keen understanding that she must look for a new vocation. Having been the first of the Unholy Trio to arrive in the film capital, she was the last to enter the gossip business. It was her good fortune, a talented nose for finding juicy stories, and insider connections that included support from MGM studio boss Louis

B. Mayer that opened the door in 1937 to Hopper's writing a column for Esquire Feature Syndicate and to what would quickly be recognized as her true calling. Her newspaper column, "Hedda Hopper's Hollywood," found a home in the *Los Angeles Times* in 1938, and *The Hedda Hopper Show* made its radio debut in 1939. With the success of both these ventures, she soon entered into contention for the title "Queen of Hollywood," and her rivalry with Louella Parsons became notorious. An initial friendship in which Hopper willingly supplied Parsons insider scoop about MGM cohorts or their entertainment industry friends turned vitriolic as these women battled it out in competing arenas for the best "dish" about the stars. Critics disagree about which woman was the most vicious purveyor of the poisonous pen and the sharpened tongue, but Hopper seemed especially to delight in such power and even named her Beverly Hills home "The House That Fear Built."

Hopper spent the next several decades relishing the kind of influence that attended the role of gossip columnist, and she broadened her voice beyond being simply the authority on the stars. Social and cultural historian Jennifer Frost notes that "the movies came to be seen by audiences, moviemakers, and government officials as 'critical carriers' of cultural meanings and messages, powerfully influencing politics," and Hopper knew this.[5] When her East Coast rival columnist Walter Winchell gravitated in the 1940s from gossip-slinging to politics as the world's stage shifted toward war, Hopper followed suit. She took a more politicized stance and exercised her power of the pen on topics far more substantial than infidelity or divorce-mill rumors or the popularity or failure of the latest film. Hollywood had set a precedent for involvement in the political scene with such film stars as Carole Lombard and Clark Gable, among others, who supported the war effort. Lombard died in a 1942 plane crash after attending a rally at which she had raised more than two million dollars for the war effort, and her death would be deemed the first American female casualty suffered for the cause. Her husband and fellow film star Clark Gable temporarily left his career shortly after her death and joined the military with an assigned special duty heading a film unit for the aerial gunnery division. Hopper closely followed and reported on these newsworthy events as well as the politically related involvement of other stars sympathetic to the war efforts.

Writer/director/producer/star Charlie Chaplin also stepped fully into the stream of social commentary, offering up in film and elsewhere his controversial liberal views, thus bringing further attention to the power of the film industry to influence national discourse. Although Hopper and

Chaplin actively embraced anti-war stances, their politics were radically different, and Hopper openly criticized Chaplin's 1940 film *The Dictator*. She acknowledged the view of those who believed foreign policy "had no place in a movie column," but she went on to say that "they are right, of course, but I was a mother long before I was a columnist." Summoning the old adage "the hand that rocks the cradle rules the world," Hopper argued that mothers should use their power to save their "babies" from the wages of war, and she used her media position to advance this point of view (Frost 172).

Sheilah Graham was arguably the least influential of the Unholy Trio, although some statistics report that her work eventually became more widely read than either that of Parsons or Hopper. Graham had come to America from England in 1933, having already achieved some success in writing popular pieces for the British press and with the intention of landing a job in journalism. With the help of John Wheeler, head of the North American Newspaper Alliance (NANA), she found opportunities simultaneously at two New York-based papers, the *Mirror* and the *Evening Journal*. For the *Evening Journal* she wrote a regular column, "SHEILAH GRAHAM SAYS." When NANA's Hollywood columnist position opened up two years after her arrival in America, Graham talked her way into the job, and on Christmas Eve in 1935 she flew to California and into her life's work.

Graham approached this segment of her career as a complete outsider, landing "in Hollywood with two left feet," as she described it. She confessed, "I had sensed at the beginning that I could reach the head of the class here in only one way – by having the sharpest, most startlingly candid column in Hollywood. Only in that way could I hope to compete with Louella Parsons, the most widely read Hollywood columnist in the country."[6] Graham gradually worked her way into the inner circles, simply showing up at parties or brashly initiating contacts and challenging Parsons's stronghold on the market through sheer pluck and a determination to write a story as she saw it. She attributed her early success to her pledge that "I would write what I saw without fear or favor, as in New York I had begun by writing outspokenly of what others knew but dared not express" (Graham 165). This technique certainly put her on the firing line but also provided an edge that attracted a readership drawn to frankness and outspokenness.

By 1937, when Fitzgerald arrived for a third and final stint in Hollywood – his previous two having been in 1927 and 1931 – Graham was well established and moving in the celebrity circles that were also open to Fitzgerald as chronicler of the Jazz Age. They met, according to Graham, at a party Robert Benchley gave on July 14, 1937, in honor of Graham's engagement to the British aristocrat Lord Donegall. Graham and Fitzgerald's mutual attraction was instant, and she soon abandoned her engagement. She and Scott almost immediately began a relationship that was to continue for three and a half years, ending only with Fitzgerald's death in December 1940.

Fitzgerald, like many acclaimed writers of the time, worked in Hollywood collaborating with other authors who churned out studio scripts for the big production companies, although Fitzgerald's relationship with the film industry was fraught with well-documented frustration. By this time in his life Fitzgerald had become relatively reclusive, and he was not generally interested in the Hollywood social scene. More often than not, after working on scripts at the studio during the day, he spent quiet evenings with Sheilah in one of his rented apartments, or in hers. Their relationship remained a quiet and mostly private affair, in part because Fitzgerald remained married to Zelda, who was institutionalized during much of the time of Fitzgerald's relationship with Graham. Other factors that contributed to the low-key quality of their relationship were Fitzgerald's declining health, his binge drinking, his diminished finances, and possibly a fear, perhaps on both their parts, that a relationship might be perceived as a professional conflict of interest for one or both of them. Graham's autobiographies – *Beloved Infidel*, *College of One: The Story of How F. Scott Fitzgerald Educated the Woman He Loved*, and *The Real F. Scott Fitzgerald: Thirty-Five Years Later* – make it evident that she considered Fitzgerald the love of her life and documented ways that her relationship with Fitzgerald had a profound influence on her life, both personally and professionally. Fitzgerald became her writing coach and personal editor, as well as a sounding board for decisions related to her career. He also took keen interest in educating her in what they would come to call a "College of One," a rigorous curriculum through which Fitzgerald helped Graham compensate for her lack of formal education.

During the period of her relationship with Fitzgerald, Graham wrote a daily column, "Hollywood Today," which she maintained for a remarkable run of thirty-five years, and she also began a radio career. Fitzgerald read the copy of her first script and "painstakingly – and completely – rewrote [the] copy" (Graham 197–98). He also served as voice coach, once flying with her to Chicago for an in-person recording after her first broadcast by phone did not carry her voice well.

Whereas Sheilah Graham enjoyed marked professional success during her relationship with Fitzgerald, one might argue that she provided little value to his career. Of his writing beyond the studio efforts, Fitzgerald published nothing from 1937 to 1939. Drawing a large salary during that time, he put aside other creative work, but when studio jobs dried up in the last eighteen months of his life he went back to writing magazine pieces, selling twenty-two of twenty-four of them to *Esquire*'s Arnold Gingrich, although at a much-reduced rate of $200 to $250, in sharp contrast to his top earnings in the 1920s of $4,000 per story. Seventeen of Fitzgerald's *Esquire* stories centered on Pat Hobby, a washed-up Hollywood hack that perhaps represented an extreme portrayal of Fitzgerald's own fear over the potential fate he and other writers had or might suffer at the hands of studio dominance over artists and their artistic license. Little or no trace of his relationship with Sheilah found its way into these stories, but his experience in Hollywood was obviously his inspiration.

Graham did play an important role in Fitzgerald's unfinished novel *The Last Tycoon*, based loosely on "boy wonder" producer Irving Thalberg. Fitzgerald used his insider knowledge of Hollywood for the material. Graham was, as Fitzgerald's secretary Frances Kroll corroborated, the model for the central female character, Kathleen Moore, and Monroe Stahr and Kathleen Moore's relationship "mirrored Scott's relationship with Sheilah, which had developed into a comfortable, trusting alliance."[7] Their affair seemed to be a stabilizing force for Fitzgerald as he settled back into novel writing, and the relationship also boosted Graham's self-confidence. After Fitzgerald's death, Graham helped Kroll see that the work was placed in the hands of Maxwell Perkins at Scribners, by whom it was published in 1941.

The Golden Age of Hollywood, a term primarily linked with the Hollywood of the 1930s, was an era known for its big-studio domination, star mills, genre films, and many classic films such as *The Wizard of Oz*, *Gone with the Wind*, *Wuthering Heights*, *Casablanca*, *King Kong*, and *Citizen Kane*. The era was also identified as the age in which gossip columnists began to reign, often helping to elevate to stardom such luminaries as Clark Gable, Norma Shearer, Greta Garbo, Joan Crawford, John Barrymore, Jean Harlow, and Gary Cooper. Chief among these columnists were Parsons, Hopper, and Graham – the "Unholy Trio" – whose names perhaps now are better known than those of the minor stars they neglected to mention. They fed the general public's yearning to peek behind the scenes and be privy to that seemingly exotic world.

NOTES

1 Figures vary widely as to the number of newspapers in which Graham, Hopper, and Parsons appeared; there is also little agreement about the number of readers or the number of people in the radio audiences of each of the three. Estimates in each case range from 100 to 600 papers and from 20,000 to tens of millions of subscribers and members of radio audiences. Such variance in statistics has partially to do with the fact that all three women had careers lasting several decades, from the 1930s into the 1950s and 1960s.

2 L. Parsons, *How to Write for the Movies* (Chicago: A. C. McClurg and Company, 1915), 3. Essanay Studios was founded in 1907, quickly became successful, and moved to California in 1913. Screenwriter Allan Dwan later became a famous Hollywood director, and founders George K. Spoor and Gilbert M. Anderson went on to win Academy Honorary Awards for their work as pioneers in the industry.

3 L. Sader, "*The First Lady of Hollywood: A Biography of Louella Parsons* by Samantha Barbas," *Quarterly Review of Film & Video* 26.I (2009), 51–55; 52.

4 S. Barbas, *The First Lady of Hollywood: A Biography of Luella Parsons* (Berkeley: University of California Press, 2005), 48–49.

5 J. Frost, "Dissent and Consent in the 'Good War': Hedda Hopper, Hollywood Gossip, and World War II Isolationism," *Film History* 22 (2010), 170–81; 174. Subsequent references to this work are included in the text.

6 S. Graham and G. Frank, *Beloved Infidel* (New York: Quality Paperback Book Club, 1989), 165. Subsequent references to this work are included in the text.

7 F. K. Ring, *Against the Current: As I Remember F. Scott Fitzgerald* (San Francisco: Donald S. Elli, 1985), 51.

Figure 40.1. Irving Thalberg, ca. 1935 (Courtesy of Mark A. Vieira and the Starlight Studio).

40

Heroes and Hollywood

Robert Sklar

At a particular moment in twentieth-century American culture the names of F. Scott Fitzgerald and Irving Thalberg appeared so closely entwined that the first biography of the motion picture producer, published in 1969, devoted its entire first chapter to the fiction writer, his story "Crazy Sunday," and his unfinished novel *The Last Tycoon*. Bob Thomas's aim in beginning *Thalberg: Life and Legend* in that manner was both to present and to negate the legend that "to a generation of students of Fitzgerald and of Film, Irving G. Thalberg (Figure 40.1.) has been The Last Tycoon." There were "obvious parallels" between Fitzgerald's fictional protagonist Monroe Stahr and Thalberg the actual human being, Thomas conceded, but ultimately the resemblance "becomes obscure."[1] The biographer wished to clear the field and narrate his own factual life story.

Times have changed. The most recent Thalberg biography, Mark A. Vieira's *Irving Thalberg: Boy Wonder to Producer Prince*, published in 2010, mentions Stahr and *The Last Tycoon* not at all. But from a perspective centered on Fitzgerald, the link remains as vital and relevant as ever. How could it be otherwise? In Fitzgerald's often-quoted September 29, 1939, letter to a *Collier's* magazine editor, Kenneth Littauer, pitching his novel-in-progress and summarizing its plot and perspectives, the author famously wrote that his principal male character, then known as Milton Stahr, "is Irving Thalberg – and *this is my great* secret ... Thalberg has always fascinated me. His peculiar charm, his extraordinary good looks, his bountiful success, the tragic end of his great adventure." Further, "I've long chosen him for a hero ... because he is one of the half-dozen men I have known who were built on the grand scale" (*C* 546, 549).

From the beginning of scholarly writing about Fitzgerald – indeed from the period following Fitzgerald's death when Edmund Wilson was assembling the author's notes and manuscripts into what became the original published version of *The Last Tycoon* – questions have been raised about Fitzgerald's use of Thalberg as a heroic model for Monroe Stahr and the particular qualities of heroism that the fictional movie producer may embody. Is the term "hero" simply a synonym for primary protagonist, or does it denote an individual's exalted status, in the fictional or actual world? Wilson had Scribners send his synopsis of the novel's unfinished part to Fitzgerald's secretary, Frances Kroll, for her comments. She responded that "Although Scott definitely told me he did not want to make Stahr a hero in the conventional sense of the word and did not want to justify Stahr's manner of thinking, he did want to present it thoroughly and show the cause of Stahr's reactions."[2] Whether or not one agrees with this formulation after reading *The Last Tycoon* – whether, in short, one may view Stahr as a hero in the conventional sense of the word and find his manner of thinking justified – it serves as a cautionary perspective both on the fictional character and its human counterpart.

The historiography of Thalberg's career remains open to revision, as does Fitzgerald's and Stahr's relations to it. To an earlier generation of Fitzgerald scholars, writing before the advent of systematic academic research on U.S. film history, Thalberg could be characterized, in Henry Dan Piper's words, as "the great organizing genius who, more than anyone else, was responsible for the transformation of a cheap form of entertainment into a billion-dollar, mass-production industry that for a time shaped the tastes and values of movie-goers throughout the world."[3] To Douglas Gomery, a scholar of the Hollywood studio system, writing some four decades later, Thalberg is summarized as "a faithful and trusted employee who knew his place" – which, to be clear, was somewhat lower on the ladder of greatness, genius, and world-historical significance.[4]

Thalberg was born in Brooklyn in 1899 to German-Jewish parents. A heart defect diagnosed in childhood worsened when he contracted rheumatic fever in his teen years, and it was feared he would not live past thirty. He found work as an assistant in the New York offices of another German Jew, Carl Laemmle, founder of the Universal Film Manufacturing Co., and quickly demonstrated his administrative abilities. Laemmle assigned him to manage the company's production facilities at Universal City in southern California, chaotic in the best of times. Thalberg was twenty years old, and the soubriquet "boy wonder" stuck with him ever after. It was a remarkable responsibility for so young a man, to be sure, but it should be remembered that the rapidly expanding movie industry, beyond its middle-aged Jewish immigrant founders, was essentially a young man's game. Within a few years Thalberg was joined in the ranks of leading producers by Hal B. Wallis, also born in 1899;

Walt Disney, born in 1901; and David O. Selznick and Darryl F. Zanuck, both born in 1902, among others.

In 1923 Louis B. Mayer recruited Thalberg as head of production at his film company. The studio system was beginning to take shape. We tend naturally to pay primary attention to its glamorous creative wing in Hollywood, but it may be better understood as an exhibition–distribution system to which the West Coast units were subordinate. The major movie companies owned theaters, for which they needed films, and distribution arms that rented films to unaffiliated theaters; New York told California how many titles were needed each year to keep the theaters running. Big-city theaters might show twenty-five to thirty pictures annually, holding them for two to three weeks if they were popular. However, small-town venues could change programs three times a week; although they were economically marginal to the major companies, they had to be served, in order to placate politicians who otherwise might pass legislation inimical to the industry. The demand for high volume shaped what Hollywood became. Some studios were tasked with producing fifty to sixty films per year, and the major companies together churned out more than three hundred annually.

Mayer and Thalberg fully integrated into the system in 1924 when several different production companies merged to form Metro-Goldwyn-Mayer (MGM), owned by the New York exhibition firm Loew's, Inc. Mayer was to manage MGM and Thalberg became head of production; both received hefty salaries and bonuses as a percentage of profits. But both were, as Gomery states, employees of Loew's and its head, Nicholas Schenck, who did not hesitate, later in the decade, to try to sell the studio out from under them to William Fox. (Fox's fortuitous auto accident and Mayer's clout with the Hoover administration's Justice Department blocked the deal.)

The Thalberg era at MGM ran for a dozen years, until his death from pneumonia in September 1936 at age 37. Perhaps because the company was not required to produce quite as many pictures as studios such as Paramount and Warner Bros., he was able to focus his business acumen on identifying, developing, and managing the appeal of movie stars. He grasped that in the high-volume, high-turnover industry that Hollywood had become, stars were the commodities that audiences recognized and responded to. His obsessive work with writers on improving stories and dialogue, his attention to details such as lighting and camera angles while viewing rushes, his multiple sneak previews in local communities, and his propensity to order retakes were all in the service of shaping narratives and images to enhance the appeal of the company's stars. He was regarded as particularly skillful in guiding the progress of female stars, although his marriage to one of them, Norma Shearer, caused others, such as Joan Crawford, to resent what she regarded as inevitable nepotism.

And speaking of resentment, Mayer's appeared to flourish along with the company's growing prestige and financial success. In 1932, in the depths of the Great Depression, MGM recorded a profit of $8 million; of Thalberg, biographer Vieira writes, "No producer had made so many innovative films, so many quality films, or so many hits in one year as he had in 1932."[5] To the world, it seemed, Thalberg *was* MGM, while Mayer merely signed the checks. Mayer wished to make clear that he was the man on top and deserved the credit; in his version of events, he loved Thalberg like a son and wanted only to prevent the producer from killing himself prematurely through overwork. In December 1932, in the midst of their struggles, Thalberg suffered a heart attack. During his recuperation, Mayer and Schenck restructured the production hierarchy, shifting to a producer unit system that curtailed Thalberg's overall supervisory role.

Others in the industry besides Mayer were reluctant to acquiesce to Thalberg's demigod status. Politically conservative, Thalberg fought with writers who were attempting to establish the Screen Writers Guild and worked with right-wing writers to create a rival company union. He was responsible for the notorious fake newsreels that attacked socialist Upton Sinclair's 1932 campaign (as the Democratic nominee) for California governor. In the culture of dependency in which highly paid performers and writers pursued their careers, antipathy inevitably bubbled up. "Thalberg, not Mayer, was the toughest and most ruthless man in the industry," actor Robert Montgomery, no liberal, later said. "He was nothing of the dreamer. He was money-mad. He was a shrewd, tough, hard, cold operator, with a complete ruthlessness toward people."[6] It is understandable that Fitzgerald could write on September 19, 1936, on learning of the producer's fatal illness, that Thalberg's "final collapse is the death of an enemy for me, though I liked the guy enormously" (*C* 451).

What, finally, has the passage of time meant for Thalberg's reputation and legacy? We are familiar with changes in canons from Fitzgerald's ascendency among American literary figures. Starting, to be sure, from a much more exalted position at his death than Fitzgerald at his, Thalberg from a canonical viewpoint has not maintained his status. After the Academy Awards began in 1927, MGM dominated the selections during the remainder of Thalberg's career, winning the best picture Oscar four out of the nine years for *The Broadway Melody* (1929),

Grand Hotel (1932), *Mutiny on the Bounty* (1935), and *The Great Ziegfeld* (1936), multi-star "prestige" pictures for which the studio was known, and which the industry continually favored as its best public face. By 1997, however, even so establishment-dominated a poll as the American Film Institute's "100 Greatest Movies" – needless to say, Hollywood titles only – included only one MGM film from the Thalberg era, *Mutiny on the Bounty*, in eighty-sixth place. In 2007, the AFI's "10th Anniversary Edition" dropped *Mutiny* but replaced it with a different Thalberg production, the Marx Brothers' first MGM effort, *A Night at the Opera* (1935), in eighty-fifth place.

Central to Thalberg's legend is his curbing of the autonomy of directors, most famously in the case of the profligate Erich von Stroheim, both at Universal with *Foolish Wives* (1922) and at MGM with *Greed* (1924). Few of MGM's directors in the Thalberg era have name recognition in the canons of film history and criticism. Who remembers the directors of *Mutiny on the Bounty* or *A Night at the Opera* (respectively, Frank Lloyd and Sam Wood)? The principal exception is King Vidor, for whom Thalberg, to his credit, facilitated the non-star classic *The Crowd* (1928) and *Hallelujah!* with its all-black cast (1929), as well as significant popular titles such as *The Big Parade* (1926) and *Show People* (1928). As directors have become the dominant creative figures in film theory and criticism, Thalberg's MGM, where producers functioned as auteurs, has become better known historically as a monument to commerce rather than to art.

Fitzgerald's own legend, and the facts of his life's last years, inevitably occupy the center of almost all discussions of *The Last Tycoon* equally with Thalberg's legend and life. From a wider perspective, the novel is also regarded as a significant contribution to the genre of fiction about Hollywood. Where it is rarely considered is in relation to expository works of its time that sought to comprehend and describe the making of motion pictures.

For decades, anecdote and hagiography, on the one hand, and innuendo and condemnation, on the other, had dominated discourses on American movies and moviemakers. Overall, among wide swaths of intellectual opinion, disdain far outweighed devotion, but there were signs of change beginning in the late 1930s, at least in terms of serious efforts of analysis. In 1939, Lewis Jacobs published a sweeping historical account of subjects and styles in U.S. filmmaking, *The Rise of the American Film: A Critical History*. Leo C. Rosten's sociological research on the motion picture community and its personnel appeared in 1941 as *Hollywood: The Movie Colony, The Movie Makers*. And the industry's economic structure was thoroughly explored in a monograph issued in 1941 by the U.S. government's Temporary National Economic Committee, *The Motion Picture Industry – A Pattern of Control*.[7]

Fitzgerald's contemplation of the process and politics of studio filmmaking also occurred in the period when these studies were being prepared and stemmed from a similar purpose of discerning the form and extent of the industry's cultural power. Wilson remarked in his 1941 foreword that *The Last Tycoon* was Fitzgerald's first novel "to deal seriously with any profession or business." He praised the work as "the best novel we have had about Hollywood" and "the only one which takes us inside."[8] From a later historical perspective, one could argue that the novel's treatment of the subject, on the strength of its detail and insight, deserves to be assessed not only among Hollywood novels but also alongside those nonfiction works of the era.[9]

Moreover, Fitzgerald faced up to a difficult subject that most other serious writers of fact or fiction sought to avoid. Hollywood may have accorded Thalberg – as Fitzgerald would also grant Stahr – the status of royalty, but in the culture at large motion picture producers were more commonly regarded condescendingly as vulgar barbarians, if not, at an extreme, as aliens gaining profit from debasing American culture. Anti-Semitism lay at the base of such views. Even sociologist Rosten, born in Poland to Jewish parents and author previously of a highly successful book on immigrant Jewish culture and the Yiddish language, shied away from the topic in his study on Hollywood. He strategically emphasized that a number of motion picture executives who were mistakenly "believed to have 'Jewish' names," such as Zanuck and MGM's Eddie Mannix, actually came from "old native stock" (Rosten, Hollywood, 178).[10]

Fitzgerald did not shrink from identifying Stahr as Jewish, but he did turn the producer's rival, the character based on Mayer, into an Irishman, Brady. "It was a time when Hitler dominated the news and Scott avoided making the villain Jewish," Frances Kroll Ring recalled. He had been rebuked for his portrait of the gangster Meyer Wolfsheim in *The Great Gatsby*, she wrote, and "was stung by the criticism which he considered unfair … sensitivities were running high in this period and Scott did not want to have any link with prejudice or anti-Semitism" (Ring 49).

Cecilia Brady, daughter of Stahr's boss and the novel's narrative voice, makes a single reference to Stahr's Jewish background. Discussing his wish to meet with a Communist organizer, she observes, "He was a rationalist who did his own reasoning without benefit of books – and he had just managed to climb out of a thousand years of Jewry into the late eighteenth century. He could not bear to see it melt away – he cherished the parvenu's passionate loyalty to an imaginary past" (*LT* 119). This is one of several instances in the work in which Cecilia seeks to capture Stahr's mind or his temperament or his indispensable role at the studio with exalted, aphoristic language. Some other examples follow:

"Though Stahr's education was founded on nothing more than a night-school course in stenography, he had a long time ago run ahead through trackless wastes of perception into fields where very few men were able to follow him" (18);

"He was a marker in industry like Edison and Lumière and Griffith and Chaplin. He led pictures way up past the range and power of the theatre, reaching a sort of golden age before the censorship" (*LT* 28);

"Stahr must be right always, not most of the time, but always – or the structure would melt down like gradual butter ... Dreams hung in fragments at the far end of the room, suffered analysis, passed – to be dreamed in crowds, or else discarded" (*LT* 56);

"Stahr like Lincoln was a leader carrying on a long war on many fronts; almost single-handed he had moved pictures sharply forward through a decade, to a point where the content of the 'A productions' was wider and richer than that of the stage. Stahr was an artist only, as Mr. Lincoln was a general, perforce and as a layman" (*LT* 107).

These are evocative, memorable (and, for critics, highly quotable) phrases, but Fitzgerald also gives readers reason to wonder to what extent his narrator can be counted on as a reliable analyst or witness. As if to foreground the question, the author periodically inserts passages in which Cecilia accounts for her sources of information, and others in which she openly admits invention or candidly states her bias. "As for me I was head over heels in love with him then," she tells us, "and you can take what I say for what it's worth" (*LT* 67). Readers at least need to keep in mind a certain skepticism about her romantic effusions, rather than simply accepting them at face value.

Beyond Cecilia's rhetorical flights, other viewpoints about Stahr are offered in her narration. For one, the producer speaks about himself in his own voice – in a less metaphoric register, more practical and also more concretely illuminating. In a conversation with Kathleen Moore, the woman he has pursued because she resembles his deceased wife, Stahr relates that when he was young he wanted to be a chief clerk. "And now you're much more than that," she says, and he replies, "No, I'm still a chief clerk ... That's my gift, if I have one" (*LT* 79). On another occasion, discussing his problems with writers and his system of putting multiple pairs of writers "working independently on the same idea," his interlocutor asks, "But what does make the – the unity?" and Stahr answers, "I'm the unity" (*LT* 58).

During his meeting with the communist organizer Brimmer, Stahr explains that although a writer might have more brains than he, the producer, does, those brains belong to him because he knows how to use them: "Like the Romans – I've heard that they never invented things but they knew what to do with them … I don't say it's right. But it's the way I've always felt – since I was a boy." Brimmer responds, "You know yourself very well, Mr. Stahr" (*LT* 126).

It is in the context of Stahr's specificity about his attributes, rather than Cecilia's soaring phrases, that we might place the one occasion in the text in which the word "hero" is broached. Following the flood at the studio, workers – "electricians, grips, truckers" – pass by Stahr and greet him. In Cecilia's words, "There is no world so but it has its heroes, and Stahr was the hero." Through the changeover to talkies and the economic crisis of the Great Depression, "he had seen that no harm came to them. The old loyalties were trembling now, there were clay feet everywhere; but still he was their man, the last of the princes" (*LT* 27). This hero is not the great genius who transforms world consciousness; he is the chief clerk who understands the company and its personnel as no one else does and has kept it afloat through hard times.

Fitzgerald stages a challenge to the hero in what may be the novel's most significant encounter. Stahr and Kathleen, after having sex at his beach house, go outside at night to watch the grunion fish running through the waves along the shore. A "negro man" is there with two pails to catch them. The man is carrying a work of Emerson inside his shirt, and also Rosicrucian literature, which he disparages. He asks Stahr what work he does, and when Stahr answers, "for the pictures," the man replies, "I never go to movies … There's no profit. I never let my children go." With his pails full, the man leaves, "unaware that he had rocked an industry" (*LT* 92–93).

There may be something a bit forced about a "negro man" with two pails to catch grunion late at night who says, "I really come out to read some Emerson" (*LT* 93). It's clear that Fitzgerald is driving home a point. Emerson is the American philosopher of "Self-Reliance." The "negro man" is a seeker who sees no profit, no benefits or gains, from movies – a medium in its Hollywood version, as Fitzgerald describes it, in which dreams are manufactured for crowds and creative artists are reduced to dependency on a prince.

"They have pictures of their own" (*LT* 94), Stahr says defensively to Kathleen, refusing at first to acknowledge the challenge. The next morning he acts: "Stahr had thrown four pictures out of his plans – one that was going into production this week. They were borderline pictures in point of interest, but at least he submitted the borderline pictures to the negro and found them trash. And he put back on the list a difficult picture that he had tossed to the wolves … He rescued it for the negro man" (*LT* 96).

It is unclear how much emphasis Fitzgerald was placing specifically on race, or whether this reader of Emerson is, so to speak, a "representative man" whose values and goals stand opposed to Stahr's, who does not allow his children to "listen to Stahr's story" (*LT* 96). In either case, the episode makes clear that Fitzgerald is not entirely conceding to Hollywood's cultural power and appeal. "There is no world so but it has its heroes," in Cecilia's uncharacteristically complicated phrasing, and in his own world Stahr is a hero to many. But just as there is more than one opinion about Irving Thalberg's historical significance, so in Fitzgerald's compelling and tantalizing fragment we are left with an open question of how much of a hero his motion picture producer is to the rest of us.

NOTES

1 Bob Thomas, *Thalberg: Life and Legend* (Garden City, NY: Doubleday, 1969), 31.

2 F. K. Ring, *Against the Current: As I Remember F. Scott Fitzgerald* (Berkeley, CA: Creative Arts, 1985), 140. Subsequent references to this work are included in the text.

3 H. D. Piper, *F. Scott Fitzgerald: A Critical Portrait* (New York: Holt, Rinehart and Winston, 1965), 261.

4 D. Gomery, *The Hollywood Studio System: A History* (London: British Film Institute, 2005), 104.

5 M. A. Viera, *Irving Thalberg: Boy Wonder to Producer Prince* (Berkeley, CA: University of California Press, 2010), 184.

6 Qtd. in S. Eyman, *Lion of Hollywood: The Life and Legend of Louis B. Mayer* (New York: Simon & Schuster, 2005), 2004.

7 L. Jacobs, *The Rise of the American Film: A Critical History* (New York: Harcourt, Brace, 1939). L. Rosten, *Hollywood: The Movie Colony, The Movie Makers* (New York: Harcourt, Brace, 1941). Subsequent references to this work are included in the text. D. Bertrand, W. D. Evans, E. L. Blanchard, *The Motion Picture Industry – A Pattern of Control*, Temporary National Economic Committee, Monograph No. 43 (Washington: Government Printing Office, 1941).

8 E. Wilson, foreword to the 1941 edition of *The Last Tycoon*, in *Three Novels of F. Scott Fitzgerald* (New York: Charles Scribner's Sons, 1953), iv.

9 Beyond the novel's text as published, Fitzgerald's notes also offer additional perspectives on the film industry. Different versions of the notes are in the Wilson version, 134–63; M. J. Bruccoli's edition of the novel, *The Love of the Last Tycoon: A Western* (Cambridge: Cambridge University Press, 1993), 131–99; and Bruccoli's *"The Last of the Novelists": F. Scott Fitzgerald and* The Last Tycoon (Carbondale, IL: Southern Illinois University Press, 1977), 129–56. References to *The Last Tycoon* in the text are to Bruccoli's *The Love of the Last Tycoon: A Western* and are included parenthetically in the text.

10 Rosten's previous book was *The Education of H*Y*M*A*N*K*A*P*L*A*N* (New York: Harcourt, Brace, 1937).

Further Reading

BIOGRAPHY

Buttitta, T. *After the Good Gay Times*. New York: Viking, 1974.

Callaghan, M. *That Summer in Paris*. New York: Coward-McCann, 1963.

Hemingway, E. *A Moveable Feast*. New York: Charles Scribner's Sons, 1964.

Milford, N. *Zelda*. New York: Harper & Row, 1970.

Wagner-Martin, L. *Zelda Sayre Fitzgerald: An American Life*. New York: Palgrave Macmillan, 2004.

INTERPRETING FITZGERALD'S LEDGER

Bruccoli, M. J., S. F. Smith, and J. P. Kerr, eds. *The Romantic Egoists*. New York: Charles Scribner's Sons, 1974.

Bruccoli, M. J., ed. with assistance of J. M. Atkinson. *As Ever Scott Fitz – Letters Between F. Scott Fitzgerald and His Literary Agent Harold Ober 1919–1940*. Philadelphia: Lippincott, 1972.

Kuehl, J. and J. R. Bryer, eds. *Dear Scott/Dear Max: The Fitzgerald – Perkins Correspondence*. New York: Charles Scribner's Sons, 1971.

LETTERS

Bruccoli, M. J., ed. with J. S. Baughman. *The Sons of Maxwell Perkins: Letters of F. Scott Fitzgerald, Ernest Hemingway, Thomas Wolfe, and Their Editor*. Columbia, SC: University of South Carolina Press, 2004.

Decker, W. M. *Epistolary Practices: Letter Writing in America Before Telecommunications*. Chapel Hill, NC: The University of North Carolina Press, 1998.

Wheelock J. H., ed. *Editor to Author: The Letters of Maxwell E. Perkins*. New York: Charles Scribner's Sons, 1950.

LITERARY STYLE

Breitwieser, M. "Jazz Fractures: F. Scott Fitzgerald and Epochal Representation," *American Literary History* 12 (Autumn 2000): 359–81.

Broun, H. "Books" in M. J. Bruccoli and J. S. Baughman, eds. *Conversations with F. Scott Fitzgerald*. Oxford, MS: University Press of Mississippi, 2003, 3–5.

Bruccoli, M. J. *Fitzgerald and Hemingway: A Dangerous Friendship*. New York: Carroll & Graff, 1995.

Curnutt, K. "*The Great Gatsby* and the 1920s" in L. Cassuto, C. V. Eby, and B. Reiss, eds. *The Cambridge History of the American Novel*. New York: Cambridge University Press, 2011, 639–52.

———. "The Short Stories of F. Scott Fitzgerald: Structure, Narrative Technique, Style" in A. Bendixen and J. Nagel, eds. *A Companion to the American Short Story*. London: Blackwell, 2010, 295–315.

———. "'A Unity Less Conventional But Not Less Serviceable': A Narratological History of *Tender Is the Night*" in W. Blazek and L. Rattray, eds. *Tender Is the Night: New Essays*. Liverpool: Liverpool Hope University Press, 2007, 121–42.

Donaldson, S. *Hemingway vs. Fitzgerald: The Rise and Fall of a Literary Friendship*. New York: Overlook Press, 1999.

Finkelstein, S. "Alienation as a Literary Style: F. Scott Fitzgerald and T. S. Eliot" in *Existentialism and Alienation in American Literature*. New York: International Publishers, 1965, 172–90.

Ford, E. *Rereading F. Scott Fitzgerald: The Authors Who Shaped His Style*. Lewiston, NY: Edwin Mellen Press, 2007.

Garrett, G. "Fire and Freshness: A Matter of Style in *The Great Gatsby*" in *The Sorrows of Fat City: A Selection of Literary Essays and Reviews*. Columbia, SC: University of South Carolina Press, 1992, 53–68.

Giltrow, J. and D. Stouck. "Style as Politics in *The Great Gatsby*," *Studies in the Novel* 29 (Winter 1997): 476–90

Horodowich, P. M. "Linguistics and Literary Style: Deriving F. Scott Fitzgerald's Linguistic Contours" in D. M. Lance and D. E. Gulstad, eds. *Papers from the 1977 Mid-America Linguistics Conference*. Columbia, MO: University of Missouri Press, 1978, 461–72.

Phillips, L. W., ed. *F. Scott Fitzgerald on Writing*. New York: Charles Scribner's Sons, 1986.

Quirk, T. "Fitzgerald and Cather: *The Great Gatsby*," *American Literature* 54 (December 1982): 576–91.

Toles, G. "The Metaphysics of Style in *Tender Is the Night*," *American Literature* 62 (September 1990): 423–44.

LITERARY INFLUENCES

Berman, R. "Reading the Past" in The Great Gatsby *and Modern Times*. Urbana, IL: University of Illinois Press, 1994. 161–94.

Bloom, H. Introduction in *Bloom's Modern Critical Views: F. Scott Fitzgerald, Updated Edition*. New York: Chelsea House, 2006. 1–5.

Bruccoli, M. J. and J. S. Baughman, eds. *F. Scott Fitzgerald on Authorship*. Columbia, SC: University of South Carolina Press, 1996.

Clayton, J. and E. Rothstein, eds. *Influence and Intertextuality in Literary History*. Madison, WI: University of Wisconsin Press, 1991.

Endres, N. "Petronius in West Egg: *The Satyricon* and *The Great Gatsby*," *F. Scott Fitzgerald Review* 7 (2009): 65–79.

Graham, S. *College of One*. New York: Viking Press, 1967.

Kuehl, J. "Scott Fitzgerald's Reading," *Princeton University Library Chronicle* 22.2 (Winter 1961): 58–89.

McGowan, P. "Reading Fitzgerald Reading Keats" in W. Blazek and L. Rattray, eds. *Twenty-First-Century Readings of* Tender Is the Night. Liverpool: Liverpool University Press, 2007, 204–20.

Miller, J. E. *F. Scott Fitzgerald: His Art and His Technique*. New York: New York University Press, 1964.

INTELLECTUAL INFLUENCES

Berman, R. *Translating Modernism: Fitzgerald and Hemingway*. Tuscaloosa, AL: University of Alabama Press, 2009.

———. *Fitzgerald's Mentors*. Tuscaloosa, AL: University of Alabama Press, 2012.

Curnutt, K. *A Historical Guide to F. Scott Fitzgerald*. New York: Oxford University Press, 2004.

Dewey, J. *The Philosophy of John Dewey*. J. J. McDermott, ed. Chicago: University of Chicago Press, 1981.

James, W. *The Writings of William James*. J. J. McDermott, ed. Chicago: University of Chicago Press, 1977.

Perret, G. *America in the Twenties*. New York: Touchstone, 1982.

Prigozy, R., ed. *The Cambridge Companion to F. Scott Fitzgerald*. Cambridge, UK: Cambridge University Press, 2002.

Santayana, G. *The Essential Santayana*. Bloomington, IN: Indiana University Press, 2009.

Whitehead, A. N. *Science and the Modern World*. New York: Macmillan, 1953.

CONTEMPORARY CRITICAL RECEPTION

Bruccoli, M. J. *Some Sort of Epic Grandeur: The Life of F. Scott Fitzgerald*. 2nd rev. ed. Columbia, SC: University of South Carolina Press, 2002.

Bruccoli, M. J. and J. R. Bryer, eds. *F. Scott Fitzgerald in His Own Time: A Miscellany*. Kent, OH: Kent State University Press, 1971.

Bryer, J. R. *The Critical Reputation of F. Scott Fitzgerald: A Bibliographical Study*. Hamden, CT: Archon, 1967.

———. *The Critical Reputation of F. Scott Fitzgerald: A Bibliographical Study – Supplement One Through 1981*. Hamden, CT: Archon, 1984.

———. "F. Scott Fitzgerald" in J. R. Bryer, ed. *Sixteen Modern American Authors: A Survey of Research and Criticism*. New York: W. W. Norton, 1973, 277–321.

Bryer, J. R., ed. *F. Scott Fitzgerald: The Critical Reception*. New York: Burt Franklin, 1978.

Claridge, H. *F. Scott Fitzgerald: Critical Assessments*. 4 vols. Robertsbridge, UK: Helm, 1991.

Curnutt, K. *The Cambridge Introduction to F. Scott Fitzgerald*. Cambridge, UK: Cambridge University Press, 2007.

Mizener, A. *The Far Side of Paradise: A Biography of F. Scott Fitzgerald*. Rev. ed. New York: Vintage, 1959.

Tanselle, G. T. and J. R. Bryer. "*The Great Gatsby*: A Study in Literary Reputation," *New Mexico Quarterly* 33.4 (1963–64): 409–25.

THE FITZGERALD REVIVAL

Berman, R. The Great Gatsby *and Fitzgerald's World of Ideas*. Tuscaloosa: University of Alabama Press, 1997.

———. The Great Gatsby *and Modern Times*. Urbana, IL: University of Illinois Press, 1994.

Bruccoli, M. J. *Some Sort of Epic Grandeur: The Life of F. Scott Fitzgerald*. Rev. ed. Columbia, SC: University of South Carolina Press, 1994.

Bryer, J. R. *The Critical Reputation of F. Scott Fitzgerald*. Hamden, CT: Archon, 1967.

———. *F. Scott Fitzgerald: The Critical Reception*. New York: Burt Franklin, 1978.

———. *The Critical Reputation of F. Scott Fitzgerald: A Bibliographical Study – Supplement One Through 1981*. Hamden, CT: Archon, 1984.

Bryer, J. R., ed. *F. Scott Fitzgerald: The Critical Reception*. New York: Burt Franklin, 1978.

Cowley, M. *Exile's Return: A Literary Odyssey of the 1920s* (1924). New York: Penguin, 1976.

———. "The Fitzgerald Revival, 1941–1953," *Fitzgerald/Hemingway Annual* 6 (1974): 11–13.

———. *A Second Flowering: Works and Days of the Lost Generation*. New York: Viking, 1973.

Fitzgerald, F. S. *The Crack-Up*. E. Wilson, ed. New York: New Directions, 1945.

Graham, S. *College of One*. New York: Viking, 1967.

Graham, S. with G. Frank, *Beloved Infidel*. New York: Henry Holt, 1958.

Hemingway, E. *A Moveable Feast*. New York: Charles Scribner's Sons, 1964.

Kazan, A. *F. Scott Fitzgerald: The Man and His Work* (1951). New York: Collier Books, 1967.

Mayfield, S. *Exiles from Paradise: Zelda and Scott Fitzgerald*. New York: Delacorte Press, 1971.

Mellow, J. R. *Invented Lives: F. Scott and Zelda Fitzgerald*. Boston: Houghton Mifflin, 1984.

Meyers, J. *F. Scott Fitzgerald: A Biography*. New York: HarperCollins, 1994.
Milford, N. *Zelda: A Biography*. New York: Harper & Row, 1970.
Mizener, A. *The Far Side of Paradise: A Biography of F. Scott Fitzgerald (1951)*. Boston: Houghton Mifflin, 1959.
Parker, D., ed. *The Portable F. Scott Fitzgerald*. New York: Viking Press, 1945.
Prigozy, Ruth. *F. Scott Fitzgerald: An Illustrated Life*. London and New York: Penguin and Overlook Press, 2002.
———. "Fitzgerald and Hemingway: A Matter of Measurement," *Commonweal* 95 (October 29, 1971): 103–09.
Prigozy R., ed. *The Cambridge Companion to F. Scott Fitzgerald*. London: Cambridge University Press, 2002.
Schulberg, B. *The Disenchanted*. New York: Random House, 1950.
———. *The Four Seasons of Success*. Garden City, NY: Doubleday, 1972.
Tompkins, C. *Living Well Is the Best Revenge*. New York: Viking, 1971.
Turnbull, A. *Scott Fitzgerald*. New York: Charles Scribner's Sons, 1962.
Wakefield, D. *New York in the Fifties*. Boston: Houghton Mifflin, 1992.

BUFFALO AND SYRACUSE, NEW YORK

P. L. Bernstein. *Wedding of the Waters: The Erie Canal and the Making of a Great Nation*. New York: W. W. Norton & Company, 2005.
Connors, D. J. *Crossroads in Time: An Illustrated History of Syracuse*. Syracuse, NY: Syracuse University Press, 2006.
Dreishpoon, D., ed. *The Long Curve: 150 Years of Visionary Collecting at the Albright-Knox Art Gallery*. Milan: Skira, 2011.
Dunn, E. T. *Buffalo's Delaware Avenue: Mansions and Families*. Buffalo, NY: Canisius College Press, 2003.
Goldman, M. *City on the Edge: Buffalo, New York*. Amherst, NY: Prometheus Books, 2007.
Logan, M. K. *Narrating Africa: George Henty and the Fiction of Empire*. New York: Garland Publishing, 1999.
Miller, S. *The President and the Assassin: McKinley, Terror, and Empire at the Dawn of the American Century*. New York: Random House, 2011.
Rydell, R. W. *All the World's a Fair: Visions of Empire at American International Expositions, 1876–1919*. Chicago: The University of Chicago Press, 1984.
Spaulding, K. L., ed. *Masterworks at the Albright-Knox Art Gallery*. New York: Hudson Hills Press, 1999.
Wilson, E. *Upstate: Records and Recollections of Northern New York*. London: Macmillan, 1971.

ST. PAUL, MINNESOTA, ST. PAUL ACADEMY, AND THE *ST. PAUL ACADEMY NOW AND THEN*

Butwin, D. "In the Days of the Ice Palace," *Saturday Review* 55 (January 29, 1972): 55–56.

Donaldson, S. "St. Paul Boy" in H. L. Weatherby and G. Core, eds. *Place in American Fiction: Excursions and Explorations*. Columbia: University of Missouri Press, 2004.

Flandrau, G. H. *Being Respectable*. New York: Harcourt, Brace, 1923.

Hampl, P. Introduction in P. Hampl and D. Page, eds. *The St. Paul Stories of F. Scott Fitzgerald*. St. Paul, MN: Borealis, 2004.

Irish, C. "The Myth of Success in Fitzgerald's Boyhood," *Studies in American Fiction* 1 (1973): 176–87.

Jacobson, M. F. *Whiteness of a Different Color: European Immigration and the Alchemy of Race*. Cambridge: Harvard University Press, 1998.

Kriel, Margot. "Fitzgerald in St. Paul: People Who Knew Him Reminisce" in proceedings of the University of Minnesota Conference on F. Scott Fitzgerald: St. Paul's Native Son and Distinguished American Writer, October 29–31, 1982, University of Minnesota.

Page, D. and J. Koblas. *F. Scott Fitzgerald in Minnesota: Toward the Summit*. St. Cloud, MN: North Star Press, 1996.

A CATHOLIC BOYHOOD: THE NEWMAN SCHOOL, THE *NEWMAN NEWS*, AND MONSIGNOR CYRIL SIGOURNEY WEBSTER FAY

Allen, J. M. *Candles and Carnival Lights: The Catholic Sensibility of F. Scott Fitzgerald*. New York: New York University, 1978.

Karabel, J. *The Chosen: The Hidden History of Admission and Exclusion at Harvard, Yale, and Princeton*. Boston: Houghton Mifflin, 2005.

Kimmel, M. *Manhood in America*. New York: Free Press, 1996.

Marsden, D. *The Long Kickline: A History of the Princeton Triangle Club*. Princeton, NJ: Princeton University Press, 1968.

Rotundo, E. A. *American Manhood: Transformations in Masculinity from the Revolution to the Modern Era*. New York: Basic Books, 1993.

PRINCETON, NEW JERSEY, PRINCETON UNIVERSITY, AND THE *NASSAU LITERARY MAGAZINE*

Fitzgerald, F. S. *The Apprentice Fiction of F. Scott Fitzgerald, 1909–1917*. J. Kuehl, ed. New Brunswick, NJ: Rutgers University Press, 1965.

Meyers, J. *Scott Fitzgerald: A Biography*. New York: HarperCollins, 1994.

Mizener, A. *The Far Side of Paradise: A Biography of F. Scott Fitzgerald*. Boston: Houghton Mifflin, 1951.

West, J. L. W. III *The Perfect Hour: The Romance of F. Scott Fitzgerald and Ginevra King, His First Love*. New York: Random House, 2005.

WORLD WAR I

Bremer, S. H. "American Dreams and American Cities in Three Post-World War Novels," *South Atlantic Quarterly* 79 (1980): 274–85.

Dyer, G. "The Missing of the Somme" in J. Hannah, ed. *The Great War Reader*. College Station, TX: Texas A&M University Press, 2000, 16–21.

Harries, M. and S. Harries. *The Last Days of Innocence: America at War, 1917–1918*. New York: Random House, 1997.

von Clausewitz, C. *On War*. M. Howard and P. Paret, eds. Princeton, NJ: Princeton University Press, 1976.

Winter, J. *Sites of Memory, Sites of Mourning: The Great War in European Cultural History*. New York: Cambridge University Press, 1995.

Zieger, R. H. *America's Great War: World War I and the American Experience*. Lanham, MD: Rowman and Littlefield, 2000.

ZELDA IN THE SHADOWS

Anderson, W. R. "Rivalry and Partnership: The Short Fiction of Zelda Sayre Fitzgerald," *Fitzgerald/Hemingway Annual* 9 (1977): 19–42.

Courbin-Tavernier, J. "Art as Women's Response and Search: Zelda Fitzgerald's *Save Me the Waltz*," *Southern Liberty Journal* 11.2 (Spring 1979): 22–42.

Harnett, K. S. *Zelda Fitzgerald and the Failure of the American Dream for Women*. New York: Lang, 1991.

Hudgins, A. "Zelda Sayre in Montgomery," *Southern Review* 20 (1984): 882–84.

Nanney, L. "Zelda Fitzgerald's *Save Me the Waltz* as Southern Novel and *Kunstlerroman*" in C. S. Manning, ed. *The Female Tradition in Southern Literature*. Urbana: University of Illinois Press, 1993, 220–32.

Petry, A. H. "Women's Work: The Case of Zelda Fitzgerald," LIT 1 (Dec. 1989): 69–83.

Wagner-Martin, L. "*Save Me the Waltz*": An Assessment in Craft," *Journal of Narrative Technique* 12 (Fall 1982): 201–09.

FITZGERALD'S SOUTHERN NARRATIVE: THE TARLETON, GEORGIA, STORIES

Fulkerson, T. N. "Ibsen in 'The Ice Palace,'" *Fitzgerald/Hemingway Annual* 11 (1979): 169–71.

Gervais, R. J. "A Miracle of Rare Device: Fitzgerald's 'The Ice Palace,'" *Notes on Modern American Literature* 5 (Summer 1981), Item 21.

Mangum, B. *A Fortune Yet: Money in the Art of F. Scott Fitzgerald's Short Stories*. New York: Garland, 1991. 32–33; 42–43; 48–49; 119–20.

Moses, E. "F. Scott Fitzgerald and the Quest to the Ice Place," *CEA Critic* 36 (January 1974): 11–14.

Seidel, K. L. *The Southern Belle in the American Novel*. Tampa, FL: University of South Florida Press, 1985.

Sklar, R. *The Last Laocoön*. New York: Oxford University Press, 1967. 87–88.

Zeitz, J. *Flapper*. New York: Three Rivers Press, 2006.

AMERICAN LITERARY REALISM

Baker, C. R. "F. Scott Fitzgerald's *The Great Gatsby*" in J. Parini, ed. *American Writers Classics*, II. New York: Charles Scribner's Sons, 2004, 109–24.

Barron, J. N. "Teaching Regionalism and Class in *The Great Gatsby*" in J. R. Bryer and N. P. VanArsdale, eds. *Approaches to Teaching Fitzgerald's* The Great Gatsby. New York: The Modern Language Association of America, 2009, 59–67.

Berman, R. "*The Great Gatsby* and the Twenties" in R. Prigozy, ed. *The Cambridge Companion to F. Scott Fitzgerald*. Cambridge, UK: Cambridge University Press, 2002, 79–94.

Bryer, J. R. and N. P. VanArsdale, eds. *Approaches to Teaching Fitzgerald's* The Great Gatsby. New York: The Modern Language Association, 2009.

Chambers, J. B. *The Novels of F. Scott Fitzgerald*. New York: St. Martin's Press, 1989.

Coleman, D. "'A World Complete in Itself': *Gatsby's* Elegiac Narration," *Journal of Narrative Technique* 27.2 (1997): 207–33.

Curnutt, K. "All That Jazz: Defining Modernity and Milieu in *The Great Gatsby*" in J. R. Bryer. and N. P. VanArsdale, eds. *Approaches to Teaching Fitzgerald's* The Great Gatsby. New York: The Modern Language Association, 2009, 41–49.

DeForest, J. W. "The Great American Novel," *Nation* 6 (January 9, 1868): 27–29.

Donaldson, S. *Critical Essays on Fitzgerald's* The Great Gatsby. Boston: G. K. Hall, 1984.

———. "The Trouble with Nick" in S. Donaldson, ed. *Critical Essays on Fitzgerald's* The Great Gatsby. Boston, MA: G. K. Hall, 1984, 131–39.

Eble, K. *F. Scott Fitzgerald*. Boston: Twayne, 1977.

Hays, P. L. "Enough Guilt to Go Around: Teaching Fitzgerald's Lesson in Morality" in J. R. Bryer and N. P. VanArsdale, eds. *Approaches to Teaching Fitzgerald's* The Great Gatsby. New York: The Modern Language Association of America, 2009, 169–74.

James, P. "Teaching *The Great Gatsby* in the Context of World War I" in S. Donaldson, ed. *Critical Essays on Fitzgerald's* The Great Gatsby. Boston: G. K. Hall, 1984, 32–39.

Kunz, H. M. "Symmetry Versus Asymmetry: Structuring *The Great Gatsby*" in J. R. Bryer and N. P. VanArsdale, eds. *Approaches to Teaching Fitzgerald's* The Great Gatsby. New York: The Modern Language Association of America, 2009, 119–25.

Lehan, R. The Great Gatsby*: The Limits of Wonder*. Boston: Twayne, 1990.

Long, R. E. *The Achieving of* The Great Gatsby. Lewisburg, PA: Bucknell University Press, 1979.

Nowlin, M. "Teaching the Racial Subtext of *The Great Gatsby*" in J. R. Bryer and N. P. VanArsdale, eds. *Approaches to Teaching Fitzgerald's* The Great Gatsby. New York: The Modern Language Association of America, 2009, 50–59.

Phelan, J. "Rhetoric and Ethics in *The Great Gatsby;* or, Fabula, Progression, and the Functions of Nick Carraway" in J. R. Bryer and N. P. VanArsdale, eds. *Approaches to Teaching Fitzgerald's* The Great Gatsby. New York: The Modern Language Association of America, 2009, 99–110.

VanArsdale, N. P. Introduction in J. R. Bryer and N. P. VanArsdale, eds. *Approaches to Teaching Fitzgerald's* The Great Gatsby. New York: The Modern Language Association, 2009, 27–31.

NATURALISM AND HIGH MODERNISM

Berman, R. "F. Scott Fitzgerald, Gerald Murphy, and the New Arts," *F. Scott Fitzgerald Review* 7 (2009): 127–41.

———. The Great Gatsby *and Modern Times*. Urbana, IL: University of Illinois Press, 1994.

Hutchinson, B. *Modernism and Style*. New York: Palgrave, 2011.

Kenner, H. *A Homemade World: The American Modernist Writers*. Baltimore: Johns Hopkins University Press, 1975.

Miller, J. E. *F. Scott Fitzgerald: His Art and His Technique*. New York: New York University Press, 1964.

Nowlin, M. *F. Scott Fitzgerald's Racial Angles and the Business of Literary Greatness*. New York: Palgrave, 2007.

Piper, H. D. *F. Scott Fitzgerald: A Critical Portrait*. Carbondale, IL: Southern Illinois University Press, 1965.

Sklar, R. *F. Scott Fitzgerald: The Last Laocoön*. New York: Oxford University Press, 1967.

AVANT-GARDE TRENDS

Berman, R. "F. Scott Fitzgerald, Gerald Murphy, and the New Arts," *F. Scott Fitzgerald Review* 7 (2009): 127–41.

———. "F. Scott Fitzgerald, Gerald Murphy, and the Practice of Modernism," *F. Scott Fitzgerald Review* 6 (2007–2008): 145–53.

———. *Fitzgerald, Hemingway, and the Twenties*. Tuscaloosa, AL: University of Alabama Press, 2001.

———. The Great Gatsby *and Modern Times*. Chicago: University of Illinois Press, 1994.

Corn, W. M. "Chapter Two: An American in Paris" in *The Great American Thing: Modern Art and National Identity, 1915–1935*. Berkeley: University of California Press, 1999.

Miller, L. P., ed. *Letters from the Lost Generation: Gerald and Sara Murphy and Friends*. Gainesville, FL: University Press of Florida, 2002.

Miller, L. P., "Gerald Murphy in Letters, Literature and Life" in Debra Rothschild, ed. *Making It New: The Art and Style of Sara and Gerald Murphy*. Berkeley, CA: University of California Press, 2007. 143–63.

Moreland, Kim. "Gerald Murphy, F. Scott Fitzgerald, and Dick Diver, The Artist's Vocation," *Journal of Modern Literature* 23 (1999–2000): 357–63.

Rothschild, Deborah, ed. *Making It New: The Art and Style of Sara and Gerald Murphy*. Berkeley, CA: University of California Press, 2007.

Rubin, W. *The Paintings of Gerald Murphy*. New York: Museum of Modern Art, 1974.

Vaill, A. *Everybody Was So Young: Gerald and Sara Murphy: A Lost Generation Love Story*. Boston: Houghton Mifflin, 1998.

PROHIBITION IN THE AGE OF JAZZ

Behr, E. *Prohibition: Thirteen Years that Changed History*. New York: Arcade Publishing, 2011.

Burns, K. and L. Novick, dirs. *Prohibition*. PBS, 2011. DVD.

Coffey, T. M. *The Long Thirst: Prohibition in America, 1920–1933*. New York: W. W. Norton, 1975.

Drowne, K. *Spirits of Defiance: National Prohibition and Jazz Age Literature, 1920–1933*. Columbus: The Ohio State University Press, 2009.

Kobler, J. *Ardent Spirits: The Rise and Fall of Prohibition*. Boston: DaCapo Press, 1993.

Okrent, D. *Last Call: The Rise and Fall of Prohibition*. New York: Charles Scribner's Sons, 2010.

Slavicek, L. C. *The Prohibition Era: Temperance in the United States*. New York: Chelsea House, 2008.

CLASS DIFFERENCES IN FITZGERALD'S WORKS

Berman, R. The Great Gatsby *and Modern Times*. Urbana: University of Illinois Press, 1994.

Marchand, R. *Advertising the American Dream: Making Way for Modernity, 1920–1940*. Berkeley: University of California Press, 1986.

Tichi, C. *Shifting Gears: Technology, Literature, Culture in Modernist America*. Chapel Hill, NC: The University of North Carolina Press, 1987.

Way, B. *F. Scott Fitzgerald and the Art of Social Fiction*. New York: St. Martin's Press, 1980.

ETHNIC STEREOTYPING

Abramson, E. A. "Aliens, Stereotypes, and Social Change: The Jews and Hollywood in F. Scott Fitzgerald's Fiction," *Studies in American Jewish Literature* 24 (2005): 116–36.

Forrey, R. "Negroes in the Fiction of F. Scott Fitzgerald," *Phylon* 28.3 (1967): 293–98.

Gidley, M. "Notes on F. Scott Fitzgerald and the Passing of the Great Race," *Journal of American Studies* 7.2 (1973): 171–81.

Gross, B. and E. Fretz. "What Fitzgerald Thought of Jews: Resisting Type in 'The Hotel Child'" in J. Bryer, ed. *New Essays of F. Scott Fitzgerald's Neglected Short Stories*. Columbia, MO: University of Missouri Press, 1996, 189–205.

Higham, J. *Strangers in the Land: Patterns of American Nativism 1860–1925*. New Brunswick, NJ: Rutgers University Press, 1988.

Joshi, S.T. *Documents of American Prejudice: An Anthology of Writings on Race from Thomas Jefferson to David Duke*. New York: Basic Books, 1999.

Margolies, A. "The Maturing of F. Scott Fitzgerald," *Twentieth-Century Literature* 43.1 (1997): 75–93.

Michaels, W. B. *Our America: Nativism, Modernism, and Pluralism*. Durham, NC: Duke University Press, 1995.

Nies, B. L. *Eugenic Fantasies: Racial Ideology in the Literature and Popular Culture of the 1920's*. New York: Routledge, 2002.

Nowlin, M. *F. Scott Fitzgerald's Racial Angles and the Business of Literary Greatness*. New York: Palgrave Macmillan, 2007.

Rohrkemper, J. "Becoming White: Race and Ethnicity in *The Great Gatsby*," *Midwestern Miscellany* 31 (Fall 2003): 22–31.

Schreier, B. "Desire's Second Act: 'Race' and *The Great Gatsby*'s Cynical Americanism," *Twentieth-Century American Literature* 53.2 (2007): 153–80.

Turlish, Lewis A. "The Rising Tide of Color: A Note on the Historicism of *The Great Gatsby*," *American Literature* 43.3 (1971): 442–44.

GENDER IN THE JAZZ AGE

Douglas, A. *The Feminization of American Culture* (1977). New York: Knopf, 1988.

Grant, J. "A 'Real Boy' and Not a Sissy: Gender, Childhood, and Masculinity 1890–1940," *Journal of Social History* 37.4 (Summer 2004): 829–51.

Rotundo, E. A. *American Manhood*. New York: HarperCollins, 1993.

POSTWAR FLAPPERS

Fryer, S. B. *Fitzgerald's New Women: Harbingers of Change*. Ann Arbor, MI: UMI Research Press, 1988.

Gourley, C. *Flappers and the New American Woman: Perceptions of Women from 1918 Through the 1920s*. Minneapolis: Twenty-First Century Books, 2008.

Latham, A. J. *Posing a Threat: Flappers, Chorus Girls, and Other Brazen Performers of the American 1920s*. Hanover, NH: Wesleyan University Press, 2000.

Matthews, J. V. *The Rise of the New Woman: The Women's Movement in America, 1875–1930*. Chicago: Ivan R. Dee Publishers, 2003.

Prigozy, R. "Fitzgerald's Flappers and Flapper Films of the Jazz Age: Behind the Morality" in Kirk Curnutt, ed. *A Historical Guide to F. Scott Fitzgerald*. New York: Oxford University Press, 2004.

Sagert, K. B. *Flappers: A Guide to an American Subculture.* Santa Barbara, CA: ABC- CLIO/Greenwood, 2010.

Sanderson, R. "Women in Fitzgerald's Fiction" in Ruth Prigozy, ed. *The Cambridge Companion to F. Scott Fitzgerald.* Cambridge, UK: Cambridge University Press, 2002.

Stevenson, E. "Flappers and Some Who Were Not Flappers" in L. R. Broer and J. D. Walther, eds. *Dancing Fools and Weary Blues: The Great Escape of the Twenties.* Bowling Green, OH: Bowling Green State University Press, 1990.

Yellis, K. A. "Prosperity's Child: Some Thoughts on the Flapper," *American Quarterly* 2.1 (1969): 44–64.

Zeitz, J. *Flapper: A Madcap Story of Sex, Style, Celebrity, and the Women Who Made America Modern.* New York: Crown Publishers, 2006.

YOUTH CULTURE

Allen, F. L. *Only Yesterday: An Informal History of the Nineteen-Twenties.* New York: Harper & Row, Publishers, 1931.

Campbell, N., ed. *The Radiant Hour: Versions of Youth in American Culture.* Exeter, Devon, UK: University of Exeter Press, 2000.

Curnutt, K. "Youth Culture and the Spectacle of Waste: *This Side of Paradise* and *The Beautiful and Damned*" in R. Prigozy, J. R. Bryer, and M. Stern, eds. *F. Scott Fitzgerald in the 21st Century.* Tuscaloosa: University of Alabama Press, 2003, 79–103.

Fass, P. S. *The Damned and the Beautiful: American Youth in the 1920's.* New York: Oxford University Press, 1977.

Graff, H. J. *Growing Up in America: Historical Experiences.* Detroit: Wayne State University Press, 1987.

Hawes, J. M. *Children Between the Wars: American Childhood 1920–1940.* New York: Twayne Publishers, 1997. 49.

Shannon, David A. *Between the Wars: America, 1919–1941.* 2nd ed. Boston: Houghton Mifflin, 1979. 109.

AMERICAN EXPATRIATES IN FRANCE

Allen, F. L. *Only Yesterday: An Informal History of the Nineteen-Twenties (1931).* New York: Harper Perennial, 1992.

Bougault, V. *Paris Montparnasse: A l'heure de l'art moderne 1910–1940.* Paris: Terrail, 1996.

Bradbury, M, ed. *The Atlas of Literature.* London: De Agostini, 1996.

Bruccoli, M. J. *Some Sort of Epic Grandeur: The Life of F. Scott Fitzgerald.* London: Cardinal, 1991.

———. *Fitzgerald and Hemingway: A Dangerous Friendship.* London: André Deutsch, 1995.

Clébert, J-P. *La Littérature à Paris: L'Histoire, les lieux, la vie littéraire*. Paris: Larousse, 1999.

Fitzgerald, F. S. *The Letters of F. Scott Fitzgerald (1963)*. A. Turnbull, ed. London: The Bodley Head, 1964.

———. "How to Live on Practically Nothing a Year" in *Afternoon of an Author*. New York: Charles Scribner's Sons, 1968. 100–16.

———. *Tender Is the Night (1934)*. New York: Charles Scribner's Sons, 1982.

Hemingway, E. *A Moveable Feast*. New York: Charles Scribner's Sons, 1964.

———. *The Sun Also Rises (1926)*. New York: Charles Scribner's Sons, 1970.

Kennedy, G. and J. R. Bryer, eds. *French Connections: Hemingway and Fitzgerald Abroad*. London: Macmillan, 1998.

Moore, L. *Anything Goes: A Biography of the Roaring Twenties*. London: Atlantic Books, 2008.

Soutif, D., ed. *Le Siècle du Jazz*. Paris: Flammarion, 2009.

Stein, G. *Paris France (1940)*. London: Peter Owen, 2003.

Tomkins, C. *Living Well Is the Best Revenge (1962)*. New York: New American Library, 1972.

Vaill, A. *Everybody Was So Young. Gerald and Sara Murphy: A Lost Generation Story*. New York: Houghton Mifflin, 1998.

POPULAR LITERARY TASTES

Berman, R. "The Great Gatsby and the Twenties" in R. Prigozy, ed. *The Cambridge Companion to F. Scott Fitzgerald*. Cambridge, UK: Cambridge University Press, 2002, 79–94.

Bradbury, M. *The American Novel and the Nineteen Twenties*. London: Edward Arnold, 1971.

Brickell, H. "The Literary Landscape," *The North American Review* 230.5 (November 1930): 628–38.

Carter, P. A. *Another Part of the Twenties*. Columbia University Press, 1977.

Cowley, M. *Exile's Return: A Literary Odyssey of the 1920s*. Harmondsworth: Penguin, 1994.

———. *The Literary Situation*. New York: The Viking Press, 1955.

Goldberg, D. J. "Rethinking the 1920s: Historians and Changing Perspectives," *Magazine of History* 21.3 (July 2007): 7–10.

Leavis, Q. D. *Fiction and the Reading Public*. London: Chatto & Windus, 1932.

Prigozy, R., ed. *The Cambridge Companion to F. Scott Fitzgerald*. Cambridge, UK: Cambridge University Press, 2002).

Radway, J. *A Feeling for Books: The Book-of-the-Month Club, Literary Taste, and Middle-Class Desire*. Chapel Hill, NC: The University of North Carolina Press, 1997.

Snowman, D. *America Since 1920*. London: Heinemann, 1978.

Tanselle, G. T. "The Historiography of American Literary Publishing," *Studies in Bibliography* 18 (1965): 3–39.

MAGAZINES

Allen, F. L. *Only Yesterday: An Informal History of the Nineteen-Twenties*. New York: Harper and Brothers, 1931.

Cohn, J. *Creating America: George Horace Lorimer and The Saturday Evening Post*. Pittsburgh: University of Pittsburgh Press, 1989.

Fitzgerald, F. S. *The Short Stories of F. Scott Fitzgerald: A New Collection*. M. J. Bruccoli, ed. New York: Charles Scribner's Sons, 1989.

Kuehl, J. *F. Scott Fitzgerald: A Study of the Short Fiction*. Boston: Twayne, 1991.

Mangum, B. *A Fortune Yet: Money in the Art of F. Scott Fitzgerald's Short Stories*. New York: Garland, 1991.

Mencken, H. L. *H. L. Mencken's* Smart Set *Criticism*. W. H. Nolte, ed. Ithaca, NY: Cornell University Press, 1968.

West, J. L. W. III "Fitzgerald and *Esquire*" in J. R. Bryer, ed. *The Short Stories of F. Scott Fitzgerald: New Approaches in Criticism*. Madison, WI: University of Wisconsin Press, 1982, 149–66.

Zeitz, J. *Flapper: A Madcap Story of Sex, Style, Celebrity, and the Women Who Made America Modern*. New York: Three Rivers Press, 2006.

BROADWAY MELODIES

Booth, M. *The Experience of Songs*. New Haven, CT: Yale University Press, 1983.

Bordman, G. *American Musical Comedy, From* Adonis *to* Dreamgirls. New York: Oxford University Press, 2001.

Breitwieser, M. "Jazz Fractures: F. Scott Fitzgerald and Epochal Representation," *American Literary History* 12 (Autumn 2000): 359–81.

Erenberg, L. *Steppin' Out: New York Nightlife and the Transformation of American Culture, 1890–1930*. Chicago: University of Chicago Press, 1981.

Ewen, D. *The Life and Death of Tin Pan Alley: The Golden Age of American Popular Music*. New York: Funk and Wagnall, 1964.

Frith, S. *Performing Rites: On the Value of Popular Music*. Cambridge, MA: Harvard University Press, 1996.

Furia, P. *The Poets of Tin Pan Alley: A History of America's Great Lyricists*. New York: Oxford University Press, 1990.

Graham, T. A. "The Literary Soundtrack: Or, F. Scott Fitzgerald's Heard and Unheard Melodies," *American Literary History* 21.3 (Fall 2009): 518–49.

Henson, K. *Beyond the Sound Barrier: The Jazz Controversy in Twentieth Century American Fiction*. New York: Routledge, 2003.

Moreland, K. "Music in *The Great Gatsby* and *The Great Gatsby* as Music" in M. J. Meyer, ed. *Literature and Musical Adaptation*. Amsterdam: Rodope, 2002.

Savran, D. *Highbrow/Lowdown: Theater, Jazz, and the Making of the New Middle Class*. Ann Arbor: University of Michigan Press, 2009.

Seldes, G. *The 7 Lively Arts: The Classic Appraisal of the Popular Arts* (1924). Mineola, NY: Dover, 2001.

STAGE AND SCREEN ENTERTAINMENT

Berman, R. *Fitzgerald, Hemingway, and the Twenties*. Tuscaloosa: University of Alabama Press, 2001.

Curnutt, K. *A Historical Guide to F. Scott Fitzgerald*. New York: Oxford University Press, 2004.

Gilbert, D. *American Vaudeville: Its Life and Times*. New York: McGraw Hill, 1940.

Prigozy, R. *The Cambridge Companion to F. Scott Fitzgerald*. Cambridge: Cambridge University Press, 2002.

Quirk, T. *Bergson and American Culture: The Worlds of Willa Cather and Wallace Stevens*. Chapel Hill, NC: The University North Carolina Press, 1990.

CONSUMER CULTURE AND ADVERTISING

Balkun, M. M. *The American Counterfeit: Authenticity and Identity in American Literature and Culture*. Tuscaloosa, AL: University of Alabama Press, 2006.

Barrett, L. "From Wonderland to Wasteland: *The Wonderful Wizard of Oz, The Great Gatsby*, and the New American Fairy Tale," *Papers on Language & Literature* 42.2 (2006): 150–80.

———. "'Material Without Being Real': Photography and the End of Reality in *The Great Gatsby*," *Studies in the Novel* 30.4 (1998): 540–47.

Berman, R. The Great Gatsby *and Fitzgerald's World of Ideas*. Tuscaloosa: University of Alabama Press, 1997.

Bicknell, J. W. "The Waste Land of F. Scott Fitzgerald" in K. Eble, ed. *F. Scott Fitzgerald*. New York: McGraw-Hill, 1973, 67–80.

Bryer, J. R. "F. Scott Fitzgerald, 1896–1940: A Brief Biography" in K. Curnutt, ed. *A Historical Guide to F. Scott Fitzgerald*. Oxford: Oxford University Press, 2004. 21–46.

del Gizzo, S. "Within and Without: F. Scott Fitzgerald and American Consumer Culture" in D. Noble, ed. *Critical Insights: F. Scott Fitzgerald*. Pasadena: Salem P, 2011. 34–54.

Donaldson, S. "Possessions in *The Great Gatsby*," *The Southern Review* 37.2 (2001): 187–210.

Douglass, A. *Terrible Honesty: Mongrel Manhattan in the 1920s*. New York: Farrar, Straus & Giroux, 1995.

Fitzgerald, F. S. *F. Scott Fitzgerald's Ledger: A Facsimile*. M. J. Bruccoli, ed. Washington: Bruccoli Clark/NCR, 1973.

———. *A Life in Letters*. M. J. Bruccoli, ed. New York: Charles Scribner's Sons, 1994.

Fussell, E. S. "Fitzgerald's Brave New World," *ELH* 19 (1952): 291–306.

Grenberg, B. L. "Fitzgerald's 'Crack-up' Essays Revisited: Fictions of the Self, Mirrors for a Nation" in J. R. Bryer, A. Margolies, and R. Prigozy, eds. *F. Scott Fitzgerald: New Perspectives*. Athens, GA: University of Georgia Press, 2000: 203–15.

Mangum, B. *A Fortune Yet: Money in the Art of F. Scott Fitzgerald's Short Stories.* New York: Garland, 1991.

Marchand, R. *Advertising the American Dream: Making Way for Modernity, 1920–1940.* Berkeley: University of California Press, 1985.

Nowlin, M. *F. Scott Fitzgerald's Racial Angles and the Business of Literary Greatness.* New York: Palgrave, 2007.

Posnock, R. "'A New World, Material Without Being Real': Fitzgerald's Critique of Capitalism in *The Great Gatsby*" in S. Donaldson, ed. *Critical Essays on F. Scott Fitzgerald's* The Great Gatsby. New York: G. K. Hall, 1984, 201–13.

Rule-Maxwell, L. "The *New Emperor's Clothes*: Keatsian Echoes and American Materialism in The Great Gatsby," *F. Scott Fitzgerald Review* 8.1 (2010): 57–78.

Veblen, T. *Theory of the Leisure Class: An Economic Study in the Evolution of Institutions.* New York: Macmillan, 1899.

West, J. L. W. III "F. Scott Fitzgerald, Professional Author" in K. Curnutt, ed. *A Historical Guide to F. Scott Fitzgerald.* Oxford, UK: Oxford University Press, 2004, 49–68.

FASHION

Breward, C. *The Culture of Fashion: A New History of Fashionable Dress.* Manchester, UK: Manchester University Press, 1995.

Driscoll, C. *Modernist Cultural Studies.* Gainesville, FL: University Press of Florida, 2010. 140–62.

Herald, J. *Fashions of a Decade: The 1920s.* New York: Facts on File, 1991.

McEvoy, A. *Costume and Fashion Source Books: The 1920s and 1930s.* New York: Chelsea House, 2009.

Peacock, J. *Fashion Sourcebook: The 1920s.* London: Thames and Hudson, 1997.

TRANSPORTATION

Armstrong, T. *Modernism, Technology, and the Body: A Cultural Study.* Cambridge, UK: Cambridge University Press, 1988.

Echevarría, L. G. "The Automobile as a Central Symbol in F. Scott Fitzgerald," *Revista Alicantina de Estudios Ingleses* 6 (1993): 73–78.

Faith, N. *The World the Railways Made.* London: Bodley Head, 1990.

Flink, J. J. *The Automobile Age.* Cambridge, MA: MIT Press, 1988.

———. *The Car Culture.* Cambridge: MIT Press, 1975.

Gartman, D. *Auto Opium: A Social History of American Automobile Design.* New York: Routledge, 1994.

McShane, C. *Down the Asphalt Path: The Automobile and the American City.* New York: Columbia University Press, 1994.

O'Meara, L. "Medium of Exchange: The Blue Coupé Dialogue in *The Great Gatsby*," *Papers in Language and Literature* 30 (1994): 73–87.

Scharff, V. *Taking the Wheel: Women and the Coming of the Motor Age*. New York: Free Press, 1991.
Seltzer, M. *Bodies and Machines*. New York: Routledge, 1992.
Thacker, A. "Traffic, Gender, Modernism," *Sociological Review* 54 (2006): 175–89.
Tichi, C. *Shifting Gears: Technology, Literature, Culture in Modernist America*. Chapel Hill, NC: University of North Carolina Press, 1987.

PARTIES

Donnelly, H. M. *Sara and Gerald: Villa America and After*. New York: Crown Publishing, 1983.
Okrent, D. *Last Call: The Rise and Fall of Prohibition*. New York: Charles Scribner's Sons, 2010.
Taylor, D. J. *Bright Young People: The Lost Generation of London's Jazz Age*. New York: Farrar, Straus & Giroux, 2009.
Tomkins, C. *Living Well Is the Best Revenge*. New York: Random House, 1998.
Walker, S. *The Night Club Era*. Baltimore, MD: Johns Hopkins University Press, 1999.

ARCHITECTURE AND DESIGN

David P. H. *American Architecture*. London: Thames & Hudson, 1985.
Gelernter, M. *A History of American Architecture: Buildings in Their Cultural and Technological Context*. Manchester, UK: Manchester University Press, 1999.
Hitchcock, H. R. and E. Kaufmann. *The Rise of an American Architecture*. New York: Praeger, 1970.
Jenkins, V. S. "A Green Velvety Carpet: The Front Lawn in America," *Journal of Popular Culture* 17.3 (Fall 1994): 43–7
Loth, C. and J. Trousdale, Jr. *The Only Proper Style: Gothic Architecture in America*. Boston: New York Graphic Society, 1975.
McCarter, R. *Frank Lloyd Wright*. London: Reaktion, 2006.
McMullen, B. S. "'This Tremendous Detail': The Oxford Stone in the House of Gatsby" in J. Assadi and W. Freedman, eds. *A Distant Drummer: Foreign Perspectives on F. Scott*. New York: Peter Lang, 2007, 11–20.
Teyssot, G., ed. *The American Lawn*. Princeton, NJ: Princeton Architectural Press, 1999.
Wilson, C. and P. Grath. *Everyday America: Cultural Landscape Studies after J. B. Jackson*. Berkeley, CA: University of California Press, 2003.

THE CRASH AND THE AFTERMATH

De Brunhoff, S. *Marx on Money*. J. Goldbloom, trans. New York: Urizen Books, 1976.
Debord, G. *The Society of the Spectacle*. D. Nicholson-Smith, trans. New York: Zone Books, 1995.

Harvey, D. "Money, Credit, and Finance" and "Financial Capital and its Contradictions" in *Limits to Capital*. London: Verso, 2006. 239–82; 283–329.
Haug, W. *Critique of Commodity Aesthetics*. R. Bock, trans. Cambridge, UK: Polity Press, 1986.
Marx, K. "Commodities and Money" in *Capital*. Volume 1. B. Fowkes, trans. Harmondsworth, UK: Penguin, 1976. 125–244.
Zizek, S. *The Sublime Object of Ideology*. London: Verso, 1988.

FITZGERALD AND THE GREAT DEPRESSION

Breidlid, A., et al., eds. *American Culture: An Anthology of Civilization Texts*. London: Routledge, 1996.
Bruccoli, M. J., ed. *Scott Fitzgerald: A Life in Letters*. New York: Charles Scribner's Sons, 1994.
Bruccoli, M. J. and J. S. Baughman, eds. *Conversations with F. Scott Fitzgerald*. Jackson, MS: University Press of Mississippi, 2004.
Cowley, M. *Exile's Return: A Literary Odyssey of the 1920s*. London: The Bodley Head, 1951.
Fitzgerald, F. S. *The Price was High: Volume 1 of the Last Uncollected Stories of F. Scott Fitzgerald*. M. J. Bruccoli, ed. London: Picador, 1981.
———. *The Crack-Up with Other Pieces and Stories*. London: Penguin, 1971.
———. *F. Scott Fitzgerald's Ledger: A Facsimile*. M. J. Bruccoli, ed. Washington: Bruccoli Clark/NCR, 1972.
Geismar, M. *Writers in Crisis: The American Novel 1925–1940*. New York: Hill and Wang, 1961.
Gervais, R. J. "The Socialist and the Silk Stockings: Fitzgerald's Double Allegiance" in H. Bloom, ed. *Modern Critical Views: F. Scott Fitzgerald*. New York: Chelsea House, 1985, 167–80.
Hemingway, E. "A Clean, Well-Lighted Place," *The First Forty-Nine Stories*. London: Cape, 1964.
———. *A Moveable Feast*. London: Cape, 1964.
Kazin, A. *Writing Was Everything*. Cambridge, MA: Harvard University Press, 1995.
Kuehl, J. *F. Scott Fitzgerald: A Study of the Short Fiction*. Boston: Twayne, 1991.
Milford, N. *Zelda Fitzgerald*. Harmondsworth, UK: Penguin, 1970.
Prigozy, R. "Fitzgerald's Short Stories and the Depression: An Artistic Crisis" in J. R. Bryer, ed. *The Short Stories of F. Scott Fitzgerald*. Madison, WI: Wisconsin University Press, 1982, 111–26.
Sklar, R. *F. Scott Fitzgerald: The Last Laocoön*. Oxford, UK: Oxford University Press, 1969.
Turnbull, A., ed. *The Letters of F. Scott Fitzgerald*. Harmondsworth, UK: Penguin, 1968.

Welland, D. "The Language of American Fiction Between the Wars" in Marcus Cunliffe, ed. *American Literature Since 1900*. London: Barrie and Jenkins, 1975, 48–72.

THE WRITER IN HOLLYWOOD

Cerasulo, T. *Authors Out Here: Fitzgerald, West, Parker and Schulberg in Hollywood*. Columbia, SC: University of South Carolina Press, 2010.

Dardis, T. *Some Time in the Sun: The Hollywood Years of Fitzgerald, Faulkner, Nathanael West, Aldous Huxley and James Agee*. New York: Charles Scribner's Sons, 1976.

Fine, R. *West of Eden: Writers in Hollywood, 1928–1940*. Washington: Smithsonian Institution Press, 1993.

Hamilton, I. *Writers in Hollywood, 1915–1951*. New York: Harper & Row, 1990.

Latham, A. *Crazy Sundays: F. Scott Fitzgerald in Hollywood*. New York: Viking Press, 1971.

Rhodes, C. *Politics, Desire and the Hollywood Novel*. Iowa City, IA: University of Iowa Press, 2008.

Schulberg, B. *The Four Seasons of Success*. Garden City, NY: Doubleday, 1972.

THE GOLDEN AGE OF HOLLYWOOD

Bruccoli, M. J., S. F. Smith, and J. P. Kerr, eds. *The Romantic Egoists: A Pictorial Autobiography From the Scrapbooks and Albums of F. Scott and Zelda Fitzgerald*. Columbia, SC: University of South Carolina Press, 2003.

Crafton, D. *The Talkies: American Cinema's Transition to Sound, 1926–1931*. Berkeley, CA: University of California Press, 1999.

Dardis, T. *Some Time in the Sun*. London: André Deutsch, 1976.

Margolies, A. "Fitzgerald and Hollywood" in R. Prigozy, ed. *The Cambridge Companion to F. Scott Fitzgerald*. Cambridge, UK: Cambridge University Press, 1992.

Shipman, D. *The Story of Cinema*. New York: St. Martin's Press, 1982.

Sklar, R. *Movie-Made America: A Social History of American Movies*. Rev. ed. New York: Vintage, 1994.

Thompson, K. and D. Bordwell, eds. *Film History: An Introduction*. 2nd ed. New York: McGraw-Hill, 2003.

HOLLYWOOD AND THE GOSSIP COLUMNISTS

Eells, G. *Hedda and Louella*. New York: Putnam, 1972.

Graham, S. *College of One: The Story of How F. Scott Fitzgerald Educated the Woman He Loved*. New York: Bantam, 1967.

———. *The Real F. Scott Fitzgerald: Thirty-five Years Later*. New York: Grosset & Dunlap, 1976.

———. *Confessions of a Hollywood Columnist*. New York: Bantam, 1969.
Parsons, L. *The Gay Illiterate*. New York: Doubleday, 1944.
———. *Tell It To Louella*. New York: Putnam, 1961.

HEROES AND HOLLYWOOD

Berg, A. S. *Goldwyn: A Biography*. New York: Alfred A. Knopf, 1989.
Didion, J. "In Hollywood" in *The White Album*. New York: Simon & Schuster, 1979.
Latham, A. *Crazy Sundays: F. Scott Fitzgerald in Hollywood*. New York: Viking, 1971.
Selznick, D. O. *Memo from David O. Selznick*. Rudy Behlme, ed. New York: Viking Press, 1972.
Sklar, R. *Movie-Made America: A Social History of American Movies (1975)*. Rev. ed. New York: Vintage, 1994.

Index